IELTS Collected Papers

Research in speaking and writing assessment

IELTS Collected Papers

Research in speaking and writing assessment

Edited by

Lynda Taylor and Peter Falvey

CAMBRIDGE
UNIVERSITY PRESS

CAMBRIDGE UNIVERSITY PRESS
Cambridge, New York, Melbourne, Madrid, Cape Town, Singapore, São Paulo

Cambridge University Press
The Edinburgh Building, Cambridge CB2 8RU, UK

www.cambridge.org
Information on this title: www.cambridge.org/9780521542487

First published 2007

Printed in the United Kingdom at the University Press, Cambridge

A catalogue record for this publication is available from the British Library

ISBN 978-0-521-542487

In memory of Peter Hargreaves
1942–2003

Contents

PART 2

Writing

Appendices

Abbreviations

ACTFL	American Council on the Teaching of Foreign Languages
AIE	Arguments, Ideas and Evidence
ALTE	Association of Language Testers in Europe
BC	British Council
BC/IDPA	British Council/International Development Programme Australia
BEC	Business English Certificates
BSS	Business Studies and Social Sciences
CAE	Certificate in Advanced English
CASE	Cambridge Assessment of Spoken English
CB	computer-based
CC	Coherence and Cohesion
CLC	Cambridge Learner Corpus
CPE	Certificate of Proficiency in English
CQ	Communicative Quality
EAP	English for Academic Purposes
EFL	English as a Foreign Language
ELICOS	English Language Intensive Courses for Overseas Students
ELT	English Language Teaching
ELTS	English Language Testing Service
ELTSVal	ELTS Validation Project
EPTB	English Proficiency Test Battery
ESL	English as a Second Language
ESOLComms	English for Speakers of Other Languages Communications (computerised test administration system)
ESP/LSP	English or Language for Specific Purposes
FCE	First Certificate in English
IDP	International Development Program
IELTS	International English Language Testing System
ILTA	International Language Testing Association
IRT	item response theory
LMS	Life and Medical Sciences
MFRA	multifaceted Rasch analysis
NS	native speaker

OET	Occupational English Test
OMR	Optical Mark Reader
OPI	Oral Proficiency Interview
PET	Preliminary English Test
PSN	Professional Support Network
PST	Physical Sciences and Technology
QPP	Question Paper Production
SEM	standard error of measurement
TE	trainee examiner
TF	Task Fulfilment
TOEFL	Test of English as a Foreign Language
UCLES	University of Cambridge Local Examinations Syndicate
VSS	Vocabulary and Sentence Structure

Contributors

Caroline Coffin is a senior lecturer in the Centre for Language and Communication at The Open University (UK). Previously she worked as a lecturer at the University of Technology, Sydney and the University of New South Wales, Australia. Her area of expertise is functional linguistics with much of her research focusing on disciplinary knowledge construction. Recent publications include *Historical Discourse: the language of time, cause and evaluation,* (Continuum, 2006), *Applying English Grammar: functional and corpus approaches* (edited with Ann Hewings and Kieran O'Halloran, Hodder-Arnold, 2004) and, of relevance to this book, 'Arguing about how the world is or how the world should be: the role of argument in IELTS Tests' (*Journal of English for Academic Purposes*, Vol 3, no. 3).

Peter Falvey, who has an MA and PhD in Applied Linguistics, is currently a Consultant with Cambridge ESOL and teaches on the MA ELT programme at the University of Nottingham. Before returning to the UK in 2001, he taught for 13 years in the Faculty of Education at the University of Hong Kong where he was a Head of Department. Before that he was a specialist British Council Officer in ELT and ELT teacher education for 14 years, working in Kuwait, Iraq, Hong Kong and Saudi Arabia. He has published six books on Testing in ELT and Literature Methodology, numerous articles and has supervised over 10 PhD students, two of whom gained international awards for their theses. He was a co-principal investigator for the Hong Kong government from 1996–2000 in the ground-breaking language benchmark initiative setting standards of English proficiency for teachers of English in Hong Kong.

Clare Furneaux teaches in the School of Languages and European Studies (formerly Centre for Applied Language Studies), the University of Reading, England. Her background is in English for academic purposes and teacher education. She teaches on the campus-based MA in English Language Teaching and is academic director of the Distance Study programme. Her current research interests are distance learning and the teaching of writing.

Ann Hewings is a senior lecturer in the Centre for Language and Communication at The Open University (UK). She previously taught English in Europe, Asia, and Australia from primary to tertiary levels. She worked for a number of years on the COBUILD project, researching and contributing to dictionaries and other English language reference material. Her current research focus is academic writing in disciplinary contexts, particularly at tertiary level and in electronic environments. Publications include 'IELTS as preparation for tertiary writing: distinctive interpersonal and textual strategies', with Caroline Coffin, in *Analysing Academic Writing* (eds Louise Ravelli and Rod Ellis, Continuum, 2004).

Professor Chris Kennedy has worked as teacher, trainer, adviser, and researcher in Africa, the Middle East, South-East Asia, and South America. His research and publications focus on Language Policy, Curriculum Innovation, and English as a Global Language, with interests also in Primary ELT, Professional Communication and Applied Corpus Linguistics. He is a Past President of IATEFL, and is Chair of the British Council's English Teaching Advisory Committee. He is Director of the Centre for English Language Studies at the University of Birmingham, UK, which runs in-house and distance Masters and PhD programmes in ELT, Applied Linguistics, and Translation Studies.

Barbara Mayor is a lecturer in the Centre for Language and Communication at The Open University (UK). She previously taught English at secondary and adult level in Europe and the Middle East. Her research interests include bilingualism and bilingual education, and the use of English as a global language of education. Recent publications include 'The English language and "global" teaching', with Joan Swann, in *Distributed Learning: Social and Cultural Approaches to Practice* (eds Mary Lea and Kathy Nicoll, Routledge Falmer, 2002) and 'Dialogic and Hortatory features in the writing of Chinese candidates for the IELTS test' (*Language, Culture and Curriculum*, Vol 19, no 1).

Sarah North is a lecturer in the Centre for Language and Communication at The Open University (UK). After teaching EAP for several years in Indonesia, Singapore, Tanzania and China, she then moved into teacher education, working with teachers and teacher trainees from a range of countries, including India, Malaysia and Mexico. Her main research interests are English for academic purposes, language and literacy, and computer-mediated communication. She has published in *ELT Journal, Applied Linguistics* and *Studies in Higher Education*, and has recently written with Theresa Lillis a chapter on academic writing in *Doing Postgraduate Research* (ed Stephen Potter, Sage, 2006, 2nd edn).

Kieran O'Loughlin is currently Senior Lecturer in TESOL at the University of Melbourne. He was employed in the same position at the time both research projects reported in this volume were completed. He has worked in the fields of applied linguistics and TESOL for many years as a teacher,

teacher educator, manager and academic. In recent years he has continued to undertake research projects under the IELTS joint-funded research program including studies on test-taker score gains after intensive English language instruction and higher education degree programs as well as the use of the test for university selection in Australia.

Mark Rignall taught on the EAP programme at the University of Reading's Centre for Applied Language Studies through the 1990s and published EAP course material with Clare Furneaux. He has been a Senior Examiner for IELTS and, with colleagues at Reading, has carried out a number of small-scale research studies of rater behaviour and the effects of rater training.

Joan Swann is a senior lecturer and currently Director of the Centre for Language and Communication at The Open University (UK). Her teaching focuses on the design of multi-media materials in English language studies for international as well as UK audiences. Her main academic area is sociolinguistics, and her research includes the study of language and gender, language and educational policy and practice, and political and cultural issues in academic writing in English. Recent books include *The Art of English: Everyday Creativity* (co-edited with Janet Maybin, Palgrave Macmillan, 2006); *A Dictionary of Sociolinguistics* (co-authored with Ana Deumert, Rajend Mesthrie and Theresa Lillis, Edinburgh University Press, 2004).

Lynda Taylor is Assistant Director of the Research and Validation Group at the University of Cambridge ESOL Examinations (part of Cambridge Assessment – a non-teaching department of the University). She assists in co-ordinating the research and validation programme to support Cambridge ESOL's wide range of language tests and teaching awards. She has extensive experience of the theoretical and practical issues involved in second language testing and assessment. She regularly writes and presents on the work of the Group and has been involved in providing expert assistance for a number of major test design and development projects in the UK and overseas.

Dilys Thorp has many years' experience of TESOL in China, Japan, Hong Kong and Britain. After thirteen years as Senior Lecturer in ELT at Thames Valley University, Ealing, London, she has worked freelance as a lecturer and researcher for a number of different universities. At the time of writing this paper she was working as a researcher with Chris Kennedy at Birmingham, whilst also teaching on the MEd TESOL at Bristol. Recently she has completed a research project for the Peninsula Medical School, Exeter, investigating the linguistic nature of reflective writing in a corpus of medical undergraduates' scripts.

Series Editors' note

This volume, the nineteenth in the *Studies in Language Testing* series, is dedicated to the memory of Dr Peter Hargreaves. Peter was appointed Chief Executive of Cambridge ESOL (known at that time as the UCLES EFL Division) in 1988; he saw its ESOL and Teacher Education Examinations and their validation and administrative services develop and grow during the 14 years he was in charge until his untimely death in January 2003. Among his many contributions to Cambridge ESOL, he encouraged the introduction of this series of language testing volumes in the early 1990s. Peter was involved with the development of IELTS from its very early stages while working with the British Council as a senior evaluation consultant and he continued this involvement for his whole time with Cambridge ESOL contributing greatly to the success of IELTS.

IELTS has developed over the years in line with theoretical and technical developments in assessment. Lynda Taylor's general introduction to this volume is a very useful guide for those who wish to learn about the beginnings of IELTS, its subsequent development and its recent changes, particularly in the Speaking and Writing components of the examination.

Since 1995, the IELTS partnership has provided funding for research into various aspects of IELTS, in particular its Speaking and Writing components. IDP Education Australia Limited (IDP) has to date published several volumes of the IDP-commissioned reports. This volume in the *Studies in Language Testing* series includes a selection of British Council as well as IDP-commissioned work. As the process of publishing hard copy takes time, often resulting in delays, it is our intention, in future, to publish more of the commissioned research studies in a web-based format. This will put recent and relevant research into the public domain more quickly, and so allow access to studies much earlier than hitherto.

The 10 studies published here provide insights into issues that were in the thoughts of those involved in the development and revision of IELTS in the late 1990s and the first half of this decade. An important rationale for this volume is to illustrate how applied research into specific issues contributed to the evolution of IELTS over this period. As such, the reader's attention will be drawn to Lynda Taylor's two chapters (5 and 12), which discuss the impact that these particular studies had on IELTS revisions. Issues investigated in Part 1 are: *interviewer style and candidate performance in the IELTS oral interview* (Brown and Hill); *the role of gender in the IELTS oral interview*

(O'Loughlin); *the rating process in the IELTS oral interview* (Brown); *examiner attitudes and behaviour in the IELTS oral interview* (Merrylees and McDowell).

The effects of interviewer style on candidate performance has been the focus of many studies in recent years. Likewise, the role of gender in assessment has become well-established over the past 10 years as an issue for discussion in assessment circles ever since attention began to focus on ethical matters. The rating process is a regular topic in direct tests of language production and surveys of examiner attitudes are always of value. What is of particular interest in this volume is that all the studies were commissioned specifically for IELTS performance tests.

Part 2 contains the six chapters focusing on various issues in writing assessment: *authenticity in Task 2 of the IELTS Academic Module Writing test* (Moore and Morton); *linguistic analysis of Chinese and Greek L1 scripts for IELTS Academic Writing Task 2* (Mayor et al); *corpus-based investigation of linguistic responses to an IELTS Academic Writing task* (Kennedy and Thorp); *task design in Academic Writing prompts* (O'Loughlin and Wigglesworth); *standardisation-training on rater-judgements for the IELTS Writing Module* (Furneaux and Rignall); *bias analysis feedback to raters for the IELTS Writing Module* (O'Sullivan and Rignall).

Once again, it is clear that the issues of authenticity, linguistic analyses of writing performance, the training of raters of writing, task design in writing prompts and feedback to raters of the IELTS Writing Module are all important topics. As Lynda Taylor shows in her chapter on the impact of these studies on the revisions to the Writing component of IELTS, all of these studies had either a direct influence on the revision process itself or provided evidence on which to base informed decisions.

A further component has been added at the end of each chapter which provides a commentary on the research methodology employed in each of the 10 research studies. These commentary sections are specifically designed to assist new/young researchers who are interested in research on assessment and assessment instruments. They were trialled with new researchers at the 2005 ALTE Conference in Berlin and were found to be helpful in stimulating questions about topics such as the formulation of research questions, the design of questionnaire-based surveys and the selection of appropriate research methodologies.

The general introduction to the volume along with Lynda Taylor's chapters on the impact of these studies on the work of IELTS and Peter Falvey's comments on the research methodology used in each study will be, we hope, a valuable contribution to the assessment community, not only for those who are already assessment professionals but particularly for new and recently-joining members of the community.

Michael Milanovic
Cyril Weir

Introduction

The IELTS Joint-funded Research Program

To support the ongoing development of the International English Language Testing System (IELTS), the IELTS partners co-ordinate a comprehensive research and validation programme. A major component of this programme is the funded research sponsored jointly by IDP: IELTS Australia and the British Council, with active support from Cambridge ESOL.

The origins of this research programme date back to 1995 when the IELTS Australia Board first set aside grant funding and invited external researchers to submit IELTS-related proposals. The Board believed that such research would complement internal research and validation activities being conducted by the IELTS partnership and would provide valuable additional information on a range of issues relating to the quality and standing of IELTS; it could also help IELTS stakeholders (including English language professionals and teachers) to develop a greater knowledge and understanding of the test.

The first round of funded studies was conducted in 1995 and a selection of these were edited and published jointly by ELICOS and IELTS Australia as *IELTS Research Reports 1998*, Volume 1. IDP later went on to publish four more edited volumes of selected reports from the period 1996–2001 and further edited volumes are in production at the time of writing.

In 1998 the British Council joined IELTS Australia in setting aside annual funds for research grants and since that time the programme has been jointly funded by these two IELTS partners. Cambridge ESOL, the third IELTS partner, supports the programme by providing data, materials, advice and many other types of assistance to approved researchers.

The annual call for research proposals is widely publicised and aims to reflect current concerns and issues relating to IELTS as a major international English language proficiency test with high-stakes value. A Joint Research Committee, comprising representatives of the three IELTS partners, agrees on research priorities and oversees the tendering process. Research proposals are reviewed and evaluated according to the following criteria:

- relevance and benefit of outcomes to IELTS
- clarity and coherence of the proposal's rationale, objectives and methodology

- feasibility of outcomes, timelines and budget (including ability to keep to deadlines)
- qualifications and experience of proposed project staff
- potential of the project to be reported in a form which would be both useful to IELTS and of interest to an international audience.

In determining the quality of the proposals and the research to be carried out, the Committee routinely consults with a panel of external reviewers. The Committee also oversees the publication and/or presentation of research findings.

Over the past decade the outcomes of the funded research programme have made a significant contribution to the monitoring, evaluation and ongoing development of IELTS, especially in the following areas:

- the assessment of speaking in IELTS: issues of task design, candidate discourse, assessment criteria, test bias, examiner/rater behaviour, examiner/rater training and monitoring
- the assessment of writing in IELTS: issues of task design, construct validity, features of writing performance, rater training and monitoring, approaches to assessment
- the impact of IELTS in education and society: stakeholder attitudes, use of test scores, score gains, impact on courses and preparation materials, with key user groups
- computer-based IELTS: approaches to rating and issues of candidate processing.

In addition, one of the most valuable outcomes of reports from joint-funded projects is the surveys of recent literature they provide; these help the IELTS test developers stay up to date with theoretical and empirical work in a wide range of fields (including some that are only indirectly linked to language testing) allowing them to take account of these in their work.

Since 1995, nearly 70 research studies and more than 120 individual researchers have received grants under the joint-funded programme. Ten years on, the Joint-funded Research Program has become a key component within the larger research and validation agenda in support of IELTS and reflects the IELTS partners' commitment to continuing improvement of the test.

The background to this volume

For some years the IELTS partners have been working towards publishing a selection of the project reports from the Joint-funded Research Program as a single volume, based around a common theme. In this way it is hoped they will become available to a wider audience and illustrate the value of this work within the larger research and validation agenda which underpins IELTS.

Many of the funded research studies conducted during the past 10 years have focused on the IELTS Speaking and Writing Modules, both of which have received considerable attention in recent years from the test developers. Findings from the funded studies complemented internal validation and research studies conducted or commissioned by the IELTS partnership, especially those undertaken by Cambridge ESOL. Such studies directly informed major revision projects for the productive components of IELTS: the IELTS Speaking Revision Project took place between 1998 and 2001, and the IELTS Writing Revision Project was carried out between 2001 and 2005.

Ten reports have therefore been selected and edited for inclusion in this volume, all focusing on the IELTS Speaking and Writing Modules. A number of the studies – those which received funding from IDP: IELTS Australia – have already appeared in one of the five volumes of *IELTS Research Reports*, or in some cases been the basis of a refereed journal article. Others have been presented at conferences but have not appeared to date in published form. All 10 studies have impacted directly on recent changes to the IELTS Speaking and Writing components so will be of interest to test stakeholders and those involved with IELTS. However, they are also likely to be of interest to anyone concerned more generally with the assessment of written and oral proficiency. (At some point in the future, it is hoped that a partner volume can be published focusing on funded studies of the IELTS Reading and Listening Modules.)

The four studies reported in Part 1 (Chapters 1–4) focus on the IELTS Speaking test or 'oral interview' as it was operationalised during the period 1989–2001 and were conducted between 1995 and 1998. Findings from these studies provided valuable insights into the language and behaviour of both candidates and examiners in the IELTS Speaking test as it was at that time, as well as useful evidence relating to the validity, reliability, practicality and impact of the Speaking test; at the same time, they highlighted specific aspects of the test needing review and possible revision. In combination with outcomes from other commissioned studies and internal validation investigations, they directly informed the IELTS Speaking Revision Project (1998–2001) and had a significant impact on the revised design and implementation of the IELTS Speaking Module which became operational in July 2001.

The six studies reported in Part 2 (Chapters 6–11) focus on the IELTS Writing test as it was operationalised during the period 1995–2004 and were conducted between 1996 and 2001. Findings from these studies offered valuable insights into the nature of candidate performance and rater behaviour; they provided useful validation evidence in support of the test and at the same time pointed to areas of concern. As with the speaking-related studies, they were able to feed directly into the IELTS Writing Revision

Project (2001–2005) and inform changes made to the assessment criteria and rating scales for the Writing Module which became operational from January 2005.

The publication of this volume is seen by the IELTS partners as a positive contribution to the field of language testing and assessment. First of all, it allows more of the IELTS-related research which has been completed over the past decade to be shared with a wider audience, not just among IELTS stakeholders but within the broader language testing and assessment community. In addition to the ten reports, the volume includes a review and appraisal (immediately following each report) of the different methodologies used by the researchers across the studies. This should make it a useful resource for anyone involved in language testing research, especially novice researchers and others who are relatively new to the field. As explained earlier in this introduction, the rationale for the IELTS Joint-funded Research Program is to promote and support research activity among test stakeholders which contributes to the ongoing validation and development of the International English Language Testing System. For this reason two additional sections (Chapters 5 and 12) have been included – at the ends of Parts 1 and 2 – explaining how the findings of the studies reported in this volume impacted directly on subsequent changes to the Speaking and Writing Modules; these sections also explain why some recommendations made in the studies were not implemented. Finally, publication of this volume is an appropriate way of celebrating 10 years of the Joint-funded Program and acknowledging its overall contribution to the quality and standing of IELTS.

The development of writing and speaking assessment in IELTS

The direct assessment of L2 writing and oral proficiency in IELTS is a long-established feature of the test; its origins can be traced back at least 30 years to the development and introduction of ELTS (English Language Testing Service) – the test which preceded IELTS. To contextualise the more recent developments in the IELTS assessment of speaking and writing proficiency it may be helpful to review here how L2 writing and speaking ability were tested in the past in IELTS and its predecessors. The remainder of this intro-ductory chapter summarises the history of the Writing and Speaking compo-nents to provide a brief chronological overview of the steady evolution of the test. For a more detailed and comprehensive account of the development of ELTS/IELTS and its role within the broader context of English language proficiency assessment for academic purposes over the past half century, the reader is recommended to consult a partner volume in the Studies in Language Testing series – Volume 23 (Davies, forthcoming).

The English Proficiency Test Battery (1966–80)

From 1966 until 1980 the British Council relied on a language proficiency test called the English Proficiency Test Battery (EPTB) as part of its procedures for recruiting overseas students into higher education in Britain. The EPTB was a traditional set of standardised tests in a multiple-choice format focusing on the receptive skills of reading, listening and grammar. At the time, the EPTB developers acknowledged the importance of writing and speaking skills; however, the practical problems of testing these skills (e.g. the requirement for skilled examiners), combined with the British Council's need for a test which could be taken in a short period of time, meant that tests of speaking and writing could not realistically be included in the EPTB (see Davies, forthcoming).

In the mid-1970s a project was established to develop a replacement for the EPTB which would address some of the problems the current test was facing (e.g. limitations on the number of parallel versions) and which could also take account of the significant changes that took place in the 1960s and 1970s in approaches to language learning and teaching. The new communicative competence paradigm had brought with it an emphasis on the use of language skills in context; this allowed a fresh discussion of whether the new test to replace the EPTB could/should include Writing and Speaking components.

The testing of writing and speaking in ELTS (1980–89)

The replacement for EPTB was a brand new test, developed jointly by the University of Cambridge Local Examinations Syndicate (UCLES) and the British Council, entitled the English Language Testing Service (ELTS). It was introduced in 1980 after a 4-year period of development. Its overall design reflected the new paradigm of communicative language teaching and testing, with its emphasis on authenticity and relevance; the new test also took account of the growing interest in English or Language for Specific Purposes (ESP/LSP). Test tasks were based on an analysis of the ways in which language was used in academic contexts and were intended to reflect the use of language in the 'real world'. The strong emphasis on needs analysis and communicative language demands in the study/work context meant that, alongside the Reading and Listening components, subtests of writing and speaking ability were allocated a place within the new test – in the form of the M2 Writing and the M3 Individual Interview. Both the M2 Writing and M3 Interview subtests were subject specific papers, i.e. they were linked to one of six academic 'domains' or areas of study (Life Sciences, Social Studies, Physical Sciences, Technology, Medicine, General Academic). Each candidate received a Source Booklet relevant to their chosen discipline from the six domains available; the

Source Booklet contained extracts from appropriate academic texts, including bibliography and index, and it formed the basis for the writing tasks in M2 as well as for the main discussion in the M3 Interview.

The M2 Writing test consisted of two questions. The first was considered to be 'divergent'; although it was based on one of the reading texts in the Source Booklet, it still required the candidate to bring in their own experience and views. The second question was considered to be 'convergent', i.e. strictly limited to the information available in the input texts. Candidates had to write at least 12 lines for Task 1 and were advised to spend about 25 of the allocated 40 minutes on it.

The M3 Interview was conducted face-to-face with the individual candidate and had three parts. In the first part the interviewer put the candidate at ease with general questions, and on the basis of the candidates' responses selected an adjacent range of three (out of the possible nine) bands which encompassed what the final oral proficiency band score for the candidate would be. In the second part of the interview the candidate was asked about one of the texts from the Source Booklet, and the interviewer narrowed the band range assigned to two. In the final part of the interview, the candidate was asked to discuss their future plans; at the end of this phase the interviewer made the final band assignment.

Although innovative in its design and implementation when compared with EPTB and other tests of a similar nature (e.g. TOEFL), the new ELTS test nevertheless presented a number of practical and administrative challenges, especially with regard to the inclusion of the direct Writing and Speaking subtests. Qualified EFL teachers had to be recruited and trained to mark the M2 essay; they also had to be trained to conduct and rate the M3 oral interview. Training for both components took several hours; in addition, each essay took around 10 minutes to mark and each oral assessment required about 15 minutes, making the whole test much lengthier than its EPTB predecessor. Even though training manuals were created for both M2 and M3, it was difficult to ensure effective training in all test centres since suitably qualified EFL staff were often in short supply, and in some centres there might be only one qualified individual to assume the role of writing/speaking assessor as well as test administrator. Practical constraints meant that marker training for M2 and M3 was largely carried out on a self-access basis, with the help of an audio/video pack for M3; marker standardisation was difficult to achieve for obvious reasons.

The assessment of Speaking and Writing in ELTS between 1980 and 1989 can be summarised as follows:

Writing test (M2)

- linked to one of six academic domains (Life Sciences, Social Studies, Physical Sciences, Technology, Medicine, General Academic)

- based on a Source Booklet of textual extracts for input
- two writing tasks
- length = 40 minutes
- assessed on a 9-band scale
- required qualified and trained EFL teachers for marking.

Individual Interview (M3)

- linked to one of six academic domains (Life Sciences, Social Studies, Physical Sciences, Technology, Medicine, General Academic)
- based on a Source Booklet of textual extracts for input
- face-to-face, one-on-one interview
- three parts
- length = 15 minutes
- assessed on a 9-band scale
- required qualified and trained EFL teachers for interview and rating.

The ELTS Revision Project (1986–89)

Shortly after its introduction in 1980, the British Council and UCLES commissioned the Institute for Applied Language Studies at the University of Edinburgh to undertake a detailed validation study of the test. The ELTS Validation Project (Criper and Davies 1988) explored aspects of the practicality, validity and reliability of the existing English Language Testing Service (ELTS) and work on the 5-year project was completed in 1986. In addition, valuable research was conducted during the early 1980s which cast light on the EAP language and literacy needs of overseas students at British universities (e.g. Geoghegan 1983, Hawkey 1982, Weir 1983).

By 1986 the producers of ELTS determined that the test was once again due for formal review and possible revision. The report of the ELTS Validation Project provided a convenient starting point for the ELTS Revision Project, a 3-year project (1986–9) set up under the direction of Professor Charles Alderson of Lancaster University; British Council management support came from a team headed by Dr Peter Hargreaves, who was at that time with the British Council and from 1988 head of the UCLES EFL Division. An Australian perspective was provided by Professor David Ingram of Griffith University, seconded to the revision project in Lancaster from 1987 with support from the International Development Program of Australian Universities and Colleges.

A large-scale, questionnaire-based consultation exercise was conducted with ELTS user groups (receiving institutions, British Council staff, overseas administrators, EAP teachers, language testers and applied linguists) to determine the perceived strengths/weaknesses of the existing test and the desirable characteristics of a revised test (see Alderson and Clapham 1992). User views were also gathered via focus group meetings. In terms of the practicality and validity of ELTS, test length and administrative complexity were considered major causes for concern by informants, especially the selection of appropriate subject-specific modules by candidates and centres. Concerns were also raised about the reliability of the examiner-marked M2 (Writing) and M3 (Interview) components.

The ELTS Validation Consultative Conference, held in July 1987, brought together language testing researchers from Britain, Australia, Canada and the USA to review the outcomes of the consultation exercise and to discuss possible options for the future (Hughes, Porter and Weir 1988). It was generally agreed that the test should be shortened, its administration simplified, and its reliability improved; financial constraints, however, dictated that the Speaking and Writing Modules would continue to be single-marked.

The questionnaire responses acknowledged the importance of the direct Speaking and Writing components though the difficulty of achieving standardised marking was also recognised. The UCLES view on this issue was expressed in their brief report to the Project Steering Committee; it commented that, although the Assessment Guides used to train markers for M2 (Writing) and M3 (Interview) were being constantly improved, and sample monitoring of M2 scripts was being implemented, with the revised ELTS 'this monitoring needed to become more rigorous and systematic and needed to be supplemented by the monitoring of sample recordings of the oral interviews' (Alderson and Clapham 1992:6).

The nature of the Speaking and Writing test content and format, especially its degree of subject specificity, was discussed at length. The Oral Interaction component was at that time subject-specific but this proved unsuccessful in cases where the interviewer and candidate were from different disciplines or where candidates did not yet have a subject discipline to draw on. It was therefore decided to transform the Speaking component from modular (M3) to general status (G3) so it would be taken by all candidates. The Writing subtest, however, would remain modular in nature – M2. The proposal was that G3 could be administered by a trained ELT or non-ELT specialist, but that both G3 and M2 would be marked by a trained ELT specialist at the local centre.

In addition, the six subject-specific modules were reduced to three:

• Physical Sciences and Technology (PST)
• Life and Medical Sciences (LMS)
• Arts and Social Sciences (ASS).

These three 'clusters' were believed to offer the best way of broadly categorising the wide range of subject areas represented within the test candidature. A fourth non-academic module was also envisaged. Reading and Writing would remain integrated so that, to some extent at least, candidates' written output depended on the reading input in the Reading subtest, though separate scores would be reported for the two skills. For more details of this first stage of the ELTS Revision Project, see Alderson and Clapham (1992).

Information gathered during the early stages of the ELTS Revision Project enabled members of the revision team to redraft the content and format of the test, trial draft tasks and analyse the results with a view to making final decisions based on a combination of expert feedback and empirical evidence (Clapham and Alderson 1997). By 1987 the proposed structure of the new ELTS envisaged:

- a general (G) component containing Grammar and Listening subtests, and a 15-minute Speaking subtest
- an academic (M) component linked to three subject-specific areas (PST, LMS and ASS) and containing integrated Reading and Writing subtests
- a non-academic component containing integrated Reading and Writing subtests.

While Grammar, Reading and Listening subtests would be clerically marked, the new Writing and Speaking subtests would require trained raters.

Redevelopment of the Speaking component focused on addressing the issues of validity, reliability and practicality which had been raised during the first stage of the project. The various considerations and constraints, informed by input from user groups, are listed by Ingram and Wylie (1993 and 1997). These included a requirement for the Speaking test to:

- contain a variety of tasks accessible to all levels and backgrounds
- include assessment of social survival skills
- maintain continuity with the existing 9-band scale for ELTS
- take account of security issues
- last 10–15 minutes
- be face-to-face, one-on-one, and audio-taped for monitoring purposes
- use a single interviewer/rater, possibly not an ELT specialist
- involve straightforward training procedures for interviewers/raters
- achieve high reliability.

A Speaking test team set about drafting test specifications, preparing draft materials and making recommendations to the Revision Project members and the Project Steering Committee. Although innovation was encouraged, it nevertheless had to remain within the considerations and constraints given above. Attention focused on issues of task design, band levels, discrimination, security, timing, interview conduct, assessment procedures, administration, and interviewer/rater training. In mid-1988 draft specifications and exemplar test materials were circulated to EAP teachers, applied linguists and EFL specialists in Britain, Australia and Canada. Feedback was received via questionnaires and face-to-face interviews and this fed into redrafting of the specifications, test materials and band scales. Trialling was used to confirm the final format of the redrafted Speaking test. The end result was a rather more structured Speaking test format than previously – 'designed to measure general proficiency in speaking' and 'to interact in social, survival and training or academic contexts without focusing specifically on technical or academic features of the language' (Ingram and Wylie 1997:14). The 10–15 minute oral interview included five phases as follows: Phase 1 (1–2') – *Introduction*; Phase 2 (3–4') – *Extended Discourse*; Phase 3 (3–4') – *Elicitation*; Phase 4 (3–4') – *Speculation and Attitudes*; Phase 5 (1') – *Conclusion*. (See Chapter 1 in this volume for more details of the test format.)

The old ELTS Oral Interaction Band Scale was redeveloped to produce a new global, holistic scale. It was anticipated that all examiners acting as interviewer/rater would be EFL/ESL teachers and that they would undergo a comprehensive training programme; a new examiner training package (face-to-face, and also in self-access mode for remote locations) was created for this purpose, and it included a standardisation video as part of the Speaking Assessment Guide. A number of other quality assurance measures were put in place at this point: after initial training all examiners had to go through a certification process to confirm their ability to mark to acceptable standards; a sample monitoring process was set up according to which all live test interviews would be audio-recorded and 1 in 10 of these would be returned to a centre in the UK or Australia for moderation. (For more details of this phase, see Ingram and Wylie 1993, 1997.)

Finally, the Speaking team listed various issues they believed merited further investigation; in some senses, this provided an ongoing and longer term research agenda for the Speaking test which came to fruition during the 1990s, both in Cambridge ESOL's work on speaking assessment in the early 1990s and in the work conducted from 1995 onwards under the funded programme.

A similar process was used to draft specifications and test materials for the Writing components – both Academic and Non-Academic (later General Training). Three teams of experts worked to create specifications and tasks which would allow for integrated Reading and Writing subtests in the three Academic Modules – PST, LMS and ASS* (see Clapham 1997, Hamp-Lyons

---

* Some time after the Arts and Social Sciences (ASS) variant for IELTS was introduced in 1989, it was renamed Business Studies and Social Sciences (BSS).

and Clapham 1997). A fourth team concentrated on producing materials for the General Training Module (see Ingram 1997). All four teams considered how purposes for writing in differing academic and general contexts should shape the nature of the writing tasks and topics. Draft specifications and tests were sent out for feedback to subject specialists in the three broad academic areas as well as to language teachers, testers and applied linguists. In response to feedback comments from informants, the development team decided that all three academic modules should contain two writing tasks and that these should be based on similar sets of specifications, with any difference being related to topic and subject matter rather than to genre or task type. The General Training Writing Module included two tasks focusing on everyday writing activities related to survival in social and training contexts, including letters and descriptive prose. All the Writing specifications were revised and new tasks piloted in Algeria, Australia and the UK. Once the format had been finalised for the two tasks, draft assessment criteria (both analytical and global) and band scale descriptors were developed; criteria and descriptors also went through successive phases of trialling and redrafting. A decision was taken to restrict the higher level for General Training to Band 6 – for two reasons: first, it was doubtful whether the GT format would allow reliable rating over the whole 9-band range; and second, there was concern that the possibility of achieving a Band 9 on General Training might attract candidates to take GT rather than Academic Modules for university access purposes (see Alderson 1997). A revised Writing Assessment Guide was produced as part of the training programme for future examiners; and, for the first time, examiner training materials included a Certification Package, i.e. a set of writing performances which all examiners had to mark to standard within acceptable limits in order to become 'licensed' ELTS examiners.

The revised ELTS test became operational in 1989 when it was renamed the International English Language Testing System (IELTS) to reflect the involvement from 1987 of the International Development Program of Australian Universities and Colleges. One important aspect of the new management partnership for IELTS from 1989 was that it ensured a fully international perspective and helped counter any tendency towards a Eurocentric bias.

The final formats of the Speaking and Writing Modules introduced for IELTS from 1989 were as follows:

IELTS Academic Writing Module

- linked to one of three academic domains (PST, LMS and ASS, later BSS)
- based on a Source Booklet of textual extracts for input

- two writing tasks
- length = 45 minutes
- assessed on a 9-band scale
- use of both analytical/profile and holistic/global criteria and descriptors
- enhanced Writing Assessment Guide for examiner training
- introduction of certification procedures for examiners
- introduction of sample monitoring for quality assurance.

IELTS General Training Writing Module

- based on a Source Booklet of textual extracts for input
- two writing tasks
- length = 45 minutes
- assessed on a 6-band scale (i.e. no higher than Band 6)
- use of both analytical/profile and holistic/global criteria and descriptors
- enhanced Writing Assessment Guide for examiner training
- introduction of certification procedures for examiners
- introduction of sample monitoring for quality assurance.

IELTS Speaking Module

- face-to-face, one-on-one interview
- five phases
- length = 10–15 minutes
- assessed on a global, 9-band scale
- enhanced Speaking Assessment Guide for examiner training
- introduction of certification procedures for examiners
- introduction of sample monitoring for quality assurance.

The testing of writing and speaking in IELTS (1989–95)

Following its introduction in 1989, IELTS gained in worldwide recognition and the candidature grew steadily to reach over 30,000 by 1993; the test was available to candidates in 186 test centres in 105 countries. In the same period organisational changes within the IELTS partnership (British Council, IDP and UCLES) paved the way for the next review and revision of the test, and developments at UCLES in the early 1990s were particularly significant in this regard.

Developments at UCLES in the early 1990s

By 1990 Dr Peter Hargreaves had moved from the British Council to head up the new EFL Division at UCLES in Cambridge. A new Evaluation Unit, headed by Dr Michael Milanovic, had been created within the EFL Division to focus on matters of validation and research for all the English language proficiency tests produced by Cambridge at that time. Particular attention was focused on improving procedures for producing test materials, and on collecting and analysing item level/task-based responses from candidates taking the Cambridge tests. This included increased pretesting of materials for item/task calibration and the creation of an electronic item banking system to enable more effective test construction and equating. More detailed information about the test-taker populations for the Cambridge EFL tests was also needed to inform an understanding of background factors and test-taker characteristics such as age, gender, first language, level of education, etc; only by gathering, storing and analysing such data would it be possible to undertake research triangulating test content, candidate background and test performance.

This led in turn to the development of scannable, Optical Mark Reader (OMR) answer sheets for objectively scored tests such as those for Reading, Listening and Use of English. OMR answer sheets captured test responses directly from candidates – either as a selected response (e.g. candidate shades in a lozenge A, B, C or D), or as a constructed response (e.g. candidate writes in a word or short phrase); in the latter case, the candidate's answers are clerically marked centrally in Cambridge and the clerical marker records whether the response is right or wrong by shading the appropriate lozenge. In both cases, the completed answer sheet then passes through a scanning machine to provide electronic datasets of test responses at item level; these in turn can be analysed in a variety of ways – using statistical software packages – to answer questions about test facility, discrimination, and other technical measurement issues. The early 1990s saw extensive exploration by Cambridge into the use of OMR technology for capturing candidate responses (to Reading, Listening and Use of English test items), examiner assessments (awarded in direct Speaking and Writing tests), as well as key information on candidate background variables.

At the same time, increased interest and energy also focused on investigating issues of performance assessment, particularly in relation to: the nature of oral interaction in assessment contexts; describing features of spoken/written language across proficiency levels (common scale); rating scale development; marking strategies; the training, standardisation and monitoring of examiners; computer marking of essays; and the building/exploitation of corpora of learner written and spoken language (for example, development of the Cambridge Learner Corpus began in collaboration with Cambridge

University Press in 1993). In 1994 Cambridge established its Oral Examiner Team Leader (TL) system to improve quality assurance measures for its face-to-face Speaking tests; the TL system comprised a hierarchical network of professionals with various levels of overlapping responsibility and a set of procedures covering minimum levels and standards for recruitment, induction, training, standardisation, monitoring and evaluation.

Research and development in all the above areas for Cambridge's Main Suite of EFL tests (i.e. KET, PET, FCE, CAE and CPE) continued in the period 1990–95 and invariably impacted on the continuing evolution of IELTS. For example, a series of projects carried out in collaboration with Professor Anne Lazaraton (now at the University of Minnesota) used conversation and discourse analysis to examine the language and behaviour of Oral Examiners (Lazaraton 2002). Research findings confirmed the value of using a highly specified interlocutor/examiner frame for standardisation of input (now a standard feature of the Cambridge tests); this work also led to the development of an Oral Examiner Monitoring Checklist for training and feedback purposes. Other studies and investigations, including some focusing specifically on the IELTS Speaking test, explored aspects of test taker language and behaviour (Lazaraton 2002); these informed our understanding of criterial features of spoken language performance and were later to help validate and revise assessment scales.

Another emerging area of interest for Cambridge and for other language testers at that time was the issue of ethics and professional standards (Kunnan 2000; Saville 2002). In 1990 UCLES began collaborating with other European institutional providers of language examinations within the context of the newly formed Association of Language Testers in Europe (ALTE); work started on articulating and communicating professional standards for language test providers. Founder members of the association agreed the importance of a Code of Practice for examination developers and examination users which would help ensure quality and fairness in developing and using assessment procedures. Discussion of what constitutes principles of good practice has continued ever since and reflects a concern for accountability in all areas of assessment. In this respect, it recognises the importance of *test validation* and the role of *research and development* in examination processes. In 1994, ALTE published its first Code of Practice which set out the standards that members of the association aimed to meet in producing their language tests; other testing-related organisations have contributed to an ongoing debate in this area, e.g. *Standards for educational and psychological testing* (AERA/APA/NCME 1999) and the International Language Testing Association's Code of Ethics (2000).

The IELTS 95 Revision Project (1993–95)

In the light of the interests and developments outlined above, the IELTS partners turned their attention once again in the early 1990s to the next stage in the evolutionary development of IELTS. This was to include not only a review of test content and format, but also a major 're-engineering' of key aspects of test delivery, administration and processing to ensure that IELTS would be able to cope with the increasing demands being placed on it; this was considered especially urgent given the opening up in the 1990s of opportunities in international education and the growing numbers of students seeking higher education in English-speaking countries such as Australia, Canada, the USA and the UK.

Results from routine test monitoring and evaluation in the period 1989–94, together with some specially commissioned and independent work conducted on IELTS by external experts (e.g. Clapham 1993; Wylie 1993) led to the IELTS 95 Revision Project (1993–95) which introduced further modifications to IELTS from April 1995. As in previous projects, the revision process involved successive and iterative cycles of review, consultation, drafting, redrafting and trialling before final decisions were confirmed. This approach was consistent with the model of test development and revision emerging at Cambridge ESOL in the early 1990s (see Saville 2002). Significant modifications were made to IELTS in seven key areas (for more details see Charge and Taylor 1997). They included:

- removal of subject-specific subtests and replacement with a single Academic Module and a non-academic General Training Module (see Clapham 1996, for further discussion of the rationale underlying this); in addition the thematic link between the Reading and Writing Modules was removed
- the extension of the General Training scales for Reading and Writing to nine bands to bring them into line with the 9-band scale used for the Academic Module
- the extension of the window for the administration of the Speaking Module to three days (instead of one) to allow greater flexibility in test centres to accommodate rising candidate numbers
- enhancement of the IELTS question paper production methodology for purposes of quality assurance
- enhancement of routine systems for capturing data on test taker performance and background to improve test processing, validation and research
- improved security measures relating to despatch, management and retirement of IELTS test versions
- a new test centre administration package (ESOLComms) and training for staff at all BC and IDP test centres.

It will be clear from this overview that many of the changes made in the IELTS 95 Revision Project were driven as much by practical concerns, administrative problems and technological developments, as by applied linguistic and measurement issues. This points to the importance of recognising the complex infrastructure which accompanies any large-scale, high-stakes assessment endeavour; the long-term usefulness and sustainability of any test will inevitably depend as much on the successful design of the systems and procedures for producing, promoting, administering and evaluating it, as on the design of test content and format.

Following a period of consultation and a review of the available research, the Revision Project team based in Cambridge drafted revised test specifications for IELTS; these were sent out for review and the International IELTS Advisory Committee (which included language testing experts from the UK, USA, Australia and New Zealand) gave feedback at a 2-day meeting in August 1993. A further round of redrafting took place in 1993–94 followed by trialling of test materials, including trialling of tasks and full test versions with pre-university, English L1 students in the UK and Australia.

For the IELTS Writing Modules, the major changes in 1995 related to:

- replacement of the three academic subject-specific modules with a single Academic Module
- removal of the thematic link between the Reading and Writing Modules
- increase in length of output required from test takers: Academic Writing Module – Task 1: 150 words (instead of 100) and Task 2: 250 words (instead of 150); General Training Writing Module – Task 1: 150 words (instead of 80) and Task 2: 250 words (instead of 120)
- increase in time allocation for both the Academic and General Training Writing Modules – extended from 45 minutes to 60 minutes
- the extension of the General Training scale for Writing to nine bands to bring it into line with the 9-band scale used for the Academic Module.

Despite the earlier reduction in 1989 from six to three subject-specific modules, even this simpler, three-way subdivision continued to cause administrative problems for test centres and receiving institutions between 1989 and 1995; they were often unclear about the appropriate subtests for different courses, and whether to match a candidate to a module based on their previous or intended discipline area. Feedback from IELTS administrators and examiners supported a reduction in the number of subtests. In addition, monitoring of subtest take-up showed that around 75% of IELTS test takers were taking Module C (Arts and Social Sciences). Results from Cambridge's internal research into a single-module option, together with results from Clapham's independent investigation into second language reading and ESP testing (Clapham 1996), suggested that one test for all academic candidates did not discriminate for or against candidates of any discipline area. For this reason, the IELTS 95 Revision Project introduced one Academic Reading Module and one Academic Writing Module.

In addition, the strong thematic link between the Reading and Writing Modules (both Academic and General Training) was removed on the grounds that such a link, though desirable in some respects, increased the potential for confusing the assessment of writing ability with the assessment of reading ability. Monitoring of candidates' writing performance suggested that the extent to which candidates exploited the reading input varied considerably. Some candidates drew heavily on the written content of the reading texts, apparently treating the writing task as a measure of their reading ability; as a result, many risked masking their actual writing ability. Other candidates chose to articulate their own ideas on the topic, either making very little reference to the reading texts or forging artificial connections for the sake of the task. In some cases candidates were confused about whether it would be better to articulate their personal point of view on the topic or to reflect a more 'authoritative' view expressed in the reading text(s). This variation in candidates' treatment of the linked writing task made the achievement of fair assessment at the marking stage a complex process so a more equitable form of task design was sought. Removal of the link also made it easier to control comparability of task difficulty across the many different test versions which needed to be produced for the IELTS Reading and Writing Modules each year.

The length of written output required from test takers was increased to a total of 400 words for the Academic and General Training Modules in order to achieve a richer sample of performance for reliable assessment purposes, and the time allocation was increased accordingly.

Finally, a decision was made to extend the scale for the General Training Writing Module to cover the full nine bands thus bringing it into line with the scale for the Academic Writing Module (and the Reading Modules); this was done on the basis that users of GT scores needed greater discrimination than was offered by the 6-band scale, and a 9-band scale already operated for GT candidates taking the Listening and Speaking Modules.

From 1995 both Academic and General Training Writing required candidates to provide two pieces of writing, one of at least 150 words and one of at least 250 words. Both tasks were to be completed in 60 minutes. Task 1 would be assessed on: *Task Fulfilment; Coherence and Cohesion; Vocabulary and Sentence Structure*; Task 2 would be assessed on: *Arguments, Ideas and Evidence; Communicative Quality; Vocabulary and Sentence Structure*. These criteria would be expressed as both global and analytical band descriptors, and examiners would be able to select the 'global' or 'profile' approach to marking according to whether a script had a 'flat' or 'uneven' profile.

Identifying a way forward for the Speaking test in the IELTS 95 Revision Project was less straightforward. Various options were considered, including the possibility of an optional, discrete, add-on Speaking component for IELTS. This option was briefly considered by the revision team on the grounds that the existing face-to-face oral interview was both financially and logistically demanding. One possibility was to replace the existing IELTS Speaking test with an optional, standalone Speaking component. During the early 1990s Cambridge had been developing just such a Speaking test, using a format which combined a number of innovative features. The Cambridge Assessment of Spoken English (CASE) was a test of oral proficiency designed to assess both the linguistic and communication skills necessary for oral communication between non-native and other speakers of English in a wide variety of contexts. CASE was a 2-stage assessment, carried out by two trained examiners with groups of six candidates. Stage 1 involved a 5-minute individual interview with each candidate to provide an impression check of their level; for Stage 2 each candidate was matched with a partner and both took part in a paired, task-based interaction lasting 13–15 minutes. (For more details of the development and format of CASE, see Lazaraton 1996a, b, 2002, Milanovic et al 1996.)

The CASE Speaking test option was included in the early draft specifications for IELTS and was considered by the IELTS Advisory Committee at their meeting in August 1993; however, committee members were unable to reach a consensus on its suitability for the IELTS context. Consultants at the Language Testing and Curriculum Centre, Griffith University, Australia, were subsequently commissioned to review the proposal to use CASE; they reported back in early 1994 raising various concerns about the CASE format and recommending the retention of an IELTS Speaking component more like the conventional Oral Proficiency Interview (OPI). The Revision Project team therefore decided not to make changes to the IELTS Speaking test format in 1995 but to continue to explore options for the future and to revise the Speaking component at a later date, after undertaking further research and development work.

The final format of the Speaking and Writing Modules introduced for IELTS in 1995 was as follows:

IELTS Academic and General Training Writing Modules

- one Academic Module and one General Training Module
- no thematic link between the Reading and Writing Modules
- two writing tasks in each Writing Module: Task 1 – minimum 150 words; Task 2 – minimum 250 words
- common assessment criteria across the Writing Modules: *Task Fulfilment*; *Coherence and Cohesion*; *Arguments, Ideas and Evidence*; *Communicative Quality*; *Vocabulary and Sentence Structure*
- length of each Module = 60 minutes

- both Academic and General Training assessed on a 9-band scale
- continuing use of both analytical/profile and holistic/global criteria and descriptors
- enhanced Writing Assessment Guide for examiner training
- continuation of certification procedures for examiners
- continuation of sample monitoring for quality assurance.

IELTS Speaking Module (no significant change to 1989 content/format)

- face-to-face, one-on-one interview
- five phases
- length = 10–15 minutes
- assessed on a global, 9-band scale
- Speaking Assessment Guide for examiner training
- continuation of certification procedures for examiners
- continuation of sample monitoring for quality assurance
- extension of the Speaking test window for administrative reasons.

IELTS research programme from 1995 onwards

Following the introduction of revised IELTS in 1995, a comprehensive research framework was established by the IELTS partners to embrace all activities related to test research and validation; these include everything from routine internal test validation and other research studies carried out by Cambridge ESOL, to the externally managed studies which receive grant funding from the IELTS Australia Board (since 1995) and the British Council (since 1998) – several of which are reported in this volume.

The IELTS Impact Study Project (1995–2003)

Growing professional and public concern about the effects of large-scale tests on educational processes, and on society more generally, stimulated Cambridge ESOL to consider how these effects might be investigated and to establish a long-term research programme exploring the concepts of test impact and consequential validity (Messick 1989). As a high-profile and high-stakes international test, IELTS was considered by Cambridge to be a prime candidate for the investigation of impact; for this reason, as soon as the revised test went live in April 1995, work began in collaboration with a team at Lancaster University to develop suitable research hypotheses, instrumentation, and procedures for monitoring the effect of the test on four key areas:

- the content and nature of classroom activity
- the content and nature of teaching materials
- the views and attitudes of user groups
- the test-taking population and use of test results.

A full account of this work to date is published as Volume 24 in the Studies in Language Testing series (Hawkey 2006).

The IELTS Speaking Revision Project (1998–2001)

As previously discussed, the IELTS 95 Revision Project left the Speaking Module unchanged for a variety of reasons: there was no clear consensus on the approach to take; a number of research studies were in progress and the findings still awaited; added to this, revision of a face-to-face Speaking test is a complex matter, requiring careful management and considerable resources to retrain examiners and re-engineer test delivery systems as well as revise test content and format. All three IELTS partners were anxious to ensure that the major changes to IELTS made in 1995 were given time to 'bed down', and that any future changes to the Speaking test could be adequately resourced and sustained.

Plans to revise the Speaking test were revisited in early 1998 with identification of the key issues which needed addressing. This was informed from a number of sources: a review of the routinely collected candidate score and test performance data for the operational IELTS Speaking test; a review of theoretical and empirical studies on the test conducted between 1992 and 1998, including several reported in this volume (e.g. Brown and Hill 1998, Merrylees and McDowell 1999); a review of other research into speaking assessment, together with work on Speaking test design and delivery for the other Cambridge EFL tests (e.g. Lazaraton 2002). Issues needing attention included those relating to test format, task design, rating scales, examiner/rater behaviour, and processes for test monitoring and validation. At the IELTS Policy Group meeting in June 1998, the IELTS partners agreed to proceed with a formal revision project.

Once again the revision process was guided by Cambridge ESOL's test development and revision methodology, but was conducted in close con-sultation with the other IELTS partners. The following timetable was envis-aged:

Phase 1   Consultation, initial planning   June–December 1998
           and design
Phase 2   Development   January–September 1999

Phase 3	Validation	October 1999–September 2000
Phase 4	Implementation	October 2000–June 2001
Phase 5	Operational	July 2001

From the outset, it was recognised that certain features of the test would remain unchanged:

- the face-to-face, one-on-one format, audio-recorded
- the overall test length (maximum 15 minutes)
- the multi-phase approach.

The revision project concentrated on several key areas in order to achieve greater standardisation of conduct and improve the validity of assessment; activities related to:

- developing a clearer specification of tasks, e.g. in terms of input and expected candidate output, and the revision of the tasks themselves for some phases of the test
- introducing an examiner frame to guide examiner language and behaviour and so increase standardisation of test management
- redeveloping the assessment criteria and rating scale to ensure that the descriptors matched more closely the output from the candidates in relation to the specified tasks
- retraining and restandardising a community of around 1,500 IELTS examiners worldwide using a face-to-face approach, and introducing ongoing quality assurance procedures for this global examiner cadre.

The 1989 Speaking test had been designed with five phases, with phases 2–4 designed to push candidates progressively to their 'linguistic ceiling'. However, analyses of the operational test indicated that Phases 3 and 4, in which the candidate was required to elicit information, to express precise meaning and attitudes, and to speculate, did not always elicit a 'richer' performance; moreover, these elicitation problems led, in turn, to variations in amounts and type of examiner talk.

No change was envisaged to the underlying construct/s of spoken language proficiency which the test producers had always attempted to operationalise in the IELTS Speaking test. Cognitive views of the speech production process at that time (e.g. Garman 1990, Levelt 1989) suggested that the proficient L2 speaker possesses the following competence:

- a wide repertoire of lexis and grammar to enable flexible, appropriate, precise construction of utterances in 'real time' (the knowledge factor)
- a set of established procedures for pronunciation and lexico-grammar, and a set of established 'chunks' of language, all of which enable fluent

performance with 'online' planning reduced to acceptable amounts and timing (the processing factor).

In addition, spoken language tends to be based in social interaction, purposeful and goal-oriented within a specific context, and, while it is capable of being routine and predictable, it also has the capacity for relative creativity and unpredictability.

Research during the late 1980s and early 1990s highlighted various features that are characteristic of oral performance at higher and lower proficiency levels; Tonkyn and Wilson (2004) list some of the key studies which can help oral test designers identify theoretically relevant and discriminating features of performance. More recently, Fulcher (2003) and Luoma (2004) have provided useful summaries of relevant research on spoken language assessment.

Progress on the Speaking Test Revision Project was regularly reported in the *IELTS Annual Review* (between 1998 and 2002). More detailed reports on various phases of the IELTS Speaking Test Revision Project can be found in Cambridge ESOL's quarterly publication *Research Notes* (see Taylor, 2001a, b, Taylor and Jones 2001) as well as other publications (Tonkyn and Wilson 2004).

The IELTS Speaking Test Revision Project was completed on schedule and the revised test became operational from 1 July 2001 in the following format:

IELTS Speaking Module (2001–present)

- face-to-face, one-on-one interview
- three parts: Part 1 – *Introduction and interview*; Part 2 – *Individual long turn*; Part 3 – *Two-way discussion*
- length = 11–14 minutes
- assessed using four analytical criteria and subscales – *Fluency and Coherence; Lexical Resource; Grammatical Range and Accuracy; Pronunciation* – over 9 bands
- new induction and training programme for examiners
- new certification programme for examiners
- continuation of sample monitoring for quality assurance.

Following introduction of the revised Speaking test format in July 2001, attention focused on monitoring its implementation and evaluating its effectiveness. Over 4,000 recordings of live IELTS Speaking tests were collected and organised in 2002–03 to form a spoken language corpus for ongoing investigation and validation of the revised test format. This dataset permits the investigation of key features of the test such as quality of candidate language, aspects of examiner language behaviour, and nature of task output. A variety of methodologies has been used to analyse the spoken language data including transcription analysis, observation checklists, and text analysis software (e.g. WordSmith Tools).

The IELTS Speaking Test Revision Project benefited greatly from the outcomes of discourse and conversation analytic (CA) studies on live test samples (Taylor 2001b); however, the transcription process involved in such studies is far too complex and time-consuming for it to be implemented on a large scale. In the light of this, efforts were made to find alternative approaches to analysis. In 2002 work was completed on developing a tailored observation checklist for use with the IELTS Speaking test (Brooks 2003) based on earlier work to develop a checklist for Cambridge's paired Speaking tests (O'Sullivan, Weir and Saville 2002); the observation checklist instrument identifies the language functions (*informational, interactional,* and *managing interaction*) associated with particular tasks and is capable of producing a profile of language elicited across several different tasks within a Speaking test. The checklist was applied to more than 70 IELTS Speaking tests in the context of two specific research studies. The first study explored the range and distribution of speech functions occurring across the three parts of the revised test format and across different test versions; the second study compared the range and distribution of speech functions occurring in the revised format and pre-2001 format (Brooks 2002). Findings from these studies confirmed that the revised format is capable of eliciting a broad range of speech functions overall and that all three categories of function are represented in varying degrees. As such, they provide useful validation evidence in support of the revised test's effectiveness and complemented earlier CA-based validation studies which took place during the revision project (Lazaraton 1998).

Both internal and externally commissioned studies continue to be undertaken to explore various aspects of the spoken language produced by IELTS test takers and examiners, and the IELTS Speaking test corpus has recently proved a valuable source of data for researchers awarded grant funding under the IELTS Joint-funded Research Program (e.g. Read and Nation 2004, Seedhouse and Egbert 2006).

The IELTS Writing Revision Project (2001–05)

The IELTS Writing Revision Project began in June 2001 with three main objectives:

- the development of revised rating scales including a definition of assessment criteria and revised band descriptors (Task 1 and Task 2 for both the General Training and the Academic Modules)
- the development of materials for training trainers and examiners

- the development of new certification/recertification sets and procedures for examiners.

No changes were envisaged to the content or format of the Writing Test Modules since these had been significantly revised under the IELTS 95 Revision Project (see p. 15). The focus instead was on revising the assessment criteria and rating scales taking into account results from internal routine validation analyses and specially designed experimental studies (including several in this volume), as well as a survey of recent literature in the area of writing assessment and feedback from stakeholder groups (e.g. trainers, examiners); the overarching aim, as always, was to improve on the validity, reliability, positive impact and practicality of the assessment procedures.

The IELTS Writing Revision Project adopted a similar approach to that used successfully for the Speaking Test Revision Project and was broken down into five phases:

Phase 1	Consultation, initial planning and design	June–December 2001
Phase 2	Development	January 2002–April 2003
Phase 3	Validation	May 2003–April 2004
Phase 4	Implementation	May–December 2004
Phase 5	Operational	January 2005

Progress on the revision project was regularly reported in the *IELTS Annual Review* (from 2001 onwards). More detailed reports on all phases appeared in Cambridge ESOL's quarterly publication *Research Notes* (Bridges and Shaw 2004, Shaw 2002a, b, 2004a, b). A full report on the completed project is available as a web-based publication (Shaw and Falvey, forthcoming).

The project was completed on schedule and the revised assessment criteria and band descriptors became operational from 1 January 2005. The revised approach for the Writing Module is shown below.

IELTS Academic Writing Module 2005

- two writing tasks: Task 1 – minimum 150 words; Task 2 – minimum 250 words
- Task 1 assessment criteria: *Task Achievement*; *Coherence and Cohesion*; *Lexical Resource*; *Grammatical Range and Accuracy*
- Task 2 assessment criteria: *Task Response*; *Coherence and Cohesion*; *Lexical Resource*; *Grammatical Range and Accuracy*
- length = 60 minutes
- assessed on a 9-band scale
- use of analytical/profile criteria and descriptors

- enhanced examiner training, certification and monitoring procedures for quality assurance.

IELTS General Training Writing Module 2005

- two writing tasks: Task 1 – minimum 150 words; Task 2 – minimum 250 words
- Task 1 assessment criteria: *Task Achievement; Coherence and Cohesion; Lexical Resource; Grammatical Range and Accuracy*
- Task 2 assessment criteria: *Task Response; Coherence and Cohesion; Lexical Resource; Grammatical Range and Accuracy*
- length = 60 minutes
- assessed on a 9-band scale
- use of analytical/profile criteria and descriptors
- enhanced examiner training, certification and monitoring procedures for quality assurance.

The current approach to assessing speaking and writing in IELTS

Extensive revisions to the IELTS Speaking and Writing components over the past 10 years have made it possible to address many of the earlier concerns raised about quality and fairness issues for these subjectively rated subtests. A comprehensive and transparent set of test production and validation procedures is now in place to support claims about the usefulness of IELTS Speaking and Writing assessment; information on technical qualities of these subtests is increasingly available in the public domain; and research studies continue to explore a range of issues in preparation for future test revision and development cycles. Some of these aspects are described in more detail in the sections which follow.

The production of IELTS Speaking and Writing test materials

The IELTS Question Paper Production (QPP) cycle involves checking all material produced for the IELTS test against quality standards. The objective is to ensure that the material in the test covers the range called for by the specifications and is of proven quality. The QPP process uses both *qualitative* standards for the production of test material involving the judgement of qualified professionals, and *quantitative*, statistical standards for the selection of suitable test material and the maintenance of consistent levels of test difficulty over time. The process is summarised in Figure 1. Initial

Figure 1 The Question Paper Production process for IELTS

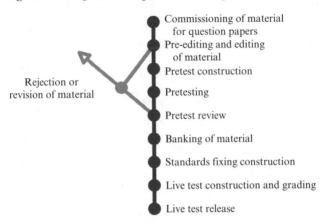

stages of commissioning, pre-editing and editing involve the selection of appropriate test content that reflects the aims of the Academic and General Training Modules. The material is then pretested (Listening and Reading) or trialled (Speaking and Writing) with representative groups of candidates, to ensure that it is appropriately challenging and that it discriminates between more and less able candidates. Finally, listening and reading material is banked before being introduced to the live test in stages through a process known as standards fixing so that it can be related to the established IELTS metric; after successful trialling and review, speaking and writing tasks are located in the test construction bank to await compilation into live sets of material.

Commissioning

There are one or two commissions each year for each of the item writing teams. These feed material into the Question Paper Production process. To reflect the international nature of IELTS, test material is written by trained groups of item writers in the United Kingdom, Australia and New Zealand and is drawn from publications sourced anywhere in the world. Overall test content is the shared responsibility of both externally commissioned language testing professionals (the Chairs of the item-writing teams for each paper – Listening, Reading, Writing and Speaking) and of Cambridge ESOL staff.

Item writers work from a version of the test specifications which details the specific characteristics of the six IELTS modules, outlines the requirements for commissions and guides writers in how to approach the item writing process including the selection of appropriate material, the development of questions and the submission of material for pre-editing and editing.

Pre-editing

Pre-editing is the first stage of the editing process and takes place when commissioned materials are initially submitted in draft form by item writers. A meeting is held involving Chairs of the papers and Cambridge ESOL staff to review the material. At this stage, guidance is given to item writers on revising items and altering texts, and advising on rejected texts and/or unsuitable item types.

The purpose of pre-editing is to ensure that all test material is suitable for editing; is culturally appropriate and accessible worldwide; and meets the test specifications. Further, it is there to suggest appropriate changes to materials requiring amendments or rewriting. With respect to these considerations, the pre-editing process includes attention to the following task features:

* topic
* topicality
* level of language
* suitability for the task
* length.

Editing

Following pre-editing feedback, material is completed and submitted for editing. Editing takes place at meetings involving Cambridge ESOL staff and Chairs of papers. Item writers are encouraged to participate in editing meetings dealing with their material. This is seen as an important part of their ongoing training. At editing, texts and selected items are approved for pretesting or are sent back to a writer for further revision. Revised material is then re-edited at a subsequent meeting.

Pretest construction and pretesting

IELTS pretests are similar to live modules, including task rubrics (instructions) and examples. Writing and Speaking pretests are administered to representative samples of candidates to assess the appropriateness of this material for use in live tests and to establish that the tasks are capable of eliciting an adequate sample of language to allow for the assessment of candidates against the scoring criteria.

Pretest review

The Research and Validation Group at Cambridge ESOL collates and analyses the pretest material. Writing pretest scripts are double-marked by experienced IELTS examiners and their comments are scrutinised to assess the suitability of tasks for inclusion in live versions. The feedback on the trialling of the Speaking tasks is reviewed and evaluated. At a pretest review meeting, the statistics, the feedback from candidates and teachers, and additional information are all reviewed; informed decisions are made on whether tasks can be accepted for construction into potential live versions. Material is then banked to await test construction. Cambridge ESOL has developed its own item banking software for managing the development of new live tests. Each speaking or writing task is banked with a comprehensive content description. This information is used to ensure that the test versions which are constructed have the required content coverage, including a balance of topic and genre.

Assuring the quality and fairness of IELTS Writing and Speaking assessment

Single rating of the performance components (Writing and Speaking) has always been a feature of IELTS as it was of the original ELTS. Concern is sometimes expressed about the extent to which an acceptable level of reliability can be achieved where a single rating approach is adopted; the challenge for any test developer, however, is to provide a level of reliability adequate to the purposes of a test while at the same time keeping the cost of the test within reasonable limits, i.e. there is a balance to be achieved between the demands of reliability and those of practicality. It would also be naive to assume that the reliability of any test resides solely in the quality of the rating involved, as reflected in a statistic; other significant factors which impact on test reliability include aspects of test format, task design, administrative conditions, assessment criteria, rating scales and rater training. It is clearly important for all these aspects to receive adequate attention during any revision project.

Interestingly, Lee, Kantor and Mollaun (2002) investigated single versus double rating in the context of the development and validation of Writing and Speaking tasks for the new TOEFL; they reported that 'adopting a single rating scheme would have a smaller effect on the score reliability than expected for both writing and speaking' and that increasing the number of tasks provides a cost efficient way to maximise the score reliability. It is precisely for this reason that there are two tasks in the IELTS Writing Module and three parts in the IELTS Speaking Module.

Evidence that satisfactory levels of reliability can be achieved using single rating models was provided during the IELTS Speaking and Writing

Revision Projects. For example, an experimental G-study carried out during the Speaking Test Revision Project produced an inter-rater reliability of 0.77, and a g-coefficient of 0.86 for the operational single-rater condition (Taylor and Jones 2001). An experimental G-study carried out during the Writing Test Revision Project produced an inter-rater reliability of 0.77 and g-coefficients of 0.85–0.93 for the operational single-rater condition (Shaw 2004b).

Reliability of rating for IELTS is partly assured through the face-to-face training and certification of IELTS examiners; all examiners must undergo a retraining and certification process every two years (Bridges and Shaw 2004, Taylor 2001b). In addition, a sample monitoring process requires selected centres worldwide to provide a representative sample of examiners' marked tapes and scripts such that all examiners working at a centre over a given period are represented. (All IELTS Speaking tests are routinely recorded for quality assurance purposes.) Tapes and scripts are then second-marked by a team of experienced IELTS examiners worldwide. Examiners monitor for quality of both test conduct and rating, and feedback is returned to each centre for follow-up with individual examiners.

Since the late 1990s, the IELTS partners have been working to build up a Professional Support Network (PSN) to manage and standardise the IELTS examiner cadre (along the lines of the TL system which has been in place for the Cambridge Speaking tests since 1994). This system includes provision for face-to-face and/or distance (i.e. cassette-based) monitoring of examiners by more experienced examiners and trainers; such an approach supplements the traditional sample monitoring which IELTS has always had and it offers an additional means of controlling potential variability of examiner conduct and assessment which can threaten reliability. The PSN system is expected to be fully in place by the end of 2006.

To maintain a further check on the worldwide reliability of IELTS perform- ance assessment, a 'jagged profile' system was introduced alongside sample monitoring in 1995. The jagged profile system involves routine targeted double marking of candidates identified as being at risk of misclassification, based on the level of divergence between their Writing and/or Speaking scores and their Reading and Listening scores. (It has been estimated that approximately 8% of candidates have their Writing or Speaking performances re-marked because their profiles are identified as jagged.) In addition, candidates who are unhappy with their results can also ask for an enquiry on results which involves any or all of the four modules being re-marked.

At the time of writing, an alternative solution is being explored at Cambridge which combines 'jagged profile' marking (to identify and double mark potentially 'at risk' candidates) with 'targeted sample monitoring' (to identify those examiners who may be putting candidates at risk by faulty rating). Such a development is consistent with the IELTS partners' ongoing commitment to improve quality management and assurance systems for IELTS as this becomes possible through improvements in technology, knowledge, expertise, etc. Assuring quality and fairness in IELTS Writing and Speaking assessment thus depends upon a multi-faceted strategy made up of various components (see Table 1).

Table 1 Systems and procedures to ensure quality and fairness in IELTS Writing and Speaking assessment

Pre live test	During live test delivery	Post live test
QP Production	*Administration*	*Jagged profile system*
• test format	• standardised procedures	
• task design		*Enquiries on results*
• trialling		
		Routine validation of:
Examiners	*Examiner conduct*	• task performance
• training	• interlocutor frame	• candidate performance
• certification	• analytical assessment	• examiner performance
• trainer-led	criteria and scales	• targeted sample
standardisation		monitoring
• 'focus on procedure'		
(FOP) video		*Public reporting*
• self-access norming		
• distance and local		
monitoring		
• recertification		

Estimating and reporting reliability of IELTS Writing and Speaking assessment

Since 2001 the IELTS Annual Review has reported the range of mean band scores for Writing (Academic and General Training) and Speaking test versions released each year; results show a very consistent pattern across different versions over time and support claims about task comparability (see below). Annual Reviews have also routinely reported inter-rater correlations for the Writing and Speaking test scores based on analyses of sample monitoring data available. Current testing practice tends to regard a figure of 0.8 or above as acceptable evidence of reliability of rating for subjectively scored performance components. In recent years this figure has been routinely achieved for the IELTS Writing and Speaking tests. Results from the most recent sample monitoring analyses available (for 2003 data) have produced an average correlation between original examiner and Senior Examiner of 0.91 for both Writing and Speaking Modules.

It is customary to use inter-rater correlations in calculating the reliability of subjectively marked tests such as the Writing and Speaking components.

Table 2 Mean, standard deviation and standard error of measurement (SEM) for Writing and Speaking

	Mean	Standard deviation	Standard error of measurement
Academic Writing	5.74	1.07	0.43
General Training Writing	5.89	1.13	0.46
Speaking	6.04	1.12	0.46

Where a single rater is employed, the Spearman-Brown formula given below can be used to generalise to the case of a single rater from the correlation found between two ratings.

$$r_{nn} = \frac{nr_{11}}{1 + (n-1)r_{11}}$$

n is the length of the test (here n = 0.5 to represent one rather than two raters)
r_{11} is the reliability of the test under the paired rating condition

This formula gives a reliability of 0.84 for the Writing and Speaking Modules.

The SEM derived from the reliability figures should be interpreted in terms of the final band scores reported for Writing and Speaking (which are currently reported as whole bands).

Performance of test materials in the Writing and Speaking Modules is routinely analysed to check on the comparability of different test versions and to ensure any variation is within the acceptable limit of 0.5 of a band. Mean band scores for the Academic Writing versions released in September 2003, and for which a sufficient sample size was available, ranged from 5.54 to 6.01 (variation of 0.47 of a band). Mean band scores for the General Training Writing versions released in September 2003 ranged from 5.62 to 6.05 (variation of 0.43 of a band). Mean band scores for Speaking versions released in September 2003 ranged from 5.94 to 6.27 (variation of 0.33 of a band). The analysis for both Writing and Speaking materials shows a consistent pattern across different test versions over time.

Information on test quality now appears routinely on the IELTS website as part of annual reporting on test performance.

Current and future developments

This introductory section has attempted to trace the development of the Speaking and Writing subtests in ELTS/IELTS from the earliest days of their existence up to the present time. Direct assessment of written/spoken language ability presents language test developers with complex theoretical and practical challenges; it is not surprising therefore that some testing agencies avoid using a direct approach for one or both of these skills. From 1980 onwards, ELTS and later IELTS chose to include mandatory Writing and Speaking components on the grounds that these are fundamental components within the overall language proficiency construct and that the direct method offers the best approach for assessing written and/or spoken ability.

The success of the ELTS/IELTS Writing and Speaking Modules has always depended upon the close and professional relationship maintained between the three IELTS partners, which reflects a willingness to regularly review the status quo and to embrace change as required as well as a readiness to share responsibility in matters of test design, production, delivery and processing: at the current time, Cambridge ESOL takes responsibility for matters of test design and production, while the British Council and IDP: IELTS Australia provide the global centre network and manage the worldwide examiner cadre. Advances in applied linguistics, language pedagogy, measurement understanding and technological capabilities constantly challenge test developers to review, refine and reshape their approaches to test design, development, delivery and evaluation; the steady evolution of ELTS/IELTS since the mid-1970s testifies to this reality and clearly demonstrates how such factors shape the life of a large-scale, high-stakes language proficiency measure. The strength of the international IELTS partnership has meant that each new era of challenge has led to creative and innovative responses which seek not only to ensure the intrinsic value of the test in terms of its contemporary relevance and continuing usefulness for immediate test stakeholders, but also to contribute more broadly to our growing understanding of the nature of language proficiency and its place within linguistics and language education.

For example, alongside the IELTS Writing Revision Project, Cambridge ESOL has been undertaking a major research study to explore the linguistic and functional relationships between levels of writing performance in IELTS and in the other Cambridge English examinations (e.g. First Certificate, Certificate of Proficiency). This work forms part of a larger endeavour to establish a common scale for second language writing ability and to determine comparability across different language proficiency measures (see Hawkey and Barker 2004); a further goal is to be able to map levels of writing performance in IELTS onto the proficiency levels of the Common European Framework of Reference (2001), and to analyse how the study-oriented 'Can Do' performance descriptors produced by ALTE can be used in relation to performance on the IELTS tests. This type of study benefits greatly from corpus-based analyses so a feasibility study was undertaken in 2002 to explore how IELTS Writing scripts could be incorporated into the existing

Cambridge Learner Corpus (CLC). The CLC is a computerised database of contemporary written learner English – developed jointly with Cambridge University Press – and, at the time of writing, stands at around 22 million words. In 2002 the IELTS partners formally agreed to allow scripts to be entered into the CLC from the middle of 2003; in time this will enable quantitative analysis of large amounts of data from the written responses of IELTS candidates.

Another major area of innovation over recent years has been the joint development by the IELTS partners of a computer-based variant of IELTS (CB IELTS) in response to the growing use of computer-based technology in language teaching and learning. CB IELTS – introduced in 2005 – is a linear (rather than adaptive), computer-based test containing a fixed number of items and offers an alternative mode for IELTS users. Candidates opting to take CB IELTS Listening and Reading tests are given the option of taking the Writing test on screen or on paper; all candidates still take the face-to-face Speaking test. As further research and development work takes place, and as ever more sophisticated technological options become available, so the future assessment of speaking and writing in IELTS is likely to evolve in new and innovative ways.

Conclusion

Nearly 20 years ago, in their introduction to the published proceedings of the conference held in October 1986 to consider the ELTS Validation Project Report, Hughes, Porter and Weir (1988) made the following comment:

> The publication of a detailed validation study represents an exercise in public accountability: the question of how far the test does the job it was intended to do is addressed, and is seen to be addressed. The information yielded by such a study is moreover of fundamental importance in the dynamic process of continuing test development. The ELTS test is itself not a static instrument . . . (1988: 4).

Hopefully, this introductory section has succeeded in demonstrating the extent to which IELTS, like its predecessor ELTS, is not a 'static instrument' but continues to experience a 'dynamic process of continuing test development'. The 10 research studies which were funded and supported by the IELTS partners and which are included in this volume represent a major contribution to that ongoing and dynamic process. As will be apparent from the discussion in the research impact sections located at the end of the sections containing the speaking and writing reports, they complement other IELTS-related research (both internal and externally commissioned) in the ongoing effort to provide a quality measurement instrument for assessing language proficiency. Like several of the other recent volumes in the Studies in Language Testing series, this volume seeks to be 'an exercise in public accountability'.

Dr Lynda Taylor
June 2006

Part 1
Speaking

1 Interviewer style and candidate performance in the IELTS oral interview

Annie Brown and Kathryn Hill

Abstract

Recent research into the validity of oral language interviews has extended the focus beyond that of statistical analysis to investigations of the structure of the interview discourse itself, and to the language produced by both candidate and interviewer. Research has indicated that, despite training, interviewer behaviour varies considerably in terms of the amount of support they give candidates, the amount of rapport raters consider them to have established with candidates and the extent to which they follow the instructions in terms of the type of discourse elicited from candidates. While several writers allude to the potential of such variable interviewer behaviour to affect the validity of tests, studies have not yet empirically investigated the relationship between interviewer behaviour and candidate performance.

This study aims first to investigate the extent to which differential behaviour by IELTS interviewers affects the scores awarded to candidates and to identify interviewers who consistently present a difficult or easy challenge to candidates. The second part of the study involves a discourse analysis of the contributions of 'difficult' and 'easy' interviewers, and aims to identify aspects of interviewer behaviour which contribute to the challenge they present.

The study is based on interviews undertaken with 32 candidates, each of whom was interviewed twice by two different interviewers. Six interviewers took part in the study. The interviews were audio-taped and multiple-rated.

The test data were analysed using the multifaceted Rasch analysis program FACETS (Linacre 1989) in order to identify cases where candidates perform differentially in the two interviews, as well as identifying interviewers who consistently elicit poorer or better performance. A total of 10 interviews from the two most difficult and two easiest interviewers were transcribed and analysed.

It was found that the easier interviewers tended to shift topic more frequently and asked simpler questions, spending longer in Phase 2 of the interview. The more difficult interviewers tended to use a broader range of interactional behaviours, such as interruption and disagreement as well as asking more challenging questions.

While the intent in the development of the IELTS interview has not been to standardise interviewer behaviour to the extent that all candidates receive exactly the same prompts, there must be some concern to ensure that all candidates are treated equally in terms of the challenge presented by the interviewer. By making explicit those features of interviewer behaviour which have the potential to affect the quality of the candidates' performance, this study is of relevance to the training of raters in terms of increasing their understanding of the effect of their performance on that of the candidate and in ensuring the comparability of the challenge presented to different candidates.

1 Introduction

This paper reports on a study into the extent to which differential behaviour by IELTS interviewers can affect the scores awarded to candidates, and which features of interviewer behaviour might contribute to this. Until recently there has been little focus on interviewer variation and the effect this might have on candidates' scores, the assumption being that variability in interviewer behaviour is not a source of unreliability in the same way as variability of rater behaviour or even of task are. Test developers have long been aware of the variability inherent in rater behaviour. Steps are generally taken to minimise this variability through the provision of explicit band descriptors, through initial and follow-up rater training, through the use of multiple ratings and, in some cases, through the use of Item Response Theory to compensate for rater harshness. Using Item Response Theory, test tasks may be equated or scores may be adjusted to compensate for variation. Little, however, is yet understood about the extent of interviewer variation and its implications. This study attempts to add some understanding to what is a growing area of concern among language testers.

Oral interviews, such as those forming part of the IELTS test, generally follow a prescribed format. Interviewer training introduces prospective interviewers to the format of the interview and to relevant interviewing techniques. Nevertheless, the intent is normally *not* to standardise interviewer behaviour to the extent that all candidates receive exactly the same prompts; however, it would seem that personality and background factors are likely to influence the interviewing style adopted by individuals (just as they have been found to affect the awarding of scores) so there must, nevertheless, be some concern to ensure that all candidates are treated equally in terms of the support and challenge offered by the interviewer. Research into the discourse produced in oral interviews and the effect of individual interviewers on candidate performance can inform interviewer training and contribute to fairness for candidates.

This study aims to explore interviewer differences in both quantitative and qualitative terms. It does this first, by identifying whether interviewer style does in fact have an effect on scores, and second by using discourse analysis to explore the features of interviewing style which characterise 'difficult' and 'easy' interviewers; 'difficult' interviewers being those with whom a candidate is more likely to receive a lower score than with an 'easy' one. It is hoped that the findings of this study will contribute to the understandings beginning to emerge from other research into interviewer behaviour, and inform the process of interviewer training.

2 Research into interviewer behaviour

In the last few years, research into oral language interviews has begun to investigate the discourse produced by the participants. This research indicates that, despite training, interviewer behaviour appears to vary considerably in terms of the amount of support given to candidates (Lazaraton and Saville 1994, Ross 1992, Ross and Berwick 1990), the amount of rapport established with candidates (Lumley and McNamara 1993), and the extent to which the interviewer guidelines are followed in terms of the type of discourse elicited from candidates (Lazaraton 1993, Lumley and Brown 1996).

Ross and Berwick (1990) demonstrated a relationship between the amount of accommodation (modification of the 'form and content of the discourse in order to facilitate communication') provided by an interviewer and the score awarded. However, there has been no research into whether different interviewers interviewing *the same candidate* vary in the amount of accommodation they make and whether this might have an effect on the score awarded; in other words, whether the candidate would get a different score depending on who the interviewer was.

Ross (1992) again investigated accommodation within oral interviews, this time identifying the causes of accommodation. Using variable rule analysis he identified four factors: interviewee response to previous question, structure of response to previous question, outcome of the interview, and use of accommodation in the previous question. Again, however, no comparison of the use of accommodation was made across interviewers.

Lazaraton and Saville's 1993 study reported on an investigation of interviewer difficulty in CASE. However, as candidates were not double tested, it is not clear how the measures of interviewer difficulty were arrived at. Nevertheless, the authors identify several aspects of interlocutor support, including supplying vocabulary, rephrasing questions, evaluating responses, echoing and correcting responses, using interview prompts that require only confirmation and drawing conclusions for candidates.

In another study Lumley and McNamara (1993) obtained multiple ratings of Occupational English Test (OET) interviews. In addition to providing ratings of the candidates using the normal test rating scale, raters were asked to provide an assessment of the rapport established between interviewer and candidate. They found that raters tended to compensate for what they perceived as poor rapport. In other words, candidates received higher scores where the interviewer was perceived by the rater as 'difficult'. This finding is relevant to the present study in that interviewer 'difficulty' may be masked because of compensation by the raters.

Lumley and Brown (1996) investigated nurses' perceptions of interviewer performance in OET role plays. They found that a wide variety of behaviours were considered 'authentic' but that different challenges were set for candidates according to the extent to which interviewers performed the role play as instructed, i.e. with some degree of conflict, rather than engaging in more 'teacher-like' behaviour and supporting and agreeing with the candidate. Again, no study was made of the effect different interviewers might have on perceptions of candidate ability. Nevertheless, a discourse analysis did indicate that certain interviewers have entrenched patterns of behaviour, that is, they consistently provided more or less support than other interviewers.

In conclusion, despite the growing literature on observed interviewer variation in terms of the discourse they produce, there has to date been little empirical analysis of the relationship between this and candidate scores. This study combines a qualitative approach, involving the analysis of actual test interactions, with a quantitative study using multiple interviews conducted by trained IELTS interviewers and multiple ratings. The stages of the study are as follows:

1. Using multifaceted Rasch analysis, determine whether different interviewers represent different 'hurdles' in terms of the difficulty of doing an IELTS interview.
2. Identify cases where candidates perform differentially in each of the two interviews they undertake.
3. Transcribe and analyse these interviews in order to identify whether there are particular interviewing styles which characterise 'easy' or 'difficult' interviewers and which may contribute to better or worse performance by candidates.

3 The IELTS interview and rating

The IELTS Speaking Module[1] takes between 10 and 15 minutes. It consists of an oral interview, a conversation between the candidate and a trained interviewer/assessor. There are five sections:

Introduction	The candidate is encouraged to talk briefly about his/her life, home, work and interests.
Extended Discourse	The candidate is encouraged to speak at length about some very familiar topic either of general interest or of relevance to their culture, place of living, or country of origin. This will involve explanation, description or narration.
Elicitation	The candidate is given a task card with some information on it and is encouraged to take the initiative and ask questions either to elicit information or to solve a problem. Tasks are based on 'information gap' type activities.
Speculation and Attitudes	The candidate is encouraged to talk about their future plans and proposed course of study. Alternatively the examiner may choose to return to a topic raised earlier.
Conclusion	The interview is concluded.

The interview is scored using a set of global band scales with 10 levels (0–9). (IELTS Handbook 1997, Cambridge: UCLES.)

4 Methodology

Thirty-two students from IELTS preparation courses and six accredited interviewers participated in this study. Each of the 32 candidates was interviewed twice by two different interviewers. In order to ensure that candidates were not exposed to the same topic twice, and to avoid any practice effect, in this study the suggested interview topics for the Extended Discourse section (Phase 2) and Speculation and Attitudes section (Phase 4) were divided into two lists. Interviewers were instructed to draw either on List A or on List B for each interview. See Appendix 1.1 for the information given to the interviewers about the phases of the interview and their content focus.

The interviews were audio-taped and each tape was later rated by four accredited IELTS raters.

The candidates were all ELICOS students who at the time of the interviews were preparing to take IELTS prior to submitting applications for tertiary study in Australia. Hence there was a high level of motivation on the part of the candidates to take part in the interviews so as to gauge their readiness to take the test. Candidates were informed that if they agreed to take part in the study, undertaking two IELTS interviews each, they would receive an informal assessment of their proficiency in the oral component of IELTS. This assessment was given at the end of the second interview rather than the first interview as this would potentially discourage the candidate from proceeding to the second interview.

The interviewers were all accredited and practising IELTS interviewers who responded to a request for assistance with an IELTS research project. In order not to affect their behaviour when interviewing, they were not given any information about the focus of the research other than that it was 'looking at' the IELTS interview; most assumed that the focus was on the candidates. After the interviews had been completed, they were informed of the aims of the study.

Each of the 32 candidates was interviewed twice, each time by different interviewers. The interviews were carefully planned so that the interviewers were equally assigned to first and second interviews, and so that they over-lapped in their pairings, i.e. they were each paired with several of the other interviewers rather than being paired with just one in order to allow for cali-bration of the interviewers against each other. Where two interviewers inter-viewed several candidates in common, the number of first and second interviews each carried out by each interviewer was balanced. As has already been mentioned, the interviews were controlled to the extent that no candi-date was subjected to the same Phase 2 and 4 topics in either interview in order to avoid a practice effect.

The interviews were audio-taped and each interview was later rated from the tape by accredited IELTS raters.[2] In order to take rater harshness into account (i.e. to compensate for it in the estimate of candidate ability), each tape was rated four times using a patterned design of any four of the seven raters employed. This overlap between raters enables the program used to analyse the data to model 'rater' as a facet and hence compensate for the effect of rater harshness.

The analysis was done in two stages:

(a) The multifaceted Rasch analysis program FACETS (Linacre 1989) was used to analyse the test data. Facets which are normally considered to contribute to a candidate's score are candidate ability and rater harshness.[3] In this study we are trying to determine whether interviewer 'difficulty' may be an additional factor. Specifically, we wanted to identify whether different interviewers represent different 'hurdles' for candidates in terms of the difficulty of doing an IELTS interview, in that they consistently elicit poorer or better performances from candidates.

Through the use of IRT analysis it is possible to compensate for rater harshness and derive candidates' 'fair scores'.[4] We were able therefore to identify cases where, after compensating for the effect of the particular raters involved, a candidate's performance in the two interviews was judged to be at two different levels of ability, and also to identify the extent of the difference.

(b) In the second part of the analysis, pairs of interviews were chosen where the same candidate performed at different levels and selected interviews were transcribed. An analysis was undertaken in order to identify whether there are particular patterns of interviewer behaviour which contribute to better or worse performance by candidates. While differential performance may be due to factors other than interviewer behaviour, such as choice of topic, motivation or other aspects of the interviewer-candidate relationship, this study attempts to isolate those features of interviewer behaviour which co-vary with candidate performance. The analysis focused on a range of potentially relevant aspects of interview technique. These were drawn to some extent from previous research into oral interview discourse and included aspects such as questioning technique and topic organisation.

5 The analysis

Question 1: Are there significant differences in interviewer difficulty?

An analysis (Analysis 1) was carried out using FACETS, with four facets: *candidate*, *interviewer*, *occasion* and *rater*, in order to estimate interviewer difficulty. The findings of this analysis are shown in Table 1.1.

The interviewer difficulty measures are presented in logits, the units of measurement used within Rasch analysis (see Appendix 1.2). As can be seen, these range from 0.75 logits (the most difficult interviewer) to −0.86 logits (the easiest interviewer). The separation information given within the FACETS analysis and reproduced in Table 1.1 confirms that there are significant differences amongst this group of interviewers in terms of their

Table 1.1 Interviewer difficulty

	Interviewer ID	Interviewer difficulty (logits)	Model SE	Model fit Infit		Outfit	
				MnSq	Std	MnSq	Std
most difficult	5	0.75	0.42	0.4	−2	0.3	−2
	6	0.48	0.45	1.1	0	1.1	0
	3	0.15	0.22	0.9	0	1.0	0
	1	0.01	0.24	1.0	0	1.0	0
	2	−0.52	0.33	1.4	1	1.4	1
easiest	4	−0.86	0.25	0.7	−1	0.7	−1

RMSE 0.33 Adj S.D. 0.44 Separation 1.34 Reliability 0.64
Fixed (all same) chi-square: 17.9 d.f.: 5 significance: .00
Random (normal) chi-square: 4.9 d.f.: 4 significance: .30

difficulty: the interviewer separation index indicates 1.34 statistically distinct interviewer strata,[5] separated with a reliability of 0.64. This means that the probability that the differences between interviewers are due to chance is low. There is a greater possibility that the differences are significant. The low reliability (generally 0.8 is considered acceptable) is most likely a consequence of the small sample size. In addition, there is a 0.00 probability that the interviewers can be considered equally severe (the 'fixed' chi-square). This means that the chances that the interviewers are equally severe are very low (0.00 probability), although this likelihood is slightly lessened by the fact that there is a 0.30 probability that they are not sampled at random from a normally distributed population (the 'random' chi-square). This latter statistic is also likely to be a consequence of the small sample size.

Turning to the fit of the interviewers to the model, as shown in Table 1.1, we can consider all the interviewers to be reasonably well fitting to the model. That is, none of the fit indices are unacceptably high (standardised scores ranging from +2 to −2 are generally considered acceptable). The highest is interviewer 2, one of the easier interviewers, at 1 and the lowest and most severe interviewer 5 at − 2.

In order to determine exactly which pairs of raters presented a significantly different level of difficulty for candidates, the following calculation was carried out:

Is the difference in difficulty measures greater than the square root of the sum of the two standard errors squared?

$$\text{Is } d1 - d2 > \checkmark (se^2 + se^2) \, ?$$

To take an example, the difference between the difficulty measures of Interviewer 5 (the most difficult) and Interviewer 4 (the easiest) is 1.61 logits. The square root of the sum of the squared standard errors of these two difficulty measures is 0.97. Therefore, as 1.61 is greater than 0.97, the two interviewers can be considered to be significantly different in difficulty.

The result of this calculation is presented in Table 1.2. Here, Interviewer 4 (the 'easiest') presents a significantly different level of difficulty from interviewers 5, 6, 3 and 1 (the four most 'difficult' interviewers). In addition, interviewer 2 (the second 'easiest') presents a significantly different level of difficulty from interviewer 5 (the most 'difficult').

It appears then, that interviewer difficulty may well affect a candidate's chances, in that the ability level construed for the candidate will be *not only* a result of his/her inherent ability, but *also* of the difficulty presented by the interviewer. This will be particularly the case where an interviewer at the extremes of the 'difficulty' continuum is used.

Table 1.2 Paired differences in interviewers

Pairs of Interviewers	Difference in Difficulty (d1–d2) (logits)	√(se² + se²)	Significant Difference
5 and 4	1.61	0.97	✓
5 and 2	1.27	1.07	✓
5 and 1	0.74	0.97	–
6 and 4	1.34	1.03	✓
6 and 2	1.00	1.12	–
3 and 4	1.01	0.67	✓
3 and 2	0.67	0.79	–
1 and 4	0.87	0.69	✓
2 and 4	0.34	0.83	–

Question 2: Can we identify pairs of interviews where the same candidate was judged as being of a different level of ability on each occasion, and to what extent are these differences consistent with interviewer difficulty?

Before comparing scores across the two interviews it was necessary to ascertain the extent of any effect for 'occasion' (first or second interview). It was conceivable that any of a number of factors may come into play here to either increase or decrease the 'difficulty' of the second interview in relation to the first. It was, for example, possible that there may be a practice effect which would make it easier for candidates to gain a higher score on the second interview. While the topics had been carefully assigned to ensure that no candidate was exposed to exactly the same Phase 2 and 4 topics, there was still the likelihood that the format would be more familiar and hence easier the second time around. On the other hand, it was also conceivable that fatigue or boredom might have the opposite effect, with candidates scoring lower on the second interview.

The FACETS analysis which included 'occasion' as a facet (Analysis 1) confirmed that occasion did indeed present a significant difficulty factor. The separation information on the facet 'occasion' was: Separation 1.99; Reliability 0.80; Fixed (all same) chi-square: 9.9; d.f.: 1; significance: 0.00.

We were able to determine the extent of the effect of occasion by comparing the mean fair score (an average score adjusted for rater harshness but not converted to a logit) for all first interviews with the mean fair score for all second interviews. In order to do this a further FACETS analysis (Analysis 2) was set up with two facets, *candidate* and *rater*. In this analysis each interview was treated independently, resulting in two scores for each candidate, i.e. one for each interview. A grouping facility was used to enable us to compare the mean of all occasion 1 scores with the mean of all occasion 2 scores. When the means of the fair scores on each occasion were compared, a difference of 0.2 of a band was found, with the first interview attracting the higher score.

In order to make the first and second interview comparable 0.2 was added to the fair score of each candidate for the second interview. We then compared pairs of interviews involving the same candidate in order to identify first, cases where candidates received a different score on each occasion, and second, whether these differences were consistent with what was known about the relative difficulty of the interviewers involved.

As not all interviewers were significantly different from each other, we only considered cases where the two interviewers were not adjacent in terms of difficulty rankings, a total of 15 pairs (Table 1.3). Of these, there were only two instances where there was no score difference and only two instances where the direction of the score difference was unexpected (i.e. the candidate got a better score with the more difficult interviewer).

Six pairs of interviews, highlighted in Table 1.3, were selected for transcription: of these, 10 interviews were used in the analysis, two each from the two most difficult interviewers (interviewers 5 and 6), two from the second easiest (interviewer 2) and four from the easiest (interviewer 4).

Table 1.3 Interview pairs: score differences

Candidate	Occasion 1 fair average	Interviewer	Occasion 2 fair average	Occasion 2 Adjusted for difficulty	Interviewer	Difference in fair score	Expected direction of difference
35	7.3	4	7.1	7.3	1	–	–
03	7.2	5	7.4	7.6	4	.4	✓
25	5.9	6	6.9	7.1	2	.8	✓
02	6.8	1	6.2	6.4	4	.4	✗
21	6.8	4	6.4	6.6	5	.2	✓
24	6.6	6	5.9	6.1	2	.5	✗
06	6.5	2	5.4	5.6	6	.9	✓
37	6.3	3	6.6	6.8	4	.5	✓
14	6.3	3	6.2	6.4	4	.1	✓
01	5.9	3	6.1	6.3	4	.4	✓
18	5.9	4	4.9	5.1	5	.8	✓
16	5.8	4	5.0	5.2	5	.6	✓
15	5.4	3	6.2	6.4	4	1.0	✓
38	5.2	2	5.0	5.2	3	–	–
19	4.3	5	4.3	4.5	3	.2	✓

6 Discourse analysis

6.1 Number and length of turns

A count was made of the total number of turns by each interviewer. These turns were classed either as 'interview' turns (turns aimed at eliciting information) or 'feedback' turns.

Types of feedback included:

- minimal feedback (mm, yes, right, is it?, etc.)
- evaluative comment, e.g.

    57.47[6]   *suits you*

    32.14   *sounds lovely*

- summary comment, e.g.

    43.21   *and I am sure you have learnt a lot from that*

    46.28   *even the women here are taller*

- echo (repeating part of previous answer)
- correction (repetition of part or whole of previous response, supplying correct grammar or more precise lexis)
- clarification questions (where the interviewer did not catch what the candidate said).

From Table 1.4 we can see that the easiest interviewer, Interviewer 4, tends to conduct longer interviews than the others in terms of the total number of turns. This interviewer also tends to ask a larger number of information-seeking questions than the other interviewers, as well as having a tendency towards more frequent use of feedback. The second easiest interviewer, Interviewer 2, in contrast with the other three, rarely provides feedback alone:

Table 1.4 Interviewer turns

Interviewer (difficult to easy)	Tape	Turns requiring response	Feedback turns	Unknown	Total number of turns
5	46	26	10	1	37
	50	42	11	3	56
6	57	38	9	1	48
	32	24	6	–	30
2	66	44	1	1	46
	8	40	1	–	41
4	43	41	26	–	67
	44	62	12	–	74
	45	59	16	–	75
	27	33	9	–	42

on the few occasions when she does provide feedback she immediately follows it up with a question:

66.03   one and a half months, ah good, um, where do you come from?
66.04   Malaysia, and have you got a family in Australia?
8.07   your dog? Ah how lovely. You have a pet too, and who's looking after it now?

The two most difficult interviewers both varied in the number of questions they asked in each of their two interviews. Given the variation shown by all four interviewers in this data, one cannot here infer any connection between length and difficulty. Further studies focusing specifically on length may, however, reveal some relationship between the amount of information supplied and the ability inferred by the assessor.

Table 1.5 presents information on the balance of talk between candidate and interviewer, and average length of turn in the interview. It shows that each interviewer is consistent in the length of their turns, and that with the exception of the second most difficult Interviewer (Interviewer 6) this is around 10 words. Interviewer 6's turns are roughly double this length. As would be expected, candidates, on the other hand, are more varied in the amount of speech they produce (weaker candidates being more likely to

Table 1.5 Interviewer and candidate turns

Interviewer	Tape	Candidate	Number of turns	Number of words	% Interviewer talk	Average length of turn (words)	Average length of response (words)
5	46	3	37	I 365	31	9.9	
				C 806			21.8
	50	18	56	I 560	60	10	
				C 381			6.8
6	57	6	48	I 945	64	19.7	
				C 527			11
	32	25	30	I 642	47	21.4	
				C 713			23.8
2	66	6	46	I 550	50	11.9	
				C 541			11.8
	8	25	41	I 424	34	10.3	
				C 807			19.7
4	27	37	42	I 495	50	11.8	
				C 1000			23.8
	44	18	74	I 786	56	10.6	
				C 623			8.4
	43	3	67	I 532	30	7.9	
				C 1263			18.8
	45	15	75	I 758	43	10.1	
				C 1021			13.6

produce shorter turns). The length of candidates' turns also tends to be similar in each of their two interviews.

6.2 Question forms

The interviewers' questions were classified according to whether they were open or closed.

Closed questions included those which:

1. Required a yes/no response:

    44.0   *Do you live in a flat?*

    27.05   *Is that near the university?*

2. Expected confirmation:

    50.33   *but sometimes you'd eat Indian?*

    44.71   *. . . you're generally quite happy here at the moment?*

3. Required the selection of one of two alternatives offered:

    9.24   *and are the marriages arranged or do the young people meet each other by themselves?*

Table 1.6 presents the findings of this analysis. There does not appear to be any marked difference between easy and difficult interviewers in their choice of question form.

6.3 Question focus

The interviewers' turns were classified according to the question focus or content. It was hypothesised that easier interviewers would be characterised

Table 1.6 Question forms

Interviewer	Tape	Candidate	Total turns requiring response	Open questions	Yes/No questions	Confirmation questions	Alternative questions
5	46	3	26	13	11	2	–
	50	18	42	22	12	2	6
6	57	6	38	15	16	7	3
	32	25	24	16	5	1	2
2	66	6	44	17	24	3	–
	8	25	40	24	12	2	2
4	43	3	41	23	16	1	1
	44	18	62	40	19	1	2
	45	15	59	31	23	5	–
	27	37	32	16	14	1	1

by more frequent use of simpler questions (those asking for simple factual information and description) rather than the more complex skills of speculating or presenting and justifying an opinion. Accordingly, questions were categorised as follows:

Type 1 Simple factual information – personal and general
   9.05   *and how many, do you have brothers and sisters?*
   57.11 *ten hours, so what time would they normally start?*
   44.32 *What are your favourite kind of movies?*

Type 2 Feelings
   45.25 *Oh dear, so you had to move did you? Are you happy at the moment?*
   45.18 *and do you like living in Melbourne city?*

Type 3 Straightforward description
   57.22 *no, so what happens to those people?*
   43.16 *What do they do at midnight?*

Type 4 Personal plans
   43–65 *So now you have this year to prepare for 1997, what are you going to do next year, X?*

Type 5 Considered response: requires judgement or analysis to select content
   43.19 *. . . so when you think of ideal living conditions for yourself what would you choose next?*
   50.38 *in commerce, right, why commerce?*
   44.67 *did you, right, so you've just been here a short time, what are your first impressions of Australia?*

Type 6 Speculation
   66.47 *Do you think it would be easy to earn a living? How far to engineering, would that be easy to get a living in Malaysia?*

Type 7 Confirmation of understanding
   50.19 *That's in [name of city] they have those?*

What we find in Table 1.7 is that of the number of turns requiring a response from the candidate, there do not appear to be any significant patterns in the number of turns allocated to each question type. However, there are three tendencies apparent in this data:

Table 1.7 Question focus

Interviewer	Tape	Candidate	Total turns requiring response	Questions						
				Type 1	Type 2	Type 3	Type 4	Type 5	Type 6	Type 7
5	46	3	26	16	1	1	3	2	2	1
	50	18	42	22	1	7	3	6	1	2
6	57	6	38	18	1	3	3	6	5	2
	32	25	24	6	1	1	4	8	4	–
2	66	6	44	25	–	2	6	4	3	3
	8	25	40	14	2	7	4	10	–	2
4	43	3	41	26	1	3	1	7	2	1
	44	18	62	34	1	16	2	9	–	–
	45	15	59	30	3	8	3	10	–	5
	27	37	33	23	–	2	1	6	–	1

1. The largest percentage of all interviewers' questions are of the simple factual type. Interviewer 4, the easiest interviewer, tends to ask more of these than the other interviewers.
2. Interviewer 4 failed to ask any speculative questions in three of the four interviews, as did interviewer 2 in one of the two she carried out.
3. Interviewer 4 asked fewer questions about the candidate's personal plans.

6.4 Topic

Table 1.8 shows the number of topics introduced in each interview as well as the number of turns and subtopics within each topic. Examples of topic and subtopic include the topic *how the candidate lives* with subtopics *the flat* and *food* (Tape 45); the topic *studying in Singapore* with subtopics *language* and *exams* (Tape 43).

What we find is that the easiest interviewer, Interviewer 4, introduces many more topics than the other interviewers. For example, candidate 18 experienced nine topic shifts with Interviewer 4 compared with two topic shifts with Interviewer 5. For the other three interviewers the smaller number of topics was accompanied by a larger number of turns within each topic. The number of subtopics within a topic does not seem to distinguish difficult and easy raters.

Table 1.8 also shows the number of turns in Phase 2 (Extended Discourse) and Phase 4 (Speculation and Attitudes) as well as the total number of turns for each interview. We find that the more difficult interviewers devoted roughly the same number of turns to each of Phases 2 and 4. In contrast, for Interviewer 4 the overwhelming majority of turns occur in Phase 2 (e.g. Tape

Table 1.8 Topics introduced in interviews

Interviewer	Tape	Candidate	Topics	Turns per topic	Sub-topics	Turns per Phase 2	Turns per Phase 4	Total turns
5	46	3	1	17	2	17	12	29
			2	12	2			
	50	18	1	29	2	29	22	51
			2	22	3			
6	57	6	1	24	7	24	18	42
			2	18	6			
	32	25	1	13	5	13	12	25
			2	12	7			
2	66	6	1	1		22	20	42
			2	21	2			
			3	20	5			
	8	25	1	22	3	24	8	32
			2	2				
			3	8	4			
4	45	15	1	12	2	69	4	73
			2	9	2			
			3	6				
			4	4				
			5	11	2			
			6	7				
			7	17	2			
			8	3				
			9	4				
	27	37	1	8	2	37	2	39
			2	2				
			3	7				
			4	2				
			5	9				
			6	9	3			
			7	2				
	43	3	1	17	1	59	4	63
			2	9	1			
			3	14	2			
			4	8				
			5	11	2			
			6	4	2			
	44	18	1	23	5	66	4	70
			2	2				
			3	5				
			4	5	1			
			5	17	3			
			6	6	1			
			7	8	1			
			8	2				
			9	2	1			

45 Phase 2 = 69 turns, Phase 4 = 4 turns). This finding is consistent with the earlier finding that interviewer 4 tends to ask more simple factual questions with fewer questions about personal plans and no questions requiring speculation.

The fact that candidates assigned the easiest interviewer experienced more frequent topic shifts means that they were not required to talk about any topic in depth. It seems then that the interview is 'easier' (or candidates appear more competent) when several topics are touched on briefly rather than fewer topics explored in depth, and where questions are possibly less 'probing'. It may also be that the more questions there are on the one topic, the more complex they become referentially and the less complete grammatically due to the shared knowledge that is being built up. A further analysis will be required in order to investigate this question. It is also worth noting that Interviewer 4's interviews are typically much longer than the others, giving candidates the opportunity to produce more language and more information, either of which may lead raters to perceive a candidate as being more able.

The difficult interviewers not only require the candidate to go into greater depth about the chosen topic, but they also appear less inclined to accommodate their questions to the candidate's level. For example, the more difficult interviewers are much more likely to persist with a topic or predetermined sequence of questioning when a candidate is obviously struggling.[7]

50.21 What about the types of architecture, what kinds of architecture, style of buildings do you see in X?
50.C Local?
50.22 Yes, any sort of traditional architecture?
50.C Yeah.
50.23 Tell me about that.
50.C Something like Malay style.
50.24 Yeah, what does that look like?
50.C There's a lot of um, um, . . . the Malay . . . they're like in Malay . . .
50.25 What does that mean though?
50.C The name of the language is Malay language.

Interviewer 4, on the other hand, rephrases and breaks the question down where the candidate has not produced the required response, either through lack of comprehension or where the interviewer's intention was not clear, as in this extract:

44.41 um, can you tell me about any special festivals that you have in Malaysia?
44.C oh, yeah.
44.42 any celebrations that everybody has at sometime during the year, can you think of one special one?

The difficult interviewers are also more likely to challenge the candidate, for example, to justify a decision. In one interview, interviewer 5 challenged the candidate consistently in relation to his study plans, first, in relation to his chosen subject:

50.43 so why accounting, isn't it better to learn management than accounting if you want to be, and have your own company?

Second, in relation to his chosen place of study:

50.45 why aren't you studying in Malaysia?
50.48 but why did you come to Australia, why didn't you stay in Malaysia?
50.49 but why Australia, why not England or America?

And third, in relation to the relevance of studying the chosen subject in the chosen country:

50.50 now if you study commerce here, I imagine the course here is very much centred around Australian business, the Australian economy, how are you going to use that in Malaysia?

Interviewer 5's questioning style could be characterised in two ways. First, he tends to use many fragments rather than complete sentences:

46.09 so the same state though?
46.12 for secondary school?
50.34 sometimes Malay?
50.38 in commerce, right, why commerce?

Second, a number of his questions are somewhat ungrammatical and potentially confusing:

50.15 ahm okay, I have a list of things to talk about here. Tell me, is Port Kelang not a big, it's a small city, if you go to KL for example, that's much bigger.
50.26 right, in Kelang is there many Malay or a lot of Chinese or what is it in Kelang?
46.21 how do you actually when speaking to the teacher how do you?

Interviewer 6 (the second most difficult) also appears to create difficulty through the syntactic complexity of her questions. Her turns, as was noted earlier, tend to be much longer than those of the other interviewers. This seems to be a consequence of a large percentage of her questions consisting of multiple formulations, any of which might be incomplete, resulting in potential confusion for candidates.

57.48 Now if you could have a career path, we are talking about after you finish your study here, if you could choose a career path that led anyway you wanted, what would you choose to do with your career, if you could work anywhere you wanted, do anything you . . .

32.17 I mean especially for an Australian to go to Japan, especially to Tokyo. Is there any way that I can overcome that, is there some way that I can live in Tokyo and be able to afford it? Do you have any advice?

57.10 Okay, can you tell me a little bit about perhaps work, I know you probably don't work in Malaysia, you look probably a bit too, you are obviously a student still, um but you probably know about work in Malaysia, generally what's what are the conditions like. Do people, you know do they work long hours? Is the pay good?

Another noteworthy aspect of Interviewer 6's behaviour is that she frequently interrupts the candidates with another question before they have completed what they want to say in their previous response.

In contrast, the easier interviewers (4 and 2) consistently use economical, complete and grammatically correct questions. While the amount of backchannelling (i.e. mm, right, oh, aha, etc.) taking place while the candidate is still talking does not appear to distinguish easy and more difficult interviewers, feedback at the beginning of a next turn or as a stand-alone turn is a characteristic of the two easier interviewers. This could be read as both acceptance of the previous answer and encouragement to elaborate, in other words a positive evaluation of the candidate's contribution, possibly contributing to increased confidence on the candidate's part or, alternatively, presenting to the raters a sense that the candidate is able to participate adequately in an interaction with a native speaker.

7 Conclusions

In this study we set out to investigate first, whether different interviewers could be said to present significantly different hurdles for candidates, and second, what features of interviewer behaviour might contribute to this. Through a research design using multiple interviews and ratings, analysed using multifaceted Rasch, we were able to demonstrate that there are indeed significant differences. Of six randomly selected interviewers, one was significantly easier than all but the second easiest, and the second easiest was significantly easier than the most difficult. In other words there is no doubt that candidates can be disadvantaged or advantaged by 'the luck of the draw' in interviewer allocation.

An initial analysis of interviewer styles showed some differences. While it is not possible from this limited study to draw any firm conclusions about which interviewer behaviours could be said to contribute to difficulty, certain tendencies were identified here which warrant further investigation.

In particular, the easier interviewers tended to shift topic more frequently, with fewer turns per topic; they also asked more questions of a simpler nature and spent considerably longer in Phase 2 than in Phase 4. Furthermore, it seems that the more structured the interview is as a straightforward question-and-answer routine, the easier it appears to be (or the more competent the candidate appears). Those interviewers identified as the most difficult in this study were, in fact, more likely to engage in more 'natural' conversational techniques such as interruption and disagreement. They were more likely to produce sentence fragments or complex ungrammatical utterances. Moreover, they were also more likely to push the candidate into a range of harder linguistic behaviours including speculating and justifying opinions.

For IELTS then, as for any other oral interview, the challenge is to decide what behaviour is appropriate and to ensure that it occurs. Is the aim to replicate authentic interaction (which would imply a lack of simplification and accommodation) or simply to elicit information (which would imply limiting the interview to a question-and-answer format and making allowances for weaker candidates)? There appear to be two types of interviewer, one (the most difficult) who makes fewer allowances and provides less support, uses more complex language, and pushes the candidates into more complex interactional skills such as speculation and justification; and the other who uses simple language and more straightforward questions and who provides more support and feedback. These findings support those of Lumley and Brown (1996), where two types of interviewer were identified, those who took on the role prescribed in the role play and acted it out in the spirit intended, and those who exhibited more 'teacher-like', or supportive, behaviour. Whatever the intention of the test developers, interviewers need to be trained accordingly as to what is and is not suitable behaviour. This could include monitoring of their own performance, discussion of how they should deal with particular situations (for example where they do not feel the candidate will cope with the speculative phase), even comparison of various interview techniques and behaviours – all these, while naturally contributing to additional expense in training, are necessary to ensure equivalence across interviews and interviewers, and hence fairness to candidates. It is after all, only as much as is done in the training of raters. Why should interviewer training warrant less attention? The findings of studies such as this demonstrate that interviewer talk is not neutral and indicate that the time is ripe to re-evaluate the emphasis we place on training for oral tests.

Notes

1   This information is quoted from the IELTS Handbook 1995 (Cambridge: UCLES). This version of the Speaking test was replaced in 2001 by a structured interview.
2   The interviewers also gave a rating (as is normal practice in IELTS administrations) but this information was not used for the present study.
3   In cases where the tasks are substantially different, task difficulty may also be

included; in this case task was not considered as it was felt that variability due to topic was considerably less likely to affect scores than variation in interviewer behaviour.

4 The fair score in a FACETS analysis represents a modification of the actual score(s), taking other variables (facets) into account. In this case, as *rater* is a facet of the analysis, it compensates for rater harshness.

5 Where these strata are defined by their centres being three measurement errors apart.

6 Numbers refer to tape and interviewer turn.

7 C = candidate response.

APPENDIX 1.1

Progress of the IELTS interview

Phase 1: Introduction

Aim: To settle the candidate down, get some background information on the candidate and make an approximate assessment of the candidate's proficiency level.

Skills: Providing personal information and general factual information.

Progress: Greet them, check who they are and how to address them, ask them one or two factual questions about self, schooling, hobbies, family or where they're from, etc.

Phase 2: Extended Discourse

Aim: To elicit extended speech.

Skills: Providing general factual information, expressing likes and dis-likes, describing and comparing, narrating or sequencing events, explaining.

Progress: You should not focus on the candidate's personal work/study history or interests in this section, but discuss the culture-related topics in general terms. You may move from one topic to another if necessary. The end of the phase should be oriented in such a way as to bridge into Phase 4.

Phase 4: Speculation and Attitudes

Aim: To elicit language at high levels by encouraging the candidate to express precise meaning, attitudes, and to speculate.

Skills: Providing general personal and factual information; expressing needs, wants, likes and dislikes; expressing opinions, intentions, attitudes, moods, possibilities, values and emotions; describing and comparing objects, events and sequences; explaining how something works and why something is the case, speculating on future events and their consequences.

Progress: Discuss in depth one of the two topic focuses. Ask them to explain, elaborate, or give reasons; agree or disagree with them, challenge them – engage them in debate.

Phase 5: Conclusion

Aim: To round off the interview.
Skills: Leave taking.
Progress: Express thanks and farewell to the candidate. Give them their score if it is their second interview.

Phase 2

List A	List B
Ceremonies (e.g. wedding, funeral, graduation)	**Festivals** (e.g. Christmas, Diwali, Chinese New Year)
City/rural life (e.g. crowds, facilities, lifestyle, buildings)	**Travel and tansport** (e.g. preferred mode, cost, availability, accidents)
Education (schools, universities, kindergartens) (e.g. equipment, size, uniforms, quality, importance, structure)	**Work** (e.g. pay, hours, unemployment, industry, etc.)
Tourism (e.g. overseas visitors and local travel – choice, effect, sights, growth, etc.)	**Pollution** (e.g. effects, cause, industry/nature)
Leisure interests (e.g. sports, hobbies)	**Family life** (e.g. upbringing, extended?, activities, relationships, etc.)
Buildings and architecture (e.g. style, age, materials)	**Wealth/poverty** (e.g. distribution of income, sufficiency, change, source of income, government support)

Phase 4

Topic A: Work plans/vocational field

What the candidate intends doing workwise.
Why?
Likely benefit to country.
What family/employer/friends think about it.
Stages in career, etc.

Topic B: Study plans/academic field

> What the candidate intends doing studywise.
> Why?
> Likely benefit of study.
> Why overseas?
> What family/employer/friends think about it.
> Importance of study, etc.

APPENDIX 1.2

Description of the multifaceted Rasch model

In multifaceted Rasch analysis, as in the standard Rasch model, the aim is to obtain a unified metric for measurement not unlike measuring length using a ruler. The scale on a ruler should not change when measuring a variety of objects. The measurement scale derived by application of the Rasch model is based on the probability of occurrence of certain phenomena (item difficulty, student ability, different judge severity–leniency levels). Once a common metric is established for measuring different phenomena, the different features can be examined and their effects controlled. The result of using a Rasch model of measurement provides, in principle, independence from situational features in a particular test, students, etc. In other words, the results can have a general meaning. Multifaceted Rasch analysis is a Rasch-based approach where various situational factors are explicitly taken into consideration in constructing measurement. The units of measurement in Rasch analysis are logits, which are centred at zero; this is the 50% probability represented by an 'item' of average difficulty. (For an overview of multifaceted Rasch analysis, the manner in which it may be conducted, and the results interpreted, the reader is referred to McNamara (1996) Chapters 5–8 for a discussion.)

Interviewer behaviour was modelled using the IRT multifaceted Rasch analysis computer program FACETS (Linacre 1994). Analysis was conducted using a three-faceted model – interviewers, assessors, and test takers. In terms of interviewers, a logit score above zero (a positive measure) indicates difficulty. In terms of assessors, a logit score above zero indicates harshness; a logit score below zero (a negative measure) indicates leniency. Similarly with test takers, a positive logit value indicates greater ability, while a score in negative logit values indicates a less able candidate.

Source: adapted from Coniam, D and Falvey, P (2002).

Methodology evaluation of Chapter 1

This chapter, which investigates Interviewer Style and Candidate Performance in the IELTS oral interview, employs two research tools in order to address two research questions. The first research question investigates 'The extent to which differential behaviour by IELTS interviewers affects the scores awarded to candidates'. A corollary of the first question is 'To identify interviewers who consistently present a difficult or easy challenge to candidates'. After ascertaining which interviewers were 'difficult' or 'easy' the second research question investigates, by means of discourse analysis, the aspects of interviewer behaviour that contribute to the challenge they present to candidates.

The first part of the study employs multi-faceted Rasch analysis to analyse test data. Multifaceted Rasch analysis is a useful research tool because it provides levels of probability involving different facets of a language situation. In this study, four facets were employed in order to estimate interviewer difficulty: candidate, interviewer, occasion and rater. The use and understanding of Rasch modeling is not easy but the description of its use in this chapter provides insights for the statistically-challenged reader and is a useful chapter for researchers and research students who might become involved in the testing and assessment of different aspects of language. The data and results demonstrate that interviewer difficulty 'may well affect a candidate's chances'. This is an important finding 'in that the ability level construed for the candidate will be not only a result of his/her inherent ability but also of the difficulty presented by the interviewer'. This finding means that the reliability of raters, enhanced by thorough training, is not the only factor in determining candidates' scores. Interviewer difficulty, it appears, is another important factor.

The study then progresses further in terms of shedding light on candidates' scores by using discourse analysis of recorded and transcribed tapes of interviews in order to determine whether there are differences in easier or more difficult interviewers' talk involving aspects such as length of candidate talk, interviewer talk, aspects of topic-shifting and turn-taking and whether these can affect candidate scores. The use of this research instrument shows that after the initial concern about interviewer difficulty demonstrated by the results of the multifaceted Rasch analysis, the follow-up analysis of interviewer data, as revealed in interview transcripts, shows tendencies towards separate patterns of behaviour by easier and more difficult interviewers.

By using complementary research instruments, Rasch analysis and discourse analysis, the study is able to address the first research question and then, by addressing the second research question, show findings which can be subsequently addressed in the training of interviewers.

In summary, the two research instruments have contributed to the identification of a problem with the Speaking component of IELTS through the use of multifaceted Rasch analysis. Subsequently, by means of a different research instrument, discourse analysis, the data which can lead to a possible solution to that problem was revealed.

2 An investigation into the role of gender in the IELTS oral interview

Kieran O'Loughlin

Abstract

This paper reports on a study into the impact of gender on the IELTS oral interview. This is a relatively underinvestigated issue in the assessment of oral proficiency. The study examines the issue of gender on two levels: first, its impact on the discourse of the interview and second, its effect on the rating process.

There is a large body of research which suggests that male and female speakers have distinctive communicative styles. Therefore, it might be anticipated that such differences would be reflected in the discourse of interviewers in the oral test interview, possibly affecting the quantity and quality of the candidate's output. Furthermore, candidates' output may vary in relation to their own gender and whether their interviewer is of the same or opposite sex. It is also possible that the gender of the rater and/or candidate may significantly influence assessment of the oral interview. In the case of tests like the IELTS interview where the interlocutor also acts as the rater this poses the question of whether a gender effect, where it exists, stems from the interview itself, the rating decision or a combination of both these 'events'.

The study is based on interviews undertaken with 16 candidates (eight female and eight male) who were each interviewed by a female and male interviewer. This yielded a total of 32 interviews. Each interview was rated by the interviewer and audiotaped. Four other raters (two females and two males), drawn from a pool of eight females and eight males, subsequently assessed each of the interviews using the audio-recordings. The audio-recordings were then transcribed and several features of language use which have been identified in previous research as key markers of gendered communication were examined, specifically the use of overlaps, interruptions and minimal responses by both interviewers and candidates. The test score data was analysed using a facility of the multi-faceted Rasch computer program FACETS (Linacre 1989–95) known as bias analysis.

In the discourse analysis of the interviews it was found that there were some gender differences between female and male interviewers and candidates, but these did not form a consistent gender pattern. In general, most interviewers and candidates adopted a supportive and collaborative speech style irrespective of their own gender or the gender of their interlocutor. Furthermore, the analysis of test scores indicated there was no evidence of significant bias in the rating process in relation to the gender of raters or candidates. Both sets of findings therefore suggest that gender does not have a significant impact on the IELTS interview.

1 Introduction

Recent research into oral language interviews has indicated that interviewers vary considerably from each other in relation to their test behaviour. Such variability includes the amount of support they give to candidates, the amount of rapport they establish with candidates and the extent to which they follow the instructions relevant to their role (e.g. Brown and Hill 1996, Lazaraton 1996, McNamara and Lumley 1997, Morton et al 1997, Young and Milanovic 1992). A previous study of the IELTS oral interview (Brown and Hill 1998; this now appears as Chapter 1 in this volume) indicates that different interviewers present different 'hurdles' for candidates and that there are particular interviewing styles which characterise 'easy' and 'difficult' interviewers. Brown and Hill found that the easier interviewers tended to shift topic more frequently and asked simpler questions. The more difficult interviewers tended to use a wider range of interactional behaviours, such as interruption and disagreement as well as asking more challenging questions.

A key issue arising from such findings is *why* interviewers vary from each other. One possibility is that such variability stems, at least partly, from gendered differences in communicative style. There is a large body of research in the field of language and gender which suggests that male and female conversational styles are quite distinct (see, for example, Coates 1993, Maltz and Borker 1982, Tannen 1990, Thwaite 1993). These studies characterise the female conversational style as collaborative, co-operative, symmetrical and supportive whereas its male equivalent is portrayed as controlling, unco-operative, asymmetrical and unsupportive.

In her book *Women, Men and Language* Jennifer Coates (1993:140), for instance, argues that women and men seem to differ in terms of their communicative competence in so far as they 'have different sets of norms for conversational interaction'. Therefore, she concludes 'women and men may constitute distinct speech communities'. Such claims may have serious implications for language testing since they imply that the construct of communicative competence is not gender neutral. Is it reasonable, for instance, to assess female and male speakers against the same set of norms? Equally, we might ask, is it fair for test takers, especially females, to be interviewed and rated by members of the opposite gender if they belong to different speech communities? On the other hand, it could be argued that a language test need not reflect all aspects of 'real-life' communications (including gendered differences) in order to be still valid.

More recently, the research which has found clear gender differences in spoken interaction has been strongly criticised for its tendency to overgeneralise its findings to all men and all women irrespective of other social identity factors (such as their age, ethnicity, occupation and sexual identity) and situational factors such as the communicative context and the gender of their interlocutors. In recent studies men and women in fact show themselves capable of using a range of conversational styles in different speech contexts. Where men and women exhibit similar conversational behaviour it may be that other aspects of their social identity which override potential gender differences are brought into play. In other words, instead of being fixed, polarised and predictable, the language use of men and women is now seen as varying across cultural, social and situational contexts, sometimes exhibiting difference and other times similarity (see, for example, Freed 1995, Freed and Greenwood 1996, Freeman and McElhinny 1996, Stubbe 1998).

Notwithstanding such critiques of fully predictable and inevitable gendered differences in spoken interaction, the potential for such differences is clearly an important issue in the testing context. In the interests of test fairness, systematic investigations into whether clearly distinct styles are consistently evident for male and female interviewers, for instance, need to be carried out together with what effects such gendered differences (if they exist) have on candidate performance.

As Sunderland (1995) suggests, differences in male and female interviewer styles *per se* can be viewed as one potential gender effect. Another possibility she identifies is that the behaviour of interviewers of either gender may vary according to whether they are paired with a male or female candidate. In both cases, it is feasible that the gendered behaviour of the interviewer will influence the outcome of the test by either strengthening or undermining the candidate's performance.

A further gender consideration in oral test interviews is that candidates' output may vary according to their own gender. As suggested above, the quantity and quality of their output may be affected positively or negatively by the gender of the interviewer.

Finally, it is also worth considering whether there is a gender effect in the rating of oral interviews. It is possible in oral interviews that male and female raters may assess differently. It is also possible that their assessments are influenced by the gender of the candidate. In the case of tests like the IELTS interview where the interlocutor also acts as the rater this poses the question of whether a gender effect, where it exists, stems from the interview itself, the rating decision or a combination of both these 'events'.

There have been a number of recent studies which have examined the possibility of a gender effect in the rating of candidates by their interviewers in oral interviews. Most of this research reveals some kind of gender effect on test scores although, interestingly, the effect is not always the same. Some studies report that test takers scored more highly with male interviewers (e.g. Locke 1984, Porter 1991a, 1991b) while others report higher scores with female interviewers (e.g. O'Sullivan 2000, Porter and Shen 1991). An interaction effect between the gender of the interviewer and interviewee has also been reported (Buckingham 1997). In this case candidates achieved a higher score when paired with an interviewer of the same gender. By virtue of their very inconsistency these findings appear to support more recent thinking about the shifting, unstable nature of gender in spoken interaction to which I have just alluded and to which I return at the conclusion of this chapter.

The study aimed therefore to address the following questions:

1. What impact does the gender of participants have on the discourse produced in the IELTS oral interview?
2. What impact does gender have on the rating of the IELTS oral interview?
3. If a gender effect is found to exist in the course of interviewing and/or rating, how might its impact on test scores be managed?

2 Methodology

2.1 The IELTS oral interview

The IELTS is a four-skill test employed in the selection of prospective students whose first language is not English to universities in such countries as Australia, Canada and the UK. The version of the Speaking subtest used at the time this study was conducted (July 1998) lasted between 10 and 15 minutes. It was described by the University of Cambridge Local Examinations Syndicate (UCLES 1998:11) as 'an oral interview, a conversation, between the candidate and an examiner' and consisted of five phases as outlined below:

Phase 1   *Introduction*
        The examiner and candidate introduce themselves. The candidate is made to feel comfortable and encouraged to talk briefly about their life, home, work and interests.

Phase 2   *Extended Discourse*
        The candidate is encouraged to speak at length about some very familiar topic either of general interest or of relevance to their

culture, place of living, or country of origin. This will involve explanation, description or narration.

Phase 3   *Elicitation*
The candidate is given a task card with some information on it and is encouraged to take the initiative and ask questions either to elicit information or to solve a problem. Tasks are based on 'information gap' type activities.

Phase 4   *Speculation and Attitudes*
The candidate is encouraged to talk about their future plans and proposed course of study. Alternatively the examiner may choose to return to a topic raised earlier.

Phase 5   *Conclusion*
The interview is concluded.

The version of the Speaking test assessed whether candidates have the necessary knowledge and skills to communicate effectively with native speakers of English. Interviewers were given an outline which includes suggested topics for Phases 2 and 4 and a prescribed task for Phase 3. The interviewers also carried out the assessment of the candidate's proficiency using a global band scale with nine increments. Assessment took into account evidence of communicative strategies, and appropriate and flexible use of grammar and vocabulary. IELTS interviewers are qualified teachers and certificated examiners appointed by individual test centres and approved by UCLES. All interviews are recorded (IELTS Handbook UCLES 1998:14). Note that the format of the IELTS Speaking test changed from 1 July 2001 (UCLES 2000:15).

2.2 Interview design

Sixteen different students (eight male and eight female) and eight accredited IELTS interviewers (four male and four female) participated in this stage of the study. Each of the candidates was interviewed on two different occasions by a male and a female interviewer yielding a total of 32 interviews. Each of the interviews was audiotaped, as they are in the official IELTS Speaking component.

The candidates were international students engaged in an IELTS preparation course with the aim of undertaking further study here in Australia. Consequently, they volunteered for this project on the basis of experiencing the interview under exam-like conditions, gauging their readiness and receiving feedback from the interviewers about possible areas to develop in their preparation for the official test. The candidates came from a range of language and cultural backgrounds. The women came from China, Indonesia, Japan and Thailand and ranged in ages from 19–31. The men came from

China, Indonesia, Japan, Korea and Thailand and were in the age range of 20–30.

The interviewers were all fully trained, current IELTS examiners ranging in age, workplace and length of time as an examiner. They were all paid Aus$60 for their participation but, like the candidates, were not given any indication of the focus of the project beyond it being a study of the discourse produced in the oral interview. As indicated above, the interviewers were each asked to provide feedback to the candidates about their strengths and weaknesses in preparation for the official test. This was done immediately after each interview.

All the students were interviewed twice, once by a female interviewer and once by a male interviewer. Half of the students were interviewed by a male interviewer first and the other half by a female interviewer first. The interviews were done at the same site on two different days. Candidates were not exposed to the same topics in the two interviews so as to minimise any potential practice effect. For this purpose two different test versions (Test A and Test B) were used as outlined below.

Test A

Phase 1 *Introduction*
Phase 2 *Extended Discourse:* Topics such as ceremonies, education, tourism, leisure interests, and building and architecture were suggested to the interviewers.
Phase 3 *Elicitation:* 'Living cheaply in the city' was the prescribed task.
Phase 4 *Speculation and attitudes:* Topics such as work plans/vocational field – intentions, benefits to home country, family and friends' attitudes, career stages were suggested to the interviewers.
Phase 5 *Conclusion*

Test B

Phase 1 *Introduction*
Phase 2 *Extended Discourse:* Topics such as travel and transport, work, pollution, family life and wealth/poverty were suggested to the interviewers.
Phase 3 *Elicitation:* 'Football match' was the prescribed task.
Phase 4 *Speculation and attitudes:* Topics such as study plans/academic field – importance, benefits, family and friends' attitudes were suggested to the interviewers.
Phase 5 *Conclusion*

2.3 Rating design

Each candidate was subsequently assessed by two female and two male accredited IELTS interviewers, again from a range of ages, workplaces and experience as IELTS examiners, using the audio-recordings of the interviews. Each was paid Aus$80 for their participation and, like the interviewers, they were not given any indication of the focus of the project beyond it being a study of the discourse produced in the oral interview. A mixed design was used for these additional ratings whereby each interview was assessed by different combinations of male and female raters drawn from a pool of eight females and eight males with each rater carrying out a total of eight assessments. This design enabled the raters to be calibrated against each other in the statistical analyses which followed. For the purposes of clarity, the reader should note that in the rest of this report 'interviewer score' refers to the rating assigned by the original interviewer and 'rater score' refers to an assessment subsequently made by one of the additional raters based on the audio-recordings of the interview.

Table 2.1 outlines the design for both the interviews and ratings.

3 Findings

3.1 Discourse analysis

The interviews were transcribed, using a broad notation system adapted from Tannen (1984) (see Appendix 2.1), and then analysed in detail in relation to effect of the different gender pairings as follows:

Interviewer	*Candidate*
Female	Female
Female	Male
Male	Male
Male	Female

Coates (1993) takes up Hymes' (1972) notion of communicative competence as a sense of knowing how language is used in a given society, i.e. it is essential to understand socio-cultural factors as well as grammar and phonology when learning a language. She acknowledges that our understanding of when to speak, when to remain silent, what to talk about and how to talk about it in different circumstances is learned. She argues that women and men seem to differ in their communicative competence: they differ in their sense of what is *appropriate* speech behaviour.

The analysis which follows focuses on three of Coates' (1993) key markers of gendered communication as used in the IELTS interviews examined in this

Table 2.1 Interview and rating design

Candidate number	Candidate gender	Interviewer number	Interviewer gender	Female raters' numbers		Male raters' numbers	
1	Male	1	Male	5	6	9	10
1	Male	2	Female	1	2	11	12
2	Male	1	Male	3	4	13	14
2	Male	2	Female	5	6	15	16
3	Female	1	Male	7	8	10	12
3	Female	2	Female	2	4	9	11
4	Female	1	Male	1	3	14	16
4	Female	2	Female	6	8	13	15
5	Male	3	Male	5	7	9	12
5	Male	4	Female	1	4	10	11
6	Male	3	Male	2	3	13	16
6	Male	4	Female	5	8	14	15
7	Female	3	Male	6	7	12	16
7	Female	4	Female	4	8	9	13
8	Female	3	Male	1	5	10	14
8	Female	4	Female	2	6	11	15
9	Male	5	Male	3	7	9	14
9	Male	6	Female	1	6	10	13
10	Male	5	Male	2	5	11	16
10	Male	6	Female	3	8	12	15
11	Female	5	Male	4	7	10	16
11	Female	6	Female	2	8	9	15
12	Female	5	Male	1	7	12	14
12	Female	6	Female	4	6	11	13
13	Male	7	Male	3	5	9	16
13	Male	8	Female	1	8	10	15
14	Male	7	Male	2	7	11	14
14	Male	8	Female	3	8	12	13
15	Female	7	Male	4	5	11	16
15	Female	8	Female	3	4	9	10
16	Female	7	Male	1	2	15	16
16	Female	8	Female	7	8	13	14

Source: 2002 Edward Arnold (publishers) Ltd.

study: overlaps, interruptions and minimal responses. These were considered to be potentially the most salient categories for comparison between females and males in this context.

3.1.1 Overlaps

Coates (1993:109) defines overlaps as 'instances of slight over-anticipation by the next speaker: instead of beginning to speak immediately following current speaker's turn, next speaker begins to speak at the very end of current speaker's turn, overlapping the last word (or part of it)'.

Coates (1993) cites studies that observed more overlaps in same-gender pairs. These studies also showed that all overlaps in mixed-gender pairs were caused by males, and that women used no overlaps with men but did in same-gender talk. She suggests women are concerned not to violate the man's turn but to wait until he has finished speaking.

The overlaps observed in the IELTS interview data collected for this study appeared to express different meanings. They have therefore been classified in two ways. There were 'positive overlaps' that seemed to be offering support for the person whose turn it was, both by confirming information and continuing the topic. Also some 'negative overlaps' were observed, particularly attempts to control the topic. Examples of both kinds of overlaps follow.

Positive interviewer overlaps[1]

i) Giving confirmation

The example below shows the interviewer confirming the candidate's idea that 'many people want to see this game'. As the candidate reformulated this (line 221), the interviewer perhaps recognised the candidate's need for support in this idea and thus joined in to confirm it:

    C: So many people want to see this game.

    I: Sure.

    C: Looking forward to [see this game.]

 * I: [lots of students] want to go and see this game.

                            Interviewer 3 (male)/Candidate 6 (male): lines 219–22

ii) Continuation of topic/supporting

In this instance, the interviewer overlaps to support the candidate by continuing the topic and supplying a word that matched what the candidate appeared to be looking for:

    C: so (.) that case Tanzanian people are very kind but not very friendly, I can say that in Ken Kenya the peoples is very friendly but ah: how can I say they try to sell many things (.) [for tourists,]

 * I: [they are more commercialised,]

    C: Commercialised yeah.

    I: I see.

    C: Yeah it looks they are just interested in our money.

                          Interviewer 2 (female)/Candidate 3 (female): lines 107–14

Negative interviewer overlaps

i) Attempt to control topic

The interviewer in this example attempts to introduce the idea of unemployment. First she refers to people losing jobs and then when the student continues by talking about government protection of industry, the interviewer overlaps with the question of the unemployment rate. Following the overlap she then reiterates the question thus reinforcing the direction she wants the discussion to go:

> C: Um (0.5) because I want to I think it's OK to trade with (.) to trade with another country. Because I think labour in Thailand have trend have trend to ah expensive in the future, yeah. so if we use (0.5) if we use ah: (.) not no (.) we can ah we can import something from the other countries?
> I: Mm,
> C: which will cheaper than in my country in the future=
> I: =but will that help your country develop? If if people lose jobs? Because you traded from outside?
> C: Um I think it doesn't matter because my government will have a policy to protect (.) um (.) some industrial in Thailand. Yes. Same [Australia (.) in here,]
> * I: [what's the unemployment] what's the unemployment rate in Thailand.
> C: Unemployed?
>
> Interviewer 4 (female)/Candidate 5 (male): lines 269–81

These examples illustrate how overlapping was used both 'positively' and 'negatively' by interviewers in the course of the interviews.

A quantitative analysis of interviewer overlaps is reported below. The total number of interviewer overlaps across all 32 interviews was only 79. This indicates a fairly sparing use of overlaps by individual interviewers.

Table 2.2 Instances of female interviewer overlaps

	Interviewer: female Candidate: male		Interviewer: female Candidate: female	
	Number of interviews	Number of overlaps	Number of interviews	Number of overlaps
Positive overlap	7	24	5	22
Negative overlap	1	1	1	1
Total	**8**	**25**	**6**	**23**

Table 2.2 shows female interviewer overlaps in the data. Column 1 indicates whether the overlaps were positive or negative. Column 2 shows the number of interviews where overlaps were found and column 3 the instances of overlaps within those interviews. Both these figures are for the female interviewer and male candidate pairing. Column 4 indicates the number of interviews with female candidates where overlaps were employed and column 5 the number of instances of use found therein. (The total number of interviews for each gender pairing is eight.)

Table 2.3 Instances of male interviewer overlaps

	Interviewer: male Candidate: male		Interviewer: male Candidate: female	
	Number of interviews	Number of overlaps	Number of interviews	Number of overlaps
Positive overlap	5	7	7	24
Negative overlap	0	0	0	0
Total	**5**	**7**	**7**	**24**

Table 2.3 summarises the incidence of male interviewer overlaps in the data. Again, column 1 indicates whether the overlaps were positive or negative. Columns 2 and 3 show the male interviewer and male candidate pairing: the number of interviews in which overlaps were observed and the number of overlaps across the number of interviews indicated. Similarly, columns 4 and 5 show the number of interviews in which overlaps were observed in the pairing of male interviewers and female candidates, and also the number of overlaps found within these.

In order to analyse the results of Table 2.3, and the other tables in this section, a Chi-square test analysis was used (for further explanation of Chi-square statistics see the Methodology evaluation section at the end of this chapter). Chi-square tests have 'probably been used more than any other in the study of linguistic phenomena' (Butler 1985). They are frequently used to compare frequencies of occurrence, in two or more samples or populations, of characteristics that cannot be measured in units (e.g. feet and inches, or centimetres and metres). In Table 2.3, for example, the overlaps of male interviewers are being compared for male and female candidates. The Chi-square test takes observed frequencies and, through a statistical formula, estimates expected frequencies in order to discover whether the observed and expected occurrences are not likely to be significantly different (a null hypothesis). This chapter uses a special form of Chi-square analysis known as 'Chi-square analysis, using a 2×2 contingency table'. The 2×2 contingency version enables the researcher to test whether two characteristics are independent or are associated in such a way that high frequencies of one tend to be coupled with high frequencies of the other.

A Chi-square analysis, using a 2×2 contingency table, was used to test the null hypothesis (Ho) that there was no relation between interviewer gender and candidate gender.

Result:

Interviewer overlaps ('positive' and 'negative' combined): $\chi^2 = 5.72, df = 1, p < 0.05$

Interviewer 'positive overlaps': $\chi^2 = 5.58, df = 1, p < 0.05$

The symbol χ^2 means Chi-square. The symbol df = means 'degrees of freedom' and p means the significance of the chi-square result. The reason for this result seems to be that the total number of 'positive overlaps' by male interviewers with male candidates is clearly lower than the other three pairings (refer to Tables 2.2 and 2.3). However, this result should be viewed cautiously in light of the very limited use of interviewer overlaps in the interviews overall.

Positive candidate overlaps

i) *Giving confirmation*

In this example of giving confirmation the candidate is affirming the interviewer's response that her home town Nagoya is well known:

> I: But everybody knows the name. [Nagoya]
> * C: [Oh yeah:] Mm hm I hope so.
>> Interviewer 1 (male)/Candidate 3 (female): lines 21–22

ii) *Continuation of topic/supporting*

Here the candidate (female) is supporting the interviewer's idea of shopping at the local supermarket and continuing this by offering examples of names of supermarkets:

> I: And and the supermarket um (0.5) the local supermarket a good idea to buy [buy food?]
> * C: [Mm: like Coles?] Target,
> I: Coles Target Safeway,
>> Interviewer 4 (female)/Candidate 8 (female): lines 162–65

In this example a male candidate is developing the topic of moving from a homestay to a shared house:

> I: Are you in a homestay?
> C: No I'm living share house.
> I: Oh [yeah well that's very cheap,]
> * C: [Yesterday] I moving.
> I: Oh you moved yesterday.
> C: From from homestay.
>> Interviewer 4 (female)/Candidate 7 (male): 131–35

These examples demonstrate the ways in which both female and male candidates used overlaps for 'positive' ends i.e., to confirm information and for topic development with their interviewers.

A quantitative analysis of candidate overlaps was also undertaken and the results reported below. The total number of candidate overlaps across all 32 interviews was only 77. As with the interviewers, this indicates a fairly sparing use of overlaps by individual candidates.

Table 2.4 shows the type of overlap, the number of interviews and the number of overlaps in those interviews for the gender pairings female candidate/male interviewer and female candidate/female interviewer.

Table 2.5 provides the same information for the gender pairings with male candidates.

A Chi-square analysis, using a 2×2 contingency table, was used to test the null hypothesis (Ho) that there was no relation between candidate gender and interviewer gender.

Result:
Candidate 'positive overlaps': $\chi^2 = 0.07$, $df = 1$, n.s.

As shown in both Tables 2.4 and 2.5 male candidates used fewer overlaps with both male and female interviewers. Again however, this result should be viewed with caution in light of the limited use of candidate overlaps in the interviews overall.

Table 2.4 Instances of female candidate overlaps

	Candidate: female Interviewer: male		Candidate: female Interviewer: female	
	Number of interviews	Number of overlaps	Number of interviews	Number of overlaps
Positive overlap	5	33	8	22
Negative overlap	0	0	0	0
Total	**5**	**33**	**8**	**22**

Table 2.5 Instances of male candidate overlaps

	Candidate: male Interviewer: male		Candidate: male Interviewer: female	
	Number of interviews	Number of overlaps	Number of interviews	Number of overlaps
Positive overlap	5	13	6	11
Negative overlap	0	0	0	0
Total	**5**	**13**	**6**	**11**

3.1.2 Interruptions

According to Coates (1993:109):

> Interruptions on the other hand are violations of the turn-taking rules of conversation. The next speaker begins to speak while the current speaker

is still speaking, at a point in the current speaker's turn which could not be defined as the last word. Interruptions break the symmetry of the conversational model; the interruptor prevents the speaker from finishing their turn, at the same time gaining a turn for themselves.

Coates (1993) also cites studies that observed few interruptions in same-gender pairs: where men rarely interrupt one another. She explains that 46 out of 48 observed interruptions in one study were performed by males in mixed-gender pairs.

Interruptions were employed in these 32 IELTS interviews seven times by interviewers and 17 times by candidates. It was also observed that these interruptions were actually functioning in a positive way by assisting in topic development and providing confirmation to support the interlocutor's understanding.

Interviewer interruptions

i) Developing topic

In this example we see the interviewer interrupting to take up and develop the first response given by the candidate:

> C: Yeah. Firstly I would like to improve my English because I think it's important for me to (.) to study English [and also,]
> * I: [Why?] Why do you think you need English?
> Interviewer 1 (male)/Candidate 2 (male): lines 245–48

ii) Attempt to control topic

In this instance the interviewer attempts to control the topic by redirecting the candidate away from discussing her husband's training in environmental protection to the broader area of environmental issues in South-East Asia and the whole world:

> C: Ah but after he graduate he plan he has a plan to have a small company like a consulting company,
> I: Right,
> C: Yeah. Because will popular I think we hope because the government will launch a new policy new law for the environment,
> I: Right,
> C: To protect the our environment,
> I: Yes,
> C: [So I think it very good next to train as,]
> * I: [Yes that that's um a very (.) significant area isn't it.]
> C: Mm. Mm.
> I: Well for all south-east,

C: Mm:.
I: Well for the whole world
C: Mm.

Interviewer 4 (female)/Candidate 7 (female): lines 194–208

In these examples both female and male interviewers encouraged topic development in the candidates.

The quantitative analysis of the number of interruptions used by interviewers is reported below. Table 2.6 shows female interviewer interruptions. Columns 2 and 3 show the number of interviews in which they were observed (out of the possible eight for each gender pairing), and how many interruptions were found in those interviews between female interviewers and male candidates. Columns 4 and 5 provide the same information for the gender pairings of female interviewer and female candidate.

Table 2.7 gives the same information of the number of interviews in which interruptions were observed, the number of interruptions found therein for each of the pairings of male interviewer with male candidate and male interviewer with female candidate.

Table 2.6 Instances of female interviewer interruptions

	Interviewer: female Candidate: male		Interviewer: female Candidate: female	
	Number of interviews	Number of interruptions	Number of interviews	Number of interruptions
Total	2	2	1	1

Table 2.7 Instances of male interviewer interruptions

	Interviewer: male Candidate: male		Interviewer: male Candidate: female	
	Number of interviews	Number of interruptions	Number of interviews	Number of interruptions
Total	1	4	0	0

A 2×2 contingency table was established based on this data. However, the expected frequencies were too small to carry out a Chi-square analysis.

Candidate interruptions

i) Continuing topic

In this example the interruption continues the topic of Melbourne's very unpredictable weather referred to in the interviewer's previous turn:

I: Because you know what Melbourne's like? Huh?=
C: =Yeah. (laughs)
I: Always very unpredictable? Um so just listen carefully to the forecast,=
C: =Mm hm,=
I: =And then take the right stuff for this [kind of weather.]
* C: [Because sometimes] we can't believe them.
I: That's right.

Interviewer 3 (male)/Candidate 8 (female): lines 232–40

ii) Confirming

In this instance the candidate is confirming for the interviewer that he has understood correctly what the candidate had previously explained:

I: How about the river. Do they use the river much for (.) local transportation for travel?
C: Yeah, (.) they always use ah (1.0) my ah my they always use ah boat but (.) it doesn't have much way to go to (.) it doesn't have much way to connect with another part,
I: Mm hm,
C: so if sometimes they use a boat (.) and (.) and then they use bus,
I: Mm hm,
C: to continue um (2.0) their (.) to continue to go to work,
I: Mm. So part of the journey [by boat]
* C: [yes]
I: then catch the OK. So do they have river taxis? Can you (.) catch a small boat just to go quickly across the river? Or
C: Mm: doesn't have private but have a (?) you go together with another person.
I: Mm.
C: Yeah.

Interviewer 3 (male)/Candidate 5 (male): lines 137–53

These examples show how both female and male candidates used interruptions to express positive responses to their interviewer's turns.

The quantitative analysis of candidate interruptions is given below. Table 2.8 shows the number of interviews in which interruptions occurred and the number of interruptions within those interviews between female candidates and male interviewers, and female candidates and female interviewers.

Table 2.8 Instances of female candidate interruptions

	Candidate: female Interviewer: male		Candidate: female Interviewer: female	
	Number of interviews	Number of interruptions	Number of interviews	Number of interruptions
Total	3	7	2	3

Table 2.9 Instances of male candidate interruptions

	Candidate: male Interviewer: male		Candidate: male Interviewer: female	
	Number of interviews	Number of interruptions	Number of interviews	Number of interruptions
Total	1	2	3	5

Table 2.9 provides the same information for the gender pairings of male candidate with male interviewer and male candidate with female interviewer.

Again, a 2×2 contingency table was established based on this data. However, the expected frequencies were too small to carry out a Chi-square analysis.

3.1.3 Minimal responses

Coates (1993:109) describes minimal responses (MRs) such as *yeah* and *mhm* as not constituting a turn. Instead, 'they are a way of indicating the listener's positive attention to the speaker, and thus a way of supporting the speaker in their choice of topic' (Coates 1993:109).

For Coates then, MRs are a way of indicating the listener's positive attention; a listener, therefore, has an active not a passive role. She also found research to be unanimous in showing that women use MRs more than men and at more appropriate moments.

In the IELTS interview data analysed here, MRs appeared to be used for encouraging the interlocutor to continue and supporting them by providing a signal to show active listening. There were many more instances of MRs throughout the 32 interviews than there were of either overlaps or interruptions. Interviewers' MRs totalled 805 and candidates' totalled 291. No delays in MRs were detected.

Interviewer MRs

i) Encouraging continuation

Here a male interviewer is encouraging the candidate to continue by displaying his positive attention through the use of MRs:

    I: Mm. And is it also the case that it's important that the other people
        in the family help each other ah when there is a problem with not
        earning enough money?
    C: Ah, (.) I I think this is the important from this time.
* I: Mm hm,
    C: Because ah in ah in ah in ah Bangkok big city in Thailand,
* I: Mm,
    C: The capital of Thailand,
* I: Mm,
    C: And now (?) not have a lot of job.
* I: Mm,
    C: So when the people when they come back to their city so they will be
        help another people,
* I: Mm hm,
    C: Around them.
    I: Mm, mm, And ah I mean I've been in Bangkok and I wasn't aware
        that there were many people begging or having to ask for money
        and so on, ah is this becoming more of a problem now because of
        unemployment? And the problems with the economy?
    C: Ah I think this is the problem of economic.

                  Interviewer 3 (male)/Candidate 6 (male): lines 100–19

The next example shows a female interviewer using MRs to encourage the
candidate to continue the idea she is trying to express:

    C: Ah I'm marketing supervisor,
* I: Mm hm,
    C: Also I still work hard. Everyday busy,
* I: Mm hm,
    C: Because I have a analyst analyst team? And ah (.) investigate (?)
        marketing information and I should do I should start I should do
        project and ah supervise the project how the progress,
* I: Mm:,
    C: And how affect in this project,
* I: Mm:,
    C: And I feel stress and too busy and ah no too much time for holiday
        yeah so I cracked,
    I: Not too much free time.

              Interviewer 6 (female)/Candidate 11 (female): lines 49–61

ii) Supporting

In this example the interviewer is supporting the candidate's development of the topic by employing the MR *right*:

    C: Mm I hope ah: (0.5) become teacher,
* I: Right,
    C: In high school,
* I: Right,
    C: High school or college,

Interviewer 5 (male)/Candidate 11 (female): lines 278–82

Alternatively, in the example below the interviewer uses the MR *mm* to support the candidate's development of the topic:

    C: Um yeah actually I really wanted to study about film,
* I: Mm:.
    C: But ah now my parents support me,
* I: Mm::,
    C: So if I insis insisted on studying movie,
* I: Mm:,
    C: Maybe they said absolutely no.

Interviewer 8 (female)/Candidate 13 (male): lines 205–11

These examples indicate that neither female nor male interviewers seemed to use MRs differently.

The quantitative analysis of interviewer MRs is reported below. Table 2.10 presents the figures for the use of MRs by female interviewers. Columns 2 and 3 show the number of interviews in which MRs were found (out of the possible eight for each gender pairing) and the number of MRs within those. Columns 4 and 5 provide this information for the gender pairing of female interviewer and female candidate.

Table 2.11 provides the parallel information for the male interviewers. A Chi-square analysis, using a 2×2 contingency table, was used to test the null hypothesis, (Ho), that there was no relation between interviewer gender and candidate gender.

Result:
Interviewer MRs: $\chi^2 = 4.09$, $df = 1$, $p < 0.05$

Table 2.10 Instances of female interviewer minimal responses

	Interviewer: female Candidate: male		Interviewer: female Candidate: female	
	Number of interviews	Number of MRs	Number of interviews	Number of MRs
Total	8	199	8	169

Table 2.11 Instances of male interviewer minimal responses

	Interviewer: male Candidate: male		Interviewer: male Candidate: female	
	Number of interviews	Number of MRs	Number of interviews	Number of MRs
Total	8	204	8	233

Although the result shows a significance level of $p = <0.05$, thus demonstrating a slight amount of significance (and thus a small link between male interviewers interviewing male and female candidates), the reason for this result seems to be that the total number of MRs used by female interviewers with female candidates is clearly lower than those used in the other three pairs, particularly male interviewers with female candidates.

Candidate MRs

i) Encouraging continuation

In this example the candidate signals that he is listening to the interviewer and is encouraging him to continue with the question:

    I: Ah ha oh I see. And um (0.5) when you go back to to Bangkok and you you work for a few years,

* C: yeah,

    I: In this sort of area, (0.5) what do you think ah will be the result of your work. Do you think that ah Bangkok needs a lot of construction? A lot of industrial (.) work?

          Interviewer 1 (male)/Candidate 1 (male): lines 206–11

The next example shows a female candidate using MRs for the same purpose:

    I: OK if you ah if you ah find that with your Australian qualification it's rather difficult to get a job in Japan,

* C: Mm hm,

    I: because as your mother said it might be easier with a Japanese qualification,

* C: Mm,

    I: Ah have you thought about other possible careers? As well as a career in hospitality? Are there other things you could do with your qualifications.

          Interviewer 5 (male)/Candidate 12 (female): lines 184–92

ii) Showing attention

Here the candidate is using MRs to indicate that he is paying attention to the information being provided by the interviewer:

> I: =Ok alright. Ah (0.5) I think motel will be cheaper than a hotel. (0.5) so if you're looking for the cheapest form then choose the motel accommodation, but if you want something even cheaper than motel, then you should look for hostel accommodation.
> * C: Mm.
> I: In the city (.) you'll find several hostels for example the YWCA? And they offer you rooms as well as dormitories.
> * C: Mm,
> I: So you have a choice there, or you have the Miami hostel (.) where a lot of students stay but tourists can stay there too. You will have to look at the Yellow Pages,=
> C: =Yeah=
> > Interviewer 2 (female)/Candidate 2 (male): lines 170–82

iii) Supporting

In this example the candidate uses MRs to show that she is listening and to provide support for the information being given by the interviewer:

> I: Well Japanese is usually expensive.
> C: Yeah I think so,
> I: Um there is a nice Japanese restaurant in the city,
> * C: Yeah,
> I: At the top of mm: (1.0) off the main at the top of Bourke Street you might know it.
> C: No I don't know it,
> I: Anyway that's about,
> * C: Yeah,
> I: That's one of the you know for value,
> * C: Oh:?
> I: That's probably the cheapest Japanese restaurant?
> * C: Yeah,
> I: But if you want Japanese you have to pay in Australia.
> > Interviewer 8 (female)/Candidate 15 (female): lines 134–47

These examples show that both female and male candidates seemed to use MRs to support, encourage and express interest in their interviewer in similar ways.

The quantitative analysis of candidate MRs is given below. All but one male candidate employed MRs, although not to the extent used by the interviewers. This is to be expected given their respective roles. Table 2.12 indicates

Table 2.12 Instances of female candidate minimal responses

	Candidate: female Interviewer: male		Candidate: female Interviewer: female	
	Number of interviews	Number of MRs	Number of interviews	Number of MRs
Total	8	48	8	115

Table 2.13 Instances of male candidate minimal responses

	Candidate: male Interviewer: male		Candidate: male Interviewer: female	
	Number of interviews	Number of MRs	Number of interviews	Number of MRs
Total	8	71	7	57

the female candidates' use of MRs. Columns 2 and 3 show the number of interviews and the number of MRs within those for the gender pairing female candidate and male interviewer. (There were eight of each gender pairing.) Columns 4 and 5 show this information for the interviews in which there were female candidates and female interviewers.

Table 2.13 expresses the same information for the male candidates and their use of MRs.

A Chi-square analysis, using a 2×2 contingency table, was used to test the null hypothesis (Ho) that there was no relation between candidate gender and interviewer gender.

Result:
Candidate MRs: $\chi^2 = 19.03$, $df = 1$, $p < 0.001$

The reason for this result seems to be that female candidates used a lot more MRs with female interviewers than in any of the other three pairings, especially female candidates with male interviewers.

Overall, the results of the Chi-square analysis for interviewer and candidate MRs do not reveal any clear gender pattern.

3.1.4 Summary

The results indicated that male and female interviewers used about the same number of overlaps, except for when male interviewers were paired with male candidates in which case the number was smaller. On the other hand, female candidates produced a larger number of overlaps than male candidates irrespective of the gender of their interlocutor. Therefore there is no consistent gender pattern across interviewers and candidates. However, these results should be viewed cautiously because of the very limited use of overlaps in the interviews overall.

Given the low incidence of interruptions used across 32 interviews it was not possible to draw any clear conclusions about the impact of gender on the IELTS oral interview from this perspective.

Female and male interviewers employed MRs more than either the female or male candidates. This is probably because of the role of the interviewer in facilitating the candidates' discussions. The Chi-square analysis for both interviewers' and candidates' use of MRs suggested there was a significant relation between interviewer and candidate gender. However, post-hoc inspection of the data showed that this relationship was not the same in the two analyses. Thus, there was no consistent gender pattern in the use of MRs by interviewers and candidates.

While the frequency of use showed no clear gender patterns, these discourse features were used by all participants in similar ways irrespective of gender. Through their use of overlaps, interruptions and MRs they sought to provide confirmation of ideas, to encourage continuation or development of a topic or question, to express support for their interlocutor's contributions and to indicate active attention to the interlocutor. The few instances where interviewers attempted to control the topic were still within the bounds of encouraging the candidate to develop the topic in another way; they were not trying to seize their turn.

On the basis of these findings, it would seem that interviewers and candidates generally adopted a more collaborative, co-operative and supportive communicative style irrespective of their gender or the gender of their interlocutor. Both participants appeared to understand that a co-operative dialogue would provide the best situation for the candidate to achieve the best possible result.

Having explored the impact of the gender of participants on the discourse produced in the IELTS oral interview, the second question the study aimed to address was the impact of gender on the rating of the interview.

3.2 Test scores

The primary focus of the analysis of test scores which follows is on the scores of the raters who assessed the audio-recordings of the interviews, rather than on the original interviewers' scores. There are several reasons for this. First, this analysis provides a more controlled investigation into possible gender bias in scoring since it is based on comparisons of four different ratings (two female and two male) of every interview (n = 32). Each interview, however, was only scored by one interviewer and it would therefore be extremely difficult to make meaningful comparisons of interviewers in respect to their scoring and possible gender bias. Furthermore, as outlined in Section 2.2 above (interview design), by using a mixed design whereby each interview was assessed by different combinations of male and female raters drawn from a pool of eight females and eight males, raters could be calibrated against each other in relation to their potential gender bias. Due to practical problems in conducting the interviews, such a design could not be employed for the interviews, thus disallowing this kind of intra-group comparison of their ratings. In any case, each interviewer only rated the four interviews they conducted, and this would provide insufficient evidence on which to make claims about any possible gender bias.

The band scores assigned to candidates by their interviewers and the other raters in each of the 32 interviews together with information about the gender of both candidate and interviewer are given in Table 2.14.

As is evident in this Table, it is interesting to note that the interviewers used a more restricted range of band scores (i.e. 5–7) than the other raters (i.e. 4–8). In addition, in 24 out of the total of 32 cases, the interviewer was more lenient than the average rater score. This may be due to a method difference in the way the assessments were carried out, i.e. in the live face-to-face context by the interviewers on the basis of audio-recordings by the raters. It may also be the case that interviewers are less harsh in their scoring because of their personal engagement with the candidate in the course of the interview. The differences between the leniency of the interviewers and that of the raters rating on audio tapes, does not affect the results as only the raters' results were analysed in this part of the study.

The scores of the raters who assessed the audio-recordings of the interviews were examined using a facility of the multi-faceted Rasch computer program FACETS (Linacre 1989–95), known as *bias analysis*.

Bias analysis in multi-faceted Rasch measurement identifies unexpected but consistent patterns of behaviour which may occur from an interaction of a particular rater or group of raters with respect to some component or 'facet' of the rating situation such as, in this study, candidate gender or interviewer gender. The output of these analyses shows first, whether individual raters are scoring say, candidates of one gender significantly more harshly or leniently than candidates of the other gender, and second, whether they are behaving consistently towards candidates of each gender. These analyses therefore assist in identifying potential important sources of measurement error in the rating process. Multi-faceted Rasch-based bias analysis has been used in a number of recent studies for this purpose (see, for example, McNamara 1996, O'Loughlin 2001, Wigglesworth 1993). Bias analysis is used in the current study to investigate the impact of candidate and rater gender on the reliability of test scores.

Table 2.14 Summary of results

Candidate		Interviewer			Raters' score			
Number	Gender	Number	Gender	Score	Female		Male	
1	Male	1	Male	5	5	6	6	5
1	Male	2	Female	6	6	5	5	4
2	Male	1	Male	6	6	7	6	6
2	Male	2	Female	7	6	6	6	7
3	Female	1	Male	7	7	7	8	7
3	Female	2	Female	7	6	6	7	7
4	Female	1	Male	5	6	5	5	5
4	Female	2	Female	7	6	5	5	6
5	Male	3	Male	6	5	4	5	5
5	Male	4	Female	5	6	5	5	4
6	Male	3	Male	6	. 5	6	5	5
6	Male	4	Female	6	5	4	5	5
7	Female	3	Male	7	6	6	6	6
7	Female	4	Female	6	6	5	6	5
8	Female	3	Male	6	6	5	7	5
8	Female	4	Female	6	5	5	5	6
9	Male	5	Male	6	4	4	5	4
9	Male	6	Female	5	4	5	5	4
10	Male	5	Male	6	5	6	5	6
10	Male	6	Female	6	6	5	6	5
11	Female	5	Male	5	5	5	5	3
11	Female	6	Female	6	5	4	6	5
12	Female	5	Male	5	5	4	5	4
12	Female	6	Female	6	5	4	4	4
13	Male	7	Male	6	5	6	5	6
13	Male	8	Female	6	7	5	5	5
14	Male	7	Male	6	5	5	5	6
14	Male	8	Female	7	6	6	7	5
15	Female	7	Male	6	5	6	5	7
15	Female	8	Female	5	7	5	5	6
16	Female	7	Male	6	5	6	6	5
16	Female	8	Female	7	5	6	6	6

Question 1: Is there a significant interaction between raters' scoring and candidate gender?

The first issue to be examined involves the interaction between raters' scores and candidate gender. In other words, do raters score candidates of either gender significantly more harshly than the other? The output from the bias analysis conducted here provides detailed information about individual raters in relation to this question.

Table 2.15 shows the output from the bias analysis. In this table, Column 1 provides the rater identity number and Column 2 candidate gender. Column 3 provides the total observed score of each rater for female and male candidates respectively, while Column 4 shows each rater's total expected score for the two versions. Column 5 shows the number of ratings given by the rater to candidates of the specified gender. Column 6 then provides the average difference between the expected and observed score. A bias logit, based on this difference, is then calculated together with its standard error (columns 7 and 8). The bias score is then converted into a standardised Z-score by dividing it by its standard error (column 9). The Z-score values are the most revealing figures in this analysis. Where the Z-score values fall between -2.0 and $+2.0$, the rater may be considered to be scoring candidates from the specified gender without significant bias. Where the value falls below -2.0 the rater is marking candidates from the specified gender significantly more leniently than the other gender. On the other hand, where the value is greater than $+2.0$ the rater is scoring candidates of the specified gender significantly more harshly compared to the way that the rater treats the other gender. Furthermore, in this analysis the infit mean square value (column 10) indicates how *similar* the rater's scoring is for the specified gender overall. Where the value is less than 0.7 the rater's scoring for candidates of that gender lacks variation, i.e. it is too similar. Conversely, where this value is greater than 1.3 the rater's scoring tends to be inconsistent for the given gender.

Since all of the Z-scores are within the range of -2 to $+2$ it can be concluded that none of the raters is significantly biased in favour of candidates of either gender. The infit mean square values, however, suggest that there are a number of raters whose scoring is too similar for female candidates overall, i.e. raters 1, 2, 4, 5, 6, 9 and 15 and for male candidates overall, i.e. raters 2, 5, 6, 7, 8, 9, 10, 11, and 16. This is perhaps not surprising given that the whole group of raters only assigned band scores between 4 and 8 and mostly, 5, 6 or 7. Conversely, raters 7, 8, 10, 11 and 16 show a significant tendency to be inconsistent in their scoring of female candidates and raters 1 and 12 in their scoring of male candidates. However, given the relatively small number of assessments carried out by each rater for candidates of either gender ($n = 2–6$) this trend towards inconsistency should be regarded with a degree of caution.

Table 2.15 Bias calibration report, rater–candidate gender interaction

Rater ID	Candidate gender	Observed score	Expected score	Observed count	Obs.-Exp. score	Bias (logit)	Error	Z-score	Infit mn sq
1	Female	22	23.0	4	−0.25	0.34	0.59	0.6	0.4
1	Male	23	22.0	4	0.25	−0.34	0.58	−0.6	1.6
2	Female	22	21.5	4	0.13	−0.19	0.59	−0.3	0.4
2	Male	20	20.6	4	−0.14	0.23	0.64	0.4	0.0
3	Female	12	11.6	2	0.19	−0.25	0.81	−0.3	1.3
3	Male	33	33.4	6	−0.06	0.09	0.49	0.2	0.8
4	Female	32	33.4	6	−0.23	0.33	0.50	0.7	0.3
4	Male	12	10.7	2	0.67	−0.92	0.81	−1.1	1.3
5	Female	11	11.4	2	−0.18	0.25	0.84	0.3	0.4
5	Male	33	32.6	6	0.06	−0.09	0.49	−0.2	0.4
6	Female	21	22.5	4	−0.37	0.54	0.62	0.9	1.0
6	Male	23	21.5	4	0.31	0.51	0.58	−0.9	0.3
7	Female	27	25.4	5	−0.54	0.48	0.54	−0.9	1.5
7	Male	13	14.6	3	0.19	0.93	0.76	1.2	0.4
8	Female	27	26.1	5	−0.33	0.28	0.54	−0.5	1.5
8	Male	14	15.0	3	0.25	0.55	0.75	0.7	0.4
9	Female	24	23.0	4	−0.25	0.33	0.57	−0.6	0.6
9	Male	21	22.0	4	−0.25	0.37	0.62	0.6	0.3
10	Female	26	23.5	4	0.62	0.82	0.58	−1.4	1.7
10	Male	20	22.5	4	−0.62	0.93	0.64	1.5	0.0
11	Female	21	20.4	4	0.14	0.21	0.62	−0.3	1.8
11	Male	19	19.6	4	−0.15	0.25	0.65	0.4	0.3
12	Female	25	23.5	4	0.37	0.49	0.57	−0.9	0.9
12	Male	21	22.5	4	−0.37	0.54	0.62	0.9	1.8
13	Female	20	20.4	4	−0.11	0.18	0.64	0.3	0.8
13	Male	20	19.6	4	0.10	0.16	0.64	−0.2	0.8
14	Female	20	21.0	4	−0.24	0.38	0.64	0.6	0.8
14	Male	21	20.1	4	0.23	0.36	0.62	−0.6	1.0
15	Female	23	23.5	4	−0.13	0.17	0.58	0.3	0.3
15	Male	23	22.5	4	0.13	0.17	0.58	−0.3	0.9
16	Female	19	22.0	4	−0.74	0.17	0.65	1.8	2.0
16	Male	24	21.1	4	0.74	0.02	0.57	−1.8	0.6

Source: 2002 Edward Arnold (publishers) Ltd.

Question 2: Is there a significant interaction between candidates' scores and rater gender?

The second bias analysis examined whether there was a significant interaction between candidate scores and rater gender. In other words, the issue here is whether raters of one gender scored candidates significantly more harshly than raters of the other gender. The results of this bias analysis are shown in Table 2.16.

The results indicate that none of the candidates was treated significantly more harshly by raters of either gender since all Z-scores fell within the range of -2 and $+2$. Once again, however, the infit mean square values indicate a tendency for raters to assess candidates either too similarly or too inconsistently. On the one hand, the scoring of female raters as a group for candidates 1, 2, 3, 4, 7, 8, 9, 10, 11, 14 and 16 and male raters as a group for candidates 2, 3, 4, 5, 6, 7, 12, 13 and 16 was too similar. As in the previous analysis, this is not unexpected given that the whole group of raters only assigned band scores between 4 and 8 and mostly, 5, 6 or 7. On the other hand, the scoring of female raters as a group for candidates 5, 6, 13 and 15 and male raters as a group for candidates 1, 8, 10, 11, 14, and 15 showed too much variability. Again, given the relatively small number of assessments carried out for each candidate by raters of either gender group (n = 4) this trend towards inconsistency should also be regarded with a degree of caution.

Question 3: Is there a significant interaction between candidate gender and rater gender?

The third bias analysis examined whether there is a significant interaction between candidate gender and rater gender. Table 2.17 summarises the output from this analysis.

The Z-score values indicate that the interaction between candidate gender and rater gender is not significant, i.e. candidate scores are not significantly affected by whether their rater is of the same or opposite sex. Furthermore, in only one gender combination, i.e. male raters with female candidates, is the infit mean square value outside the acceptable range: in this case a value of 1.4 suggests that male raters tended to score female candidates less consistently than the three other gender pairings overall.

From the above analyses it appears that the impact of both candidate and rater gender on test scores in the IELTS oral interview is not significant. However, this conclusion should be regarded with some caution given the relatively small data set available for analysis. Furthermore, the findings here do not imply that the measurement process

Table 2.16 Bias calibration report, candidate–rater gender interaction

Candidate ID	Rater gender	Observed score	Expected score	Observed count	Obs.-Exp. score	Bias (logit)	Error	Z-score	Infit mn sq
1	Female	22	20.9	4	0.26	−0.71	0.79	−0.9	0.6
2	Female	25	24.9	4	0.02	−0.05	0.74	−0.1	0.4
3	Female	26	27.4	4	−0.35	0.91	0.77	1.2	0.6
4	Female	22	21.4	4	0.14	−0.37	0.79	−0.5	0.6
5	Female	20	19.5	4	0.13	−0.43	0.90	−0.5	1.6
6	Female	20	20.0	4	0.01	−0.03	0.90	0.0	1.6
7	Female	23	22.9	4	0.02	−0.05	0.75	−0.1	0.4
8	Female	21	21.9	4	−0.23	0.62	0.85	0.7	0.5
9	Female	17	17.5	4	−0.12	0.32	0.82	0.4	0.5
10	Female	22	22.4	4	−0.10	0.25	0.79	0.3	0.6
11	Female	19	19.0	4	0.01	−0.02	0.87	0.0	0.6
12	Female	18	17.5	4	0.13	−0.36	0.83	−0.4	0.7
13	Female	23	21.9	4	0.27	−0.63	0.75	−0.8	1.5
14	Female	22	22.4	4	−0.10	0.25	0.79	0.3	0.6
15	Female	23	22.9	4	0.02	−0.05	0.75	−0.1	1.5
16	Female	22	22.4	4	−0.10	0.25	0.79	0.3	0.6
1	Male	20	21.1	4	−0.26	0.81	0.90	0.9	1.6
2	Male	25	25.0	4	−0.01	0.03	0.75	0.0	0.4
3	Male	29	27.5	4	0.37	−1.10	0.88	−1.3	0.6
4	Male	21	21.6	4	−0.14	0.38	0.85	0.4	0.5
5	Male	19	19.6	4	−0.14	0.45	0.87	0.5	0.6
6	Male	20	20.1	4	−0.02	0.05	0.90	0.1	0.0
7	Male	23	23.1	4	−0.01	0.03	0.75	0.0	0.4
8	Male	23	22.1	4	0.24	−0.55	0.75	0.7	1.5
9	Male	18	17.6	4	0.10	−0.28	0.83	0.3	0.7
10	Male	23	22.6	4	0.11	−0.25	0.75	0.3	1.5
11	Male	19	19.1	4	−0.02	0.06	0.87	0.1	3.6
12	Male	17	17.6	4	−0.15	0.40	0.82	0.5	0.5
13	Male	21	22.1	4	−0.26	0.70	0.85	0.8	0.5
14	Male	23	22.6	4	0.11	−0.25	0.75	0.3	1.5
15	Male	23	23.1	4	−0.01	0.03	0.75	0.0	1.5
16	Male	23	22.6	4	0.11	−0.25	0.75	−0.3	0.4

Source: 2002 Edward Arnold (publishers) Ltd.

can be considered flawless: it could still be true that certain candidates are rated significantly more harshly or leniently by individual raters compared to the way that rater treats other candidates irrespective of candidate or rater gender.

Table 2.17 Bias calibration report, candidate gender–rater gender interaction

Candidate gender	Rater gender	Observed score	Expected score	Observed count	Obs.-Exp. score	Bias (logit)	Error	Z-score	Infit mn sq
Female	Female	174	175.4	32	−0.04	0.06	0.20	0.3	0.8
Male	Female	171	169.7	32	0.04	−0.06	0.20	−0.3	0.9
Female	Male	178	176.4	32	0.05	−0.06	0.20	−0.3	1.4
Male	Male	169	170.6	32	−0.05	0.07	0.21	0.3	0.9

Source: 2002 Edward Arnold (publishers) Ltd.

Table 2.18 Bias calibration report, significant interactions between candidates and raters

Candidate ID	Rater ID	Observed score	Expected score	Observed count	Obs.-Exp. score	Bias (logit)	Error	Z-score	Infit mn sq
1	12	4	5.3	1	−1.3	5.07	1.92	2.6	0.0
11	16	3	4.7	1	−1.71	4.47	1.93	2.3	0.7

Source: 2002 Edward Arnold (publishers) Ltd.

Question 4: Is there a significant interaction between individual candidates and raters?

The final bias analysis therefore examined whether there were any candidates who were treated by a particular rater significantly more or less harshly than that rater would treat other candidates. The output from this analysis revealed there were only two such occurrences. Table 2.18 provides the output from the analysis for these cases.

In both instances, since the Z-score values are greater than +2, the raters are marking the specified candidate significantly more harshly than they would other candidates. Considering there were only two such occurrences out of a total of 128 ratings it can be concluded that there was a high degree of intra-rater reliability in this study.

4 Conclusions

To sum up the findings: the results from both the discourse and test score analyses suggested that gender did not have a significant impact on the IELTS oral interview in this study. The discourse analysis indicated, first, in relative terms, that there was limited use of overlap, negligible use of interruptions and widespread use of minimal responses in the interviews. Second, the use of these features did not appear to follow any clear gendered pattern. Third, there was a high degree of variability in the use of overlaps and especially minimal responses within the different gender pairings. Most importantly, perhaps, both female and male participants indicated their ability to make supportive contributions to the interviews through their use of positive overlaps and minimal responses in particular. A collaborative style is therefore clearly not exclusively the province of female speakers in the testing context.

The test scores analyses also revealed that the gender of candidates and raters did not have a significant impact on the rating process. This finding, in particular, conflicts with other recent studies which have reported a significant gender effect in the rating of test takers, although, as noted earlier in this article, the direction of this effect has not been consistent.

Why there was little or no discernible gender effect in either the interviews or subsequent ratings in this study is difficult to determine. Some of the possible reasons will now be examined. In terms of the interview process, perhaps the test tasks used and/or the roles of interviewer and candidate are particularly gender neutral in the IELTS test. Might a clearer gender effect emerge in oral tests where candidates are paired? Alternatively, in terms of methodology, is it possible that pre-selecting the discourse features used to examine the interviews in this study meant that the analysis ignored other ways in which gender may have had an impact on the oral interview?

In terms of the rating process, could it be that the global band scale used in the test is not sensitive enough to register a gender effect amongst raters where it does exist? Or else, does focusing on the scores of raters who were not the original interviewers in this study mask a gender effect that results from the interaction between the interviewing and rating processes under normal conditions? Would there have been evidence of a gender effect in the ratings if the test performances had been video-taped rather than audio-taped? Any one or combination of these factors may account for the observed lack of gender effect in this study.

However, another way to understand why this and other studies into the impact of gender in speaking tests seem to contradict each other is to speculate from a broader social perspective about characteristics of the context and participants which might bring gender differences into play rather than simply on the test instrument itself. It is highly possible that aspects of the testing context itself, such as the purpose of the test, the language being tested, the country where it is administered as well as the social identities of the interviewer and test taker (including their gender, age, ethnicity and perceived status), may determine whether significant gender differences emerge in both the interviewing and rating processes. For instance, in Australia the IELTS oral interview is conducted by experienced ESL teachers of the host country who often work with international students on a regular basis. Their behaviour in the interviews may be most strongly influenced by how they view their task. If they consider it to be closely aligned to their teaching role then it is possible they will adopt a supportive, facilitative interviewer style. If they view it as more distant from their teaching role – more in terms of say impartial judge or gatekeeper – they may use a much less supportive style. This, in turn, could affect the way the candidate responds to them. In other words, the professional orientation of the teacher-as-interviewer may influence their behaviour more strongly than gender differences.

Furthermore, the fact that gendered differences amongst interviewers and candidates were not clearly evident in the interviews may have reduced the salience of gender to the raters who subsequently scored the audio-taped performances without significant gender bias. However, in other test settings where interviewers are not trained language teachers, then perhaps both the interviewing and rating processes may be more significantly affected by gender differences. Further research on these issues needs to be undertaken.

It would appear, therefore, that gendered differences are not inevitable in the testing context. This is consistent with recent thinking in the fields of both gender studies and applied linguistics suggesting that gender competes with other aspects of an individual's social identity in a fluid and dynamic fashion. In one situation it may be strongly foregrounded, in another much less so. In short, we cannot always easily predict when gender will have a significant impact on speaking tests, and this seems to be equally true for both the interviewing and rating processes.

Acknowledgements

A version of this paper was previously published in 2002 in *Language Testing* 19, 167–90: The impact of gender in oral proficiency testing, by Kieran O'Loughlin.

I wish to thank IELTS Australia for the research grant which enabled me to undertake the study, the language centre in Melbourne which provided the facilities for the data collection, as well as the candidates, interviewers and raters who participated in the study. I am also extremely grateful to Jeanette Carter for her assistance in many aspects of this research project.

Note

1   In each of the examples * indicates the focus of analysis, I = Interviewer and C = Candidate.

APPENDIX 2.1

Transcription notation

1. *Unfilled pauses and gaps*: periods of silence are timed in tenths of a second by counting 'beats' of elapsed time in accordance with the rhythm of the preceding speech. Micropauses, those of less than 0.2 seconds are symbolised (.); longer pauses appear as time within parentheses: e.g. (0.8) = 0.8 seconds. Where 'real' time is indicated (e.g. in between the end of task instructions and the beginning of the candidate's response brackets { } are used.

2. *Repair phenomena*: reformulations are indicated by a hyphen -.

3. *Intonation*: a period . indicates a falling intonation, a question mark ? marks a rising intonation and a comma , is used for continuing intonation.

4. *Overlapping talk*: brackets [ ] are used to indicate overlaps, i.e. where utterances start and/or end simultaneously.

5. *Transcription doubt or uncertainty*: these are marked by a question mark within parentheses (?)

6. *Quiet talk*: percent signs %% are used to mark the boundaries of quiet talk.

7. *Latched utterances*: i.e. where there is no interval between utterances: equal signs = are used at the end of the first utterance and at the beginning of the second utterance.

8. *Lengthened sounds or syllables*: a colon : is used; more colons prolong the stretch.

9. *Speakers*: The interviewer is indicated by I and the candidate by C.

Methodology evaluation of Chapter 2

Chapter 2 contains two approaches to a discussion of the effect of gender in the assessment of speaking in IELTS. First, it uses a discourse analysis approach to three categories of rater/candidate and candidate/rater interaction. The three categories are: interaction overlaps between the interviewer and the candidate or the candidate and the interviewer; interruptions from the interviewer or from the candidate; and minimal responses either from the interviewer or from the candidate. The author has taken these categories from the work of Coates (1993) and investigates whether commonly-accepted views on rater gender judgements can be substantiated. On the whole, the findings are that gender differences are not significant in IELTS oral examining.

In order to analyse the results of the discourse analysis section of the study, a very common set of statistics is used. This is the Chi-square test which Butler (1985) has described as probably being 'used more than any other in the study of linguistic phenomena' (page 113). The Chi-square test is used when the significance of differences between non-quantitative measures needs to be calculated. Other statistical instruments are used when the significance of the differences between quantitative measures is being calculated (see the research methodology comments for Chapter 6). The Chi-square test is thus an extremely useful tool when researchers are dealing with non-quantitative measures such as the frequency of present-tense verbs, or the frequency of nouns in a text. It is thus an indispensable tool for language and language test researchers. The normal Chi-square test compares observed frequencies of an occurrence with the expected frequencies of an occurrence and decides whether or not a comparison of those frequencies is significant. If it is not, the default expectation known as the null hypothesis (Ho) – where significance is not expected – has been proven and it can be said, confidently, that there is no significant difference between the categories being analysed.

In this chapter a different form of the Chi-square test is used. This is known as a Chi-square 2×2 contingency analysis. Whereas the normal Chi-square test deals with frequencies of occurrence of a number of categories (e.g. whether a number of trains are running on time and whether the differences are significant or not), the 2×2 contingency version enables the research to 'test whether two characteristics are independent or are associated in such a way that high frequencies of one tend to be coupled with high frequencies of the other' (Butler 1995:118).

In the second part of this chapter, the author analyses the results of an assessment of speaking ability in IELTS. The candidates, of both genders, are assessed by raters of different genders using audio-recordings of interviews as the data. The increasingly common statistical tool used in this section of the chapter is the multifaceted Rasch computer program

FACETS. This tool was used in Chapter 1 and an explanation of its major categories was presented. In this chapter, somewhat more explanation is presented by the author himself. Thus, the chapter provides a good example of the use of multi-faceted Rasch analysis for language and language testing researchers who might want to familiarise themselves with this analytical tool before beginning to use it for their own research.

The chapter demonstrates that complementary methods can be used successfully when investigating linked research questions. The first section deals with the analysis of discourse while the second section deals with the scores that raters of different genders give to candidates of different genders.

One issue involving the validity of the study is the decision to provide feedback to candidates by interviewers immediately after the interview. This issue occurs frequently in research when the co-operation of 'subjects/data points' is sought by researchers. If asked whether they will take part in an activity linked to a test they are about to take in the future, candidates will often volunteer but a condition of their co-operation usually includes a, quite natural, request for feedback so that they can gauge how well or how badly they have done on the test. The problem with agreeing to give feedback is that the results of the second interview (each candidate had an interview with a male and female rater) might be contaminated by the initial feedback. Researchers might wish to consider two methods where this possibility of contamination by feedback can be resolved or, at least, mitigated.

The first, and preferred, method is to leave all forms of feedback until after the second interview. This would resolve the problem at once. The second method would be to avoid mention of the categories of discourse being investigated after the initial interview. Thus, in this study, if it was thought necessary to give feedback after the initial interview, any mention of Coates' (1993) three categories of overlap, interruption and minimal response could be omitted from the feedback provided by the interviewer. If the interviewer thinks that the use or lack of use of these three categories of discourse might be a problem for the candidate in a 'live' IELTS test, comments could be withheld until after the second interview has been completed.

3 An investigation of the rating process in the IELTS oral interview

Annie Brown

Abstract

Holistic assessments of oral language proficiency are often made in relation to performance in conversational language proficiency interviews, one such example of which is the IELTS oral interview. This study seeks to explore the rating practices of trained and accredited IELTS raters when judging candidates' performance in IELTS interviews. In particular, it aims to address questions such as:

- How do raters cope with the task of having to base an assessment of *ability* on a single *performance*?
- What is the relationship of linguistic and non-linguistic aspects of the performance?
- How is the *interlocutor's* performance dealt with in the assessment of the *candidate's* ability?
- Do raters focus on criteria other than those specifically mentioned in the descriptors?
- How salient are the stated criteria?
- Does the same performance elicit judgements of the same kind from different raters?

This study adds to a small but growing body of qualitative research into the judgements made in assessments of second language speaking proficiency. Using data (taped IELTS interviews) collected in an earlier study (Brown and Hill 1998; this now appears as Chapter 1 in this volume), eight IELTS raters each rated four interviews selected from a set of eight using the IELTS band scales. For each interview they provided a verbal protocol where they first summarised the reasons for the score they had awarded and then reviewed the tape in order to identify those features of the rating procedure which influenced their scoring. This methodology is known as stimulated verbal recall (di Pardo 1994). In these interviews, the raters were asked to talk about the judging process and to identify the salient decision-making points of the interview.

The raters were all accredited and practising IELTS interviewers. The candidates were all overseas students drawn from a pre-university (Foundation) course. At the time of the interviews they were preparing to take IELTS prior to submitting applications for tertiary study in Australia.

The protocols were transcribed and coded. Findings are discussed and implications are drawn regarding the validity of this test format.

1 Introduction

The conversational language proficiency interview, a face-to-face interview in which an interviewer questions a learner on a number of specified topics, is a popular technique for the assessment of oral language proficiency. The popularity of this technique derives to a large extent from the belief that it provides a context in which candidates' *communicative* and *interactional* skills can be tested. The IELTS oral interview is one example of this test genre.

The discourse produced in conversational language proficiency interviews has been the focus of a number of studies, often in response to questions of authenticity or the conversational nature of the interaction (see, for example, Cafarella 1994, Filipi 1994, Lazaraton 1993, 1996b, 1997, Neeson 1985, Perrett 1990, Ross 1992, Ross and Berwick 1992, Young and Milanovic 1992). However, despite claims that interactional skills and communicative skills (for example the ability to negotiate meaning, the ability to maintain a conversation) are tapped in conversational interviews, there are as yet relatively few studies of the *rating* process, investigating just what raters take into account when awarding scores, despite a growing interest in general in what raters do (see Brown 1995, Chalhoub-Deville 1995, Lazaraton 1993, 1996, McNamara and Lumley 1997, Meiron 1998, Pollitt and Murray 1996). In particular, in contrast with research into raters' decision-making processes in the assessment of writing, there are as yet few published studies which use verbal protocols.

Verbal protocol studies can provide valuable information on aspects of the rating process which quantitative studies of test scores cannot necessarily explore. For example: How do raters cope with the task of having to base a general assessment of *ability* on a single, co-constructed *performance*? How is the *interlocutor's* performance dealt with in the assessment of a *candidate's* ability? and What is the relationship between *linguistic* and *non-linguistic* aspects of the performance?

This study adds to a small but growing body of qualitative research into the judgements made in assessments of second language speaking proficiency. Retrospective verbal protocols provided by a group of trained IELTS raters are analysed in order to investigate how the construct of oral language ability is understood, how linguistic and other criteria contribute to raters' judgements, and which aspects of candidates' performances are salient to these judgements. In other words, it seeks to shed some light on the question *What does it mean to be proficient?* in the context of the IELTS oral interview.

The study seeks in particular to respond to a range of questions raised in earlier studies of both speaking and writing assessment. Researchers have commented, for example, on the existence of 'implicit' criteria, criteria which are not explicitly stated in the band descriptors. They have also commented on the fact that of the stated criteria, some may be more salient than others, and that judgements may in fact be based on one or two particular language behaviours rather than on the whole range of features included in the band descriptors. It appears also to be the case that different features may be more or less salient at different levels of proficiency.

As noted, conversational interviews are generally considered appropriate means of assessing not only traditional linguistic criteria (such as accuracy, syntactic and vocabulary breadth, and pronunciation) but also aspects of what is commonly termed *communicative competence*. The influence of less narrowly linguistic factors (such as sensitivity to audience, interactive skill, personal style, etc.) in performance-based language assessment has long been acknowledged and discussed by language testers (see, for example, Jones 1985, McNamara 1990, Upshur 1979, Wesche 1992), although there is considerable disagreement on what should or shouldn't be included in second language proficiency tests. Absalom and Brice (1997), for example, consider pragmatic skills such as affecting and responding to an interlocutor, expressing one's self (ideas and emotions), initiating and controlling dialogue, cuing topic shifts and listening actively to be important aspects of the oral proficiency construct. Similarly, Bennett and Slaughter refer to the importance of interactional skills in determining 'conversational proficiency' over and above the 'linguistic skills', for example in ensuring coherence through 'the provision of adequate background information and specific pronoun reference' (1983:19). Others argue that not all aspects of the performance are necessarily relevant to the construct of second language proficiency. 'Interpersonal skills and other affective components', for example, are rejected by Stansfield and Powers (1983) as dimensions of second language communicative competence. De Jong and van Ginkel (1992:187) similarly argue that 'productive skills are observable, but not everything that can be observed in performance data is necessarily skill related'.

A few studies have attempted to identify aspects of the construct of second language speaking proficiency within the context of specific tests. Hadden (1991), for example, found linguistic ability to be but one of five factors contributing to global assessments of oral communicative proficiency, the others being comprehensibility, social acceptability, personality and body language, and argues that there is, therefore, a lack of a direct relationship between linguistic ability and communicative proficiency. Chalhoub-Deville (1995) found that as well as the more linguistic features (grammar and pronunciation) raters focused upon creativity and content (for example, the extent to which the speaker engages the listener) and on detail (for example, the ability to provide information unassisted, the length of the answer and the amount of elaboration). However, while such studies depend upon the analysis of analytic scores, many language proficiency interviews (like IELTS) are based upon a single holistic rating which is not amenable to such analysis.

This shift away from a focus on narrowly linguistic skills towards communicative skill appears to have created an assessment climate where raters, in order to make judgements about learners' communicative skills, need to make *inferences* about candidates on the basis of their communicative behaviours. Pollitt and Murray (1996), in a study of the Certificate of Proficiency in English examination raters' perceptions using a type of verbal protocol, found that many of the raters' statements consisted of inferences about candidates based on their behaviour. Raters referred, for example, to the candidates' exam-consciousness, apparent lack of intelligence, maturity, willingness or reluctance to converse and sex-related comfort or discomfort. In fact, Pollitt and Murray conclude, raters are 'as concerned with their interpretation of what they observed as with those objective features evident in the performances and equally accessible to all judges'.

While most would agree that inferences are not a suitable basis for judgements, it is nevertheless clear that the assessment of communicative skill is a complex task, made all the more complex because of the general lack of agreement and clarity about what aspects of performance are relevant. Shohamy and Walton (1992) point out, 'The degree of uncertainty about which categories are relevant [to judging the success of the communication] and which kinds of distinctions should be made only increases as we move further away from a purely linguistic description.' We believe that in the IELTS oral interview, which espouses a communicative model (Ingram and Wylie 1996) and which aims to evaluate candidates' ability to cope with the communicative demands of tertiary study, non-linguistic aspects of the performance will inevitably be drawn into the raters' judgements. One aim of this study will be to identify those aspects of the performance and the performer, both linguistic and non-linguistic, which contribute to the raters' perceptions of proficiency.

A further complexity in the assessment of speaking proficiency in a conversational interview concerns the question *Whose ability?* While the potential for variation amongst interviewers in how they manage the interview and construct the 'task' for the candidate has long been acknowledged, it is only recently that studies investigating the form and effect of this variation have begun to appear (e.g. Brown and Hill 1998, Brown and Lumley 1997, Halleck and Reed 1996, Lazaraton 1996a, 1996b, Ross 1996). Variation in interviewer style, of course, means that aspects of the task will not be the same for all candidates. It also appears to be the case that interviewers support the candidates (i.e. accommodate their language to that of the candidate) to differing extents and scaffold the task differently. Although raters are required to make a single judgement of the candidate alone, it is inevitable that interviewers' behaviour will impact on their scoring.

In a study of the role of interviewer quality in tape-based ratings of second language interviews, for example, McNamara and Lumley (1997) found that raters compensated for what they considered to be poor interviewing technique. This finding is supported by a similar study by Morton et al (1997), and also by Pollitt and Murray (1996) who found that raters made reference to interviewers being encouraging or not. Brown and Hill (1998; this now appears as Chapter 1 in this volume) found that raters appeared also to be unconsciously affected by the interviewer when scoring candidates, in that with certain raters candidates were likely to be awarded lower scores than they would receive with others. The present study therefore investigates the extent to which raters include or refer to the interviewer when making judgements of candidates' ability, and what aspects of interviewer behaviour in particular are commented upon.

Findings regarding the nature of holistic assessment of writing as revealed through protocol studies are also likely to be of relevance to this study. Vaughan, in one such study, argues that 'holistic assessment . . . rests on the assumption that trained raters will respond to an essay in the same way if they are given a set of characteristics to guide them' (1991:111), yet she found that raters did not apply the same criteria to each performance when making holistic judgements. In addition, she reports that when the holistic scales don't fit, they 'fall back on their own styles of judging'. Given the holistic nature of the IELTS band scales, and the vagueness of meaning in terms used within them (e.g. 'communicates effectively'), it may well be that raters make individual interpretations of what the scales mean. In addition, the communicative focus of the scales may lead raters to evaluate aspects of the performance which are the least controlled (the interactive aspect) and which may vary considerably from interview to interview.

So, it seems that however tightly defined the criteria or scales are, it is not necessarily the case that all raters will react to the same performance in the same way. There are grounds for empirical investigation of the rating process in order to provide a more thorough understanding of the features of performances which impact on the scores awarded. Such a study can also serve as a type of validation of the test construct: if raters are unable to interpret the scales or apply their own criteria rather than those of the test developer, the validity of the whole exercise will come into question. Agreement between raters is particularly likely to be an issue where, as is the case with IELTS, rater re-accreditation does not necessarily involve retraining, but simply the re-rating of a set of tapes. It may be, in fact, that raters are in agreement in the scores they award but disagree as to why they awarded them. This in itself, whilst not an issue of test reliability, is certainly of interest with regard to test validity.

Finally, the dearth of protocol studies of oral proficiency assessment means that the way in which raters go about the task of rating oral performance is somewhat less well known than that of rating writing. One study, by Pollitt and Murray (1996), which used a methodology based on Kelly's (1954) Personal Construct Theory, found that the six raters used two contrastive approaches to assessment:

(a) A 'synthetic' process in which a holistic image is formed which derives from the individual's preconstructed understanding of language learners. 'Some aspect of the performance serves as a primary indicator of level, and the observed performance is then compared with the judge's memory of a person at that level; if it fits reasonably then all of the traits in the judge's repertoire become part of the description of the individual.'

(b) A process whereby raters limited their comments to observed behaviour – 'a more objective, less natural mode signalling perhaps a greater effort to think within a strictly assessment-oriented framework. The impression is that they scored the candidate intuitively for each observed utterance, and somehow added these up.'

Meiron (1998) found that similar approaches were adopted by the raters in a study of assessments made in relation to the Test of Spoken English. It is anticipated that the present study will provide some evidence of raters' approaches to rating the IELTS oral interview.

2 Overview of the study

The aims of this study are to investigate the orientations of trained IELTS raters when holistically rating the IELTS oral interview. The particular aims are to gather, present and discuss retrospective protocol data in relation to:

- the construct of oral proficiency as perceived by IELTS raters
- the constituent aspects of specific categories of linguistic features
- the extent to which the same performance elicits judgements of the same type
- features of interviewer behaviour which may impact on raters' judgements of candidate proficiency.

Using data (taped IELTS interviews) collected in an earlier study (Brown and Hill 1998), raters were asked to rate a series of interviews using the IELTS band scales and to identify those features of the performance which influenced the scores they awarded. In retrospective verbal protocols, elicited after each tape had been rated, they were asked to identify the salient decision-making points of the interview, to describe why they awarded the score they did, and to talk about the judging process. These protocol data were then transcribed, coded and analysed.

3 The IELTS oral interview

This section provides an overview of the IELTS oral interview, both the developers' intentions and the test itself. The test consists of two aspects, the task and the band scales, although we would argue that the criteria (and, in particular, the raters' interpretations of them) more properly reflect the operational construct. Below we consider firstly the construct from the test developers' perspective, as specified in a review of the developmental process (Ingram and Wylie 1996). This is followed by a description of the interview format and band scales.

3.1 The development of the IELTS oral interview

Ingram and Wylie (1996) report on the development of the IELTS oral interview in what appears to be the most comprehensive publicly available document pertaining to the interview. The following excerpts provide something of a picture of the construct from the 'task' aspect (the complementary aspect to this being the criteria contained in the scales which will be discussed subsequently):

> The three main phases of the interview were sequenced to give candidates the initiative from the start, to encourage them to become <u>active participants in the conversational exchange</u> rather than just provide minimal responses to a series of questions, and to enable them to demonstrate their ability to produce a variety of eliciting functions . . . Phase 3 [later Phase 2] was designed to give candidates the opportunity to produce <u>extended speech</u>, describing, narrating, explaining or speculating on a familiar topic generally relating to their own experience. Phase 4 was to be a 'dialogue', a classic oral interview situation in which interviewers used brief 'c.v.' forms that had been filled in by candidates before the interview as a basis on which to engage them in discussions (including speculative discussions) about future intentions. This phase was intended to personalise the test, provide something familiar on which candidates could be questioned and could <u>respond at length</u>, and allow scope for more complex, speculative language . . . the principal reason for the test

was to require candidates <u>to take the initiative</u>, <u>seek information</u>, and <u>speak at length</u>'.

[Phase 4]: Activities require the candidate to speculate; to express ideas, attitudes, and plans with some precision; to demonstrate the ability to <u>switch register</u>; and to use language relevant to their particular academic, vocational, or other interests' (Ingram and Wylie 1996: 3–4, 11).

As we can deduce from these excerpts, the oral interview was based largely upon a functional view of language. A range of functions are nominated, and the distinction between phases of the interview is based primarily on the different functions to be elicited from the candidate in each phase.

The expectation is also stated that the candidates will demonstrate 'inter-actional' skills, such as taking the initiative. However, exactly what 'active participant' means is unclear and is perhaps what lies behind the criticisms of oral interviews in general as 'conversations' (cf. van Lier 1989). Taking the initiative and being 'active' imply some sort of equality in determining the flow of the conversation, yet this has been argued to be unlikely, to say the least, in an institutional event such as a test where the interviewer is the more powerful participant (e.g. Neeson 1985, Perrett 1990).

As well as functions and interactional skills, there is also a focus on the complexity of language ('more complex, speculative language'). Additionally, mention is made of precision in expressing ideas and of ability to vary register.

In summary, oral proficiency as interpreted from the description provided in Ingram and Wylie (1996) may be seen as being on a continuum with the following aspects to it:

less evidence of   ⟵————————⟶   more evidence of
functional range
complexity of language
initiative
extended speech
precision of meaning
register variation
field-specific vocabulary

3.2 The test

3.2.1 The interview structure[1]

The IELTS Speaking Module takes between 10 and 15 minutes. It consists of an oral interview, a conversation between the candidate and a trained interviewer/assessor. There are five sections:

Introduction	The candidate is encouraged to talk briefly about his/her life, home, work and interests.
Extended Discourse	The candidate is encouraged to speak at length about some very familiar topic either of general interest or of relevance to their [sic] culture, place of living, or country of origin. This will involve explanation, description or narration.
Elicitation	The candidate is given a task card with some information on it and is encouraged to take the initiative and ask questions either to elicit information or to solve a problem. Tasks are based on 'information gap' type activities.
Speculation and Attitudes	The candidate is encouraged to talk about their [sic] future plans and proposed course of study. Alternatively the examiner may choose to return to a topic raised earlier.
Conclusion	The interview is concluded.

The present study is concerned particularly with the assessment of interview skills and for this reason the Phase 3 role-play was not included in the interview (see Brown and Hill 1998).

3.2.2 The band descriptors

As in any oral test, the task itself is only one half of the story. The other half is the criteria or scales, which are designed to 'exert control on observations both through directing the observer and by providing the language with which to describe an observation' (Griffin and McKay 1992:17). In this respect the criteria *are* the construct.

The IELTS scales include the following features:

- effectiveness of communication (in relation to a specified range of topic types)
- grammatical range and accuracy
- the ability to talk at length
- functional range.

Other features referred to at specific levels only are circumlocution, accent/pronunciation and fluency. The study will investigate the status of these nominated criteria *vis-à-vis* other (non-specified) linguistic and non-linguistic criteria in the assessments made by the raters. In particular it seeks to determine what is understood by the term 'effective communicator'.

4 Methodology

4.1 Protocol analysis

Protocol analysis has long been acknowledged as a suitable technique for investigating the construct validity of tests (see Cronbach 1970, 1971, for example). The application of verbal protocols in language test validation is discussed by Cohen and Hosenfeld (1981), and a range of studies report on their use in investigations of rater perceptions of composition or writing ability (e.g. Cumming 1990, Delaruelle 1997, Huot 1990, Milanovic and Saville 1994, Milanovic et al 1993, Vaughan 1991, Weigle 1994).

Of the various types of verbal protocol, *concurrent* verbal reports have been widely used in studies involving test data, especially in the investigation of reading skills and the judging of written scripts. This study however, uses a type of *retrospective* verbal protocol known as stimulated verbal recall (di Pardo 1994, Smagorinsky 1994). Stimulated verbal recalls are claimed to have 'a unique capacity to probe the reasons for particular decisions' (Smagorinsky 1994:xiv). They have been widely used in studies in the fields of psychology, sociology, anthropology and linguistics. The validity of this methodology is premised on the belief that the subject is likely to remember or relive the original behaviour if presented with the same stimulus (Ericsson and Simon 1984). The advantage of retrospective over concurrent protocols is that they are less intrusive; they allow access to the participants' thoughts while avoiding interruption (and hence possible contamination) of the behaviour of interest. This is particularly of concern in the present study where raters cannot be expected to monitor the performance at the same time as verbalising their thoughts, so that protocols could only be gathered concurrently with constant stopping and starting of the taped interview; verbalisations are likely to interrupt the 'online' listening and rating process and seriously distort it.

As the scores themselves are awarded under normal conditions, that is without the interruption of verbalisations, we can assume that the ratings and processes of rating will be consistent with normal rating behaviour as it is undertaken in rater training and re-accreditation, for example. On the other hand, the ratings do not reflect operational IELTS ratings in one respect. Operational ratings are awarded by the interviewer herself, so in the present study there is likely to be an additional focus on the interviewer which is not present in IELTS interviews which are rated 'live'.

The fact that the protocols are gathered immediately after each rating allows us to assume that raters will still have access to their 'working memory' (Green 1997:6). We are not, however, claiming the protocol to be an exact replication of the cognitive processes of the interviewer while rating;

the task is far too complex for this to be possible. Nevertheless, we can reasonably assume that comments made during these protocols will have some basis in the earlier rating event. Raters were first asked to nominate and justify a score; this justification can only be made by drawing on their earlier thoughts and perceptions. In addition, they were explicitly requested to point out aspects of the performance which contributed to their judgement in the subsequent review of the tape.

The retrospective protocol procedure does, of course, have drawbacks. Obviously time is a consideration: the more delayed the recall, the more likely the subject is to 'reinvent' their earlier behaviour rather than remember. Green discusses this in terms of two phenomena: tidying up one's comments, and saying what one thinks the interviewer wants to hear. In this study we anticipated particularly that raters would tidy up their comments in order to appear to be adhering to the criteria (the band descriptors). Steps were taken to ensure that this did not happen by indicating to participants beforehand that it was expected that they would consider features not included in the scales, and that one of the purposes of the study was to find out exactly *what* experienced raters considered relevant. Care was taken to refer to the raters as the experts, and the study was framed as an investigation of the nature of this expertise. In this way the importance of conforming to the scales was downplayed. In fact, the range of features referred to in raters' comments, and the fact that they at times explicitly acknowledged that they considered factors other than those mentioned in the band descriptors, indicated that this strategy worked.

4.2 Procedure

This study is linked to an earlier one investigating interviewer variability (Brown and Hill 1998; this now appears as Chapter 1 in this volume), and draws on the same data. The test candidates are overseas students taking part in a pre-university Foundation Program. At the time of the interviews they were preparing to take IELTS prior to submitting applications for tertiary study in Australia. For the present study, a sub-set of eight from the total of 42 interviews was selected.

Eight accredited IELTS examiners were recruited by letter to take part in the study. They had been IELTS raters for between one and nine years. Each was to rate and provide a verbal protocol for four of the eight tapes, a total of 32 protocols in all.

The raters were scheduled to provide the protocols individually. At the start of each rater's session they were told that they would be asked to listen to four interviews and rate them in the normal way. After each one had been rated they would then be asked to talk about their reasons for awarding the score they gave. As well as these verbal instructions, they were also given them in written form (Appendix 3.1), which they were asked to read through before asking any clarificatory questions. They were also given a copy of the IELTS band descriptors to read through before listening to the first tape. The room was set up with two tape recorders, one to play back the IELTS interview tape for rating, and one to record the subsequent retrospective verbal protocol.

During each protocol session, that is after nominating the score awarded and providing a brief justification, the rater was invited to replay the tape from the beginning, stopping wherever they felt some comment was in order. The researcher was present during these events, providing an audience for the comments, but minimal intervention. Most of the researcher's participation consisted of minimal feedback and encouragement to continue. At times, however, intervention was necessary, for example where a comment was unclear, or where the interviewer appeared to react strongly to something in the interview but did not stop the tape.[2]

A short break was offered between each protocol session and the rating of the next interview. Each rater's full session lasted for between three and four hours.

5 The data

5.1 Scores

Table 3.1 shows the ratings awarded to the performances. As can be seen, and is perhaps to be expected given the nature of the assessment (a single rating using an holistic scale), there was a considerable level of disagreement amongst raters. Variation in scores awarded to individual candidates ranged from two band levels (tapes 48, 57 and 66) to three band levels (all other tapes).

Table 3.1 Ratings

Tape	Raters								Range	Mean score
	1	2	3	4	5	6	7	8		
8		8		6		8		8	6–8	7
32	6		6		8		6		6–8	6.5
40	6	4				5	5		4–6	5
44			5	6			7	6	5–7	6
48			4	5			5	4	4–5	4.5
50	6	5			5	6			4–6	5
57		5		5		4		5	4–5	4.75
66	5		6		6		6		5–6	5.75

5.2 Protocols

All but one of the protocols (Interviewer 4, Interview 8) were recorded successfully. The data set therefore consists of 31 protocols. The shaded cell in Table 3.1 indicates the missing protocol.

At the start of each protocol session the rater started by nominating a score for the candidate and briefly justifying it. Further comments were invited once raters had completed the stimulated recall. These comments, which served to sum up the reasons for the particular score awarded, are henceforth referred to as summary comments. All other comments, i.e. those which took place *during* the stimulated recall, the review of the interview, are referred to as review turns.

Contributions varied enormously, with the longest protocol, 2,207 words, being produced by Rater 3 in response to Interview 44, and the shortest, 326 words, being produced by Rater 4 in response to Interview 48. Rater 3 produced the longest protocols on average (1,542 words) which was more than twice the average amount produced by Raters 4 (718 words) and 2 (756 words).

The number of review turns (that is, the number of times the rater stops the tape to comment) also varies enormously, ranging from 7 for Rater 2 (Interview 50) to 28 for Rater 3 (Interview 32). In fact, Rater 2 produced the shortest reviews on average (363 words) and Rater 3 the longest (1,281 words). Averages for each rater are presented in Table 3.2. The number of summary words (the justification of score) varied from a low of 72 (Rater 4, Interview 48) to a high of 753 (Rater 8, also Interview 48). Rater 4 produced the shortest summaries on average (255 words) and Rater 8 the longest (558 words).

In summary, Rater 3 had the most to say during the reviews. Although she didn't have the most to say in the summaries (in fact she produced the second shortest on average), she compensated for this with frequent stops for

Table 3.2 Averages for each rater

Rater	Av. protocol length (words)	Av. summary length (words)	Av. review length (words)	Av. number of review turns	Av. review turn length (words)
1	1374	482	892	18	50
2	756	393	363	9	40
3	1542	269	1281	28	46
4*	718	255	462	11	42
5	1425	539	886	18	49
6	1100	368	732	13	56
7	1066	403	663	14	47
8	1239	558	1047	17	62

*Note: * 3 interviews only.*

comments (average 28) during the review. Raters 2 and 4, in contrast, between them produce the two shortest protocols, with Rater 4 producing the shortest summary turns, and Rater 2 the shortest reviews. In addition, Raters 2 and 4 produced the least number of turns per interview on average, and the shortest review turns (as measured by average number of words produced).

6 The analysis

Transcripts of the protocol session were reviewed carefully in order to get a feeling for both possible units of analysis and possible coding categories, although there was clearly an expectation that these would reflect, at least to some extent, the contents of the band scales. The unit of analysis decided upon was 'a single or several utterances with a single aspect of the event as the focus' (Green 1997). Additional items which elaborated on the central comment in some way (for example, providing justification, amelioration, evaluation and exemplification) were not treated as separate units for the purposes of this analysis. Because of the complexity of the comments and the overlap between categories (the result to some extent of a lack of clarity or ambiguity in raters' comments, but also attributable to a difficulty in separating aspects of performance conceptually, such as the organisation and content of candidates' contributions), the process of coding was an iterative process, requiring constant revision until most comments were classifiable in a way which appeared intuitively adequate and was also relatively straight-forward to do.

In general, three types of comment occurred – *evaluative*, which focused on some aspect of the candidates' language; *non-evaluative*, which referred often to affective aspects of the interview such as the relationship between the two participants; and *interviewer-focused*, consisting of comments on the interviewer or their behaviour. We first consider the evaluative comments.

A total of 413 evaluative comments were made. Evaluative comments include both explicit and implicit evaluations. Examples of explicit evaluations include:[3]

40–6 So she explains all that quite clearly.
66–7 Yeah: *I think my cousin or my sister is in fifth year*. That's alright, that's okay.
44–8 Now that's not a bad answer: *a lot of development and a good place to study*.
32–5 A bit inappropriate: *animal bashing*.

Implicit evaluations were less frequent, but occurred particularly in relation to sentence level syntax and vocabulary, and tended to include quotations of errors (negative evaluations) or sophisticated language (positive evaluations). The evaluative nature of the comment was often to be inferred from the way the rater uttered the comment, or from the context in which it appeared:

57–8 *One of my uncles are engineering.*
32–5 See that? Another aside: *It's got lots of shops, quite expensive.*
8–8 *They're pretty old.*
32–1 *Not really hotel.*

Of the evaluative comments, 151 (37%) were positive and 262 (63%) were negative, in other words the majority of comments were negative. Starting initially with aspects of linguistic skill included in the band descriptors and following an iterative procedure, comments were ultimately grouped according to the following categories: (sentence level) syntax, discourse, vocabulary, production, comprehensibility, use of strategies, and comprehension. Each of these will be discussed in more detail in following sections.

6.1 Validity of the protocols

A check was made upon the validity of the retrospective protocol data as a representation of raters' actual assessment processes. We hypothesised that the proportion of positive comments would increase as the score increased. The ranking of the eight interviews according to their mean score was compared with their rankings based on the proportion of 'positive' to 'negative' comments.

The distribution of positive and negative comments on the whole reflected the rankings based on scores. We can reasonably conclude, therefore, that the comments are adequately representative of raters' views. There was only one interview where the score ranking appeared to be out of line with the polarity of the comments, and that was for Interview 8 (mean score ranking = 1, ranking according to polarity of comments = 4). For this interview, the scores awarded were 8, 8 and 6. The fourth score, awarded by Rater 4, is not considered here (as the protocol recording was faulty and could not be included in the analysis), and the candidate was hence ranked the highest by score, but sixth based on polarity of comments. We reviewed the comments themselves in order to seek a reason for this discrepancy.

We found that the two raters who gave the highest scores actually presented more negative comments than positive (Table 3.3). While the main reason Rater 2 gives in her summary statement for awarding an 8 was a certain 'nativeness', particularly in the use of markers such as *like* and *hopefully*, this is not in fact mentioned in the band descriptors. Perhaps this is why she avoided further mention of this in the review section, choosing instead to comment overwhelmingly on the candidate's syntax and fluency, both being categories which are explicitly mentioned in the descriptors. She comments

Table 3.3 Protocol validation: rankings

Interview	Total no. of evaluative comments	Negative comments		Positive comments			Mean Score	Mean Score ranking
		No.	%	No.	%	Ranking		
8	42	27	64	15	36	4	7	1
32	83	41	49	42	51	1	6.5	2
40	57	38	67	19	33	6	5	5
44	53	33	62	20	38	3	6	3
48	41	32	78	9	22	8	4.5	8
50	43	26	60	17	40	2	5	5
57	44	32	73	12	27	7	4.75	7
66	50	33	66	17	34	5	5.75	4

positively five times, all on syntax, and negatively six times, all on fluency. However, each time she comments on fluency she provides non-linguistic justification for the candidate's disfluency – embarrassment ('She doesn't know how to put it delicately'), thinking of ideas ('I think it's difficult to speak fluently and readily about the same topic for . . . yeah, you're running out of ideas'), or personal style of speaking ('It's a personal trait probably'; 'That's her style of speaking'). In short, although the comments were negative, they did not lead to a negative evaluation of candidate ability.

Rater 6 also awarded an 8, yet provided eight negative comments and only two positive ones. Again, this rater's judgement was not, as she acknowledged, something that was clearly based on the scales, but was instead to do with the extent to which she would have to modify her speech: 'If I were talking to her, I wouldn't adjust my language . . . it doesn't say anything like that in the bands, but that's a sort of a gut feeling you have when you first listen to someone'. In fact the negative comments, the weaknesses that she points out, are probably examples of the 'few inappropriacies' she refers to in her summary. And again the candidate's hesitancy is perceived as non-linguistic: 'the sort of hesitancy that native speakers have just speaking appropriate words and searching through the brain'.

6.2 The comments by category

The largest group of comments (31% of all evaluative comments) relates to sentence level syntax, and just over half of these (55%) are negative (Table 3.4). The heavy focus on grammar reflects the findings of a number of other studies. McNamara (1990), for example, in an analysis of the relationship between an 'overall' score and specific linguistic analytic criteria in a speaking test for medical professionals, found that grammar contributed more than any other category to the overall assessments. This may well be because grammar is quantifiable and systematically taught, so that for a language expert, as Wall,

Table 3.4 Positive and negative comments by category

	Syntax	Discourse	Production	Compre-hensibility	Vocabulary	Strategies	Compre-hension
Total	130	89	75	39	36	33	11
%	31	22	18	9	9	8	3
Polarity	+ −	+ −	+ −	+ −	+ −	+ −	+ −
Total	58 72	36 53	14 61	2 37	12 24	27 6	2 9
%	45 55	40 60	19 81	5 95	33 67	82 18	18 82

Clapham and Alderson (1994:334) point out, 'grammar is less difficult to judge than the language skills'. Comments on the discourse (including content) account for 22% and are the second largest category, and again over half (60%) are negative. Production is the third largest category, with 18% of all comments, of which an overwhelming majority (81%) are negative.

The next three groups each account for just less than 10% of all comments – comprehensibility, strategies and vocabulary. While the overwhelming majority of comprehensibility-related comments are negative (95%), the comments on strategies are overwhelmingly positive (82%). Comments on vocabulary are also mainly negative (67%). The candidate's comprehension accounts for only 3% of comments, and most of these are negative.

The fact that comments in the production, comprehensibility, comprehension and strategies categories are mainly negative deserves comment. This will be done as each category is discussed in turn.

6.2.1 Syntax

Positive reference was made to syntactic accuracy and maturity, and negative reference to syntactic error, immaturity and limited range. Whereas some comments made reference to the candidate's overall syntactic ability, others made reference to occurrences of specific aspects of syntax. Thus positive general comments tended to refer to 'structural competence', to infrequency or lack of impact of errors on comprehensibility, or to sophistication, naturalness or maturity of expression. Negative but general comments tended to refer to lack of structural control, the occurrence of errors or the narrowness of the range of structures used. Positive specific comments referred typically to the occurrence of structures which were presumably considered evidence of a developing syntactic maturity (discussed below) and negative specific comments typically referred to syntactic errors (also discussed below). Examples of comments in the syntax category include:

> 40–1 But still, I mean, she's keeping utterances going without making any terrible mistakes, without mistakes which really do interfere with communication. They're pretty thin on the ground. (*general positive*)

66–3 He doesn't display any degree of flexibility in, or creativity in his sentence structures. They're very sort of simple, really. (*general negative*)

50–2 *More easily than other subjects*, I thought was quite good. (*specific positive*)

32–1 Again *youth hostel* there wasn't an article. (*specific negative*)

In order to increase our understanding of what *specific* aspects of grammar raters consider relevant, comments were coded according to the aspect of grammar referred to. Positive comments referred to conditionals and verb tense (seven comments each), adverbs (six comments), relative clauses (four), modals (three), and the comparative and use of connectives (two each). Negative comments, references to grammatical errors, overwhelmingly concerned verbs, and in particular tense (18 comments). Other negative comments concerned the comparative (five comments), connectives, articles and prepositions (three each), word order, adverbs and pronouns (two each), and adjective order, conditionals, relative clauses, reported speech and the subjunctive (one each).

While the use of connectives is explicitly referred to in the band descriptors, and the use of the conditional is implied (as a task feature in relation to the function of speculation), the other grammatical categories commented upon here derive presumably from teachers' experience of and expectations regarding the acquisition of English grammar. While the number of comments is admittedly low for many categories, it seems reasonable to assume that the fact they are commented on indicates that the occurrence and accurate use of these specific aspects of grammar is considered to be an indicator of syntactic maturity. It is interesting to note that tense appears to be a most salient indicator, being commented on at some point by all raters.

6.2.2 Discourse

Comments in this category included reference both to the *discourse structure and organisation* and to the *content* of the candidate's speech. Positive comments made reference to the adequacy of the sample of speech in relation to specific functions (narrating, describing, speculating, hypothesising, and so on), to the ability to produce extended discourse, or to the sophistication or maturity of the ideas or their organisation. While some of the comments were readily identifiable as one or the other of these three categories – functional skill, discourse complexity, and maturity of ideas – many of the raters' comments did not appear to distinguish content and means of expression, perhaps because the two notions, sophistication of content and discoursal sophistication, tend to go hand in hand, or perhaps because it is not always possible to disambiguate content and organisation.[4]

Because of the difficulty in assigning all comments to one or another of these discourse-related categories, this analysis does not distinguish between them. A further analysis, or perhaps a different study where raters are asked to elaborate and expand on their comments, may be able to tease out more subtle distinctions than has been possible here given the scope of the current research project. The examples below reflect the range of comments in the discourse category:

Discourse: positive comments

66–1 I suppose again he's managing to get out quite a complex discussion there about the advantages and disadvantages of pharmacy. It's taking him a long time to get it out, but it's reasonably sophisticated.

57–6 He's not too bad there. He explains it . . . he's linking his ideas and explaining why he chose it, so you know, it's not too bad.

50–1 Okay, well there she challenges the interviewer, which I thought was sort of fairly critical because I think that is part of communicating effectively, that you are able to challenge.

32–5 You can see that she's trying to say something more than the obvious. You know, she's trying to think of something: *well everyone knows it's big, and everyone knows it's got lots of cars . . . What else can I say that's, you know, interesting, that people don't already know*, you know, she's sort of excusing herself for saying something so ordinary when she says *of course*.

50–1 Again, that's sort of, it's reasonable reasoning. Okay, maybe business is culturally bound, but accounting? It seems a reasonable suggestion that accounting is –

Discourse: negative comments

8–8 See, she could have expanded there. She could have said: Yeah my grandfather, my father, even though, you know, my grandfather is older and would normally have more respect because my father was an important businessman or something. She didn't. She had a chance to say more there, but she didn't.

32–3 See the descriptions fall down.

32–3 Okay so when he's here and she says: *Tell me something about it,* he starts saying: *it's very beautiful and it's a beautiful island.* Then he says: *there's a lot of Chinese,* and then he says *the food's good,* and it just seems to me that these are the words he knows. It's not a very sophisticated way of describing where you live. You could see he was – perhaps if he started to talk about the Chinese if he could get involved in the politics of what it feels like to be living there, and he never gets there so you think okay, he knows those words, that's why he's using them. So I really felt he was limited in what he could explain.

40–2 She can manage a conversation, but still the nature of what she's saying is not going much – not advancing.

44–8 So she says it reasonably well, but there's no sort of opening general comment following, oh you know: *Oh when I go to Singapore, oh there's*, you know, *lots to do*, or, you know, *I do a whole range of things*, you know, nothing like that. It's just, you know, *I visit my auntie and I* – It's like kids.

66–1 He gave very minimalist answers. He was very unforthcoming.

While functional skill and extended discourse are explicitly referred to in the band descriptors and/or in the test and task specifications, the quality of ideas is not explicitly referred to. It is interesting that some raters, particularly Raters 4 and 8 made relatively frequent reference to the maturity of ideas expressed by the candidate (or lack thereof), particularly in the more cognitively demanding functions of hypothesising and speculating. It seems that for such raters content is indeed an aspect of the construct. This may well be because the purpose of the test, to screen tertiary applicants, leads some raters at least to consider intellectual maturity as well as linguistic maturity, the two being relevant to success at university.

The complexity of the relationship between length of output, complexity of ideas and complexity/precision of expression is further compounded when we note that while in some instances immaturity of ideas was attributed to a lack of linguistic resources, in other instances the apparent youth or immaturity of the candidate was used to justify the lack of extended or complex response. In fact, inferences about the candidates' personality, maturity, world knowledge, and so on, occurred frequently in comments falling into this category. This is perhaps inevitable given the references in the band descriptors to 'effectiveness of communication' and 'precision of meaning', terms which are abstract, which do not themselves make the distinction between language and content clear. A lack of extended discourse was attributed variously:

To the interviewer's style:

44–3 I think she jumps in pretty quickly.

To the interviewer's failure to elicit extended discourse:

44–3 And again those yes/no questions . . . rather than general questions 'Tell me about your life'.

50–5 You know, they're not questions that are making her actually – you know, you just need something like 'Tell me', or 'Go on and tell me a bit more about that' or – Yeah, I think he's trying to make her talk by switching topic, but actually, that's making it worse because every time there's a new topic, it's only a short answer again instead of maybe digging deeper and saying 'Well tell me about that then' or 'Tell me in detail' . . . Yeah, because until a topic is established, you don't really know what's relevant and what isn't, but he keeps changing topics and there's no time to work out what we're going to talk about.

To the candidate's personality or youth:

44–4 It could be, again, a young person who doesn't really like to talk too much.

44–3 There's never any attempt to fill in the details the whole way through. So, again, it's a bit of immaturity too a little bit I think, but she's just answering the questions rather than filling in any of the details or describing or explaining or, you know –

To affective factors:

8–7 She had a chance to say more there, but she didn't. But I think it was a confidence thing by the end of the interview.

To test wiseness:

50–5 She just didn't add information, and I don't know whether that was a cultural thing because she, maybe she was shy, but I don't think it was that. Maybe lack of preparation.

And to the choice of topic:

44–4 The topic doesn't really extend them either.

Even within the same performance, raters do not agree in their interpretations of particular behaviours. We draw on the summary comments provided for interview 44 to illustrate this. Rater 3 who gave the lowest score (5) felt that the candidate was *not able* to produce extended discourse or speculation, whereas of the two raters who awarded a score of 6, Rater 6 justified the limited discourse with reference to the skill of the *interviewer* and Rater 8 with reference to the *candidate's youth* or immaturity. Rater 7, who awarded a score of 7, attributed the lack of extended discourse to *both* the skill of the interviewer *and* the youth of the candidate.

Raters frequently made reference to the functional skills displayed by the candidates, a feature of the band descriptors. However, again, inferences were made regarding non-satisfaction of the functional demands, and reasons given were both linguistic and non-linguistic (see Section 6.2). Rater 1, for example, interpreted the candidate's failure to speculate in Interview 32 as a result of linguistic weaknesses; he justifies this interpretation on the grounds that the candidate has (to him) clearly thought about the issue:

32–1 Judging from what she said about her commitment against animal testing, I felt that it probably wasn't a lack of having actually thought about the issue, which was causing a problem here . . . It was some difficulty in presenting complex ideas and language that was causing it to break down.

In other instances, non-linguistic reasons were inferred for lack of speculative language. These drew on maturity:

40–1 . . . taking into account the fact that X was 17 years of age, and that therefore, sort of cognitively, just in terms of real-world knowledge her ability to speculate would be a little bit limited.

The difficulty of the questions:

32–8 Okay, she's having some difficulty speculating about how she can help her country . . . I think it's quite a difficult question if you haven't thought about it before.

Lack of speculative questions:

44–7 I really feel like the interviewer doesn't challenge enough in terms of the speculative, argumentative.

66–3 . . . there wasn't a lot of speculative language elicited.

And lack of comparison of real-world and test context:

32–9 I always think about it in context of the university situation, and I think, usually you do have time to prepare for those sorts of responses, and you're dealing with the issue all the time, so you're becoming very familiar with the vocabulary, it's all at the tip of your tongue. Just off the cuff like that it's hard to think about those things.

It was also clear that raters perceive the status of functions, particularly speculation, as an assessment focus to be somewhat problematic. This appears to be because it is not entirely clear whether they are to focus on the *linguistic* exponents of the function (e.g. the conditional, the subjunctive) or the ability to respond to such questions with *appropriate content*. The reasons for this are undoubtedly because of the common association of certain grammatical features with particular functional uses of language in the teaching of language. The use of the conditional, for example, is typical of speculation and hypothesising, and at times raters commented specifically on the candidate's use of the conditional:

40–2 I think I heard one conditional, and that was a first conditional.

Comments such as these have been coded in the syntax category (see Section 6.2.1). Other comments refer more generally to the candidates' failure to respond to a speculative question, seeing it as a consequence of immaturity, rather than linguistic limitations, in one case:

40–2 It's all description even though she's asked her what – about the future and her plans, and even – She is actually in theory talking about the future, but it's still description.

32–2 . . . the younger ones tend not to be able to deal with that sort of speculation very easily. So I think the more mature candidates do have an advantage in that way.

It appears then that different raters look for different evidence of ability to hypothesise or speculate; some for specific linguistic structures, others for fulfilment of the functional task (i.e. answering the interviewer's question adequately in terms of meaning) *regardless* of the linguistic forms used. The tension between these two perspectives is evident to at least some of the raters themselves, as the following excerpt shows:

66–3 He's tried to ask him some speculative questions, and rather than using conditionals or hypothetical language, he actually just takes off: *Because all my sisters are over here*, and that's quite natural way of speaking really. So I don't know whether he can use it or not, but it's quite natural. 'Would you have studied over here anyway?' 'Yeah, because my brothers have.' I wouldn't say 'Yes I *would have* studied even if I hadn't done' – you know, that sounds unnatural in the conversation that's going on. So, even though there wasn't a lot of speculative language elicited, I think that he dealt with it. Whether he could, his response was appropriate, even if we're not sure whether he can use speculation.

While this ambiguity is, as noted, of concern in the classification of comments, more importantly it highlights an underlying lack of consistency in the ways raters focus on functional skills, which in itself reflects the lack of explicitness in the assessment guidelines.

6.2.3 Production

Comments in this category referred to fluency, rhythm and intonation, and pronunciation.

Fluency

Fluency was in some (five) instances referred to in a non-specific way, for example:

44–8 Yeah, so she's sort of quite fluent with sort of answering the questions.

44–7 See this is tending to lose fluency here.

40–1 There you see, on the one hand it's definitely not fluent . . .

Other references (a total of 56) were more specific and concerned features such as hesitation or speed of delivery, the use of fillers, and repetition:

Hesitancy and speed of delivery (30 comments)

Most comments in this category were negative (27) and every interview received at least one or two:

40–1 And also there was a certain hesitancy *always* there.

32–3 It's a little bit slow I guess for an interview process.

8–2 The only thing that is irritating is that it takes her so long to actually spit it out. She's taking a lot of thinking time.

The three positive comments were all made by the same rater, Rater 7, two of them in relation to the same interview:

44–7 And she's just, she's like a native speaker in her retorts so quickly and with her amusement. I mean she, there's no hesitation. She's very quick.

44–7 See, when she's asked: *What are the main things you've learned?* she says: *Independence.* She says it very quickly. I mean it's just a – she knows the response straight away, and she can articulate it.

66–7 Okay now see, he responds to that quickly and capably. Now is that because he's been asked that question five thousand times before, and he's got the answer down pat, or is it something that he . . . not like that and he just formulates it quite capably? I don't know what it is.

It is interesting to note that the raters often made inferences about the reasons for hesitation. Lack of fluency was at times seen as a *linguistic* feature, that is, the candidate was searching for words or structures:

32–3 I think her biggest limitation is a lack of vocabulary and she tries to cover that a lot by using phrases like *something like* and *you know.*

48–2 There's so much hesitation as she's trying to find words or the form of the words as with, *Malay, Malay.*

It was also frequently attributed to *non-linguistic* features such as:

Personality:

8–2 I think that's a personality thing rather than a linguistic thing . . .

8–6 I know a lot of slow native speakers . . .

Affective aspects of the encounter:

8–2 Maybe she's embarrassed here . . .

57–4 And so much hesitation, you know . . . but that's stage fright . . .

Interest in the topic:

8–2 In terms of content, I think that it's difficult to speak fluently and readily about the same topic for . . . yeah, you're running out of ideas . . .

8–2 She's speeding up a little bit now because she's got something different to say.

A result of (native-like) cognitive planning:

8–6 The sort of hesitancy that native speakers have just speaking appropriate words and searching through the brain . . .

32–7 See, all this hesitation I feel is because she's thinking, not because she's trying to think of the word.

8–6 So there's a lot of pausing here, but I think this is really hard for her to explain.

It seems therefore that, as predicted, raters routinely infer the reason for particular behaviours and, moreover, that they realise that they have to make inferences. At one point one rater says:

66–7 . . . but why is he hesitating? I don't know why he's hesitating so much . . . and I'm asking myself why is he hesitating so much . . .

And later on she comments:

66–7 I don't know whether he's buying time – he repeats, you know, *How long have I*, that technique in conversation when you repeat the question like you want to buy time to formulate your answer. Now are you doing that because you're trying to do it to think of an opinion or think of answer or because you're just thinking I'm trying to process these words that you're giving to me? See the two different things that might be happening and I'm trying to think about which is happening because obviously it affects how you score it.

A major problem with performance tests is the fact that while evidence of a particular behaviour can clearly be taken as an indication of mastery, lack of evidence cannot always be assumed to indicate non-mastery. So in the case of fluency the question arises 'Is the lack of fluency evidence of linguistic shortcomings (i.e. a search for words) or simply evidence of cognitive planning, a consequence of the type of task or question?' Whatever the case, it is likely that the inference drawn by the rater as to the cause of hesitation will affect the way the perception of fluency is integrated into the final judgement. The same issue of how to interpret non-production of particular grammatical features (in this case the lack of a conditional) applies also to the comment by Rater 3 in relation to the use of 'would' (in section 6.2.2 on discourse above). Non-use of 'would' in the context of a hypothesising statement may indicate that the candidate is *unable* to produce conditionals; it may however simply be that she has *chosen* not to use this particular form (as, in fact, Rater 3 assumes).

Fillers (12 comments)

Comments on the use of fillers were made in relation to four of the interviews. These are particularly interesting, as raters appear to draw different conclusions about candidate proficiency when fillers are a feature of their speech. Some cases were considered to be native-like, indicative of a certain ease with the language, and hence a positive feature. In these instances the assumption is that fillers are used as native-speakers use them, that is, while the speaker is thinking *what* to say. In other cases, however, the use of fillers is interpreted as evidence of limited vocabulary. In these cases the assumption is that they indicate that the candidate is thinking *how* to say it, i.e. searching for words. The following two comments are illustrative of these two viewpoints (and both were made in relation to the same interview):

> 32–3 Okay, there when she's filling in she continues to do this all during the tape. I think her biggest limitation is a lack of vocabulary and she tries to cover that a lot by using phrases like *something like* and *you know* and she's got lots of fillers like that so she's fluent enough to be able to use those but I think really does hide a limited vocabulary and not being able to extend herself . . .

> 32–7 *What I mean is like.* . . The fact she says *like*, shows a degree of sophistication. You know, she's heard Australians talking, or she's picked that up – 'like I can da da da'.

Stress, rhythm and intonation (10 comments)

Five positive comments were made regarding intonation and five negative. It is interesting that all the positive comments were made in relation to one interview, Interview 32, and were made by all four raters. These positive assessments of intonation were typically associated with nativeness:

> 32–5 Now it's really – that's a classic (rising intonation) and you do this or you do that, that's really Australian intonation. You get carried into her conversation.

> 32–7 See, there where she's talking about animal bashing, the intonation rises just the way that a native speaker does when we're trying to, you know . . . You know, she's picked up those little nuances of native speaker language . . .

> 32–3 . . . her intonation is also very good, so and that's just the rhythm of her speech . . . I like the way she used that *of course* . . . Quite naturalistic sort of . . .

Negative assessments were made in relation to Interviews 44 (two comments) and 40 (three comments) and were typically associated with interference from the L1:

40–5 I reckon that intonation is just annoying me. It's just 'na na na na' [*undulating*]. It's Hong Kong.

44–8 It's a combination of the stress and the way she occasionally leaves a word out that gives her this machine gun effect rather than a nice smooth speaking style.

Repetition

Only four comments were found in relation to repetition, all of them negative. Three were made by the one interviewer in relation to a single interview (Interview 48, Rater 7). Repetition appears to be interpreted as a failed self-repair strategy:

48–7 See, she has to try about three ways to say something, you know, *Some people, some students, some* . . . And then there's a lot of rephrasing until she finally – and even then she doesn't necessarily get it right. Whereas I'd take it as some form of mastery that they could self-correct quickly and get it right. But she's still at that stage where she's exploring three or four options and still not necessarily coming out with the right one.

Pronunciation (14 comments)

Comments in this category referred both to general traits:

57–4 And his pronunciation is a little bit difficult.

57–5 You're sort of initially thrown off guard because his pronunciation's bad . . .

And to specific instances where the pronunciation was noticed as being problematic:

48–7 And – first of all I thought she said: *no clothes*, and couldn't work out what she was saying . . .

40–1 Yes, the play/pray problem.

The fact that there was only one instance of a positive comment:

48–3 . . . but the pronunciation's really good . . .

provides evidence for the claim that pronunciation is likely to be salient to the rater only when it causes problems. All but one of the interviews received one or two comments regarding the quality of pronunciation. Interview 57 received the most, five (negative) comments made by three of the raters.

6.2.4 Vocabulary

Comments falling into this category were of three broad types:

Drawing attention to specific words:

8–8 She seemed to have trouble describing the company, like she didn't know the vocabulary for the – she couldn't say it was a stationery or whatever it was . . . Yeah, she had to say what it was. She couldn't generalise about it, but then she countered that with something that was quite – what did she say after that? *She told me that she was going to quit.* Now even that is pretty natural sort of English. Usually they don't know that, you know, the bad ones don't know the word *quit*.

32–1 *Small house*, so again, and this was the point where I decided well this is definitely not a 8.

32–5 A bit inappropriate, *animal bashing*.

Drawing attention to lexical sets in relation to a particular topic:

57–8 Okay, so that's not very impressive, you know, Describe it . . . *beautiful island, surrounded*. That *surrounded* was good, but he hasn't got very many adjectives, so his vocabulary is not too fantastic.

66–5 He's got words like *increase, the chance, applying, job* . . .

General comments on vocabulary range or usage:

40–6 So she's got limited vocabulary.

44–3 She misuses the vocab too occasionally.

Only in one instance is there general comment on the same vocabulary item – 'seldom'. Otherwise raters appear to be idiosyncratic in choosing lexical items to comment on.

44–8 *Seldom's* a rather good word. [laughs]

44–4 Yeah, I love this little use of *seldom* that she has there.

44–7 *I seldom go*, you know, that's sophisticated. I mean who says *seldom*? I mean she's learned English well, I feel.

Negative comments on vocabulary (24) outweighed positive ones (12), and three interviews in particular received a rather large proportion of negative ones, Interview 40, Interview 32 and Interview 50.

6.2.5 Comprehensibility

The comments included in this category relate primarily to the effect on the listener, unlike those classified in the production category which do not explicitly refer to the raters' understanding.[5] They are, however, as for pronunciation, almost entirely negative; out of a total of 40 comments only two were positive assessments. While in some cases it is possible to infer where the cause of the comprehensibility problem lies, it is more often not clear. Mishearing may be due to an attention lapse of the rater as much as to the candidate's production:

40–6 Yeah I've lost this bit. I don't know what she's talking about.

66–1 I wasn't sure what he said there: *I like to play pigs tennis?*

Some comments refer to a lack of coherence:

48–8 Not a lot of coherence there, not a lot of cohesion and I don't have the vaguest idea what on earth she's talking about. I think she's trying to say that people have different types of jobs and they have different working hours, but it's sort of quite, very, very sort of unclear.

50–6 Okay, one of the problems she's got here is that she's so concerned about what she's saying that she's actually not able to engage in conversation, so she doesn't – for the listener she's not actually putting it in context. So she's not saying: *In KL compared to Klang, where I come from, this happens.* So she's just getting those: *Oh, there's light rail.* And as a listener, you've got to try and work out she's talking about KL now and not Klang.

In other instances comprehension problems appear to be the result of poor syntax:

48–3 I found it hard to understand her there. I think she said: *so Hong Kong people would make friends not always*, something like that, so she was trying to put that across, but it didn't come across clearly.

On the whole, however, comments in this category are not specific, referring simply to an inability to understand:

32–1 Okay she's clear and she's easy to understand right from the start.

48–4 It's very unclear for me. I can't really understand what the student's saying.

66–5 Can't really understand a word he's saying actually.

Two interviews received a particularly high number of negative comments in relation to comprehensibility – Interview 48 (nine comments) and Interview 66 (eleven comments). It is interesting that in each case a disproportionate number of these comments came from one particular rater (Rater 3 in Interview 48: six comments; and Rater 1 in Interview 66: seven comments). It is also the case that these two raters each awarded scores a band lower than the median score, so it appears that comprehensibility (or lack thereof) is particularly salient to raters when awarding scores. It also appears to be the case that some raters are more able to follow learners' speech than others.

6.2.6 Strategies

A further group of comments referred to what are generally termed communication strategies. These were nearly all positive. In particular, reference was made to:

Self-correction (10 comments):

40–2 She corrects herself. She does say *eaten*. She corrects herself, so that's good.

38–1 She – this is a good feature – this is one reason why I thought she was definitely a 6. She corrects herself quickly when she makes a slip: *I went to there, I went there when I was 16 for a school trip.*

Clarification strategies (eight comments):

44–7 Asking for clarification, which is good.

32–5 Like there she says *You mean for accommodation?* That's a kind of clarification that makes such a natural conversation, and such a fluent conversation, because she does it a few times you know, and then she goes off, you know, she's –

40–6 But quite good in terms of conversation, she checks with the interviewer: *oh you mean what time? you mean my homework?* So she's got those sort of conversational skills.

Circumlocution (five comments):

44–7 I really like this *double-decker bed*, you know, she's not going to have a bunk, she calls it a *double-decker bed*. (It's creative.) She knows she can get around it, so she can, you know, get around that.

32–7 'Can use circumlocution to cover gaps.' To me she can do this.

44–4 Bit of circumlocution there. But you get the point of what she says, she goes around the words.

Rehearsal (five comments, negative):

66–5 This sounds really rehearsed.

48–3 That sounded almost memorised. That sort of word, by, word, really either translating or really almost sort of memorised. And then the final: *this is my plan.*

Other strategy-related comments referred to the use of feedback tokens (1), deflecting a question (1) and paraphrasing the interviewer's words (3):

32–3 Again that *mhm* she's got good communication in that way. (*feedback*)

57–2 *Get a job?* That's good. *Actually, I haven't thought about this.* That's very good. Yeah, it's probably a really bad thing to say, but it's well put. (*deflecting*)

57–6 When he says there: *I'd like to do*, he's listening to her to repeat what she says because he hasn't got it himself and he gets a little bit stumbled there because then it's: *I'd like to do* and he can't get it all out and so he gets into a bit of a tangle. If his English were better, he would have opened with his own introductory phrase. (*para-phrasing*)

Despite the fact that circumlocution is the only communication strategy referred to in the band descriptors, it appears that such strategies are nevertheless salient to raters – perhaps they view them as relevant aspects of being a 'good communicator' (a general focus of the scales). Given however that they are not construed as part of the construct in terms of the task (in that no provision is made for specific checking of these strategies), there are grounds for concern if indeed raters are taking their occurrence into account when awarding scores. Observations are likely to be made only when there is a noticeable use of (or failure to use) a relevant strategy, rather than on a basis which applies across all candidates. On the other hand, the data here does not indicate a close relationship between the number of positive comments on strategies and the final score (Interview 32 received the most, nine positive comments). It remains unclear as to how or to what extent raters take strategies into account when awarding scores.

6.2.7 Comprehension

Nine negative and two positive comments were made regarding the candidates' comprehension of the interviewer. Negative assessments of comprehension refer to simple mishearing as well as language-related inability to understand (such as not knowing specific vocabulary), and miscomprehension of the intent of the interviewer's question (misinterpretation). It is also clear from the comments below that raters appear not to put too much weight on the importance of individual instances of miscomprehension:

50–6   That's right. So, okay, so she misunderstood what he said, but that's not an issue, I don't think. He came back to it, and she answered it.

48–7   See, she lacks the – she doesn't understand that question, which is what's important. I mean she's relating it to herself. I don't think she understood that at all.

44–7   I think she misunderstands here. She says: *What's your first impression?* and she said: *Oh, I came here before.* She thinks she means the first trip. So that comprehension thing comes into it, but I think it's a minor sort of error in communication.

32–7   See, she's just lost – hasn't understood that at all, has been thrown by the concept of stages and got a bit lost I think in what the interviewer was saying because it's quite a long explanation of what she meant, and hasn't answered appropriately, but I don't think we can give her the chop for that.

Comprehension appears to have an ambiguous status as an assessment focus. One rater (in fact the rater who comments the most on comprehension) comments explicitly on this:

32–7 I always have a problem with the issue of comprehension because when we did our training I got the distinct impression that we shouldn't be testing the comprehension, that comprehension was looked after in the listening section, but I don't see how you can possibly cut your mind off from comprehension even though it doesn't say anything here about comprehension. And I have a problem with that. Well if you ignore that they haven't comprehended what you've said, then it isn't real communication, and this is supposed to be a test of some sort of communicative ability, so yeah . . .

We turn now to the two categories of non-evaluative comments, the interviewer and affective factors.

6.2.8 The interviewer

A considerable number of comments (95) were devoted to the interviewer. These included reference to the difficulty of questions, the lack of speculative questions (Phase 4), the number of closed questions, the interviewer 'talking down' to the candidate, the labouring of particular topics, the inappropriateness of certain topics ('delicate', 'boring') the interviewer interrupting the candidate, the time allowed for the candidate to respond, and the interviewer's failure to pick up on points made by the candidate. Examples include:

44–7 I don't think it really reflects an extended conversation, and I really feel like the interviewer doesn't challenge enough in terms of the speculative, argumentative.

8–2 It's getting a bit laboured now. I'm ready to move on.

8–2 I think that there has been a missed opportunity here to get her to talk about why she wants to do the multicultural course and where that might lead her then in the future. I'm not saying that the interviewer's done the wrong thing. It's just I would like to have heard her expand on that because she might have been a bit more enthusiastic, but: *now we're going to talk about Melbourne.*

32–6 That is the first of a series of interruptions which I found really off-putting at the beginning. She does it three or four times, and she interrupts so badly that she even apologises at one stage. She goes: *Oh sorry.*

32–7 See, she's just lost – hasn't understood that at all, has been thrown by the concept of *stages* and got a bit lost I think in what the interviewer was saying because it's quite a long explanation of what she meant.

40–6 I wish the interviewer had said more 'Tell me about the subjects you studied'. She's giving her the opportunity give single answers all the time.

40–6 So disapproving. Don't you think it's a really sort of, not . . . Yeah, she can't work out what to do. So then she does something and then the interviewer doesn't like it. So then she says: *BUT, you're seventeen.* What do you do? . . .

44–4 . . . but the examiner really gives me the shits, that she's very condescending.

50–1 That's a rather delicate question, and he then goes on with it.

50–5 Students hate talking about architecture usually. Maybe it's because they don't have the vocab. That could be a reason as well. And often, people don't walk around looking at their architecture, like people living in modern cities and people who are coming to Australia, they're more interested in, you know, high-rise and shopping complexes.

66–5 She leaves plenty of time for him to talk. She's just silent [*laughs*] letting him get over the gaps . . . I think the fact that she leaves a silence and he has to fix it means he's got more chance of showing that he's a 6.

66–3 She's already asked this question. He's already answered the question previously. He already said there's shortage of engineers in Malaysia, therefore it'd be easy to get a job. So she's lost concentration, which throws the candidate a bit.

6.2.9 Affective comments

A number of non-evaluative comments concerning the attitude of the candidate or the relationship between the two participants were made, for example:

44–3 She seems to be relaxed. The candidate seems to be relaxing a little bit more here when she's talking about her mother and her home. She's obviously feeling easier and feels comfortable talking about that sort of thing.

40–6 Okay. When she starts, she actually interacts – tries to interact – with the interviewer – she says *How are you?* So that makes you think 'okay, she's got a bit of confidence', and that immediately puts her in maybe – okay, she's not going to be down low. And then she starts talking, and the tone of her voice initially is confident. So I'm still thinking because she sounds confident. I know you shouldn't think that, but I – it does prejudice me if someone sounds confident. I think okay they're not going to be too . . .

8–8 They've lost the momentum in this interview. They started off quite well and she sounded happy and the interviewer sounded happy but they've both lost the momentum a bit, and it's tapering off to a nothing interview. Do you know what I mean? It's like she's lost interest in what they're talking about, and the interviewer doesn't sound very interested any more either. You know how some . . . Yeah, yeah, I don't know exactly what's going on, but somehow the interview's not working now. She's lost confidence, the girl, the interviewee, the Japanese girl's lost confidence, and she's sounding a lot more unsure now than she did when she started off. She sounded quite happy when she started.

32–3 . . . although you can see the relationship there, she was obviously sort of having a bit of a giggle with a laugh with the interviewer, so she was relating quite well from what I see here.

6.3 Distribution of comments by interview

Our next question concerns the extent to which the assessment focus differed in the eight interviews. For each interview the number of turns in each category across the four raters was calculated as a percentage of the total number of comments. This was then compared with the average across all interviews (Table 3.5).

For any one category, percentages which were found to be more than one standard deviation higher than the mean are indicated in bold type. In these instances, the particular assessment feature appears to be more salient to raters than is usual in this particular interview.

We also compared these findings with the reasons the raters stated for awarding their scores, to see if the number of comments actually reflected their main concern when awarding the score. Interview 8 received a greater number of comments on syntax than average. In fact all three raters also referred to the candidate's syntax when summarising their scores. Interview 40 received proportionally more comments on vocabulary, and again two of the raters referred explicitly to the candidate's limited vocabulary in

Table 3.5 Comments by category for each interview (%)

Interview	Syntax	Discourse	Production	Compre-hensibility	Vocabulary	Strategies	Compre-hension
8	**52**	12	21	5	7	2	–
32	26	24	23	4	7	12	4
40	24	19	23	7	**16**	11	–
44	36	**26**	17	2	8	9	2
48	22	17	24	**22**	5	3	**7**
50	39	19	2	14	**14**	7	5
57	29	25	16	7	5	**14**	5
66	28	**26**	14	**22**	8	2	–
Mean %	32	21	17.5	10.4	8.8	7.5	2.9
S.D.	9.9	5.1	7.3	8	4.1	4.8	2.8

their summaries. Interview 44 received more comments on discourse, and all the raters made reference to the lack of extended discourse in this interview. Interview 48 received more comments in the comprehensibility and comprehension categories, and two raters focused on a lack of comprehensibility (coherence). All the raters commented on the candidate's vocabulary in relation to Interview 50, and this interview received more comments than average in this category. Interview 57 received more comments than average on strategies, but this (as has already been discussed) was *not* a focus of the summary comments. Interview 66 received more comments on discourse and comprehensibility, and again the lack of extended discourse was the focus of all raters' summary comments. It seems, therefore, that there is in general a relationship between the comments the raters make while reviewing the interview tapes and their overall focus when awarding a score, at least with regards to linguistic features.

In Table 3.5 the mean percentage indicates the frequency with which raters made comments in that category across all interviews. Raters commented more on syntax (32% of all comments) than on any other category. One must be careful, however, of interpreting this as an indication that syntax is the most salient feature when rating performance. It may well be that such a distribution simply reflects how easy raters find it to draw attention to and comment on particular features (cf. the extent to which handwriting is commented upon in studies of the rating of first and second language writing). It may be that aspects of sentence level syntax received a disproportionately high level of attention in their comments because raters, who are first and foremost teachers, are more at ease with talking about highly discrete items of grammar than the 'fuzzier' notion of discourse or content.

6.4 The process of rating

It was difficult to draw any conclusions regarding the raters' process of rating from what they said during the protocols. However, there does appear to be evidence to suggest that the two approaches identified by Pollitt and Murray (1996) are followed at least to some extent by the raters in this study.

In the first approach, evidence is sought to defend or disprove the initial choice of level by considering various aspects of the performance – fluency, vocabulary, structures, discourse – and the initial assessment is then retained or revised in the light of this. The final judgement appears to weigh up the various aspects of the performance in order to decide on one level or another. Of course, as has been pointed out above, it is not simply a case of identifying relevant levels of performance on the various features, but inferences may also be drawn regarding the type and level of performance which are integrated into the final judgement.

8–8   When she started, I thought 'Okay, she's a good 6'. . . but then later on when she actually got a chance to talk, she didn't do as well as I thought she was going to . . . It was like, it was as though she didn't have the language to say anything particularly brilliant. She just came out with the standard sort of answers. So she didn't show a wonderful range of vocabulary, or she didn't change the structures very much, so by the end of the interview I was wondering whether she was really only a 5 . . . She didn't have enough vocabulary. She was saying such standard things, you know, nothing particularly precise, just the usual trite sort of remarks. But she was still using verbs quite well, and she still had that naturalness about her English, and that's why I made her a 6.

In the second approach raters assessed sections of the test independently; thus comments were frequently made that a particular passage was 5-ish, or that another section was 6-ish. In this approach raters often commented that they revised their earlier assessment in the light of performance on the final section of the test, where evidence of the ability to perform functions such as hypothesising, arguing, and speculating is required. In other words, each *section* is assessed independently and these are then weighed up in order to award the score.

32–3   I gave her a 6 in the end although I was tossing up between in the first section between a 7 and a 6 and maybe going towards a 7 after section 1, but by section 4 I'd taken her back to a 6.

40–1   This is not a terribly good sequence. It's one of the more 5-ey sort of passages . . . This section, you see, this comparison didn't seem to be bad at all, so she then goes back into being 6-ish . . . I thought (that section) not bad at all, and I felt unconsciously the interviewer was almost saying that when she said: *That's good, Julie.*

However, in general raters show evidence of using both these approaches; they discuss 'sections', 'passages' and 'phases', as well as evaluating individual aspects of the interaction. Given that raters are instructed to base their assessment on the candidate's best performance (i.e. a 'section' focus), plus the fact that features are described in the scales in relation to particular levels (i.e. a 'features' focus), it is hardly surprising that the two co-exist.

6.5 Interviewer agreement

An analysis of raters' summary statements, that is responses to the task of briefly justifying the score awarded, was carried out in order to ascertain (impressionistically) whether raters agree on their interpretations of candidate performance but rate to different standards, or whether they also focus on different aspects of the performance. It was generally found to be the case that raters focus on different aspects of a performance, and that this may well be the reason for their awarding different scores. In Interview 8 (which we have discussed earlier) two raters awarded scores of 8 on the basis of the 'naturalness' of the candidate's speech, whereas the third rater[6] awarded a score of 6, primarily on the basis of perceived limitations in the candidate's syntax and vocabulary which led to 'limited precision' in expressing meaning. Similarly, in Interview 32, the rater who awarded the higher score of 8 did so because of the naturalness of the candidate's speech and because she appeared mature (because of her interests). The other raters, who all awarded scores of 6, did not refer to these as factors influencing their scores.

7 Discussion

We review here and comment further on the main findings of the study. Implications are drawn both for IELTS, and for oral proficiency testing in general.

7.1 Validity of protocols and agreement between raters

There is some evidence in the present study that the protocols provide valid insights into the rating process. An initial validation check revealed that the percentage of positive and negative comments produced in relation to specific interviews was correlated with the score awarded to the interview, as would be hoped. In addition, raters' summaries of why they awarded particular scores in general reflected the orientation of the comments produced in the protocols.

On the other hand, raters frequently awarded different scores. This seemed to be a consequence of their focusing on different aspects of performance. In addition, some raters appeared to be more performance-oriented, focusing more narrowly on the criteria, and others more inference-oriented, drawing more conclusions about the candidates' ability to cope in other contexts, a result presumably of the raters' familiarity (or assumptions about) the requirements of tertiary study. It is worth commenting here that the most recently trained rater focused more exclusively on features referred to in the scales, and made fewer inferences about candidates. A follow-up study comparing the rating styles of recently-trained and experienced raters would be of interest in this regard.

Given the level of disagreement between raters in relation to the same performance, there is obviously a question of reliability here. Holistic scales, by their very nature, rely on raters' expertise to appropriately identify and weight relevant aspects of behaviour, while at the same time giving little support in terms of explicitness and detail of descriptors. The varied nature of performance across interviews, attributable to some extent to different interviewers' techniques, adds to the difficulty of making comparable judgements in every case. It may be that raters would be more likely to agree if the criteria were more discretely and clearly specified, for example through analytic scales. This would however, not only add to the complexity of the raters' task (and perhaps be impossible in a context where interaction has to be maintained at the same time as rating is carried out) but would remove what is presumably the basis of holistic scales, a 'gut-reaction', albeit guided, and by experts, to a naturalistic and variable (although supposedly equivalent) performance. Perhaps the only way to ensure reliability in contexts such as IELTS is to base candidate scores on more ratings than one.

7.2 Analytic categories

Raters commented on a range of linguistic and non-linguistic features. As was perhaps to be expected given the findings of previous studies, syntax appeared to be highly salient to raters; the largest category of comments related to syntax, both its sophistication and its accuracy. In the discourse category we noted that comments referred either to the *content* of candidates' talk (its sophistication or lack thereof) or to the *organisation* of the discourse (again its sophistication or lack thereof). However, in many other instances it was not clear which of these raters were talking about, so we have not been able to separate out comments on sophistication of linguistic *vis-à-vis* cognitive tasks. While this ambiguity was in some cases due to a lack of specificity in the raters' choice of words, it points also to the difficulties raters might have in separating out purely linguistic skills (or more properly *second-language* linguistic skills) from the non-linguistic (such as cognitive and affective). This tension is perhaps inevitable in a communicative performance test where the language is both the focus and the medium of assessment.

Comprehensibility and production typically received comments only where there was a problem. This finding reflects those of previous studies which have found either that they are salient at the lower levels in particular, or that they are salient only when they create problems of understanding for the listener. An interesting finding with regard to comprehensibility is that raters appear to have different 'tolerance' levels for the quality of candidate talk, so such an assessment category (that is, an *interviewer*-oriented one, one which focuses on the impact on the rater of candidate talk) cannot fail to contribute to differences between raters. This is perhaps more of a concern where comprehensibility is stated explicitly as one of the criteria. Within the category of production, raters without exception commented on fluency, despite it not being specifically referred to in the band descriptors. Where there was disfluency, raters inferred reasons for this. These inferences often differed from rater to rater, even for the same performance. It may be, then, that this particular feature of learner performance contributes much of the variation in scores from rater to rater. In addition, fluency is also likely to vary from interview to interview, or from topic to topic, being attributable to the nature of the interaction (i.e. a performance feature) rather than an inherent aspect of ability. Where tasks vary as much as they do in tests such as IELTS (in part because of the interviewer) it is clearly not appropriate to rely on fluency as a measure of proficiency. However, despite the fact that it is not an explicit indicator in the IELTS band scales, raters still focus on fluency. Where there is disfluency they tend to make judgements about candidate ability on the basis of their inferences regarding the reasons for disfluency. In this respect, fluency is a problem category – clearly salient to raters and yet potentially performance-specific and differently interpretable.

Comprehension was also commented upon where candidates experienced problems understanding the interviewer, but, as they are instructed, they tend not to penalise students for misunderstanding.

Finally, it is interesting that raters comment on the communication strategies used by candidates, particularly as the elicitation of such strategies is neither prescribed within the interview format, nor consistent across performances, and, indeed, is generally a result of problems in the communication. While most of the comments are positive, it is not clear to what extent the raters take their occurrence into account in awarding scores. While there is an explicit acknowledgement of their relevance in the band descriptors, at least in terms of circumlocution, they are not addressed systematically either in the test or the descriptors. It may be time to consider either their explicit and systematic inclusion or their removal from consideration in general.

7.3 Interpretations of candidate behaviour

We would concur with the findings reported by Pollitt and Murray (1996) that many of the raters' comments consisted of inferences based on the candidates' behaviour, and that these inferences often differed from rater to rater. We have commented more than once before now on the amount of interpretation that raters engage in. Inferences were frequent, and typically used to excuse or explain certain patterns of behaviour and to justify certain scores. They occurred particularly in relation to fluency, the use of speculative language and the production of extended discourse, and were often concerned with the candidates' maturity.

While we would agree with Pollitt and Murray's statement that 'Given the subjective nature of the interpretative process, there is, then, clearly room for variability in the ways in which different judges perceive a performance', we feel it is important to consider why it happens and, in the interests of fairness, how it can be constrained. As with the assessment of any complex performance, some ambiguity arises when certain required aspects of performance are not demonstrated: Is the candidate not capable of this skill, or is the candidate capable but did not display it for another reason? Given the frequent (and typically negative) evaluations of the interviewer, coupled with the interpretations referred to above, it appears to be the case here that raters tended to give the candidate the benefit of the doubt, particularly in relation to lack of evidence of extended discourse and speculation. Perhaps the time has come to tighten up the elicitation process in performance tests such as IELTS in order to ensure that *all* candidates are required to demonstrate specific skills, even those candidates who are not familiar with the test requirements, so that assessments can be based more directly on what does occur rather than what doesn't occur. This would mean, for example, that candidates are *explicitly* instructed to produce extended discourse, rather than its production being a result of test wiseness or personality, as often appears to be the case now.

7.4 The interviewer

The raters in this study were constantly aware of the fact that the interviewer is implicated in a candidate's performance. Given the extent to which interviewers' behaviour varies from interview to interview, part of the raters' dilemma in tape-based assessments is an attempt to disentangle the two so that a score can be awarded to the candidate *alone*. A further complication lies in the fact that each performance (each *interaction*) is unique, and that certain behaviours which will be noticed by the rater may occur in one performance and not in another, for example, failure of the candidate to comprehend, the chance/need to demonstrate certain communication strategies. In addition, the choice of topic and the way it is addressed will vary, as will the interviewers' interviewing style, and these will have implications for the candidate's performance.

While operational ratings of IELTS do not require raters to assess from tape so the question of how to compensate for the interviewer does not arise, it does lead us to ask to what extent performances elicited by two different interviewers will differ, and what the implications of this may be for candidates. This is the subject of a current study (Brown 1998).

7.5 The band scales

Finally, as this study has shown, the rating of complex communicative performances such as that exhibited in the IELTS interview is a difficult task, especially where they are guided by brief and necessarily vague holistic band scales. It is and will always remain an 'imprecise science' and raters deserve to be given credit for their attempts to make sense of the interaction and quantify it as they are required to do. We are perhaps over-ambitious to expect patterns of rating which are consistent across interviews and across raters. Perhaps we must in the end accept that raters of performances such as these must be allowed their individuality and their internal variability, and that the best we can hope for is that they ultimately conform to some notional standard of *reliability*. Perhaps we should look for other ways to ensure fairness for candidates. One way, of course, is to use more constrained and explicit tasks and criteria, but the danger here is the potential loss of communicativeness, or at least interactiveness. Another is the use of multiple ratings, which would avoid putting the entire responsibility on a single rater and expecting them to perform the impossible and produce a replicable and justifiable single score.

Notes

1   This information is taken from the *IELTS Handbook* (1997). Note that the format of the IELTS Speaking test changed from 1 July 2001.
2   As we shall see, the result of this is that some comments which appeared obvious at the time were less meaningful later. The question of how much intervention and clarification should be allowed in verbal protocols is a difficult and unresolvable issue.
3   In all extracts the first number refers to the tape or interview number, the second to the rater. Thus 40–6 refers to Tape 40 Rater 6. Within the extracts, direct quotes from candidate speech are in italics.
4   On the other hand it may be that the raters themselves were clear on what they were commenting upon, but were simply not explicit enough. As was mentioned earlier, a decision was made not to ask for clarification or elaboration as it was felt that this intervention may influence the direction of subsequent talk by the interviewer. Such are the difficulties of this type of research!
5   Obviously such comments are related; their classification into different categories is unfortunately a consequence of the necessity of imposing categorical distinctions on such speech data.
6   The recording of the fourth protocol for this interview failed.

Appendix 3.1
Instructions to raters

For each tape you will first be asked to award a score using the IELTS bandscales.

Please note: these IELTS interviews do not contain Phase 3 (asking questions).

After you have awarded a score, you will be asked to summarise the reasons you gave the score you did.

You will then be asked to play the tape through again and describe in much more detail your process of rating. You should stop the tape and comment whenever you come across anything that contributed to your perceptions of the candidate.

You may comment both on behaviours that reflect the final score you gave, and on behaviours which reflect other levels on the bandscales. Other comments may not be linked directly to band levels (i.e. the link may not be so direct as 'this behaviour here was a six'), but may simply refer to some aspect of the performance, either good or bad, that you particularly noticed when scoring the interview.

Stop as frequently as you can and comment on anything you like. You may also comment on the frequency of certain behaviours, i.e. performance over an extended time, rather than individual instances of a behaviour.

(When the tape has ended I'd like you to add any 'overall' perceptions which you have not yet commented on.)

Please say as much as you can; don't leave anything out because you think it's irrelevant – everything is relevant.

Methodology evaluation of Chapter 3

In this section three elements of the study are discussed: abstract, research literature, and research methodology.

The abstract in this study is slightly unusual in that it does not refer to the major findings of the study. This is not an accident because, in the last paragraph of the abstract, the author states, 'Findings are discussed and implications are drawn regarding the validity of this test format'. However, this is such a well-written paper that the author manages to provide the reader with enough access to the study and its findings in the main text that they need not feel hampered by this lack of information in the abstract. Generally, however, it is unlikely that such practice should be encouraged among new researchers.

New researchers will note that the author has researched the topic thoroughly and that she includes recent and relevant references plus key older references (e.g. Kelly 1955, Munby 1978) to underpin her background to the research study. Unless they are writing up their doctoral thesis, new researchers will not normally have a comprehensive set of references to draw on. However, as they gain experience, they will notice that important references in their specialist field crop up regularly so that they can draw upon these to provide the research context of their study while they continue to report recent references. An example of this occurs in section 4.1 of this chapter, where the researcher cites the author of the fifth volume in this series (Green 1997). Researchers should note that this volume provides an excellent introduction to the theory and practice of verbal protocol analysis.

Section 4 of this Chapter is in two parts: Protocol analysis; and Procedure. Researchers do not always describe fully their choice of research methods. This study does, however, by providing a short but useful outline of protocol analysis, mentioning that concurrent verbal reports are widely used but clarifying, for the reader, the alternative technique that will be used in this study: retrospective verbal reports. The author explains why retrospective verbal reports have drawbacks, namely the effects of time lapse between the rating and its report and the tendency of the subject to say what the researcher wants to hear. But she also explains, convincingly, why concurrent verbal reports would seriously interfere with the subjects' ability to carry out real time, ongoing assessment of the IELTS Speaking test. This is because each of her subjects is the sole rater for each interview. Concurrent verbal reports would thus make the subject's prime role as assessor impossible.

In terms of avoiding the 'tidying up' of subjects' comments, Brown, in the last paragraph of section 4.1 explains clearly what steps were taken to minimise the 'tidying up' effect. This was both procedural 'by indicating to participants beforehand that it was expected that they would consider features not included in the scales' and attitudinal where 'care was taken to refer to the raters as experts, and the study was framed as an investigation of the nature of this expertise'. This is a methodological procedure that every researcher should heed: the preparation and role of subjects, particularly when investigating raters' perspectives of assessing spoken and written language.

The second part of the chapter's methodology section describes the procedures that were carried out using retrospective verbal reports. An interesting point for new researchers is that this study was able to access data from an existing study (Brown and Hill 1998). This demonstrates that useful and complete data sets can be 'mined' fruitfully when a new research question, quite different from that in the original study, becomes salient.

In the second part of the research methodology section (on Procedure) the author explains every step that took place: contact by letter, the number of interview tasks to be completed, what the subjects should read, how they would respond to the tape, and the role of the researcher (minimal wherever possible). This is a procedure that all researchers should adhere to when reporting what takes place during an investigation. This Chapter serves as a useful, thorough example for researchers in this area.

4

A survey of examiner attitudes and behaviour in the IELTS oral interview

Brent Merrylees and Clare McDowell

Abstract

This research project was designed to complement research being carried out at the time by the University of Cambridge Local Examinations Syndicate (UCLES) into candidate and examiner discourse produced in the Speaking Module of the test. The researchers felt that analysis of this kind was funda- mental to informed discussion of any possible changes to the test format and that the debate would be further enhanced by consulting IELTS examiners, the practitioners who are actually required to apply the Speaking test instru- ment. At the time there had been no large-scale survey of IELTS examiners to establish their attitudes to either the Speaking test format or to the band descriptors in their current form.

The research project investigated examiner attitude to the Speaking test by carrying out a survey of IELTS examiners working at test centres in Australia, New Zealand, Malaysia, Thailand, Indonesia, Hong Kong, the Philippines and Taiwan. The survey was delivered in a 2-page questionnaire and was divided into the three broad sections of IELTS interview format, IELTS band descriptors and the different interview phases. The final sample size for the survey was 151 respondents.

1 Background to the research project

The prime motivation for the design of this research project was to comple- ment existing research being carried out at the time by UCLES. The research commissioned by UCLES concentrated on the Speaking Module through a linguistic analysis of the discourse produced. The researchers felt that analysis of this kind was fundamental to having informed discussions on any possible changes to the test format and the debate would be further enhanced by con- sulting IELTS examiners, the practitioners who are actually required to apply the Speaking test instrument. At the time there had been no large scale survey of IELTS examiners to establish their attitudes to either the Speaking test format or to the band descriptors in their current form and it was important that any investigations into these examiner attitudes be informed by input from both IELTS Australia and the British Council examiners. Given the fact that UCLES was currently carrying out research, the researchers thought it apposite to carry out a survey which would dovetail in with the UCLES research and produce a clearer picture of how the Speaking Module was performing.

Australia has more than 40% of the IELTS worldwide cohort and the team for this had considerable experience, both through training of examiners and in the delivery of the test, of the issues/problems involved with the current Speaking Module.

The overall objectives were therefore:

* to establish examiner attitude to format, usability and perceived reliability of the Speaking Module
* to establish examiner attitudes to the speaking band descriptors focusing on the examiner ability to interpret the band descriptors consistently and reliably
* to critically review the band descriptors in order to provide data which will then be used to inform collaborative research with UCLES to investigate the effectiveness and reliability of the Speaking Module.

When the questionnaire was designed, it was deemed relevant that it be precise, contain no ambiguities and that it could be completed in a time frame of under five minutes. The authors were keenly aware of the pitfalls of designing prompts in any questionnaire and paid particular attention to having prompt precision while not overly burdening the respondent with complex and ambiguous language. Once the design was finalised after a brief trial on a group of Sydney based examiners, the questionnaire (see Appendix 4.1) was able to be printed on two sides of one page, back to back for ease of distribution and handling, and ultimately contained 39 short questions. Respondents were asked to rate on a scale of 1–4 a number of aspects of the IELTS Speaking test. Some space was provided for examiners to include, in their own words, their views on certain aspects of the Speaking test and to the Speaking test as a whole. The survey was divided into three broad sections:

* IELTS interview format
* IELTS band descriptors
* the interview phases.

It should be noted that the willingness with which the respondents were prepared to comment at the end of each section of the questionnaire is encouraging but also points to a perceived need to discuss such issues. Clearly respondents have jumped at the opportunity to express an opinion, albeit under cover of anonymity, on how they feel they manage an IELTS interview. The comments are both illuminating and helpful.

2 The cohort

In January and February of 1997, all Australian IELTS Test Centres were telephoned and asked to participate in the survey of IELTS examiners to ascertain examiner attitude to the Speaking Module. Administrators were asked to seek the co-operation of their examiners by having them complete an anonymous questionnaire. This instrument was, wherever possible, given to examiners on the day that they were examining, to ensure that the responses were based on fresh recollection of the exercise.

The Australian data was drawn from 113 respondents across the following centres: Sydney, Brisbane, Perth, Armidale, Launceston, Townsville, Wagga Wagga, Darwin, Melbourne, Gold Coast, Canberra, Newcastle and Wollongong. Following the success of the initial Australia-based survey which had yielded both interesting and insightful results, and in accordance with the original research brief, further data was gathered during May and June 1997 at IELTS Australia and Asia-Pacific centres to add to the preliminary findings. Centres in Malaysia, Thailand, Indonesia, New Zealand, Hong Kong, the Philippines and Taiwan were invited to participate and 38 responses were received from the first five countries; the findings were then analysed in the same manner as those received from the Australian centres. A bar graph was drawn up to illustrate the responses to each question for both cohorts and these can be viewed on pages 145–162. A comparison between the two sets of data follows on an item by item basis. The countries surveyed are not identified separately but rather the responses from the countries involved have been collated to produce the results from the Asia-Pacific centres. It would be possible to further identify the responses on a country by country basis but as the cohort is approximately a third the size of the Australian cohort it was felt this would not yield representative results if fragmented.

3 Methodology

The initial phase of the project required a survey of a sample of examiners to investigate a number of issues:

- how the examiners feel about the format and the phases of the Speaking Module
- what changes, if any, to the Speaking Module format the examiners would like to see
- whether the examiners felt the current descriptors were easy to use
- how often the examiners refer to the descriptors when giving their rating of a candidate's performance in an interview
- whether there are areas, if any, of the descriptors examiners would like to see changed.

All examiners were surveyed on an anonymous basis, their permission having been first obtained for the research project. The survey was, wherever possible, given to examiners by the Test Administrator on the day that they were examining to ensure that the responses were based on fresh experience.

4 Analysis of the data

The information captured on the completed questionnaires was entered onto a database and then analysed to produce a statistical overview of the responses. The individual questions are produced in Appendix 4.1 together with the responses received, presented in statistical form and accompanied by the researchers' interpretation of the data. In addition to the statistical data and the analysis, a summary of the respondents' individual comments is also attached at the end of each section.

4.1 Section 1: The IELTS interview format

Respondents were asked to rate the following propositions from 1 to 4 with 1 being 'strongly agree' and 4 being 'strongly disagree'.

Question 1 The interview format is easy to manage

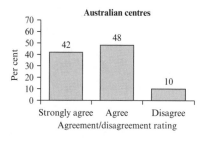 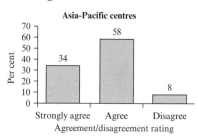

The vast majority of respondents from both cohorts agreed that this was true though 10% disagreed. We can assume from this that the format is generally acceptable to examiners.

Question 2 The interview format is effective in generating assessable discourse

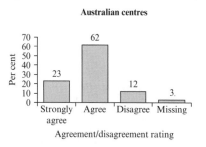 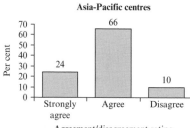

Over three-quarters of the respondents felt this to be the case. In other words, the language produced by the candidates in response to the tasks is adequate for an assessment to be made.

Question 3 The interview is of a manageable length

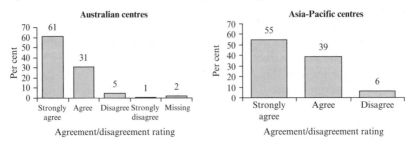

All but a handful of respondents felt the length of the interview was manageable.

Question 4 The taping of all interviews is a good idea

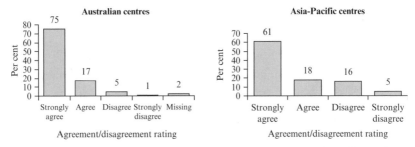

The vast majority of examiners had no problem with the taping of interviews though it can be seen that the responses from the Asia-Pacific centres reflect the fact that some examiners are not in favour of the taping. This may stem from a lack of understanding of the rationale for taping interviews.

Question 5 The interview should be less structured than it currently is

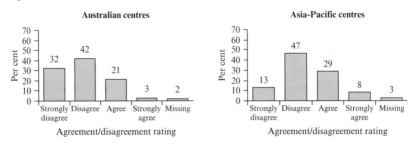

While 74% of the Australian respondents felt happy with the interview format, almost a quarter of them admitted that they would like it to be less structured than at present. This contrasts with the smaller number of 10% who answered in Q1 that it was not easy to manage. Those respondents from the Asia-Pacific centres who would like a less structured format constituted a larger percentage of their cohort.

Question 6 The interview should include picture and/or photo prompts

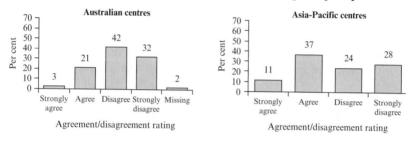

One quarter of the Australian respondents agreed with this proposition but the majority felt that pictures would not enhance the interview. Just under half of those who did not want pictures felt strongly about this. On the other hand, examiner comments included one remark which was strongly in favour of using pictures so this is an area of dispute. The responses from the Asia-Pacific centres are noticeably different and have produced a favourable response to the idea of picture prompts from almost half the group, though the field is clearly divided here.

Question 7 The interview should include a negotiated task

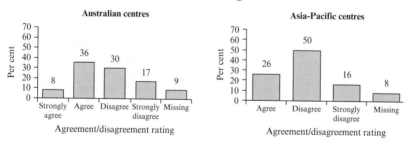

Here the Australian respondents were fairly evenly divided with 44% in favour and the rest against. However, those who were in favour were almost as great in number as those who were against the proposition, indicating that this is an area of contention. It seems that the overseas respondents were generally not in favour. It may be that some examiners misunderstood the proposition.

Question 8 There should be two examiners (one interlocutor and one assessor)

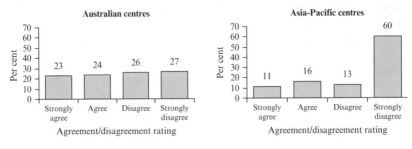

Again here we see a very evenly distributed field in Australia with almost half in favour of the idea of having two examiners present while slightly over half were against. Those who strongly disagreed with the proposition were in the majority at 27% of the cohort. One respondent suggested that this approach was essential for new examiners. However, in the Asia-Pacific centres, the idea was apparently not well received.

Question 9 The interview should be in a paired format with two examiners

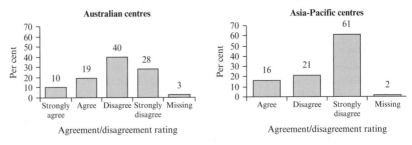

The responses to this question varied considerably from the previous question. Only 29% were in favour in Australia while almost 70% disagreed with the proposition. In the Asia-Pacific centres we see a similar pattern with the paired interview with two examiners being firmly rejected by the overseas examiners. Since all UCLES Main Suite exams now prescribe this format for the oral component of the tests, it is interesting to note the response from the IELTS examiners. It may be that those in favour were already familiar with the UCLES model.

4.1.1 Summary of respondents' comments: Questions 1–9

The general feeling from the examiners is that the format is good and quite manageable. Many comments related to the administrative difficulties that would be involved in changing the format to include more than one examiner, highlighting how organisational concerns often inform decisions. For a full listing of examiner comments on the interview format, please refer to Appendices 4.2 and 4.3.

4.2 Section 2: The IELTS band descriptors

The questions in this section of the questionnaire were designed to probe examiner behaviour and the authors acknowledge this is a difficult area to deal with as respondents often give answers which they think are appropriate or expected. Nevertheless, it was considered important to investigate the issue. Respondents were asked to rate the following propositions from 1 to 4 with 1 being 'always' and 4 being 'never'.

Question 10 I refer to the descriptors before every examination session

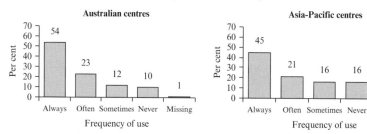

It was interesting to note that over half of Australian respondents were sure that they referred to the descriptors, though the fact that 10% admitted to never doing so is cause for concern. The overseas responses reflect the same pattern though the 16% who never refer is more alarming. Since a further 12% in Australia and 16% from the Asia-Pacific centres replied that they only did this on some occasions, we can assume that approximately 25% of examiners are not referring regularly to the descriptors before an exam session.

Question 11 I refer to the descriptors before every interview

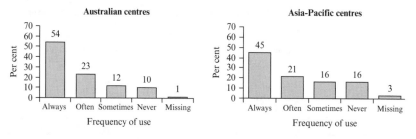

Very similar patterns to Question 10 were revealed by this question.

Question 12 I refer to the descriptors during the interview

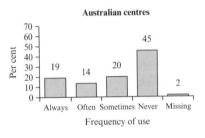

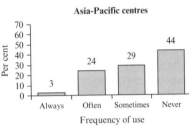

As expected fewer respondents indicated this pattern and, in fact, almost half pointedly registered that they do not do so, possibly because they would consider this to be intrusive examiner behaviour during the interview.

Question 13 I refer to the descriptors after every interview when rating

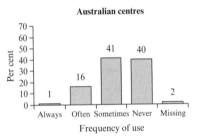

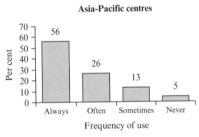

The overwhelming majority of respondents in Australian centres claim that they do not always refer to the descriptors after an interview. Since half have responded that they do not refer to them at the start, either, this response is disturbing. The examiners from the Asia-Pacific centres, on the other hand, appear to be far more likely to refer to them at the end.

Question 14 I am thoroughly familiar with the descriptors and rarely refer to them

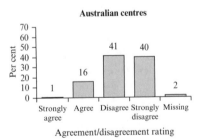

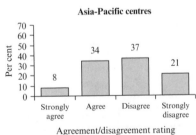

This question could have been thought of as a 'trick' question which no one wished to get caught by. Most responded that they often refer to them which is in apparent contrast to the responses to the previous three questions.

Question 15 I find the descriptors easy to interpret/apply

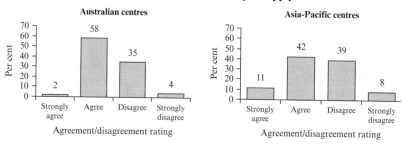

Over half of the respondents indicated that the descriptors were easy to apply but a large number in both groups (40–45%) did not agree and admitted to having difficulty using them. This is a disturbingly high proportion since the application of the rating scale is the key to reliable marking.

Question 16 I feel confident that my ratings are accurate when applying the scale

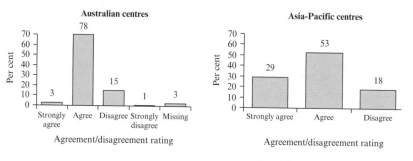

Well over three-quarters of the examiners felt confident about their own marking. This is encouraging and what one would expect. Nevertheless we find just under 20% who are not confident.

Question 17 The descriptors discriminate clearly between the levels of proficiency

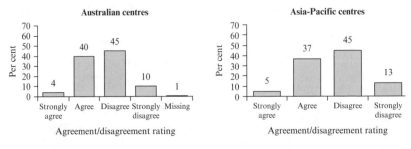

Here the field was clearly divided with just under half agreeing with the proposition and slightly over half disagreeing in both cohorts. The responses here appear to point to the need to review the descriptors as these findings would indicate that examiners are having difficulty applying them with reference to the bands.

Question 18 The descriptors are adequate for all phases of the interview

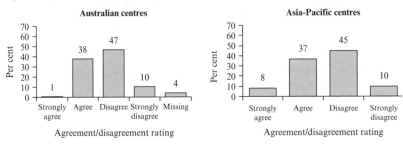

Over half of the respondents felt that the descriptors were inadequate for all phases. Both groups produced very similar split responses.

Question 19 I would like to use a profile scale, as with Writing, where individual aspects of performance are assessed (e.g. pronunciation, structure, fluency, etc.)

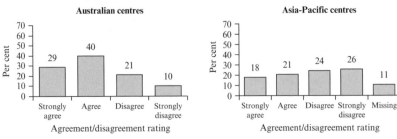

The responses to this proposition ranged across the spectrum with well over half of the Australian examiners (69%) indicating a preference for a profile scale but those not in favour also being split. Some 10% strongly disagreed with the proposition. However, the fact that nearly three-quarters of the respondents would welcome such a scale is significant. The examiners from the Asia-Pacific centres, however, would appear not to be in favour.

Question 20 I would like to use a combination of global and profile descriptors

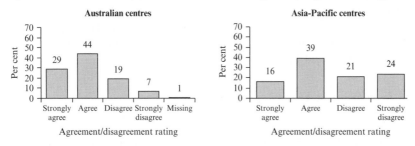

The responses to this were, as expected, very similar to the previous question though slightly more examiners were in favour of this arrangement than simply a profile approach. Significantly, the proportion of Australian examiners strongly opposed to the profile approach was slightly less when the opportunity to combine it with a global score was given. The examiners from the Asia-Pacific centres were divided on this issue.

Question 21 I am quite comfortable using the global descriptors

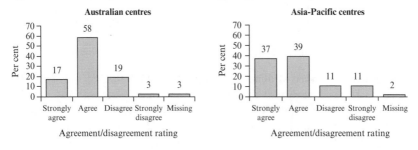

It is significant that only 20% said they were not comfortable with the global descriptors when 75% of the Australian group had claimed that they would like to see a profile approach adopted. This would indicate that while respondents showed a preference for the profile approach, they were also quite comfortable using the global descriptors.

4.2.1 Summary of respondents' comments: Questions 10–21

The comments were wide-ranging and illuminating. Many respondents commented that they found it hard to differentiate between bands 5 and 6 as far as the descriptors were concerned and that clearer indicators were needed to guide the examiners in this area. Some people offered strong views about how profile descriptors would help enormously, particularly in areas such as pronunciation which is ignored in the descriptors for bands 5, 6 and 7. Others felt profiling would be time consuming. Many respondents made reference to the vagueness of the descriptors and the difficulties of interpretation which therefore arose. Terms such as 'fairly' and 'usually' were deemed unhelpful. For a full listing of examiner comments on the descriptors, please refer to Appendices 4.2 and 4.3.

4.3 Section 3: The interview phases

Phase 1 – Introduction

Respondents were asked to rate the following propositions from 1 to 4 with 1 being 'very' and 4 being 'not at all'.

Question 22 How useful is the candidate's CV/application form in Phase 1?

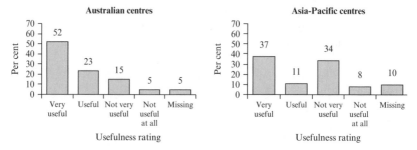

Three-quarters of Australian respondents advised that they found this useful with the majority of that group saying that it was very useful. This would indicate that the CV acts as a crutch or at least as a safety net for both the examiner and candidate. Only 20% felt that it was of little use or no use at all. Unlike the Australian based examiners who were in favour of the CV, the overseas cohort was equally divided on this question. As it is standard practice in the Australian centres to use a CV but not so at British Council centres, this question may not have been viewed equally by all respondents.

**Question 23 How much does candidate performance in Phase 1 influence
your final score?**

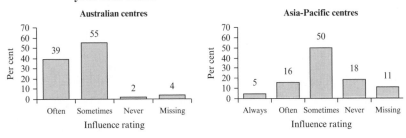

In Australia the vast majority 'admitted' to being influenced by the first
impressions gleaned in Phase 1 of the interview when technically no assessment should be taking place. The overseas examiners were not so revealing
and quite a few chose not to answer this question.

Phase 2 – Extended discourse

Question 24 How appropriate is the choice of topics for Phase 2?

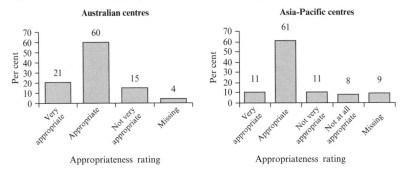

Over 80% felt that the choice of topics in Phase 2 was appropriate. This is an
interesting finding as it now appears that these topics are 'public knowledge'
and therefore can theoretically be practised in advance.

Question 25   How effective are Phase 2 topics at producing assessable discourse?

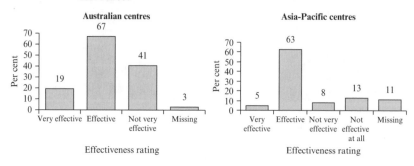

Most respondents felt that Phase 2 topics were effective at producing assessable discourse.

Question 26   How rigidly do you stick to the prescribed Phase 2 topics?

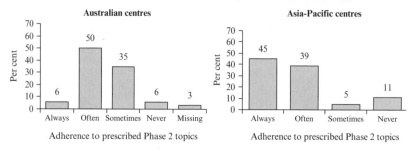

Only a very small number (6%) of the Australian examiners claim to use only the prescribed topics while for the Asia-Pacific centres this number was 45%. It appears that the Asia-Pacific respondents stick to the guidelines more than the Australian examiners.

Question 27   How often do you 'stray' into Phase 4 topics in Phase 2?

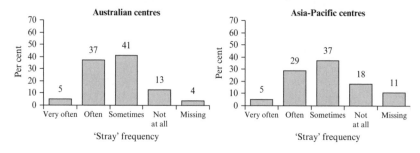

The pattern of responses is very similar from both groups. Again, the response indicates that examiners may touch on topics such as academic plans in Phase 2, which would tend to skew the format of the interview, as the Phase 4 topics have then been used. A survey such as this is revealing but also allows us to remind examiners of the way in which they should be proceeding.

Question 28 How often do candidates reach their linguistic ceiling in Phase 2?

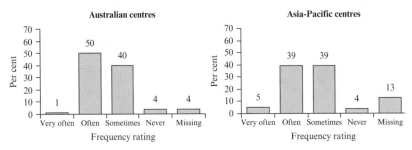

The response to this question would indicate that examiners feel that candidates often show their best performance by the end of Phase 2. This could be interpreted to mean that they are not sufficiently pushed in the latter part of the interview to show a higher level, or that indeed many candidates reach a performance plateau early in the interview.

Question 29 How much does candidate performance in Phase 2 influence your final score?

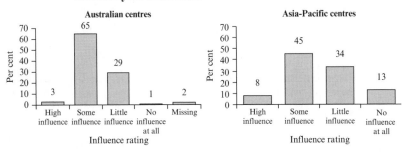

It would appear from the response to this question that many examiners effectively make up their mind about the rating by the end of Phase 2.

Phase 3 – Elicitation based on tasks

Question 30 How comfortable do you feel about the interaction in Phase 3?

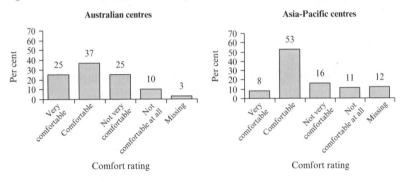

The response here was varied. Exactly 25% of Australian respondents felt very comfortable with the interaction, while an equal number expressed the view that they felt uncomfortable with it. The remaining 50% were mostly happy with the Phase 3 interaction though some 10% expressed a very negative view. The responses from the Asia-Pacific examiners were similar though less extreme.

Question 31 How often do you skip Phase 3 if candidate is struggling in Phase 2?

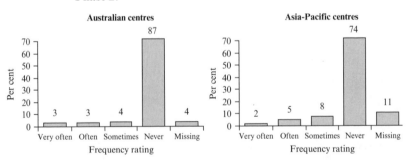

Since examiners are not supposed to skip any of the phases of the IELTS interview, and examiners are trained not to do so, the responses here are revealing. While only a few respondents admitted to skipping Phase 3, the fact that only 87% in Australia and 74% in the Asia-Pacific centres answered that they never do so confirms some administrators' suspicions. Moreover, these results are worrying for what they suggest about procedural standardisation and therefore test validity more generally.

Question 32 How easy do you find it to play the prescribed roles?

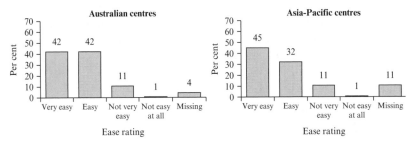

The responses from both groups are very similar. It seems that most examiners have little trouble playing the role that is expected of them in the Phase 3 elicitation phase. Slightly over 10% are not happy with the role-playing aspect of the elicitation phase.

Question 33 How effective are the tasks at producing assessable discourse?

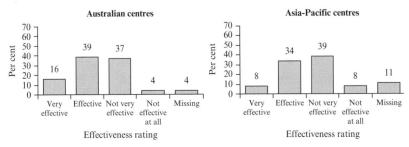

Here the field was evenly divided between those who find them effective and those who do not. In other words opinions about the merit of Phase 3 cover the full range. This demonstrates that examiner attitude to this part of the test varies enormously.

Question 34 How much does candidate performance in Phase 3 influence your final score?

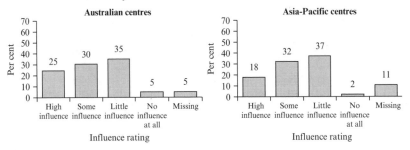

Again, the field is very divided here. We find that slightly over half of the examiners are influenced by the Phase 3 interaction and approximately 40% are not. These findings apply to both groups. This effectively means that the exercise is wasted in many cases. A significant number of respondents from Asia-Pacific centres did not offer a response.

Question 35 Do you have favourite tasks for phase 3?

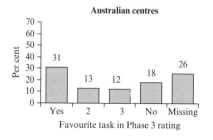

Here the responses were varied with less than 40% claiming to have favourite tasks. Those cited by examiners again covered the full range. Many examiners mentioned the 'Visiting a friend' task because of its authenticity as with the 'Wedding' and 'Evening course' (see Appendices 4.2 and 4.3 for a full overview of examiner comments).

Phase 4 – speculation and attitudes

Question 36 was intended to probe the issue of how examiners get back on track after the Phase 3 interaction, and how best to prepare examiners for this in the training situation. The responses were varied enough to warrant looking at this issue further. Both groups gave very similar responses.

Question 36 How often do you return to Phase 2 topics to generate Phase 4 discourse?

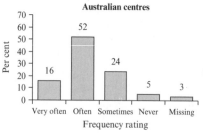
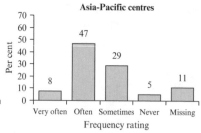

Question 37 How easy do you find it to establish a useful Phase 4 topic?

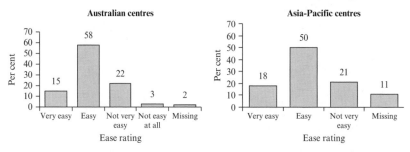

Approximately 70% of examiners claimed to have little or no trouble finding a suitable topic in Phase 4. This is encouraging and possibly what one would expect from experienced interviewers. The fact that 22% admitted to having difficulty would point to a need to include techniques for finding and establishing a suitable topic for Phase 4 in the training procedure in order to provide a framework. Some candidates are inevitably more difficult to interview than others, regardless of level, and examiners need to be able to deal with the more reticent ones.

Question 38 How often do candidates reach their linguistic ceiling in Phase 4?

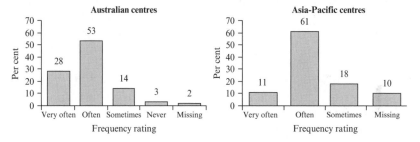

This question was included to find out how many examiners felt that they were able to take a candidate to his or her linguistic ceiling in the fourth phase. A very high proportion felt that they could do this. This is encouraging and should point to the view that Phase 4 is working. However, another interpretation of these responses would be to say that, ideally, fewer respondents should be so sure that they are achieving this and so it may actually point to the fact that they are unaware of their shortcomings as interviewers. The researchers wonder whether this is often the case.

Question 39 How much does candidate performance in Phase 4 influence your final score?

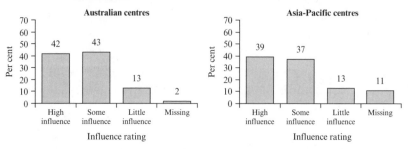

The responses to this question reflect those of the previous question (Q38) in that 85% of the examiners surveyed felt that the candidate's performance in Phase 4 was significant in arriving at their final rating. Nevertheless, the 13% of the Australian group who felt that it was not useful is significant enough to cause some concern, as is the fact that 11% in the Asia-Pacific centres chose not to answer.

4.3.1 Summary of respondents' comments: Questions 22–39

The comments vary enormously, from those who are happy with the *status quo*, to those who would eagerly accept change. This is inevitable and hardly surprising. However, the number of respondents who have commented on the non-academic nature of the interview is worth noting. Several respondents commented that candidates are now presenting for the test extremely 'test-wise' having rehearsed nearly all the topics and Phase 3 tasks. Many examiners were prepared to volunteer the information that they found Phase 3 false and that it did little to focus their rating. Others, however, felt that it provided a break between phases and perhaps it should be seen as such. For a full listing of examiner comments on the interview phases please refer to Appendices 4.2 and 4.3.

Some of the comments were revealing in that they highlighted the individuality of approach. One respondent offered the information that they did not agree with basing a rating on the candidate's peak performance but rather relied on the 'whole performance'. Some expressed a strong desire to see profile-type descriptors while others are clearly opposed to this approach.

5 Overall comments on survey findings

The responses appear to have been supplied in a very open manner and the overall feeling of the research team was that they are honest and authentic. It is therefore felt that they should be taken seriously with regard to possible improvements to the IELTS Speaking test since the respondents are the very people implementing the instrument. Several related issues were probed and now need attention.

1. There appears to be some divergence from the examiner guidelines with examiners sometimes taking liberties both with the format and the rating procedure. This can be addressed in refresher training for current examiners and also in training sessions for new examiners. It might be useful to produce a 'Reminder Checklist' for examiners which is circulated by administrators at regular intervals.

2. It is evident that examiners would welcome amendments to the descriptors to provide clearer demarcation between a band 5 and 6 which are, to all intents and purposes, the critical levels.

3. There are clear differences of opinion about the merits of profile as opposed to global descriptors which stem possibly from experience in the field and from an adherence to a linguistic philosophy. The point was made, however, by a number of respondents, that it is difficult to operate a profile approach if they are playing the role of interlocutor as well as assessor.

4. Individual comments from the examiners from Asia-Pacific centres reflected a scepticism about Phase 3 in terms of its actual usefulness. One or two commented that it interrupts the flow of the interview. These comments echo those of the Australian examiners. The question which prompted them to think about how often they embark on Phase 4 topics in Phase 2 has also pinpointed an inherent problem which needs to be addressed in training.

5. The research team would like to suggest that the examiners working in Asia-Pacific centres may be intimidated by the idea of a two-examiner system because it is an unfamiliar approach and also because it poses potential constraints on their interview style with a 'watch dog' implication built in. Even if it is not adopted, there is certainly a need to monitor examiners more often than is currently occurring.

6. Since all tests are a balance between what is practical in terms of relia-bility and what is best practice, and for reasons of administrative ease and expediency, an approach to the IELTS Speaking test which allowed for ease of delivery was adopted. The rationale for this decision must not be overlooked. IELTS is available practically on demand on a worldwide basis and must therefore be easy to administer. On the other hand, we do not want to lose sight of the importance of maintaining a reliable instrument simply in order to keep administrative arrangements to a minimum.

6 Further research

There are clear grounds for undertaking further research in the area of interest covered by this study building on the original data gathered for this
research. Suggestions for further research are listed below.

1. In the area of examiner attitude, it would be useful to undertake trials
   with a set of profile descriptors which differentiate more clearly between
   the critical levels of bands 5, 6 and 7.

2. There is an apparent need to monitor examiner performance with
   regard to standards of test delivery, both in the area of timing and also
   in the requirement to bring candidates to their linguistic ceiling in Phase
   4. At the present time examiner monitoring takes the form of checking
   to see whether the assessment is within acceptable levels of accuracy and
   does not effectively address whether correct IELTS interview procedures
   are being followed.

3. There is scope for investigating whether more prescriptive examiner
   language could be introduced into the interview format. Introducing
   more tightly controlled examiner language or even an interlocutor frame
   in the form of a finite list of specific phrases or questions to be used by
   the examiner could be one method for standardising examiner
   discourse. In addition, examiners need to follow the guidelines with the
   aim of bringing the candidates to their true linguistic ceiling in Phase 4.

APPENDIX 4.1

IELTS SPEAKING TEST – EXAMINER QUESTIONNAIRE

Confidential – Please do not give your name
Base your answers on your overall experience as an IELTS examiner.

Training Mode:	Face to face training?	Self access training?
Centre where you examine		
Number of years experience as an IELTS examiner		
Number of years experience as an EFL/ESL teacher		

IELTS INTERVIEW FORMAT

The following is understood by the term 'format':
The one to one, face to face, taped interview lasting between 12 and 15 minutes consisting of five discrete Phases.

FORMAT Tick ✓ 1 = Strongly agree . . . 4 = Strongly disagree	1	2	3	4	
The interview format is easy to manage.					1
The interview format is effective in generating assessable discourse.					2
The interview is of a manageable length.					3
The taping of all interviews is a good idea.					4
The interview should be less structured than it currently is.					5
The interview should include picture and/or photo prompts.					6
The interview should include a negotiated task.					7
There should be two examiners (one interlocutor and one assessor).					8
The interview should be in a paired format with two examiners.					9
Comments on format:					

165

The IELTS BAND DESCRIPTORS

Rating is currently by means of a 9-point scale, each level being defined by a global descriptor encompassing many aspects of language performance.

DESCRIPTORS Tick ✓ 1 = Always . . . 4 = Never	1	2	3	4	
I refer to the descriptors before every examination session.					10
I refer to the descriptors before every interview.					11
I refer to the descriptors during the interview.					12
I refer to the descriptors after every interview when rating.					13
Tick ✓ 1 = Strongly agree . . . 4 = Strongly disagree	1	2	3	4	
I am thoroughly familiar with the descriptors and rarely refer to them.					14
I find the descriptors easy to interpret / apply.					15
I feel confident that my ratings are accurate when applying the scale.					16
The descriptors discriminate clearly between the levels of proficiency.					17
The descriptors are adequate for all Phases of the interview.					18
I would like to use a profile scale, as with the writing, where individual aspects of performance are assessed (eg pron, structure, fluency etc).					19
I would like to use a combination of global and profile descriptors.					20
I am quite comfortable using the global descriptors.					21
Comments on descriptors:					

THE INTERVIEW PHASES: Tick ✓ 1 = Very . . . 4 = Not at all	1	2	3	4	
Phase 1 – Introduction					
How useful is the candidate's CV/application form in Phase 1?					22
How much does candidate performance in Phase 1 influence your final score?					23
Phase 2 – Extended discourse					
How appropriate is the choice of topics for Phase 2?					24
How effective are Phase 2 topics at producing assessable discourse?					25
How rigidly do you stick to the prescribed Phase 2 topics?					26
How often do you 'stray' into Phase 4 topics in Phase 2? (i.e. future plans)					27
How often do candidates reach their linguistic ceiling in Phase 2?					28
How much does candidate performance in Phase 2 influence your final score?					29
Phase 3 – Elicitation – based on tasks					
How comfortable do you feel about the interaction in Phase 3?					30
How often do you skip Phase 3 if candidate is struggling in Phase 2?					31
How easy do you find it to play the prescribed roles?					32
How effective are the tasks at producing assessable discourse?					33
How much does candidate performance in Phase 3 influence your final score?					34
Do you have 'favourite' tasks for Phase 3? (If *yes* tick 1 and complete box below)					35
My preferred Phase 3 tasks are: .... Use an additional sheet if necessary					

Phase 4 – Speculation & Attitudes Tick ✓ 1 = Very . . . 4 = Not at all					
How often do you return to Phase 2 topics to generate Phase 4 discourse?					36
How easy do you find it to establish a useful Phase 4 topic?					37
How often do candidates reach their linguistic ceiling in Phase 4?					38
How much does candidate performance in Phase 4 influence your final score?					39

General comments about the IELTS Speaking test	
....	Thank you very much for completing the question-naire. ***LTC*** Language & Testing Consultants Sydney

APPENDIX 4.2
Individual comments made by IELTS examiners on questionnaire – Australian centres

Comments on format

'I feel that the format is okay. Not all the tasks for Phase 3 are immediately clear to interviewees and quite often rely on a higher reading capacity than the interviewee has. I feel that two interviewers would be intimidating.'

'I find Phase 3 too structured and that it does little to clarify my ratings. I would prefer to add a more focused academic discourse task after Phase 4.'

'Stage 3 ("role play") could be dumped.'

'One to one is likely to be the least threatening of designs. Picture/Photos prompts = excellent idea, especially for elicitation Phase.'

'Definitely should be 2 examiners for the first 3–6 months of experience after training.'

'I like it – it gives a structure and the role play provides a break between asking questions and before pushing the testee.'

'Test wiseness seems to play much too important a role in the present format. Format produces unrealistic and largely non-academic discourse.'

'Questioning/role play occasionally rigid and structured. Some students who have not done preparation classes are put at a disadvantage in this Phase.'

'The role play is often rehearsed, so those who do IELTS preparation courses do it better than those who don't do these courses.'

'Don't feel that the interview should be paired with 2 examiners but feel that this format should be trialled and compared with the current format results.'

'The inclusion of Phase 3 is useful in giving another angle on the candidates' English, but awkward to manage.'

'The situational role play is fine for students up to a 6/7 threshold; above that it is forced and unnatural.'

'This of course, would assist in giving a more objective score but very difficult to organise always having 2 people to interview one candidate. The candidate might be more nervous with 2 "threats".'

'Two examiners would be more objective and save time. Like structure.'

'Phase 3 topics often put candidates in situations they can only respond to if they are already competent/fluent language in which this Phase is presented, needs to be less formal.'

'Photo prompt only for lower levels but this is not suitable for "one size fits all".'

'Some students may have some English but they do not speculate, or have much to discuss – it makes Phase 5 difficult.'

'2 examiners may benefit assessment reliability but may intimidate candidates and inhibit best performance.'

'Format does present a problem when the interviewee volunteers speculation etc. in Phase 2, i.e. interruption is necessary.'

'It's okay but has its limitations.'

'The current format is not perfect, but it works. It already contains some flexibility of approach.'

'Do not always find it easy or appropriate to slide into role play – often I do not find it easy for candidate to do – very noticeable when they have/have not had IELTS prep. training.'

'There is sufficient choice to suit the ability of all students.'

'A slight loosening of structure might be helpful in generating "unplanned" discourse from very rigorously prepared candidates. Otherwise fine.'

'There is nothing about the format that is effective XXXX dependent on interviewer.'

'I would like the interview to be a little longer maybe 20 minutes.'

'I think having two examiners would intimidate the students even more. It is easier to establish a good rapport with the student on a one-to-one basis.'

'I think the format is okay – but find candidates do disproportionately poorly on Phase 3. (How much weighting should this be given?)'

'I feel the format is adequate. I feel students would be even more nervous with two examiners. Experience some difficulty with Phase 3 if students have not been prepared.'

'Two examiners per interview would require longer timespan overall or more examiners.'

'The part where the interviewee asks the interviewer questions is artificial and situations weak.'

'If the band descriptors were to change, for example, to include profile descriptors it would be difficult for one person to manage the lot. This would be a case for having an interlocutor and an assessor.'

'One-on-one is workable – interviewer/interlocutor would make the test more exact.'

'Format is okay – I don't think two examiners would improve it.'

'Perhaps there could be pairing every now and then.'

'The combination of structure/format and timing is a little difficult, especially for students at slightly lower levels.'

'Two interviewers would be so difficult to schedule. We should be able to omit Phase 3 very competent speakers – nature proficiency.'

'I like it the way it is although one could argue that Phase 3 is artificial and disruptive of the natural flow of the discussion.'

'Explanation please.'

'The Phase 3 activity is always a little unnatural in the conversation an examiner XXXX to develop. While research shows that question formation (plus negatives) and the verb "to be" are structures non-native speakers find difficult to acquire.'

'The format is not bad as it is.'

'The question and answer section is certainly useful, but introducing it takes time. Suggestion – a picture (group activity e.g.) here, which candidate must find out about. "ask me about this . . ." '

'9+10 – This maybe preferable but often we find it difficult to get enough interviewers – we'd be stretched.'

'Interview is stressful enough for student, two examiners would make it worse.'

'I am comfortable with the format and find it offers a change of pace.'

'I think the format works well.'

Comments on descriptors

'Borderline cases are very hard to handle. Descriptors for 8 and 9 are too broad and non-specific.'

'8 and 9 could be developed more or at least 8.'

'Generally okay but band 7 is thin and there could be more on pronunciation.'

'Better descriptors needed for elicitation Phase. Some proficiency might be useful e.g. extended discourse. Elicitation and Speculation okay, but some interference from XXXX.'

'More aspects of performance should be included.'

'If we had profile descriptors I think it would be too time consuming – we'd need another 5 minutes per interview.'

'Question/role play phase occasionally inappropriate.'

'Not enough difference between band descriptors for 5 and 6.'

'In two minds about the profiles – at a gross level I'm fairly confident about my global bands and there probably isn't time for profiling, but . . .'

'There are minor errors not covered by the descriptors, where personal judgement, coupled with common sense, comes into operation.'

'Profiles including pronunciation would be great. Also, inclusion of quest. form. Guidance in bands 5, 6 would be helpful.'

'Question of pron. needs referring to all levels. Differences between levels (e.g. 5 and 6) needs to be clearer. Question of listening skills needs incorporating in some way. Quick/accurate comprehension means candidate responds appropriately (though not XXXX').

'I feel the descriptors are too general which results in significant differences in candidates who may receive the same band score. I'd like to see the descriptors rewritten to be more specific, especially between bands.'

'Admissibility of .5 scores (as in other components) would allow more accurate rating of borderline candidates.'

'Familiarity depends on frequency of use.'

'Candidates' speaking abilities often fall between 2 bands and therefore very difficult to assess accurately – hence a good idea to profile as well.'

'I am familiar with the descriptors, but always refer back to them as a check. The tricky one is 5/6.'

'The descriptors do not accommodate assessment of the candidates' comprehension skills and how they affect the interview.'

'Can be vague and or explicit in certain areas, however I've learned to work within their parameters.'

'Occasionally students can be extremely interesting and communicative, and they are able to transmit information despite grammatical mistake etc. This could be due to personality and/or the ability to select pertinent points which are interesting . . .'

'2 parts – I am familiar with descriptors but do refer to them.'

'Guidelines on the meaning of words like "usually", "fairly", "occasionally" would be helpful!'

'They need much more teasing out or changed to be competency related.'

'Sometimes it is very difficult to decide between band 5 and 6. Many candidates share characteristics of each band. Yet discrimination in scoring here is critical.'

'Perhaps there are too many.'

'Very necessary – but sometimes they are not clear enough between bands – especially 5 and 6.'

'It is difficult to distinguish the grey areas e.g. good 5, low 6. Either a .5 score or a profile scale would help with these areas.'

'As with the writing, a profile scale would be useful for borderline cases.'

'Some student performances fit descriptors easily others are more difficult to match e.g. 5/6.'

'Comfortable with descriptors only when they fit accurately.'

'The bands do not always take into account a very proficient communicator with severe pronunciation problems.'

'As above this would take into account factors such as pronunciation, which is not mentioned after Band 4. However, this could be difficult for one person to manage.'

'With profile assessment, an assessor/interlocutor setup would be more effective.'

'I am comfortable with present descriptors but the option of profile rating would be useful for difficult interviewees.'

'I find the descriptors too vague and general.'

'I much prefer the Cambridge 2:2 interview format but do see that academic require a candidate to produce less social English. This question is too philosophically complex for me to answer so easily. I am familiar with the descriptors but do nevertheless ...'

'More reference should be made to pronunciation in the medium to higher ranges.'

'Not perfect, but very thoughtfully devised and reasonably easy to administer.'

'Would like to see some reference to pronunciation in descriptors for bands 5, 6, 7.'

'Useful, but rather verbose: what I do is highlight and summarise on separate card.'

'Profile descriptors would encompass those performances of fluent-speakers whose accuracy and/or pronunciation are problematic. If simply expressed, discrete profiles would be easier for assessors to be familiar with and remember ...'

'Pronunciation should have greater prominence among the criteria. Unclear how Phase 3 performance should affect assessment.'

'Appropriate and useful. Examiners may need to apply their own discretion or common sense, but this is inevitable in any system – speaking is communicating with other people, and written descriptors do not alone assess that communication.'

'There seems to be considerable overlap. Sometimes it's clear what band students should get – otherwise a profile scale would help immensely.'

'There is often an overlap. The descriptors can be ambiguous.'

'Different people understand terms like "communicates effectively" differently, but it is hard, perhaps impossible, to avoid terms like these.'

'Adequate, but each new candidate is an individual who may "fit" the descriptors differently.'

'I sometimes feel candidates fall between two band descriptors.'

'The subjective and modal nature of the descriptors is problematic.'

General comments about the IELTS Speaking test

'I find Phase 3 an intrusion and then difficult to get back onto a train of thought. Phase 4 seems to follow naturally from Phase 2 while Phase 3 seems to be an artificial interruption. I don't usually base results on Phase 3 but if it's especially bad . . .'

'I'd like to delete Phase 3 and add more guidance to interviewers on extending candidates in Phase 4. I'd also like to see more specific descriptors in bands 5, 6, and 7 and more linguistic characteristics in 8 and 9.'

'Introducing two examiners and a greater example of language elicited through the one of two candidates. Some of the Phase 3 tasks are bizarre.'

'Elicitation Phase – I never use the personalised role plays where testees have to ask assessor re. assessor's life etc.'

'The risk to reliability the isolation of examiners acting alone in their closed rooms, with no official system for reflecting on their own performance as interlocutors or their accuracy as assessors.'

'Phase 3 can be difficult in getting anything from the candidate. Often I feel I am saying more than he is. I think it should be more optimal to test the ceiling of the more capable candidates.'

'Phase 3 needs to be looked at – I don't think it's so realistic. Visuals sounds like they could be a useful alternative. There should be a team marker for beginners.'

'I find it well structured balanced – I feel uncomfortable with most of Phase 3 tasks – and usually use my favourites. But I like Phase 3 to break up conversation if the level is low or the testee is not a good communicator.'

'Would like to see two assessors and two candidates interacting with each other – would produce much more realistic, assessable discourse and get rid of the problems of inter and intra-rater reliability that plague this section of the test.'

'Phase 3 topics need update urgently.'

'It's hard to dissolve the nervousness that the students have and to avoid prepared responses especially in Phase 3. Some more general tasks i.e. more real-world tasks in Phase 3 would be welcome.'

'Test structure appropriate and effective. However, subject to skills of examiner and can be influenced by examiner bias XXXX etc.'

'I'm not confident about rater reliability. I only use 3 or 4 of the Phase 2 topics most not useful at all. The variation in acceptability of straying from format from interviewer to interviewer worries me.'

'I would like the flexibility and quasi-naturalness of the present format to be made more rigid, whether through the introduction of picture prompts or a fixed list of topics in Phase 2. Ideas are always useful, but not prescriptions.'

'A problem in Phase 4 is that candidates (especially Asian) don't have much worldly knowledge to answer questions about current issues. It is difficult to get them to talk in any depth on a topic because they just don't know much about it.'

'More detailed descriptors would be appreciated especially for Bands 4, 5, 6, 7. Phase 3 is often at odds with other phases – another form for eliciting questions, students often get even more stressed in this stage.'

'Difficult to distinguish between Band 5 and 6. Students can be very communicative, yet not use complex sentences. They can speculate well in simple language.'

'Question of tertiary study and its requirements as well as ability to survive while living here, need focussing on as criteria for assessing. What do we have in mind when assessing candidates, language for studying and surviving or language that fits band . . . ?'

'The task often generates readily assessable discourse because the higher scoring students will use this opportunity to elicit information and so further "settle down" for Phase 3 and 4. (They can "take control" at the start of Phase 3.)'

'I am reasonably satisfied with it as it is and not anxious for change.'

'Needs new band descriptors possibly profile marking and a more detailed description for each band – making bands more easily distinguished.'

'CV sheet needs development should include age, sex, more information on candidates' interests or should be encouraged to fill it out more seriously. Age and sex would help examiners to partially pre-select Phase 2 topics.'

'Phase 4 clarifies the final score especially if the candidate is a borderline case.'

'A reasonable test.'

'Generally the test suits more mature students who have a wide variety of "life" experiences. A significant number of IELTS students don't fall into this category. i.e. they find it difficult to talk.'

'The performance of the candidate is obviously influenced both by personality and state of mind (nervousness particularly) make accurate assessment difficult at times.'

'Having a profile scale would perhaps make rating easier for a candidate who is either shy, reticent or nervous and may not perform as well as another with a more outgoing personality.'

'It's a very general test for testing academic candidates it doesn't test their ability to present work orally for example, but it would be very difficult to create and assess such a task. As a general test it is very good provided it is conducted correctly.'

'I am quite happy with it. A lot of time and debate has gone into the current format. There always will be accusations of subjectivity, but this argument may be neutered by reference to experience and qual. status of the tester.'

'Would like more moderation on speaking test. Maybe use interlocutor and assessor combination now and then.'

'The more a candidate is relaxed the more interactive and confidently they deliver. I believe interviewer interaction has a huge influence on candidate performance and capacity to demonstrate ability with confidence. This ultimately impacts strongly on assessment.'

'The range of scores used in Australia is very limited – generally 4–7, descriptors need to be more specific and perhaps reviewed to expand this range more realistically 5.5 perhaps 6.5 etc. These are scores I would often like to be able to give.'

'Should include some scope for assessment of listening proficiency – only chance that candidates have to demonstrate listening proficiency in a real world situation.'

'Generally speaking I am comfortable. However, I feel extra refinement of the descriptors would help. In particular, I seem to find it hard to use evidence from Phase 3 to help distinguish between bands of 6 and over.'

'It is more difficult now than it was a year ago to avoid rehearsed answers. Students are very familiar with the topics and format of the test.'

'Sometimes very difficult to determine whether it is a particular band score – perhaps 0.5 needed to differentiate. Even though Task 3 is most difficult for many candidates, I think it's useful for seeing the really good ones and being certain they are 7 and 8.'

'The information on the personal details should be elicited and not provided by candidate. Phase 3 fares better as a role play if the examiner plays out experiences not what is on the card. Levels 6 and 7 are not well defined – without using a profile they will . . .'

'I am always most concerned about grading between 5/6, given the similarity of the descriptors. My second big concern is to what degree I suddenly let my grading be influenced by performance being poor in Phase 3 given candidates often do disproportionately . . .'

'Very young candidates often have little to say/ little experience of the Phase 2 topics.'

'Phase 3 is not a smooth transition from Phase 2. Phase 2 and 4 need to be together to create a more realistic discourse for candidates.'

'Students who are prepared do much better. I feel that bands are broad and a .5 would be very useful.'

'I do think Phase 3 can be quite artificial in its format and sometimes it's the wording of the prompts that confuse them. Perhaps they a need a less structured format in which they can show more initiative in problem-solving skills.'

'With some candidates Phase 3 is not helpful there are often misunderstandings about the task or they are not comfortable with it.'

'Phase 3 elicitation is not "information gap" according to me. Two examiners would be great.'

'I have always had some reservations about Phase 3 – which often shows a mismatch against the other Phases. It sometimes seems false, especially for competent speakers, and does not always display the same level of proficiency. Much depends on the initiative.'

'Once interviewer is used to the routine it becomes easier to focus on descriptors.'

'A difficult task to relax the student and make fairly natural conversations while at the same time closely monitoring their language ability and proceeding through the various Phases of the test. But you get better at it the more you do it of course.'

'Students often find Task 3 to be difficult.'

'I really do think that it needs to be more similar to the two candidate/assessor/ interlocutor format for other Cambridge exams.'

'I think it is potentially a fair test, but it does vary depending on the extent to which the examiner makes the student feel at ease. Nerves can be an immense obstacle. Training is essential for examiners in this respect.'

'Generally quite a good test.'

'I find it works well with the vast majority of candidates. I would be very strongly against the introduction of assessment through individual aspects of performance.'

'Would like to be able to give levels between the present bands e.g. 5.5 as a number of students don't fit the exact bands.'

'I would like to see some differentiation within Bands 5 to 7, as these are vital for university entrance and most of our students fall between these bands e.g. a low 5 = 5-high; 7– 7+ and most important, 6+ or 6– or use 5.5.'

'The comprehensiveness of the test is good if examiners say little and place the onus on candidates in all but very difficult situations. Phase 3 does interfere with the natural flow of the conversation. The long-winded descriptors and the absence of Pronunciation.'

'I have doubts about assigning a score based on a candidate's highest level reached in the interview. I'm inclined to take into account the whole performance.'

'I enjoy the test – I think it is an opportunity to relieve the IELTS "examination" atmosphere for the candidate. The progression from easier to more complex language works, and does enable (for me) confident assessment on the scale.'

'Phase 3 tasks vary considerably – some don't seem to produce much assessable discourse I have my favourites and use them.'

'Least comfortable with Phase 3 – even very competent examinees can misunderstand what to do.'

'Students are least comfortable with Phase 3. Whole exercise is partially false. Our job is to have students relax enough to be able to use language skills to maximum of their potential.'

'IELTS for some reason are strident that Phase 3 is not a role play, while in reality it is. I believe the elicitation based tasks should be as real as possible e.g. questions about the interviewer, e.g. background, current lifestyle etc. . . .'

'Sometimes it feels like the student has rehearsed, particularly Phases 1 and 4. Nervousness is hard to judge its impact on speaking. More real naturalistic setting would be helpful.'

'Determining what a linguistic ceiling for some candidates is very difficult. A truly objective assessment of speaking is obviously very difficult. As an administrator problems can occur if students are not marked as highly as on a previous test.'

APPENDIX 4.3
Individual comments made by IELTS examiners on questionnaire – Asia–Pacific centres

Comments on format

'My reservations are about the Phase 3 questioning – I feel its position in the middle of the interview and the difficulty in leading into it present problems. It is also misunderstood frequently by those who have not undergone a preparation course.'

'The timing for each Phase should be more flexible.'

'The Phase 3 role play tends to interrupt the overall flow of the interview.

'Elicitation breaks flow.'

'I find the format manageable, however with a lower level student the interview can be extremely difficult.'

'Photo prompts could be a good means of improving what is already a flexible and manageable format.'

'I find the tape inhibiting for the students; I don't mind it myself as I am already used to it. Nobody likes being recorded.'

'Sometimes Phase 4 seems unnecessary because it has already been covered in Phase 1 or 2 or I stop in Phase 2 to pick up again later in Phase 4.'

'Two examiners would be more intimidating. Pictures/photos would be more stimulating, negotiated task is not clear/too vague.

'Two examiners would add to reliability, but two are not necessary. A second opinion on a section of the taped interview would be helpful before making a final assessment.'

'Agreement by two raters on tape.'

'The format is good but perhaps it is too known. Why not versions as with writing.'

'It's a bit artificial to break with two if they're discussing their work/study and go back to it in step 4, but I manage w/o much difficulty. With weaker Ss, the option of pix is good.'

'It wouldn't be necessary to tape all interviews if there were two examiners.'

'Phase 3 is awkward and interrupts the flow from Phase 2 to Phase 4.'

'It would be difficult to design a negotiated task manageable for all levels when a candidate's level is very low, the speculation part is XXXX.'

'Really should be seen as 3 Phases. Phase 1 and 5 aren't really Phases at all. Hello and goodbye.'

'It's XXXX on the whole.'

'Present format is too unreliable in terms of XXXX variability. Role play is not a good task type for oral assessment.'

'The Phases: OK but need to be interchangeable/flexible to match the unpredictability/digressions of natural discourse.

Comments on descriptors

'Question 18 – I don't think it's always possible. There will always be borderline cases.'

'Sometimes problems arise when an assessor is unwilling to give the same score for an interview that's better than a previous one, even if they're really within the same band. Half-bands as are given for listening and reading, should be considered.'

'Phase 3 is somewhat difficult to assess using the descriptors.'

'Being a relatively new assessor I find the bands very helpful and all in all a fair guide.'

'Good system – don't change it.'

'Speculation/Extended argument/Complex description tend to discriminate against younger and less experienced candidates, even though they have a very good level of English.'

'Distinctions between 5/6 (and 7/8) are often difficult.'

'Quite subjective – but this is a difficult dilemma for the XXXX of a test.'

'Speaking is a more ephemeral phenomenon where a global impression is what remains.'

'Sometimes I find that a S's performance can be characterised by various descriptors in 2 bands. It is not so much the descriptors themselves which enable me to assign band scores as what I and other examiners have negotiated them to mean.'

'I would prefer to allocate half band scores.'

'There is nothing about pronunciation in the descriptors for many bands. The descriptors are not very good.'

'Categories are often rather vague – but this is probably unavoidable.'

'Clean and easy to follow.'

'Generally OK – though don't really take into account enthusiasm/sincerity and genuine attempt of communication despite errors of certain candidates.'

General comments about the IELTS Speaking test

'I find Phase 3 almost useless.'

'Could be more like FCE/CPE exams – UK. I'm an IELTS and FCE/CPE examiner, and I enjoy both but photos are a good focus point and relax the very nervous student. I'd like a change in scores to follow like the old FCE/CPE format (prior Dec. 96).'

'I generally find the test easy to administer and can usually generate a fair amount of language from the participant.'

'Some students cannot adapt to the role play section. Sometimes they are quite good speakers but have had little test practice. This section tends to influence my grading – often lowering the score, perhaps because the candidate has poor Q. forms ...'

'If there can't be an assessor and interlocutor there should be a XXXX assessment of the first candidate of each session to set a standard.'

'Phase 3 interrupts what would be a natural (and logical) progression from Phase 2 to Phase 4. Artificiality of Phase 3 tasks sometimes disrupts easy relationship established/developed in Phases 1 and 2.'

'With some candidates I find the prescribed topics in Phase 2 too limiting. I find Phase 3 a little awkward, but I think it is important to include the opportunity for a candidate to ask questions. I would like to experiment with using both profile and global.'

'I would like different tasks for Phase 2 (i.e. a range) and I would like more variety of format.'

'As a XXXX text on the whole. However, sometimes I find the role play a little bit artificial.'

'Phases do often seem to merge naturally and difficult to maintain strict order and maintain a fairly natural type conversation. Role play if at all should go at the end.'

'I feel that most examiners can consistently distinguish borderline 4/5 from 5/6 etc. thus, half bands should be considered. Similarly, half bands should be considered for the Writing test.'

'Candidates need intellectual ability and experience as well as language competence to get a high score. Not suitable for younger candidates.'

'Do not like the order. The Phase 3 tasks often disrupt the flow. Often difficult for candidates to "get into" the role. Sometimes I go 1–2–4–3. Also find the borderline between band 5 and 6 sometimes difficult to judge. In Malaysia many are in this area.'

Methodology evaluation of Chapter 4

This chapter presents interesting findings and is to be commended for the attempt to shed light on examiners' attitudes. However, in terms of research methodology, there are a number of issues that require discussion. Foremost among these are the issues of survey research, questionnaire design and the basic processes and procedures that are required to ensure that the purposes of the questionnaire are fulfilled.

The first issue is the lack of references in this chapter. In such a study, it is customary for researchers to cite their sources, thus justifying the theoretical and practical underpinning to their approach to questionnaire design. Included below are a number of websites that new researchers may wish to consult before attempting survey research.

www.tardis.ed.ac.uk/~kate/qmcweb/ql0.htm – a short, useful list of check
    questions
www.cc.gatech.edu/classes/cs675 1_97_winter/Topics/quest-design/
marketing-bulletin.massey.ac.nz/article9/article3b.asp – this
    website presents a theory of questionnaire design and contains useful
    references
www.soc.surrey.ac.uk/~scslps/SOC103%20Lecture%202%20
    questionnaire%20design%201.pdf – a sensible, amusing introduction to
    questionnaire design
www.leeds.ac.uk/iss/documentation/top/top2.pdf – this website from the
    University of Leeds (2003), is a pdf file in nine sections. It presents a
    very useful account of approaches to questionnaire design and contains
    an up-to-date reference section and two appendices providing examples
    of questionnaire design and examples of questionnaires.

It will be noted that many of the sites refer to one of the major works on questionnaire design: Foddy, W (1994) *Constructing Questions for Interviews and Questionnaires: Theory and Practice in Social Research*, Cambridge: Cambridge University Press.

Some detailed, small, but important points may be made about the design of the questionnaire itself. In the bar chart for Question 5 'The interview should be less structured than it currently is', readers will note that the Lickert scale categories have been reversed. All of the previous questions and the remaining four questions from 6–10 move from the left-hand side of the scale 'strongly agree' to the right-hand side of the scale 'strongly disagree' (except for the 'missing' category on the extreme left-hand side). In the bar chart for Question 5, however, the scales are reversed, beginning with 'strongly disagree' and moving to 'strongly agree'. It should also be noted, paradoxically, that in Appendix 4.1 which sets out the questionnaire, the scale for Question 5 runs from 'strongly agree' to 'strongly disagree'. This is not a practice usually followed in questionnaire design and new researchers should be discouraged from following such practice.

Another point concerns 'check' questions. These are questions designed to weed out respondents who are not focusing on the responses to the questionnaire or to those who are inconsistent. This questionnaire contains no such check questions.

Another example of a question that would have benefited from a pilot administration and moderation is Question 14 'I am thoroughly familiar with the descriptors and rarely refer to them'. The authors themselves comment: 'This question could have been thought of as a "trick" question which no one wished to get caught by. Most responded that they often refer to them, which is in apparent contrast to the responses to the previous three questions.' The problem, however, is more likely to be that there are two questions to be answered not one. Questions should never consist of two questions, as such a practice renders the question invalid. Question 15 also makes demands of the respondent by asking about two matters: interpretation and application.

Overall, it can be said that the design and creation of questionnaires is much more than sitting down and brainstorming to produce some questions. It is always necessary to specify the purpose of the questionnaire, to outline the major areas that the questionnaire should cover, to formulate questions (checking that they are neither ambiguous or double questions), and to create some check questions. In the final stages of design, the questionnaire should be moderated, piloted and moderated again before the first administration.

5 The impact of the joint-funded research studies on the IELTS Speaking Module

Lynda Taylor

As explained in the introduction to this volume, the rationale for the IELTS Joint-funded Research Program is to promote and support research activity among test stakeholders which will contribute to the validation and ongoing development of the International English Language Testing System (IELTS).

The four funded research studies reported in Part 1 of this volume were all conducted between 1995 and 1998 and focused on the IELTS Speaking test (or 'oral interview') as it was operationalised during the period 1989–2001. Findings from these four studies provided the IELTS partners with valuable insights into the language and behaviour of both candidates and examiners in the IELTS Speaking test as it was at that time, and gathered useful evidence relating to the validity, reliability, practicality and impact of the test; they also highlighted specific aspects of the Speaking test needing closer review and possible future revision. As a result, they directly informed the IELTS Speaking Revision Project (1998–2001) and, in combination with outcomes from other commissioned studies and internal validation investigations, had a significant impact on the revised design and implementation of the IELTS Speaking Module which became operational in July 2001. The specific contribution of each of these four studies to the process of ongoing IELTS Speaking test development and validation, as well as to the broader language testing field, is reviewed and evaluated in the sections which follow. Much of the work carried out within the IELTS Speaking Revision Project was reported in a series of articles in Cambridge ESOL's quarterly publication *Research Notes*.

Chapter 1: Interviewer style and candidate performance in the IELTS oral interview (Brown and Hill)

In the early 1990s researchers into oral proficiency assessment began to focus their efforts on investigating the structure of the oral proficiency interview using innovative, and often complementary, methodological techniques to analyse test score and spoken language data (e.g. multi-faceted Rasch analysis, conversation analysis). Such studies provided applied linguists and language testers with rich insights into the linguistic behaviour of both the interviewer and the test candidate (see, for example, Lazaraton 1993; Ross and Berwick 1992; Young and Milanovic 1992). Brown and Hill's study was conducted in 1996 and first published in Volume 1 of the IELTS Research Reports 1998. It was a good example of the mixed-method (i.e. combined quantitative and qualitative) approach to research in this field and gave us a much better understanding of the oral interview which constituted the IELTS Speaking test at that time. Their study was instrumental in highlighting key features of IELTS interviewer behaviour which had the potential to affect the quality of candidate performance and so put at risk the validity and reliability of the Speaking assessment.

Findings from the Brown and Hill study, together with outcomes from other relevant research – including other studies reported in this volume – directly informed changes to the IELTS Speaking Module when it was revised in the late 1990s.

In particular, the test format was redesigned to ensure more standardised management of the IELTS Speaking test event. The original 5-phase format – which Brown and Hill noted was sometimes adapted by individual examiners – was replaced with a more structured 3-part test; each of the three parts is clearly defined and designed to fulfil a specific function in terms of interaction pattern, task input and candidate output. In Part 1 (4–5 minutes), candidates answer general questions about themselves, their homes/families, their jobs/studies, their interests, and a range of similar topic areas. In Part 2 (3–4 minutes), candidates are given a short written prompt and asked to talk on a particular topic for one to two minutes after one minute's preparation time. In Part 3 (4–5 minutes), examiner and candidate engage in a discussion of more general or abstract issues which are thematically linked to the topic in Part 2.

Test tasks and content are designed to reflect a progression from familiar topics to more unfamiliar topics – a move from less to more challenging subject matter. The long turn in Part 2 provides an opportunity for sustained language production on the part of the candidate, including taking the initiative and holding the floor. This revised test format is more structured, allowing for greater standardisation of examiner behaviour within the Speaking test and hence comparability of the challenge presented to IELTS candidates, e.g. in relation to topic management, timing of parts, and types of talk elicited. It therefore addresses several of the issues which the Brown and Hill report raised concerning examiners' management of the structure, timing and content of the IELTS Speaking test event.

In addition, an examiner frame was introduced to ensure greater standardisation of the language produced by IELTS examiners and thus address some of the concerns highlighted by Brown and Hill relating to potential variation in individual examiner speech, both in terms of its linguistic complexity and in terms of the degree of support and/or feedback provided to candidates. The examiner frame is a carefully designed script for the examiner's role in the interaction with the candidate and it guides the management of the test as it progresses through each of the three parts. The wording in the frame is carefully controlled in Parts 1 and 2 to ensure that all candidates receive similar input and to help control timing. In Part 3 (the two-way discussion) the frame is looser and the examiner has some flexibility to accommodate their language to the level of the candidate by fashioning appropriate questions from graded prompts; this flexibility is important in a speaking test which assesses across a fairly broad proficiency continuum. In this way, the frame provides support for lower level candidates while still allowing higher-level candidates the opportunity to demonstrate their proficiency. In designing the examiner frame an appropriate balance was sought between a straightforward question/answer routine and opportunities for the use of more 'natural' conversational techniques.

Finally, the Brown and Hill study fed directly into revised IELTS examiner training and standardisation procedures which accompanied the introduction of the revised Speaking test in July 2001; in particular, it allowed IELTS examiner-trainers and examiners to develop their understanding of how interlocutor conduct and language can impact on candidate performance and how to adjust their behaviour accordingly.

Chapter 2: An investigation into the role of gender in the IELTS oral interview (O'Loughlin)

Applied linguists have long recognised that individual background characteristics (e.g. age, gender, ethnicity) can influence how people behave and how they use language. In recent years language testers have investigated how such background characteristics impact on language and behaviour in the testing context (Bachman 1990; Bachman and Palmer 1996; Alderson, Clapham and Wall 1995; O'Sullivan 2000). Test-taker characteristics tend to be the main focus of interest (see, for example, work by Kunnan 1995 on test-taker background characteristics and test performance). Background variables such as age, gender, and L1 are all normally taken into account when designing language tests or monitoring their score outcomes. In performance-based tests of writing and speaking the background characteristics of raters as well as test takers are clearly of interest. In writing assessment examiner/rater background characteristics (gender, age, L1) may influence the process of rating. In speaking assessment, especially where there is face-to-face interaction between interviewer and test taker, background characteristics can affect both the language and behaviour of an interviewer/rater; they have the potential to influence both the discourse of the interview and the process of rating and its outcomes. Test developers strive to reduce construct-irrelevant variance and test bias to a minimum; investigation of the various potential effects of background characteristics is part of this process.

O'Loughlin's study was conducted in 1998 and first published in Volume 3 of the IELTS Research Reports 2000. It contributes to the growing body of research focusing on the potential impact of gender in the context of oral proficiency assessment (O'Sullivan 2000, Porter 1991a, Porter and Shen Shu Hung 1991) and does so in the context of the IELTS oral interview. The risk of test bias due to gendered differences in communicative style (i.e. between male and female interviewers) is clearly a concern in a high-stakes test such as IELTS; and, as O'Loughlin rightly points out, the interaction of variables is a particularly complex one in the IELTS oral interview where the interviewer acts as both interlocutor and rater.

His study of the language produced by the participants in the IELTS oral interview found no evidence that the test was a strongly gender differentiated event. Instead, he concluded that IELTS 'interviewers and candidates generally adopted a more collaborative, co-operative and supportive communicative style irrespective of their gender or the gender of their interlocutor' (p. 85). It seems that both participants understand that a co-operative dialogue will produce the best possible speech sample and thus best possible outcome for the candidate. Furthermore, no evidence was found of significant bias due to the gender of raters or candidates with regard to the rating process and the scores awarded.

O'Loughlin's findings were encouraging for the IELTS Speaking test developers as they support the view that gender does not have a significant impact in the IELTS oral interview. He concludes that it is unnecessary to allow candidate gender to determine the gender of the interviewer/rater. It is interesting to speculate, however, whether – had the findings been different – it would be feasible to administer an international speaking test in which the gender of test taker, interviewer and rater could be regulated in order to avoid potential bias. Practically speaking, such an arrangement is logistically problematic for tests of speaking and writing; matching test takers and interviewers/raters by gender might even lead to the introduction of another form of bias. Test producers nevertheless have a responsibility to design and administer their tests so that any potential for bias is reduced to a minimum. How is this achieved in the context of the IELTS Speaking and Writing Modules?

The careful design of any speaking test format and the establishment of comprehensive procedures for training and standardising interviewers and raters are instrumental in ensuring that potential sources of bias are removed or that their impact is minimised. This was a key motivation for changing the conduct and assessment of the IELTS Speaking Module when it was revised in the late 1990s and it also underpinned changes to assessment introduced for the IELTS Writing Module in 2005. As discussed earlier, the introduction of a frame or 'script' for the examiner ensures greater standardisation of IELTS examiner language, especially in Parts 1 and 3 of the revised IELTS Speaking test. The use of the frame helps to reduce the potential negative effects of 'overlap' and 'interruption' – two of the features investigated in the O'Loughlin study. In Part 3 the frame is looser for reasons already explained, so overlaps and interruptions can still occur. Extensive examiner training seeks to ensure that examiners' use of these features is positive rather than negative; examiners are also trained to use minimal responses in an appropriate way and to avoid using backchannelling expressions such as 'good' and 'fine' which candidates may misinterpret as an evaluative comment on their performance.

Finally it is worth remarking once more on the value of using both qualitative and quantitative analytical techniques with IELTS Speaking test data. Like the Brown and Hill study, O'Loughlin's research shows how discourse analysis of IELTS transcripts can offer us rich insights into the language of both the interviewer and the test taker (see also other studies reported in Lazaraton 2002); in addition, it highlights the value of using multi-faceted Rasch analysis with IELTS score data to investigate potential rater bias – an approach which has been used in similar studies conducted with IELTS Writing (see the O'Sullivan and Rignall study, Chapter 11 of this volume).

Chapter 3: An investigation of the rating process in the IELTS oral interview (Brown)

From the early 1990s language testing researchers became increasingly interested in the nature of the rating process, in particular the decision-making strategies used by raters in both speaking and writing assessment (see, for example, Lazaraton 1996b, Meiron and Schick 2000, Milanovic, Saville and Shuhong 1996, Pollitt and Murray 1996).

The need to investigate what raters take into account when awarding scores in oral proficiency assessment is essential for informing the design of test tasks, the choice of criteria for assessment, and the construction of rating scales; furthermore, an understanding of rater behaviour helps shape effective procedures for rater training and standardisation ensuring that these are as valid and reliable as possible. Specific questions of interest to test developers are: *How do raters understand the construct of oral proficiency? Which aspects of performance do they find salient? Are these aspects more or less salient at different levels of proficiency? What is the best way to train/standardise raters?* The availability of new and effective methodological approaches, such as conversation analysis, discourse analysis, and in particular, verbal protocol analysis, has made it easier over the past decade to investigate the questions above and to provide some answers. Today, verbal protocol studies are widely regarded as an effective way of gaining rich insights into how raters make their judgements when assessing oral and written language proficiency, and what factors are likely to constrain this process (see Green 1998).

The second study by Brown in this volume was conducted in 1998 and published in Volume 3 of the IELTS Research Reports 2000. It builds upon the researcher's earlier study exploring aspects of 'interviewer style'. Findings from this second study provided the IELTS test development and validation team with valuable insights to help inform the IELTS Speaking Revision Project (1998–2001) as they redeveloped the speaking assessment criteria and rating scales. For example, the study highlights the potential for variability in how raters assign their scores and suggests that an analytic rather than a holistic approach may help to enhance reliability: 'It may be that raters would be more likely to agree if the criteria were more discretely and clearly specified, for example through analytic scales' (p. 135). The study goes on to suggest various analytic categories that raters seem to find salient when assessing oral proficiency and to indicate those categories that may be especially salient for them higher up or lower down the proficiency scale.

The decision in the Speaking Revision Project to replace the earlier holistic criteria with a set of analytical criteria was based upon findings from this and similar studies. A move from holistic to analytic scales was perceived to offer three main advantages: first, it would allow for more consistent and visible treatment of features throughout the scale; secondly, it would permit recognition of the complex and variable ways in which features can interact to build up an overall performance profile; and finally, it would help to improve the reliability of ratings, requiring a number of potentially independent judgements of a performance rather than just one. Many of the analytic categories identified in the Brown study are reflected in the way the current IELTS Speaking assessment criteria and subscales were conceived and defined: *Fluency and Coherence, Lexical Resource, Grammatical Range and Accuracy*, and *Pronunciation*. Furthermore, the wording of the band descriptors for the nine proficiency bands in each subscale draws upon observations of what raters say they find particularly salient in performance at different levels, as well as what the research literature suggests are characteristic features of oral proficiency higher up and lower down the continuum (see Tonkyn and Wilson 2004).

The Brown study sensibly notes the complexity and challenges faced when analytic criteria and scales are used in a test context where the rater is playing a dual role, i.e. providing an assessment at the same time as conducting the test and maintaining interaction with the candidate. For this reason, the trialling phases of the revision project took care to explore the practicability of raters using several analytic scales rather than a single holistic scale when fulfilling this dual role. Four analytical scales proved to be manageable in the

IELTS Speaking test and raters often perceive the candidate's long uninterrupted turn in Part 2 as an important stage during which they can focus more strongly on their assessment role.

Findings from this study also confirmed the need to tighten up the elicitation process to ensure that all candidates are offered the same opportunity to demonstrate their skills. The introduction of a more standardised test format and an examiner frame was specifically to reduce the potential for interlocutor language and/or behaviour to impact negatively on scores, and this has already been discussed in more detail above.

Finally, the Brown study helped to inform the development of rater training and standardisation materials. The differences observed in the behaviour of newly-trained and experienced raters highlights the importance of regular *re*training and *re*standardisation. Following recruitment, all IELTS examiners are required to undergo an initial training and certification process which licenses them to examine for a period of two years. After this, they must retrain and re-certificate in order to continue examining. This approach to IELTS rater training and certification has been in operation since IELTS was first introduced in 1989 and the training guidelines and procedures have been regularly updated and enhanced since then. Over time, standard face-to-face training based around trainer-led standardisation packs and a Focus-on-Procedure video has replaced the earlier mix of face-to-face and self-access procedures for all examiners. Additional forms of ongoing support for IELTS examiners have been introduced, including a self-access standardisation video pack; this pack enables trained examiners to refamiliarise themselves with test procedure/format and to restandardise their assessments at any time between initial certification and re-certification. Such procedures form part of the developing IELTS Professional Support Network (PSN) – a global system that integrates all aspects of IELTS examiner management including recruitment, training, certification, standardisation, monitoring and conduct.

The Brown study makes several references to the desirability of having multiple ratings in performance assessment. Historically, the IELTS Speaking test (and ELTS before it) has always relied on a single-rater model underpinned by a range of measures and procedures to ensure reliability (including examiner monitoring programmes, checks on uneven performance profiles, etc). Routine double rating is both expensive and logistically complex, and single rating was believed to provide a level of reliability adequate to the purpose of IELTS while keeping the cost of the test within reasonable limits; in other words, it balances aspects of practicality and reliability. In recent years, information on the reliability of IELTS Speaking and Writing assessment has been collected through experimental generalisability studies as well as operationally, via analyses of sample monitoring. Targeted double marking is routinely used in the case of IELTS candidates identified as being at risk of misclassification, i.e. those candidates whose scores on the Speaking and Writing components of IELTS appear significantly different from their Reading and Listening scores. In addition, candidates who are unhappy with their results may ask for an enquiry on their results which involves a re-mark of any or all of the four test modules.

A major factor in achieving acceptable reliability is the gathering of multiple observations. Simply having more than one rater (double rating) is undoubtedly one way of achieving this though the financial and logistical implications need to be carefully considered. Another approach is to elicit several samples of language for assessment and to rate these samples using multiple assessment scales or criteria; using this method it becomes possible to achieve positive benefits and to avoid the increased costs or administration usually associated with double rating. The move to using analytical criteria for the IELTS Speaking test was in part for this reason, as previously discussed. Interestingly, as reported in the Introduction to this volume, Lee, Kantor and Mollaun (2002) investigated single versus double rating in the context of the development and validation of writing and speaking tasks for the new TOEFL project. They observed that adopting a single rating scheme had a smaller effect on the score reliability than expected for both writing and speaking; instead, they reported that increasing the number of tasks provided a cost efficient way to maximise score reliability. It is precisely for this reason that there are three parts in the IELTS Speaking test and two tasks in the IELTS Writing test. Recent technological advances (i.e. digital audio) are likely to make a more sophisticated form of a multiple rating model increasingly viable in the future and possible options are being actively explored by the IELTS partners for both the Speaking and the Writing tests.

Chapter 4: A survey of examiner attitudes and behaviour in the IELTS oral interview (Merrylees and McDowell)

The final speaking-focused study in this volume reports on a survey of examiner attitudes and practice relating to the IELTS oral interview. Conducted in 1997, this study appeared in Volume 2 of the IELTS Research Reports 1999. This project complemented other internal projects on the IELTS Speaking test being carried out at that time by the EFL Division (now Cambridge ESOL) within UCLES (now known as Cambridge Assessment). As the IELTS partner with primary responsibility for test development and validation, UCLES was already undertaking studies to analyse candidate and examiner discourse in the IELTS Speaking test (e.g. Lazaraton 2002); in addition, it was important to explore the attitudes of IELTS examiners towards the existing test format and the band descriptors, and their perceived use of them, in order to inform discussion of any changes.

This type of stakeholder consultation is a fundamental element of the test production methodology which underpins IELTS and all other tests produced by Cambridge ESOL Examinations. The test production methodology allows for various cycles of activity (planning, trialling, monitoring, evaluation) within the overall lifecycle of a test; each of these cycles involves periodic consultation with a wide range of test stakeholders (for further discussion of this approach see the chapter by Saville in Weir and Milanovic 2003). It is also worth noting that this project was undertaken by an IELTS Test Administrator and his colleagues working in one of the largest IELTS test centres in the world at that time. Test stakeholders such as teachers, senior examiners and test administrators have a direct involvement and stake in IELTS and are often well-placed to identify and investigate specific research questions. They also benefit from being in close and regular contact with other test stakeholders, such as students and examiners, who may be potential informants for applied research studies. The Merrylees and McDowell study is therefore a good example of the type of research partnership which can take place with those who have a direct interest and stake in IELTS, in addition to partnerships with members of the more traditional academic research community. Collaboration with test stakeholders has always been part of the underlying rationale for the Joint-funded IELTS Research Program and it makes an important contribution to the development and validation of the test, balancing a more theoretical/measurement-focused perspective with one which takes account of issues of practicality and impact in the field.

One interesting issue raised in the survey of examiner attitudes and behaviour was the possibility of replacing the traditional one-on-one format in the IELTS Speaking test with a paired format (i.e. two candidates and two examiners); the paired format is widely used today in many Cambridge ESOL tests of oral proficiency (e.g. First Certificate in English, Certificate of Proficiency in English). In the early 1990s Cambridge ESOL explored the issues of the paired format through a prototype speaking test known as the Cambridge Assessment of Spoken English or CASE (see Milanovic and Saville 1996). Serious consideration was given to whether such an approach could be implemented for IELTS but the revision project team decided against this for a number of reasons relating to the test qualities of validity, reliability, impact and practicality. The paired format is normally used in tests that are targeted around a particular level of proficiency and candidates are therefore paired with others who have entered at the same level; though some may be relatively weaker or stronger in their oral proficiency, the difference between candidates is unlikely to be great. IELTS, however, is designed to measure across a much broader proficiency continuum and so makes the acceptable pairing of candidates at a more or less similar proficiency level very difficult. Given the practical considerations, combined with its high-stakes nature, the individual Speaking test format has remained a more appropriate format for IELTS.

Although the Merrylees and McDowell study may not conform in all respects to traditional expectations of research methodology and presentation, it nevertheless made a valuable contribution to the IELTS Speaking Revision Project. Insights into examiner attitudes to test format, content and length informed discussions within the revision project team about how best to redevelop these aspects of the test, especially in relation to the different phases of the test; they also provided further support for the decision to constrain the examiner language and behaviour through the introduction of an examiner frame. Examiner perceptions of the strengths and weaknesses of the current band descriptors fed into consideration of how these might be improved and supported the move towards an analytic rather than holistic approach. Finally, the study's findings informed the redevelopment of the training and standardisation procedures for IELTS examiners, and pointed to the need to tighten up procedures in future for monitoring examiner performance more closely for both assessment and conduct.

Part 2
Writing

6 Authenticity in the IELTS Academic Module Writing test: a comparative study of Task 2 items and university assignments[1]

Tim Moore and Janne Morton

Abstract

The study reported here investigated the authenticity of the Task 2 component of the IELTS Writing test (Academic Module) by examining the extent to which this component of the test corresponds to the writing requirements of university study. This was researched in two ways: through a survey of writing tasks set in the two domains, and through interviews with academic staff. In the task survey, a total of 155 assignment tasks from a range of undergraduate and postgraduate courses were compared with a corpus of 20 IELTS Task 2 items according to four dimensions of difference: genre; information source; rhetorical function; object of enquiry. While the IELTS tasks were found to bear some resemblance to the predominant genre of university study – the essay, a number of important differences were observed:

1. The use of prior knowledge as the basis for writing in the IELTS tasks, compared with the prescription of a variety of research processes in the university assignments.
2. A restricted range of rhetorical functions in the IELTS items (with a focus on hortation), compared with a diversity of functions in the university tasks.
3. An emphasis on 'real-world' entities (situations, actions, practices) in the objects of enquiry of IELTS items compared with a greater focus on abstract entities (theories, ideas, methods) in the university tasks.

The staff survey – a supplement to the task analysis – consisted of interviews with twelve lecturers of first year undergraduate subjects. Overall, lecturers were positive about the nature of the IELTS Task 2 format and also the type of language instruction they imagined students would receive in preparing for it. Most however, identified some substantive differences in writing requirements in the two domains which in general terms, were of a similar order to those found in the task analysis, including IELTS' emphasis on opinionative styles of writing as opposed to the careful use and evaluation of sources required in many university tasks.

In the final section of the report, recommendations are made for modifications to the format of Task 2 items. If implemented, these changes would bring this component of the test more into line with the requirements of university writing and in so doing improve the test's washback effect on pre-tertiary English programmes.

1 Introduction

A central issue in validating direct assessments of writing is the authenticity of test tasks. Authentic test tasks are those which correspond closely to tasks which a language user is likely to encounter in the target situation (Bachman and Palmer 1996). A second, related issue concerned with validity is that of a test's impact. When a test influences programmes of instruction, this impact is referred to as washback. Washback is said to have a harmful or negative effect on classroom practice if the teaching concentrates solely on preparing students to pass a test rather than for the broader demands of real-world or target language use tasks. The washback effect is seen as particularly relevant in the case of large-scale public tests which have become the focus of teaching programmes (McNamara 1996:23). In such circumstances, when tests are used for making important decisions about large numbers of people, the potential for impact on instruction or washback is high and therefore the authenticity of test tasks is of utmost importance (Bachman and Palmer 1996:262).

The IELTS is an example of a large-scale public test, one which is used for university entrance selection. The expanded use of the IELTS test in recent years has been the result of an increase in the numbers of international students intending to study at English-speaking universities, along with an increase in the number of universities requiring IELTS band scores as a pre-requisite. A consequence of this situation is that many English language centres now include IELTS preparation within their EAP programmes. In a recent Australian survey of teachers' attitudes to IELTS (Deakin 1997), it was found that despite an overall positive response to the test, almost half of those surveyed believed that IELTS had a less than efficacious washback effect on EAP teaching and university preparation. The increasing influence of IELTS and the apparent concerns about its washback effect on EAP programmes highlights the need for the test to be as authentic as possible.

The current study takes up the issue of authenticity of test tasks on the IELTS Academic Writing Module. Specifically, its purpose was to investigate the degree of correspondence between tasks in the IELTS Writing test and target language use tasks, i.e. those that students are required to undertake in university study.

The IELTS test (Academic Module) is made up of four components: Listening, Reading, Writing and Speaking. The Writing component is a direct test of writing, requiring candidates to produce two samples of writing in the 60 minutes allocated. In Task 1, candidates write a short description of information presented in the form of a diagram, table, etc. Task 2 requires candidates to write a composition, usually an essay, in response to a proposition or question. In both tasks, candidates are assessed on their ability to write with 'appropriate register, rhetorical organisation, style and content' (UCLES 1996).

In the present study, it was considered too large an undertaking to investigate the authenticity of both tasks in the Writing test. A decision was made to focus only on Task 2; this was partly because 'this component carries a heavier weighting on the test and also because anecdotal evidence suggests that this task is given greater attention in test preparation classes.

2 Previous studies of university writing requirements

The study of writing requirements in different domains has been an active strand of applied language research over the last three decades – motivated largely by the imperatives of needs analysis and the development of communicative pedagogies (Munby 1978). In the domain of higher education, a number of large-scale surveys have been conducted in recent times to develop a picture of the type of writing required by students on university courses. While most of these studies have been undertaken for the purpose of EAP syllabus design (e.g. Braine 1995, Canesco and Byrd 1989, Carson et al 1992, Horowitz 1986, Johns 1981), others have been designed specifically for test validation purposes (e.g. Bridgeman and Carlson 1983, Hale et al 1996). Two studies which reflect theoretical approaches to academic writing are Bereiter and Scardamalia (1987) and Grabe and Kaplan (1996).

The methods and data used in these writing surveys have been of two types: there are those studies which have drawn on academic staff (or students) as the main source of data and those which have focused on the actual writing tasks set by these academics. The first type has involved surveying academic staff to obtain their impressions of writing requirements and practices in their faculties (Bridgeman and Carlson 1983, Johns 1981, Ostler 1980). These studies have used interview or questionnaire methods and usually included in their design some rank ordering of academic skills or tasks with respect to their frequency and importance. Academic staff, who are the ones who actually 'create' the writing requirements of university study, are obviously an important source of information in writing research.

These survey studies however, have not been without their critics. Horowitz draws attention to one problem (also identified by Johns (1981) in her own survey study): the difficulty of knowing whether survey data reflects 'what academics do, what they think they do, or what they want the researcher to think they do'(Horowitz 1986:448). Another problem concerns the metalanguage that is used unavoidably in this type of research. Many of the terms needed by researchers to characterise aspects of academic tasks (e.g. genre, rhetorical function and the like) may not be readily comprehensible to survey respondents and can be a source of confusion.

These shortcomings of the academic staff survey have been the spur for the other type of study mentioned – surveys of academic tasks – with those by Hale et al (1996) and Horowitz (1986), the most substantial to date. A key element of this type of research has been the development of classification systems used for the analysis of task corpora (Hamp-Lyons 1986). For example, Horowitz's (1986) study, which analysed a total of 54 writing tasks from one US university, employed a classification system based mainly on the type of information sources to be used in the preparation of the task. Horowitz identified seven categories: 1) summary/reaction to reading; 2) annotated bibliography; 3) report on a specific participatory experience; 4) connection of theory and data; 5) case study; 6) synthesis of multiple sources and 7) research project. The main finding from this work was that almost all tasks collected involved research processes of some kind, requiring students to collect and reorganise some specified source material. Very few tasks, by contrast, required students to draw exclusively on personal experience.

Hale et al (1996) was a considerably larger study, involving the collection and analysis of tasks from 162 undergraduate and postgraduate courses at eight US universities. As mentioned, this study was conducted for test validation purposes, specifically for the development of future versions of the TOEFL test. The classification system used was considerably more elaborate than that used in Horowitz (1986) involving six broad 'dimensions of difference': *locus of task* (i.e. in class; out of class); *prescribed length of product*; *genre*; *cognitive demands*; *rhetorical task*; *pattern of exposition*. Under each of these dimensions was a set of subcategories. For example, included under *cognitive demands* were the following: *retrieve/organise* and *apply/analyse/synthesise*. While this study is impressive in scope, its findings are a little inconclusive. This is due in part to the complexity of the classification scheme used, as well as the difficulty of achieving interjudge agreement across the six researchers on the project.

The rationale for the 'task survey' study is that the tasks themselves, rather than the lecturers who set them, are able to reveal more directly what students are required to do in their university writing. We are also of this view, but note that this approach is not without its own shortcomings. The researcher in this type of study must engage in a good deal of interpretation. This interpretation enters not only into the process of analysing tasks according to the classification system used, but also into the development of this system in the first place. Despite the claim that these classification systems are data-driven (Horowitz 1986), it needs to be acknowledged that the system decided upon will invariably reflect the researcher's notions of what is salient in a task, which may or may not be identical with those of the task's designer. Clearly, there is a place for both the task-based and the staff-based approach.

The present study is, in essence, a task survey study and borrows to some extent from the work of Hale et al (1996) and Horowitz (1986), especially for the development of the classification system used. However, it does not rely exclusively on writing tasks as data. In the second part of the study, a small scale survey of academic staff was conducted as a means of supplementing the findings from the task analysis. Our study also differs from these previous works in several other ways. First it is a comparative study, with comparisons drawn between writing requirements in two distinct domains: university courses and on the IELTS Writing test. Second, it is more linguistically based than these previous studies, drawing to a greater extent on the methods of discourse analysis. Finally, to our knowledge, it is the first wide-scale survey of this kind which uses Australian data.

3 Method

This section describes the two stages of the study: the task survey and the interviews with academic staff.

3.1 Task survey

For the task survey section of the study, assignment handouts were collected from a range of courses taught at two Australian universities, Monash University and the University of Melbourne. Assignments were obtained from first year undergraduate, and postgraduate subjects (excluding degrees by research only). For the study, it was important that the sample of tasks represented the types of writing international students can expect to encounter in tertiary study. There was therefore, some targeting of subject areas with high enrolments of international students, including economics, computing and management.

Letters were sent to academic staff from selected disciplines requesting two writing tasks from a subject they teach. Of the 98 academic staff contacted, 79 provided tasks, yielding an overall response rate of 81% across the two universities. This rate compares very favourably with those obtained in previous task surveys (Hale et al 1996; Horowitz 1986). The sample consisted of 155 tasks; 125 from undergraduate and 30 from postgraduate courses. Table 6.1 shows the distribution of the sample according to discipline areas.

Table 6.1 Number of tasks collected (by discipline)

Discipline areas	Total	Undergraduate	Postgraduate
Accounting	5	3	2
Agriculture	3	3	
Anthropology	2	2	
Architecture	4	4	
Biology	5	5	
Business development	4	4	
Chemistry	2	2	
Communication	2	2	
Computing	12	11	1
Economics	11	11	
Education	7	7	
Engineering	7	3	4
English literature	1	1	
Geography	1	1	
History	6	6	
Law*	16	15	1
Linguistics**	8	5	3
Management	18	11	7
Marketing	3	–	3
Medicine	8	3	5
Philosophy***	7	7	
Physics	2	2	
Politics	10	10	
Psychology	1	1	
Social work	2	1	1
Sociology	3	3	
Tourism	3	–	3
Visual Arts	2	2	
Total	**155**	**125**	**30**

* *Includes a range of subjects offered in the Faculties of Law (Torts, Legal Process, Jurisprudence) and Business (Business Law).*

** *Includes Japanese Linguistics.*

*** *Includes History and Philosophy of Science, Bioethics.*

For the comparison with IELTS, a total of 20 Task 2 items was used. The IELTS corpus consisted of two items from IELTS Specimen Materials (1995) as well as a sample taken from recent commercially produced materials (see Appendix 6.1 for details of the IELTS corpus). The use of the specimen tasks and the commercial tasks was required because 'live' and 'retired' Task 2 items were unavailable to the researchers. It was assumed that the items from these sources would reflect the nature of those used in the official versions of the test.

Tasks from the two domains were analysed and compared using a classification scheme developed for the study. The formulation of a scheme which would enable useful comparisons of the two sets of data represented a major challenge in the project. The one eventually settled on was derived from several sources, including previous survey studies of academic writing (discussed above), taxonomic frameworks from the field of discourse analysis, and a preliminary survey of our own data. Details of the classification scheme as well as the process by which it was formulated are provided in Section 3.3.

3.2 Staff survey

In stage two of the study, interviews were conducted with 12 of the academic staff who had provided tasks in stage one. The aims of these interviews were:

- to provide an alternative perspective on the task analysis
- to obtain feedback on the suitability of the IELTS Writing test in relation to the writing demands of various subjects
- in a more general way to gain further information about the nature of university writing tasks.

Interviews were conducted with first year teaching staff from the following discipline areas: chemistry, computing, economics, engineering, geography, law, linguistics, management, politics, and communications. Prior to the interviews, a schedule of questions including two sample IELTS tasks was sent to each interviewee (see Appendix 6.2 for interview schedule). The interviews were approximately 20 minutes in length and were tape recorded.

The interview was divided into two sections. In the first part, staff were asked to elaborate on the task(s) they provided for stage one of the study – including:

- characteristics distinguishing the assignment from other academic genres
- sources of information students were expected to consult
- criteria used in assessing students' work.

The questions in the second section were designed to probe staff perceptions of Task 2 items and their suitability with respect to the writing demands of their subject. Interviewees were asked to comment on the degree of correspondence between characteristics of tasks in the two domains.

3.3 The classification scheme

The methods used in stage one of the study to analyse and compare assessment tasks were based to an extent on the methods used in the field of discourse analysis to analyse whole written texts. While there are obvious differences between these two types of written data, we believe there are reasonable grounds for analysing them in similar ways. First, the rubrics of assessment tasks *do* constitute texts in themselves, even though by their nature they are much shorter than whole texts. The second reason relates to the special communicative function of assessment tasks, which is to prescribe the composition of another text, i.e. an essay, report, etc. From the nature of the task in question, it is possible, to varying degrees, to make informed predictions about the type of text that will be produced in response to it. It needs to be acknowledged however, that this predicting involves an act of interpretation on the part of the analyst, a point that will be taken up in more detail later in the discussion of the results of the study.

The field of discourse analysis offers many different frameworks and taxonomies for analysing written texts including, for example, Systemic Functional Linguistics (Halliday 1985), Rhetorical Structure Theory (Mann and Thompson 1989), Genre Analysis (Swales 1990). In our study, we did not seek to employ any single taxonomic framework, believing that a syncretic approach would be more useful to deal with the specialist data used. Furthermore, it was thought sensible not to begin with any a priori set of theoretical categories, but to draw initially on the data to establish broad 'dimensions of difference' (Hale et al 1996) and then to refer to relevant theoretical frameworks later to refine the classification scheme.

The classification scheme was developed in the first place through analysis of a selection of university assignment tasks and IELTS Task 2 items. From this process, the following broad categories were generated:

A   Genre
B   Information source
C   Rhetorical function
D   Object of enquiry

Figure 6.1 shows an example of an IELTS Task 2 item and indicates, in a preliminary way, how each of these categories was derived from the task rubric.[2]

Figure 6.1 Sample IELTS Task 2

TASK 2

You should spend about 40 minutes on this task:

A Genre

Present a written argument or case to an educated non-specialist audience on the following topic.

It is inevitable that as technology develops so traditional cultures must be lost. Technology and tradition are incompatible – you cannot have both together.

C Rhetorical function

D Objects of enquiry

To what extent do you agree or disagree with this statement?

You should write at least 250 words.

You should use your own ideas, knowledge and experience and support your arguments with examples and relevant evidence.

B Information source

Source: IELTS Handbook 1996.

In the section that follows, explanations are provided for each of the categories A, B, C, D as well as the subcategories included under each. An outline of the overall classification scheme is given in Table 6.2.

Table 6.2 The classification scheme

A	**Genre [G]**

By what name is the task described? (Select one category)

1.	Case Study Report	[G-CaseR]
2.	Essay	[G-Ess]
3.	Exercise	[G-Ex]
4.	Experimental Report	[G-ExR]
5.	Literature Review	[G-LitR]
6.	Research Report (other)	[G-ResR]
7.	Research Proposal	[G-ResP]
8.	Review	[G-Rev]
9.	Short Answer	[G-SAns]
10.	Summary	[G-Sum]
11.	Written argument or case	[G-Arg]
12.	Other	[G-Oth]

B Information source [I]

On what information source(s) is the written product to be based?
(Select one category)

1.	Prior knowledge	[I-pk]
2.	Primary sources	[I-ps]
	2.1 provided in task	[I-ps-p]
	2.2 collected by student	[I-ps-c]
3.	Secondary sources	[I-s]
4.	Primary/secondary source*	[I-p/s]
5.	No specification of source	[I-n]

*Categories 2.1 and 2.2 were also applied to the *primary source* component of these tasks

C. Rhetorical function [R]

What is the task (or component of the task) instructing students to do?
(Select one or more categories)

1. Epistemic [R-E]

1.1	Comparison	[R-E-co]
1.2	Description	[R-E-d]
1.3	Explanation	[R-E-ex]
1.4	Evaluation	[R-E-ev]
1.5	Prediction	[R-E-p]
1.6	Summarisation	[R-E-s]

2. Deontic [R-D]

2.1	Hortation	[R-D-h]
2.2	Instruction	[R-D-i]
2.3	Recommendation	[R-D-r]

D. Object of enquiry [O]

With which type of phenomenon is the task mainly concerned?
(Select one category)

1.	Phenomenal	[O-p]
2.	Metaphenomenal	[O-m]

3.3.1 Genre

Genre, the first category used in the classification scheme, has become a difficult concept in discourse analysis, with a variety of definitions being offered for the term (e.g. Swales 1990; Martin 1989), as well as disagreement about how this concept might relate to associated concepts, such as 'text-type' and 'speech event' (Levinson 1979; Paltridge 1996). Another source of complexity is the variety of genre taxonomies that have been generated by analysts. For example, Martin's (1984) categories of report; recount; explanation, etc. bear no obvious correspondence to the categories used by other genre theorists such as Swales (1990), e.g. research article; reprint request, etc. In the present study, we sought to avoid these theoretical difficulties. As the first category in the analysis, the concept of genre was used in an unproblematical, self-referential way – that is, the genre of a task was taken to be the name given to the required written product as outlined in the task rubric, i.e. whether students were asked to write an essay, a literature review, etc. In reference to the variable taxonomies above, it should be noted that such a methodology generates a set of categories related more closely to those of Swales (1990) than to Martin's (1984). The category *Written argument or case* was a genre designation peculiar to the IELTS data. Its relationship to the university genres is discussed later in section 4.1.1. The category *Other* refers to genres that appeared only once in the data. These included the following: *annotated reference, computer program, education program proposal, homepage, letter, project brief, resume.* Our survey of the collected tasks generated the following genre categories: *essay; review; literature review; experimental report; case study report; research report (other); research proposal; summary; exercise; short answer; written argument/case; other.*

The analysis of the data according to *genre* was mainly an empirical procedure, but not in all instances. In a number of tasks, no genre term was specified in the task rubric. In these cases, a category was assigned, if there was other contextual information that enabled a plausible judgement to be made about the genre-type. For example, if a task instructed students to write up the results of a laboratory experiment, this task was assigned to the category *experimental report.* To assist in the process of allocating unspecified tasks, the following rough definitions of genre categories were drawn up. These were based on information provided in those tasks that were genre-explicit:

Essay	A task with a variety of features and specifications. In its prototypical form, an essay is a task requiring the presentation of an argument in response to a given proposition or question.
Review	A task requiring the summarisation and appraisal of a single text (including non-verbal texts, e.g. film, painting).

Literature review	A task requiring the identification, summarisation and appraisal of a range of texts relevant to a specific field of knowledge.
Experimental report	A task requiring the description and analysis of data obtained from an empirical research procedure.
Case study report	A task involving identification and discussion of a problem(s) arising from a given situation, along with suggested ways for solving the problem.
Research report (other)	A task similar in many respects to the *experimental report*, but requiring the description and analysis of information of a non-empirical nature, e.g. that obtained from interview or participant observation.
Research proposal	A task requiring the description of an intended research project, including a statement of its rationale.
Summary	A task requiring the representation of the main contents of a text or texts.
Exercise	A task requiring the application of some discipline-specific tool or model to a given situation.
Short answer	A task requiring mainly the reproduction of previously provided items of knowledge, e.g. from lectures or textbooks.

3.3.2 Information source

The second dimension of difference used in the classification scheme was *information source*. This category was concerned with the type of information that was to be used in the completion of a task; for example, whether students were required to read from a list of prescribed readings or to analyse data obtained from an experimental procedure or to examine case material. The following subcategories were included under this dimension, derived in part from the classification of Taylor (1989):

1. Prior knowledge
2. Primary sources
   2.1 *provided in task*
   2.2 *collected by student*
3. Secondary sources
4. Primary/secondary source*
5. No specification of source

*Categories 2.1 and 2.2 were also applied to the *primary source* component of these tasks.

The first category – *Prior knowledge* – was used for tasks which did not require students to draw on any external sources of information. For tasks in this category, the contents of the piece were to be based exclusively on the writer's pre-existing knowledge, experience, beliefs, intuitions and the like.

The two categories *primary sources* and *secondary sources* were applied to those tasks which required the use of external sources of information; in other words, tasks which involved research of some kind. The category *primary sources*, denoted those sources which might otherwise be called 'data'. Examples of primary sources in our corpus included:

(i)   The documents provided for analysis in a history assignment.

(ii) The details of a case given in a law assignment.

(iii) The experimental data to be collected and analysed in a chemistry practical.

The category *primary sources* was further divided into two types: those *provided in the task* itself and those to be *collected by students* via some pre-scribed research procedure. Of the sample sources above, (i) and (ii) would be classified as *provided* and (iii) as *collected*. The category *secondary sources* was used for those tasks which required students to engage with and incorpo-rate in their writing works of an 'interpretative' nature – monographs, research articles and so on.

The combined category *primary/secondary sources* was assigned to tasks which prescribed sources of both varieties. Examples from the corpus here were various research tasks which required students to collect and analyse their own data (*primary source*), but also to situate their work within previ-ous research (*secondary sources*). Similarly, in a number of case study tasks, students needed to analyse case material (*primary sources*) but also to draw on relevant theoretical frameworks to help resolve issues raised in the case (*secondary sources*). The category *no specification of sources* was used when there was no mention of information sources in the assignment guidelines and when it was not possible to infer from the task itself the nature of sources to be used.

3.3.3 Rhetorical function

The concept of rhetorical function has been used widely in the field of discourse analysis (e.g. Hoey 1983; Lackstrom et al 1973; Meyer 1975) and has led to the generation of an array of functional categories, e.g. *com-parison/contrast*; *cause/effect*; *definition*; *problem/solution*. By one definition, the rhetorical function of a text is 'that which a given unit of discourse is trying to do' (Trimble 1985), e.g. *comparing* entities, *explaining the cause* of an entity. Applied to the study of academic tasks, the concept can be modified to mean 'that which a task (or unit of a task) is instructing students to do'.

Our attempts to develop a systematic set of rhetorical categories began with an initial distinction being drawn between tasks that involved a more 'analytical' rhetoric and those with a more 'practical' orientation. This difference can be illustrated in the following two tasks, the first from the pure discipline of sociology and the other from its applied counterpart, social work:

1. Write an essay on the following topic: Do young people from different class backgrounds experience the world differently?
2. Discuss some of the problems currently facing youth in Australia. Using a social theory, discuss how the situation of youth could be improved in Australian society.

The first task requires the writer to 'analyse' a situation and to assert whether something *does* (or *does not*) happen – in this case whether class has a bearing on young people's experience of the world. The focus of the second task, at least the second part of it, is not on what *does* happen, but rather on what *could* be done to change what happens – by way of a solution to the problems identified.

The rhetorical difference noted in these two tasks is captured in the distinction traditionally drawn in semantics between epistemic and deontic modality. An epistemic clause, as Huddleston (1982) explains, has the status of a proposition; it asserts whether something is true, partly true, false, etc. A deontic clause, in contrast, has the character of an action: 'what is at issue is not whether something is true but whether something is going to be done' (Huddleston 1982:168).[3] The difference between these two modal meanings can be illustrated in the following ambiguous sentence (with epistemic and deontic interpretations given below):

> *This task must be an essay.*
>> 'I am forced to conclude that this task is an essay' (epistemic)
>> 'This task **is required** to be an essay' (deontic)

The distinction between the deontic and epistemic was used in the study to establish a first level of rhetorical categories. Under these two broad categories, the following sets of sub-categories were generated.

Epistemic categories

Comparison This category was applied to tasks (or components of tasks) which required students to identify the similarities and/or differences between two or more entities or phenomena. The prototypical 'comparative' question was in the form: *What are the similarities and/or differences between X and Y?*

Description | This category was applied to tasks (or components of tasks) which required students to give an account of the nature of a given entity or phenomenon. The prototypical 'descriptive' question was in the form: *What is the nature of X?*

Explanation | This category was applied to tasks (or components of tasks) which required students to give an account of the causes for a given entity or phenomenon. Note that both non-volitional causation (eg. cause, reason) and volitional causation (e.g. purpose, motive) were included under this category. The prototypical 'explanatory' question was in the form: *What is the cause of X?*

Evaluation | This category was applied to tasks (or components of tasks) which required students to make a judgement about the value of a given entity or phenomenon with respect to its validity, importance, relevance, etc. The prototypical 'evaluative' question was in the form: *How valid/important/relevant is X?*

Prediction | This category was used for tasks (or components of tasks) which required students to speculate about the future state of a given phenomenon or entity. The prototypical 'predictive' question was in the form: *What will happen to X?*

Summarisation | This category was used for tasks (or components of tasks) which required students to give an account of an author's views on a given entity or phenomenon. The prototypical 'summary' question was in the form: *What is author A's view of X?*

Deontic categories

Hortation | This category was used for tasks (or components of tasks) which required students to make a judgement about the desirability of a given entity or phenomenon, especially those concerned with actions and states of affairs. The prototypical 'hortatory' question was in the form: *Should X happen/be done?*

Recommendation | This category was used for tasks (or components of tasks) which required students to suggest ways of dealing with a given entity or phenomenon, usually presented in the form of a problem. The prototypical 'recommendatory' question was in the form: *What can be done about X?*[4]

Instruction | This category was used for tasks (or components of tasks) which required students to outline a sequence of procedures for a given entity or phenomenon. The prototypical 'instructional' question was in the form: *What must be done to achieve X?*

3.3.4 Object of enquiry

A final dimension of difference, one that to our knowledge has not been considered in studies of this kind, is what we have referred to as *object of enquiry*. This dimension was concerned with probing the nature of the variable X referred to in the discussion of *rhetorical function* categories above. The need for this additional category arose from our observation that some tasks in the corpus, of their nature, required a more 'abstract' form of writing than others. This difference can be illustrated in the following two topics from a first year management subject:

1. Discuss the role of the manager in Australia in the 1990s.
2. Are there significant differences between 'systems' and 'classical' views of management?

These topics, it can be argued, deal with two distinct domains. In the first, the 'object of enquiry' might be regarded as the real world of the manager (i.e. what managers do or need to do, in their real-world activities). The second topic, in contrast is concerned less with the world of managers and more with the abstract or 'metaphenomenal' world of management theorists (i.e. how these theorists *view* the world). This difference in our view is not trivial; we would argue that the pattern of discourse elicited by each topic is likely to be of a different kind. In terms of Hallidayan grammatical categories (1985), responses to the first topic are likely to include a preponderance of clauses with the following configuration:

managers   do
actor   process: material

In contrast, the predominant clauses in responses to the second topic are more likely to be of the following form:

management theorists   believe
actor   process: mental

In the classification scheme, this difference in the objects of enquiry was captured in the following two categories, using additional terms from Halliday (1985: 229):

Phenomenal

Metaphenomenal

The *phenomenal* category was used for those tasks which directed students primarily to consider such 'real-world' entities as events, actions, processes, situations, practices, etc. The *metaphenomenal* category, in contrast, was applied to tasks concerned mainly with the abstract entities of ideas, theories, methods, laws, etc.[5]

3.4 Sample analyses

In the following section, the way in which we applied the classification system to our data is demonstrated through the analysis of four tasks: one sample IELTS Task 2 item and three university tasks from the disciplines of sociology, chemistry and management. These tasks were selected for the range of disciplines they cover, as well as for the variety of their generic forms. Among other things, this discussion is intended to demonstrate the interpretative nature of the task analysis.

In the analysis of this task (Sample 1), the first two categories *genre* [G] and *information source* [I] can be applied unproblematically. For the category *genre*, the task instructs students to present 'a written argument or case' and is thus allocated to the category [G-Arg]. For *information source*, students are instructed to draw on their 'own ideas, knowledge and experience' which would mean allocation to the category *prior knowledge* [I-Pk].

Analysing tasks according to the remaining dimensions of difference is a more interpretative activity. For *rhetorical function* [R], the principal modality of the topic is *deontic* [R-D], signalled by the auxiliary 'should'. Further to this, students are asked to express a view about the desirability of a social practice, (i.e. whether alternative forms of transport should be encouraged), hence the task is classified as *hortatory* [R-D-h]. The task however, also

Figure 6.2 Sample 1: IELTS Task 2 item

TASK 2

You should spend about 40 minutes on this task:

Present a written argument or case to an educated non-specialist audience on the following topic.

The first car appeared on British roads in 1888. By the year 2000 there may be as many as 29 million vehicles on British roads.

Should alternative forms of transport be encouraged and international laws introduced to control car ownership and use?

You should write at least 250 words.

You should use your own ideas, knowledge and experience and support your arguments with examples and relevant evidence.

Source: IELTS Specimen Materials, 1995.

includes an *epistemic* element [R-E], which relates to the requirement of 'supporting the argument with relevant evidence'. To support their arguments, students would need to state the advantages and/or disadvantages of alternative forms of transport. The task therefore also includes the rhetorical category of *evaluation* [R-E-ev]. For *object of enquiry*, the task is concerned with a real-world activity, namely transportation usage, and hence is classified as *phenomenal* [O-p]. The above analysis thus gives the following configuration of categories:

Genre:	written argument or case
Information source:	prior knowledge
Rhetorical function:	hortation, evaluation
Object of enquiry:	phenomenal

This task from a first year sociology subject (Figure 6.3) prescribes an *essay* [G-Ess]. The task instructs students to use a wide range of 'references', hence *information source* would be classified as *secondary* [I-s]. For *rhetorical function*, the modality is *epistemic*, glossed in the following question: *What **are** the similarities and differences between the two approaches?* For specific functions, clearly the task involves *comparison* [R-E-co]. Implicit in this part of the task however, is also *summarisation* [R-E-s]; presumably a summary of the two approaches would be necessary before they could be compared. In the final part of the task, students are asked to *evaluate* the two approaches [R-E-ev]. Finally the *object of enquiry* is *metaphenomenal* [O-m], with students being asked to focus on two theoretical approaches to the subject matter, 'work'. This analysis of the task gives the following configuration of categories:

Genre:	essay
Information source:	secondary
Rhetorical function:	summarisation, comparison, evaluation
Object of enquiry:	metaphenomenal

Figure 6.3 Sample 2: Sociology

Essay question

Compare and contrast Scientific Management with the Human Relations approach to work. Which in your view is the more valid approach?

Essays should be approximately 2,000 words. You are encouraged to read more widely than the references provided. Also do not forget to read the 'Departmental Policy on Plagiarism' in this booklet.

Sample Task 3 (Figure 6.4) from a first year chemistry subject prescribes a 'formal report of an experiment', and is thus classified under the genre category of *experimental report* [G-ExR]. The principal *source of information* for

Figure 6.4 Sample 3: Chemistry

> This exercise is intended to give you an introduction to an important aspect of research in chemistry by writing a short formal report of an experiment you have done. You will be assigned by your demonstrator, either the analysis of Hortico or cement to write up in full.
>
> Your report should include:
> i) a description of the problem and its background
> ii) a description of the important principles and approaches
> iii) a description of resources and procedures used to obtain results
> iv) a well-ordered presentation of experimental observations
> v) consideration and explanation of results

the task is the data collected from the experimental procedure and so is classified as a *primary source – collected* [I-ps-c]. The *rhetorical functions* of the task are clearly epistemic [R-E], glossed in the following questions (*What* **was** *the experimental procedure? What* **were** *the results? What* **might be** *the explanations for the results?*). As can be seen in the task rubric, the *rhetorical functions* are mainly *descriptive* [R-E-d] i.e. descriptions of the problem, the procedure and the results. The final component of the task (v) asks students to explain the results, hence *explanation* [R-E-ex]. For the *object of enquiry*, the experiment involves analysing one of two substances 'Hortico or cement', which are categorised as *phenomenal* [O-p]. This analysis of the task gives the following configuration of categories:

Genre: experimental report
Information source: primary – collected
Rhetorical function: description, explanation
Object of enquiry: phenomenal

This final task (Figure 6.5) from a postgraduate management subject instructs students to prepare a *case study report* [G-CaseR]. The main *information source* is in the form of survey data provided for analysis, and thus would be allocated to the category *primary source – provided* [I-ps-p]. The *rhetorical functions* in the task include both *epistemic* and *deontic* elements. The *epistemic* elements are those concerned with providing background information about the company, i.e. *description* [R-E-d] and with then identifying the 'strengths and problems' in the CAR Department, i.e. *evaluation* [R-E-ev]. The *deontic* elements are those concerned with making suggestions for resolving problems, i.e. *recommendation* [R-D-r] and then with outlining the specific 'actions' to be taken, i.e. *instruction* [R-D-i]. Finally, for the *object of enquiry*, the task would be classified as *phenomenal*, concerned as it is with real-world problems in an organisation. This analysis of the task gives the following configuration of categories:

Figure 6.5 Sample 4: Management (abridged version)

Case study

JP Hunt is a large department store. Senior management has become
concerned about a high turnover rate in the Credit and Accounts Receivable
(CAR) Department of the store. As a first step towards addressing the problem,
JP Hunt has contracted a consulting firm to conduct a survey of (CAR)
Department employees

Your syndicate has now been contracted by the consulting firm to prepare a
report which:
1. Provides background about the company;
2. Analyses the survey data shown in the summary table. (On the basis
   of this analysis identify and diagnose strengths and problem areas in the
   (CAR) Department);
3. Makes suggestions for resolving problems;
4. Develops an action plan for feedback to the CAR department.

Genre: case study report
Information source: primary – provided
Rhetorical function: description, evaluation, recommendation, instruction
Object of enquiry: phenomenal

4 Results and discussion

4.1 Task survey

In this section, the findings from the analysis of the total university corpus
are presented under the four dimensions of difference in the classification
scheme. Each set of findings is then considered in relation to those obtained
from the analysis of the IELTS corpus. While the data presented includes
that of a quantitative nature, it needs to be acknowledged that the analysis
was not a strictly empirical one. As mentioned previously, the process of
analysing tasks involved a degree of interpretation and inference on the part
of the researchers. Thus, it is intended that the numerical data not be seen as
a definitive set of results; rather it is designed to provide a broad picture of
the types of writing required in the two domains.

The analysis of the university corpus found a great diversity of writing
requirements, both within and across disciplines. While in all subjects,
written work of some kind had to be submitted, this varied considerably
with respect to the type and the amount required, ranging from a single
short report in engineering to a series of lengthy essays in philosophy. Some
interdisciplinary variations are discussed below.

4.1.1 Genre

The diverse nature of university writing is evidenced in the wide range of genres identified in the university corpus (see Table 6.3). Of these types however, the *essay* was clearly the most common, accounting for almost 60% of tasks. This assignment type appeared most frequently in subjects in the humanities and social sciences, but was also prescribed in a range of other disciplines, including biology, computing and medicine. As a generic form, the essay was characterised in a variety of ways in assignment handouts; common to most definitions however, was the requirement that students argue for a particular position in relation to a given question or proposition. The following is a comprehensive account provided for students in a history subject:

> The term 'essay' comes from the French word 'essayer' meaning to try or to attempt. From this older form we get our terms 'assay' or 'test'. An essay therefore asks you to answer a question by constructing and testing an argument. You will be assessed on the quality of your attempt . . . We look to you to convince us that your consideration of the question is the most convincing.

The next most common genre was the *case study report* (10% of tasks), confined to subjects in certain applied disciplines: management, accounting, law, computing, and engineering. Case studies typically required students to analyse case material (in narrative and/or statistical form) and to suggest ways of resolving the issues raised in the case. Sample Task 4 (Figure 6.5) is an example of a case study report from the corpus.

The genre category *exercise* (8% of tasks) included a range of minor tasks often set as a first piece of work in subjects and usually requiring students to

Table 6.3 Genres of university assignments

Genre	Number	%
Essay	90	58
Case Study Report	15	10
Exercise	12	8
Research Report (other)	10	6
Review	7	5
Experimental Report	6	4
Literature Review	2	1
Research Proposal	2	1
Summary	2	1
Short Answer	2	1
Other*	7	5
Total	**155**	**100**

* *Annotated reference, letter, project brief, resume, homepage, computer program, educational programme proposal.*

demonstrate their understanding of a particular concept or technique by applying it to an exemplary situation. The following is one such task from the corpus, set in a literature/cultural studies subject:

> Choose a television program (e.g. news broadcast, quiz show) and develop an analysis of this program in terms of its i) mode of address ii) programming iii) genre iv) internal organisation.

The only other genre to appear with any frequency was the *research report* (non-experimental). In these tasks, students were required to collect their own data and to describe and explain it. Research reports of this kind were set in a broad range of disciplines. The following is an example from a linguistics subject:

> Write a report which examines the structure of greetings in a wide sample of languages. What are the most common types of information used in greetings? Can you construct a grammar that represents the first moves of the greeting sequence?

The corpus also included a small number of *experimental reports*. These were confined to the disciplines of physics, chemistry and psychology.

Analysis of the IELTS corpus found that the genre specifications were standard for all items. In each case, students were instructed to 'present a written argument or case' on a given topic, taken from the rubric used in official versions of the test. The 'topic' part of all items consisted either of a question or a proposition often followed by a prompt asking students to indicate the extent of their agreement or disagreement with the proposition.

While the *written argument* nomenclature does not correspond exactly to any of the genre terms identified in the university corpus, clearly IELTS Task 2 items most resemble the format of the university essay. Indeed, in earlier versions of the official test, the Task 2 was referred to as an *essay*. The avoidance of the *essay* label in current versions of the official test suggests, however, that test developers have been mindful of certain differences between the university essay and the IELTS version of this form. The differences we have found are discussed below under the remaining categories considered in the task survey.

4.1.2 Information source

Table 6.4 shows the results from the analysis of *information sources* prescribed in the tasks from the university corpus. The most notable finding is that almost all tasks involved a research component of some kind, requiring the use of either *primary* or *secondary* sources or a combination of the two. The most frequently prescribed sources were *secondary sources* (55% of the

Table 6.4 Information sources prescribed in university assignments

Information sources	Number	%
Secondary	85	55
Primary/secondary	33	21
Primary	28	18
Prior knowledge	5	3
No specification of sources	4	3
Total	**155**	**100**

corpus), usually described in tasks as 'references'. These included monographs, journal articles and textbooks. The use of *secondary sources* was required in tasks from a broad range of disciplines, but with a higher aggregation in disciplines from the humanities and social sciences. There was a good deal of variation in the amount of information provided about the *secondary sources* to be used, ranging from tasks which included a simple exhortation for students to base their work on 'wide reading', to those which provided a specific list of references to be incorporated in the written product. One feature common to most tasks prescribing the use of *secondary sources* was the inclusion of information about citation practices in the discipline, along with warnings about plagiarism.

Tasks prescribing the use of *primary sources* (or data) were also from a wide range of disciplines, but especially in the more research-oriented, as opposed to theoretical, disciplines. As suggested in section 3.3.2, there was a good deal of variation in the types of primary sources prescribed. These ranged from quantitative and qualitative data in the natural and social sciences, to case study material typically used in the disciplines of law, management and economics. As mentioned, a distinction was made in the classification scheme between *primary sources* that needed to be *collected* by students and those that were *provided* in the task itself. In the latter type, students were not required to collect data but only to be engaged in their interpretation. The results from this analysis are shown in Table 6.5. It is of some interest that the majority of prescribed primary sources were of the *provided* type, both at undergraduate and postgraduate (coursework) level. A possible

Table 6.5 Primary source-types prescribed in university assignments

Primary source*	Number	%
Provided in task	36	59
Collected by student	25	41
Total	**61**	**100**

* *Note that sources from both the categories* primary source *and* primary/secondary source *were considered in this analysis.*

explanation for this is that in certain discipline areas, lecturers may not have wanted their first year students, with limited grounding in research methods in the discipline, to be conducting their own research.

As can be seen in Table 6.4, a fair proportion of tasks (21%) required the use of a combination of *primary* and *secondary* sources. These tasks tended to be of two types: research projects which required students to compare their findings with literature in the field and case studies which required reference to theoretical frameworks to resolve the issues in the case. The following two tasks are examples of these respective assignment types:

> Play is an important area of development for children aged 2–5. Piaget called it 'the child's work'. Discuss play as observed in your study child and compare your observations to the literature.   (Medicine)

> Your advice has been sought to settle the following dispute in Company X (Case study material provided about dispute). Referring to appropriate accounting principles, write a report advising the company on the best course of action to adopt.   (Accounting)

As can be seen in Table 6.4, the category *prior knowledge* represented the least frequently prescribed information source. The very small number of tasks in the corpus that fell under this category (3%) tended to be minor pieces of work in the overall assignment requirements of subjects, including, for example, the following task set as the first piece of writing in a history subject:

> Write a paragraph explaining what you know about your own family's experience of World War II.

Other *prior knowledge* tasks tended not to be generically typical of the corpus, including a *personal resume* set in a communications subject and the text for a *homepage* in a computing subject.

Unlike the assignments in the university corpus, IELTS Task 2 items were found not to be framed around the use of external sources. All items in the IELTS sample included the following instruction to students, taken from the standard rubric in the official versions of the test.

> You should use your own ideas, knowledge and experience and support your arguments with examples and relevant evidence.

This specification meant that all tasks in the sample were allocated to the category *prior knowledge*.

These findings point to a major difference in the nature of writing in the two domains; even if it is one that can be readily accounted for. In a test of writing, the task must be completed, of necessity, within a restricted time frame (in the case of IELTS Task 2 it is 40 minutes). This restriction means it is not possible to incorporate a substantial research component in writing tasks. For university tasks, this time restriction does not usually apply. The difference in prescribed *information sources* can also be related to the different nature of writing assessment in the two domains. In a writing test, the task is used to elicit a written sample which is then assessed primarily in terms of its linguistic proficiency. In university study, writing is assessed according to far broader criteria, including a student's understandings of key knowledge in a discipline, the modes of analysis used, as well as the discipline's discursive practices, much of which will come from an engagement with sources. In short, in the university context, the content of a piece of writing is salient; in a language testing context it is often incidental.

The reasons for the differences in prescribed information sources are understandable enough. It needs to be recognised however, that preparation for the IELTS Writing test (Task 2) may not give students an entirely accurate view of the nature of academic argumentation, especially with respect to what constitutes adequate evidence in a piece of writing. In the IELTS test, students learn that it is sufficient to base their assertions on 'their own ideas, knowledge and experience'. In the university context – where valid evidence is usually seen as the findings of research or the authoritative pronouncements of disciplinary scholars – a student who relies exclusively on *prior knowledge* will usually be criticised for being 'anecdotal' and for not having read adequately for the task. Another point to be made is that the IELTS Task 2, as it is framed, does not suggest any need for students to be taught about the conventions for citing the ideas of other writers.

4.1.3 Rhetorical function

Table 6.6 shows the results from the analysis of rhetorical functions in tasks from the university corpus. As explained in the sample analyses (see Section 3.4), assignments were generally found to prescribe more than a single rhetorical function. A total of 393 functions were identified in the corpus of 155 tasks (see Table 6.6, column 3). The first point to note from this table is that the epistemic functions were considerably more common than the deontic. In general terms, tasks specifying exclusively epistemic functions tended to be from the more 'pure' disciplines, e.g. the physical and social sciences. In contrast, those tasks that included deontic elements were clustered around disciplines of a more applied nature, e.g. agriculture, computing, engineering, education, law, management. This, of course, is not a surprising result, given that it is the nature of the applied disciplines to be concerned as much with practical knowledge as theoretical knowledge; the 'knowing how' in addition to the 'knowing that', as knowledge in these fields is sometimes characterised (Becher 1989).

Table 6.6 Rhetorical functions in university assignments

Rhetorical Function	Modality E = Epistemic D = Deontic	No. of tasks incorporating function	% of tasks incorporating function
Evaluation	E	104	67
Description	E	71	49
Summarisation	E	55	35
Comparison	E	54	35
Explanation	E	43	28
Recommendation	D	35	23
Hortation	D	15	15
Prediction	E	11	7
Instruction	D	5	3
Total functions		**393**	

The epistemic category of evaluation was found to be the most common, with about two-thirds of tasks in the corpus adjudged to involve this function. Evaluation was found to be characteristic of tasks across a wide range of disciplines in the corpus. Tasks (or components of tasks) prescribing evaluation required students to make a judgement of the value of some entity or phenomenon with respect to its validity, importance, relevance, etc. The following are two sample 'evaluative' questions taken from tasks set in sociology and management.

> How plausible do you find Marx's account of social inequality?
> (Sociology)

> To what extent can people be regarded as the most important resource of an organisation? (Management)

It was noted that there was some variation in the nature of entities to be evaluated in tasks. This can be seen in the two sample questions above. In the first question, it is the views of a particular writer (Marx) which are to be evaluated; the second in contrast requires an evaluation to be made of a particular state of affairs, namely 'human resources in an organisation'. This difference corresponds to the distinction drawn earlier between *metaphenomenal and phenomenal objects of enquiry* and is considered in greater detail in Section 4.1.4.

As can be seen in Table 6.6, the next most common functions were also epistemic in nature: *description, summarisation, comparison, explanation.* Several sample questions under each of these categories are given below.

> Description
> What is the biology of toxoplasmosis? (Biology)

Describe what is meant by international, domestic and mass tourism?
(Tourism)

Summarisation

Explain Plato's theory of the tripartite soul.   (Philosophy)

What are the main points Christine Halliwell is making about the status of women in society in her chapter 'Women in Asia: Anthropology and the study of women'?   (Anthropology)

Comparison

What differences and what similarities emerge from a comparison of Egyptian and Mesopotamian temples?   (Architecture)

Where do the arguments of Oakey and Gati differ?   (History)

Explanation

What are the causes of the current high levels of unemployment in Australia?   (Economics)

Adolescent mental health is a growth industry. Discuss factors which have contributed to this growth.   (Medicine)

As mentioned, the deontic functions – *recommendation, hortation, instruction* – were less frequent in the corpus than the epistemic. Of these, *recommendation* was clearly the most common and was especially prominent in the more applied disciplines. In tasks involving *recommendation*, the entity to be analysed was presented as being problematic in some sense and students were required to suggest ways in which it could be resolved. 'Recommendatory' questions tended to be framed around the notion of possible action (or 'can-ness') as in the following examples:

What strategies can be used to make internet contributors self-regulating?
(Computing)

How can the land degradation problems of the Parwan Valley be overcome?   (Agriculture)

The other deontic category that appeared in the data, though to a much lesser extent than *recommendation*, was what we have termed *hortation*. In hortatory tasks students were asked to comment on the desirability of a given course of action or state of affairs. These tasks were framed around the notion of necessary action (or 'should-ness') and were most characteristic of disciplines with an ethical or polemical element to their contents, including law, medicine, politics, philosophy. The following are sample hortatory questions:

Since no person is an island, society should regulate private behaviour. Discuss.   (Politics)

People subject to the power of the state need the protection of a bill of rights. Discuss.   (Law)

The remaining categories used in the classification scheme – *prediction* and *instruction* – appeared infrequently in the corpus. The following are single examples of each of these respective categories:

What major changes in the Australian business environment are likely to impact on managers over the next decade?   (Management)

In an assignment requiring the writing of a computer program:

Outline to any potential users precisely how the program is to be used.
                                                                        (Computing)

A similar analysis of rhetorical functions was made of the IELTS items, the results of which are shown in Table 6.7. All items, it can be seen, involved *evaluation* of some kind. (This is a finding consistent with the 'argumentative' nature of the Task 2 genre, as it is described in official versions of the test). In the following example, taken from the IELTS specimen materials (UCLES 1995), the quality to be evaluated is 'compatibility'. (It needs to be noted that this task also comprises the function of *comparison*.)

It is inevitable that as technology develops so traditional cultures must be lost. Technology and tradition are incompatible – you cannot have both together. To what extent do you agree or disagree with this statement?

Table 6.7 Rhetorical functions in IELTS items

Rhetorical function	No. of IELTS items incorporating function (n=20)	% of items incorporating function
Evaluation	20	100
Hortation	14	70
Prediction	3	15
Comparison	3	15
Explanation	3	15
Recommendation	2	10
Description	–	–
Summarisation	–	–
Instruction	–	–

While all tasks involved some form of *evaluation*, in many instances this was found to be accompanied by another function, namely hortation. As mentioned, hortatory elements in tasks were those framed around the notion of necessity (or should-ness). The following three tasks are representative of the 14 tasks which were found to incorporate this function:

> Higher mammals such as monkeys have rights and should not be used in laboratory experiments. (Source 5)

> A government's role is only to provide defence capability and urban infrastructure (roads, water, supplies etc.) All other services (education, health and social security) should be provided by private groups or individuals in the community. (Source 7)

> Television nowadays features many programs of a violent nature. For this reason, it is necessary for parents to impose strict controls on their children's viewing habits. (Source 8)

The other rhetorical functions that showed up in the analysis were *prediction, comparison, explanation* and *recommendation,* although each of these was confined to a total of only two or three tasks. The following are examples of tasks (or components of tasks) which incorporated these functions:

> Prediction
> The idea of having a single career is becoming an old fashioned one. The new fashion will be to have several careers or ways of earning money and further education will be something that continues throughout life. (Source 6)

> Comparison
> . . . Which subjects can be better taught using computers? (Source 7)

> Explanation
> News editors decide what to broadcast on television and what to print in newspapers. What factors do you think influence these decisions?. . . (Source 6)

> Recommendation
> . . . What are the most effective ways of reducing population growth? (Source 8)

The patterns of rhetorical functions identified in the IELTS Task 2 items were clearly different from those in the university corpus, as Table 6.8 shows. The more notable differences can be summarised thus:

1. The functions of *summarisation* and *description,* which were common in the university corpus, did not appear in the IELTS sample.
2. The functions of *comparison, explanation* and *recommendation* were less frequent in the IELTS sample.

Table 6.8 Comparison of rhetorical functions in university tasks and IELTS items

Rhetorical function	University assignments (% incorporating rhetorical function)	IELTS items (% incorporating rhetorical function)
Evaluation	67	100
Description	49	–
Summarisation	35	–
Comparison	35	15
Explanation	28	15
Recommendation	23	10
Hortation	15	70
Prediction	7	15
Instruction	3	–
Total number of functions identified in corpus	**393**	**45**

3. The function of *hortation*, which was relatively rare in the university corpus, was, along with *evaluation*, the predominant rhetorical mode in the IELTS sample.

Of these findings, the last is perhaps the most significant. Indeed it is interesting to speculate about why *hortation* should figure so prominently in IELTS items. We can posit only one explanation here – this is that writing in a hortatory mode, of its nature, may not require the same amount of background knowledge that is needed to engage with topics of an epistemic nature. To take the topic area of animal experimentation as an example, it seems fair to assume that students in a testing context would be able to write more readily about the moral desirability (or not) of this practice (*hortation*), rather than, for example, about the reasons why the practice is employed (*explanation*) or about its scientific validity (*evaluation*) or about the views of various animal rights proponents (*summarisation*). While the prominence given to *hortation* in IELTS Task 2 items is probably attributable to certain test-specific exigencies, this feature nevertheless represents a substantial difference in the nature of writing in the two domains, one that is likely to have implications for students whose pre-entry English language instruction is mainly concerned with test preparation.

4.1.4 Object of enquiry

Analysis was made of the objects of enquiry (or topic areas) of tasks – specifically whether these were of a *phenomenal* or *metaphenomenal* nature. The results of this analysis are shown in Table 6.9. While a majority of tasks were concerned with topics of a phenomenal nature, there was also a fair proportion of what may be termed *metaphenomenal* tasks. The latter category was particularly characteristic of disciplines in the humanities, some of which

Table 6.9 Objects of enquiry in university assignments

Object of enquiry	Number	%
Phenomenal	95	61
Metaphenomenal	60	39

may be said to be concerned exclusively with the metaphenomenal, e.g. philosophy and literature. Examples of metaphenomenal tasks however, were found in a range of disciplines, including, surprisingly, the following rather demanding task set for first year agriculture undergraduates:

> Present a critical review of literature relating to a scientific topic which interests you. Summarise the principal ideas presented in a collection of scientific papers, highlighting the validity of the claims made, the conclusions and other important features.

No attempt was made to analyse the objects of enquiry further within each of the two broad categories; the topics were found to be too diverse and of too discipline-specific a nature to allow for such an endeavour. A sense of the diversity of topics covered in the corpus is captured in Table 6.10 which presents a representative sample of objects of enquiry under the *phenomenal* and *metaphenomenal* categories.

Table 6.10 Sample objects of enquiry in university assignments

Phenomenal	Metaphenomenal
1. Land degradation (agriculture)	1. Barthes' theoretical model (literature)
2. The Roman arch (architecture)	2. Methods for calculating household incomes (economics)
3. Atmospheric pollution (biology)	3. Theoretical approaches to child's play (education)
4. Graphical user interfaces (computing)	4. The Aboriginal Protection Act (law)
5. Children's acquisition of speech (education)	5. Speech act theory (linguistics)
6. Public water supply systems (engineering)	6. Freud's views of the feminine (medicine)
7. The Vietnam war (history)	7. Systems and classical views of management (management)
8. Adolescent mental health (medicine)	8. Utilitarian and retributive theories of punishment (philosophy)
9. The vibration of strings (physics)	9. Machiavelli's political thought (politics)
10. Developments in international tourism (tourism)	10. The Chicago school of sociology (sociology)

In contrast to the university tasks, the object of enquiry in all IELTS items was found to be of a *phenomenal* nature. A complete list of these is provided in Table 6.11. The lack of *metaphenomena* in IELTS tasks can again be related to the issue of necessary background knowledge. Clearly the sorts of metaphenomenal topics from the university corpus given above (Table 6.10) would be unsuitable in a language testing context. For example, an account of 'Barthes' theoretical model' could only be attempted after a careful reading of Barthes' text (and even then, in this case, there may be no guarantee of success!). Similarly it would not be possible to discuss different 'methods for calculating household incomes' without first being familiar with these accounting methods.

Table 6.11 Objects of enquiry in total IELTS corpus

1.   The relationship between technology and tradition
2.   Government regulation of motor car usage
3.   Retirement age
4.   Telecommuting
5.   Studying abroad
6.   Paternal responsibilities in child care
7.   Government regulation of new technology
8.   Government provision of health care
9.   The use of animals in scientific experiments
10. Studying abroad
11. Government funding of tertiary education
12. Editorial policies of newspapers
13. The future of work
14. Provision of aid by wealthy nations
15. Patient attitudes to medical treatment
16. Government provision of social services
17. Computers in education
18. Capital punishment
19. Parental regulation of children's television habits
20. Population growth

While the objects of enquiry in the IELTS items shown in Table 6.11 are of a diverse nature they were found to be more amenable to further analysis than the university tasks. If there is any recurring theme to be discerned among these items, it is that of the social responsibilities of various agents of authority, especially with respect to the provision of services and the regulation of behaviours.

On our analysis the following items would fall within this overarching theme – items 2, 6, 7, 8, 9, 11, 12, 14, 16, 18, 19. In most instances, the agent in question is 'the government'; others include 'wealthy nations' (14), the scientific community (9), parents (19), fathers (6). This focus on the responsibilities of certain authorities is clearly connected to the rhetorical function of *hortation* and can be adduced here as additional evidence for the fairly restricted nature of Task 2 items.

4.1.5 Summary of findings

The main findings from the comparative task analysis can be summarised thus:

1. The predominant *genre* in the university corpus was the *essay*. While this term is not used to refer to IELTS Task 2 items, the genre that is specified – a *written argument* – is thought to resemble most closely the university essay.

2. Almost all university tasks required for their completion the use of external sources – either *primary* or *secondary* sources or a combination of the two. IELTS Task 2 items in contrast were framed around the use of *prior knowledge.*

3. The university tasks covered a broad range of *rhetorical functions*, mainly of an epistemic nature. The most common categories were *evaluation, description, summarisation, comparison* and *explanation*. Of the deontic functions, *recommendation* was the most common. Like the university corpus, *evaluation* was the predominant category in IELTS items. A distinctive feature of the IELTS corpus, however, was the disproportionately high number of *hortatory* tasks.

4. The objects of *enquiry* in the university corpus were mainly of a *phenomenal* nature; but there was also a fair proportion of *metaphenomenal* tasks. The IELTS items in contrast, were all of a *phenomenal* nature.

These differences in the two corpora appear rather technical in the terms described above. Taken in combination however, they suggest a distinction that can be characterised in broader terms. University tasks, by definition, prescribe academic modes of discourse, or to be precise, the discipline-specific discourses required of novice scholars. While the IELTS items clearly share features with those set at university, the form of writing they prescribe, on analysis, would appear to bear a closer resemblance to certain public forms of discourse. In particular, the emphasis placed on the spontaneous expression of opinion is suggestive of such public, non-academic genres as the letter to the editor or the newspaper editorial.

This section of the report concludes with a final comparison of tasks, one that captures well some of the differences discussed above. The first task is an IELTS item and the second an assignment from a bioethics subject. The comparison here is instructive, because the two tasks, on face value, appear similar in a number of respects. Both are concerned with a similar content area (i.e. government provision of health care) and seemingly with a similar rhetorical focus (hortatory – *should*); yet they are quite different.

IELTS item
The most advanced medical treatment tends to be expensive. However, people's access to good health care should not depend on social factors such as their level of income or social status. Discuss.

Bioethics essay
Should a just state provide health care for its citizens? How can relevant ethical theories help to resolve this question?

What is required in the IELTS task above is that candidates express a point of view on the issue; one that is based on their own beliefs and knowledge. The bioethics task, in contrast, is concerned not so much with students expressing a point of view, but with them discussing the theoretical means by which a point of view might be reached. This difference can be understood in terms of some of the contrasts that have been considered so far; that is between *prior knowledge* and *research*; between a *deontic* and an *epistemic* rhetoric and between the *phenomenal* and the *metaphenomenal*. The nature of the two tasks is different, and it is fair to say that the language skills needed for the fulfilment of each will also be different.

4.2 Staff survey

While the task survey was the main part of this study, follow-up interviews with a sample of the lecturers who had submitted tasks, provided an alternative data source representing a different perspective on the university tasks. In addition, in the interviews the lecturers gave feedback on the suitability of the IELTS in relation to the writing demands of their disciplines (see Appendix 6.2 for interview schedule). In the staff survey, 12 lecturers were interviewed from ten discipline areas with comments provided on a total of 19 tasks submitted for the first stage of the study. The distribution of the genres of these tasks was similar to that in the corpus overall, with essays being the most common. Table 6.12 is a list of the tasks which formed the basis of the interviews.

The following discussion focuses on common themes arising from the interviews. It begins with a summary of the more notable features of the university tasks as perceived by those who set them, and then deals with perceptions of the sample IELTS tasks.

4.2.1 University assignments

Rhetorical function was one of the categories used by the researchers to analyse university assignments in the first stage of the study and was also the subject of a specific question in the interviews. The main rhetorical functions required in university assignment tasks were identified by the lecturers; the

Table 6.12 Interview data: Number and types of tasks from each discipline

Discipline area	Genre	Number
Chemistry	Experimental report	1
Computing	Computer program	1
Economics	Essay	2
Engineering	Case study report	1
Geography	Essay	2
Law	Essay	3
	Case study report	1
Linguistics	Research report (other)	2
Management	Essay	3
Politics	Essay	2
Communications	Research report (other)	2

results of this process are shown in Table 6.13 together with the results from the task analysis. This comparison reveals a surprising degree of correspondence between the results from the two stages with the order of frequencies almost the same. The only variation in order was a greater number of tasks requiring *recommendation* than *explanation* in the lecturers' analyses.

Table 6.13 Rhetorical functions in university assignments: A comparison of interview and task analysis results

RHETORICAL FUNCTION	Lecturer perceptions Stage 2 (% of tasks incorporating function)	Task analysis Stage 1 (% of tasks incorporating function)
Evaluation	63	67
Description	63	49
Comparison	53	35
Summarisation	37	35
Recommendation	32	23
Explanation	26	28
Hortation	16	15
Prediction	11	7
Instruction	5	3

In the interviews, the lecturers were also asked to comment on the key characteristics of their tasks and on the qualities that would distinguish an outstanding assignment. Their comments fell into two main areas – those concerned with the research process and those with features of the written product. Almost all lecturers, regardless of discipline, emphasised the importance of research skills and many noted that a discriminating feature of outstanding assignments was evidence of extensive independent research. The following comments give a sense of the value lecturers placed on the use of sources. The first from a geography lecturer is interesting for the number of references recommended as well as the detail he provides on acceptability of different types of references; the second, from a politics lecturer, specifies the research skills and types of sources one could expect from a 'better' essay in the subject he teaches:

> A minimum of at least 10 references are required – really good essays would use 20 or more . . . students should avoid encyclopedias and textbooks if possible . . . and should probably avoid using www pages as they are very difficult to verify. Students need to recognise that New Scientist and Scientific American are not exactly refereed journals . . . books by single authors are fine, as long as they are not university level textbooks . . . dictionaries are unacceptable . . . if they're using them repeatedly to define terms.

> Students need to show the ability to use footnotes and bibliographies to jump off into other texts . . . [and] a familiarity with other kinds of cultural documents, perhaps literary works, works of visual art, an understanding or familiarity with architecture of the period, as a way of giving the historical framework.

Another aspect of assignments that many lecturers considered important was the structure and organisation of the written product. Students were expected to be aware of and to conform to the structural conventions of the relevant genre, such as the different sections of a research report (introduction, methodology, etc.) or of an essay (introduction, body and conclusion).

4.2.2 Comparison with IELTS Task 2

In the interviews, lecturers were asked to make comparisons between their tasks and two sample IELTS tasks (items 1 and 2 in Appendix 6.1), and then to consider whether training for IELTS Task 2 items would be useful preparation for writing tasks in their disciplines.

In their discussion of the degree of correspondence between the tasks (academic and sample IELTS) comments about intrinsic similarities were most common among those lecturers from disciplines in which the task *genre* was an essay. The similarities noted by these lecturers tended to be of a general nature, especially in relation to the broad area of argumentation in writing. The following were two observations of similarities:

> In short I don't think there are big differences. I'm asking them to write a coherent piece of work, not a set of dot points or scattered ideas . . . it is essential that they construct the arguments that they present with examples and relevant evidence . . . The tasks that I set . . . usually ask them to compare and contrast, do you agree or disagree, to what extent is this statement relevant, or I have a quote, do you agree. So in many ways the sorts of tasks I set are quite similar . . .   (Economics)

> The requirements of the IELTS tasks arguing two sides of an issue, responding to a proposition seem similar to the requirements of my subject. (Law)

The focus of staff responses, however, was more frequently on differences. IELTS tasks tended to be perceived as much simpler than academic tasks, with several lecturers comparing them to secondary school tasks.

> The major assignments in my subject are more difficult and comprehensive. We're asking for 2,000 words, in depth. IELTS tasks of 250 words are more like school rather than university level. (Management)

> The IELTS tasks remind me of Year 12 essays which don't require much background work. There's certainly no scope for rigorous attention to getting the detail right that we require. (Law)

An exception was the comment by a chemistry lecturer who observed that experimental reports in chemistry required:

> A lower level [of interpretation] than the IELTS, which [requires] fairly high-level interpretation skills . . . In Chemistry practical reports students are asked for a fairly operational description of what they've done so that someone else can do it. (Chemistry)

In their comments about the requirements of their own assignments, lecturers emphasised the importance of research. This was considered to be a major difference between the academic and IELTS tasks. A law lecturer emphasised the reflective nature of university writing with tasks integrally related to course content:

> The sample IELTS questions are asking people to use their background knowledge and whatever has come to them from life, whereas we're expecting them to use material that we've taught and they've read.

A similar observation was made by a geography lecturer:

> Our assignments are research essays and focus on students researching a given question, whereas the IELTS tasks don't have this focus on research.

Some discussed this disparity in terms of the differing nature of evaluation and opinion in the two domains. It was mentioned that both types of tasks require the expression of a point of view, however a qualification was made that the only valid opinions in university writing were those based on reading and research:

> Students are asked to be critical and evaluate what they found in their research, what their informants said, what the literature says, we don't ask them for their personal values or opinion.   (Linguistics)

Although lecturers were not specifically asked about what we have termed 'the object of enquiry' of tasks, several noted a difference in the topic areas of university and IELTS tasks, similar to the *phenomenal/metaphenomenal* distinction noted in the task analysis:

> [In the IELTS tasks] students are being asked to develop an argument . . . about entities, objects . . . and make predictions and policy prescriptions . . . the discipline I teach deals with writers and ideas . . . In my own questions the students are not so much being asked to develop an argument, as to show how an argument was constructed by others in the past, and also to show the kinds of features that bring about that construction, whether it's logical or not, in its own context.   (Politics)

While most lecturers identified differences in the two types of tasks, some were aware of reasons for these differences, i.e. the different assessment contexts of the two tasks. The constraints imposed by test conditions were summed up by a law lecturer in the following comment:

> IELTS tasks [are] designed for a specific testing situation, so they've got limited time, limited words and no possibility of research, so they have to sit down and write an essay based on their own knowledge.

All lecturers, even those who emphasised the differences between the two types of tasks acknowledged that training for IELTS Task 2 items could be useful preparation for university writing. Some lecturers spoke in a general way of training in writing skills being relevant, thus lending support for direct tests of writing:

> Any training in clear writing is useful preparation.   (Communications)

> For writing overall for this subject – IELTS training would be useful preparation.   (Chemistry)

Others remarked on how IELTS would be a useful framework for teaching conventions of essay writing, such as paragraph structure and coherence:

> How to structure an essay and how to argue a case . . . will serve the students well for the questions we have here.   (Geography)

> Training in how to unravel a question . . . how to make sure every paragraph relates to the question, how to make each paragraph flow from the one before . . . introductions and conclusions . . . some preparation for IELTS questions could be of great use.   (Law)

4.2.3 Summary of findings

Overall, lecturers were positive about the nature of the IELTS Task 2 format and the type of language instruction they imagined students would receive in preparing for it. Indeed some who were previously unfamiliar with the test and also with general issues related to language screening of prospective students expressed surprise at the quality of the test instrument. Most lecturers however, could identify substantial differences between the writing needed for the test and that required in their respective subjects. In general terms, these differences were similar to those found in the task analysis. Lecturers noted the limited rhetorical range of IELTS, especially its emphasis on an opinionative style of writing based on 'lived experience' – or what was described as *hortation* in the task analysis. In contrast, they stressed the overriding importance of 'content' in their students' work, content that is acquired through processes of teaching, reading and researching in their subjects. The reasons for these differences were understood by some. As one lecturer succinctly put it:

> My writing requirements are totally different. My students have got eight weeks to do the assignment. They're not expected to have much knowledge of their own at the start – and we don't really want to hear too much about their preconceptions of the issues. They're expected to do a lot of research and they've got eight weeks to mull over it. In IELTS they've only got an instant. I guess the only problem is that students coming from this background may not realise how much needs to happen before they start their drafting.

5 Conclusions and recommendations

In this final section, we draw on the results of the two stages of the study to suggest ways in which the IELTS Task 2 format might be adapted to resemble more closely the requirements of university writing. Optimising the 'authenticity' of a test is an important objective of any test development process (Bachman and Palmer 1996). In the case of the IELTS test, with its increasing use as a university selection instrument and its corresponding influence on programmes of English for academic purposes, this objective seems especially pressing. Any recommendations for enhanced authenticity however, need to take account of the special constraints imposed on writing in a test situation. For the IELTS Writing test in its existing format, these constraints can be outlined as follows:

1. It must be possible to perform the task in the time frame available (40 minutes).
2. The task must not make unwarranted assumptions about the background knowledge of candidates.

3. The task must be, as far as possible, a test of candidates' writing skills, and should not require to any major extent the use of other skills for its completion.
4. The task should elicit a sample of writing that is assessable according to the existing criteria used on the test.

The suggestions which follow are organised around the categories used in the classification scheme.

5.1 Genre

The study found that the *essay* is the pre-eminent written genre of university study. It was also found that the standard Task 2 item resembles the *essay* genre more closely than any of the other generic forms identified in the university corpus, a point also made by a number of academic staff in interview. For this reason, the current format of the IELTS Task 2, requiring candidates to 'present a written argument or case' in relation to a given topic, would appear to be the most suitable. Within this basic format however, a number of modifications are suggested.

5.2 Information source

One of the main findings of the study was the difference in prescribed information sources in the two domains, with the extensive use of sources required in university tasks and a contrasting reliance on *prior knowledge* in the IELTS Task 2 format. This was a difference also identified by staff in the interviews.

There are several options which might be considered to deal with this disparity. The two discussed here involve what might be termed a strong and a weak reading–writing link. In the 'strong link' option, writing tasks could be accompanied by a range of reading materials (secondary source), with candidates *required* to incorporate these materials in their responses. Such an approach, which would represent a close simulation of university essay tasks, is already used in a number of university entrance tests, including, for example, the Faculty of Arts Essay Admission Test used at Monash University (see Appendix 6.3). While the strong link option, in our view, represents an optimal task design, it does not fit well with some of the constraints on the IELTS Writing test listed above. This format, for example, would require more time than the currently prescribed 40 minutes. Furthermore, the obligation to include source material in responses would make this as much a test of reading as of writing.

An alternative option would be to draw on the framework used in the pre-1995 version of the IELTS Task 2. In this former version, at least one text in the Reading test was thematically linked to the Writing task and candidates were given the *option* of referring to this text in their written response. Included in the task rubric was the following instruction to candidates:

> *You may use ideas from Reading Passage 1, but do not copy directly from it.*

In the light of the study's findings, a return to such a framework would seem to be an option worth considering. Inclusion of this kind of reading–writing link would serve to enhance the test's authenticity and would also be compatible with test constraints. In terms of test washback, a link between the Reading and Writing components of the test would provide a basis in EAP programmes for the teaching of the important academic skills associated with citation.

5.3 Rhetorical function

The task analysis found a restricted range of rhetorical functions in the IELTS corpus, with a disproportionately high number of *hortatory* tasks and a corresponding lack of *summarisation, comparison, explanation, recommendation*. (This was a finding supported in the interviews, although not discussed by informants in the same precise terms.) These results, it needs to be acknowledged, are only strictly relevant to the sample of IELTS practice materials used in the study. As mentioned, official Task 2 items – live or retired – were not available to the study and so it is difficult to know the extent to which the findings might apply to them. Nevertheless, the study's recognition of the need for rhetorical diversity in Task 2 items is a point that probably needs to be heeded by test developers.

It was mentioned earlier that writing in an epistemic mode (e.g. *summarisation, comparison, explanation*) will normally require more specialised knowledge. If such functions are to be incorporated to a greater extent in IELTS items, it is important that topic areas are chosen carefully to ensure that candidates have sufficient background knowledge to be able to engage with the task (constraint 2). One way of dealing with this would be to use tasks which draw on candidates' knowledge of their country of origin. The following is an example of a possible *explanatory* task employing such an approach:

> What is the pattern of population shift in your country? From rural to urban areas or from urban to rural areas? What are some of the possible reasons for this pattern?

It should also be pointed out that the inclusion of relevant reading materials (discussed in the previous section) could also serve to provide necessary epistemic content, as well as allowing for the incorporation of the function of *summarisation* in tasks.

5.4 Object of enquiry

The task survey found that university tasks were concerned with both *phenomenal* and *metaphenomenal* entities, whereas tasks in the IELTS corpus were all of a *phenomenal* nature. This was a difference also noted by several staff in interviews. While it is clearly not possible in a testing context to use a given theory (e.g. a particular ethical theory) as the basis for topics, it may be possible to frame tasks so that they at least elicit a more *metaphenomenal* form of discourse. This could be achieved by incorporating in tasks propositions which are attributed either to individual scholars or to a general school of thought, as in the following two examples:

> **Ballard and Clanchy argue that** students preparing to study abroad need to do more than develop their English language skills. They also need to learn about the academic culture of English-speaking universities. To what extent do you agree with this view?

> **Some educationists argue that** a student's success at school is mainly due to the quality of learning that takes place in the home. To what extent do you agree with this view?

While such modifications in wording may appear minor, tasks framed in this way would be formally more akin to many set in the university domain. We would also argue that 'attributed tasks' like the examples above would encourage a more academic style of writing, one that would be more focused on the metaphenomenal lexis of 'views', 'arguments', 'beliefs' and the like.

5.5 Summary of recommendations

The suggestions made in the foregoing discussion are summarised in the following set of specific recommendations:

1. It is recommended that the subject of Task 2 items be thematically linked to at least one passage from the Reading test and that candidates be given the option of making reference to this reading passage in their written response.
2. It is recommended that a minimal number of Task 2 items be framed around what we have termed a 'hortatory rhetoric', that is items that require candidates to discuss the desirability (or not) of a particular social practice, public policy and the like.

3. Following on from 2, it is recommended that Task 2 items be designed to incorporate a diverse range of rhetorical functions. An effort should be made to include the following functions, either singly or in combination: *description*; *summarisation*; *comparison*; *explanation*; *recommendation*.

4. It is recommended that some Task 2 items be framed to include an attributed proposition in the task rubric. These propositions could either have a generic attribution (e.g. *many psychologists argue, some educationists believe*, etc.) or be attributed to a specific scholar.

5.6 Implications for teaching programmes

The results of the present study have been used as a basis for assessing the authenticity of the IELTS Writing Task 2 format and also for suggesting ways in which the test might be modified to enhance this authenticity. We believe the study also has implications for the design of pre-enrolment EAP language programmes which seek to prepare students simultaneously for the IELTS test and for university study. In this section we discuss briefly two issues:

1. The likely impact of the Task 2 component of the test on teaching programmes.

2. How programme designers and teachers might best approach test preparation within the broader context of pre-tertiary EAP.

The issue of a test's impact on teaching programmes (or washback effect) is a complex one. Alderson and Wall (1993) suggest that our thinking about washback should not be restricted to some 'general' and 'vague' notion of influence (either positive or negative). Instead, they argue, we need to refine the concept to take account of a variety of possible specific effects, including *inter alia*, effects on:

1. How teachers teach.

2. How learners learn.

3. What teachers teach.

4. What learners learn.

The results of the present study can shed no light on the way IELTS Task 2 might impact on matters of teaching methodologies and learning processes (i.e. effects 1 and 2); but they do suggest a likely effect on curriculum (i.e. effects 3 and 4). On this score, we would conclude that the writing curriculum implicit in the current Task 2 format is a comparatively narrow one. While the test would appear to provide a basis for the teaching of a number of important aspects of academic writing (e.g. structuring of paragraphs, writing coherently, arguing a case), there are other important areas which are unlikely to receive coverage in test preparation programmes. Perhaps the most significant of these are the skills, both linguistic and cognitive, associated with the integrating of other writers' ideas into one's own writing. We would also point to the limited rhetorical range intrinsic to the IELTS writing curriculum.

The best way to handle IELTS preparation within the broader context of pre-enrolment EAP language programmes represents a significant challenge for teachers and programme designers. In a survey of Australian language centres, Deakin (1997) identified a number of different models currently in use, including:

1. 'Integrated' models, where IELTS preparation is incorporated into EAP courses.
2. 'Separated' models, where IELTS preparation courses and EAP courses are run separately.
3. 'Exclusive' models, where IELTS preparation courses only are run, with no option of EAP for students.

Deakin (1997) points out that programme design decisions in language centres are motivated by a number of factors, some of which are administratively based and some educationally. We believe the present research can provide some guidance for the design of IELTS/EAP programmes, at least in those situations where decisions can be based primarily on educational imperatives. The first point to be made is that preparation for the IELTS Writing test should not be seen as adequate preparation in itself for the literacy demands of tertiary study. In this regard, the 'exclusive' model, from the alternatives above, should be viewed as the least adequate. Of the other options mentioned, the study's findings probably lend greater support to the 'separated' model. As we have suggested, the IELTS Task 2 prescribes a form of writing which is distinct from that required in the academy, one which is arguably more akin to certain public non-academic genres, e.g. the letter to the editor. For this reason, the more prudent option would appear to be to run two separate programmes. While 'integration' of IELTS and university preparation may be a worthwhile objective, without systematic attention given to the distinctions discussed above, such programmes run the risk of presenting students with a confusing model of university writing.

5.7 Further research

This report concludes with some suggestions for further research. These can be divided into areas; those related specifically to the IELTS Writing test and those concerned with broader issues of writing research. In the first area, this study has only considered the Task 2 format of the IELTS Writing test; clearly there is an equally pressing need to investigate the authenticity of the Task 1 format with respect to university writing requirements. The methodology used in the present study, in our view, would also be suitable for any study of this other component of the test. An additional objective in a survey of Task 1 items could be to investigate how it fits with the Task 2 format and also the extent to which it might fill some of the rhetorical and linguistic gaps identified in the present study.

The present study has discussed the advantages and also shortcomings of each of the sources of data used, i.e. the tasks themselves and staff perceptions of tasks. An additional source of data which might be drawn on in further authenticity studies is the actual written texts (particularly exemplary texts) produced in response to university and test tasks. This data would lend itself to more conventional 'discourse analysis' procedures and, as Hale et al (1996) suggest, would enable one to obtain 'an even more concrete picture' of the nature of writing in the university and testing domains.

In the broader area of writing research, the present study has made some contribution to that field of discourse analysis concerned with the classification and analysis of writing tasks. One limitation however, of the taxonomic procedures used is that our dimensions of difference were all considered independently of each other. Clearly there is a need to investigate in what ways these dimensions might relate to each other systematically; and in particular, to find out the extent to which categories of genre can be understood in terms of specific configurations of the other dimensions used: *information sources*; *rhetorical functions*; *objects of enquiry*. A better understanding of the nature of academic genres, as this study suggests, will have obvious benefits for the field of language testing – to improve the way in which students are selected for university study. But it is likely to have even greater benefits for the field of language teaching – to help students to be better prepared for their studies.

Acknowledgements

The researchers wish to thank the following people for their assistance with this project: the staff at Monash University and the University of Melbourne who provided copies of their writing assignments, and also those staff who agreed to be interviewed; Associate Professor Gordon Taylor, Associate Professor Brian Lynch and Dr Brian Paltridge who provided advice on a range of methodological issues; Judith Bishop and Caryn Nery, who acted as research assistants in the collection of data and the interviewing of academic staff. The researchers also wish to thank IELTS, Australia for their support of this project.

Notes

1   A modified version of this paper has been published as follows: Moore, T and Morton, J (2005) Dimensions of difference: Academic writing and IELTS writing, *Journal of English for Academic Purposes* 4 (1), 43–66.

2   Note that data was not collected for such variables as *length of product* and *time allowed on task*. This was because the differences between IELTS and university tasks with respect to these variables were thought to be self-evident. A very cursory analysis of the data showed that university tasks were considerably longer and also that extended time was allowed for their completion.

3   A similar distinction is found in Halliday's (1985) modal categories of 'propositions' (which are concerned with the functions of asserting and denying) and 'proposals' (concerned with prescribing and proscribing).

4   Our category of 'recommendation' resembles in some respects the rhetorical pattern of 'problem-solution' analysed at length by Hoey (1983). In our study however, we sought to draw a distinction between tasks (or sub-tasks) which require students to describe an existing solution (epistemic-description) and those which require students to propose their own solution (deontic-recommendation).

5   This distinction corresponds roughly to Lyons' (1977) semantic categories – 'first-order, second-order and third-order entities'. Under Lyons' schema, first-order entities refer to entities which exist in both time and space, i.e. physical objects or beings. Second-order entities also exist in time, but rather than *exist* in space they are said to *take place* or *occur* within it; they refer to such entities as events, processes, situations, activities, practices, etc. Third-order entities, on the other hand, are said to be unobservable and have no spatio-temporal location; they refer to abstract entities such as propositions, facts, etc. The classification scheme used in the study has conflated the first and second-order categories into the single *phenomenal* category. This was for the sake of simplicity, but also because the two-way *phenomena–metaphenomenal* distinction appears to be the more significant.

APPENDIX 6.1

Sources of IELTS Task 2 items used in the study

1. IELTS (1996) *The IELTS Handbook*, Cambridge: UCLES.
2. IELTS (1995) *IELTS Specimen Materials*, Cambridge: UCLES.
3. E van Bemmel and J Tucker (1996) *IELTS to Success: Preparation Tips and Practice Tests*, Brisbane: Jacaranda Wiley.
4. G Deakin (ed) (1996) *Practice Tests for IELTS* (2nd edition), Hawthorn: LTS.
5. R De Witt (1995) *How to Prepare for IELTS* (2nd edition), London: British Council.
6. V Jakeman and C MacDowell (1996) *Cambridge Practice Tests for IELTS*, Cambridge: Cambridge University Press.
7. V Todd and P Cameron (1996) *Prepare for IELTS: Academic modules*, Sydney: Insearch Language Centre.
8. Unpublished IELTS practice materials used at one Melbourne English language centre.

Sample IELTS Task 2 items used in the study

All sample items used the following template taken from official versions of the test.

The topic components of items are listed below.

WRITING TASK 2

You should spend about 40 minutes on this task.

Present a written argument or case to an educated non-specialist audience on the following topic:

TOPIC

You should write at least 250 words.

You should use your own ideas, knowledge and experience and support your arguments with examples and relevant evidence.

Topics

1. It is inevitable that as technology develops so traditional cultures must be lost. Technology and tradition are incompatible – you cannot have both together. To what extent do you agree or disagree with this statement? Give reasons for your answer.   (Source 1)

2. The first car appeared on British roads in 1888. By the year 2000 there may be as many as 29 million vehicles on British roads. Should alternative forms of transport be encouraged and international laws be introduced to control car ownership and use?   (Source 2)

3. In some countries the average worker is obliged to retire at the age of 50, while in others people can work until they are 65 or 70. Meanwhile we see some politicians enjoying power well into their nineties. Clearly there is little agreement on an appropriate retirement age. Until what age do you think people should be encouraged to remain in paid employment. Give reasons for your answer.   (Source 3)

4. Telecommuting refers to workers doing their jobs from home for part of each week and communicating with their office using computer technology. Telecommuting is growing in many countries and is expected to be common for most office workers in the coming decades. How do you think society will be affected by the growth of telecommuting?   (Source 3)

5. The idea of going overseas for university study is an exciting prospect for many people. But while it may offer some advantages, it is probably better to stay at home because of the difficulties a student inevitably encounters living and studying in a different culture. To what extent do you agree or disagree with this statement? Give reasons for your answer.   (Source 3)

6. Fathers are just as capable as mothers of taking care of children, so men should share parenting work more equally with women. (Source 4)

7. Technology can bring many benefits, but it can also cause social and environmental problems. In relation to new technology, the primary duty of governments should be to focus on potential problems, rather than benefits.   (Source 4)

8. The most advanced medical treatment tends to be expensive. However, people's access to good health care should not depend on social factors such as their level of income or social status.   (Source 4)

9. Higher mammals such as monkeys have rights and should not be used in laboratory experiments.   (Source 5)

10. More and more young people are studying and working overseas and this will help to bring about greater international co-operation in the future.   (Source 5)

11. As most postgraduate research today is funded by industry, then student grants should also come from the same source.   (Source 5)

12. News editors decide what to broadcast on television and what to print in newspapers. What factors do you think influence these decisions? Do we become used to bad news? Would it be better if more good news was reported?   (Source 6)

13. The idea of having a single career is becoming an old fashioned one. The new fashion will be to have several careers or ways of earning money and further education will be something that continues throughout life.   (Source 6)

14. Should wealthy nations be required to share their wealth among poorer nations by providing such things as food and education. Or is it the responsibility of the governments of poorer nations to look after themselves?   (Source 6)

15. A number of different medical traditions are now widely known and used: Western medicine (using drugs and surgery) herbal medicine, acupuncture (using needles at certain points of the body) homoeopathy (using minute doses of poisons) and so on.

    How important is the patient's mental attitude toward his/her treatment in determining the effectiveness of the treatment?   (Source 7)

16. A government's role is only to provide defence capability and urban infrastructure (roads, water, supplies etc.) All other services (education, health and social security) should be provided by private groups or individuals in the community.   (Source 7)

17. Are computers an essential feature of modern education? What subjects can be better taught using computers? Are there aspects of a good education that cannot be taught using computers?   (Source 7)

18. Should capital punishment (the death penalty) be used as a way of reducing violence in society?   (Source 8)

19. Television nowadays features many programs of a violent nature. For this reason it is necessary for parents to impose strict controls on their children's viewing habits.   (Source 8)

20. The world's expanding population is increasingly seen as a problem. What are the most effective ways of reducing population growth?   (Source 8)

APPENDIX 6.2

Interview schedule

The following questions will form the basis of the interview.

Section 1

The questions in this section refer to the assignment task(s) you provided:

1. You've called one of your written assignments an *essay/report/review* etc. What do you think are the key characteristics of this type of assignment?

2. What in your judgement would distinguish an outstanding from an ordinary student response to this assignment?

3. What sources of information would you expect students to use in preparing this assignment? What types of references, how many etc.?

4. The following categories represent some of the 'rhetorical demands' that might be included in a university writing task.

   (a) Which of these categories, if any, would you say best characterise the assignment(s) you have provided?

   (b) Are there any additional categories (not listed here) that you would use to characterise the assignment(s) you have provided?

       i)   *Explanatory focus* – the writer is required to give an account of the causes/reasons for a given entity or phenomenon.

       ii) *Problem-solution focus* – the writer is required to discuss a problem and to suggest possible ways of dealing with the problem.

       iii) *Descriptive focus* – the writer is required to indicate the distinguishing characteristics of a given entity/phenomenon.

       iv) *Comparative focus* – the writer is required to identify the similarities and/or differences between two or more entities/phenomena.

       v) *Hortatory focus* – the writer is required to make a judgement about whether a course of action should or should not be pursued.

vi) *Evaluative focus* – the writer is required to indicate the value of a given entity/phenomenon with respect to its usefulness, relevance, rightness etc.

vii) *Predictive focus* – the writer is required to speculate about what might happen to a given entity/phenomenon at some point in the future.

viii) *Summary focus* – the writer is required to give an account of what an author has said about a given entity or phenomenon.

ix) *Instructional focus* – the writer is required to outline a procedure to be followed.

Section 2

Questions in this section concern comparisons between the assignment tasks you provided and the attached sample IELTS tasks.   (Appendix 6.1)

5. What do you see as the main similarities and/or differences between the assignment tasks you provided and the sample IELTS tasks?

6. On the evidence of these IELTS tasks, to what extent do you think training for the IELTS Writing test would be useful preparation for the writing demands of your subject? Explain.

APPENDIX 6.3

MONASH UNIVERSITY
FACULTY OF ARTS ESSAY ADMISSION TEST (FAEAT)

General Instructions

For this test you must write an essay on ONE of the following topics below:

Time allowed: 3 hours

Length: Approximately 700 words

Attached is a set of extracts from books and newspapers[6] which deal with various questions concerning refugees. Using this material as fully as you can, you are required to write on ONE of these topics:

Topic 1:

What is a 'refugee'? Is the traditional definition of a refugee still fruitful in a world which often discriminates between economic and political refugees? Do you think it is possible to define a refugee in such a way that a humane and consistent international policy could be developed for dealing with the world's refugees?

Topic 2

Loescher and Scanlon observe in their book __Calculated Kindness__ (see extracts) that in recent times the United States (and other countries) have begun 'to limit the opportunities for refugee migration'. What factors can you suggest for this change of approach? What are likely to be some of the effects of restricted refugee policies on the various parties involved?

In assessing your essay the examiners will take into account the following:

1. the success with which you select and focus on the arguments and evidence in the reading matter most <u>relevant</u> to your answer;

2. the success with which you <u>integrate</u> your reading into the development of your own ideas. Use your own words rather than those in the readings, unless for some reason you especially want to quote them.

---

[6]Extracts not included here.

3. the <u>fluency</u> with which you develop your argument and sustain it with evidence.

4. the <u>organisation</u> of the writing, especially the success with which you use paragraphs to keep the lines of your argument clear.

5. the <u>clarity</u> and <u>accuracy</u> of your English (grammar, word choice and so on).

A dictionary will be supplied.

© Language and Learning Unit, Monash University

Methodology evaluation of Chapter 6

The methodology used in this chapter reflects the ways in which the research methodology of many current doctoral and research studies are designed viz: a complementary approach in which a survey is followed by in-depth interviews. Such an approach provides two perspectives to a study, making the overall study richer in its findings.

The methods used in this chapter follow this broad and currently popular approach but differ in the greater emphasis given to the first research instrument – the survey. Most current studies use the first instrument to establish a wide perspective for the research questions. The second instrument – the interviews – is usually used to provide deeper descriptions and insights, ones that the survey is not always able to reveal.

In this chapter, however, the methodological emphases are reversed but this strategy is undoubtedly appropriate. The survey provides the major part of the study because it is a detailed, comparative study of IELTS Writing tasks and the writing tasks used in universities. In this instance the interviews serve a complementary and confirmatory role. It is also appropriate for the survey to be given greater weight because it describes the development of a new research tool, a taxonomy of tasks.

The development of the taxonomy provides an excellent example for researchers of the ways to approach the development of a research instrument when it is not always possible, or appropriate, to use an existing research instrument. The authors detail the sources which exist: Systemic Functional Linguistics; Rhetorical Structure Theory; and Genre Analysis. However, in an exemplary approach to their research, they do not rely on any one of these instruments alone. Instead, as the authors state:

> . . . it was thought sensible not to begin with any a priori set of theoretical categories, but to draw initially on the data to establish 'broad dimensions of difference' (Hale et al 1996) and then to refer to relevant theoretical frameworks later to refine the classification scheme.

This is an approach which commends itself to all researchers into writing and writing tasks.

Thus the research methodology used in the chapter provides two examples of approaches to research:

1. The use of complementary research approaches – the survey and the interview.
2. The development of a purpose-built taxonomic research instrument.

7 A linguistic analysis of Chinese and Greek L1 scripts for IELTS Academic Writing Task 2

Principal researchers:
Barbara Mayor, Ann Hewings, Sarah North and
Joan Swann with Caroline Coffin

Abstract

This chapter differs from research studies that focus on IELTS test design and specific task design by examining the linguistic features of candidate output, specifically output for the Academic Writing Task 2 component. The research aims were to investigate how high-scoring scripts differ from low-scoring scripts; the extent to which candidates' writing might be related to the topic or wording of the task; and the extent to which candidates' prior linguistic, cultural and educational experience might lead them to write in distinct ways.

The data came from high-scoring and low-scoring Chinese L1 and Greek L1 IELTS candidates. The five forms of analysis, moving from smaller to larger units of analysis, and from more formal and quantitative to more functional and qualitative approaches consisted of: error analysis; sentence structure; argument structure at the sentence level; argument structure at the discourse level; and tenor and interpersonal meaning.

With regard to levels of performance (as measured by the specific task score) the major finding was that high and low-scoring scripts were differentiated not by a single feature, but rather by a constellation of features. The study indicates that markers appear to be responding to scripts in a holistic rather than a strictly analytic way. However, 'incomplete' argument structures, which typically lack a 'thesis' or an 'issue' stage, or include limited evidence in their 'argument' stage, were concentrated among low-scoring candidates.

In terms of test design, the instruction to write for 'an educated reader' and to 'use your own words' elicited a strikingly high level of interpersonal reference among all groups of candidates, implying that the generic test prompt itself may be cueing candidates into adopting a style of writing which is both heavily interpersonal and relatively polemical.

The investigation into the influence of candidates' prior linguistic, cultural and educational experiences indicated that low-scoring Chinese L1 candidates made significantly more grammatical errors than Greek L1 at the same level of performance, with the latter making proportionately more of the remaining categories of error. In terms of argument structure, there is little difference between Chinese L1 and Greek L1 candidates in their preference for expository over discussion argument genres. However, whereas the Greek L1 candidates strongly favour hortatory argument genres, the Chinese L1 have a slight preference for arguments that are formally analytic in genre. The Chinese L1 candidates also have a greater tendency to directly address the reader and to speak in the collective voice.

In terms of the style as opposed to the structure of their arguments, there is evidence that the candidates diverge widely from the normal tenor of (professional) academic texts, particularly in their excessive and qualitatively different use of the collective 'we', in the high incidence of 'I' in Theme position among Greek L1 candidates, and in the high incidence of dialogic features among the Chinese L1 candidates. Again, it may be that the generic task prompt, coupled with the lack of source material on which to base their argument, may account for this more personal style.

In complying with the rubric to '*present an argument . . . to an educated reader*', candidates are thrown back on their own resources, which is not a situation similar to that encountered in academic writing at tertiary level. However, it may well be that candidates who can cope successfully in this situation will also be successful in more traditional forms of academic writing in English.

1 Introduction

1.1 Research rationale

There is an established body of research on the linguistic and/or rhetorical analysis of academic writing. Much of this research has focused on professional academic discourse (for example, Bazerman 1988, Bazerman and Paradis 1991, Berkenkotter and Huckin 1995, Dudley-Evans and Henderson 1990, Swales 1990). There is also a body of work on student writing in general (for example, Drury and Webb 1991, Hewings 1999a, 1999b, Ivanic 1998, Prosser and Webb 1994) and on student writing in English as an additional language (for example, Atkinson and Ramanathan 1995, 2000, Connor 1996, Kachru 1995, 1997). The output produced by candidates for the IELTS Academic Writing tasks differs from other forms of student academic writing, not least because it is produced under test conditions and as a display of language proficiency rather than of academic knowledge. For these reasons, it constitutes a distinct form of writing produced for a specific academic purpose.

Much of the research on the IELTS tests conducted thus far focuses on overall test design and specific task design, including such issues as: the discipline specificity of test content and the effect of background knowledge on reading comprehension (Clapham 1996); the rationale behind the redesign of IELTS (Alderson and Clapham 1992, Charge and Taylor 1997) and content validity (Fulcher 1999). The present research differs from all of these in that it turns attention from the design and content of the test itself towards the linguistic features of candidate output.

The research focuses specifically on Academic Writing Task 2, the generic prompt for which is as follows:

> Present a written argument or case to an educated reader with no specialist knowledge of the following topic.
>
> [Controversial proposition]
>
> To what extent do you agree or disagree with this opinion?
> You should write at least 250 words.
> You should use your own ideas, knowledge and experience and support your arguments with examples and relevant evidence.

1.2 Research aims

The specific aims of the research were to analyse some of the linguistic features of candidate output for Academic Writing Task 2, and to establish the extent to which these features are associated with the task score awarded for the task, the declared first language group of the writer, the version of the test used and, where available, comparable corpora of tertiary-level academic writing. We thus set out to investigate:

- how high-scoring scripts differ from low-scoring scripts
- the extent to which candidates' writing may be related to the topic or wording of the task
- the extent to which candidates' prior linguistic, cultural and educational experiences may lead them to write in distinct ways

in order to make explicit:

- some of the valued linguistic features of currently successful scripts
- any possible intrusive effects of the design of the test
- any signs of cross-cultural variation in the way the task is approached
- the extent to which the language produced under test conditions approximates to the target genre(s) of tertiary-level English-medium academic writing (where comparative data is available).

Our assumption was that the outcomes of the research would have implications for:

- pedagogical interventions prior to the test
- more sensitive test design
- enhanced marking criteria
- staff development for those who grade the tests.

2 Methodology

2.1 The data sample

The data sample consisted of 186 candidate scripts produced in response to two different versions of IELTS Academic Writing Task 2 (referred to here as Versions A and B). The scripts were divided roughly equally between 'high'-scoring (defined as a score of 7–8 on the specific task) and 'low'-scoring (defined as a score of 5), and between first-language Chinese and first-language Greek candidates (referred to as Chinese L1 and Greek L1). It was decided to focus on Chinese L1 and Greek L1 candidates both for reasons of principle, because these language groups represent two of the largest groups of IELTS candidates, and also for pragmatic reasons, because they are concentrated in some of the largest test centres, thus simplifying access to an appropriate sample of scripts.

The original aim had been to work with 200 scripts, 100 of which would be at Band 8 or above, but in practice it proved difficult to obtain a sufficient supply of high-scoring scripts in the relevant test versions, particularly from Chinese L1 candidates. Moreover it proved necessary to draw on a disproportionate number of high-scoring scripts from Hong Kong rather than mainland China. The final tally for Chinese L1 candidates was five scripts at Band 8 and 35 scripts at Band 7, and for Greek L1 candidates 19 scripts at Band 8 and 27 scripts at Band 7. The full sample of scripts subjected to analysis was distributed as shown in Figure 7.1 (with the breakdown of 'high-scoring' scripts into Bands 7 and 8 bracketed in italics).

For certain of the analyses, a subset of scripts was used. Except in the case of the error analysis and the analysis of argument structure (both of which were conducted before a full sample of scripts was available) and some of the more qualitative analyses, this subset consisted of seven scripts from each of the cells (i.e. 56 scripts in all). The maximum possible number of Band 8 scripts for each cell were included in this analysis.

All scripts were keyed in retaining original errors. Each was given a unique identifier in the form GR/A/8/201 (indicating a Greek L1 candidate who took Version A of the task and obtained a score of 8, with a unique identifying number of 201). All references to individual scripts are given in this form.

Figure 7.1 Distribution of scripts according to test version, task score and language group

Language group	Test version	Task score		Word count	Clause count	t-unit count
Chinese L1	A	High-scoring (7+8)	19 *(18+1)*	6596	721	471
		Low-scoring (5)	25	7468	903	627
	B	High-scoring (7+8)	21 *(17+4)*	6593	731	449
		Low-scoring (5)	25	6536	758	504
Greek L1	A	High-scoring (7+8)	25 *(12+13)*	8594	859	502
		Low-scoring (5)	25	6888	783	492
	B	High-scoring (7+8)	21 *(15+6)*	6853	747	402
		Low-scoring (5)	25	6626	784	405
Totals			**186**	**56,154**	**6286**	**3852**

2.2 The analyses

The scripts were subjected to the following types of analysis, moving roughly from smaller to larger units of analysis and from more formal to more functional approaches.

Error analysis (section 3)

Sentence-level errors seemed one of the more obvious categories to include. These are highly salient features, frequently commented on by teachers at tertiary level in their assessment of the quality of student writing. They are therefore likely to be related to IELTS test scores. We felt also that there might be specific differences between candidates from different first language groups in relation to the types of sentence-level errors encountered.

Lexis was included in the error analysis but, while it was possible to count occurrences of unsuitable lexical items, it proved more difficult to find a revealing approach to the range and delicacy of the candidates' vocabulary. A preliminary attempt was made to investigate type/token ratio, word length, lexical density and vocabulary range in a small number of scripts. However, the more quantifiable features seemed to have little significance in themselves, but rather to interact in potentially complex ways with other aspects of the candidates' writing. (There is scope for further research on the nature of this interaction.)

Sentence structure (section 4)

Like surface errors, sentence structure seemed to be a relatively salient feature of language that might be attended to by markers: we hypothesised that high-scoring scripts would show evidence of greater complexity in their sentence structure. Our initial analysis of the full data set focused on candidates' use of embedded or dependent clauses. This was followed by a more open-ended qualitative analysis of sentence structure in a small subset of scripts.

Argument structure: sentence-level features (section 5)

The prompt for Academic Writing Task 2 specifically asks candidates to present an 'argument or case' and so how students rhetorically structured their answers was expected to be significant in whether the answers were awarded high or low scores. We look in this section at signals of text organisation at the level of the sentence or clause-complex ('t-unit') and particularly at ways in which the writers signal their argument in sentence-initial position (Theme).

Argument structure: discourse-level features (section 6)

In this section we pursue the analysis of the scripts in terms of how they function as argumentative writing. We look at paragraph and whole text organisation using the concept of genre. The expectation was that the high-scoring scripts would use impersonal argument structures similar to those found in other studies of academic texts.

Tenor and interpersonal meaning (section 7)

A striking aspect of the corpus was the apparently high incidence of dialogic features such as first and second person reference and the use of questions and commands. These represent aspects of the Tenor system in Systemic Functional Linguistics, which is concerned with the manifestation of relative status and formality of exchange, as well as the expression of personal engagement and point of view. Our initial hypothesis was that high-scoring scripts would construe a Tenor whereby solidarity between writer and reader was *not* assumed.

3 Error analysis

Error analysis was carried out on a subset of 108 scripts, of which 92 had been graded at Band 5 and 16 at Band 8 (the low number of Band 8 scripts reflects the shortage of these scripts in the relevant test versions at the time of this analysis). The distribution of scripts was as shown in Figure 7.2.

Errors were initially classified into four categories: spelling, punctuation, grammar, and lexis/idiom. After preliminary analysis, a separate category was added for prepositions, as such errors were frequently indeterminate between grammar and lexis/idiom. The final classification system was as follows:

Spelling   errors in spelling and word division
Punctuation   errors in the use of punctuation marks, capitals, and sentence-
              initial conjunctions; run-on sentences

Grammar   errors in word class, tense, voice, use of modals, non-finite forms, concord, number, countability, article usage, and word order; faulty cohesion (failure to agree with antecedent); lack of conjunction
Preposition   inappropriate or omitted preposition
Lexis/idiom   incorrect or inappropriate vocabulary; unclear reference; excessive parataxis.

Figure 7.2

Language group	Test version	Task score	No. of scripts
Chinese L1	A	High-scoring	–
		Low-scoring	20
	B	High-scoring	–
		Low-scoring	25
Greek L1	A	High-scoring	16
		Low-scoring	25
	B	High-scoring	–
		Low-scoring	22

Means and standard deviations were calculated for the length of each essay (word count) and for the different categories of error. These were then analysed for significance using Fisher's t-test for uncorrelated samples. Pearson product-moment correlation coefficients were also calculated between error categories.

In interpreting the results of the error analysis, it should be recognised that identifying, classifying and quantifying errors is not a straightforward process. It is not always obvious what precisely counts as an error, or how it should be categorised. In particular, we were forced to evaluate errors against our own interpretation of what the writer intended to say. In consequence our judgements were to some extent subjective, and the less comprehensible the writing, the less reliable the analysis becomes. In Appendix 7.1 we describe the problems in categorising error which need to be borne in mind when interpreting the error statistics discussed in the following sections.

3.1 Analysis by task score

The small sample of high-scoring scripts, and its disparity with the low-scoring sample, make statistical analysis difficult. Nevertheless, clear differences can be seen between these two samples (see Figure 7.3).

The average word count of high-scoring scripts was 336.9, compared to 265.8 for low-scoring scripts. This difference was highly significant, with less than 0.1% probability of occurring by chance ($p < .001$).

In every category of error the frequency of errors was lower in high-scoring scripts, which had an overall average of 5.6 errors every 100 words, compared with 15.9 in low-scoring scripts. All these differences were highly significant (p < .001), except for punctuation (where p < .002).

Figure 7.3 Frequency of errors (per 100 words) in high- and low-scoring scripts

	Word count	Spelling	Punctuation	Grammar	Prepositions	Lexis	Overall
High n = 16							
Average	336.94	0.65	0.54	2.03	0.48	1.94	5.64
SD	58.58	0.70	0.52	1.21	0.45	1.23	2.00
Low n = 92							
Average	265.76	2.21	1.17	7.74	1.29	3.55	15.97
SD	59.50	2.09	1.56	3.03	0.80	1.47	5.11
t =	4.48***	5.61***	3.39**	13.07***	5.74***	4.67***	14.14***

* p < .05; **p < .01; ***p < .001

As Figure 7.4 indicates, overall error frequency was negatively correlated with task score, with grammar as the most significant error category. Punctuation was the only category which did not correlate significantly with task score. Word count, however, was more strongly correlated with task score than any of the error categories. These results are in line with those for the t-test, but should still be regarded cautiously in view of the small sample size and skewed distribution of high-scoring scripts.

Figure 7.4 Correlation of task score with word count and frequency of errors, in descending order of significance

Total errors	−0.611**
Grammar	−0.584**
Word count	0.395**
Lexis/idiom	−0.372**
Prepositions	−0.356**
Spelling	−0.276**
Punctuation	−0.184

n = 108; ** p < .01

3.2 Analysis by language group

Owing to the small number and skewed distribution of high-scoring scripts available, analysis by candidates' language group has been carried out only on low-scoring scripts, 47 of which were by Greek L1 candidates and 45 by Chinese L1 candidates. Although Greek L1 candidates tended to make slightly fewer errors, these differences were generally not significant

Figure 7.5 Frequency of errors (per 100 words) in Greek L1 and Chinese L1 scripts

	Word count	Spelling	Punctuation	Grammar	Prepositions	Lexis	Overall
Chinese L1 n=45							
Average	271.62	1.82	1.27	8.91	1.20	3.55	16.74
SD	50.33	1.24	1.22	3.00	0.69	1.19	4.39
Greek L1 n=47							
Average	260.15	2.60	1.09	6.63	1.37	3.55	15.24
SD	67.19	2.62	1.37	2.64	0.89	1.71	5.66
Significance							
t=		0.93	1.84	−0.65	−3.88***	1.07	0.01	−1.43

*$p < .05$; ** $p < .01$; *** $p < .001$

(see Figure 7.5). The only exception to this was in grammar, where Chinese L1 candidates averaged 8.9 errors every 100 words, compared with 6.6 for Greek L1 candidates. This difference was highly significant ($p < .001$), but was sufficiently balanced in other categories for there to be no significant difference in overall error frequency. The calculations were repeated with preposition errors included in the grammar category but, although this combined category produced a less significant difference, the probability of a chance result was still lower than 1%.

3.3 Analysis by test version

The scripts represented two different versions of the test, with 45 scripts relating to Version A, and 47 relating to Version B. Parallel versions of the test should be equally reliable, so we would not expect to find significant differences in the results. As Figure 7.6 indicates, the results were generally comparable, but there were significant differences in two categories, with Version B producing slightly more preposition errors, and slightly fewer errors of lexis/idiom ($p < .05$). It is possible that the nature of the topic could lead to variations in the type of writing demanded of students, or to variations in the application of the classification system.

3.4 Analysis of error categories

As Figure 7.7 shows, grammar errors were by far the most frequent of the five categories, accounting for half of all errors in low-scoring scripts.

The picture changes dramatically, however, with high-scoring scripts, where lexis/idiom errors become almost as frequent as grammar errors, each accounting for just over a third of all errors (see Figure 7.8). While this sug-

Figure 7.6   Frequency of errors (per 100 words) in test Versions A and B

	Word count	Spelling	Punctuation	Grammar	Prepositions	Lexis	Overall
Version A n=45							
Average	272.04	2.51	1.43	7.69	1.10	3.91	16.64
SD	67.11	2.60	1.64	3.49	0.64	1.44	6.22
Version B n=47							
Average	259.74	1.93	0.93	7.80	1.46	3.20	15.33
SD	51.18	1.41	0.80	2.56	0.89	1.43	3.71
Significance							
t =	0.99	1.34	1.84	−0.170	−2.28*	2.38*	1.24

$* p < .05; ** p < .01; *** p < .001$

Figure 7.7 Proportion of errors in low-scoring scripts, by category

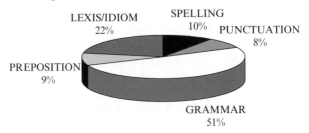

Figure 7.8 Proportion of errors in high-scoring scripts, by category

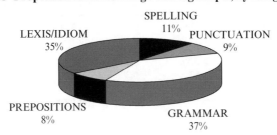

gests that grammar is less obtrusive in higher level scripts, with lexical and stylistic choices becoming more discriminative, the small sample size for Band 8
makes any conclusions tentative.

The relationship between different categories of error was examined using
Pearson product-moment correlation. The results for the 92 low-scoring
scripts show significant correlations between grammar and punctuation,
grammar and prepositions, and grammar and lexis/idiom (see Figure 7.9).
Spelling did not correlate with other types of error. Not surprisingly, all categories were strongly correlated with the overall total, and grammar, which
accounted for half of all errors, showed the strongest correlation.

Figure 7.9 Correlation of error frequency between categories for low-scoring scripts

n=92	Spelling	Punctuation	Grammar	Prepositions	Lexis/idiom	Total
Spelling		0.141	0.035	0.104	−0.023	0.383**
Punctuation	0.141		0.401**	0.125	0.146	0.588**
Grammar	0.035	0.401**		0.272**	0.235*	0.832**
Prepositions	0.104	0.125	0.272**		0.164	0.445**
Lexis/idiom	−0.023	0.146	0.235*	0.164		0.512**
Total	0.383**	0.588**	0.832**	0.445**	0.512**	

$* p < .05; ** p < .01$

There are striking differences, however, in high-scoring scripts, where there were no significant positive correlations between error categories, and both spelling and punctuation were negatively correlated with other categories and with the overall total (see Figure 7.10). Although only one of these negative correlations reached the 5% significance level, the result is still surprising, suggesting that candidates who made more errors in spelling and punctuation tended to make fewer errors in grammar, prepositions and lexis/idiom.

Figure 7.10 Correlation of error frequency between categories for high-scoring scripts

n=16	Spelling	Punctuation	Grammar	Prepositions	Lexis/idiom	Total
Spelling		−0.117	−0.420	−0.320	−0.472*	−0.358
Punctuation	−0.117		−0.197	−0.100	−0.313	−0.114
Grammar	−0.420	−0.197		0.167	0.306	0.828**
Prepositions	−0.320	−0.100	0.167		0.319	0.402
Lexis/idiom	−0.472*	−0.313	0.306	0.319		0.655**
Total	−0.358	−0.114	0.828**	0.402	0.655**	

$* p < .05; ** p < .01$

One possible interpretation is that spelling and punctuation, as relatively mechanical features, contribute little to the construction of meaning in a text at the production stage. This view also suggests a link with the reduced proportion of grammar errors in high-scoring scripts. Higher-level writers generally have a greater degree of control over the mechanical aspects of writing, including spelling, punctuation, and basic grammatical patterns. At this level, therefore, mechanical errors become less significant to the writer, yielding place to those aspects of composition which involve semantic and stylistic choices. Given the small sample size of high-scoring scripts, however, these conclusions must remain speculative.

3.5 Summary of findings from error analysis

The results of this analysis can be summarised as follows.

In relation to task score

- High-scoring scripts were significantly longer than low-scoring scripts; word count was therefore strongly correlated with task score.
- High-scoring scripts had significantly fewer errors overall than low-scoring scripts; overall errors were therefore a good predictor of task score.
- Grammar errors were the most frequent in low-scoring scripts, accounting for about half of all errors.
- Errors in grammar and lexis/idiom were the most frequent in high-scoring scripts, each accounting for about one third of all errors.

In relation to language group

- There was no significant overall difference between the error rate in Chinese L1 and Greek L1 scripts.
- However, low-scoring Chinese L1 scripts had significantly more grammatical errors than comparable Greek L1 scripts.

In relation to test version

- Error frequency in different categories was comparable across the two versions of the test with the exception of prepositions and lexis/idiom, which may reflect the different demands of the controversial propositions within the task prompt.

As noted in our discussion of the problems associated with error analysis (see Appendix 7.1), it is often not one particular error that is notable, but rather constellations of error. This finding is also pertinent to other analyses and to the combination of linguistic variables that make up texts.

4 Sentence structure

In order to investigate sentence structure in IELTS scripts, we carried out a quantitative analysis of the full data set, followed by a qualitative analysis of a subset of 16 scripts.

For the quantitative analysis we needed a measure of sentence complexity that could be coded and quantified relatively unambiguously. We decided to focus on candidates' use of embedded or dependent clauses. An initial scan of a small sample of scripts had suggested that, in some cases at least, high-scoring scripts made greater use of complex sentence structures that included one or more dependent clauses. Furthermore, complex embedding is often regarded as a 'higher order' linguistic skill, taught and learnt later in the language learning process. We might expect candidates with less confidence in English to 'play safe' – for instance, using a higher proportion of sentences that consist simply of an independent (or main) clause. Our follow-up qualitative analysis allowed us to focus in greater detail on a smaller set of scripts in an attempt to identify further aspects of sentence structure that might be associated with candidates' task score.

4.1 Quantitative analysis: independent and dependent clauses

We took as our unit of analysis the 't-unit', or clause complex: i.e. an independent clause along with any dependent clauses. While t-units may coincide with sentence boundaries, as marked by punctuation, they need not necessarily do so. In IELTS scripts punctuation is not used consistently across (or sometimes within) scripts, and candidates also make errors in punctuation (see discussion of punctuation errors in Section 3). Because t-units are based on clauses, they may be identified independently of punctuation, and this made them particularly appropriate to our analysis.

We adopted a 'hard' definition of the clause as a structure that contains a finite verb. This was robust enough to allow us to identify clauses relatively unambiguously. Following this definition, the examples below illustrate t-units that consist respectively of an independent clause only, an independent clause plus one (finite) dependent clause, and an independent clause plus two (finite) dependent clauses:

> We are living in a period of change.
>
> Everyday it is highly debatable if the quality of our lives is changing.
>
> When somebody realises that his life does not satisfy him it is his duty to re-estimate the value of life . . .   (all from GR/A/8/204)

We should note at this point that this is a highly restrictive definition. 'Non-finite' clauses (e.g. *to* or *-ing* forms; 'elliptical' forms) would not be counted separately as clauses within this analysis. So, examples such as the following would be excluded from the analysis:

> Moreover, some other countries, less powerful than the above, like China, India or Mexico are willing to participate in such researches, *ignoring their own internal unresolved problems.*   (GR/B/7/501)
>
> *. . . in order to follow these changes,* people are expected to do more in a shorter time period.
>
> This is a good reason *for complaining about the lack of time.*
>   (GR/A/8/202)

We return to this issue below in Section 4.2.

4.1.1 Findings from quantitative analysis

Figure 7.11 shows the distribution of different types of t-unit within our data. It distinguishes between scripts from Greek L1 and Chinese L1 candidates, between different test versions and between different task scores, indicating the mean percentage within each group for the use of different t-unit types. Types of t-unit are:

Single clause	t-unit that consists of a single, independent clause
2+ clauses	t-unit consisting of an independent clause plus one or more dependent clauses
3+ clauses	t-unit consisting of an independent clause plus two or more dependent clauses (i.e. a subset of '2+ clauses').

Figure 7.11 shows that the distribution of t-unit types is uneven across groups of candidates. There are some differences in the use of dependent clauses between high- and low-scoring candidates; between candidates from different language groups; and between different test versions. In order to assess the statistical significance of these differences we used two-way factorial analyses of variance. The first analysis took the percentage of t-units with one or more dependent clauses (i.e. '2+ clauses') as the dependent variable. The dependent variable in the second analysis was the percentage of t-units consisting of clauses with two or more dependent clauses (i.e. '3+ clauses'). In each analysis the independent variables were task score (high- versus low-scoring), language group, and test version.

Figure 7.11 Mean percentages of different t-unit types in Greek L1 and Chinese L1 high- and low-scoring scripts, in test Versions A and B (standard deviations are given in brackets)

Language group	Test version	Task score	Single clause	2+ clauses	3+ clauses
Chinese L1	A	High-scoring	59.03 (13.37)	40.96 (13.27)	12.52 (11.38)
		Low-scoring	65.00 (15.99)	35.01 (15.99)	10.69 (8.72)
	B	High-scoring	54.47 (12.62)	45.53 (12.62)	15.02 (8.80)
		Low-scoring	61.06 (10.37)	38.94 (10.37)	10.65 (6.52)
Greek L1	A	High-scoring	52.43 (15.21)	47.57 (15.21)	18.49 (10.13)
		Low-scoring	54.85 (13.49)	45.15 (13.49)	13.98 (11.85)
	B	High-scoring	42.26 (12.09)	57.74 (12.09)	21.23 (9.70)
		Low-scoring	37.33 (13.91)	62.67 (13.91)	25.25 (13.49)

The results for percentage of t-units with one or more dependent clauses show statistically significant effects for language group (p < .001); test version (p < .001); and the interaction between language group and test version (p < .05). The effect of task score was not significant. The interaction between language group and task score was close to statistical significance.

The statistically significant effect of language group derives from the fact that Greek L1 candidates tended to use a greater percentage of t-units containing at least one dependent clause than did Chinese L1 candidates. Figure 7.11 shows that this is a consistent pattern that operates within each test version and among both high- and low-scoring candidates. The test version effect comes about because Version B elicited a greater percentage of t-units consisting of at least one dependent clause than Version A. Figure 7.11 shows that this pattern operates within each language group and among both high- and low-scoring candidates. This tendency was, however, more pronounced with Greek L1 candidates than with Chinese L1 candidates, giving rise to the significant interaction between language and test version referred to above. This pattern is illustrated in Figure 7.12.

Figure 7.12 Use of t-units containing at least one dependent clause by Chinese L1 and Greek L1 candidates on test Versions A and B

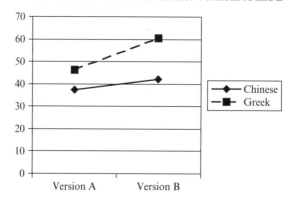

The interaction between language and task score, although not statistically significant, is noteworthy. In line with our prediction, high-scoring Chinese L1 candidates used a greater percentage of t-units containing at least one dependent clause than did low-scoring Chinese L1 candidates (43.4% and 36.9% respectively). However, the reverse was the case for Greek L1 candidates. In fact, overall, low-scoring Greek L1 candidates' use of dependent clauses was slightly higher than that of high-scoring candidates (53.9% as opposed to 52.2%). This is illustrated in Figure 7.13 below. T-tests revealed that the difference between high- and low-scoring Chinese L1 candidates was statistically significant (t = 2.32, df = 90, p < .05). By contrast,

Figure 7.13 Use of t-units containing at least one dependent clause by Chinese L1 and Greek L1 candidates with high and low task scores

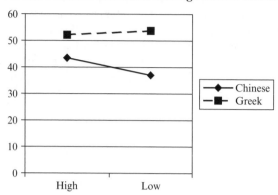

the difference between high- and low-scoring Greek L1 candidates was not significant.

These general patterns were mirrored, although in a weaker form, in candidates' use of t-units with two or more dependent clauses. Our analysis of the distribution of these showed statistically significant effects for language group ($p < .001$); and for test version ($p < .01$). There were no other statistically significant effects, although the interaction between language group and test version was close to statistical significance.

4.1.2 Summary of findings on sentence structure

Sentence structure in relation to task score

These results offer only partial support for our hypothesis that complexity in sentence structure (at least insofar as use of finite dependent clauses is an indicator of this) is positively associated with task score. This association holds for Chinese L1, but not for Greek L1 candidates. The results do suggest, however, that a candidate's language background, and the particular version of the test taken, may affect their choice of sentence structures. The reasons for this are by no means clear, but we offer some speculative suggestions below.

Sentence structure in relation to language group

It is possible that the tendency towards parataxis in Chinese (in which relations between clauses need not always be explicitly expressed) may contribute towards Chinese L1 candidates' lower use of dependent clauses in English. It is also possible that certain teaching practices (e.g. teaching sentence structure in a relatively decontextualised manner) may leave some Chinese L1 candidates uncertain about the use of dependent clauses in particular contexts. (We are grateful to Xiao Junhong from Shantou Radio and Television University for these suggestions.)

Sentence structure in relation to test version

Our analysis showed that Version B was associated with greater use of t-units that included dependent clauses; and that this effect was greater for Greek L1 than for Chinese L1 candidates. As in the case of influences from candidates' language backgrounds, the relationship here is probably between the test and the particular measure of complexity we adopted, i.e. certain factors associated with the test may have encouraged greater use of dependent clauses. Test factors may include:

- the topic candidates had to write about; however it is not clear to us why space exploration (Version B) should encourage greater use of dependent clauses than the pace of modern life (Version A). Furthermore, scrutiny of test scripts did not suggest the prevalence of any particular structures (e.g. if . . . then structures) that might be associated with one topic rather than another
- the wording of the specific test question or prompt
- structures used in any practice tests on similar topics that candidates have access to
- factors related to candidates' geographical location rather than to the topic of the test – e.g. the Greek L1 candidates who attended centres where test Version B was used may have had access to resources/support material that encouraged the use of dependent clauses.

There are no doubt other possible factors. However, while there does seem to have been a test effect, it is not immediately clear which factors (or which combination of factors) influenced candidates' use of different types of t-units.

Our discussion so far suggests that the relationship between candidates' use of dependent clauses and their task score is far from straightforward. Also relevant is the degree of variability within each cell. For instance, although there is a significant difference between high- and low-scoring Chinese L1 candidates' use of dependent clauses, with high-scoring candidates making greater use of these, some Chinese L1 candidates obtain high scores with only limited use of dependent clauses and some Chinese L1 candidates obtain low scores despite a relatively high use.

4.2 Qualitative analysis

In order to examine more closely candidates' use of aspects of sentence structure that might be associated with a high or low task score, we decided to focus on a subset of 16 scripts. We selected, from each cell, two scripts with a high and low (usually the highest and lowest) percentage of t-units containing dependent clauses. Our sample of scripts is set out in Figure 7.14.

Figure 7.14 Sample of scripts used for qualitative analysis of sentence structure

IELTS test version/task score	Chinese L1 candidates		Greek L1 candidates	
	Greater use of dependent clauses	Lesser use of dependent clauses	Greater use of dependent clauses	Lesser use of dependent clauses
Version A high-scoring	CH/A/8/298	CH/A/7/281	GR/A/7/218	GR/A/8/250
Version A low-scoring	CH/A/5/132	CH/A/5/102	GR/A/5/055	GR/A/5/059
Version B high-scoring	CH/B/7/256	CH/B/7/253	GR/B/7/506	GR/B/7/547
Version B low-scoring	CH/B/5/018	CH/B/5/025	GR/B/5/165	GR/B/5/160

Because our analysis was exploratory and involved only a small number of scripts it was open-ended and qualitative. Within this sample of scripts, we looked first at clause length (number of words per clause) since this seemed (impressionistically) to vary between scripts. In this sample, scripts that obtained a high task score had a slightly higher mean clause length than low-scoring scripts (10.3 as opposed to 9.0). Within each script pair (i.e. scripts in each cell with greater and lesser use of subordination), the script with less sub-ordination usually had a higher mean clause length, though differences were not always great. Clause length is clearly not a measure of complexity, but it may serve as an indirect indicator of features other than finite dependent clauses (such as degree of modification, non-finite clauses and similar structures) that, in combination, contribute to an impression of greater complexity.

We also looked at the range of clause types used in each script. High-scoring scripts in particular often used a wide variety of dependent clauses, and they sometimes used relatively complex forms of embedding, as in the following constructions from a Chinese L1 script:

> In analysing whether the complaint that people nowadays never have enough time is valid . . .
> It is submitted that while technological advances have saved much time for people, working hours and the amount of work to be done has likely surpassed any time saved by technological advances.
>
> (CH/A/8/298)

Scripts often made effective use of non-finite clauses and similar structures. Examples from one Greek L1 and one Chinese L1 script include:

> To catch up with the fast-evolving, information-booming world, we are required to be more competative, to learn more and keep updated continuously.

[. . .]

In order to meet their requirement, you have to increase your competitiveness by acquiring more useful skills and knowledge, and you often have to work overtime to meet the deadlines.

(both from CH/A/7/281)

The introduction of technology has considerably fascilitated life by satisfying certain needs . . .

[. . .]

As a result of this hard competition, people often complain of being always under pressure.   (both from GR/A/8/250)

With this last example, contrast the following from its 'partner' script that showed a high use of dependent clauses:

Nowadays, people complain that they are constantly under pressure . . .

(GR/A/7/218)

Many scripts made effective use of nominalisation. While this is a device frequently associated with academic writing in English, it may reduce the number of embedded clauses in a text. Examples in our data (from a Greek L1 and a Chinese L1 script) include:

In my opinion the exploration of space is very important.

(GR/B/7/547)

So the utilization of resources and the financial support are necessary and important.

[. . .]

As aside, the achievements made from space research and exploration will give a great many advantages to human being.

(both from CH/B/7/253)

In low-scoring scripts, the use of dependent clauses may be associated with errors. In some cases it is possible that attempts to use relatively complex structures may lead to errors, with candidates 'over-reaching' themselves. The Chinese L1 script below provides examples:

Furthermore, the past people who had relaxed lives but they couldn't earn more money . . .

[. . .]

If you want to be a past year people so that you can only earn a little money on your life and no competition in the society.   (CH/A/5/132)

Finally, as we discussed in Section 3, low-scoring scripts contain a large number of errors at different linguistic levels. A high – and even effective – use of embedded clauses would be unlikely to 'rescue' such scripts.

Our qualitative scrutiny of scripts suggests that a wide range of grammatical features may be associated with task score. High-scoring candidates may demonstrate effective use of English by drawing on different combinations of grammatical structures. The grammatical structures drawn on may vary between groups of candidates and between individual candidates: they are not always predictable. Similarly, markers are likely to respond to sentence structure in an impressionistic (and complex) way, so that any one of a number of features may count towards candidates' eventual grades. Other factors will also be important. For instance, grammatical, spelling and other errors are likely to be highly salient: they may obscure candidates' attempts to use complex sentence structures, so that these go unrecognised by markers.

5 Argument structure: sentence-level features

Having looked at aspects of what we have described as formal features in the corpus of IELTS scripts, we now turn to analyses that are broadly functional and concerned, in various ways, with candidates' construction of an academic argument. Argument is a useful focus for analysis because of its salience in IELTS tasks. Candidates are explicitly asked in Academic Writing Task 2 to 'present a written argument', and published guidance on IELTS tends to foreground argument (alongside correct grammar, etc.) in providing advice and practice exercises for candidates (e.g. de Witt 1997, Garbutt and O'Sullivan 1996, Hopkins and Nettle 1998, Jakeman and McDowell 1996). In the remaining sections of this chapter we look at the significance of the beginning of the clause and paragraph for framing candidates' arguments, at a broader classification of argument types, at the role of pronouns in anchoring those arguments in the writer's own perspective, and finally at the role of commands and questions in establishing a relationship with the reader. We start with an outline of the functions that can be fulfilled by the beginning of the clause.

5.1 Analytical framework

Functional analysis of the beginning of the clause has used the term Theme to refer to initial elements and Rheme to refer to the rest of the clause (Halliday 1994). The significance of Theme lies in its central role in creating coherence throughout a text and in presenting the writer's 'angle' on what comes in the Rheme. This can be observed in the example below (where Themes are italicised):

> *The pollution, the change of climate all* push us the change the situation. *Maybe one day all these problems* will be solved as a result of space research successful. (CH/B/5/006)

In the second sentence we can see that the writer by using 'Maybe one day' is expressing a level of doubt about the positive outcomes of space research, in other words setting up his or her angle on the message. Secondly, 'all these problems' serves to link the second sentence back to the first where two of the problems are noted. An analysis of Theme therefore allows us to investigate the function and complexity of information being encoded in this slot as possibly indicative of patterning across the scripts as a whole and also to allow comparisons with similar analyses of other corpora.

5.2 Analysing Theme

The concept of Theme used here comes from within the tradition of systemic functional linguistics (SFL). Within this tradition, the variety of messages that texts can convey are grouped into a tripartite system of functions. The first function conveys information about content (the ideational function), the second about relationships (the interpersonal function) and the third about how items within the text are to be interpreted in context to convey a coherent message (the textual function). Within the Theme, the first part of a clause, there will always be some element of content meaning and in addition there may be interpersonal and textual meanings as well. This allows varying degrees of complexity to be expressed.

Themes can be either *simple*, containing only a content element (topical Theme), often a noun phrase, for example:

> *This image* is contrasted to the old model of carefree individuals enjoying relaxed lives. (GR/A/8/203)

or they may be *complex*, including information from two or more of the functions. In the following example, the sentence opens with a marker of the argument in the text (textual Theme) before moving on to the topical Theme. (Different types of Theme are divided by '/'.)

> *On the other hand, / the rythm of life in big centre* has become extremely rapid. (GR/A/8/208)

At its most complex, Theme can include interpersonal, textual and ideational (topical) components as in the example below:

Furthermore,	I believe that	there	is another important reason in favor of the establish-ment of human colonies in space, which is totally realistic.
textual	interpersonal	ideational (topical)	
Theme			Rheme (GR/B/8/509)

Themes can also be classified according to whether they are *unmarked*, that is, the elements are in the most expected positions, or *marked* where, for example, information about a circumstance such as time or location is fore-grounded as in the next example:

> *Especially in Greece*, long wars covered the first half of the 20th century.
> (GR/A/8/208)

Manipulation of marked and unmarked Themes and simple and complex Themes allows writers to build greater cohesion into their text structure and to signal the development of their own viewpoint. This brings us to the second facet of Theme analysis.

Theme is an organising device which signals the method of development of a text. A variety of patterns of thematic development have been identified. At their simplest, Themes may be repetitive showing a constant Theme pattern:

> *Some people* support on this while others think that it is unrealistic to spend our resources on space research and exploration. *Some people* think that more money should be spent on space research and exploration. (CH/B/8/212)

> *Education* helps people cope with the problems of everyday life. *Education* is what stays when what has been learnt is forgotten. *Education* helps people resist to the challenges of our material world and under-stand the true meaning of life. (GR/A/8/204)

Commonly, Themes link back to previous Rhemes:

> So, *children and adolescents* are actually spending most of their time being at schools, attending classes, learning foreign languages and gen-erally doing nothing else but studying. *This* is due to an increased demand for qualifications set by the potential employer.
> (GR/A/8/206)

This patterning between Themes and Rhemes also occurs at paragraph and whole text level. These wider thematic organising devices are discussed in Section 6.1.

5.3 Theme analysis findings

The 186 essays in the full set ranged in length from 93 to 667 words. The unit of analysis was the t-unit (independently conjoined clause complex). The overall average number of t-units per essay was 19.7, and the range was from 4 to 44. Pearson product-moment correlation coefficients were calculated between types of Theme and other variables, including task score.

5.3.1 Analysis by task score

In Figure 7.15 and the following tables, the different combinations of elements in Theme are shown. Simple topical Theme (To), where Theme and subject are the same, is the most common while a marked Theme (M) preceded by a textual (T) and interpersonal (I) Theme is the least common. This is in line with other studies of Theme (Fries 1994, Ghadessy 1999).

The results comparing the different bands show no statistically significant results. However, they demonstrate the pattern of overall Theme choice across the whole corpus. We can see that the majority of Themes are unmarked ideational Themes, where all or part of the Theme is the same as the subject of the clause as in the following examples.

Figure 7.15 Comparison of Theme choices in low- and high-scoring scripts

		To	M	T/To	T/M	I/To	I/M	T/I/To	T/I/M
High-scoring (n=86 t-units 20.38)	Average instances*	7.99	3.79	4.98	0.85	1.62	0.26	0.83	0.06
	% of total Themes**	39.21	18.61	24.43	4.17	7.95	1.30	4.06	0.28
Low-scoring (n=100 t-units 19.13)	Average instances*	7.60	3.29	4.81	0.96	1.48	0.36	0.55	0.08
	% of total Themes**	39.73	17.05	25.14	5.02	7.74	1.88	2.88	0.42

Notes:
To: topical Theme
M: marked Theme
T: textual Theme
I: interpersonal Theme
* Average instances refers to the numbers of Theme types and combinations within each sub-sample.
** In order to provide a standard point of comparison the average figures were calculated as percentages of the total number of Themes in each sub-sample.

> *The adults* also face more competition, including continue education and
> employment. (CH/A/5/143)

> *So* / *he* could only take a leisure journey. (CH/A/5/142)

> *In my opinion,* / *I* would like to have some pressure because it can make
> you more energetic sometimes, and even stimulate your potential energy.
> (CH/A/5/144)

In the first example above, the Theme is simply the sentence subject; it supplies the information on what the message of the clause is about. In the second, preceding the ideational Theme, *he*, there is a textual Theme, *so*, which indicates a logical connection with what has gone before in the text. In the final example, we see an interpersonal Theme preceding the ideational Theme, *I*. The interpersonal Theme serves to strengthen the focus on the writer and highlight the message as personal.

Marked Themes are, as would be expected, less common overall, accounting for around 24–25% of Themes in the corpus as a whole. Typically these consist of references to time, place or manner (as in the first example below), sometimes premodified by a textual (as in the second example) or interpersonal Theme.

> *In the 60's*, the conquer of space was presented as one of the most biggest
> efforts of human beings. (GR/B/8/510)

> *But,* / *in small cities and villages* people don't face this problem.
> (GR/A/5/051)

Of interest is the relatively high number of multiple Themes, that is where two or more types of Theme are used together. For both bands, slightly over 42% of Themes are of this type. This compares with a study by Ghadessy (1999:134), which found 40.5% for academic prose and 25.5% in biographies. Use of multiple Theme demonstrates an awareness of the resources available at the start of the clause and a willingness to exploit them. Its significance in this corpus is discussed further in Section 5.4 below.

5.3.2 Analysis by language group

Scripts were grouped and compared on the basis of Theme choices made by candidates from each first language group (see Figure 7.16). Three areas showed significant correlations at the $p = <.01$ level. The first of these was the number of t-units used by the different groups of candidates. On average, Chinese L1 candidates' scripts contained more clauses and therefore Themes. The distribution of these Themes differed significantly from the

Figure 7.16 Comparison of Theme choices in Chinese L1 and Greek L1 scripts

		To	M	T/To	T/M	I/To	I/M	T/I/To	T/I/M
Chinese L1 (n=90 t-units 21.21)	Average instances	8.30	4.20	5.04	0.89	1.89	0.29	0.48	0.07
	% of total Themes	39.27	19.90	23.76	4.20	8.91	1.35	2.28	0.31
Greek L1 (n=96 t-units 18.29)	Average instances	7.23	2.90	4.73	0.09	1.22	0.34	0.86	0.07
	% of total Themes	39.53	15.86	25.86	5.07	6.66	1.88	4.73	0.40

Themes in Greek L1 scripts in two categories. The Chinese L1 candidates used more single Themes, marked and unmarked, than Greek L1 candidates; that is, they had fewer preceding textual and interpersonal Themes. They were, therefore, using fewer overt cohesive ties such as 'therefore', 'so', 'and', and so on. In addition, they showed less interpersonal marking at the beginning of clauses. Overall, therefore, Chinese L1 candidates were exploiting the varied possibilities of the beginning of the clause in terms of Theme categories less than Greek L1 candidates. In contrast, however, they made greater use of marked Themes (as in the examples below). This shows a tendency to use time and place markers and conditionals to organise texts.

> *In these 30 years*, we see more and more money and resources has been spent on space research and exploration for investigating the possibility of establishing human colonies in space for the future.   (CH/B/7/271)

> *If the amount of money used for space development in the US are diverted to fighting against poverty*, the whole Africa can be benefited.
> (CH/B/7/252)

It should be noted in this description of Theme choices that the personal pronouns 'I' and 'we', which may occur as a simple ideational Theme, would not count as interpersonal, despite their use in this type of text being mainly to signal attitude towards the content or the reader. This is a function of the Theme categorisation used and, therefore, to make sure that the significance of these pronouns was not ignored, they were analysed separately (see Section 7.1).

5.3.3 Analysis by test version

In terms of Theme choices, there is little overall variation between the two test versions (see Figure 7.17). The only area of noticeable difference is in the use of interpersonal Theme which is higher in test Version B. If all uses are combined, 14.99% of clauses use interpersonal Theme in Version B as opposed to 11.70% in Version A. More of these occur in the Greek L1 scripts than in the Chinese L1 scripts.

Figure 7.17 Comparison of Theme choices in test Versions A and B

		To	M	T/To	T/M	I/To	I/M	T/I/To	T/I/M
Version A (n = 94 t-units 20.90)	Average instances	8.53	3.74	5.23	0.96	1.37	0.40	0.59	0.09
	% of total Themes	40.81	17.89	25.02	4.58	6.56	1.93	2.80	0.41
Version B (n = 93 t-units 18.51)	Average instances	6.98	3.33	4.56	0.86	1.72	0.23	0.77	0.05
	% of total Themes	37.71	17.99	24.63	4.65	9.30	1.22	4.18	0.29

> *Maybe / there* is life in other planets. (GR/B/5/152)

> *It is now believed that / all this* should be stop. (GR/B/5/153)

Some, as in the first example above, are the result of probability markers. The test prompt on space exploration encourages speculation and therefore such markers are more likely. In addition, phrases such as 'In my opinion', 'I think' and empty *it*-clauses, as in the second example above, all show a greater degree of interpersonal involvement in arguing a case. This may well reflect the advice the students are given when preparing for the test. A number of books of guidance (e.g. de Witt 1997, Garbutt and O'Sullivan 1996, Hopkins and Nettle 1998, Jakeman and McDowell 1996) stress the importance of expressing a clear opinion and explicitly teach phrases such as *In my view . . ., I think . . .* This concern with developing an argument is explored further in Section 6, in discussing the writer's involvement or angle on the message as it relates to Theme and discourse organisation.

5.4 Discussion of findings from Theme analysis

Before moving on to the wider implications and applications of the notion of Theme, it is useful to see how the IELTS scripts compared with other similar studies. In addition to the comparisons made between Theme choices in different bands, language groups and test versions, Theme as a whole in the IELTS scripts was compared to two other similar studies (Figure 7.18): a corpus of academic prose analysed by Ghadessy (1999) and a corpus of undergraduate geography essays analysed by Hewings (1999a and b). Different coding conventions have meant that in order to make valid comparisons the data has been reduced to two categories. Simple Theme is any Theme, either marked or unmarked which occurs without any preceding textual or interpersonal Theme. Multiple Theme, as its name implies, always consists of at least two elements one of which is textual or interpersonal Theme.

Figure 7.18 Comparison of major Theme categories with other research corpora

Corpora	Simple theme	Multiple Theme
IELTS	56.32	41.99
Undergraduate essays	76.58	24.42
Academic prose	59.50	40.50

The statistics for the IELTS scripts described here showed a higher use of multiple Theme than either of the two other corpora. The difference is most noticeable between the undergraduate student essays and the IELTS scripts. From the point of view of Theme choice and exploitation of Theme position, IELTS candidates were closer to published academic writing than student writing. This may be the result of the test preparation that many have received. It seems likely, on the basis of published materials, that students are taught to overtly signal coherence and argumentation. This may account for why they are actually using it even more than any of the norms for native speaker writing would suggest.

Theme in relation to task score

There was little overall difference in the Theme choices of the high and low-scoring scripts with unmarked simple topical Theme being the most common starting point. The overall proportion of multiple Theme was also similar across the different bands.

Theme in relation to language group

Significant differences were noted between Chinese L1 speakers and Greek L1 speakers. Chinese L1 scripts contained more t-units and therefore more Themes. The Chinese L1 scripts contained more single Themes (that is, not multiple Themes) and also more marked Themes. Greek L1 scripts contained more interpersonal Themes (but see also Section 7.1 below).

Theme in relation to test version

There was little overall variation between test versions with the exception of a slight increase in the use of interpersonal Theme in Version B which was attributed to the more speculative nature of the prompt.

To summarise, the analysis of Theme has demonstrated a level of sophistication in the use of the beginning of the clause by all groups of IELTS students. They use a high proportion of multiple Themes and, particularly the Chinese L1 students, a lot of marked Theme. This allows writers to give overt signals of coherence (textual Theme), comment (interpersonal Theme) and alternative starting points for the clause (marked Theme). In addition to these overall findings, there were some significant inter-corpus variations, most notably in the use of multiple and marked Themes. The Chinese L1 group used less multiple Theme but more marked Theme than Greek L1 students. Thematic analysis across the corpus also showed a relatively high level of interpersonal Theme use.

6 Argument structure: discourse-level features

6.1 Theme and discourse organisation

The generic IELTS test prompt (*Present a written argument or case . . . To what extent do you agree or disagree. . . .?*) was a starting point for the analysis of argument structure at discourse level. In addition, the findings on the frequent use of multiple Theme indicated the use of rhetorical structuring within the corpus as a whole. The initial investigation of discourse organisation is based on an extension of the notion of Theme to paragraph and whole text level which begins to shed light on the organisation of the essays as argumentative texts. This is followed by a categorisation of scripts into different argumentative genres.

Martin (1992:453–6) discusses the opening generalisations commonly found at the beginning of paragraphs as hyper-Themes. Traditionally, in pedagogic contexts, these have been referred to as topic sentences. In addition, the final sentence or sentences of a paragraph often pull together or summarise information built up in the rest of the paragraph. Martin refers to these as the hyper-New. When considering whole discourse organisation they are referred to as macro-Theme and macro-New. The classification for different text levels is given in Figure 7.19.

Figure 7.19 Theme terminology at different text levels

	Clause	Paragraph	Whole text
First element	Theme	Hyper-Theme	Macro-Theme
Final element	Rheme	Hyper-New	Macro-New

6.1.1 Qualitative findings

Analysis of such wider text organisational features is not amenable to statistical analysis in the same way as Theme choice in clauses. What we report below is based on a qualitative view of the corpus and identifies examples of hyper-Theme and hyper-New used to signal writer viewpoint and discourse organisation.

Qualitative analysis of the scripts identified more coherent use of hyper-Theme and hyper-New in high-scoring scripts. As noted in the discussion on errors, it is likely to be aspects affecting the whole text that markers are reflecting when they award marks to particular scripts. Thus, signals of argumentation or organisation at levels higher than the clause are valuable.

Example A shows the penultimate and final paragraphs of an essay, paragraphs 4 and 5. At the beginning of paragraph 4 there is an example of hyper-Theme with the writer indicating the subject matter of the paragraph – establishing human colonies in space. At the close of paragraph 5, we see a final concluding sentence, which not only pulls together and summarises, but also makes prominent the writer's own personal stance (*I very much hope . . .*). (Hyper-Theme and hyper-New are in italics.)

Example A

Secondly, I would like to throw some light on idea that establishing human colonies in space is unrealistic. Up to this present moment, no one can tell the research result (hyper-Theme). It is not substantial to abandon the programmes now. People have always said 'What can be imagined can be achieved'. Imagine for how many times of failure Addison experienced before he invented light bulbs. I think we should allow time for the research since outer space is a new subject and the research has only been going on for 30 years.

We must not forget if it comes to the time when the food is not edible or the water is not drinkable on Earth than we do research, the comment will be very simple. It is really too late. *I very much hope that this article help clarify some of the sceptical views on outer space research and funding* (hyper-New). (CH/B/7/271)

Such a pattern of hyper-Theme and hyper-New is not unique to this essay. Other high-scoring texts employ similar patterns, with authorial viewpoints being frequently made salient through their strategic location in the overall structure of the argument. Such a texturing of authorial stance serves to inject a strong subjective orientation – both prospectively and retrospectively – to the unfolding arguments and evidence. The following skeleton essays, all high-scoring, provide further illustration. (The extracts from the essays are labelled hyper-Theme, hyper-New and so on, and in addition, the overt markers of interpersonal angle or argument are in italics. Ordinary clause Themes are not in italics in these examples.)

Example B

In my view, space research and exploration should be encouraged. (hyper-New, end of paragraph 1)

Firstly, space research and exploration is of great importance to human's work and life. (hyper-Theme, beginning of paragraph 2)

From this point of view, space research and exploration is a very important channel. (hyper-New, mid–paragraph 2)

Another reason is that space research and exploration has brought about and will continue to bring about benefit to human kind. (hyper-Theme mid-paragraph 2)

When the theory is applied to practice, it has made great benefit to human, for example, we can utilize the nuclear power to generate electricity. (hyper-New end of paragraph 2)

Secondly, we can not judge that establishing human colonies in space is unrealistic only because this goal seems impossible. (hyper-Theme beginning of paragraph 3)

In my view, establishing human colonies in space is a very challenging idea, it is very possible to be realized, and this will solve the problem that the earth will not undertake the heavy burden of population-exploding. (hyper-New end of paragraph 3)

In conclusion, space research and exploration should be encouraged and establishing human colonies in space is a good idea and it may be realized. (macro-New final paragraph)   (CH/B/7/251)

Example C
The establishing of human colonies in space has created conflict among many people. *I personally believe* that money should be spend on space research and exploration, provided that each state has taken care of certain more important priorities. (hyper-Theme, opening paragraph)

Furthermore, *I believe* that there is another important reason in favor of the establishment of human colonies in space, which is totally realistic. (hyper-Theme, paragraph 2)

Apart from this option, *I strongly believe* that it is our natural charisma to have the willingness to learn new things. (hyper-Theme, mid-paragraph 2)

In concluding my agreement with this opinion I would like to add the fact that money should be spend on space since it constitutes an important aspect of human life and of our world specifically. (macro-New, final paragraph)   (GR/B/8/509)

In Example B, we can see a pattern of organisation outlining and summing up the arguments being made. It also allows us to note where there should arguably have been a new paragraph in paragraph 2 as the sentence is functioning as a hyper-Theme but occurs in the middle of a paragraph. Example C has a similarly signalled organisational pattern, though with less use of hyper-New to round off paragraphs. In this example, the writer makes greater use of personal pronouns to signal opinion and argument (an aspect which is explored further in Section 7.1 below).

The qualitative work reported here concentrated on only high-scoring scripts and demonstrates the level of sophistication of discourse organisation in those scripts examined. Within hyper-Theme and hyper-New the arguments being put forward by students were highlighted often through the use of personal reference. The significance of flagging the essay's argument probably reflects the test prompt and the advice available in published test preparation texts as discussed earlier. The following section pursues the focus on argument through an examination of the different argumentative genres students used.

6.2 Analysis of argument genres

In our analysis of argument genres, scripts were classified according to their precise argumentative purpose and text structure. This was an exploratory analysis, carried out on the subset of 56 scripts (giving us seven scripts per cell) to allow for the greater time needed for this type of qualitative analysis. In identifying and classifying different generic structures we were often working, therefore, with relatively small numbers. We have not carried out any statistical analysis of argument structure, and some of the findings we discuss must be regarded as tentative.

Drawing on the work of Martin and Coffin (see, for example, Martin 1989; Coffin 2004, 2006), our analysis of the scripts suggested that candidates organised their texts in four main ways depending on whether they wished to:

- put forward a single point of view (referred to as analytical exposition)
- put forward a single point of view and recommend a course of action (referred to as hortatory exposition)
- consider alternative perspectives prior to reaching an interpretation (referred to as analytical discussion)
- consider alternative perspectives prior to recommending a course of action (referred to as hortatory discussion).

Figure 7.20 outlines the stages that typically make up each of these argument genres.

Example D below is a complete IELTS essay analysed to show the stages that comprise a hortatory exposition.

Example D
[Thesis]
This year marks the 30th anniversary of man landing the moon. In these 30 years, we see more and more money and resources has been spent on space research and exploration for investigating the possibility of establishing human colonies in space for the future.

However, some people think that further funding the research is a waste of resources. This article aims at clarifying some of the views and tries to establish and reiterate the importance of further research on outer space.

[Argument]

First of all, we talk about resources. Resources is said to be misused if the balance of 'supply and demand' is not reached. Most of the researches, if

Figure 7.20 Types of argument genre identified

Genre	Social purpose	Staging
Analytical exposition	To put forward a point of view or argument	(Background) Thesis Arguments + evidence Reinforcement of thesis
Hortatory exposition	To put forward a point of view and recommend a course of action	(Background) Thesis Arguments + evidence Recommendation
Analytical discussion	To argue the case for two or more points of view about an issue	(Background) Issue Arguments/perspectives + Evidence Judgement/Position
Hortatory discussion	To argue the case for two or more points of view about an issue and recommend a course of action	(Background) Issue Arguments/perspectives + evidence Recommendation

not all, are being carried out by developed countries which they hold a great bundle of reserves, should it be money, gold or natural resources. Up till now, there is no one report or any evidence to suggest that there are people starved because of the ongoing research. Yet the research has not produced any known environment pollutants that would adversely affect human existence. Those countries only use their 'excess' resources for the research, nevertheless, we must not forget (demand) the researches may lead to new job opportunities or new resources found in outer space or even lead up to human beings being able to emigrate to the outer space in case the Earth is not suitable for human living resulting from increasing environmental pollution problems because of industrialization and modernization. We could say the researches some form of investment, yet we don't know whether we will gain or lose. But we cannot say we are wasting the resources since we are not spending at the expense of others, let alone sacrifice.

[Argument]

Secondly, I would like to throw some light on idea that establishing human colonies in space is unrealistic. Up to this present moment, no one can tell the research result. It is not substantial to abandon the programmes now. People have always said 'What can be imagined can be achieved'. Imagine for how many times of failure Addison experienced before he invented light bulbs. I think we should allow time for the research since outer space is a new subject and the research has only been going on for 30 years.

[Recommendation]

We must not forget if it comes to the time when the food is not edible or the water is not drinkable on Earth than we do research, the comment will be very simple. It is really too late. I very much hope that this article help clarify some of the sceptical views on outer space research and funding.   (CH/B/8/271)

Figure 7.21 indicates how the different types of argument structure identified above were distributed between high- and low-scoring scripts; candidates from different language groups; and candidates taking test Versions A and B.

Figure 7.21 Distribution of argument genres between different groups

Argument genre	Hortatory exposition	Analytical exposition	Hortatory discussion	Analytical discussion	Total exposition/ discussion	Total hortatory/ analytical
All groups	22	18	10	6	40/16	32/24
High-scoring	11	5	6	6	16/12	17/11
Low-scoring	11	13	4	0	24/4	15/13
Chinese L1	9	12	3	4	21/7	12/16
Greek L1	13	6	7	2	19/9	20/8
Version A	12	9	2	5	21/7	14/14
Version B	10	9	8	1	19/9	18/10

These findings suggest the following patterns:

General patterns

- Candidates show an overall preference for expository over discussion argument genres: hortatory expositions are preferred over hortatory discussions; and analytical expositions over analytical discussions.
- Although this is less marked, there is also a preference for hortatory over analytical arguments; this is more pronounced in the case of discussion genres.

In relation to task score

- The preference for expository over discussion argument genres is stronger among low-scoring candidates.
- There is little difference between high- and low-scoring candidates in their preference for hortatory over analytical arguments.

In relation to language group

- There is little difference between Greek L1 and Chinese L1 candidates in their preference for expository over discussion argument genres.

- Greek L1 candidates prefer hortatory arguments, whereas Chinese L1 candidates have a slight preference for analytic arguments.

In relation to test version

- There is little difference between test versions in candidates' preference for expository over analytical genres.
- In Version B there is a greater preference for hortatory arguments than in Version A.

Our analysis also assessed the extent to which candidates' argument structure was complete: 'incomplete' argument structures typically lacked a 'thesis' or an 'issue' stage, or included limited evidence in their 'argument' stage. Of the 56 scripts in our sample, 24 were identified as incomplete. Perhaps not surprisingly, these were concentrated among low-scoring candidates: 21 low-scoring candidates produced incomplete arguments, compared to only three high-scoring candidates. There was however a difference between language groups: whereas all (14/14) low-scoring Greek L1 candidates produced incomplete arguments, only half (7/14) low-scoring Chinese L1 candidates did so. There were no differences between test versions A and B.

While it is not clear what specific guidance is available to candidates in our sample, published IELTS guidance (e.g. de Witt 1997, Garbutt and O'Sullivan 1996, Hopkins and Nettle 1998, Jakeman and McDowell 1996) suggests that candidates are encouraged to evaluate/contrast different positions – so it may seem surprising that candidates produce more expository arguments. However, the advice also emphasises the need to give one's own point of view. It may be that weaker candidates, in particular, are more attracted to this and do not consider different positions. The fact that even high-scoring candidates make slightly greater use of expository genres than discussion genres indicates that, despite the emphasis in published advice on weighing up different positions, it is possible to gain a high task score without following this advice.

Advice to candidates to give their own point of view may also explain the slight preference for hortatory over analytical arguments. Analysis of published academic writing indicates that professional writers are rarely seen to recommend a course of action and that, where they do so in more practice-based disciplines, this is often substantially hedged (Hewings and Hewings 2002). It is analytical arguments that are more usually associated with writing at university level (i.e. analysing and arguing about how the world 'is' rather than recommending how the world 'ought to be' – on this see Martin 1989). Our analysis suggests that, in this respect, IELTS writing may differ from other forms of academic writing. It is not clear to us why Greek L1 candidates should use proportionately more hortatory arguments, or why test Version B should produce more hortatory arguments.

The difference between high- and low-scoring candidates in terms of completeness of their arguments is predictable. While examiners may not consciously award marks according to genre type or organisational structure, they may be predisposed to essays that conform to a clear generic structure. This accords with our overall finding that many aspects of a script are graded holistically rather than analytically.

7 Tenor and interpersonal meaning

The Tenor system in Systemic Functional Linguistics is concerned with the linguistic manifestation of relative status and formality of exchange between writer and reader (referred to as the *negotiation* system), as well as the expression of personal engagement, point of view, etc. (referred to as the *engagement* system). In other words, it aims to describe how language is drawn on as a resource for constructing a dialogic relationship between writer and reader. (For a fuller treatment, see, for example, Coffin 1997, Martin 1997, 2000, White 1997, 1998.)

One of the chief ways in which this dialogic relationship may be construed is through the use of interpersonal reference – an aspect which, as we have seen in Section 5, may not be fully captured by a traditional interpersonal Theme analysis. An apparently high incidence of interpersonal pronouns was a striking feature of the IELTS test corpus as a whole, and so this seemed an obvious feature to consider first.

7.1 Interpersonal pronominal reference

The full set of scripts were analysed for instances of first and second person reference, regardless of whether this was realised in the form of pronouns (such as *I/me/my/myself/mine*, etc.) or possessive determiners (such as *my/your/our*). In addition to the obvious forms, occasional instances of 'each other' were coded, according to context, as equivalent to 'ourselves' or 'yourselves'. Third person *one* was also coded, as arguably representing a more formal alternative to the generic use of 'we' or 'you' (or to the use of the passive, which falls outside the scope of the present study). Together these features represent a subset of what Berry (1995) defined as Writer-orientation or Reader-orientation and what Ghadessy (1999) refers to as the lexico-semantic property of Speaker/Hearer. Rare instances of imaginary direct speech were included in the quantitative analyses on the grounds that this realisation was selected by the writer in preference to reported speech.

The incidence of each interpersonal pronominal reference group was then calculated, both as an absolute figure and in relation to the word length of the scripts in each cell. In order to assess the significance of the findings an analysis of variance was carried out, with the dependent variable being the incidence of each pronominal reference group and the independent variables being task score (high- versus low-scoring), language group, and test version. The findings were then compared with a large-scale corpus in the *Longman Grammar of Spoken and Written English* (Biber et al 1999).

The distribution of interpersonal pronominal reference according to the task score is shown in Figure 7.22. It can be seen that there is a tendency for low-scoring candidates to make a greater use of the first person singular and of the second person, although this was not statistically significant. Usage of 'one', however, is virtually restricted to the high-scoring group ($p = <.01$).

Figure 7.22 Instances of interpersonal pronominal reference (recalculated as instances per 1000 words) according to task score

	1st person singular	1st person plural	2nd person	3rd person 'one'
High-scoring (28,636 words)	175 (6.1 per 1000)	671 (23.4 per 1000)	110 (3.8 per 1000)	13** (0.5 per 1000)
Low-scoring (27,518 words)	248 (9.0 per 1000)	651 (23.7 per 1000)	137 (5.0 per 1000)	1 (0.04 per 1000)

Note: Asterisks are used in the figures throughout this section to indicate cases where the relative occurrence of the given feature between the two sub-groups of candidates is statistically significant, as follows:
* $p = <.05$
** $p = <.01$
*** $p = <.001$

The distribution of interpersonal pronominal reference according to the first language group of the candidates is shown in Figure 7.23. It can be seen that there is a tendency for Chinese L1 candidates to make a greater use of the first person singular ($p = <.01$) and of the second person ($p = <.05$). On the other hand, the Greek L1 candidates predominate in the use of 'one', although this failed to reach statistical significance.

Figure 7.23 Instances of interpersonal pronominal reference (recalculated as instances per 1000 words) according to language group

	1st person singular	1st person plural	2nd person	3rd person 'one'
Chinese L1 (27,193 words)	256** (9.4 per 1000)	644 (23.7 per 1000)	169* (6.2 per 1000)	3 (0.1 per 1000)
Greek L1 (28,961 words)	167 (5.8 per 1000)	678 (23.4 per 1000)	78 (2.7 per 1000)	11 (0.4 per 1000)

The distribution of interpersonal pronominal reference according to the test version is shown in Figure 7.24. It can be seen that there is a highly significant tendency for Version A to elicit greater use of the second person (p = <.001). The analysis of variance revealed that this was particularly associated with Chinese L1 candidates (p = <.01). There was also a significant tendency for Version A to elicit greater use of 'one' (p = <.01). The analysis of variance revealed that this was particularly associated with high-scoring candidates (p = <.05). Version B, on the other hand, tended to elicit rather more of the first person plural (p = <.05).

Figure 7.24 Instances of interpersonal pronominal reference (recalculated as instances per 1000 words) according to test version

	1st person singular	1st person plural	2nd person	3rd person 'one'
Version A	210	575	216***	13**
(29,546 words)	(7.1 per 1000)	(19.5 per 1000)	(7.3 per 1000)	(0.4 per 1000)
Version B	213	747*	31	1
(26,608 words)	(8.0 per 1000)	(28.1 per 1000)	(1.2 per 1000)	(0.04 per 1000)

It can be seen from the above data that usage of the first person plural is high among all groups, particularly in Version B. However, an additional factor which does not emerge from the conflated data is that individual usage varies greatly, with many candidates favouring a particular pronoun throughout the text. The highest incidence of individual first person plural usage is to be found in high-scoring scripts (the record being 44 instances in a Greek L1 script). Conversely, a high-level of first person singular usage was most common among the low-scoring Chinese candidates (the record being 20 instances in a single script). Second person usage was predominantly to be found among Chinese L1 candidates at both levels (the record being 37 instances in a high-scoring script). Although a handful of candidates across all groups use a more varied inventory, in general the pronouns *we/you/one* appear to be in complementary distribution. Specifically there is only a single instance (in a high-scoring Greek L1 script) of 'one' co-existing with 'you'.

Why is it that the relatively inexperienced academic writers who take the IELTS test feel obliged to foreground interpersonal reference in this way? It is possible that this could be an effect of the generic test prompt (*Present a written argument or case to an educated reader . . . You should use your own ideas, knowledge and experience . . .*) but, if so, it does not apply evenly across the language groups, with the Chinese L1 candidates displaying a significantly higher use of first person singular and of second person reference. On the other hand, the high usage of first person plural across all groups may be a result of coaching for the test. It is indeed true that 'we'-usage is high in academic writing compared with other genres; Thompson (2001:63) has argued that this may be a way of mitigating the possibly face-threatening implications of challenging a proposition which the reader holds dear. In their overuse of the first person plural, it is possible that IELTS candidates may simply be overshooting the target.

Given the lack of a strictly comparable corpus of texts by novice undergraduate writers, we compare the IELTS scripts with data drawn from the *Longman Grammar of Spoken and Written English* (Biber et al 1999) on general conversation and on the writing of professional academics. The Longman figures for first person reference in academic prose are broadly confirmed by a more detailed recent study by Hyland (2001). The Hyland study, however, reveals significant differences in self-reference between academic disciplines, the range for which is given in brackets in Figure 7.25.

Figure 7.25 Comparative frequency of interpersonal reference in different corpora (normalised to instances per thousand words)

	1st person singular	1st person plural	2nd person
Longman academic prose corpus (Hyland 2001)	2.5 (0.01–4.9 #)	4 (0.2–5.3 #)	1
Longman conversation corpus	45	8.5	33
All IELTS scripts (56,154 words)	7.5	23.5	4.4
Chinese L1 scripts (27,193 words)	9.4	23.7	6.2
Greek L1 scripts (28,961 words)	5.8	23.4	2.7

Notes: The Longman grammar codes data on each pronoun separately, so the figures here represent combined data for all forms of the type I/me/my/mine/myself.
 # The analytic categories used by Hyland are slightly broader than those used in the Longman grammar, in that they include nominal reference in the form 'the writer', 'the research team', etc.

It can be seen from Figure 7.25 that usage of first person singular in the test corpus overall was three times the average for professional academic prose (exceeding the most self-referential discipline in Hyland's study), and usage of the second person over four times the average. More starkly, usage of first person plural was almost eight times the average for the Longman corpus and over four times that of even the most self-referential discipline in Hyland's study, greatly exceeding even the level of usage in general conversation. When the figures were calculated separately for the language groups, some of the disparities became still more apparent among the Chinese L1 candidates, with usage of the first person singular almost four times the average and of the second person over six times the average for the professional academic texts.

We went on to map pronoun usage on to Theme, since this is an area for which comparative data is available. In a traditional Theme analysis (see Section 5), pronoun use would be generally captured as an ideational element (i.e. with 'I', 'we' or 'you' typically playing a Participant role) within topical Theme. However, as a way of providing insight into the full range of interpersonal relationship that may be foregrounded, we found it revealing to analyse the instances of interpersonal pronominal reference that are located within all types of Theme.

When interpersonal reference was mapped onto Theme in the subset of 56 scripts, the pattern shown in Figure 7.26 emerged. It can be seen that average figures for interpersonal pronominal reference in Theme position range between 33% second person to 65% first person singular, rising to 70% first person singular in Theme position among the Greek L1 candidates. This contrasts sharply with a corpus of academic prose studied by Ghadessy (1999), which found that only 5.3% of Themes foregrounded the Speaker/Hearer. In interpreting these figures, we need of course to bear in mind that usage across individual subjects is variable, and so the figures for such a small sample are indicative only. Conversely, however, Ghadessy's total included nominal as well as pronominal reference ('the writer', 'the reader', etc.), so the actual degree of disparity for pronouns alone is likely to be wider still.

Figure 7.26 Percentage of interpersonal pronominal reference in Theme position in sub-sample of scripts

		1st person singular	1st person plural	2nd person
All 56 scripts		64.8%	37.3%	33.1%
Chinese L1 scripts	high-scoring	64.9%	41.1%	34.3%
	low-scoring	50%	41%	37.5%
Greek L1 scripts	high-scoring	70.4%	35.6%	(50% #)
	low-scoring	69.6%	31.9%	17.6%

Note: # This figure is based on only two instances of the feature in a single script.

Martin (1989) contends that a high degree of such interpersonal reference is characteristic both of spoken language and of the style of writing he terms Hortatory Exposition (see Section 6.2 above). Comparing texts written in archetypally different styles, Martin (1989:41) found that interpersonal reference was not only more frequent in itself but three times as likely to occur in Theme position in a text of the Hortatory Exposition than the Analytical Exposition type. Taken together, these findings may imply that IELTS test candidates may be adopting a relatively hortatory *style* in their writing, even when the *structure* of their arguments (see Section 6.2) may be formally of the Analytical type. (For a fuller treatment of these issues, see Coffin and Mayor 2004.)

A qualitative analysis of the nature of the interpersonal pronoun usage in the test scripts reveals further significant differences from conventional academic usage. The conventional academic usage of 'we', for example, normally stands either for collective authorship (as in '*We* have found that . . .') or for the co-option of a 'reader-in-the-text' (Thompson and Thetela 1995) into the stages of the textual argument (as in 'As *we* have seen above . . .'). Although we do find such instances in the test corpus, many instances of *we* appear to be references to a collective identity or experience in the world beyond-the-text. For example, in the following text, we may observe the slippage from the textual/academic to the experiential/collective 'we':

> If *we* first take a glance in the disadvantages of space research and exploration *we* will mention the enormous amounts that are spent every year for these 'trips'. There is the question if *we* could make better use of these amounts to find new resources here on earth and not seeking for new habitant planets. Moreover, doing this, *we* spent the resources *we* already have and *we* all know of how much value they are.
>
> (GR/B/8/508)

Other examples, particularly among Chinese L1 candidates, show more unambiguously the use of the 'we' to appeal to collective experience:

> Thirdly, *we* can image if there is only human being in space, *we* will feel so lonely. If *we* can find alien in other place in universe, it will be a exciting thing. *We* can communicate with them.   (CH/B/5/001)

> *We* should take responsible attitude to our grandsons. *We* must find more energy form to leave with them.   (CH/B/7/251)

This lends support to a claim by Shen (1989) that those who have been acculturated and educated in Chinese prefer to speak in the collective voice: ' "I" is always subordinated to "We" ' (quoted in Connor 1996:73). In the context of the test corpus, however, 'we'-usage occurs alongside a still relatively high level of 'I' usage.

'You' may be used with either a specific reference to the reader, as illustrated by the following example:

> If *you* think that space research and exploration cost much and the hope of establishing human colonies in space is unrealistic, I will tell *you* that *you* are wrong.   (CH/B/5/004)

or, more commonly, with a generic reference, as in the following:

> If *you* don't look before *you* leap, *you* may get into big trouble.
>
> (CH/A/5/103)

In general, generic 'you' is in complementary distribution to 'we' (or, more rarely, 'one'), and seems to be the preferred choice of some individual writers, especially the low-scoring candidates and the Chinese L1 candidates more generally, as an alternative way of referring to shared experience or shared knowledge. It is also consistently more common in test Version A. Usage among high-scoring Greek L1 candidates, on the other hand, is virtually nil.

Usage of specific 'you' to address the reader is relatively low and concentrated predominantly among the low-scoring Chinese L1 in test Version B, where it frequently coincides with the dialogic use of interrogatives (which we discuss in Section 7.2 below).

7.2 Verb form and speech function

Another major way in which the Tenor of a text (see Section 7.1 above) is manifested is through the choice of verb mood to express speech functions, specifically the use of interrogatives and imperatives as a dialogic device. In a traditional grammar, verb mood is usually classified according to its *form* as declarative, interrogative, imperative or exclamative. The last of these categories accounts for a very small percentage of any corpus and is usually realised by a clause fragment without a verb. In the present data there was only a single instance of a formally exclamative clause:

> How unrealistic it is! (CH/B/5/025)

All other independent clauses which were not interrogative or imperative in form were therefore coded as declarative. In practice, of course, many of the formally declarative verbs were modalised or otherwise semantically mitigated in expressions ranging from:

> Everyone can see . . . (CH/B/5/001)

to:

> One could logically assume . . . (GR/B/7/507)

but our concern at this point was solely with verb mood.

Setting aside for a moment considerations of function, we began by considering the relative frequency of usage of the verb mood forms in the corpus. In order to assess the significance of the findings, an analysis of variance was carried out, with the dependent variable being the incidence of interrogative and imperative verb forms and the independent variables being task score (high- versus low-scoring), language group, and test version.

It can be seen from Figure 7.27 that high-scoring candidates produced more interrogatives and slightly more imperatives than low-scoring candidates, although neither of these reached statistical significance. The analysis of variance revealed that the use of interrogatives among high-scoring candidates was particularly associated with Chinese L1 candidates, although this again failed to reach statistical significance.

The Imperative category includes instances of 'Let's' plus one instance of 'So be it'. The single Exclamative clause in the data is acknowledged in the calculations for low-scoring Chinese L1 Version A.

Figure 7.27 Instances of each verb form (as percentage of t-units) according to task score

	Total t-units	Interrogative	Imperative	Declarative
High-scoring	1824	40 (2.2%)	20 (1.1%)	1764 (96.7%)
Low-scoring	2028	33 (1.6%)	17 (0.8%)	1977 (97.5%)

Note: Percentages in brackets represent the incidence of the given verb form relative to the total number of t-units in the relevant cell.

It can be seen from Figure 7.28 that the Chinese L1 candidates used significantly more imperatives ($p = <.001$) and interrogatives ($p = <.01$) than the Greek L1 candidates. As noted above, there was also a strong association between the use of interrogatives, language group and task score, although this failed to reach statistical significance.

Figure 7.28 Instances of each verb form (as percentage of t-units) according to language group

	Total t-units	Interrogative	Imperative	Declarative
Chinese L1	2051	53 (2.6%)**	30 (1.5%)***	1967 (95.9%)
Greek L1	1801	20 (1.1%)	7 (0.4%)	1774 (98.5%)

It can be seen from Figure 7.29 that Test B elicited twice as many interrogatives and rather more imperatives than Test A, although neither reached statistical significance.

When the IELTS scripts were compared with the Longman corpus (Biber et al 1999 – see also Section 7.1 above), the pattern shown in Figure 7.30 emerged.

It can be seen from the above that the overall incidence of imperatives in the test corpus and the incidence of interrogatives among Greek L1 candidates does not differ greatly from that in professional academic prose. The only striking difference lies in the relatively high incidence of interrogatives among Chinese L1 candidates.

Figure 7.29 Instances of each verb form (as percentage of t-units) according to test version

	Total t-units	Interrogative	Imperative	Declarative
Version A	2092	28 (1.3%)	18 (0.9%)	2046 (97.8%)
Version B	1760	45 (2.6%)	19 (1.1%)	1695 (96.3%)

Figure 7.30 Comparative frequency of verb forms (per thousand words) in different corpora

	Interrogative	Imperative
Longman academic prose corpus	0.5	1
Longman conversation corpus	23.5	10
All IELTS scripts (56,154 words)	1.3	0.7
Chinese L1 scripts (27,193 words)	1.9	1.1
Greek L1 scripts (28,961 words)	0.7	0.2

It is equally important, however, to understand whether verb mood is being used in any distinctive ways in the IELTS corpus. We discuss this aspect below.

Functional grammar places less emphasis on the form than the *function* of the verb, which Halliday (1994) has characterised in broad terms as the giving or demanding of information or goods and services. Three of these speech functions may be coded 'congruently' in language, as in Figure 7.31, where the giving of information – the Statement – is realised by a Declarative

Figure 7.31 The relationship between form and function: congruent realisations (based on Iedema et al 1995:108)

	Goods and Services	Information
Giving	*Offer:* Let.me start my explanation (CH/A/5/135) I would like to throw some light on . . . (CH/B/8/271)	*Statement:* It's never too late to do the right thing for our health. (GR/A/5/063) It is widely accepted nowadays that time is never enough. (GR/A/8/201)
Demanding	*Command:* Emagine a world with no electric. (GR/A/5/051) Stop space race! (CH/B/7/252)	*Question:* What's difference between human and animals? (CH/B/5/010) But to what extent this sacrifices are beneficial for the humanity? (GR/B/7/502)

and the demand for goods and services – the Command – by an Imperative etc.; the Offer, on the other hand, appears to have no 'congruent' form.

It is not only the Offer, however, which may be incongruently coded. Incongruence between the semantic function of an utterance and its grammatical form is widespread, so that Commands, Questions and Statements can all be realised grammatically as declaratives, interrogatives, or imperatives. Thus, for example, an implicit Command may be realised formally as a declarative, as in:

> It is necessy to people to pay more attention on space research.
> (CH/B/5/012)

or as an interrogative, as in:

> If we can use it on the study which can benefitial people, why not afraid of that spend . . .? (CH/B/5/006)

Particularly striking in the corpus was the wide variety of grammatical ways in which demands for goods and services, and to a lesser extent demands for information, were realised, and it is to these that we turn in greater detail.

Not surprisingly, there were qualitative differences in the data which were not captured by the quantitative analysis. In particular, the use of interrogatives appeared to vary in a similar way to the use of specific vs general 'you' (see Section 7.1 above). A few interrogatives, largely confined to the Greek L1 candidates, appeared to be genuine questions addressed to the reader or to an imaginary third party, as in:

> 'There is no time.' How often have you heard that?   (GR/A/8/209)

> But the serious question is 'do I need all this comfortable?'
> (GR/A/5/058)

> I would only like to ask the NASA researchers, 'how do you relieve the starvation in the so called 3rd World?'   (GR/B/7/501)

whereas the majority of the interrogatives used by Chinese L1 candidates appeared to be purely rhetorical devices and thus not strictly demands for 'information' at all, as in:

> Compare with many years before, who knows it will be like nowadays?
> (CH/A/5/121)

> (I)f we spend every minutes on work and learn, what's the life for?
> (CH/A/5/140)

> We have paid a lot of money on it to research and explore. Is it worthy of
> this money? (CH/B/5/025)

It was beyond the scope of this study to investigate fully the range and distribution of question functions. A more systematic analysis would be required to establish whether or not the above patterns are consistent.

Given the widespread hortatory tone of the scripts (see Section 6 above), demands for 'goods and services' were frequent. In general, these were incongruently coded, in other words the incidence of straightforward imperatives was low. However, we noted many modals of necessity or obligation, as in:

> We *must* realise that the past years aren't the same, and also that the
> future years aren't going to be the same. (GR/A/5/068)

> Thus people *should* stop complaining and do something about it!
> (GR/A/7/216)

> So, we *need* to find a new place out of earth to move part of present 6
> billion persons. (CH/B/5/001)

> We'd *better* spent our money on overcome the pollution, to make our
> earth better and better. (CH/B/5/007)

It was further observed that many of the implied demands, especially among the Chinese L1 candidates, were realised as positive or negative conditions of the form *If we don't do x, y will follow* or *If we do z, all will be well*, as in:

> If we can explore these vast resources and use them, problems such as
> depletion of fossil fuel, environmental pollution can be largely avoided.
> (CH/51/7/267)

> If we keep a well-balanced timetable . . . it will improve our efficiency of
> work. (CH/45/5/140)

There were also many weaker formulations to be found such as *important to. . ., worthwhile, a mistake (not) to . . .* etc, as in:

> It is *very necessary* for us to have a plan to cope with something happened in the future. (CH/B/5/023)

> Proper time management and stress relaxation is *recommended* to those
> on stress. (CH/A/7/290)

> And definitely *the best way* to achieve this goal is to have the
> cooperation. (GR/B/5/165)

It is everybody's *duty* to develop compromises between the two
extremes. (GR/A/8/204)

It is just *urgent* to find a clean and full energy enviorment for human to
survive. (CH/B/5/003)

Because of the wide variety in their surface realisations, no attempt was made
to code such 'weak' demands quantitatively. However, they added to the
hortatory impression given by the texts.

When the incidence of these demand forms between the language groups
was compared, the results were as in Figure 7.32.

**Figure 7.32 Comparative incidence of demands for goods and services between
language groups**

			Total clauses	Imperatives	Modals of obligation	Conditionals	Total demands
Chinese L1	A	High-scoring	471	5 (1.1%)	12 (2.5%)	2 (0.4%)	19 (4.0%)
		Low-scoring	627	8 (1.3%)	20 (3.2%)	7 (1.1%)	35 (5.6%)
	B	High-scoring	449	11 (2.4%)	28 (6.2%)	9 (2.0%)	48 (10.7%)
		Low-scoring	504	6 (1.2%)	48 (9.5%)	9 (1.8%)	63 (12.5%)
Greek L1	A	High-scoring	502	3 (0.6%)	21 (4.2%)	4 (0.8%)	28 (5.6%)
		Low-scoring	492	2 (0.4%)	22 (4.5%)	8 (1.6%)	32 (6.5%)
	B	High-scoring	402	1 (0.25%)	42 (10.4%)	5 (1.2%)	48 (11.9%)
		Low-scoring	405	1 (0.25%)	37 (9.1%)	1 (0.2%)	39 (9.6%)

As already observed, the Chinese L1 group are distinctive in their relatively high use of the imperative. Across both language groups, however, the
most common form of demand was the modal of necessity or obligation.
This is the only demand form where the level of use among Greek L1 candidates frequently exceeds that of the Chinese L1 candidates. Usage of the
modals was particularly high overall on Test Version B. Version B, especially
among Chinese L1 candidates, tended in general to elicit more varied grammatical forms, including speculations and recommendations. Furthermore,
individual Chinese L1 candidates tend to use a wider *range* of demand forms,
including many of the 'weaker' formulations described above.

It is only rarely, however – and predominantly among the high-scoring
candidates – that we find a realisation of the demand which might be
regarded as archetypal of academic writing in English, namely the weak negative as in *It is not a good idea to . . .* or *It is not a waste of time to . . .* The sum
total of examples in the corpus was as follows:

It is *not substantial* to abandon the programmes now. (CH/B/8/271)

Spending money on visions is *not futile or a waste*. (GR/B/7/542)

> With such problems remaining unresolved, it is *not so mindful* to spend
> so much money on research and exploration of space.

> It is *not worthless* to try for the establishment of human colonies in space
> (both GR/B/7/546)

> It is *not normal thing* to spend money for space research . . .
> (GR/B/5/162)

Furthermore, the nature of the demands appeared to differ between the language groups, with the Greek L1 candidates apparently favouring appeals to mental action, as in:

> People *should think carefully* and re-evaluate their needs and put priorities.
> (GR/A/8/201)

> (W)e should try to find a mid-point between time we spent working and
> relaxing. (GR/A/5/075)

While such examples are also to be found among the Chinese L1 candidates, the latter are equally likely to call for a physical response on the part of some unspecified collective such as 'we', 'mankind' or 'society', as in:

> We *must work hard* to earn more money and develop ourself in the pres-
> sure situation. (CH/A/5/139)

> (H)ave *a better control* of your time, then your live will become more
> relax. (CH/A/5/137)

It was beyond the scope of this study to investigate this aspect fully. (For a fuller discussion, see Mayor 2006.)

8 Conclusions and recommendations

As outlined in Section 1, the aims of this study, in summary, were to investigate:

- how high-scoring scripts differ from low-scoring scripts
- the extent to which candidates' writing may be related to the topic or wording of the task
- the extent to which candidates' prior linguistic, cultural and educational experiences may lead them to write in distinct ways.

These issues were studied in order to expose:

- the extent to which the language produced under test conditions approximates to the target genre(s) of tertiary-level English-medium academic writing (where comparative data is available)

- any implications for pedagogical interventions, test design, marking criteria or staff development.

We consider each of these aspects in turn.

8.1 How high-scoring scripts differ from low-scoring scripts

What are the valued linguistic features of currently successful scripts? As observed in several sections of the report, it is often not the prevalence of a particular feature that determines a candidate's score but rather constellations of features. Markers appear to be responding to scripts in a holistic rather than strictly analytic way and, all other things being equal, stylistic variety may itself add to the perceived effectiveness of a script. Nonetheless, it is possible to make some very general statements about the characteristics of high-scoring scripts.

Not surprisingly perhaps, the strongest current predictors of a high task score are high word length and low formal error rate (Section 3), complexity in sentence structure (Section 4) and occasional use of the impersonal pronoun 'one' (Section 7). Interestingly, as observed in Section 3, candidates who made fewer errors in grammar, prepositions and lexis/idiom tended to make more errors in spelling and punctuation – one possible interpretation being that spelling and punctuation, as relatively mechanical features, contribute little to the construction of meaning in a text. At the higher level, therefore, mechanical errors may become less significant to the writer, yielding place to those aspects of composition which involve semantic and stylistic choices. Conversely, in low-scoring scripts, because grammatical, spelling and other errors are likely to be highly salient, they may obscure candidates' attempts to use complex sentence structures, so that these go unrecognised by markers. As noted in Section 4, the notion of 'complexity' in sentence structure is in any case an elusive one, which cannot be reduced merely to a single measure. There is indeed some evidence that the mean clause length of a script may be in inverse proportion to use of dependent clauses, reflecting the higher use among some writers of features such as non-finite clauses and nominalisation.

In addition to the formal features discussed above, there are more functional features which appear to correlate positively with task score. These include Thematic structure (Section 5), argument genre (Section 6) and some of the more subtle ways of expressing the interpersonal tenor of the text (Section 7). Scripts at both levels showed cohesive patterning between Themes and Rhemes and the foregrounding of argument through the use of evaluative interpersonal Themes. However, high-scoring candidates made greater use of rhetorical structuring devices (macro- and hyper-Theme and macro- and hyper-New) which showed patterns of organisation throughout the whole text and at paragraph level. 'Incomplete' argument structures, which typically lacked a 'thesis' or an 'issue' stage, or included limited evidence in their 'argument' stage, were concentrated among low-scoring candidates. The differences between high- and low-scoring candidates in terms of completeness of their arguments is predictable. While examiners may not consciously award marks according to genre type or organisational structure, they may be predisposed to essays that conform to a clear generic structure. This accords with our overall finding that many aspects of a script are graded holistically rather than analytically.

8.2 The extent to which candidates' writing for the test may be related to the topic or wording of the task

Were there any possible intrusive effects of the design of the test, either in its generic framing or in the specific version prompt? We began with the assumption that alternative versions of the test should be equally reliable, so we would not expect to find significant differences in the results. This was, by and large, the case. However, the specific wording of the prompt did appear to 'cue' students in to use certain linguistic forms rather than others, for example the significantly greater use of 'you' and 'one' in Version A and of 'we' and the interrogative in Version B (Section 7). It was less obvious why the frequency of errors in the use of prepositions and lexis/idiom should differ between the versions, particularly as the tendency was not in the same direction, with significantly more errors of lexis/idiom in Version A and of preposition use in Version B (Section 3). We can only speculate that the different nature of the topics could have led to differential gaps in candidates' knowledge of the relevant vocabulary. Alternatively, it is conceivable that there may have been variations in the classification of specific errors associated with one version rather than the other (see Appendix 7.1).

More puzzlingly, our analysis showed that Version B was associated with significantly greater use of t-units that included dependent clauses (Section 4). It is not clear to us from the topic alone why Version B should encourage greater use of dependent clauses than Version A. Furthermore, scrutiny of test scripts did not suggest the prevalence of any particular grammatical structures that might be associated with one topic rather than another. So, while there does seem to have been a test effect, it is not immediately clear which factors (or which combination of factors) influenced candidates' use of different types of t-units. The decision to look at functional categories and particularly those relating to argument drew its rationale from the generic test prompt (*Present a written argument or case to an educated reader . . .*) rather than the specific test version. The significance of 'presenting a written argument' was seen as central to how the scripts would be evaluated, and there were indeed no significant differences between the test versions in terms of argument structure. At the level of the clause complex, our Thematic analysis highlighted the relative sophistication of most of the candidates at both levels of performance. They were able to utilise the beginning of the clause to mark both ideational, textual and interpersonal meaning. In particular, the texts showed cohesive patterning between Themes and Rhemes, and argument was foregrounded through the use of evaluative interpersonal Themes.

On the other hand, at the outset of the research, we had hypothesised that the high-scoring scripts would adopt an interpersonal tenor whereby solidarity between writer and reader was not assumed. Given that highly opinionated and non negotiable argumentative styles are generally not valued characteristics of academic writing at tertiary level, we reasoned that the test would award higher marks for a rhetorical strategy which acknowledged alternative positions and viewpoints, objectively presented. However, possibly due to the nature of the generic test prompt (*Present a written argument or case to an educated reader . . . you should use your own ideas, knowledge and experience . . .*), which emphasises the personal nature of the dialogue, there was in reality a strikingly high level of interpersonal reference among all groups of candidates, with only very limited use of the impersonal alternatives (Section 7). We speculate that the high usage of first person plural across all groups may be a result of coaching for the test, since this may be seen as a characteristic of academic writing. However, 'we' appears to be used in some very different ways in the test corpus (Section 7). In their overuse of this pronoun, it is possible that candidates may simply be overshooting the target, attempting to speak with an authoritative voice without always having the evidence to back it up. There may also be distinctive cultural influences here (see 8.3 below). However, it is equally possible that the generic test prompt itself may be cueing candidates into adopting a style of writing which is both heavily interpersonal and relatively polemical.

8.3 The influence of candidates' prior linguistic, cultural and educational experiences on their writing

Were there any signs of cross-cultural variation in the way the task is approached? In other words, to what extent do students' prior linguistic, cultural and educational experiences affect the way that they write?

Findings from the sub-sample of scripts (analysed in Section 3) indicate that low-scoring Chinese L1 candidates make significantly more grammatical errors than Greek L1 at the same level of performance, with the latter making proportionately more of the remaining categories of error. Greek L1 candidates at both levels, but particularly the low-scoring, tend significantly more than the Chinese L1 candidates towards syntactic 'complexity' as measured by the use of dependent clauses (Section 4). The reasons for this are by no means clear. However, we speculate that the tendency towards parataxis in Chinese (in which relations between clauses need not always be explicitly expressed) may contribute towards the Chinese L1 candidates' lower use of dependent clauses in English. It is also possible that certain teaching practices (e.g. teaching sentence grammar in a relatively decontextualised manner) may leave some Chinese L1 candidates uncertain about the use of English dependent clauses in context.

In terms of Thematic structure (Section 5), Chinese L1 candidates produce more clauses and therefore Themes than the Greek L1. However, these are significantly more likely to be single Themes, in other words there are fewer preceding textual and interpersonal Themes than among Greek L1 candidates. As a consequence the Chinese L1 candidates use fewer overt cohesive ties such as 'therefore', 'so', 'and' and so on. In addition, they show less interpersonal marking at the beginning of clauses. Overall, therefore, Chinese L1 candidates exploit the varied possibilities of the beginning of the clause in terms of Theme categories less than Greek L1 candidates. In contrast, however, they make greater use of 'marked' Themes, including the use of time and place markers and conditionals to organise texts.

So far as argument structure is concerned (Section 6), there is little difference between Chinese L1 and Greek L1 candidates in their preference for expository over discussion argument genres. However, whereas the Greek L1 candidates strongly favour hortatory argument genres, the Chinese L1 have a slight preference for arguments which are formally analytical in genre, although they may nonetheless be hortatory in tenor (see below). In terms of completion of their arguments, all low-scoring Greek L1 candidates in the sub-sample produced incomplete arguments, whereas only half the low-scoring Chinese L1 did so, implying that other features of the Chinese L1 candidates' writing were influencing their relatively low score.

In terms of the tenor of their writing (Section 7), all the dialogic features that we have observed in the test corpus are manifested more starkly among the Chinese L1 than the Greek L1 candidates, with the Chinese L1 group using both a larger amount and a wider variety of interpersonal reference, as well as a higher proportion of interrogatives and imperatives. Furthermore, we suggest tentatively that the Chinese L1 candidates appear more likely than the Greek L1 candidates to call for an active response on the part of the individual reader or the collective. This confirms observations elsewhere (Thompson 2001; Shen 1989) that Chinese L1 writers have a greater tendency to directly address the reader and to speak in the collective voice.

8.4 The relationship between the test and the academic writing skills required of tertiary education

To what extent does the test develop and measure the academic writing skills required of tertiary education? There are two reasons why our conclusions in this regard need to be tentative. First, comparisons with the 'target genre' have not been attempted in all sections of the report. Second, the comparative corpora available to us are frequently drawn from professional rather than student academic writing and are undifferentiated according to academic discipline, thus possibly conflating key variables. Nonetheless some observations are possible, particularly with regard to the more functional and discourse-level features of the scripts.

Our findings from the subset of data analysed in Section 6 indicate that candidates use more of the exposition than the discussion genre of argument and frequently recommend a course of action. This ran counter to our expectations of academic writing. Studies of professional academic writing and the writing of students indicates that a more objective stance is favoured. However, IELTS candidates used a much more personal, involved style of argumentation which was nevertheless successful in terms of task score.

In terms of the style as opposed to the structure of their arguments (Section 7), there is evidence that the candidates are also diverging widely from the normal tenor of (professional) academic texts, particularly in their excessive and qualitatively different use of the collective 'we', in the high incidence of 'I' in Theme position among Greek L1 candidates, and in the high incidence of dialogic features among the Chinese L1 candidates. As we indicate in 8.2 above, the generic test prompt, coupled with the lack of source material on which to base their argument, may account for this more personal style. In complying with the rubric to *'present an argument . . . to an educated reader'*, candidates are thrown back on their own resources, which is not a situation similar to that encountered in academic writing at tertiary level. However, it may well be that candidates who can cope successfully in this situation will also be successful in more traditional forms of academic writing in English.

8.5 Implications for pedagogical interventions, test design, marking criteria or staff development

Writing Task 2 appears to discriminate effectively and consistently between candidates in terms of the more formal features of their writing such as accuracy and complexity at the sentence level (Sections 3 and 4), as well as clarity of argument structure (Sections 5 and 6). We note that different versions of the test elicit somewhat different formal features, but this does not appear to affect scores in any serious way.

On the other hand, the generic prompt appears to trigger in candidates an overly personal and often hortatory style of writing, which may lead them into making strong claims without the necessary supporting evidence. The resultant tenor of their writing is often more reminiscent of letters to the press than of academic prose. It seems logical and desirable to us that candidates should aim towards, and be judged against, a model which approximates more closely to the styles of writing which are commonly expected of students in higher education (see Section 1 and *passim*), in particular in relation to generic argument structures (Section 6), the need for objectivity and the use of evidence (Section 7). We would therefore encourage a closer correspondence between the growing research evidence on academic writing in English and language testing practices. Specifically, in terms of IELTS test design, it may be advisable:

(a) to revise the wording of the generic prompt to encourage a more neutral tenor (e.g. by assuming a wider and preferably more academic readership, such as a seminar group)

(b) to consider re-introducing the provision of background information to stimulate the greater use of evidence (e.g. by announcing the topic in advance, or circulating additional material outside of the exam room).

Finally, it is important to bear in mind that English, as an increasingly global language of education, may have played a greater or lesser role in IELTS candidates' previous educational experiences. Vassileva (2001:8) has argued that those writing in a second language may 'try to preserve their cultural identity . . . irrespective of the language they use' by the retention of certain pragmatic features in the discourse. Our findings suggest that there are indeed some significant differences in the writing of candidates from different linguistic and cultural backgrounds, especially in their use of grammatical form, argumentative structure and interpersonal tenor. Currently the IELTS marking criteria are applied sufficiently flexibly to allow for this, and it is important that test designers and script markers remain sensitive to this kind of cross-cultural variation in the use of English.

Acknowledgements

We are grateful for additional contributions from Carolyn McKinney, Will Swann and Xiao Junhong, and for secretarial assistance from Freda Barnfield and Rita Chidley.

APPENDIX 7.1
Problems of reliability in analysing language errors

The identification, classification and quantification of errors in a written text depends on two fundamental assumptions. The first is that we can recognise what the writer was trying to say. It is only by comparing what the writer intended with what was actually written that the analyst can determine the nature of any discrepancy between them. However, there is an inherent paradox here, since the only way of determining the writer's intention is through reading what he or she has written, and if this contains error, then the message is correspondingly distorted. The second assumption is that we can itemise elements of the linguistic system. However, the linguistic system itself is neither determinate (since many rules are variable and context-dependent) nor atomistic (since it consists of interlocking and overlapping sub-systems).

The problematic nature of these two assumptions means that error analysis can never be completely exact and reliable. The following discussion considers some specific difficulties arising from the analysis of the IELTS scripts, grouping them under the headings identification, classification and quantification.

Identification

Transcription

In handwritten scripts, particularly those produced under time pressure, it may not be easy to decipher what the candidate has written, or where paragraph breaks are intended. In the example below, it seems likely that the candidate's intended meaning was 'for us'. However, this is unclear and it has been transcribed as 'forms':

> It is very necessary forms to have a plan to cope with something happened in the future.   (CH/B/023)

Occasionally the handwriting may be impossible to decipher, resulting in a mutilated sentence which resists analysis. In these cases it is clear that the 'errors' are unlikely to be what they appear, yet there may be other cases where similar transcription problems occur, but are not recognised as such by the analyst.

Variable rules

Assuming that we can read accurately what the candidate wrote, there are still problems in determining what should be counted as an error. In many cases language rules are not clear-cut, and there may be a cline of acceptability, with intermediate positions which become difficult to classify. Is it, for example, acceptable to use 'have not' in any of the following cases?

> They always try to acquire more and more money to cover their needs and they have not the available time to deal with themselves and other people.   (CH/A/5/083)

> Reasonably, people have not enough time to relax, because of the work pressure.   (CH/A/5/104)

> Consequently, effect from that is that Children have not happy and free childhood.   (CH/A/5/113)

And in what circumstances can it be regarded as correct to begin a sentence with a co-ordinating conjunction, as in the following cases?

> This problem takes plase mostly in big cities where trafic overcomes the agees. But in small cities and vilages people don't face this problem.
>   (CH/A/5/051)

> To sum up, the working tasks of modern people can't be changed, you have to accept it. But you can make your life a little more relaxed by doing less unforced chores and making fewer plans in your spare time.
>   (CH/A/5/103)

> People against the idea of exploring the space have based their argument on an invest-and-then-gain criteria. Given the large amount of money we have invested in space programmes, they haven't seen any proportional outcome yet. But if their logic holds true, I believe we would still sail from China to North American today.   (CH/A/8/214)

A similar problem occurs in the following script, where the repeated use of 'a lot of' becomes increasingly less acceptable. At what point, though, should we regard it as an error?

> Nowadays, people have a lot of works to do. They need a lot of time to achieve their aims. Their lives are very complex. It is acceptable that they face a lot of problems.   (CH/A/5/064)

The selection of an appropriate grammatical or lexical item often depends upon the writer's judgement of the overall context, and is to that extent subjective. IELTS candidates, moreover, are writing in an unusual and underspecified context, and may differ in their interpretations of that context. Stylistic choices are for this reason particularly difficult to categorise as correct or incorrect.

Content and coherence

In some cases error is obvious because a morphological or syntactic rule has manifestly been broken. Often, however, recognising that an error has been made is more complex, involving decisions about the writer's intended meaning. Consider the examples below:

> Undering [*Under?*] pressure, people are able to try their best, and they can do everything as well as they can. (CH/A/5/104)

> When you have something it is more creative to manage it as it worths [*deserves?*] and then you must care about something else.
> (CH/B/5/154)

Ignoring the errors indicated, these sentences are superficially correct, and yet in each case there is something odd about their meaning. Candidate 104 is perhaps repeating in the second clause information already given in the first clause, while candidate 154 may be trying to express the idea that you should give a problem only the attention it deserves, then move on to something else. When a sentence appears to be nonsense, is the analyst justified in translating it into a meaningful proposition, and then identifying in what respect the language fails to convey that proposition? In other words, where do we draw the line between errors of language and errors of logic?

The same question arises in connection with coherence. Sentences which on their own are superficially correct may seem unacceptable if their relation to surrounding sentences is obscure, as in the last sentence of the following extract:

> However, it is necessary for people to continue the researching in space. From this, we can learn the lesson and find out the failure. It is said that the failure is the mother of success.
> In conclusion, the problem is not the result of money itself, but the result of the science learning. (CH/B/5/005)

A more extended example is shown below, where the language is largely free of mechanical error, but fails to communicate clearly. If we attempt to identify errors here we are in danger of confusing language with content, yet if we accept this extract as (largely) correct, we seem to be ignoring its communicative vacuity.

'There is no time'. How often have you heard that? It's true that today people complain that there is not enough time.

Comming to think of it, we must wonder 'time for what?'; the question we must think of is 'Why time?'

It is true that the conditions of life have changed. Much the same happened to the cost of living. Our society has divided itself to six major categories: a. Information b. Productivity c. Services d. Education e. Family and Values f. economics.

Any one of us, today, must pursue all six of the above, in order to be a part of a modern society. (CH/A/8/209)

Classification

Uncertain aetiology

Once a decision has been made that an item counts as an error, there is then the task of classifying what kind of error it is, and again, this is often problematic. Consider for example the error below:

Undering pressure, people are able to try their best, and they can do everything as well as they can. (CH/A/5/104)

Has the candidate here made a mistake with the form of a preposition, or tried to use 'under' as a verb, or misspelt 'enduring', or made a faulty lexical selection? Or perhaps the error was caused by some combination of these factors? Similarly, should the error below be classified under punctuation, spelling or grammar?

Then he must do other things such as prepare he's work for the next day and at the end of the day he have some time to spend but he is so exusted that the only thing he want is to sleep. (CH/A/5/059)

Clearly the punctuation is faulty in that there is an unwanted apostrophe. Yet the candidate does show an understanding of punctuation, since surely this is how the possessive pronoun would be punctuated, if only it had the same morphology as a noun. On the other hand, how could the candidate make such a mistake in morphology unless he also had problems relating spelling to pronunciation? The aetiology of error may resist neat classifications, particularly when there is no way of examining the thinking behind such forms.

Intended meaning

The writer's intended meaning is evident only through what is written, and if this is unclear, the nature of any error may remain inscrutable. What, for example, did the candidate intend in the second sentence below – that people are forced to pay more attention to their jobs, or that they ought to regard their jobs as more important? Is there an error with the modal, with the lexis, or perhaps with some other aspect?

> It is commonly believed by all the people that in our days the Free time has disapear From our lives. The people must care more about their jobs that their own lives. (CH/A/5/056)

Consider also the example below:

> Nowadays a lot of people are always under pressure to do more in a shorter time period because they have stress how they afford to have a family, for the destroy of the war or for nowdays disease such as AIDS. (CH/A/5/079)

In this case the relationship between the various sentence components is not clear enough to allow a confident reconstruction of the intended meaning. Yet without such an interpretation, it is difficult to identify how the sentence should be corrected. Any decisions that the analyst takes are necessarily subjective and tentative.

Interdependent forms

Other problems of classification occur when language forms are interdependent. The sentence below provides two examples of this.

> He/she do not have the time for taking care of him/herselfs. (GR/A/5/060)

The subject pronoun could be amended to 'They', in which case the verb form is correct, or the verb form could be amended to 'does', in which case the pronoun is correct. More complex is the postmodifier, which seems to vary according to the absence or presence of a determiner:

> They do not have the time to take care of themselves.

> They do not have time for taking care of themselves.

In this case the alternatives – pronoun or verb, determiner or non-finite verb – all fall within the grammar category. In other cases, however, interdependent errors span different categories. For example, the sentence below could be corrected either by changing the lexical item 'true' to 'possible', or by changing the grammatical form 'to live on the moon' to 'that man can live on the moon'.

> There are also some people may be pessimistic and wonder whether it will be turn out to be true to live on the moon. (CH/B/5/010)

In the following example, we can either link the two clauses grammatically with a conjunction or amend the punctuation to create two sentences.

> If you waste time you will loss the money, also finally you will not adapt
> the modern society.   (CH/A/5/105)

The final example illustrates a choice between lexis and grammar: either replacing 'turn to' with 'come to', or replacing the verb 'hate' with the noun 'hatred (of)'.

> Therefore the children cannot grow up by their parnent, they will turn to
> hate their farther, mother and others.   (CH/A/5/114)

In such cases, the analyst's decisions are necessarily arbitrary, yet they determine the way errors are classified, and may have a cumulative effect which impinges significantly on the frequency of errors in each category.

Quantification

Alternative corrections

When a text is corrigible in different ways, it may become difficult to count how many errors are involved. For example, 'necessy' in the sentence below may be followed by either a finite or non-finite clause:

> It is necessy to people pay more attention on space research.
>   (CH/B/5/012)

However, the finite clause involves one change more than the non-finite clause:

> It is necessary that people pay more attention to space research.
> It is necessary for people to pay more attention to space research.

In the example below, the final clause may be intended either as a general statement about experiments in space, or a specific statement about what happened on one particular aircraft:

> The seeds which were load on the aircraft may be changed . . .
>   (CH/B/5/012)

These two possible interpretations suggest different reformulations, one involving more extensive correction:

> The seeds which were loaded on the aircraft may have been changed . . .
> Seeds which are loaded on aircraft may be changed . . .

Persistent errors

Another quantification problem occurs when the same error is repeated, for example a spelling mistake:

> And science said that it would be possible be some kind of transport which was used by an extra terestrial. Not only objects, but the same extra terestrial we saw two years later in our television dead.
>
> (GR/B/5/151)

Some errors may be extremely persistent, as in the following example:

> Most of people work in order to pay his rent, phone, cable tv, car etc. and the more he need the more he works in order to buy these things.
>
> (GR/A/5/062)

In practice, each separate error has been counted in order to maintain consistency throughout coding, since any decision to ignore a certain type of error would entail a number of further subjective decisions. However, counting persistent errors may lead to some distortion both of error frequency and the proportion of different types of error.

Multiple errors

In a large number of scripts, errors are so numerous that it can at times be difficult to disentangle them. Compare for example the following two sentences with their suggested 'corrections':

> The first reason which is almost people belives time just like money it is the important for every one.   (CH/A/5/112)

> *The first reason is that most people believe that time, just like money, is important for everyone.*

> Human must to understand that they live many other families in their own 'homes' and not only his family.   (CH/B/5/154)

> *Humans must understand that the "home" they live in is shared, not only with their own family, but with many others.*

When the writer's intended meaning is obscure, amending the language to express a reasonable proposition may require so many changes that again it is difficult to enumerate the errors involved, for example:

> Even though the exploration is completely the cost of today, we also should to do it for futhur and next generation.   (CH/B/5/013)

> *Even if the exploration involves all our current resources, we should still carry it out for the benefit of future generations.*

In a few cases, the language is so mangled that the meaning is incomprehensible, and counting errors becomes quite impossible, as in:

> eather disagree my opinion is beside these tw.　　　　　(CH/A/5/081)

Such examples illustrate some of the problems outlined earlier: uncertain aetiology, unclear meaning, interdependent forms and alternative corrections. When errors are multiplied, however, these problems are compounded, with the result that error analysis is considerably more difficult, and hence less reliable, with lower-standard scripts.

Error gravity

Error analysis typically involves counting different categories of error and comparing their frequency. This procedure suggests, however, that all errors are equally serious, when it is clear that this is not so. A run-on sentence, for example, may represent a serious breakdown in sentence structure or a minor slip of the pen. Spelling errors may range from barely noticeable slips such as 'existance' and 'satelite' to forms that may affect comprehensibility, such as 'hurt attack', 'laph', 'bahouvor', and 'paise'. The same is true of grammatical errors, as in the contrasting examples below:

> It is a good use of our resource.　　　　　(CH/B/5/003)

> Those managers and employer are very troubles . . .　　(CH/A/5/118)

A further difficulty is that counting errors does not reflect the complexity of the language that the candidate is attempting to produce. Candidates who feel uncertain of their ability to use certain structures and lexis may avoid them, thus producing language which is relatively error-free, but restricted. Consider, for example, the following two extracts. The number of errors in each extract is comparable, but it is clear that the first candidate has used a wider and more demanding range of language than the second.

> Many years before man was only dreamt about living on the moon. It was believed that the earth was the only place with life and untill then it was impossible for people to think that a great deal of money could be spent for researches in space. A lot or organizations were being built, for example the 'NASA', who were able to find out what way really happening at the rest space.　　　　　(CH/B/5/164)

As the time pass we must understand that everything becomes different. Space was a field that scientist didn't know everything. They had to work to discover it. On the other hand they knew about physics, maths. But they didn't know about the space. In consequence, think how important is to combine the space with the other sciences.

(CH/B/5/168)

Error analysis: a caveat

The results of error analysis are often reported without reference to the procedures by which they were obtained. Yet analysing errors is, as we have described above, far from straightforward. Error itself is not an absolute linguistic construct, but is evaluated as such by readers in relation to their construction of the relevant norms, contexts, and expectations. It follows that error analysis is itself subjective, and may vary from one analyst to another.

The issue is not resolved by focusing only on surface errors, since these are not clearly delimited from other types of error. Grammatical choices reflect options which are available to writers to convey their message, and are therefore interwoven with meaning. While there are some linguistic features that may be regarded as mechanical, such as subject/verb concord or the agreement of a pronoun with its antecedent, these features are themselves dependent on other choices that the writer makes. Surface features interpenetrate other aspects of writing, including coherence, information structure, and rhetorical structure.

Nor is it easy to demarcate categories of error. The use of prepositions, for example, may be grammatically determined by another sentence element, or may represent a semantic choice, and it is frequently difficult to make this distinction. Punctuation errors appear to be of two main types. 'Local' punctuation errors relate to lexis, involving faulty capitalisation of common/proper nouns, word division and hyphenation. 'Global' punctuation errors relate to sentence structure, involving problems with sentence-initial capitals and the use of full stops and commas. Even spelling turns out to be a permeable category. Should morphological errors such as 'payed' be classified under spelling or grammar? And how mutilated can a word be before it has to be regarded as a case of poor vocabulary rather than poor spelling?

Spelling, punctuation, grammar, and vocabulary are traditional linguistic categories which may not necessarily represent the most useful classification when dealing with the evaluation of written text. There appear to be, for instance, certain constellations of error which cut across these divisions. One such error constellation relates to clause structure, when candidates have trouble with the way finite and non-finite clauses combine to form sentences. This leads to errors in punctuation and grammatical errors such as omission or faulty placement of clause components, and faulty use of conjunctions. Some of these features can be seen in the extract below:

> This happening, that man landed on the moon, have had many opposite opinion, that is not worth it such a resources, because it can not be possible to leave any human species. In my opinion I totally agree with these kind of resources. It can not be possible only on earth to have human beings, maybe somewhere very far from earth exists. And this after many years of resource, which until now they will try to find out if this is true that they are human colonies in space. (CH/B/5/151)

Another error constellation clusters around the use of thematic focus. This involves grammatical errors in, for example, the use of pronouns and other cohesive features, and also inappropriate stylistic and lexical choices resulting in lack of a clear antecedent and misleading connectors. Problems with thematic focus also overlap with content, as the reader is left unsure what the writer was intending to convey, as the following example illustrates:

> Firstly scientists want to discover, as much information as possible, about different environments and see the possibility for human being to live in such conditions. For instance moon, we would never know that a step could be much bigger than a common one, before a man landed there. Moreover informed us that there is no living there and soone earth human being would be able to live without an oxygen mask.
>
> Secondly the first step has been already done. As a result moon might be the ticket to other planets and the challenge in order to move on, and discover other planets, such as Mars. Supposing that somewhere else there is life everyone would be interested to know about them and meet them. However this is not the easiest and the cheapest travel, but T.V. and radio will inform people.
>
> On the other hand, might be unrealistic and people believe that there is no chance of establishing human colonies, but researchers have created and Found many statements that previous people from us couldn't imagine or believe. That kind of miracles happen frequently.
> (GR/B/5/160)

As noted before, it is difficult to draw conclusions about the source of error without access to the mental processes involved in composition. While there does appear to be a difference between the types of error made by these two candidates, it would be rash to assume that the error constellations suggested here reflect any cognitive reality. Nevertheless, the problems associated with an atomistic and classificatory approach to error analysis suggests that it may be useful to consider an alternative approach in which 'surface' linguistic features are seen not as a discrete phenomenon but as a closely intertwined part of the making of meaning in written text.

Methodology evaluation of Chapter 7

In this section the research methodology is discussed and a possible problem with the research design debated.

Overall, the study provides an excellent introduction for the new researcher into the methods and processes of the analysis of written texts. The reader will note that this is one of the longer chapters in the book. This is because the topic 'A linguistic analysis of Chinese and Greek L1 scripts for IELTS Academic Writing Task 2' involves detailed, meticulous analysis of written texts (IELTS Task 2 scripts). This type of study invariably takes considerable time for the analysis of the data and considerable space for the recording of results, particularly the results of qualitative analysis.

The term 'discourse analysis' is usually used to describe the analysis of both spoken and written data. The term 'pragmatics' has evolved to describe the analysis of spoken text and the term 'text linguistics' has evolved over the past 30 years to describe the analysis of written text above the level of the sentence. This detailed study consists of: linguistic analysis at the level of errors, sentence structure, and argument structure at the sentence level; and text analysis at the level of argument structure at discourse level, and tenor and personal meaning.

The study analyses quantitative data, such as errors, types of clauses, sentence structure, and word count, all of which can be counted and analysed using common statistical tools. In the authors' own words:

> Means and standard deviations were calculated for the length of each essay (word count) and for the different categories of error. These were then analysed for significance using Fisher's t-test for uncorrelated samples. Pearson product-moment correlation coefficients were also calculated between error categories (p. 256).

The study also uses qualitative analysis, specifically for categories employed in the application of Systemic Functional Grammar (see Halliday 1994) in Sections 6 and 7. The ways in which the analysis is carried out and the samples used are a very good introduction to this form of analysis and classification for new researchers. As the authors themselves state on page 293: 'Not surprisingly, there were qualitative differences in the data which were not captured by the quantitative analysis'.

The above statement is meant to apply to the findings of the analysis of demands for information, but it can be taken to apply to almost all qualitative data when contrasted with quantitative data. Qualitative data invariably provides 'richer' data in the analysis of text but the price of 'richer' data is a greater investment of time and resources (and, therefore, cost) than that required for the analysis of quantitative data. Further problems with the analysis of qualitative data are: the coding of text; the subjectivity of categorisation which can lead to lack of reliability in the analysis; and the discernment of patterns in the text. These problems can be overcome by the training of analysts. Usually, the main researcher does the first analysis, then asks colleagues (working on the same or similar projects) to apply their taxonomy of categories. This process must be maintained until overall agreement is reached. The main researcher must then carry out spot checks to ensure that standards of analysis are being maintained. New researchers of qualitative data will find that adherence to the processes described above will prevent problems with the reliability and the validity of their research project.

Further useful information for researchers involved with the analysis of written errors is contained in Appendix 7.1: Problems of reliability in analysing language errors.

A problem with the design of the study, which the authors readily acknowledge (p. 253) involves the lack of high-scoring texts of L1 Chinese writers. It is clear that no high-scoring texts were available at the time but the absence of such texts can be considered a potential flaw and a risk to the validity of the study and its findings. New and young researchers should note this and try, in the early stages of their research design, to ensure that the data they wish to collect is or will be available. In this study, the lack of high-scoring scripts means that statements about high-scoring L1 Chinese writers are based on those who scored Band 7 on Writing Task 2 instead of those who scored Band 8. In addition, the problem is compounded by having to use high-scoring texts for L1 Chinese writers from candidates in Hong Kong for whom English was closer to a second language than a foreign language until the handover of sovereignty in 1997. Indeed, it is likely that many of the Hong Kong candidates will have been educated in English-medium secondary schools instead of Chinese-medium schools.

Nevertheless, a study such as this can be very useful for new researchers. It demonstrates clearly how such analysis can be designed, the processes involved in the analysis, and the need to ensure that the analysts of qualitative data, which provide 'rich' sources for analysis, are standardised.

It is sometimes claimed that the resources required for the analysis of qualitative data outweigh the usefulness of the data. This was, perhaps, a reasonable claim before the analytical tools for such analysis were developed 30 years ago. Now that the tools exist for text analysis, the claim cannot be substantiated. As the authors themselves imply, qualitative data provide us with new and richer insights into written text. Thus, it is more and more common to read of research projects, such as this, when a mixture of quantitative and qualitative data complement each other.

It is further claimed that a linguistic analysis such as this does not necessarily enhance our knowledge of language for testing purposes. This claim too can be rejected because it is only after linguistic analysis has been carried out that a theoretical linguistic position can be assumed in order to underpin the practices on which tests, questions, bands and descriptors are based.

8 A corpus-based investigation of linguistic responses to an IELTS Academic Writing task

Chris Kennedy and Dilys Thorp

Abstract

This study is based on a corpus created from 130 scripts responding to the same task from IELTS Academic Writing Task 2 in order to investigate the linguistic nature of the answers at three proficiency levels – 8 (expert user), 6 (competent user), and 4 (limited user). Both manual analysis and WordSmith Tools Concordancing programs were used for the analysis of the data.

The scripts were first transcribed into Word documents with the retention of original script layout and mistakes. They were initially coded manually. The initial manual coding took an ethno-methodological approach, 'letting the data speak for itself'. The scripts were first colour-coded for features of note and then further colour-coded for features suggested by relevant research literature. Features which lent themselves to statistical analysis were then subjected to computer analysis using WordSmith Tools. Subsequently, those features that did not lend themselves to being analysed statistically were analysed manually. The discussion summarises features of each level and then exemplifies each feature through the analysis of one script at each level.

Eleven main findings in relation to differences and similarities in the three levels are reported on. The eleven findings relate to: minimum word length, length of paragraphs and length of sentences at the three levels; the proportion of different words in the scripts; the number of words taken from the question; the organisation and numbers of lexico-grammatical errors at different levels; the use of markers at different levels; the use of hedging; the ability of higher level users to interact with the reader; the greater use of boosters and downtoners at higher levels; and the assumption of shared world knowledge by higher-level writers.

1 Introduction

Our aims were to create a corpus of answers to Academic Writing Task 2 of the IELTS examination and to investigate the linguistic nature of those answers. We analysed 130 scripts in answer to the same question (see Appendix 8.1) in Academic Writing Task 2 of the IELTS examination. We investigated the language differences at three levels – 8 (expert user), 6 (competent user), and 4 (limited user). We used both manual analysis and WordSmith Tools Concordancing programs.

The main results were as follows.

1. Level 4 writers find it difficult to reach the minimum word level required (250 words) whereas level 8 writers generally write above it.

2. Paragraphs and sentences are generally longer at level 8 than at either 6 or 4 (which tend to be similar in length).

3. Level 6 /4 writers use a similar proportion of different words in their answers; level 8 writers have a much higher level of different words and use a greater proportion of once-only words – i.e. they have both a richer vocabulary and a greater use of techniques to avoid same-word repetition.

4. There is a higher number, at levels 6 and 4 compared to level 8, of words taken from the question. Whether this means that the lexis and grammar of levels 6/4 is impoverished or that these writers find it difficult to present an argument, or whether both elements are present is difficult to say.

5. Level 4 writers try to get some main ideas across with little apparent organisation and with a high number of lexico-grammatical errors. Level 6 writers are more organised and will often provide examples of disadvantages and advantages to the proposition formulated in the question-prompt. They also have fewer lexico-grammatical errors. Level 8 writers are able to present a complex argument with detailed exemplification and with few language errors.

6. Writers at levels 6/4 use markers (e.g. *however*) more frequently. Level 8 writers rely on them less, and appear to be nearer to native-speaker use in this respect. Enumerative markers (*firstly*, etc.) are used twice as much by level 6/4 writers as level 8 writers. Subordinators are used slightly less by level 8 writers than by levels 6/4. The two lower levels appear to need overt lexico-grammatical markers to structure their argument. Level 8 writers have other means at their disposal.

7. Level 8 use more idiomatic language than levels 6/4, possibly more frequently than native speakers would. There is almost a delight in idiomatic phrasing, a form of linguistic celebration of their competence, but perhaps misplaced in the relatively formal register the question demands. Their answers may be nearer to aspects of spoken English than written in this respect.

8. Lower level scripts (6/4) are more categorical and content is less modified by hedging. Expressions of (dis)agreement and opinion tend to be more directly expressed (*I agree/disagree/in my opinion*, etc.) at level 4.

9. Level 8 writers have both the confidence and the linguistic expertise to interact with the reader to a greater extent than levels 6/4. Rhetorical questions, for example, are used at level 8 both to structure the discourse and involve the reader (perhaps a rhetorical device used more in certain registers of spoken English than in formal written English). Lower level writers (6/4) use rhetorical questions less but answer them more than level 8 writers; the latter use their questions to imply to the reader that the answer is self evident. Level 4 writers tend to set up a question and then answer it – a simple way of constructing an argument.

10. Boosters and downtoners are used at level 8 and decreasingly at the lower levels to submodify propositions and show more involvement with the reader.

11. Level 8 writers interact more with the reader by referring to assumed shared world knowledge; using interpersonal asides to the reader; and exploiting exhortations and exclamations, the two latter strategies having perhaps more in common with a more informal presentation of ideas.

2 Literature review

There have been a number of studies relevant to this research project, and they fall into the following two areas:

- cohesion and coherence of students' essays – work in L1 and in L2, comparing good and poor essays
- hedging, politeness, and stance.

2.1 Cohesion and coherence

Work in this area goes back over more than 20 years, and has been carried out through studies of good and poor writing within L1 as well as within L2. Much of the research was carried out in America in the 1980s, on small data-bases, on the writing of high school students as well as undergraduates. Most of the results show that the use of cohesive devices has little relation to overall coherence.

2.1.1 L1 studies

Eiler (1979) looking at the writing of 15 ninth grade students, found that lexical cohesion was the best indicator of students' response to literature;

reference cohesion was the best evidence 'of ability to sustain a self-sufficient text without appeal to the non-textual environment'.

Hartnett (1980) used counts of different kinds of cohesive ties as a criterion for the evaluation of essays. Her results were mixed – there was no significant difference in the writing of those who had been taught cohesion to those who had not. She pointed out that there is a difference between using cohesive ties, and using them successfully.

Cherry and Cooper (1980, cited in Neuner 1987) looked at 'average and superior' writers in a wide age range. They concluded that writers rely more on lexis and less on reference and conjunction as they mature.

Pritchard (1980) looked at the good and poor compositions of 44 eleventh grade students, and had two main conclusions:

*   The average use or frequency of lexical or grammatical ties did not distinguish the good from the poor essays; a count of devices was no indicator of the efficacy of their use.
*   Sections which readers considered 'problematic' varied from other sections in their proportional use of grammatical and lexical cohesive devices: although poor writers used such devices, their use either created, or failed to resolve, coherence problems.

Witte and Faigley (1981) took five good and five poor freshman essays, and counted the frequency of cohesive ties. Their results were similar to those of Cherry and Cooper (1980). About two-thirds of the ties were lexical, and good essays had a greater density of all types. They conclude that 'cohesion and coherence interact to a great degree, but a cohesive text may be only minimally coherent.' (1981:200).

Crowhurst (1981, cited in Neuner 1987) looked at argument essays of pupils from a wide age range. Similar numbers of students at each level used each kind of tie; surprisingly, the most common type in all categories were repetitions of the same lexical item. She had expected that older students would have a wider vocabulary and thus use fewer exact repetitions.

Tierney and Mosenthal (1983) looked at 24 essays (either a biographical sketch or a thematic essay). They found that cohesion was pervasive in all texts but causally unrelated to coherence.

McCulley (1985) looked at the relation between quality, coherence and cohesion in persuasive essays written by 17-year-olds. His findings contradict those of Tierney and Mosenthal (1983). Some of the cohesion frequencies (noun substitution and ellipsis, demonstrative reference, lexical repetition, lexical synonym, hyponym and collocation) did seem to be related to quality of writing. However, while textual cohesion represented 15% of the variance in writing quality, coherence represented 41%, and coherence also represented 53% of the variance in textual cohesion.

Neuner (1987) looked at a slightly larger sample: 40 freshman essays, of which half were good and half poor. His results reconfirm the findings of many previous researchers: a simple counting of ties does not distinguish good from poor writing at this level. The percentage of ties does not vary radically from good to poor essays. Neuner also looked at cohesive distance, and found that the distance of individual ties did not distinguish good and poor essays, if essay length was held constant. However, the length of cohesive chains did do so: chains in good essays extended over a greater distance and involved a larger proportion of the whole text. Moreover, good writers used a significantly greater number of different words in all chains as well as in each individual chain. There was also a difference in the type of words used: good writers used words in their chains that were less than half as frequent in the language as a whole. He concludes that although cohesive devices do not distinguish good from poor writing, there are several characteristics of cohesive chains which do make a difference – longer chains, greater variety of words, and greater maturity of word choice, though it is not clear what he means by the last category, nor how it is discrete from 'greater variety of words'.

Each of these L1 research studies, carried out in the ten or so years following the publication of Halliday and Hasan's (1976) *Cohesion in English*, focused on aspects of cohesion. The studies all followed a quantitative approach, and were all small scale: the largest looked at only 40 or so essays. The results are generally inconclusive, but suggest that the use of cohesive markers is not necessarily linked to quality of writing

2.1.2 L2 studies

Carrell (1982) criticises the idea that cohesion is a measure of coherence. She argues that text analytic procedures (such as Halliday and Hasan's concept of cohesion) cannot account for textual coherence. She concludes that 'Cohesion is not the cause of coherence; if anything it's the effect of coherence' (1982:486). This is a theoretical paper in which she reviews Halliday and Hasan's cohesion concept and criticisms of it. There is no empirical work of her own.

Connor (1984) compared cohesion and coherence in ESL learners' writing with that of native English speakers. Again her sample was small: she looked at six argument essays. She concluded that 'general cohesion density was not found to be a discriminating factor between the native speakers and ESL writers' (1984:301). ESL learners 'lacked the variety of cohesive devices that good native speaker writers exhibit'. This, she suggests, indicates that the use of cohesion may be developmental, particularly as poor native-speaker writers do not have the variety either. There was also a large difference in the coherence of ESL versus native-speaker writing. ESL writers did not supply sufficient support for claims in their arguments, and also did not link their conclusions to the preceding subtopics (1984:311).

Khalil (1990) investigated the relation of cohesion to coherence in 20 one-paragraph compositions by Arab freshmen EFL students. He found that Arab students overused reiteration of the same lexical item as a cohesive device, but underused other lexical and grammatical cohesive devices. His results for the percentage of lexical cohesive ties and for grammatical cohesive ties in good and poor essays were similar to those of Neuner (1987) and Cherry and Cooper (1980) – in all cases showing little difference between good and poor essays.

In the case of coherence, he found that in the most coherent essay (evaluated by native speakers on the basis of Grice's maxims), the writer elaborated on the main topic by giving specific examples. Cohesive ties such as *therefore, also, as, for*, were used to link the main topic and subtopics. 'Text coherence is achieved by a successful elaboration of the main topic' (Khalil 1990:364). In the weakest essay the writer provided no specifics, and even the generalities were unclear. Main topics were not backed up with specific details. On the analysis based on the Gricean maxims, the maxim of quantity – reflecting the informativeness of the text – had the lowest score, showing that writers did not give enough information. This reinforces similar findings by Atari (1983, cited in Khalil 1990).

Khalil's statistical analysis shows that there is a weak correlation between the number of cohesive ties and the coherence score. He agrees with Carrell's conclusions (see above).

Crewe (1990) argues that logical connectives are frequently misused by ESL students. His ideas are based on the essays of students in Hong Kong (it is not clear how many – there is no clear database). He argues that propositions are linked together not by 'an objectively correct item but by a subjective assessment of the relationship between them by the writer' (1990:316). He takes up the idea stated by others (e.g. Hartnett 1986, Mosenthal and Tierney 1984) that the presence of cohesive devices does not necessarily improve the readability and coherence of a text, and that used badly they are confusing. He provides evidence of both the overuse and misuse of connectors from the essays of his students. He argues that students have a misconception that the more connectives they use the better, but in fact, 'Discourse connectives are difficult to process in any case, but if they are both misused and overused the task becomes virtually impossible' (1990:320). He shows that 'the clutter of connectives makes the argument extremely tortuous', and that by over-relying on these ties the writer is trying to impose a veneer of logicality where actually there is none. In fact the ties can make the text harder for the reader to process, as the connective can be leading in an opposite direction to the thread of the argument. He takes this point further and suggests that an increase in ties is almost an attempt to disguise poor writing: it seems to indicate an area of difficulty for the writer, which the plethora of surface links is an attempt to overcome. He concludes that using ties too often at best clutters the text and at worst completely confuses the argument. Non-use of ties is better than misuse, since all readers can make their own logical links in an argument if there are none there, whereas misuse obfuscates the message.

Other studies of the writing of Chinese speakers (e.g. Field and Yip 1992) show that Cantonese writers use a significantly higher frequency of devices than do native English speakers, and also tend to use them in sentence or paragraph initial position rather than within a sentence.

The study by Granger and Tyson (1996) is one of the more recent in the area of connector usage. It differs from previous studies in that it is on a larger scale, based on the International Corpus of Learner English. This is a corpus of written essays by advanced learners of English (i.e. third- and fourth-year university students) from ten different language backgrounds (Granger 1993). Granger and Tyson tested the hypothesis that there would be a general overuse of connectors by learners, but in fact did not find this. They emphasise the importance of using both quantitative and qualitative approaches, and find that a qualitative analysis of their data shows a more complex picture. There is evidence of both overuse and underuse of individual connectors, and misuse of them semantically, stylistically and syntactically. The underuse of connectors is of those which contrast (*however*, *though*, *yet*) and develop the argument (*therefore*, *thus*, *then*). Learners tended to use connectors which added to a point, illustrated it, or emphasised it, but did not use them significantly either to signal a change in direction of the argument or to take it forward. They note that little work has been done on the underuse of connectors.

Flowerdew (1998) presents one of the first studies to use corpus linguistics to compare native- and non-native-speaker data. She looks at a Hong Kong learner corpus of similar size to the data we present here: 80 assignments of 500 words each, and a native-speaker (NS) corpus of a similar size. She has a number of interesting findings of relevance to our own research.

She uses an analytical approach (based on Crombie 1985a, 1985b, Hoey 1983, 1986, Winter 1977, 1978 – all cited in Flowerdew 1998:331), which as well as examining the connections between clauses and sentences also looks at the relations across larger stretches of text. In this way text coherence at both a local and global level is accounted for. She looks at the overuse, underuse and misuse of a number of causative devices. She finds that there is an interesting difference in the frequency of use of logical connectors – *because* and *therefore* occur about twice as often in the learner corpus (LC) as in the NS corpus. This is a similar finding to that of others looking at Hong Kong students, but differs from Granger and Tyson's findings (1996) with French students, that there was overuse of additive and appositive connectors, but underuse of connectors which developed the argument.

Flowerdew also found a marked difference in the positioning of connectors. In the learner corpus *therefore* (and other similar words) was, in 99% of the cases, in sentence-initial position; whereas in the NS data there was only one instance of such words in sentence-initial position, and in the other instances it 'indicated a stage of a wider process where the construction *and therefore* + *verb* with the subject ellipted was common.' (1998:332).

The grammatical patterning of *because* was another difference between the two corpora. Just over a quarter of the occurrences of *because* occurred as *It is because*, a pattern which did not occur at all in the NS corpus. Not only is the anaphoric reference wrongly signalled here (it should be *this*), but it is in a marked thematic position over-emphasising the cause or reason. There was also a problem in the learner corpus of the use of double connectors like *because . . . so that.*

Flowerdew makes an important point in her conclusion about the production of overall coherence in a text. She finds that in the NS corpus the logical connectors *so, thus,* and *then* had a summative function. The concluding summary in the NS data was also evaluative, with writers offering a viewpoint based on what they had written. This seemed to give global coherence to the text. In the LC data, there were hardly any instances of connectors used anaphorically in this way: in the LC data they were used at the local level to link adjacent clauses or sentences. Flowerdew cites Evenson's suggestion that 'the difference between poor and more proficient writers may . . . be due to the poor writer's over-reliance on local uses of these connectors and their lack of exploitation at the mesolevel' (Evenson 1990, cited in Flowerdew 1998:337).

The L2 studies looking at cohesion and coherence include some that are larger scale (Flowerdew 1998; Granger and Tyson 1996) and one that takes both a qualitative and quantitative approach (Granger and Tyson 1996). Apart from Khalil (1990), they almost all compare the writing of non-native speakers with that of native speakers of English. None compares advanced with less advanced second language learners. The studies all look at the *way* in which cohesive markers are used: they all report misuse of markers, as well as overuse of some and underuse of others. Some of these studies also look at the positioning of connectors: both Field and Yip (1992) and Flowerdew (1998) comment on the propensity of learners to use them in sentence initial position, in contrast to the way in which native speakers use them. Some of these studies (e.g. Crewe 1990, Khalil 1990) also highlight the fact that coherence in essays is achieved by means other than connectives, for example through elaboration or exemplification of the main point. Good writing seems to have an internal coherence of its own, independent of the use of cohesive markers. Interestingly, Granger and Tyson's qualitative analysis suggests a greater complexity in the use of connectors than is revealed through quantitative research. This suggests to us that there is scope for further qualitative research in this area, and into aspects of writing other than the use of cohesive ties.

2.2 Hedging, politeness, and stance

The work of Myers, Flowerdew, Hyland, Thompson and Hunston, Conrad and Biber, and Hewings have a bearing on our research.

Looking at the genre of scientific articles (a different genre from that of the essays we investigated, but nonetheless of relevance), Myers (1989) argues that features which are normally seen as scientific norms can be better understood as politeness strategies – in other words, as ways of dealing with the social interactions involved in writing an article for publication. He finds examples of both positive politeness, emphasising solidarity between writer and reader, and negative politeness in the form of hedging. Forms of positive politeness include pronouns, modifiers assuming common ground, emotional responses to indicate solidarity, and joking. Jokes can establish a sense of shared knowledge or assumptions. Forms of negative or deference politeness include hedging, impersonal constructions and assertion of general rules as well as constructions which emphasise a personal point of view. Forms of hedging include modal verbs, making a conditional statement, modifiers (e.g. probably) and any device which suggests that there are alternatives (e.g. use of indefinite article as opposed to definite). Apologies are another, though less common way, of showing deference.

Hyland (1994) also emphasises the importance of tentative language in academic writing, and considers that insufficient attention is given to it in teaching materials, particularly since it is 'an important source of pragmatic failure in the writing of second language science students' (1994:239). He endorses Stubbs' view that 'all sentences encode a point of view' (Stubbs 1986:1), and argues that 'writing is a social act': to be effective, academic writing must show recognition of the importance of interaction between writer and reader. Central to this is the use of hedging, since '. . . hedges are an important means of both supporting the writer's position and building writer–reader relations' (1994:241).

Flowerdew's work, (1997, 1998 – see also above) is important to our research in that, as we have seen, she looks at a large corpus of native-speaker and non-native-speaker data. In her 1997 paper she looks at aspects of pragmatic failure in a learner corpus (LC), and considers how much 'tentative language continues to be an important source of pragmatic failure in L2 science students' writing' (p. 77). She looks at hedging and what she terms 'boosters' (e.g. *very, far, extremely*) and 'downtoners'(e.g. *somewhat, fairly, quite*). She finds that students 'lack finesse in using intensifying or mitigating markers' (p. 77) except for *very* and *only* which were both overused and misused. She found few hedges in the LC; and while there was frequent use of the modals *may* and *could* with verbs signalling explanation in the NS corpus, there was a complete absence of such modals in the LC. The LC also shows evidence of overuse of lexical speech act verbs such as *I think* which, when used, are also misused (1977:79). The overall effect of this and of the absence of modals is that in the LC the analysis and interpretation of results tends to be presented as though 'based on certain knowledge rather than plausible reasoning' (pp. 79–80). This would seem to support the findings of Bazerman (1988) and Hyland (1994) that undergraduate writing is direct and unhedged. Flowerdew (1997) also has a useful concluding paragraph on the merits and demerits of using concordancers for analysis.

Flowerdew (1998) finds an interesting difference in the illocutionary force of causative verbs, results which confirm a similar pattern in her 1997 study. In the NS corpus just over a quarter of causative verbs were modified by use of a modal, whereas there were few such mitigators (about one tenth) in the LC. Similarly, other causal expressions such as *due to* and *because of* were modified in the NS corpus by adverbs like *largely/partly* (cf. Channell 1994 on vague language) but there was no such modification in the LC. Another use of mitigation markers was found with the items *by* and *through* to indicate means–result. In most cases in the NS corpus, the causative verb preceding *by + present participle/noun phrase* was attenuated by a marker such as *probably/possibly*. These were much less used in the LC.

Thompson and Hunston (2000) convincingly argue that greater recognition should be given to the importance of the expression of a writer's opinion in language. They show through careful analysis that this is a complex matter and lies at a far deeper level than the simple phrase-book expression *in my opinion*. They use the term 'evaluation' as a:

> . . . broad cover term for the expression of the speaker or writer's attitude or stance towards, viewpoint on, or feelings about the entities or propositions that he or she is talking about. That attitude may relate to certainty or obligation or desirability or any number of other sets of values (2000:5).

They illustrate three ways in which evaluation is important: it is a way of writers giving their opinion, and thereby also expressing or reflecting the ideology of society; it is a way of establishing and maintaining interaction with the reader; and thirdly it is a way of organising the discourse. Of particular relevance to our analysis is the way writers promote their own academic credibility: 'writers demonstrate that the topic they have chosen is interesting, important, and the subject of investigation by many other researchers' (2000:8).

Another interesting feature discussed by Thompson and Hunston (2000) is the way in which information that is expressed evaluatively may be presented as 'given' rather than 'new'. This, they suggest, makes it harder for a reader to dispute the evaluation: acceptance is taken for granted, and the reader is quietly manipulated.

Conrad and Biber's (2000) work is interesting not only for the content of their research but also for the methodology. They use a corpus to study different ways in which speakers and writers use adverbials to mark their 'stance', or attitude, towards what they are saying. The adverbials cover a range of different grammatical forms, and express three types of meaning:

- to do with certainty – 'epistemic', e.g. *probably*
- to do with feelings and judgements – 'attitudinal', e.g. *surprisingly*
- to do with how something is said – 'style', e.g. *briefly*.

Conrad and Biber's corpus comprises texts from three different genres: conversation, academic writing and newspaper reports. They find that adverbials are used twice as often in academic writing as in newspaper reports, and that epistemic adverbials are the most common in all three registers. All three types can be realised by many different grammatical structures, but prepositional phrases are the most common form of stance adverbials in academic writing. These, they discover, are particularly used to limit the extent to which a claim can be generalised, through such phrases as *on the whole* and *in most cases*.

Conrad and Biber point out the value of corpus-based analyses, arguing that such methods can 'complement more intensive studies of particular texts'. Moreover, such analyses can reveal what is 'distinctive about language use in particular contexts and identify useful directions for future investigations' (2000:73). We have found both these aspects invaluable in the present research. Hewings (1999:82), contrasts British first and third-year undergraduate geography essays and comments:

> Rhetorical motivations such as evaluation and persuasion are seen as central to academic discourses . . . Such motivations, if perceived by the student, will influence the whole discourse by changing the task of essay writing from one of disinterested knowledge display to one of involved analysis.

She argues that one way a writer presents an 'angle' on the topic is by using interpersonal theme, also showing an awareness of the reader. Interpersonal themes, which were more common in third-year essays than those of the first year, were especially evident in those essays which had been highly rated by markers. Hewings comments that the use of interpersonal themes such as *it is fair to say* or *perhaps* marks out writers who do more than present factual information; they are creating an argument for a reader. Use of interpersonal themes highlights the engagement of the writer in the persuasive dialogue that underlines the pseudo-objectivity of much academic writing.

> Comments such as 'in general' mediate the amount of commitment a writer shows to a statement. They allow the writer's opinion to be intruded into the text and . . . show a more evaluative or persuasive

rhetorical motivation. It is one way in which relevant criticism . . .
textual argument, imaginative discussion . . . were manifested in the
texts (Hewings 1999:255).

Third-year students in Hewings' data showed that they realised that the
'message' in their writing involved not just ideational content, but text building (using textual themes) and social relationships – awareness of reader –
through interpersonal themes. The first-year essays, which tended to use
more simple topical themes and fewer multiple themes, had shorter sentences, fewer co-ordinated clauses, with fewer instances of *and* and *but*, and
more subordinated clauses.

Hewings also discusses the use of 'sentences which function as rhetorical
questions and thus as discourse organisers'. They only occur in 6% of her
data. Hewings (1999:204) refers to academic style guides, such as Smyth
(1994:15), which advise students not to use rhetorical questions. Hewings
also points out that Smyth implies that such rhetorical devices are para-
graph-initial, which is not the case in her data.

One aspect of Hewings' grammatical subject analysis of particular relevance to our analysis is the role of anticipatory *it*-clauses. This is a useful way
of combining two important functions in academic writing: being persuasive
and also appearing to be 'objective and impersonal'. Hewings found more evidence of anticipatory *it*-clauses in the third-year essays than the first-year
essays. Most instances provide evaluation, often in a form concealing the view
that is being expressed. Following a Hallidayan model, Hewings discusses
metaphors of modality, and gives the example of 'it is (clear/possible/likely
obvious) that . . .' as a grammatical metaphor for 'I think/in my opinion'. She
writes, 'the use of grammatical metaphor allows the speaker/writer to present
the opinion as objective – not associated with the speaker/writer' (1999:223),
thus masking the overt expression of opinion.

She discusses the views of a number of linguists (e.g. Quirk et al 1985,
Thompson 1994) about the use of *it*-clauses. There are three different uses of
anticipatory *it*, all of which are recognised as 'hedging' devices: 'comment
clauses, *it is said/reported/claimed* as well as *it seems/appears*; complementation by extraposed subject *that*-clause and *to*-infinitive clause; and adjectival
complementation' (1999:224). Quirk, reported in Hewings, classifies the
adjectives into three patterns: those relating to truth or knowledge (e.g.
certain, evident, obvious); relating to modality and volition (e.g. *important,
essential*); and emotive adjectives (e.g. *surprising, fortunate*).

Hewings takes this research further by concordancing *it*-clauses and
analysing them grammatically. She identifies four different patterns:

* clauses with modal finites (e.g. *must, may, might*)
* impersonal projecting clauses with verbs of verbal and mental processes,
  or *seem* and *appear* (*it seems*)

- other modal constructions (*it is possible that, it is likely that*)
- comment clauses (*it is important that, it is difficult to*).

Hewings argues that these types of clauses have both 'a strongly rhetorical purpose allowing evaluation of many types to be expressed 'explicitly' and 'objectively', and they may also have a text-organising function' (1999:238). Her analysis of the undergraduate essays shows that third-year writers use both a greater number and greater variety of these clauses than do the first-year writers.

Hewings also looks at the prevalence of metadiscoursal *it*-clauses, and finds that there are almost twice as many in third-year essays as in first-year essays. Hedges were the most frequent type used, but almost as frequent in the third-year writing were attitude markers, which show the writer's judgement about the significance of the proposition (e.g. *it is important, it is fair to say* 1999:242, 245).

What is of particular interest to our present research is Hewings' conclusion, from her analysis, that *it*-clauses serve a rhetorical purpose. Most importantly they are a way by which writers convey an impersonal stance to their judgements or opinions:

> The use of it-clauses is one way in which students can present their opinions to their audience while maintaining an impersonal, deferential stance. As grammatical metaphors, many it-clauses encode the politeness and deference to the research community that may be expected given the difference in role and status between the writer and the reader (Hewings 1999:247).

The research reviewed in this section all emphasise, in different ways, the importance of audience awareness and of the social, interactive nature of writing in a variety of genres, from scientific articles to academic writing. It seems that the more advanced writers are skilled in the use of tentative language, and in conveying their attitude, expressing an opinion, or creating an argument in a variety of covert ways. Examples of this include presenting information with which they agree as given, so that it appears indisputable; using various adverbials, in particular those relating to certainty; using interpersonal theme; and using anticipatory 'it' clauses to appear objective and impersonal while in fact subtly conveying an opinion or stance.

3 Research methodology

In this section we discuss the transcription of our data and how we approached the manual and statistical analyses of the data. Statistical and manual analyses were done cyclically rather than sequentially. We used each approach to suggest areas of further investigation for the other. Similarly, our research went hand in hand with our reference to the literature: our initial reading suggested areas of possible analysis; in turn our analysis showed patterns that we wanted to investigate by reference to other research.

3.1 Transcription of data

The 130 handwritten scripts were typed into Word documents, with one script per file. Each script was answering the same question on the IELTS written examination. (See Appendix 8.1.) Original script layout and mistakes were retained, with a few exceptions. Where, particularly at the higher level, the spelling of a word had a small error such as failure to cross a 't', we corrected it. 'Pseudo' full stops – which appeared more as pencil rests – were ignored. Where a word was illegible, particularly at level 4, we made the best sense we could of it.

We also typed, as separate files, 'corrected' versions of the same texts – i.e. with clear spelling errors corrected, as a 'corrected' version was preferable in calculating the type/token ratio and the count of single instances of the same word, particularly at level 4 where misspellings are frequent.

3.2 Manual analysis of data

Starting with the level 8 scripts, we read all the scripts through to see what features were of potential interest. Then, taking an ethnographic approach and letting the data 'speak for itself', we colour-coded those features which were of particular note. We carried out further colour-coding on features suggested by relevant literature (e.g. the use of hedges). A second stage was to extend this colour-coding to levels 4 and 6. In this way we listed the features that were of note at each level. We then carried out computer analysis (using WordSmith Tools) of features of particular interest.

We summarise features of each level, and then, to exemplify, analyse one script at each of the three levels. Though it cannot be said that any one particular script is strictly 'typical', it is, in the ethnographic tradition, 'illuminating' or 'telling' to look at one in closer detail. As Evans (1988:7) says of his own qualitative studies, 'the validity . . . does not depend on numbers but on . . . necessarily subjective efforts to understand the whole through close attention to individuals'.

3.3 Computer analysis of data

After carrying out basic computer analysis based on length of essays, we used the Concord and Wordlist tools of the WordSmith Tools program to look at word frequency, concordances and collocates. We based the analysis on all the 130 files: 50 at level 4, 50 at level 6, and 30 at level 8. (Since it was difficult to find the full number of level 8 scripts, 'level 8' in fact refers to 18 scripts at level 8 and 12 at level 9). We calculated percentages for all the data. Statistical tests of significance were not carried out, and it is in any case doubtful whether such statistics resulting from relatively few scripts at each level could have been accepted as reliable and valid.

We used WordSmith Tools to look at the following features:

Use of rhetorical questions

Investigation of this aspect was achieved by using a concordance of question marks, but because of poor punctuation we had to go through all 130 scripts manually. Manual analysis also had to be carried out for the detail as to whether a rhetorical question was answered or not, and for its position within the text.

Modals, modal lexical verbs, and words like 'possibly'

First, we noticed, from a manual analysis, that there were many occurrences of modals in the scripts. In order to obtain confirmation of this and a more accurate figure, a wordlist and concordance of modals was obtained.

Discourse markers

We noticed that these were prevalent at levels 6 and 4, but not as frequent at level 8. We sought statistical confirmation through WordSmith, and found more interesting patterns. Both Wordlist and Concordancer were used to check on the use of markers: Wordlist gave us the frequency of use of markers at each level; Concordancer enabled us to see the context in which each marker was used, and to check on whether or not it was used correctly.

Subordinators and co-ordinators: number and use

Computer analysis was invaluable, not only to retrieve statistical counts, but also to investigate, through the Concordancer, actual use. It is important not to rely on counts, but, in the absence of tagging procedures, to check from the context that the word is actually being used as a clause co-ordinator (e.g. many uses of *and* are to link two nouns rather than two clauses).

'Boosters' and 'downtoners'

We looked at these to investigate differential use at the different levels.

Lexis

We considered type:token ratio and number of 'once only' words including a wordlist plus concordancing.

Proportion of title words in texts

A combination of computer and manual analysis was used. We had a subjective impression that at levels 4 and 6 there was a good deal of lexis from the essay title. We then used Wordlist to confirm this through a frequency count. We returned to a manual analysis, looked in detail at level 6, and found large chunks that were identical to the essay title.

Collocates of *I*

We looked at these in order to see which verbs are associated with this personal pronoun at each level.

Use of *it*-clauses

The Concordancer searched for *it*, and the resultant data was 'zapped' to eliminate pronoun and non-initial occurrences of *it*.

The following features could not be analysed using WordSmith and so were analysed manually.

* content: knowledge of the outside world
* content: topics
* content: exemplification
* passivisation
* interpersonal comments/asides to examiner
* the way in which rhetorical questions were answered within a text
* the use of paraphrase/identical copying of chunks from essay title.

3.4 Analysis of the three levels of answer

An account of typical features at each level was provided by studying the texts manually, although based on knowledge from the computer analysis. Similarly, a detailed analysis of one script at each of the three levels was carried out.

Although our data analysis was carried out on the entire corpus, our discussion focuses particularly on the advanced level (IELTS level 8), as the difference between this level and levels 6 and 4 is striking. We also focused on this level as we were interested in what constitutes a 'good' answer. We have therefore contrasted level 8 with the lower levels.

4 Results

4.1 Statistics relating to length

One of the apparent differences between the scripts at the higher level (8) and those at the two lower levels is in overall length of answers. This subjective impression is confirmed by the statistics. The average length of a level 8 answer is 333 words, whereas the average length at level 4 is 233 words, and

277 words at level 6. According to these averages the level 4 scripts are nearly one-third shorter than the level 8 scripts. Such figures do not tell the whole story, however, and mask greater differences, for instance, there are two untypically long scripts at the lower levels: script 6/24 (485 words) and script 4/19 (370 words). Table 8.1 shows the difference in range of length at each level. While the greatest range of length is at level 6, the shortest range is at level 8. The table also shows clearly that the bulk of level 4 scripts are below the minimum required length (250 words), while the majority of level 8 scripts are above that.

Table 8.1 Range of length of essays at each level

Level 8	Level 6	Level 4
239–457 words (range of 218)	184–485 words (range of 301)	111–370 words (range of 259)

The two sets of figures in Tables 8.2a and b are interesting. We can see from Table 8.2a that 34% of the total level 4 essays are below 200 words while there are none under 200 words at level 8. Table 8.2b shows that nearly two thirds of level 4 essays (60%) are short, below the IELTS stated minimum length of 250 words. Only 40% of level 4 essays are over this stated minimum length. By contrast at level 8 nearly two-thirds (60%) of the essays are 250–350 words, with only a mere 7% below 250. Level 6 differs interestingly from both levels 4 and 8: while 30% are below 250 words, only two (4%) are below 200 words; nearly two-thirds are 250–350 words – a similar proportion to level 8, but there are far fewer long essays – only 6% over 350 words, as opposed to 33% at level 8.

Tables 8.2 (a) and 8.2 (b) Number of essays at each level at different lengths

(a)

	100–200 words	200–300 words	300–400 words	400+ words
Level 8	0 (0%)	11/30 (37%)	14/30 (47%)	5/30 (17%)
Level 6	2/50 (4%)	34/50 (68%)	12/50 (24%)	2/50 (4%)
Level 4	17/50 (34%)	25/50 (50%)	8/50 (16%)	0

(b)

	Below 250 words	250–350 words	350–450 words	450+ words
Level 8	2/30 (7%)	18/30 (60%)	10/30 (33.3%)	0
Level 6	15/50 (30%)	31/50 (62%)	3/50 (6%)	1/50 (2%)
Level 4	30/50 (60%)	18/50 (36%)	2/50 (4%)	0

This difference in length in itself seems an indicator – but only one such – of success or failure in the IELTS Writing exam. The crucial difference in essay word length between levels 4 and 6 is striking.

Computer analysis of the data shows differences in sentence and paragraph length (in terms of the number of words in each case) between the three levels. Table 8.3 shows that levels 4 and 6 are similar in both respects, but both are different from level 8. At level 8 the average paragraph is twice as long as at level 4.

Table 8.3 Difference between sentence and paragraph length

Sentence length	Level 8 26.53	Level 6 19.45	Level 4 19.85
Paragraph length	Level 8 121.70	Level 6 69.16	Level 4 62.09

Statistics from WordSmith, using 'corrected' versions of the texts, show the following difference in type:token ratio:

Level 8: 18.57   **Level 6:** 11.01   **Level 4:** 10.93

'Types' are the different words, and 'tokens' are the total number of words. So this ratio shows that there is a higher proportion of different words in the level 8 texts than in the lower levels, as might be expected. We can see that levels 4 and 6 are similar in this respect. A more detailed examination of the word frequency lists shows that there is a greater proportion of words used once only in the level 8 texts than in the lower levels (using 'corrected' versions of the texts).

Level 8: 10.8%   **Level 6:** 4.8%   **Level 4:** 5%

Wordsmith also allows us to compare the number of words of different lengths at each level. While the number of shorter length words (1–5 letters) is fairly similar between the three levels, it is in the longer words, particularly those over 12 letters, that the difference is most striking. Level 8 texts have a total of 82 words of more than 12 letters, while level 4 texts have 34 and level 6 texts have 56. Similarity between the three levels in the frequency of words with more than eight letters is, we suggest, explained by the use, particularly at the lower levels, of key words of this length from the essay title (e.g. *computers, language, learning*).

We can see from these statistics that the level 8 essays are longer overall, have longer sentences, longer paragraphs, and use a greater variety of lexis and a higher proportion of longer words. These findings are of no surprise since variety of language is one of the criteria on which the essays are assessed – and the statistics confirm this.

Behind the statistics on paragraph length lies a greater difference that emerges from counting the number of paragraphs per essay at each level. These figures are shown in Tables 8.4 and 8.5.

Table 8.4 Number of paragraphs per essay at levels 8, 6 and 4

Number of paragraphs per essay	1	2	3	4	5	6	7	8	9	10
Number of level 8 essays/30	0	2	4	5	8	4	5	1	0	1
Number of level 6 essays/50	1	0	3	24	13	7	1	0	1	0
Number of level 4 essays/50	5	4	9	12	11	7	2	0	0	0

Table 8.5 Number of paragraphs in essays at levels 8, 6 and 4 (in percentages)

No. of paragraphs per essay	1	2	3	4	5	6	7	8	9	10+
No. of level 8 essays %	0	6.6	13.3	16	26.6	13.3	16.6	3.3	0	3.3
No. of level 6 essays %	2	0	6	48	26	14	2	0	2	0
No. of level 4 essays %	10	8	18	24	22	14	4	0	0	0

The figures show one of the few clear differences between the level 6 and level 4 scripts. Ten per cent of the level 4 scripts had only one single paragraph for the whole essay, compared to only 2% of those at level 6. If we look at the figures for up to two paragraphs per essay, then this includes 18% of the level 4 scripts, compared to only 2% of those at level 6.

These statistics also mask the fact that at level 4 there are a great number of one sentence paragraphs.

4.2 Content and internal cohesion

4.2.1 Proportion of key words from essay title in data

A subjective impression suggests that, in the lower-level texts, (levels 6 and 4), a considerable proportion of the vocabulary consists of lexical items from the essay title, in contrast to the higher-level essays. WordSmith analysis was carried out on the data to obtain a quantitative measurement of this impression. Table 8.6 confirms that lexical items from the essay title do indeed constitute a higher proportion of the texts at levels 6 and 4 than at level 8. This is also likely to account for the relatively high proportion of words with eight or more letters at levels 6 and 4, as suggested above.

At level 8, the total percentage of keywords from the title is 6.89%, whereas at level 6 and at level 4 it is nearly one third higher, at 9.97% and 9.71% respectively. For some lexical items, such as *children*, the proportion is double at levels 6 and 4 compared to level 8. Similarly the phrase 'foreign

Table 8.6 Proportion of keywords taken from the essay question and used in answers at each level

Word/phrase from question	Level 8		Level 6		Level 4	
	Frequency	%	Frequency	%	Frequency	%
children	53	0.53	135	0.97	134	1.15
computer	102	1.02	268	1.93	290	2.54
computers	99	0.99	135	0.97	88	0.75
foreign	75	0.75	204	1.47	156	1.34
language	143	1.43	190	1.37	128	1.10
languages	87	0.87	192	1.39	131	1.12
learning	66	0.66	85	0.61	72	0.62
quality	9	0.09	34	0.25	34	0.29
translation/s	53	0.53	139	1.00	100	0.86
Total	**687**	**6.89%**	**1382**	**9.97%**	**1133**	**9.71%**
foreign languages	37		124		90	
foreign language	66		188		148	
	= 103	1.00%	= 312	2.25%	= 238	2.00%

language/s' occurs twice as frequently in the level 6 and level 4 data. Table 8.6 shows the results of the WordSmith wordlist taking words from the essay question; these are highlighted in bold.

> *Every year the **quality** of **translation** by **computer** improves. In the future there will be no point in our **children learning foreign languages**, because **computers** will be able to provide immediate **translation** whenever it is needed.*

4.2.2 Topic analysis at each level

A crude manual analysis of topic was carried out at levels 4 and 6. At level 6 we identified the main topics in the first 27 of the 50 scripts to get an indication of the number of ideas per script at that level. We did the same for level 4, but for only the first 11 scripts, partly because of constraints of time, partly because of difficulty in distinguishing/comprehending the ideas, and mainly since we felt 11 scripts were sufficiently representative. It was difficult to separate out the ideas in level 4 scripts, and particularly hard to separate them out into arguments either supporting or criticising the use of computers for translation. We have attempted to simply list the main ideas.

We have not treated level 8 in the same way, as a simple listing of 'topics' would not do justice to the density and complexity of ideas and argumentation at that level. Instead, it seemed more appropriate at level 8 to list instances of detailed exemplification of main ideas. The results can be seen in Tables 8.7, 8.8, and 8.9 in Appendix 8.2.

At level 4 (see Table 8.7), there is little apparent organisation of topics, although it can be seen – e.g. from 4–01, 4–02 and 4–09 – that the writers have several interesting and relevant ideas. At level 6 there is more apparent organisation, often – though not always – arguments supporting or opposing the use of computers for translation. There is little detailed exemplification (see Table 8.9) at either level 4 or level 6. We shall return to level 8 in the further section on world knowledge.

4.2.3 Use of markers

Intuitive impressions from reading the essays are that there is considerable difference in the use of markers at the three levels. This is confirmed by statistical analysis from WordSmith. Our results bear out the conclusions of others (e.g. Crewe 1990, Field and Yip 1992, Flowerdew 1998, Granger and Tyson 1996), that there is overuse of additive markers by lower-level learners, and that all markers are used more in sentence-initial position by learners than by more advanced writers.

Table 8.10 compares the use of discourse markers between the three IELTS levels. It shows a number of interesting features.

1. Overall there is a greater preponderance of markers at levels 6 and 4 than at level 8. The two lower levels are similar in the extent of their use. At levels 4 and 6 there are almost twice the number of markers (per 10,000 words) as at level 8.

2. The use of *however* is more frequent at level 6 than at level 8, and all occurrences at level 6 are in sentence-initial position. This contrasts with the level 8 texts where only 14 out of 23 are in sentence-initial position. At level 4 there are fewer instances of *however*, though we can see from Table 8.11 that level 4 candidates use *but* more than the other two levels. *However* may therefore be a marker of relative linguistic sophistication, (or at least perceived to be so by more advanced writers), with less-skilled writers resorting to a 'prototypical' or 'core' *but* when wishing to express contrast, with more advanced writers using *however* as a more formal or register-specific item.

3. There is little difference in the frequency with which *therefore* is used between level 8 and the two lower levels. However, the use of *so* to express consequence is much more prevalent with level 4, less so with level 6, and even less so with level 8. The word *thus* is a favourite in level 8 answers, occurring 13 times, although only four out of 13 are in sentence-initial position. This word is only used once at level 4. *Thus* may be a perceived marker of sophistication (as we have called *however*, above), with level 4 writers using the more informal *so*.

4. The additive markers taken together (*moreover/in addition/furthermore*) show another marked difference between level 8 writers, who use them infrequently (7 per 10,000 words) and level 4 and 6 writers (14.5 and 18.1 per 10,000 words respectively).

Table 8.10 Frequency of markers

Marker	Level 8	per 10,000	Sentence initial position	Level 6	per 10,000	Sentence initial position	Level 4	per 10,000	Sentence initial position
however	23	23.1	14/23	42	30.4	42/42	21	18.0	18/21
therefore	7	7.0	4/7	13	9.4	10/13	11	9.4	10/11
so (= therefore)	12	12.0	8/12	32	23.0	19/32	44	37.7	31/44
thus	13	13.0	4/13	5	3.6	4/5	1	0.9	1/1
moreover	3	3.0	2/3	7	5.1	7/7	6	5.1	5/6
in addition	2	2.0	2/2	8	5.8	8/8	6	5.1	6/6
furthermore	2	2.0	2/2	11	7.2	10/11	5	4.3	5/5
firstly	6	6.0	6/6	21	15.2	21/21	17	14.6	17/17
secondly	7	7.0	7/7	17	12.3	17/17	11	9.4	11/11
thirdly	2	2.0	2/2	8	5.8	8/8	7	6.0	7/7
finally	1	1.0	1/1	4	2.9	4/4	10	8.6	10/10
in conclusion	3	3.0	3/3	19	13.7	18/19	19	16.3	18/18
Total	**81**	**81.2**	–	**187**	**134.9**	–	**158**	**135.3**	–

Table 8.11 Co-ordinators

	Level 8		Level 6		Level 4	
Co-ordinator	No. of occurrences	Frequency (%)	No. of occurrences	Frequency (%)	No. of occurrences	Frequency (%)
and	148	1.48	134	0.97	152	1.28
but	51	0.51	64	0.46	85	0.73
or	15	0.15	7	0.35	13	0.11
Total	**214**	**2.15%**	**205**	**1.48%**	**250**	**2.14%**

5. The use of enumerative markers (*firstly/secondly/thirdly*) is interesting: the subtotals show that at level 4 and level 6 there are twice as many (30 and 33.3 per 10,000 words respectively) as at level 8 (15 per 10,000 words).

6. The summation markers (*finally/in conclusion*) show the same pattern as we have noticed with the other markers. While there are only four occurrences per 10,000 words at level 8, the figures at levels 4 and 6 are six times and four times greater respectively.

The less frequent use of markers at level 8 does not of course mean that the more advanced writers are not communicating the logical content signalled by such markers. In fact, we shall see later that level 6 and particularly level 4 writers, although they signal more, typically find it more difficult to express arguments and opinions than level 8 writers. Level 8 writers clearly have other devices at their disposal apart from overt discourse markers by which they structure their ideas and convey them logically. It would be an appropriate future research objective to discover what such alternative devices might be. In the case of levels 6 and 4, the overuse of markers gives an impression that the writing is logically expressed and ordered and may mislead a reader into thinking that the writers have control over content which is not always the case. Why the less skilful writers should overuse the markers and why skilful writers do not feel the need to use them to the same extent is an interesting question. It may well be that novice writers in a second language, who, in an examination such as IELTS, are having to grapple in real time with ideational content and the lexico-grammar through which it is expressed, find the use of textual markers a useful and relatively simple way of overtly organising their discourse. It may also be that overt training (by tutors and textbooks) encourages weaker writers to use these devices. The combination of both influences might account for this phenomenon. The other intriguing question is how writers move from level 6 use (with respect to discourse markers) to level 8 use. Certainly in pedagogic terms, a comparison of a 'typical' level 8 essay with a level 6 essay (in a similar way as we do later in this report) might well be a useful exercise for the IELTS classroom, though we suspect that it will be difficult to separate discourse marker use from other strategies that level 8 writers use.

4.2.4 Use of co-ordinators and subordinators

The lower-level writers use *because* almost four times as frequently as the writers at level 8. These results are in keeping with Flowerdew's (1998) findings, namely that *because* occurred about twice as often in her learner corpus as in her native-speaker corpus. Such differential use of this subordinator (see Table 8.12) may be a useful indicator therefore of 'expert' and 'non-expert' use in the written language. There are similar differentials in the use of *if*.

Our general findings are similar to those of Hewings (1999), who found that first-year undergraduates used more subordinators (and fewer co-ordinators – though this latter use is not shown by our data) than the third-year students. In our data, the level 8 writers use more co-ordinators than levels 6 writers (though the same percentage as level 4). Level 8 writers use fewer subordinators than either levels 4 or 6.

Table 8.12 Subordinators

Subordinator	Level 8	Level 6	Level 4
if	33	62	88
when	27	37	34
because	19	79	69
so that	2	1	5
before	3	3	5
after	4	6	4
although	5	11	5
though	3	15	5
since	2	2	3
as (= since)	6	6	4
till	0	0	0
unless	0	1	1
until	1	2	2
whatever	2	5	2
whenever	11	15	11
wherever	2	0	2
where	9	1	0
whereas	0	2	0
while	4	5	4
while	3	0	0
provided that	1	0	0
Total	**137 (1.37%)**	**253 (1.82%)**	**244 (2.09%)**

4.2.5 Idiomatic language

A feature that is striking at level 8 is the use of idiomatic language. Table 8.13 lists the most interesting examples from 22 out of the 30 writers. In each case, we suggest, the choices are those of confident writers, showing versatility in the use of a wide range of lexis. This is discussed in greater detail below (see pp. 359–63). The use of expressions such as those in Table 8.13 is absent from

Table 8.13 Idiomatic language

8–01
I am all ears
prides itself
remains to be seen
if you ask me

8–02
word for word
and so forth

8–04
lumbering towards us like a charging rhino
every nook and corner
and such like

8–05
months of hard labour
at our fingertips
human touch
nuances

8–06
made rapid strides
science . . . giving birth to
ventured into
breaking the barriers
eyes of the world
day in and day out
it has added more colour
'user-friendly'
shrinks the person's world to a single room

8–07
no denying the fact
stripped of all its colouring
the years to come

8–08
the future is at hand
silicon and stainless steel filter

8–09
a boon
the same can be said
peace and harmony

8–10
curb the intrusion

8–11
opens up a world of other cultures
the lack-lustreness of some poetry
glean from others

8–12
the question arises

Table 8.13 (continued)

8–14
human touch
in a matter of weeks
technology is the key

8–15
if and only if
idioms and idiosyncrasies
and so on

8–16
looming large
at the touch of a button
explore more avenues (re career)

8–21
second only to
through the rigors of
having said this

8–22
human touch
hardly the best way

8–23
leaps and bounds
matter of moments
go through the bother
another side to this coin
GIGA principle (garbage in garbage out)

8–25
Further compelling arguments
No matter how advanced

8–26
I beg to differ
opens the doors to a vast and hitherto unknown storehouse of literature
I would say just one thing

8–27
guard against
taking a stand
state of flux
overwhelming majority
more pressing concerns

8–29
take a back seat
. . . and tv are the culprits
whole host of opportunities

8-30
handy

level 4 scripts and there are only a few examples in level 6 scripts. The use of idiomatic phrasing does raise the question whether some of the expressions are appropriate for an academic task. We shall return to this question of appropriacy later.

4.3 Writer stance: interaction between writer and reader

A number of researchers (among them Hyland 1994, Conrad and Biber 2000, Stubbs 1986, Thompson and Ye 1991) discuss the importance of 'stance', or attitude by a writer towards the point being made (see also the literature review on pp. 324–28).

Hyland (1994:240) suggests that there are eight features through which hedging, an aspect of stance, is typically expressed:

1. modal auxiliary verbs, e.g. *may/might/could*
2. adjectival/adverbial nominal modal expressions (*possibly*, *perhaps*, *probably*)
3. modal lexical verbs (*believe*, *assume*)
4. *if*-clauses
5. question forms
6. passivisation
7. impersonal phrases
8. time reference.

We have looked for evidence of these features in our data, and have analysed five of them:1 to 3, 5 and 6. We found little evidence of time phrases in the data, and analysis of *if*-clauses is unfinished. We have also concordanced all anticipatory *it*-clauses, generally recognised as hedging devices (Hewings 1999, Quirk et al 1985, Thompson 1984) and analysed them grammatically. We have classified them into patterns similar (but not identical) to those used by Hewings 1999 (see literature review on pp. 326–28). The results and discussion of our analyses follow in the next sections.

4.3.1 Use of modal auxiliary verbs, adjectival/adverbial nominal modal expressions, modal lexical verbs, and *it*-clauses

In the light of recognition of the importance of interaction between writer and reader, (see for example Hyland 1994, Myers 1989) it is interesting that we see – and have statistical evidence for – greater awareness of the reader in the level 8 texts. One indicator of effective academic writing and its interactional elements is the use of hedging. There is more hedging in the level 8 scripts than in the lower levels (6 and 4), confirmed by the greater frequency of modal auxiliary verbs, adjectival or adverbial nominal modal expressions (e.g. *possibly*), modal lexical verbs (e.g. *believe*) and question forms. These are some of the main features suggested by Hyland as typical expressions of hedging.

Table 8.14 shows the frequency of various modal auxiliary verbs and of adjectival/adverbial modal expressions at the three different levels. The greater frequency in the use of *would* at level 8 compared to the two lower levels is striking: it is four times more frequent than at level 6, and five times more than at level 4. This contrasts with the greater use at both the lower levels (6 and 4) of *can* compared to the use at level 8. There is also greater use at levels 6 and 4 of *maybe*. There is also a difference in the use of modal lexical verbs: *believe* as a correlate of *I* is hardly used at level 4, where the overuse of *think* is apparent. *Think* as a correlate of *I* is used notably less frequently at levels 8 and 6 than at level 4. *I think* and *maybe* are perhaps the most basic devices a novice writer can use to communicate hedging, (together with *can* and *will*) and it is therefore not surprising we should find level 4 writers using these items, with level 8 writers using more complex items such as *would* and *may*.

Table 8.14 Frequency of hedging words (modal auxiliaries, nominal modal expressions and modal lexical verbs)

Word	Level 8		Level 6		Level 4	
	Raw no.	%	Raw no.	%	Raw no.	%
would	56	0.56	22	0.16	12	0.10
may	33	0.33	27	0.19	9	0.07
might	2	0.02	9	0.06	5	0.04
could	16	0.16	22	0.16	17	0.15
should	28	0.28	21	0.15	21	0.18
can	76	0.76	201	1.45	176	1.51
will	68	0.68	165	1.19	147	1.26
possible	9	0.09	13	0.09	3	0.03
possibly	1	0.01	–	–	2	0.02
possibility	2	0.02	3	0.02	–	–
probably	6	0.06	5	0.04	3	0.03
maybe	3	0.03	11	0.07	18	0.15
perhaps	2	0.02	2	0.01	–	–
believe*	8	0.08	4	0.02	1	0.00
think*	5	0.05	9	0.06	40	0.34
Total	**315**	**3.1%**	**514**	**3.67%**	**454**	**3.88%**

* *as correlates of* I.

Table 8.15 shows that our findings differ from those of Hewings, (see literature review on pp. 326–28) as, apart from modal finites where there is a greater use at level 8, the greatest use of *it*-clauses occurs at level 6, and *it*-comment clauses are used least by the higher-level (level 8) students. This area of 'stance' would repay further analysis and investigation of possible reasons for the patterns we have discovered.

Table 8.15 Number of occurrences of different patterns of *it*-clauses

	Level 8	Level 6	Level 4
Modal finites (e.g. *it may, might*)	11	6	7
Verbal and mental processes (e.g. *it seems/it appears/it is believed/it is suggested*)	4	7	2
It- clauses relating to truth or knowledge (e.g. *it is inevitable/likely/true/possible*)	13	23	10
Comment clauses (e.g. *it is important/necessary/difficult*)	13	26	21
Total	**41**	**62**	**40**

4.3.2 Use of set phrases/categorical statements

The lower-level scripts (both levels 6 and 4) appear more categorical than level 8, with more use of verbs in the simple present tense unmitigated by modals, and more statements of certain fact (e.g. *It is X*). This is reflected in the frequency statistics for unmodified, unmitigated *is* (Table 8.16). While *seems* is used with similar frequency at levels 6 and 8, it is less evident at level 4, and this adds to the overall effect of certainty and lack of hedging at this level. As Hyland states (2000:179), the use of hedges such as *might, probably* and *seem*, 'signal a tentative assessment of referential information and *convey collegial respect for the views of colleagues*' (our italics). Where such hedging is present in the IELTS scripts, it may be evaluated positively by assessors, and its absence may be negatively evaluated, though we have no evidence for this.

Table 8.16 Number of occurrences and percentage use of *is* and *seems* at levels 8, 6 and 4

	Level 8		Level 6		Level 4	
	No.	**%**	**No.**	**%**	**No.**	**%**
is	173	1.73	322	2.32	230	1.97
seem/s	4	0.04	7	0.05	2	0.02

Table 8.17, showing the collocates of *I*, reveals that *disagree* features more prominently at level 4 than at level 8. There is also a greater frequency of *I agree* at level 4 than at level 6 or level 8, confirming the greater use of 'bald on record' strategies at level 4. At level 8 the writers convey their opinion more indirectly through the use of argumentation rather than stating it overtly.

The number of writers using the phrase 'in my opinion' also seems to bear out this last point (Table 8.18).

4.3.3 Question forms – rhetorical questions

Another aspect of the interactional nature of the level 8 answers is the use of rhetorical questions. As many as 12 out of 30 (40%) of the writers at level 8

Table 8.17 Collocates of *I*

Collocate	Level 8		Level 6		Level 4	
	No.	%	No.	%	No.	%
disagree (including 'do not agree')	6	0.06	10	0.07	18	0.15
agree	1	0.01	4	0.03	7	0.06

No. = number of occurrences as a collocate of 'I'

Table 8.18 Use of *in my opinion*

Phrase	Level 8	Level 6	Level 4
in my opinion	4/30 (13%)	8/50 (16%)	16/50 (32%)

use questions in their text, compared with only 10 out of 50 (20%) at level 6, and 13 out of 50 (26%) at level 4 – interestingly, more than at level 6. There are two broad functions of questions in the text: to structure the discourse and to involve the reader. The use of question forms in academic discourse is one of the ways mentioned by Hyland (1994) in which writers 'hedge', or avoid stating total certainty about a given proposition.

It is clear from the use of questions in the level 8 data that the writers are using them both to construct an argument and to involve the reader. In 18 out of 28 questions (64.3%), the writer does not answer the question, but rather implies that the answer is obvious and does not need to be stated. In the remaining 10 questions (35.7%), the writer answers the question (Table 8.19). Frequently the question is posed in order to set up an argument, or to indirectly convey an opinion.

Table 8.19 Question use

Function of Question	Level 8	Level 6	Level 4
Answered by writer	35.7%	62.5%	65.4%
Implied that answer is obvious to reader	64.3%	37.5%	34.6%

The two functions are also reflected in the position of questions within the essays. Ten questions end paragraphs, and two of these conclude the essay. In only one of these paragraph-final questions does the writer provide an answer – in the next paragraph. In this instance the question is a way of structuring the essay, providing a link between the end of one paragraph and the beginning of the next. Five questions open paragraphs, and four of these are answered by the writer. The remaining 13 questions are mid-paragraph, or a penultimate sentence in a paragraph, and are clearly used as part of the writer's argument, whether they are explicitly answered by the writer (five instances) or not (eight instances). Where they occur at the end of a paragraph they seem to function retrospectively, and in effect sum up an argument: in other words they imply that the answer is obvious to the reader given the preceding arguments. An example of this is found in 8–01 (our italics indicate the rhetorical question):

> No computer I have ever worked on has the feeling, the intuition or genius to say or place just the right word at just the right time. No computer has the ability to create subtleties like puns or intertextual references like an author does. You could feed Virgil's 'Aenead' through a computer, and I am absolutely positive it would hand you a translation, but *could it ever reflecht any of the atmosphere, created by Virgil's brilliance at construing a sentence so perfect and detailed that every syllable in every word adds to the value of his work?*   (8–01)

Here, in the first two sentences (two general statements) and the first clause of the third sentence (an exemplification), the writer sets up an argument about the limitations of the computer, so that the rhetorical question in the final clause strongly implies a negative answer. The use of a question form here establishes common ground with the reader, and implies the 'reasonableness' of the preceding argument and of the writer's opinion. Similar capping arguments are provided by rhetorical questions at the ends of paragraphs in the following two extracts:

> Although computers can translate into whatever language you want but it will help you only when you will be siting in front of your computer like in office or doing some work at home. *What happens when to want to talk or discuss something with your boss or friends or if you want to travel?*   (8–01)

> In addition, those dependent on the translation of computers will also not be bale to do anything if they are given a task in rural areas of developing countries for example. Nowadays many of the third world countries do not have computers for many of their important ofices or businesses. So if the future generations of these countries rely on computers and its translation, *what will happen if the government of these generations can not afford to provide such facilities?*   (8–18)

It is interesting that at the lower levels questions are also used. They are, however, used by a smaller number of writers (about a fifth), they are often ill-formed, (grammatically inaccurate), or without a question mark, but they are nevertheless in evidence. The writers do not, however, show the same skill in using them as the level 8 writers. This is particularly so at level 4, where the intended meaning is at times obscured.

Analysis of the function of questions in level 4 texts shows a converse pattern to level 8 (Table 8.19). While two-thirds of the level 8 questions are unanswered, implying to the reader that there is an obvious answer, at level 4 two thirds (65.4%) of the questions are answered by the writer, and only one third (34.6%) are unanswered with an answer implied. Many of the level 4 and 6 texts have an informal style, where the writers are almost conversational with themselves or the reader, asking and immediately answering their own questions. The following extracts illustrate this. While the extract from text 4–04 shows a style directly interactive with the reader, the writer in 4–14 seems to be asking questions of himself, almost holding a conversation with himself:

> *Do you really think looking through the computers are good idea?* I mean almost defenately sure that, that can cause people's eyes quite bad too.
>
> (4–04)

> *When you got the information but you don't know languages what can you do?* That's doesn't matter, because the comput have a system called 'translation', it can translate to your own language or you want the language. So the language doesn't matter. *But is this system good or bad?* I think for some people is good, some people not.   (4–14)

At level 4, in three of the essays where questions are posed and then answered, they are repetitions of the essay title, and the question is posed in the opening paragraph as a way of starting the essay. The first paragraph of 4–03 illustrates this:

> Every year the quality of translation by computer has improved. *The question is should children learn foreign language?* Because computer will be able to provide immediate translation whenever it is needed.   (4–03)

It is difficult to provide any sound analysis of the position of questions within the text at level 4 as in many of the essays paragraphing is absent or unclear.

In a manner similar to level 4, at level 6, four out of 10 people pose part of the essay title as a question in their opening section, and then answer it in the essay. Two of these question the 'truth' of the assertion:

> Some people will then argue that in the future, our children do not need to learn foreign languages, they could translate foreign languages through PC. *Is that true?* The argument for that sentence has some particular points.   (6–36)

> Some people think, in the future, our children do not need to learn foreign languages because computers can do this immediately for human beings. *Is it true?* My answer is 'No'.   (6–39)

There is one untypical essay, 6–48, which we shall exclude as it would otherwise skew the pattern. This essay has no questions in it until the final paragraph, which consists solely of 7 consecutive questions. Leaving this essay aside, of the other 16 questions posed in the level 6 texts, 10 are answered by the writer (62.5%) while six (37.5%) imply to the reader that the answer is obvious (Table 8.19). We see here that the statistics are similar to those of level 4, although tending slightly more towards level 8.

As far as the position of questions within the paragraph is concerned, it is hard to discern a reliable pattern as the writers' paragraphing is often poor. The three questions which are rephrasings of the essay title all occur in the opening section, and there is one implied question that ends a paragraph. Apart from these, all the other questions (both types) are mid-paragraph.

It seems clear from this analysis that questions which are posed and *not* answered by the writer are more interactive. They assume shared knowledge and values with the reader, and as such suggest solidarity and positive politeness. They involve the reader more than questions which are set up to be answered by the writer in the text, which have a stronger discourse structuring function. The unanswered rhetorical questions are used more by the level 8 writers than by the level 6 and 4 writers. The rhetorical device of asking a question in a text, whether answered by the writer or the reader, is relatively unusual, certainly in British cultures, and tends to be a feature of a small number of genres, for example spoken political speeches and sermons, though even in these genres, there is no obligatory use. The question has to be raised therefore of the appropriacy of this rhetorical device in the IELTS test. Questions are unlikely to be found in academic text for which the testees are presumably being prepared. However, the rubric of the written question we are investigating here (see Appendix 8.1) states that answers should be written for an educated readership, and does not mention particularly that the register should be academic. The use of rhetorical questions cannot therefore be criticised in terms of the rubric, though one could argue that those questions which the writer answers are more typical of less advanced writers. There remains the question, however, of the relative frequency of rhetorical questions in written text, which, we have argued, are infrequent. We suspect this is another difference between the 'expert' second language writers represented in our database, and expert first language writers. The expert L2 writers are displaying their expertise and facility in the language more overtly than we imagine an L1 writer would in a similar context, though we cannot entirely discount that the genre of an examination answer would probably influence L1 writers faced with a similar question.

4.3.4 Passivisation

At level 8 all except one of the 30 scripts contain passives. The following instances from 11 different writers (36.7%) are used to 'manage' the discourse, and relate to providing an opinion/line of argument, and are clear hedges:

> remains to be seen (8–01)
> the answer to this question should be settled (8–06)
> it cannot validly be concluded (8–10)
> reasons . . . cannot be reduced to (8–10)
> another point to be taken into consideration (8–16)
> a dispute has been raised (8–19)
> cannot be overemphasised (8–21)
> an opinion has been expressed (8–26)
> above mentioned problems (8–27) (*a nominalisation*)
> where foreign language is concerned (8–29)
> computer translator should be seen as (8–30)

Examples of passivisation without hedging are:

> created by Virgil
> nursery rhymes translated into Dutch
> the subtle humour was lost   (8–01)
>
> our children are taught
> computers are now equipped   (8–02)

At level 6 the picture is rather different. Fourteen of the 50 writers (28%) use no passives at all. However, if we add to this the number of people (18) who use only one or at most two passives in the whole essay (eight use one, 10 use just two – often 'the computer is used/the computer is made'), we can see that there is less use of the passive at this level. However, of those who do use the passive, nine out of 50 (18%) make use of it in the same sort of hedging way as we have seen at level 8.

The level 6 instances are listed below:

> It cannot be denied (6–05)
> As is well known (6–14)
> A number of reasons should be considered (6–16)
> . . . money is the next thing should be concerned (6–16)
> . . . it can clearly be seen (6–17)
> it has been believed (6–22)
> it is commonly believed (6–22)
> the education of foreign languages should not be ignored (6–38)
> It has been said (6–40)

It is suggested (6–40)
It has been worried (6–40)
it can be imagined . . . (6–40)
it can not be underestimated . . . (6–40)
This could be shown . . . (6–47)
who think like mentioned above (6–47)

At level 4, only 18 of the writers (36%) use any passives at all, and none of them use more than two within an essay. Moreover, where passive constructions are used, they are almost all grammatically inaccurate. Interestingly there is one student who does use passive constructions to manage the discourse, as shown below:

educator may be considered
learning process must not be point out   (4–34)

As at level 6, where the writers use only one or two passives, they are commonly *the computer is used/the computer is made*.

Interestingly, at level 6, as alternatives to passivisation, 12 of the writers (24%) use the phrase *some people think/believe/argue* or the phrase *some think*. None of the writers at either level 8 or level 4 do this.

Table 8.20 Number of students using passives

Level 8		Level 6		Level 4	
29/30	96.7%	36/50	72%	18/50	36%

Table 8.21 Number of students using more than two passives

Level 8		Level 6		Level 4	
29/30	96.7%	18/50	36%	0	0%

Table 8.22 Number of students using passives for discourse organisation/ hedging

Level 8		Level 6		Level 4	
11/30	36.7%	9/50	18%	1/50	2%

4.3.5 Use of 'boosters' and 'downtoners'

'Amplifiers' and 'downtoners' are grammatical terms introduced by Quirk and Greenbaum (1973) as subcategories of intensifiers. Amplifiers (boosters and maximisers) 'scale upwards from an assumed norm' whereas 'downtoners have a lowering effect, usually scaling downwards from an assumed norm' (1973:214). Other writers (Flowerdew 1997, Holmes 1984, 1990, Hyland 2000) have used the terms, though with varying definitions.

Our findings are consistent with those of Flowerdew (1997), who claims that an important source of pragmatic failure in the writing of science students is their lack of tentative language. They 'lack finesse in using intensifying or mitigating markers' – what she calls 'boosters and downtoners'. The results of our analysis show a marked difference between levels in the use of boosters and downtoners.

At level 8, more than 12 different emphasisers (e.g. *definitely, certainly, clearly, really*) and more than 20 different amplifiers (maximisers and boosters) are used: *alarmingly, considerably, dramatically, enormously, extensively, significantly, tremendously*. Downtoners are almost equally varied: *merely, hardly, rather, practically, simply, slightly, relatively, supposedly*. The two words which Flowerdew found were overused and misused in her learner corpus – *very* and *only* – occur as 0.15% and 0.25% of the level 8 data.

At level 6 the range and frequency of occurrence of intensifiers is noticeably less than at level 8. There are 8 different emphasisers and 14 different amplifiers (maximisers and boosters) while there is greater use of *very* (0.32%). The use of *only* (0.21%) is similar.

At level 4, only four different emphasisers and seven different amplifiers (maximisers and boosters) were used, and only two downtoners – *quite* and *almost. Only* is used more – at 0.40%, while *very* occurs 60 times – a % lemma of 0.51%.

Hyland points out that boosters 'allow writers to express conviction and to mark their involvement and solidarity with an audience' (Hyland 2000:179). The greater use of boosters by level 8 writers in our data is another indication of their higher level of audience awareness.

4.3.6 Additional elements

We would add three additional factors which we have found to be important in the context of an IELTS Writing exam:

- the reference, by the writer, to what is assumed to be shared knowledge with the reader/examiner
- the use of personal asides to the reader/examiner
- the use of imperatives, exclamations and exhortations/extreme examples.

Each of these features is evident in level 8 scripts, but not in the lower levels.

At level 8, 14/30 (46%) of writers refer to shared knowledge of the outside world. Examples are:

> Virgil's Aenead/Roald Dahl's Nursery Rhymes (8–01)
> Mademoiselle (e.g. of translation into French) (8–02)
> Exotic locations, e.g. Hawaii or India (8–04)
> Eskimos 20 words for describing ice/Shakespeare (8–07)
> Everest/Sherpa guides/Nepal *Etymology i.e.* sym = with, pathos = pain
> (8–08)
> Idioms . . . poetry (8–11)
> Third world countries/millennium bug/creation of God (8–18)
> Backpacking in Italy (8–20)
> Man landing on the moon (8–21)
> American forest (8–22)
> GIGA principle (garbage in garbage out)/George Orwell's New Speak
> (8–23)
> Shakespeare (8–26)
> Liverpool accent/Shakespeare/Marlowe (8–27)
> Terms of address (kin relationships) (8–29)
> Hitchhiker's guide/Star Trek/Tower of Babel /Esperanto (8–30)

Examples of interpersonal asides to examiners include:

> English – Dutch, although you wouldn't say so if you saw me sitting
> here, doing an IELTS test (8–01)
> I was a doctor (who is sitting this exam to be able to work in the UK)
> (8–08)
> So . . . (as I have run out of room) it is quite clear (8–11)

At Level 8, there are a number of examples of the use of rhetoric (exhortations; imperatives; exclamation marks):

> Giving up learning languages is giving up your history! (8–01)
> Let the computers do the paperwork and let our children live and learn
> about their planet by their own efforts and experiences, whether it be
> learning a new language or living in a foreign country. (8–04)
> We must curb the intrusion of these devices into the richness of our
> human experience! (8–10)
> What a tragic thought – a world divest of the many benefits of being bi-
> lingual or multi-lingual. (8–11)
> Just think how many idioms are lost in translation! (8–11)
> And don't forget the millions of people who travel to other countries for
> work– to contribute what they can and to glean from others in a
> foreign land. (8–11)
> As an analogy, when the computers came to the market, some may have
> thought that there may not be a need for the children to learn the table
> of multiplication! (8–13)
> . . . just to save time because doing them by hand it takes a lot of time!
> (8–13)

There is this thought that one day, in future, it may be possible to make a
computer that will be able to think! (8–13)

Let us take literature for instance (8–17)

Imagine reading a Chinese book with a pocket translator by your side!
(8–23)

If we stop doing that we may one day descend to the extent of adapting
George Orwell's 'New Speak' as the official and only language of the
world! (8–23)

We will still continue to do the things that give us happiness, even if the
computer can do them for us! (8–26)

Witness the difference between a Liverpool accent and an accent from
the south east of England. (8–27)

Witness also the difference in English as spoken in the time of
Shakespeare and Marlow to the present day form. (8–27)

Let the computer translator bring us together (8–30)

Look at CD players . . . (8–30)

The overall effect is that the level 8 writer puts across an identity as a competent linguist; an educated, knowledgeable professional; a reasonable and fair seeker of the truth; and above all, as a member of the academic community, writing to a fellow member.

As a conclusion to this section, we now move to a general summary discussion of the three levels, based on the results we have described.

4.4 Characteristics of the three levels

4.4.1 Characteristics of level 8: content, relevance and coherence

The level 8 scripts are characterised by the presentation of well organised, substantial arguments. They can be seen to follow the rubric of the question: they use their own 'ideas, knowledge and experience' and 'support . . . arguments with examples and relevant experience'. The second paragraph of script 8–27 illustrates this (the numbers indicate individual sentences):

[1]Languages are dynamic and change, often rapidly, with time. [2]They are often spoken in different accents and dialects which can change dramatically from region to region within a country and between different countries. [3]Witness the difference between a Liverpool accent and an accent from the South east of England. [4]Both are different to the way the language would be spoken by a native of the United States. [5]Dialects often vary within countries to such an extent that language as spoken in one area of the country may be understood with difficulty by individuals from a separate area. [6]Witness also the difference in English as spoken in the time of Shakespeare and Marlowe to the present day form. [7]The point here is that languages are constantly in a state of flux and whilst I have No knowledge of the intricacies of modern computer technology I

find it hard to concieve that programs could be made to overcome the above mentioned problems.

The opening topic sentence about language change is illustrated in connection with geographical change in sentences three and four, and further expanded on in sentence five; it is then illustrated with regard to change over time in sentence six, before the point about constant change is reiterated in sentence seven and brought round to a concluding point for this paragraph about the limitations of computers.

This paragraph is also typical in the way in which the writer's references to Shakespeare and Marlowe draw on outside world knowledge that could be expected to be shared by the 'educated reader' specified by IELTS as the audience for the essay. Other scripts at this level bring in personal experience in a more direct way, such as the second paragraph in essay 8–09:

> I am an Indian national and in India different states have different languages. As a child, I learnt 5 different languages, and I have realised that although it was quite difficult at that stage of life, I have not only learnt five languages, but in the process of learning those languages I have been exposed to five different cultures, and different life styles. Now, I feel comfortable interacting with people from different cultures and different walks of life. It makes things much easier.

This paragraph also, incidentally, creates the impression of a highly competent, cultured linguist. Indeed, most of the level 8 writers convey an impression of themselves as educated, well travelled intellectuals, members of the same community as the audience for whom they are writing.

Script 8–07 (paragraphs 3 and 4) also conveys linguistic knowledge and a love of languages, and also includes a reference to Shakespeare:

> However, I do not see this as the main reason why people learn other languages. Other languages give us the ability to 'see' the world differently. We have all heard that the Eskimos have 20 different words for describing ice. I would much rather express the many nuances to the word 'love' in French than stare at a symbol on my black and white computer screen.
>
> Language is more than a means of instruction, it is a means of expression. Even if computers could interpret the works of Shakespeare to Italians, I would like the Italians to have the opportunity to *enjoy* him in English.

These writers could almost be said to be boasting of their knowledge and enjoyment of languages and of English – there is an element of display in the writing that may differentiate expert L1 writers from expert L2 writers.

We have already seen how level 8 writers make use of idiomatic, colourful language. We have also remarked on the extent to which level 8 writers show awareness of the reader, and use a number of features (e.g. modals, rhetorical questions, passives) to express hedging. They also use downtoners and boosters to express their attitude towards a point indirectly or tentatively, again indicating awareness of the 'educated reader' for whom IELTS has asked them to write.

The level 8 essays all appear structured through the use of elaboration and exemplification of their arguments, with clear paragraphing and no extraneous material. The content all seems highly relevant. Interestingly, few level 8 writers use the exact words or even close paraphrase of the essay question, unlike writers at levels 6 and 4. Occasionally, as in sentence seven in 8–27 above, the writer will ostensibly state the relevance of a point.

The level 8 essays have an internal coherence in themselves with fewer discourse markers than levels 6 and 4. Coherence is the means by which text 'hangs together' or contains 'texture' – with the intended meaning apparent to the reader. Where the level 8 writers use cohesive words such as *however*, *therefore*, and *thus*, they tend to use them in the same way as native speakers, not in sentence initial position, unlike levels 6 and 4.

4.4.2 Characteristics of level 6: content, relevance and coherence

In contrast to the level 8 scripts, there is only one reference to knowledge of the outside world in the level 6 scripts. It is a reference to Keats, and is quoted below:

> One day I tried to translate Keats from english to french on internet. If
> you want to laugh, it is a good way.   (6–48)

This is also one of the few occurrences in level 6 data where the writer uses an interactional style – whether or not the pronoun has a general or specific meaning.

The level 6 scripts appear to have more content than those at level 4. We have analysed the scripts for topic, and found that there are at least three ideas in each essay. The structure of argument in level 6 essays is unlike that at either level 4 or level 8. At level 4, the points tend to be made in isolation with no exemplification, whereas at level 8 a point is expanded or exemplified in some depth and detail. At level 6, a main point is made and supporting points are mentioned briefly. For example, in 6–27, the main point is made that software makes jobs easier. Three supporting examples are then given of this – memory, dictionaries, and software:

> The invention of translation softwares makes jobs more easier for some
> people, particularly children in foreign language class. They don't have

to memorize the meaning of the word, which they want to know. Moreover they don't have to look up their dictionary to find out the meaning of the word. It makes easier for them to use translation software in computer.

There is, then, some attempt at exemplification or support for a main idea, but in most cases, the content appears to be thin. There are several reasons for this. Sometimes a writer seems to be trying to illustrate a point, but inability to foreground information, manipulate given–new structures, or show the relationship between clauses suggests that the same point is being made several times in a number of ways. The main body of text in 6–01 exemplifies this:

> Computer industry develops very fast. It can be introduced into many areas, even into translation more translation work has been done by computer. Especially, computers provide immediate translation whenever it is needed. It brings much convenience to human. More and more people rely on it to do many works. Espesially the people who don't understand foreign language use it to do translation work. Sometimes they think that they can get information from foreign language even they don't know the language. So they think there will be no point in our children learning foreign languages in the future, because computers will be able to provide immediate translation whenever it is needed.
>
> The above opinion is truly wrong. It is true that computer can do translation work, even sometimes it does faster than a translater.

This script also exemplifies a further feature of the level 6 data which, we suggest, accounts for our view that the content is thinner than an initial surface impression might suggest. This is the fact that at level 6 there is extensive repetition of the words of the essay title, not only in the introductions, but also in the main body of the essays. Script 6–01 is reproduced again below, this time with the introduction. Words or phrases that are identical to the essay title are shown in bold, and close paraphrases to the title are in italics.

> **In recent years** more and more **translation work is done by computer**, and the *translation quality also improves*. Even though **our children still need to learn foreign language**.
>
> Computer industry develops very fast. It can be introduced into many areas, even into **translation more translation work has been done by computer**. Especially, **computers provide immediate translation whenever it is needed**. It brings much convenience to human. More and more people rely on it to do many works. Espesially the people who don't understand foreign language use it to do translation work. Sometimes they think that they can get information from foreign language even

they don't know the language. So they think **there will be no point in our children learning foreign languages in the future, because computers will be able to provide immediate translation whenever it is needed.**

The above opinion is truly wrong. It is true that *computer can do translation work*, even sometimes it does faster than a translater.

We can see that half of the first two paragraphs are repetitions or rephrasings of the title. The title:

> Every year the quality of translation by computer improves. In the future there will be no point in our children learning foreign languages, because computers will be able to provide immediate translation whenever it is needed.

can be broken down into three related ideas:

- the quality of computer translation keeps improving
- computers provide immediate translation
- our children won't need to learn foreign languages.

The three phrases that we find repeated in the scripts are:

- 'every year the quality of translation improves'
- 'computers . . . immediate translation'
- 'our children learning foreign languages'.

We have manually analysed all the level 6 scripts to see the extent to which these words are repeated exactly or paraphrased. In 48% of the level 6 scripts (24/50) at least one of these phrases is repeated exactly; a further 9/50 writers (18%) use a close paraphrase of at least one of the ideas, bringing the figure to 66%. This is in marked contrast to the level 8 scripts, where only 4/30 (13.3%) have either the exact words or close paraphrase. One writer, 8–07, puts the phrase in quotation marks.

A third reason for the impression that the essays are of a reasonable standard is that they appear well-formed in terms of paragraphing. After a brief introduction, almost all the level 6 writers consider both sides of the argument, (a paragraph for each, sometimes even discussed as 'advantages' and 'disadvantages'), then give a conclusion. This is a different pattern from that of the level 8 essays. As we have already seen, the level 6 writers are also more direct in giving their opinion ('bald on record'), often in the introduction, as in the following examples:

> Beginning with my own opinion, I disagree that there will be no point in our children learning foreign languages because of the computer technology. However I admit that recent computers play important and significant roll in our everyday life.   (6–24)

> Every year the quality of translation by computer improves. I agree with this opinion. However I disagree that in the future our children won't need to learn foreign languages because of translation by computer.
>
> (6–13)

The level 6 writers, (apart from 6–12, 6–13, 6–33, and 6–49) use few modals, passives or other forms of hedging.

At level 6 writers do not have the same problem with relevance as do writers at level 4. As we have seen, there is some repetition of set phrases from the title, but on the whole the essays appear focused on the topic and are not hard to understand – in contrast to level 4 essays.

The level 6 essays are striking in their use of cohesion devices, particularly sequencers such as *firstly*, *secondly*, *thirdly* – in contrast to level 8.

4.4.3 Characteristics of level 4: content, relevance and coherence

The level 4 scripts say little. There is an average of only two or three ideas in each script and these tend to be expressed as simple statements without either elaboration, explanation or exemplification. This is partly because the writers do not make it clear what the connection is between sentences. There are few cohesive ties and the coherence is not immediately apparent. For example, in 4–02:

> Computer will destroy our life and our natural. We have to do something with our future and we have to study.

And in 4–45, the third paragraph comprises four short sentences without any textual marking of the relationship between them:

> On the other hand, the computer is very convinient. It could be such as math, to save something work by disk, science. Now a lots of companies have many computers. I think if our society do not have the computer, we can not live to work all over the world.

The relevance of the level 4 writers' ideas is often unclear to the reader, and students may be writing whatever they can on the general topic of computers/machines/technology/television. For example in 4–03:

> Nowsaday american have tried to communate from the other plant to the earth, but I didn't heared about result, even it did not successful.

The main point of another script, 4–04, is the health risk of computers to our eyesight, while another writer (4–15) is worried about the harmful effects on children's bodies of the 'x-ram' from computers. The topic of children in general, often linked to their use of computer games, is a favourite one in the level 4 scripts.

The level 4 essays are marked by an apparent lack of coherence and any clear link between ideas. The next section analyses a sample script from each level.

5 Discussion

5.1 Analysis of a sample level 8 script

We have chosen script 8–01 for detailed analysis for two reasons: at 356 words, it is of average length and it exhibits the features that we have found prevalent in level 8 essays. The essay follows:

Paragraph 1
When the topic of languages is raised, I am all ears. Jan I am from Belgium, the country that prides itself on having the best languages education available. Wether this is so, remains to be seen, but nonetheless, I am able to communicate in to different modern languages (English, Dutch, French and German) on leaving secondary school.

Paragraph 2
In combination with the fact that I am also bi-lingual (English-Dutch, allthough you wouldn't say so if you saw me sitting here, doing an IELTS-test!) this makes my opinion on this matter quite pronounced. Only recently I have done some work for a company, translating articles of law about archiving from Dutch into English. The computer I worked on had a very handy dictionnary installed, just for this purpose.

Paragraph 3
All I needed to do was type in a word and the computer would immediately come up with any possible translation, therefor I am the last person to deny a computers usefulness. But who's to choose which translation fits the context or the style of the text?

Paragraph 4
No computer I have ever worked on has the feeling, the intuition or genious to say or place just the right word at just the right time. No computer has the ability to create subtleties like puns or intertextual references like an author does. you could feed Virgils 'Aenead' through a computer, and I am absolutely positive it would hand you a translation, but could it ever reflecht any of the atmosphere, created by Virgil's brilliance at construing a sentence so perfect and detailed that every syllable in every word adds to the value of his work.

Paragraph 5
I have seen Roald Dahl's magic 'Nursery Rhimes' translated into Dutch and was appaled at how all the subtle humour was lost.

Paragraph 6
The best authors of the world could not, if you ask me, translate any text whithout damaging it slightly so how could a computer, who has no knowledge of the author's life, experiences, background . . . all the things that make a text what it is.

Paragraph 7
Theire is nothing more beautiful than a language, any language. Giving up learning languages is giving up your history!

The use of idioms is striking in this essay, partly on account of slightly inappropriate use. For example, the use of the idiom 'I am all ears' in the opening sentence, is perhaps infelicitous, since it is an idiom more commonly associated with spoken language and informal conversation, (indeed, it would be interesting to interrogate a large native-speaker corpus to see to what extent such idioms are used at all in everyday conversation). Similarly, the personal introduction 'Jan I am from Belgium' is not academic in style, rather it is more literary in its fronting. Colourful language, metaphor and personification are evidenced in, 'You could feed Virgil's Aenead through a computer . . . it would hand you . . .' This sentence also provides instances of the use of the generic 'you'; there are several other instances of inclusive pronoun reference. Other idioms or set phrases in this text are 'remains to be seen' (paragraph 1), and 'I am the last person to deny' (paragraph 3). There are also instances of vague language, which Channell (1994) has argued characterises native-speaker texts: '*different* modern languages' (paragraph 1); 'done *some* work' (paragraph 3); '*things*' (paragraph 6).

The writer of 8–01 has a strong sense of audience, and writes interactively. A personal aside to the examiner in the second paragraph is just one aspect of this: 'allthough you wouldn't say so if you saw me sitting here, doing an IELTS test!'

Other aspects are the colloquialisms we have already mentioned, together with the informal 'if you ask me'; three rhetorical questions, each at the end of a paragraph (discussed further below); and a final exclamation to conclude the essay.

There is substantial content in this essay, with the writer building a convincing argument about the limitations of computers. The content is highly relevant, without referring directly to the title of the question, and has internal cohesion without the use of any overt discourse markers. In this respect it is typical of level 8 texts, and is in marked contrast to the lower levels.

The first topic, stretching over the first three orthographic paragraphs, is introductory: the writer introduces himself, his country and his bilingual background. Description of the writer's own computer experience then leads, in the third paragraph, to a discussion of computer translation and its limitations, which takes up the rest of the essay. His main argument is that computer translation, although useful, is limited in the extent to which it can capture the 'style', 'subtleties', or 'atmosphere' of the original text. The argument is built up well and developed with the use of supporting statements and examples, and, as already mentioned, without the use of discourse markers.

The writer uses three detailed examples in his argument. First, he draws on his own experience translating articles of law. This statement also has the effect, at another level, of conveying to the reader that he is a competent – if not accomplished – user of English. He acknowledges the usefulness of computer translation, but in the concluding sentence of the paragraph poses the rhetorical question, 'But who's to choose which translation fits the context or the style of the text?' This question has the additional effect of showing the reader that the writer's own language is sophisticated enough for him to be aware of this problem.

Paragraph 4 opens with a topic sentence about the limitations of computer translation: 'No computer I have ever worked on has the feeling, the intuition or genius to say or place just the right word at just the right time.' This is followed, in paragraph 4, sentence 2, with a supporting statement, 'No computer has the ability to create subtleties like puns or intertextual references like an author does.' The rest of the paragraph then provides a detailed example about Virgil (bringing in knowledge of the outside world) to support sentence 1 and sentence 2, ending with another rhetorical question (though without the punctuation):

> you could feed Virgils 'Aenead' through a computer, and I am absolutely positive it would hand you a translation, but would it ever reflecht any of the atmosphere, created by Virgil's brilliance at construing a sentence so perfect and detailed that every syllable in every word add to the value of its work.

Paragraph 5 provides another example in support of the same point, again referring to knowledge of the outside world, this time about Dahl: 'I have seen Roald Dahl's magic "Nursery Rhimes" translated into Dutch and was appaled at how all the subtle humour was lost.'

The sixth paragraph brings the argument together, using the superordinates *'authors'* to create lexical cohesion, with a strong concluding point that if the best authors lose something of a flavour of a text in translation, then it is even more problematic for the computer.

> The best authors of the world could not, if you ask me, translate any text whithout damaging it slightly so how could a computer, who has no knowledge of the author's life, experiences, background . . . all the things that make a text what it is.

The writer again uses the device of a rhetorical question to make this point. The final paragraph comes as a sort of coda, and an exclamation: 'Theire is nothing more beautiful than a language, any language. Giving up learning languages is giving up your history.'

There are two interesting ways in which this writer achieves internal cohesion in this essay. First, there is lexical cohesion through the use of, for example, superordinates. Secondly, there are instances of parallelism, as in the first two sentences of paragraph 4, for example: '*No computer I have ever worked on has the feeling*, the intuition or genious *to say* or place *just* the right word at *just* the right time. *No computer has the ability to create* subtleties *like* puns . . . *like* an author does.' The parallelism with 'computer' here is created by the use of fronting in the first clause. There are other instances where the writer uses fronting to effect, as for example, in the opening sentence of the essay: 'When the topic of language is raised, I am all ears' and the third sentence in paragraph 1: 'Wether this is so, remains to be seen'.

This writer shows that he is able to use both short and long sentences effectively. He uses complex clause structures such as '. . . created by Virgil's brilliance at construing a sentence so perfect and detailed that every syllable in every word adds to the value of his work' in paragraph 4, or sentence 3 in paragraph 1: 'Wether this is so, remains to be seen, but nonetheless, I am able to communicate in to different modern languages (English Dutch French and German) on leaving secondary school.' He clearly has command of a range of grammatical structures, from gerunds to the use of 'would' for past tense habitual action (paragraph 3 'the computer would immediately come up with') and passives. He uses a number of phrasal verbs ('come up with', 'give up') and colloquial items ('handy') as well as sophisticated vocabulary ('construing', 'subtleties', 'archiving'). He also uses boosters – 'absolutely positive'; 'quite pronounced'.

There are several instances of modals in this essay: the modal auxiliaries 'could' (x3), 'could not', 'would', and 'would not'; and the adjectival modal expression 'possible'. All are examples of hedging, and provide further evidence of this writer's awareness that 'writing is a social act' (Hyland 1994:241).

There are errors of form in this essay, although none detract from the strength of the writer's argument. The seven orthographic paragraphs do not entirely tally with the development of the argument, and some consist of only one sentence. We have already observed how the first two paragraphs are introductory: similarly the final two paragraphs form a conclusion. The second and fifth paragraphs are only one sentence long. There are ten spelling errors in English: 'wether', 'whithout', 'reflecht', 'dictionnary', 'allthough', 'rhimes', 'appaled', 'therfor', 'theire', 'genious'. There is also a mistake of tense in the last sentence of paragraph 1, as well as a superfluous preposition: 'I am able to communicate in to different modern languages . . .

on leaving secondary school . . .' A slightly odd collocation ends paragraph 2: 'this makes my opinion on this matter quite pronounced'.

The overriding impression from this essay is that the writer has a convincing argument and writes fluently. We also have a strong sense of the writer's identity, as one professional writing to another. This is conveyed partly through the devices discussed above, and partly through references to what is assumed to be shared knowledge, between educated writer and educated reader, of the outside world. It is this aspect which is particularly striking in level 8 texts, and noticeably absent from those at the lower levels.

5.1.2 Analysis of a sample level 6 script

We have chosen essay 6–29 for detailed analysis based on an impression that it seems typical. The essay follows:

Paragraph 1
Some people say every year the quality of translation by computer improves. In the future there will be no point in our children learning foreign languages. However, may people agree with the quality of translation by computer improves because it is faster, better, etc. In my opinion, I suggest, computer is a very good for translation. In this essay, I will explore about it and I will give some examples.

Paragraph 2
In the future there will be no point in our children learning foreign languages because the children do not need to study foreign languages that is the big problems for the next generation in terms of education.

Paragraph 3
However, translation by computer is faster then by people because on computer, there are a high technology such as vocabulary, etc.

Paragraph 4
Secondly, computers will be able to provide immediate translation whenever it is needed. Moreover, computers are a good quality in terms of spelling so, the computer's spelling is more correctly than hand writing. For example, after I finished writing on computer I can check by the spelling's button.

Paragraph 5
Finally, it is common knowledge, translation by computer is more faster and more correctly than translators, so, therefore we have a lot of time to do some thing. For example, if I am a translator, I will use the computer for translation because it is better than I check in dictionary in terms of spelling or grammar, so, I have many time to study or work, etc.

Paragraph 6
In conclusion, translation by computer improves in the recent years because there have the high technology which help the people too much

in terms education, business or . . . etc. In my opinion, I hope in the near future, the scientist of technology will reative more and more high technology than computer. It will help the people all over the world, there are not only translation but also knowledge.

At 309 words it is above the average length (277) of a level 6 essay but it is within the band of the commonest length. It has none of the features listed as prominent in level 8 essays: no passives, no hedging, no idioms or colourful language. It does have many discourse markers and clear, 'bald on record' statements of opinion. We shall discuss these features as well as look at the structure, content and linguistic accuracy.

There are six paragraphs in this essay, some of which are very short. In particular, paragraphs 2 and 3 are each of only one sentence.

The first paragraph is clearly introductory: the writer's first two sentences have been lifted directly from the IELTS question, but with no quotation marks to indicate this. We indicate in italics what is exact repetition from the title: '[1]Some people say *every year the quality of translation by computer improves.* [2]*In the future there will be no point in our children learning foreign languages.*

This seems to be the writer's way of getting started, and is a pattern followed by many other level 6 writers as we have seen above. The third sentence, starting with 'However' indicates that a contrary idea is to follow. But the idea is actually a support for sentence 1, giving reasons ('it is faster, better etc') why 'may (i.e. many) people agree with the quality of translation by computer improves'. The next sentence is introduced by 'in my opinion' and coming as it does in sentence initial position immediately after sentence 3, we are led to expect a different idea contradicting the previous one. However the writer's opinion, 'computer is a very good for translation' supports the general statement about the use of computers for translation. The final sentence of the introduction shows an awareness of the need to indicate a statement of intent for the rest of the essay. However, the choice of the verb 'explore', the inaccurate use of the preposition 'about' and the vagueness of 'I will give some examples' detracts from the favourable impression created by the opening 'in this essay I will'.

The second paragraph seems to start the essay again, with a repetition of sentence 2, again a copy from the question. The tautologous reason given for this assertion is that 'children do not need to study foreign languages'. A new point is made within the same sentence: 'that is the big problems for the next generation in terms of education'. But there is no indication, from either a discourse marker or punctuation, that this is a new point, and the referent of 'that' is unclear. Although this paragraph might appear moderately fluent to an IELTS marker, it seems that the second paragraph is saying little. So the first two paragraphs – the first third of the essay – have minimal content and minimal original language from the writer.

Paragraph 3 begins with another marker 'However', leading the reader to expect a point against the advantages of computer translation, but instead the writer makes the point that 'translation by computer is faster than by people because on computer, there are a high technology such as vocabulary'. The propositional content here is, once again, that the computer is faster than people (for translation). This point has already been made in paragraph 1, sentence 3; it is in any case implied in the essay question with which the writer seems to agree. The dependent clause, 'there are a high technology such as vocabulary', is again tautologous: the computer is good because the computer has/is high technology. The phrase 'high technology such as vocabulary' is difficult to understand: taken literally, vocabulary is not an example of high technology. The reader is left to infer, with additional information from the IELTS question, that the computer can translate lexis.

Paragraph 4 opens with 'Secondly' – but the reader has not been given a 'firstly'. The point seems little different from the previous one. There is as yet no clear line of argument. We have seen that the writer seems sympathetic to computers, while admitting that if children do not study foreign languages it will present educational problems in the future. It is unclear, at this stage, to what the 'Secondly' might refer. In fact, it refers to the second of the propositions in the IELTS essay title, copied exactly from the title in the opening sentence of paragraph 4: 'computers will be able to provide immediate translation whenever it is needed'.

The next sentence in this paragraph opens with the additive marker 'moreover', leading the reader to expect an additional comment, of equal weight to the argument about the immediacy of translation. The point that is made is that 'computers are a good quality in terms of spelling'. While this is a valid argument, it would carry more weight were it of an equally *general* nature to the argument about speed of translation: in other words, were it about accuracy in general. The generalisation could be exemplified with regard to spelling, just as speed of translation could be exemplified. The writer then brings in personal experience by citing the instance of his own use of the spellchecker. There are a number of language errors in this paragraph (as in others): use of tenses, article, adjective/adverb, punctuation, although these do not detract from the overall meaning.

Paragraph 5 begins with 'Finally' and repeats a proposition from the IELTS title: 'translation by computer is more faster and more correctly than translators'. The point the writer goes on to make is: 'so, therefore, we have a lot of time to do something'. What the 'something' is seems unclear at this stage, but this is clarified by the exemplification that follows: 'For example, if I am translator, I will use the computer for translation because it is better than I check in dictionary in terms of spelling or grammar, so, I have many time to study or work, etc.'

The concluding paragraph, introduced by the phrase 'In conclusion' paraphrases one of the main ideas from the IELTS title: 'translation by computer improves in the recent years' giving as the reason, 'because there have the high technology which help the people too much in terms education, business or . . .' In fact it could be argued that the reason why computers in general have improved (i.e. because of technology) is of little relevance to the essay. The penultimate sentence is a bald on record 'In my opinion', the meaning of which is unclear. The final sentence is also unclear: we do not know to what the sentence initial 'it' refers, and the final clause 'there are not only translation but also knowledge' needs a context and a more specific referent.

This essay, at 309 words, appears 'not too bad'. It has a clear structure, with six clear paragraphs, and it seems relevant. However, a closer scrutiny suggests that there is little of substance here. The writer seems to agree with the IELTS statement, but provides one counter-argument ('big problems for the next generation in terms of education') and little support for the argument. We raise the question of whether the use of markers (albeit misuse) and of chunks of language from the essay title may suggest to IELTS markers that the essay is better than a closer scrutiny suggests.

5.1.3 Analysis of a sample level 4 script

We have chosen script 4–01 for detailed analysis on the grounds that it typifies this level: it is of average length, has a number of mistakes of form, and exemplifies problems relating particularly to coherence. The essay follows:

Paragraph 1
The question out of in the future there will be no point in our children learning foreign languages becaus of computers' transfermission. it is needed or not is complicated one. There are a lot of factors invoved and it is not easy to see which is the best view to take.

Paragraph 2
Agains the proposal there is a number of other points. Firstly. The beginnig of computers inventor. Nobody could mesure what would be done next generation.

Paragraph 3
Prabably, next genereation neednt to study foreign langue. At this time, we will reduce our burden which means we can speak freely though computer. Secondly, when we communicat fruently through computers we can travell every country, make friend easily any nations. That reason. the earth will be more peaceful than last century.

Paragraph 4
In support of the proposal, there are a number of important points. Firstly, many small sect of languge will be appeared influence by large

part of share languge e.g. English, French. More importanly, I feel that
the own languge cements their national united and national identity. If
they lost their own languge, they can not handed out their curture,
identification to decendents.

Paragraph 5
In conclusion, however, I feel that it is prabably best way.
We must teach our own languge in our children
Although, it is the simple way to use the computers
New millenium need a new identification in the world.

At 229 words, this essay is of average length for level 4: while the raw
average is 223 words, 50% are between 200–300 words, and 60% are below
the minimum required of 250 words. The essay shows an attempt at structuring: there are five short paragraphs, including a clearly introductory first
paragraph and a final paragraph marked as conclusion. Three orthographic
middle paragraphs form the body of the text, with two points *apparently*
arguing against the proposition and two in favour of it.

The first paragraph lifts a chunk straight from the IELTS question, but
without the use of quotation marks to acknowledge this. The italic type indicates what is exact repetition from the title: 'The question out of *in the future
there will be no point in our children learning foreign languages because* of computer's transfermission.' The writer then attempts to paraphrase the reason
for the proposition in the title, coining the word 'transfermission'. In the rest
of this paragraph he tries to make a general opening point that it is a difficult
issue with many sides to the argument, but the meaning is impeded by the use
of 'it' with an unclear referent. It is also unclear what noun the proform 'one'
is substituting.

The second paragraph shows an apparent lack of coherence: '⁴Agains the
proposal there is a number of other points. ⁵ Firstly. ⁶The beginnig of computers inventor. ⁷Nobody could mesure what would be done next generation.'

The first sentence of this paragraph, sentence 4, is highly confusing to the
reader. The word 'proposal' is presumably intended to mean the 'proposition' (i.e. that it will not be necessary for children to learn foreign languages).
The use of 'a number of other points' sets up the expectation that several consecutive points will be made in this paragraph yet there seems to be only one;
it also suggests that an argument against this has already been given, yet the
only 'point' (or reason) so far made is the writer's paraphrase ('computers'
transfermission') of the reason given in the title, which does not seem to be
'against' the proposition at all. Mistakes of form in sentence 5 and sentence 6
obscure the meaning so that it is not clear what this first point is, nor how it is
an argument against the suggestion in the question prompt that there will be
no point in children learning foreign languages in the future. Sentence 7 is
equally unclear, as is the connection between it and sentence 6.

The paragraphing also creates confusion: the third orthographic paragraph would seem to be a continuation of the meaning from the second paragraph. Indeed, sentence 8 seems to be an expansion of sentence 7. In sentence 9, the referent of 'this time' is unclear, as is the exact meaning of 'our burden' – presumably having to study foreign languages. Further confusion comes with the second point, in sentence 10, which far from being 'agains the proposal' would seem to support the use of computers for translation:

> [8]Prabably, next genereation neednt to study foreign language. [9]At this time, we will reduce our burden which means we can speak freely through computer. [10]Secondly when we communicat fruently though computers we can travell every country, make friend easily any nations. [11]That reason. the earth will be more peaceful than last century.'

The same problem of confusion occurs in the next paragraph:

> [12]In support of the proposal there are a number of important points. [13]Firstly, many small sect of language will be appeared influence by large part of share language e.g. English, French. [14]More importantly, I feel that the own language cements their national united and national identity. [15] If they lost their own language, they can not handed out their curture, identification to decedents.

It takes effort on the part of the reader to follow the argument in this paragraph, which, far from supporting the proposal, seems to be against using computers for translation. The use of 'a number of points' (sentence 12) sets up expectations for the reader which are unfulfilled. Here, as in the first paragraph, the use of 'firstly' (sentence 13) also leads one to expect subsequent points, which are not given. The use of 'more importantly', introducing sentence 14, suggests a contrast, when in fact sentence 14 is probably an exemplification or expansion of the point in sentence 13.

Coherence is clouded by the problematic use of pronominal referents, a weakness we found in several level 4 scripts. The use of 'the' premodifying 'own language' and the unclear use of 'their' and 'they' together with mistakes of spelling/lexis render the meaning unclear.

The writer's overall viewpoint in the conclusion is equally unclear, masked by the misuse of markers 'however' and 'although', and an unclear referent 'it':

> [16]In conclusion, however, I feel that it is prabably best way.
> [17]We must teach our own language in our children
> [18]Although, it is the simple way to use computers
> [19]New millenium need a new identification in the world.
> *(original layout kept)*

In the absence of a clear anaphoric referent to 'it', one assumes that the reference must be prospective to sentence 17. But then the sentence seems strange, as children will grow up learning – or rather acquiring – the L1 anyway. The point of the final sentence and its connection to what precedes it is also unclear. The conclusion leaves the reader with some frustration, struggling to understand the intended meaning.

5.2 Strengths and weaknesses of the research

5.2.1 Strengths

- We have analysed a large authentic corpus (one of the largest reported in this area of research): 130 scripts, with a total of 35,464 words, increasing the validity of our findings.
- We have used the WordSmith Tools Concordancing program giving us a powerful means of analysing the data.
- We have combined qualitative and quantitative methods of analysis.
- We based our analysis on 130 answers to the same question, allowing us to make valid generalisations about the data.
- We have created a permanent performance database which can be used for future further analysis.
- We identified the three levels (8, 6, and 4) as valid levels to distinguish different candidates.
- We have been able to identify the writing strategies and tactics adopted by writers at each of the three levels and have described the linguistic exponents of those strategies, information that can act as useful feedback for IELTS tutors, candidates, and materials writers.
- We have reviewed recent research in the area of academic writing.
- We have identified areas for further investigation.
- In the course of the research we have developed a methodology for undertaking investigative work of this sort that can be of assistance to future researchers.

5.2.2 Weaknesses

- The database has an unequal number of scripts at the different levels: 50 scripts at levels 4 and 6, but only 30 scripts at level 8 and above. All figures were however converted to percentages for comparability. We have assumed the reliability and validity of the marking system.
- Although we have kept the question-prompt common to all 130 scripts, we were not able to ascertain the first-language backgrounds of the testees, nor their IELTS teaching/learning history. This lack of

information was not crucial in this research, as it was never our intention to correlate such factors with linguistic performance.

- The higher-level scripts are a mixture of levels 8 and 9: 18 scripts are at level 8, and 12 at level 9, although this difference in level did not appear to affect the results of the analysis.

- We have not carried out any statistical tests of significance and in any case such tests are unlikely to be productive with the relatively small sub-samples we had.

- There were problems with the initial typing up of the scripts, e.g.
  - the interpretation of dubious features, (e.g. punctuation, capitals, paragraphs) was subjective.

5.3 Future research

Some suggestions for future research would include:

- matching testee information (e.g. first-language background/years of learning English/gender/age/IELTS language classes attended including methodology adopted) with test performance

- comparing lexical/grammatical use at each of the three levels (8, 6 and 4) (using Wordsmith Keyword for example) with 'native-speaker' performance on the same test

- investigating whether the results of such analyses as those reported here correlate in any way with marker strategies (using 'mark-aloud' techniques)

- continuing to build up an IELTS corpus for future research purposes, now that the value of corpus-related analyses has been demonstrated.

6 Main conclusions

The findings confirm other research (e.g. Flowerdew 1998) that the higher-level 8 essays have internal coherence without overt cohesive ties. The lower-level essays (6 and 4), by contrast, have cohesive markers, but little content.

The higher-level essays are interactive and almost conversational in style. This raises the question of whether level 8 writers use the appropriate register. They clearly do in one sense in that they achieve high marks (though see areas of further research above for ideas in this area), but we wonder whether an expert level native speaker in this context would adopt the informal conversational tone that many of the level 8 writers do (see areas of further research). However, there are two points to make here. First, it may be inappropriate to use L1 performance as a norm, and it may be sufficient to continue to categorise the performance of levels 8 upwards as expert users and use their performance as a norm. Second, although the conversational and overtly interactive style may seem inappropriate for written academic discourse, (some of the interactional features are more likely to be found in spoken academic genres such as lectures), the IELTS rubric (see Appendix 8.1) clearly states that answers should be written for an educated reader with no expertise in the subject. Measured against this rubric, the overtly interactive nature of level 8 would not seem inappropriate. Were the rubric to require testees to conform to a strictly academic written discourse genre, then there might be a case for looking at IELTS marking schemes.

Interactivity combined with a strongly-developed reader awareness is a major feature of level 8 scripts. The writers are able to use linguistic devices to modify and qualify their statements, unlike level 4 and to some extent level 6 writers, who find it difficult to do more than present propositions with little evidence of the stance they wish to take or wish the reader to take towards the propositional content.

Level 8 writers also present considerable content: they have something to say, whereas the lower-level essays are thin on content. This is reflected in a basic measurement like length, with few of the level 4 writers able to reach the required minimum number of words.

The keywords from the question-prompt make up a greater proportion of lower-level essays, and there are fewer single occurrence words. The level 8 writers draw on a wide experience and are able to transfer this experience into appropriate lexical elements with a wide range of vocabulary.

The level 6 essays show greater resemblance to the level 4 essays than to the level 8 ones: they are better versions of the level 4 essays, but substantially different from level 8 both in terms of content and the linguistic and discoursal strategies used to present that content.

Acknowledgements

We wish to thank Tony Dudley-Evans who worked with us on the research, and Philip King who gave freely of his time and expertise to assist us.

Please note the following:

- We have used '*he*' to refer to the writer of a script.
- We have used the term '*native speaker*' to distinguish a user of English as a first language from the IELTS examinees.
- Extracts from the scripts used in our report retain the candidates' original spelling/grammatical errors, etc.

APPENDIX 8.1
Academic Writing Task 2: the question prompt

You should spend about 40 minutes on this task.

Present a written argument or case to an educated reader with no specialist knowledge of the following topic:

Every year the quality of translation by computer improves. In the future there will be no point in our children learning foreign languages, because computers will be able to provide immediate translation whenever it is needed.

To what extent do you agree or disagree with this opinion?

You should write at least 250 words.

You should use your own ideas, knowledge and experience and support your arguments with examples and relevant evidence.

APPENDIX 8.2
Topic analysis at each level

Table 8.7 Main ideas in level 4 scripts

4–01	<ul><li>the invention of computers – no-one could measure what the next generation would do</li><li>computer translation will enable us to travel more easily and so the earth will become more peaceful</li><li>language cements national unity and identity</li><li>importance of keeping own languages and identity</li></ul>
4–02	<ul><li>people are lazy</li><li>computers can make mistakes – so better to know languages</li><li>if computers translate, people won't study and humans will become less intelligent</li><li>computers can destroy our life, we must be independent</li></ul>
4–03	<ul><li>computers depend on people</li><li>we mustn't depend on computers, must trust ourselves</li><li>good to learn lots of foreign languages</li></ul>
4–04	<ul><li>better to learn languages (or anything else) at first hand – learn it better</li><li>lots of health risks with computers</li><li>computers = bad influence on children from 'the world'</li></ul>
4–05	<ul><li>people have invented a lot of things throughout history without the computer</li><li>need to learn from teachers – if use computers no teachers</li><li>not necessary to learn languages</li></ul>
4–06	<ul><li>influence of computers on children</li><li>computers = various computer games</li></ul>
4–07	<ul><li>our lives will improve because of a lot of machines</li><li>computers can save time</li><li>danger of computer virus</li></ul>
4–08	<ul><li>computers for translation is very fast</li><li>affects children's way of thinking</li></ul>
4–09	<ul><li>computers are important but can't do everything – can't speak, can't be taken everywhere</li><li>must be careful with our habits</li><li>in future everyone could speak one language e.g. English</li><li>people must become more intelligent</li><li>children should learn computer language</li></ul>
4–10	<ul><li>foreign language is important</li><li>can't always rely on computers – need to be face to face</li></ul>
4–11	<ul><li>can communicate more easily</li><li>economy will develop</li></ul>

Table 8.8 Topics in level 6 scripts

	Benefits of computers for translation	Problems with computers for translation
6–01	• computer industry developing • convenient	• computer translation – depends on programmer • computer not always there
6–02	• saves time • good sound effects	• no interaction with people • language includes culture
6–03	• speed	• not a close match with words and can't get context
6–04	• improvements in technology • computers are faster • good quality translation	• computers break down and depend on man
6–05		• also need to learn culture • controlled by man • children need to make friends and can't take computers with them
6–06		• need more time to improve technology • can't have a conversation • can't express feelings • computers can go wrong
6–07	• save time • fewer faults	• may break
6–08	• speed • accuracy	• language helps people have social contact and friends • humans can use explanation to solve misunderstandings
6–09	• large information resource and big storage • computers in general useful • hotmail is useful	
6–10	• good trend for high technology • saves time	• increase children's confidence if they can communicate without computer • children can show real feelings
6–11		• likely to have misunderstandings and problems • government officials need languages • languages needed for travelling and culture, trade and business
6–12	• speed of translation	• can't take it with you • can't use it to speak • languages change and computers may not keep up with that
6–13		• language and culture • languages change

Table 8.8 (Continued)

	Benefits of computers for translation	Problems with computers for translation
		• computer might go wrong
6–14		• too many languages to translate all • language and culture • languages change
6–15	• computers in general – much used and convenient	• we must learn by ourselves • need to speak and listen • children become lazy with computer • computer bad for health • learning foreign languages is valuable for thinking
6–16	• save time • save money (don't need to pay to learn languages or study abroad)	
6–17	• save time	• can't understand body language
6–18	• computer ok for simple things	• teachers better, need teachers
6–19	• fast	• need to communicate with people, can't always carry computer • only translates word for word, not sentences • price increasing • culture
6–20	• increasing role of computer generally • better to learn own L1 • wastes time to learn English	
6–21	• analogy with calculators and maths	• language = access to culture • language = knowledge re other parts of world • can't always use computer
6–22	• speed • children like computers so increases motivation	• have to learn re computers
6–23	• computers in general have improved	• children become lazy – become more independent if learn languages on own • affect health • many jobs (e.g. translator) will disappear • people need more time translating
6–24	• important role and general improvement in computers	• conversation with people – emotional aspects • machines can go wrong • general education. Value in learning languages

Table 8.8 (Continued)

	Benefits of computers for translation	Problems with computers for translation
		• learning languages will lead to more peaceful world
6–25	• general improvement in computers • convenient for reading	• no good for speaking to people • only basic – can't deal with sentences • enjoyable experience to learn a foreign language
6–26	• computers generally fast and convenient	• computer not perfect – lacks vocabulary • programmed by humans • conversation with people
6–27	• software (3 things) makes jobs easier	• limitations – no interaction with a teacher • teachers are better

Table 8.9   Use of detailed exemplification in level 8 scripts *

8–01	prsnl experience translating articles of law (paragraph)
	translations of Aenead and Roald Dahl (paragraph)
8–02	context of business . . . imports exports
	discussion of translation of 'I miss you' into English from French
8–04	exotic locations Hawaii or India
8–05	Spanish song with its nuances
8–06	Spanish (language) in South America medical book in Italian
8–07	Eskimos 20 words for ice
	nuances of 'love' in French
	Shakespeare to Italians
8–08	(hypothetical situation of) breaking bad news to a patient
	etymology of word 'sympathy'
	beer in a Hofbräuhaus Berlin,
	hiking in English countryside,
	Sherpa guides Nepal, Nepali language, Everest (paragraph)
8–09	personal experience of multilingualism in India (paragraph)
8–11	the fun of holidaying (if know the language) (paragraph)
8–13	calculators and maths (analogy)
8–14	own experience of 9-year-old son learning language (paragraph)
8–15	poem translated (only brief example)
8–17	detailed discussion of literature in translation (paragraph)
8–20	backpacking in Italy; spontaneity lost in jokes
8–22	hypothetical e.g. of computer breaking down in US forest
8–25	interracial relationships and bilingual children (paragraph)
	personal experience of pleasure learning a language (paragraph)
8–26	French translation of Shakespeare, personal experience
	being a foreigner in UK
8–27	Liverpool accent v SE England v USA
	Shakespeare and Marlowe
	situation in Third World (paragraph)
8–28	foreign film analogy (paragraph)
8–29	kinship and terms of address – Western v Chinese society (paragraph)

*This is of main/substantial instances rather than fully comprehensive. See section on shared world knowledge.

Methodology evaluation of Chapter 8

In ways similar to Chapter 7, this is a very long study. It demonstrates to new researchers that the discourse analysis of texts takes up a lot of time and human resources even though partial analysis of texts can be done automatically with computers and relevant software (Wordsmith Tools). In spite of the use of concordancers, both the initial analysis (categorisation of linguistic features), and the subsequent analysis of linguistic features that cannot be statistically analysed, must be done manually. However, if researchers need to investigate text at the text (supra-sentential) level – and, after 30 years of discourse studies no-one can reasonably disagree that text analysis has added power to the applied linguist's set of analytical tools and provided rich insights into how text works – human resources must be committed and the time-consuming analysis that ensues must take place.

The substantial Literature Review in this chapter is very useful and sets a good example for the new researcher or research student. An unusual but interesting feature of the literature review is the use of summaries at the end of each of the three main sections: Cohesion and coherence – 2.1.1 – L1 studies; Cohesion and coherence – 2.1.2. – L2 studies; and Hedging, politeness and stance – 2.2. Summaries such as these are not common in most journal articles or book chapters but, as is clear when reading the chapter, they serve the reader well. Such a practice could be a particular strength if employed in long articles or postgraduate and doctoral theses.

The methodological section is another example of exemplary practice. The methodological processes and the research instruments that are employed are described thoroughly so that it would be relatively easy for other researchers to replicate the study with new data. It should be noted that, initially, manual analysis is carried out in two separate processes. First, using an ethnomethodological approach, 'letting the data speak for itself', features (or categories) arising from a close study of the texts are colour-coded. After the initial analysis, a further process of categorisation, using new colour-coding, is carried out. In this step, the researchers attempt to match features in the text with features noted in the research literature. The third step involves using Wordsmith to analyse the linguistic features that have been identified and that can be analysed statistically. When the statistical analysis is completed, the fourth step involves the manual analysis of the remaining features – those that cannot be analysed by the concordancer. In this painstaking, meticulous way, genuine insights into the texts of IELTS writers emerge and can then be considered by the IELTS partners and IELTS professionals when contemplating changes to the IELTS writing component.

9 Investigating task design in Academic Writing prompts

Kieran O'Loughlin and Gillian Wigglesworth

Abstract

This paper reports on a study into task difficulty in the IELTS Academic Writing Task 1. The study examined first, the extent to which the difficulty of the task is affected by the *amount* of information provided to the candidate and second, the extent to which the difficulty of the task is affected by the *presentation* of the information to the candidate.

In the Academic Writing Task 1 candidates are required to examine a diagram or table, and to present the information in their own words (IELTS 2000). Four tasks, which differed in terms of the amount of information the candidates were required to process to complete the task, were developed for the study. Two of the tasks included less information on which candidates could base their responses and the other two included more information. Within each of these two types of tasks, one was designated as the control, and the other was designated as the experimental task. Five different versions of each of the two experimental tasks were developed. These versions differed in the way the stimulus material was presented to candidates. The control tasks were designed as benchmark tasks and administered to all candidates. The experimental tasks were administered to selected subgroups of the cohort.

Two hundred and ten students, who were enrolled in English for Academic Purposes (EAP) courses in Melbourne or Sydney, completed four of the writing tasks (the two control tasks and two other experimental tasks). All scripts were double rated by trained and qualified IELTS raters. Analyses of the test scores and the scripts themselves were then undertaken.

The test-score analyses indicated that there were no substantial differences in difficulty between the tasks, either in terms of the amount of information presented or in terms of the differences in presentation of the tasks. Analyses of the written texts produced by the students focused on whether there were any systematic differences in their written performances across different proficiency levels (high, middle and low). Responses from all three proficiency groups to the task with less information showed greater complexity overall than the task with more information. The trend was less clear overall in relation to accuracy. However, the high proficiency group showed a strong tendency to display greater accuracy in response to the task with more information. It appears, therefore, that tasks providing less information actually elicit more complex language. Since the goal of these tasks is to produce as high a performance from the candidate as possible it can be concluded that this is best achieved through using simpler tasks.

1 Introduction

Written assessment tasks are designed with a view to providing an adequate sample of written discourse to make appropriate and reliable assessments of the linguistic skill of the candidate. In high-stakes tests, such as IELTS, where important decisions are made on the test results, it is critical that the tasks are all comparably difficult. Thus, one of the goals in developing assessment tasks must be to ensure comparability across different administrations. In order to do this it is essential that we know much more about the tasks, how candidates approach them, and what makes a task more or less difficult. This study was designed to investigate these issues.

Previous research into the impact of task variability in oral language has suggested that relatively small variations in task design can influence the linguistic output of learners (Foster 1996, Foster and Skehan 1996, Mehnert 1998, Ortega 1999, Skehan and Foster 1997). As has been the case with much investigation of the effects of task design, for the most part these studies have been carried out in the classroom context. The focus of these studies has been on how different tasks can influence different aspects of learner language – for example, do particular task types promote more fluent language, or more accurate language? To shed insight into these questions, these studies have involved highly detailed analyses of the oral linguistic output of the learners. A range of measures have been used to examine these differences, and while general conclusions may be drawn, the necessarily small scale of such studies, and the lack of comparability of measures (see Foster, Tonkyn and Wigglesworth 2000 for further discussion of this issue), has limited the conclusions which may be drawn.

Recent investigation of these phenomena in the testing situation, however, have allowed a different approach. Because most testing situations allow substantial numbers, it has sometimes been possible to examine both rater perceptions of differences according to task, and to include a more detailed analysis at the discoursal level. These recent studies have suggested that, once again, relatively small-scale variations in the task can influence the output (see for example, Wigglesworth 1997, 2001). To date, however, these studies have investigated oral language, rather than written language.

The question of the extent to which the specific task prompt affects writing in a second language is a vexed one. In the first language literature studies have argued that both the quality and quantity of an essay's content can be influenced by the topic, although other studies have argued that the topic has little effect on scores (Hamp-Lyons 1990). The large and much cited study by Carlson et al (1985) which investigated the Test of Written English (TWE) and looked at the effect of topic on scores, claimed that the correlations suggested no significant differences in how the different topics and task types were ranking students. However, Carlson (1986, cited in Polio and Glew 1996) found that there were significant differences in the means of scores on different types of writing tasks but not on different topics.

One of the problems with the assessment of productive language skills, and the ability to determine which type of task is more or less difficult is that there are a series of interactions which take place. First, the test taker, or candidate, interacts with the task. Thus, there may be an issue of familiarity with the content of the task. There may be more or less supporting material provided with the task. There may be a choice of which task to choose. The second major interaction which takes place is the rater's interaction with the candidate's writing. The rater approaches the writing using either a holistic or an analytic scale or a mixture of the two. But the rater does not only interact with the student's writing; the rater also interacts with the task itself. The rater may consider the task to be more or less difficult than another task, and may compensate for this in applying the score to the writing. As Polio and Glew (1996) point out, this raises a problem for studies which investigate how the prompt affects writing. This is because conclusions about writing quality are almost invariably based on the score provided by the rater which has not taken into account the way in which the rater may or may not compensate for the perceived difficulty of the task.

Kroll (1998) has argued that a great deal more research needs to be conducted in the writing assessment area on a number of critical variables, of which she identifies the writing task as one. She suggests that we need to develop a greater understanding of both how to control the range of variables, and of what to assess.

Investigations into whether different task prompts elicit language which is different in quantity and quality have been controversial (Hamp-Lyons and Kroll 1996). A number of studies have claimed that the topic does affect language differentially, while others have argued that there are no significant differences as a result of topic content. However, these studies have not examined the written output of the candidate at the level of the language – thus ratings have been conducted but there has to date been little investigation of the actual writing itself.

Various studies have examined the discourse of learner writing, and the focus of some has been the investigation of linguistic accuracy. These have included studies which have examined the written output of learners to determine whether the writer's accuracy changes under different conditions (e.g. Koyabashi and Rinnert 1992, Kroll 1990). However, these studies have looked only at the written output and the essays have not been rated.

Wigglesworth (1999) undertook a detailed examination of four different tasks administered to the same 15 candidates where each was rated by two independent raters as part of a larger batch of assessed scripts (so as to ensure that the raters would not recognise the same candidates from their scripts). Of the four tasks, two required the learners to write a report, whilst two required them to write a recount of a recent event. In addition, an analysis was undertaken which identified error-free T-units and clauses. The analyses suggested that in the report tasks, candidates used more complex, but less accurate language, whereas in the recount tasks the language was less complex but more accurate. This concords with the now substantial investigations of the language used in oral tasks, where it has been argued that there is a trade-off effect between accuracy and complexity (Skehan 1998). This conclusion has resulted from a substantial number of studies which have been carried out in second language classrooms although many of these have focused on oral language.

The brief findings reported above indicate that there is a need for further in-depth investigation of a variety of aspects of the testing situation and that these may make important contributions to our understanding of the testing process. Quantitative analyses are required for the purposes of determining reliability and validity of the testing instrument. However, more detailed qualitative analyses of the discourse are also necessary. These can inform our understanding of how candidates approach the task and of the extent to which different variables in tasks can be manipulated to affect different outcomes for candidates. Additionally, they will contribute to the process of task development through providing insights into how the language produced by the candidates may vary with the task. This project was designed to investigate some of these issues in relation to Academic Writing Task 1 in IELTS, in a study which addresses the issues from both a quantitative and a qualitative point of view. Two specific research questions were addressed in this study:

1. To what extent is the difficulty of the task affected by the *amount* of information provided to the candidate?
2. To what extent is the difficulty of the task affected by the *presentation* of the information to the candidate?

2 Methodology

2.1 Phase 1: task development

Four tasks were developed which met the criteria for Academic Writing Task 1 where candidates are required to examine a diagram or table, and to present the information in their own words (IELTS 2000). These were based on topics and task designs used in the Academic Writing Module over the last five years. Permission to do this was granted by IELTS and the tasks were submitted to IELTS test development personnel for comment.

The tasks differed in terms of the amount of information the candidates were required to process to complete the task. Two of the tasks developed were less complex. This was operationalised as tasks in which the diagram or graph represented 16 pieces of information. The remaining two tasks were developed to be more complex, operationalised as having 32 pieces of information. From each of these two types of task, one was designated as the control, and the other was designated as the experimental task. The control tasks are provided in Appendix 9.1.

Five different versions of each of the two experimental tasks were developed. The input material was in the form of graphs or tables. The different versions varied along the following dimensions:

- bar graph/dates on x axis
- reverse bar graph/dates on y axis
- line graph/dates on x axis
- reverse line graph/dates on y axis
- table.

The experimental tasks are provided in Appendix 9.2.

The control tasks were designed as benchmark tasks and administered to all candidates. The experimental tasks were administered to subgroups of the cohort (see Section 2.2).

2.2 Phase 2: data collection

Subjects

Data was collected from students enrolled in English for Academic Purposes (EAP) courses with the intention of undertaking tertiary studies in Australia. The students came from a range of language backgrounds and were enrolled in pre-university IELTS preparation classes at either La Trobe University Language Centre, The University of Melbourne English Language Centre (Hawthorn), the Centre for English Language Learning at the RMIT University or English Language Services at the National Centre for English Language Teaching and Research, Macquarie University.

Two hundred and twenty students were recruited, approximately one-third in New South Wales, and two-thirds in Victoria. To ensure anonymity all students were assigned an identification number between one and 220. Ten students did not complete all four tasks (e.g. disappeared during the break). Their data was omitted from the data set, leaving 210 students who attempted all tasks.

Research design

The two benchmark tasks, one more complex and one less complex, were administered to all students. Approximately 40 students were administered one of the variable tasks from each of the manipulated experimental tasks. This is outlined below. (The research design is provided in greater detail in Appendix 9.3.)

1. Less complex

Benchmark task (control 1)	210 candidates

Experimental task 1/1 (Bar graph)	41 candidates
Experimental task 1/2 (Reverse bar graph)	40 candidates
Experimental task 1/3 (Line graph)	43 candidates
Experimental task 1/4 (Reverse line graph)	43 candidates
Experimental task 1/5 (Table)	43 candidates

2. More complex

Benchmark task (control 2)	210 candidates

Experimental task 2/1 (Bar graph)	41 candidates
Experimental task 2/2 (Reverse bar graph)	42 candidates
Experimental task 2/3 (Line graph)	41 candidates
Experimental task 2/4 (Reverse line graph)	42 candidates
Experimental task 2/5 (Table)	44 candidates

Tasks were administered to candidates in two sessions of approximately one hour. Two tasks were administered per session. Candidates were allowed 20 minutes per task, with a 10 minute break before the next task was presented. Order of task presentation was randomised so that both control and experimental tasks occurred in all possible orders. Half the candidates did the more complex tasks first, while half did the less complex tasks first. Assignment of the various manipulated tasks was random to counteract practice and/or other effects of multiple task presentation (e.g. boredom, tiredness). This meant that of the candidates who took, for example, variable 1 in task 2, approximately eight completed one of each of the variables for task 4.

2.3 Rating

All tasks were double rated by trained and qualified IELTS raters using both the global and analytic IELTS profile band descriptors for Academic and General Training Writing Modules Task 1. This was because, for the purposes of this research, scalar measures, in addition to the global measures of task difficulty were required which would be as sensitive as possible to the range of variation within any particular feature of performance. Thus both global band scores and analytic measures were obtained for each candidate from each rater.

3 Results

3.1 Analysis of test scores

The scores assigned by raters to the tasks were subjected to both classical analyses and multifaceted Rasch analyses (using the program FACETS).

3.2 Analysis of pre-existing group differences

In order to determine whether there were any pre-existing differences between the groups in terms of candidate ability, the scores obtained by the candidates on the control tasks were analysed by allocating the learners into groups according to the experimental task they had taken. Using classical analysis for the comparison of means (Analysis of Variance and post hoc t-tests) it was found that there were no significant differences in the scores obtained by the groups on the control tasks, although it does appear that those learners assigned to the experimental task 1/1 variable were slightly more proficient than the remaining groups. Similarly, those assigned to the experimental tasks (ET) 2/2 and 2/3 may also have been slightly more proficient. These differences were not, however, significant. Table 9.1 below shows the mean scores across the two control tasks for candidates in each experimental group including both the global and analytic scores. Analysis of variance and post hoc t-tests were also used for the comparison of means in Tables 9.2–9.4.

Table 9.1 Comparison of experimental groups on control tasks

Less information	Global score	Analytic score (average)
ET 1/1	5.260	5.239
ET 1/2	4.896	4.884
ET 1/3	4.965	4.980
ET 1/4	4.728	4.760
ET 1/5	4.643	4.627
More information		
ET 2/1	4.719	4.848
ET 2/2	5.134	5.075
ET 2/3	5.024	5.024
ET 2/4	4.795	4.838
ET 2/5	4.722	4.832

3.3 Analysis of experimental tasks

Comparison of the overall results on the experimental variations were obtained from several sources. First, raw scores were available on the global measures, as well as each of the three analytic measures of (i) Task Fulfilment, (ii) Coherence and Cohesion, and (iii) Vocabulary and Grammar. In addition to this, a measure of task difficulty for each individual task was obtained from the FACETS analyses.

3.4 Raw score comparisons

Comparison of the overall results on the different experimental variations indicated that there were no substantial differences across the tasks, either in terms of the amount of information presented (the difference between the 'Less information' and the 'More information' tasks) or in terms of the differences in presentation of the tasks. Table 9.2 shows the mean figures on the experimental tasks based on the global scores.

Table 9.2 Comparison of global scores

Task	Less information	More information
Bar graph	5.037	4.792
Reverse bar graph	5.026	4.915
Line diagram	4.904	4.850
Reverse line diagram	4.707	4.678
Table	4.986	4.884

Differences across groups were minimal on the global scores, and none were significant. Table 9.3 shows the mean figures on the specified task based on the analytic scores. Once again there were no significant differences on any of these measures.

Table 9.3 Comparison of average analytic scores

Task	Less information	More information
Bar graph	5.057	4.863
Reverse bar graph	5.033	4.948
Line diagram	4.874	4.938
Reverse line diagram	4.800	4.745
Table	5.015	4.918

Table 9.4 shows the mean figures for the different experimental tasks in relation to the three analytic criteria (Task Fulfilment, Coherence and Cohesion, and Vocabulary and Sentence Structure) according to task. Once again there were no significant differences between the scores on any of the criteria, either across presentation types or amount of information.

Table 9.4 Comparison of analytic scores by criteria

	Less information	More information
Task Fulfilment		
Bar graph	4.94	4.70
Reverse bar graph	4.99	4.94
Line diagram	4.62	4.88
Reverse line diagram	4.62	4.65
Table	5.02	4.68
Coherence and Cohesion		
Bar graph	5.10	4.88
Reverse bar graph	5.10	5.10
Line diagram	4.95	4.94
Reverse line diagram	4.83	4.81
Table	5.10	4.89
Vocabulary and Sentence Structure		
Bar graph	5.02	4.77
Reverse bar graph	4.95	5.06
Line diagram	4.93	4.99
Reverse line diagram	4.89	4.74
Table	4.91	4.97

In view of the lack of differences elicited by these tasks, two additional analyses of the raw score data were undertaken. First, an examination was made of the 50 top-scoring candidates and the 50 bottom-scoring candidates to determine whether there were any differences in the scores on the experimental tasks within either of these groups. Second, candidates who had obtained three similar scores on the tasks, but who had one outlier score, were identified, and extracted from the data set in order to examine whether there were any systematic differences in the outlier scores.

3.5 High- and low-scoring candidates

The top 50 candidates, and the bottom 50 candidates, as determined by the scores from the FACETS output, were identified. An analysis of the raw scores for each of the variable tasks was conducted for the global score and the individual analytic criteria. The results of the high-scoring candidates are given in Table 9.5, and those of the low-scoring candidates in Table 9.6. Once again there are no significant differences between the performances on the different variables for the high-scoring candidates.

Although the differences are not significant, it appears that the candidates found the line diagram presentations more difficult than the remaining types of presentation. The means for the line diagrams have been highlighted in bold.

Table 9.5 High-scoring candidates

	Less information	More information
Global		
Bar graph	5.93	5.91
Reverse bar graph	6.11	5.89
Line diagram	**6.00**	**5.79**
Reverse line diagram	**5.73**	**5.64**
Table	5.73	5.37
Task Fulfilment		
Bar graph	6.13	5.86
Reverse bar graph	6.25	5.75
Line diagram	**5.83**	**5.89**
Reverse line diagram	**5.77**	**5.42**
Table	5.77	5.38
Cohesion and Coherence		
Bar graph	5.87	6.00
Reverse bar graph	6.37	5.90
Line diagram	**6.08**	**5.67**
Reverse line diagram	**5.68**	**5.50**
Table	5.82	5.25
Vocabulary and Sentence Structure		
Bar graph	6.00	5.86
Reverse bar graph	6.00	6.00
Line diagram	**5.71**	**5.75**
Reverse line diagram	**5.73**	**5.64**
Table	5.50	5.43

3.6 Outlier score analysis

The individual raw scores for each candidate on each of the four tasks they had taken were compared. Two criteria had to be met for a score to be identified as an outlier. First, the score had to differ by nine points or more from at least one of the other three scores; second it had to differ by at least six points from its nearest score. Thirty candidates had score patterns which matched these criteria. Of these, 14 had a score which was markedly higher than their other scores, and 16 had scores which were markedly lower than their other scores. There did not appear to be any systematicity in the patterning of these scores as shown in Table 9.7.

3.7 Task difficulty analysis

A FACETS analysis was conducted on all scores from all performances to obtain a measure of the task difficulty. FACETS uses a mean of zero to calculate task difficulty. Therefore measures above zero are higher than average difficulty, whereas measures below zero (i.e. minus scores) are lower than the average difficulty. (Note: in order to understand the figures in the three

Table 9.6 Low-scoring candidates

	Less information	More information
Global		
Bar graph	4.00	4.14
Reverse bar graph	4.23	4.16
Line diagram	**3.84**	**3.55**
Reverse line diagram	**3.50**	**3.91**
Table	4.15	4.14
Task Fulfilment		
Bar graph	3.90	4.00
Reverse bar graph	4.19	4.00
Line diagram	**3.54**	**3.55**
Reverse line diagram	**3.45**	**3.83**
Table	4.00	3.78
Coherence and Cohesion		
Bar graph	4.40	4.43
Reverse bar graph	4.37	4.39
Line diagram	**4.00**	**3.72**
Reverse line diagram	**3.60**	**4.04**
Table	4.20	4.28
Vocabulary and Sentence Structure		
Bar graph	4.70	4.25
Reverse bar graph	4.31	4.22
Line diagram	**4.15**	**3.78**
Reverse line diagram	**3.85**	**4.08**
Table	4.30	4.36

Table 9.7 Number of outlier scores by task

	High outlier	Low outlier
Control task 1	3	3
Bar graph, less info	0	0
Reverse bar, less info	1	0
Line graph, less info	0	0
Reverse line, less info	1	2
Table, less info	1	0
Control task 2	3	6
Bar graph, more info	1	0
Reverse bar, more info	1	0
Line graph, more info	0	2
Reverse line, more info	0	2
Table, more info	0	1

columns in Table 9.8, the reader is advised to consult the explanation of Rasch model statistics provided in Chapters 1 and 11.) These results indicated that there were three groups of tasks although none of the differences were very substantial. The two tasks ranked easiest were the less complex

Table 9.8 FACETS measures of task difficulty

	Difficulty Measure	Standard Error	Infit MnSq
ET 1/5 Table	−0.31	0.08	0.9
ET 1/2 Reverse bar	−0.30	0.09	1.0
ET 1/1 Bar	−0.05	0.09	0.8
ET 2/1 Bar	−0.01	0.09	1.0
ET 2/5 Table	−0.01	0.09	1.0
ET 2/2 Reverse bar	0.08	0.09	1.1
ET 2/4 Reverse line	0.10	0.09	0.8
ET 1/3 Line	0.11	0.09	0.9
ET 1/4 Reverse line	0.15	0.09	1.1
ET 2/3 Line	0.16	0.09	1.1

reverse bar graph, and the less complex table. In the next group were the bar graphs, both the more and less complex, and the more complex table. The final group consisted of the remaining tasks – the more complex reverse bar graph and both types of line graphs.

These figures suggest that the line diagrams are marginally more difficult than the other types of graphs used as indicated by the small score differences obtained on the raw score analysis.

In general, however, the results of these quantitative analyses reveal that the differences elicited by the different amounts of information provided in these tasks, and the different types of presentation are very small. The difficulty measures range from −0.31 for the easiest task, to 0.16 for the most difficult task, an overall difference of 0.47, which is well below a whole logit where the separation between tasks would be significant. The standard errors are virtually identical. This suggests that such differences as those provided here need not be of major concern in designing tasks for writing assessment.

4 Discourse analysis

Given that there were only minimal score differences between the different variations in the task presentations, it was decided to examine the data from a different angle, and to try to determine whether there were any systematic differences in the written performances of candidates across different proficiency levels of candidates. Because of the large number of candidates who had taken both control task 1 and control task 2, it was possible to clearly identify different proficiency levels. Thus the scripts of the 20 top-scoring candidates, the 20 medium-scoring candidates and the bottom 20 candidates (as identified by the FACETS program in the previous stage of the study) were selected for further analysis. A detailed discourse analysis, outlined below, was conducted on the two control tasks that each of these candidates had completed. The total number of scripts examined therefore was 120.

A range of different measures related to the three analytic scoring criteria were identified. The three criteria were first, Task Fulfilment, second, Coherence and Cohesion and third, Vocabulary and Sentence Structure. The following measures were used to examine the quality of the written texts.

Task Fulfilment
- number of words
- accuracy of information

Coherence and Cohesion
- coherence (structure and organisation of the body)
- cohesion (conjunctive and referential)

Vocabulary and Sentence Structure
- number of clauses
- types of clauses (subordinate and non-finite)
- number of T-units
- number of error-free clauses and T-units
- repetition of key words.

The methodologies adopted for examining each of these categories is discussed below.

4.1 Task Fulfilment

In carrying out the word count, a word was regarded as a series of letters with a space before and after it. Text titles (where used) were included in the count. The following were counted as one word: calendar years (e.g. 1985), ages (e.g. 16 years old), times (e.g. 12 p.m.) and contractions (e.g. it's). The following were counted as two words: age range (e.g. 16–27 years old), time span (e.g. 6 a.m.–12 a.m.; 1895–1990) and words separated by a hyphen (e.g. twenty-one). Symbols (e.g. % or $) were not counted.

Table 9.9 provides the mean and standard deviation figures for the three proficiency groups (high, medium and low) on the two benchmark tasks (control task 1 and control task 2).

Although the differences are fairly minimal, control task 2, on average, elicited fewer words from students at all three proficiency levels. However, standard deviations are considerably higher in the Medium and Low groups on control task 2 indicating a greater range of variability. The standard deviation on both tasks is very high for the High group, which suggests there is wide variation in terms of length of text produced by this group.

Table 9.9 Word count

	Control task 1 N	Control task 2 N
High		
Mean	207.25	201.95
Standard deviation	53.49	54.66
Medium		
Mean	155.15	134.35
Standard deviation	21.96	30.82
Low		
Mean	109.15	107.00
Standard deviation	30.60	40.55

The minimum word requirement for each task was 150 words. Table 9.10 shows the proportion of texts which met this minimum word requirement for each task.

Table 9.10 Proportion of texts which met the minimum word limit of 150 words for each task

	Control task 1		Control task 2	
	N	% of total scripts	N	% of total scripts
High				
> 150	16	80	17	85
< 150	4	20	3	15
Medium				
> 150	12	60	6	30
< 150	8	40	14	70
Low				
> 150	3	15	3	15
< 150	17	85	17	85

The results in this table suggest that the high groups meet this criterion well on both tasks. The medium group meets this criterion only on control task 1, the task in which there is less information to process. The low group does not meet this criterion on either control task 1 or 2. These findings suggest that there may be a constraint associated with the different levels of information that the candidates are required to process.

The other measure of Task Fulfilment adopted was the proportion of accurate information from the source material. The following method was used to make these calculations. For each task, the information that would be expected to be included in a comprehensive report was identified. Nine pieces of information were identified for control task 1 and eleven pieces for control task 2. These were:

Control task 1

No. of pieces of information	Age group	Content required
2	16–27	highest level of unemployment in all years slowly increased by about 5% over the 15 years
1	28–39	essentially stable (slight fluctuation of about 1%)
2	40–51	1985–95 – drop of about 3% in 1990 1995–2000 – increase of about 5%
2	52–65	essentially stable from 1985 to 1990 (about 1% decrease) sharp rise from 1990 to 2000 (rise of about 6% across 1990–5, and about 8% across 1995–2000)
1	Overall	1995–2000 – greatest increase of all, with highest rates of unemployment among 16–27s and 52–65s
1		1985–2000 – unemployment increasing, in all age groups except 28–39s

Control task 2

No. of pieces of information		Content required
3	Heating	highest use of heating is in winter winter patterns differs from summer times of greatest demand = 12–6 p.m., 6–12 a.m.
1	Lighting	similar consumption patterns for summer and winter, though winter is slightly higher
2	Hot Water	similar consumption patterns for summer and winter, though winter is slightly higher greatest use of electricity in summer is for hot water
2	Appliances	similar consumption patterns for summer and winter, though winter is slightly higher 6–12 p.m. = time when usage is greatest
3	Overall	more electricity is used in winter than in summer usage of electricity varies with time of day the greatest demand for electricity is for heating

Each text was scrutinised and the proportion of the required information included in each text was calculated. There were several issues that influenced decisions about what information should be expected to occur in the responses to each of the tasks. First, for both tasks, but especially control task 2, there were a variety of possible ways of presenting the information contained in the graphs, and the basis of organisation influenced what could be expected to be mentioned. This is related to a second issue, that of the interpretation, or understanding of what the tasks required writers to do.

Writing a report could be considered to involve synthesising the information presented in the graphs, not merely listing information already available to the reader from the graph. This leads to a third issue, of what is actually meant by 'factual information'. These issues can be illustrated by considering the following constructed sentences, based on one of the tasks:

> The level of unemployment for 28–39 year-olds goes from 7% in 1985 to 8% in 1990 and back to 7% in 1995.
> The level of unemployment amongst 28–39 year-olds is stable from 1985–1995.

Both of these sentences are correct in relation to the graph in control task 1, although the first might be considered more 'factual' in that it gives percentages from the graph. The second statement does not give figures from the graph, is less specific, but reflects a higher degree of synthesis of information provided in the graph. For this analysis, both these types of sentences were considered to 'contain accurate, factual information from the source material'.

For each script the amount of correct information was calculated and then converted to a percentage of the total number of pieces of information. Table 9.11 shows the mean and standard deviation for these percentage figures.

Table 9.11 Proportion of accurate information (%)

	Control task 1 (%)	Control task 2 (%)
High		
Mean	68.75	62.00
Standard deviation	12.13	14.27
Medium		
Mean	61.75	53.25
Standard deviation	12.70	19.82
Low		
Mean	44.75	31.50
Standard deviation	19.50	16.55

All three proficiency groups performed better on control task 1 using this measure. This is probably partly the result of the fact that there was less information to be incorporated into the responses on control task 1 than control task 2 (i.e. nine as opposed to eleven pieces of information) which means that the task is less onerous. However, it is interesting to note that the differences between the performances on control task 1 and control task 2 become greater with decreasing proficiency, suggesting once more that the lower proficiency groups may be finding the 'more information' task more challenging.

4.2 Coherence

For the purposes of carrying out the following analyses, the overlapping concepts of 'coherence' and 'cohesion' were considered separately. Coherence refers to the relationships which link the meanings of sentences in a written text.

Texts were coded into one of five categories according to which of the three main structural elements were included in the text, i.e. Introduction, Body and Conclusion:

5 Introduction, Body and Conclusion

4 Introduction and Body only (no Conclusion)

3 Body and Conclusion only (no Introduction)

2 Body only

1 Nil

A text was considered to include an Introduction if it opened with a clear orienting statement as to what the text was about, and, in some cases, how it would be organised. The Introduction sometimes took the form of a meta-textual statement. Some introductions were an exact or close repetition of the prompt; others provided an indication of the main theme of the report as well. In the examples that follow, the numbers such as 2/210 indicate the number of the control task and candidate, hence 2/210 = control task 2, candidate 210.

> I will discuss the different uses for electricity at different times of the day in kilowatt hours during winter and summer in this paper.   (2/210)

> The two graphs show the different uses for electricity at four different times a day in winter and summer. The demands for electricity in winter is higher than in summer.   (2/43)

A text was coded as having a Conclusion if it had a final paragraph or even a sentence which provided a summary of the main idea(s) of the text, usually introduced by an overt marker of conclusion, such as 'In conclusion', 'In short', or 'To sum up'. For example:

> In short, it seems that more electricity is used winter than in summer.
> (2/21)

> In conclusion, in winter heating during 12pm–6pm has the highest kilowatt hours. In summer, hot water is the major use for electricity. The resemblance between winter and summer is the use of appliances.
> (2/114)

> Through the graph, I think that the demands for electricity for heating is the most obvious difference between winter and summer.   (2/210)

Where texts had an Introduction and/or Conclusion, the remainder of the text was considered to be the Body. Texts without an Introduction or Conclusion were coded as having a Body only. Any text where the student had not attempted the task was coded as Nil. Table 9.12 shows the results of the text structure analysis.

Table 9.12 Analysis of text structure

	Control task 1		Control task 2	
	Total scripts	% of scripts	Total scripts	% of scripts
Introduction/Body/Conclusion				
High	16	80	9	45
Medium	10	50	6	30
Low	1	5	0	0
Introduction/Body				
High	4	20	9	45
Medium	7	35	11	55
Low	6	30	9	45
Body/Conclusion				
High	0	0	0	0
Medium	0	0	0	0
Low	1	5	1	5
Body only				
High	0	0	2	10
Medium	3	15	3	15
Low	12	60	9	45
Nil				
High	0	0	0	0
Medium	0	0	0	0
Low	0	0	1	5

On average, the scripts of all three proficiency groups were less complete in terms of structure on control task 2 than on control task 1. The high group also outperformed the other groups on this measure, where overall, the number of elements incorporated into the texts reduces by proficiency level.

A further measure of coherence was whether or not there was a clear, logical principle of organisation evident in the way the information in the body of the text was presented. Texts were coded as either having, or not having a clear principle of organisation, of information in the body of the text:

2 Yes, there was a clear basis of organisation evident.
1 No, the basis of organisation was not evident.

There were a number of different principles of organisation used by the participants. Some used a set of sequential organisers (e.g. *firstly, secondly, thirdly* to introduce successive sections). Others used sets of organisers, based on an aspect of topic. For example, for control task 1, common patterns of topical organisation were age groups (people aged 16–27 years/people aged 28–39 years), or calendar year (*in* 1985/*in* 1990). For control task 2, common patterns of organisation were seasons (*in winter/in summer*), time of day (*between 0 and 6 a.m.*), or when the greatest demand for different categories of electricity usage occurred. Contrastive organisers (*on the one hand/on the other hand, however*) were also employed by a few writers, usually in addition to one of the other sets of organisers. Table 9.13 shows the results of this analysis.

Table 9.13 Organisation of the body of the texts

	Control task 1		Control task 2	
	Total scripts	% of scripts	Total scripts	% of scripts
High				
Evident	16	80	14	70
Not evident	4	20	6	30
Medium				
Evident	12	60	11	55
Not evident	8	40	9	45
Low				
Evident	5	25	9	45
Not Evident	15	75	11	55

The results of this measure are interesting. The high proficiency group perform considerably better on control task 1 than on control task 2. The medium proficiency group perform similarly on both tasks, while the low proficiency group perform better on control task 2.

4.3 Cohesion

Cohesion refers to the formal (i.e. grammatical and/or lexical) relationships between the different elements of a text.

Halliday and Hasan (1976) identify four conjunctive categories. These are additive, adversative, causal and temporal. Each category was counted to provide an indication of the range of conjunctive use. The most common additive conjunctions in these data were: *and, also, for example, in addition,* and *similarly*. Examples are:

> They occupy the big portion and increase in number steadily. Also percentage of 52–65 year old unemployed people was low in 1985.   (1/131)

> In 1985, only 6% of them didn't have a job. And it decreased a bit in 1990. (1/161)

The most common adversative conjunctions in these data were: *but, however, in fact, in contrast, on the one hand/on the other hand, on the contrary.* Examples are:

> With the advance technology and science, people now lead a much better life than ever before. *On the other hand,* much automation cause more unemployed people in the world. (1/114)

> And it decreased a bit in 1990. *However,* since then, it rose rapidly to 18% . . . (1/161)

The most common causal conjunctions in these data were: *as a result, so, therefore.* Examples are:

> In fact, modern's social is very difficult for get a good job. *So* many young people stay home after university. (1/35)

> I think that this generation is including highschool and university students. *Therefore,* the percentage of unemployed people is relatively low. (1/210)

The most common temporal conjunctions in these data were: *first(ly), second(ly), third(ly), finally, in conclusion, meanwhile, next, then to sum up.* Examples are:

> *First,* I will consider the percentage of unemployed people . . . *Second* the percentage of unemployed people . . . is low constantly. (1/210)

> The number of unemployed people at the age of sixteen to twenty seven rose in 1990 with the percentage of eighteen percent. *Meanwhile,* the rate of unemployed people from . . . stayed the same as in 1985 . . . (1/21)

The total number of inter-sentential (here inter-T-unit) conjunctions was counted. In Table 9.14 the results are expressed as a percentage of the total T-units used by the three proficiency groups (high, medium and low) on each of the tasks (control tasks 1 and 2). The use of conjunctions is fairly similar within each task for the proficiency groups, but while the high and medium groups use more in control task 1, the low group uses marginally more in control task 2.

Tables 9.15 and 9.16 below show the breakdown by percentage of total T-units for the four types of conjunction used in control task 1 and control task 2 respectively.

Table 9.14 Total use of conjunctions

	Control task 1			Control task 2		
	Total T-units	Conjunctions	%	Total T-units	Conjunctions	%
High	227	77	33.92	212	55	25.94
Medium	202	68	33.66	181	45	24.86
Low	183	51	27.87	145	43	29.66

Table 9.15 Use of conjunctions by type, control task 1

	Additive	Adversative	Causal	Temporal
High	10.13	8.81	1.32	13.66
Medium	8.42	12.87	0.00	12.38
Low	9.29	9.84	4.92	3.83

Table 9.16 Use of conjunctions by type, control task 2

	Additive	Adversative	Casual	Temporal
High	7.55	8.49	1.89	8.02
Medium	5.52	12.15	1.66	5.52
Low	9.66	11.03	4.14	4.83

Causal links are used very little by any of the proficiency groups in either task. Temporal links are used most by the medium- and high-proficiency groups in control task 1, and most by the high group in control task 2. Additive and adversative conjunctions are used most by all proficiency levels on both tasks.

The total number of inter-sentential (here inter-T-unit) reference connections was counted (pronominal, demonstrative, definite article and comparative). Some of the examples below are drawn from the scripts and others from Halliday and Hasan (1976):

Pronominal
The distinctive feature is *16–27 year old people. They* occupy the big portion and increase in number steadily.   (1/131)

Demonstrative
From *1985 to 2000* the people who are the most touch by unemployment are the 16–27 years old. In the case a slise increase in unemployment appears between those years as an irregular rate.   (1/103)

Definite article
Last year we went to Devon *for a holiday. The holiday* we had there was
the best we've ever had. (Halliday and Hasan 1976:73)

Comparative
The little dog barked as noisily as the big one.
(Halliday and Hasan 1976:82)

The calculations did not include the following uses of the definite article:
generic, unique reference, definite noun phrase with specifying modifier,
because such uses are not anaphoric. The actual number of references used
in many of the texts is greater than the figures shown, but those references could not be included because they were intra-sentential, rather than
inter-sentential.

Table 9.17 below shows the results for the use of referential cohesion
expressed as percentages of the total relevant number of T-units.

Table 9.17 Total use of reference

	Control task 1		Control task 2	
	Total	% total	Total	% total
Proficiency group	references	T-units	references	T-units
High	103	45.37	61	28.77
Medium	42	20.79	33	18.23
Low	43	23.50	36	24.83

The high proficiency group exhibit much greater control of referential
cohesion than the medium and low groups, particularly on control task 1.
This difference is not reflected across tasks by the lower proficiency levels.

4.4 Vocabulary and Sentence Structure

In undertaking the clause count calculation a clause was defined as consisting
of an overt subject and a finite verb (cf. Polio 1997). Therefore:

Firstly, I will consider the demands for electricity for heating.
(2/210) = one clause

We use a lot of electricity for heating in winter/because it is very cold in
winter.
(2/210) = two clauses (one independent or main; one dependent or
subordinate)

. . . that during the 0–6 a.m., the number of kilowatt hours increases
more than 10000, and reduces to 5000 during 12 p.m.–6 p.m.

(2/114) = one clause (one dependent clause, with two finite verbs, but only one overt subject)

Table 9.18 provides means and standard deviations based on number of clauses in the scripts. As expected, the high group produce more clauses than the other two groups, with very similar numbers on both tasks. The medium and low groups tend to produce more clauses on control task 1.

Table 9.18 Clause count

	Control task 1		Control task 2	
	Mean	Standard deviation	Mean	Standard deviation
High	14.90	6.38	15.30	4.75
Medium	13.15	3.28	11.00	3.03
Low	10.80	4.30	8.80	6.00

Both dependent and non-finite clauses were coded and counted. Following Wolfe-Quintero, Inagaki and Kim (1998) no distinction was made between dependent and embedded clauses, meaning that adverbial, nominal and relative clauses were all coded as dependent (subordinate) clauses. For example:

Adverbial clauses
We use a lot of electricity for heating in *winter because it is very cold in winter. Especially while we are working during the day from six am to six pm*, the demand for electricity for heating is big . . .   (7/210)

In these texts, adverbial clauses were most commonly, though not exclusively, introduced by *because*, *while*, and *when*:

Nominal
Through this graph, *I think that the demands for electricity for heating is the most obvious difference between summer and winter.*   (7/210)

Relative
The percentage of people *who are 16–27 years old.*   (1/114)

Non-finite
The chart illustrates the number of unemployers grouped in age living in London between 1985 and 2000.   (1/91)

In Table 9.19 the number of subordinate clauses used in the texts are expressed as a percentage of total clauses. Table 9.20 then shows the proportion of total clauses containing a non-finite clause.

Table 9.19 Use of subordinate clauses

	Control task 1			Control task 2		
Proficiency group	Total clauses	Subord clauses	%	Total clauses	Subord clauses	%
High	308	77	25.00	306	65	21.24
Medium	263	35	13.31	220	35	15.91
Low	216	40	18.52	175	21	12.00

Table 9.20 Use of non-finite clauses

	Control task 1			Control task 2		
Proficiency group	Total clauses	Subord clauses	%	Total clauses	Subord clauses	%
High	308	9	3.92	306	4	1.31
Medium	263	0	0.00	220	0	0.00
Low	216	3	1.39	175	0	0.00

In Table 9.19 patterns of use across the two task types are very similar for the high and medium group, with the low group using rather more subordinators in control task 1. The use of non-finite clauses, as shown in Table 9.20, was too restricted for a clear pattern to emerge.

T-units were then counted. A T-unit consists of one independent clause and any dependent clauses or sentence fragments attached to it. For example:

> First, I will consider the demands for electricity for heating.
> (2/210) = one T-unit, consisting of one clause (one independent, or main, clause).

> We use a lot of electricity for heating in winter because it is very cold in winter.
> (2/210) = one T-unit, consisting of two clauses (one independent, or main, and one dependent, or subordinate)

> The graph shows that during the 0–6am, the number of kilowatt hours increases more than 10,000, and reduces to 5000 during 12 p.m.–6 p.m.
> (2/114 = one T-unit, consisting of two clauses (one independent, or main, and one dependent, or subordinate)

Table 9.21 shows the mean and standard deviation figures based on the counting of T-units in the scripts. This table indicates that the number of T-units used by all proficiency groups is similar across both tasks.

Table 9.21 T-unit count

Proficiency group	Control task 1		Control task 2	
	Mean	SD	Mean	SD
High	11.35	4.67	11.80	3.15
Medium	10.10	2.15	9.05	3.32
Low	8.65	3.48	7.25	4.71

The number of error-free clauses and T-units in all of the texts were then calculated to obtain a measure of grammatical accuracy. Error-free clauses (EFC) were defined as clauses without errors, expressed as a proportion of total clauses. Any error excluded a clause from being classified as error free. Error-free T-units (EFT) were defined as T-units without errors, expressed as a proportion of total clauses. Any error excluded a T-unit from being classified as error free. It is possible, and indeed common for some clauses in T-units to be error free, but due to an error in one clause, the T-unit cannot be coded as error free.

The focus of EFC/EFT analysis was primarily linguistic accuracy, but decisions about accuracy or correctness (e.g. lexical choice) cannot be divorced completely from context of use, that is, what is appropriate or correct in the context, and therefore the coding indirectly incorporates aspects of discourse level competence.

In carrying out this analysis fundamental decisions had to be made about what would be counted as an error. For this study verb, article and lexical/phrasal errors were included:

- subject–verb agreement: use of a singular verb with a plural subject, or vice versa
- other verb: this included incorrect participle form, incorrect tense, incorrect form of an auxiliary or modal verb
- article: omission of an article or inclusion of an article when not required, as well as incorrect or inappropriate article (e.g. 'these' instead of 'this')
- lexical/phrasal: this category included:
  - inappropriate or infelicitous choice of words or expressions (this category reflects the use of a word or expression which conveys the idea the writer appears to be seeking to communicate, i.e. it makes sense in context, but is not what a native speaker would use (e.g. 'no job people' instead of 'the unemployed')
  - incorrect words or phrases (e.g. 'come' instead of 'go') incorrect forms of idioms or fixed expressions (e.g. 'In the other hand' instead of 'On the other hand')

- preposition errors
- word order errors, i.e. where all the correct words were present, but were not in the correct order.

Tables 9.22 and 9.23 provide the figures on error-free clauses and T-units respectively. As would be expected, the results indicate that, overall, the high-proficiency group had a higher percentage of error-free clauses than the other two groups. In addition, this group performed better on control task 2 than control task 1, whereas the reverse was true for the medium and lower groups.

Table 9.22 Error-free clauses

| Proficiency group | Control task 1 | | | Control task 2 | | |
	Total clauses	Error-free clauses	%	Total clauses	Error-free clauses	%
High	308	99	32.14	306	129	42.16
Medium	263	68	25.86	220	33	15.00
Low	216	39	18.06	175	29	16.57

Table 9.23 Error-free T-units

| | Control task 1 | | | Control task 2 | | |
	Total clauses	Error-free clauses	%	Total clauses	Error-free clauses	%
High	227	57	25.11	212	83	39.15
Medium	202	36	17.82	181	14	7.74
Low	183	15	8.20	145	16	11.04

Similarly to Table 9.22, the high-proficiency group have a greater percentage of error-free clauses in control task 2, and outperform the other groups on both tasks. Although the medium group have a greater percentage of error-free clauses in control task 1, for the low group, there are marginally more error-free clauses in control task 2, but this difference is minimal.

4.5 Repetition of key words

This measure is adapted from the work of Lawe Davies (1998), who found that exact lexical repetition of key words from the prompt distinguished high from low rated texts. Key words from the prompt were identified for each task (see Appendices 9.1 and 9.2) as shown below. ('Year-olds' was accepted as exact repetition if the context required that form.)

Key words from the task prompts

Control task 1	*Control task 2*
graph	graphs
percentage	differing
unemployed people	different
age	demands
London	uses
1985	electricity
1990	kilowatt hours
1995	winter
2000	summer
16–27 years old	0–6 a.m.
28–39 years old	6 a.m.–12 p.m.
40–51 years old	12 p.m.–6 p.m.
52–65 years old	6 p.m.–12 a.m.
	heating
	hot water
	appliances
	lighting
	time(s) of day

Each text was then coded on the basis of whether all of the key words were used at least once in the text, or whether only some of them were repeated. For this analysis, a binary coding was used:

1 key words incomplete

2 key words complete

Table 9.24 shows the results of this analysis including the percentages of texts in which use of key words was complete and incomplete in relation to the different proficiency groups and tasks.

Table 9.24 Use of key word repetition

	Control task 1				Control task 2			
	Complete		Incomplete		Complete		Incomplete	
Proficiency group	n	%	n	%	n	%	n	%
High	15	75	5	25	11	55	9	45
Medium	15	75	5	25	8	40	12	60
Low	2	10	18	19	0	0	20	100

On this final measure all three proficiency groups performed better on control task 2. This is probably because there are more keywords in this task, and therefore greater opportunity to do so.

5 Conclusion

The test-score analyses showed no differences in task difficulty in terms of the amount or presentation of information to the candidate. The fact that no significant differences were found in the scores given by the raters on the tasks may be considered to be a positive finding. This means that the types of variations in presentation incorporated into these tasks can be shown not to influence candidate outcome. This means that a variety of presentation types can be encouraged and manipulated.

On the other hand, the discourse analyses revealed some interesting differences between the two control tasks which differed in terms of the amount of information presented to candidates. The responses from all three proficiency groups to control task 1 showed greater complexity overall on most of the relevant measures (structure, organisation, cohesion, subordination and repetition of key words). The trend was less clear overall in relation to the categories for accuracy (error-free clauses and T-units). Here there was greater variability in relation to both the tasks and proficiency levels of the candidates. However, it is worth noting that the high proficiency group showed greater accuracy in response to control task 2 on most measures of accuracy.

It appears, therefore, that tasks providing less information actually elicit more complex language. Since the goal of these tasks is to produce as high a performance from the candidate as possible it can be concluded that this is best achieved through using simpler tasks.

In line with Polio and Glew (1996) the results on the complexity measures in particular also suggest that the raters may have compensated for perceiving the tasks with more information to be more difficult since the differences in the quality of the responses on the two control tasks, from the discourse analytic perspective, were not reflected in the test scores. This underscores the importance of combining test-score and discourse analyses in investigations of task difficulty in language testing.

APPENDIX 9.1
Control tasks

Control task 1 (less complex)

You should spend about 20 minutes on this task.

The graph below shows the percentages of unemployed people by age living in London between 1985 and 2000.

Write a report for a university lecturer describing the information shown below.

You should write at least 150 words.

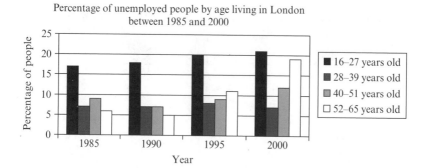

Percentage of unemployed people by age living in London between 1985 and 2000

Control task 2 (more complex)

You should spend about 20 minutes on this task.

The graphs below show the differing demand for electricity in winter and summer according to time of day.

Write a report for a university lecturer describing the information shown below.

You should write at least 150 words.

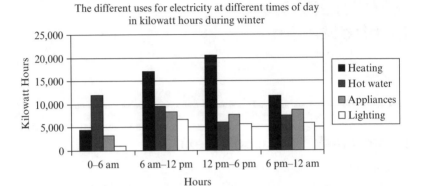

The different uses for electricity at different times of day in kilowatt hours during winter

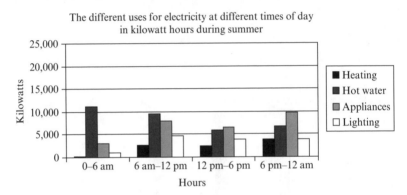

The different uses for electricity at different times of day in kilowatt hours during summer

APPENDIX 9.2
Experimental tasks

Experimental task 1 (less complex): Bar graph (ET1/1)

You should spend about 20 minutes on this task.

The graph below shows the number of people attending places of entertainment in Melbourne, Australia, between 1985 and 2000.

Write a report for a university lecturer describing the information shown below.

You should write at least 150 words.

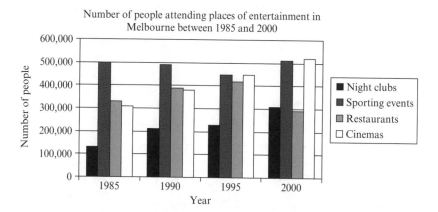

Experimental task 2 (less complex): Reverse bar graph (ET1/2)

You should spend about 20 minutes on this task.

The graph below shows the number of people attending places of entertainment in Melbourne, Australia, between 1985 and 2000.

Write a report for a university lecturer describing the information shown below.

You should write at least 150 words.

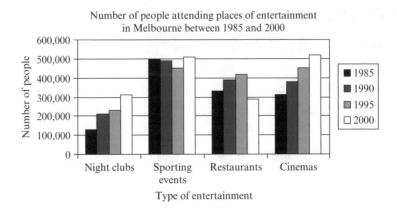

Number of people attending places of entertainment
in Melbourne between 1985 and 2000

Experimental task 3 (less complex): Line graph (ET1/3)

You should spend about 20 minutes on this task.

The graph below shows the number of people attending places of entertainment in Melbourne, Australia, between 1985 and 2000.

Write a report for a university lecturer describing the information shown below.

You should write at least 150 words.

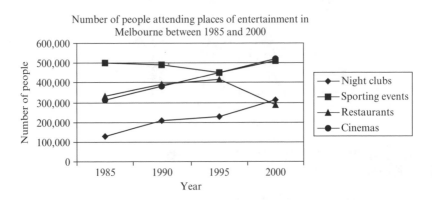

Number of people attending places of entertainment in
Melbourne between 1985 and 2000

Experimental task 4 (less complex): Reverse line graph (ET1/4)

You should spend about 20 minutes on this task.

The graph below shows the number of people attending places of entertainment in Melbourne, Australia, between 1985 and 2000.

Write a report for a university lecturer describing the information shown below.
You should write at least 150 words.

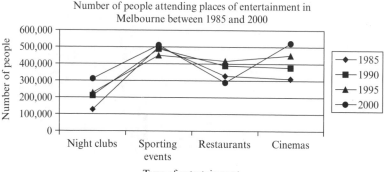

Number of people attending places of entertainment in Melbourne between 1985 and 2000

Experimental task 5 (less complex): Table (ET1/5)

You should spend about 20 minutes on this task.

The table below shows the number of people attending places of entertainment in Melbourne, Australia, between 1985 and 2000.

Write a report for a university lecturer describing the information shown below.
You should write at least 150 words.

Number of people attending places of entertainment in Melbourne between 1985 and 2000

	1985	1990	1995	2000
Night clubs	130,000	210,000	240,000	320,000
Sporting events	500,000	490,000	450,000	510,000
Restaurants	340,000	390,000	435,000	290,000
Cinemas	310,000	370,000	450,000	530,000

Experimental task 1 (more complex): Bar graph (ET2/1)

You should spend about 20 minutes on this task.

The graphs below show the numbers of women and men studying post-graduate courses in an Australian university between 1985 and 2000.

Write a report for a university lecturer describing the information shown below.

You should write at least 150 words.

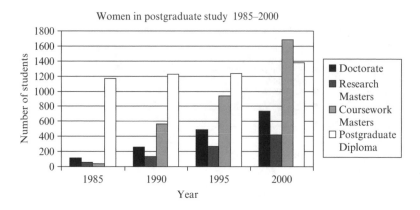

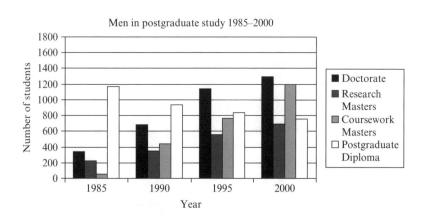

Experimental task 2 (more complex): Reverse bar graph (ET2/2)

You should spend about 20 minutes on this task.

The graphs below show the numbers of women and men studying post-graduate courses in an Australian university between 1985 and 2000.

Write a report for a university lecturer describing the information shown below.

You should write at least 150 words.

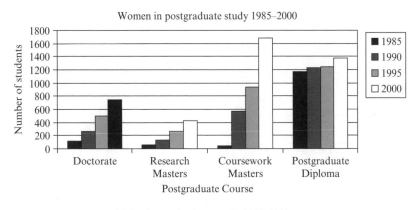

Women in postgraduate study 1985–2000

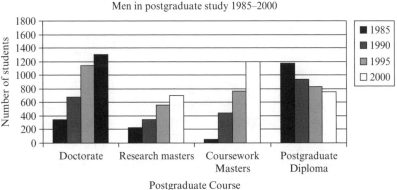

Men in postgraduate study 1985–2000

Experimental task 3 (more complex): Line graph (ET2/3)

You should spend about 20 minutes on this task.

The graphs below show the numbers of women and men studying post-graduate courses in an Australian university between 1985 and 2000.

Write a report for a university lecturer describing the information shown below.

You should write at least 150 words.

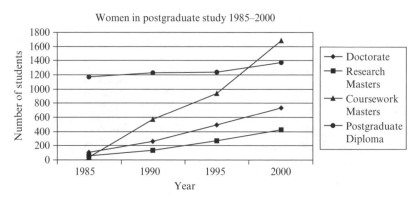

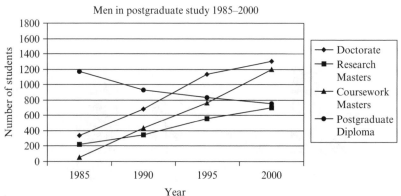

Experimental task 4 (more complex): Line graph (ET2/4)

You should spend about 20 minutes on this task.

The graphs below show the numbers of women and men studying postgraduate courses in an Australian university between 1985 and 2000.

Write a report for a university lecturer describing the information shown below.

You should write at least 150 words.

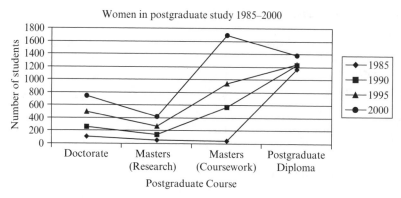

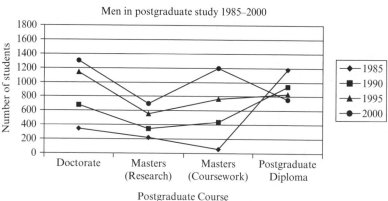

Experimental task 5 (more complex): Table (ET2/5)

You should spend about 20 minutes on this task.

The tables below show the numbers of women and men studying post-graduate courses in an Australian university between 1985 and 2000.

Write a report for a university lecturer describing the information shown below.

You should write at least 150 words.

Women in postgraduate study 1985–2000

	1985	1990	1995	2000
Doctorate	111	259	492	740
Masters (Research)	59	138	267	423
Masters (Coursework)	39	567	943	1688
Postgraduate Diploma	1167	1226	1237	1375

Men in postgraduate study 1985–2000

	1985	1990	1995	2000
Doctorate	341	681	1139	1300
Masters (Research)	222	349	557	697
Masters (Coursework)	54	438	763	1194
Postgraduate Diploma	1173	935	834	753

APPENDIX 9.3
Research design for administration of control and experimental tasks

The two benchmark tasks, one more complex and one less complex, were administered to all students. Approximately 40 students were administered one of the variable tasks from each of the manipulated experimental tasks.

Tasks	1/1	1/2	1/3	1/4	1/5
2/1	59 201 60 183 1 2 101 124 164	61 62 19 20 102 111 144 184	77 78 27 28 112 121 161	83 84 35 36 122 162 181	95 216 96 215 43 44 123 142 163 182
2/2	51 220 52 205 3 206 4 128 146 168	63 64 11 12 103 147	79 80 29 30 104 113 125 165	85 214 86 188 37 38 114 126 148 166	97 98 45 46 127 145 167 185
2/3	53 54 5 6 129 149 189	65 66 13 14 130 150 190 204 219	71 72 192 21 22 131 151 152 191 213	87 88 39 40 105 115 132 172	99 100 47 48 106 116 210
2/4	55 56 7 8 107 118	7 67 212 68 193 15 16 134 136 153 174	73 74 23 24 108 154 194 203	89 90 31 32 135 155 175 195 202 209	91 92 49 50 117 133 156 173

Tasks	1/1	1/2	1/3	1/4	1/5
2/5	57	69	75	81	93
	58	70	76	82	94
	9	17	25	33	41
	10	18	26	34	42
	119	120	137	109	110
	138	140	157	158	139
	160	180	177	198	159
	178		197	217	179
	200		208		199
			211		218

In this Appendix Student 59, for example, completed 'less complex' task 1 and 'more complex' task 1, while Student 51 completed 'less complex' task 1 and 'more complex' task 2.

APPENDIX 9.4
Ethics consent

Date

Dear Student,

We are conducting a study called 'Task design in IELTS academic writing task 1'. We are looking at the effects on student writing of (a) the way the information is presented and (b) the amount of information that has to be included in the essay.

The research is being done by Gillian Wigglesworth, Department of Linguistics, Macquarie University (ph: 02 9850 8724) and Kieran O'Loughlin, Department of Language, Literacy and Arts Education, University of Melbourne (ph: 03 8344 8377).

You will be asked to write four short essays like those in the academic writing task 1 of IELTS. Your performance on these tasks will not influence your test results in the official IELTS examination. Neither will they be considered in assessment exercises you do for your classes. Names will be removed from the essays so that your confidentiality will be ensured. The data will be kept in a locked filing cabinet to which only the researchers have access. If you would like to find out about the results of this research, these will be available from the researchers in approximately one year from now. This research project is funded by the IELTS research program.

Please note that you have the right to withdraw from further participation in this research at any time without having to give a reason and without any negative consequences.

Yours sincerely,

Gillian Wigglesworth and Kieran O'Loughlin

I agree to participate in this research.

Signed (Participant) ——————— Date ———————

Signed (Investigators) ——————— Date ———————

The ethical aspects of this study have been approved by the Macquarie University Ethics Review Committee (Human Research). If you have any complaints or reservations about any ethical aspect of your participation in this research, you may contact the Committee through the Research Ethics Officer (telephone [02] 9850 7854, fax [02] 9850 8799, email: rachael.krinks@ mq.edu.au). Any complaint you make will be treated in confidence and investigated, and you will be informed of the outcome.

Methodology evaluation of Chapter 9

Apart from presenting findings on an interesting and relevant topic, this paper also demonstrates many of the features of a well-designed and well-executed research study. Researchers will note that the Methodology section of the chapter is detailed and very clear. In some studies, the research design is not always presented as clearly as readers would wish. This is often because the researchers are completely familiar with the content and design of the study and assume that the reader knows what they mean. Often they are not as explicit as they should be. For readers to fully understand the planning that goes into a research design and the methodological processes that take place, it is always worthwhile providing a detailed description of the choices that have been made and an explanation of why they have been made.

A detailed description of the research design is particularly important in this chapter because there are two parts to the study and three separate forms of analysis, each used for different purposes. The first part of the study uses two forms of quantitative data consisting first of classical theory analysis when experimental and control group means are compared, followed by Rasch analysis using the computer program FACETS to analyse task difficulty. The second part of the study uses qualitative data to 'determine whether there were any systematic differences in the written performance of candidates across different proficiency levels of candidates' and provides a detailed discourse analysis of the candidates' texts using nine elements grouped under the three criteria of Task Fulfilment, Coherence and Cohesion, and Vocabulary and Sentence Structure that reveals how well three groups, each of different proficiency, respond to the nine elements. In order to retain the reader's attention the research process is described comprehensively because of the complexity of the analysis that follows.

Qualitative analysis, as we have seen in earlier chapters, is painstaking, detailed work that is often used to complement the findings arising from statistical analyses. In this chapter, it is used differently. It is still detailed and painstaking but, instead of enhancing the results of the first part by providing 'rich' data, the authors have used qualitative data analysis to examine a separate question – how candidate responses differ in terms of the three major criteria outlined above.

The first part of the study did not reveal significant findings. This should not be considered a problem. Researchers should not be daunted if the result of a well-developed research study reveals no significant findings in what is being investigated. As Lynda Taylor will show in Chapter 12, the non-significant findings revealed in this study are good news not bad news for IELTS. The findings remove concerns about a variable that, if proven to be significant, could affect the scores of candidates. Good research designs set out specifically to discover not to confirm prejudices or hunches. Good research is neutral. It is only once results have been presented that we can begin to discuss, explain and interpret them.

A small but important limitation in the research design of this chapter concerns the training of analysts. It is clear that the raters in the first part of the study were trained and certificated IELTS examiners. What is not clear is how much the results in the second part of the chapter, the qualitative study, were reliable, based on the adequate training of analysts. In this case, the usual method is for the researcher(s) to agree on the analytical tools and their application, to specify how the results will be presented. They then need to ensure the reliability of the analytical tools. This is done by getting others (one or two other analysts) to apply the analytical tools to a sample of the data. A comparison is then made between the results of the researcher(s) and the accuracy of other analysts on the same pieces of data. If the findings are similar one can have confidence in the reliability of the analytical tools. If they are not, the analytical tools must be revisited and modified after which further analysis must take place using analysts who have not been involved in the study.

Another important point for new researchers to note is the inclusion, in Appendix 9.4, of an ethics consent form. The agreement by an ethics committee that the proposed research is ethical is becoming standard practice around the world. The form used in this study could be used as a template for those who have not before had to ask participants for their consent.

10 The effect of standardisation-training on rater judgements for the IELTS Writing Module

Clare Furneaux and Mark Rignall

Abstract

Recent research has found evidence of the failure of rater training to eliminate variation between raters. The limited understanding of rating processes, and of how training affects raters, is seen as an obstacle to the development of an effective training programme. It has been argued that training is incapable of reducing variation to an acceptable level and that its proper function is to improve raters' self-consistency.

This study investigates the judgements made by 12 trainee examiners (TEs) for the IELTS Writing Module. On successive occasions, before and during training, the TEs rated a set of eight scripts and wrote brief retrospective reports about their rating of four of the scripts.

Analysis of the group's scores reveals a modest gain in standardisation over the period. The percentage of scores on or within one band of the standard rating rose from 83% to 92%. Three of the four aberrant scores on the final occasion were given by raters who had not yet applied to take the certification task.

Analysis of the reports suggests that some individuals' rating procedures evolved gradually over the period to conform to the prescribed scoring method. On the first occasion certain criteria featured in many more reports than other criteria. This suggests that for some raters certain of the prescribed criteria may be more difficult than others to apply. Even on the final occasion reference to the criterion of Coherence and Cohesion was markedly less common than that to other criteria such as Vocabulary and Sentence Structure or Task Fulfilment. The percentage of reports referring to all three criteria doubled over the period, to 50%. The fact that it was not higher than 50% at the end of training may indicate that raters sometimes neglected some of the prescribed criteria in their rating. If further research shows this to be the case with trained examiners, the exam board could consider incorporating additional feedback to raters in the training programme or, if this is unsuccessful, altering the prescribed scoring method to require profile scoring of all scripts.

1 Introduction

Rater variation is a potentially serious weakness in tests of language performance. Rater training has been widely recommended as a means of keeping this variation within acceptable limits:

> The training of examiners is a crucial component of any testing programme since if the marking of a test is not valid and reliable, then all of the other work undertaken earlier to construct a 'quality' instrument will have been a waste of time (Alderson et al 1995:105).

The content and methodology of rater training have not been subject to the scrutiny normal in longer-established fields such as teacher education, where the various components of training, their levels of impact and their effectiveness have been much analysed (for example by Joyce and Showers 1980). Indeed, as Weigle (1998) observes, 'little is known about what actually occurs during rater training and how it affects the raters themselves'. Much of the rater training referred to in the literature seems to follow the six steps outlined by Bachman and Palmer as 'a general procedure for training raters' (1996:222). This is the case, for instance, with the 'norming sessions' studied by Weigle (1994) and the 'rater training kit' described by Kenyon (1997:260), although the latter is concerned with self-access training by individual raters.

Two broad areas of concern relating to rater training have been prominent in the research literature in recent years. One is the need for a better understanding of the processes by which a rater arrives at a rating: 'lack of knowledge in this area makes it more difficult to train markers to make valid and reliable assessments' (Milanovic et al 1996:93). The second concern is with the effects of training – is it capable, in practice, of bringing about the necessary change in rater behaviour?

Milanovic et al used group interviews and retrospective written and introspective verbal reports to investigate the judgements made by 16 raters of FCE and CPE scripts. They were able to identify in their data four different approaches used by the raters: '1) principled two-scan read; 2) pragmatic two-scan read; 3) read through; 4) provisional mark' (p. 98). The researchers also commented on the striking diversity of the composition elements referred to by raters in explaining their judgements.

Pollitt and Murray (1996) also investigated raters' decision-making processes, this time using repertory grid procedure and paired comparisons to analyse the judgements made by six raters (all EFL teachers) of recorded CPE interviews. They found two contrasting approaches to assessment, each used by three of the raters: a 'synthetic' approach in which the rater's perception is formed primarily by their preconceived notions about language learners, and secondly a more objective approach in which raters 'limited their comments to observed behaviour, . . . signalling perhaps a greater effort to think within a strictly assessment-oriented framework' (p. 87).

A number of studies have focused on the effects of training on rater behaviour. Weigle (1994) analysed the scores and verbal protocols of four inexperienced raters of the ESL composition placement test at UCLA, before and after training. She found that training was effective in bringing the four new, initially aberrant raters 'more or less in line with the rest' in terms of scores and the procedure by which they arrived at those scores. In her later study (1998), however, which looked at the scores of eight new and eight experienced raters before and after training, she found that, although training succeeded in helping raters to be self-consistent, it was less successful in achieving inter-rater reliability: significant differences in severity remained between raters after training.

Lumley and McNamara (1995) used multifaceted Rasch analysis to compare the ratings given on three occasions, before and after training, by experienced raters for the speaking subtest of the Occupational English Test. They found 'a substantial variation in rater harshness, which training has by no means eliminated, nor even reduced to a level which should permit reporting of raw scores for candidate performance' (p. 69). They raise the question of the stability of rater characteristics over time, and point to evidence suggesting that the beneficial effects of training may not last long after a training session.

Reviewing the research evidence of differences in severity between raters after training, McNamara (1996) concludes that 'assessment procedures which rely on single ratings by trained and qualified raters are hard to defend' (p. 235). He argues that the traditional aim of rater training – 'to eliminate as far as possible differences between raters – is unachievable and possibly undesirable' (p. 232). The proper aim of training, he believes, is to get new raters to concentrate and to become self-consistent.

An alternative response to the evidence that existing training procedures fail to eliminate rater differences is to investigate techniques or interventions that could make training more effective. The quality of feedback to the trainee is likely to be one important factor in the success or failure of training. Wigglesworth (1993) experimented with detailed, analytical feedback to raters of an oral interaction test. The feedback was based on an analysis of the biases in individual raters' previous ratings, in terms of task type and rating criterion. Working with a small dataset, she found some evidence that bias was reduced following this feedback and that rater consistency improved.

The purpose of the present study is to investigate the judgements made by raters as they train to examine for the IELTS Writing Module. In particular it looks at the following questions:

1. What change is there during training in the scores given by raters?
2. What change is there in the procedure by which raters decide on a particular score?

2 Context of the study[1]

2.1 IELTS Writing Module[2]

For the IELTS Writing Module candidates are required to complete two tasks in one hour. For Task 1 they have to write at least 150 words presenting information from a table or diagram. For Task 2 they have to write at least 250 words in response to a given view of a topic.

The three criteria on which Task 1 scripts are assessed are Task Fulfilment (TF), Coherence and Cohesion (CC) and Vocabulary and Sentence Structure (VSS). For Task 2 the three criteria are Arguments, Ideas and Evidence (AIE), Communicative Quality (CQ) and Vocabulary and Sentence Structure (VSS). To rate a script, the examiner decides which of the descriptors on a 9-band scale most accurately describes the candidate's performance, and assigns a band score (from 0 to 9) accordingly.

2.2 IELTS examiner training and certification

To qualify as an IELTS examiner, it is necessary to complete the training and certification procedure, whose main stages are outlined in Figure 10.1. Applicants for training are vetted to ensure that they meet the requirements laid down for examiners in the IELTS Code of Practice. These include, for example, a stipulation that examiners will be 'native speakers of English or non-native speakers of an overall band 9', and that they will hold one of the teaching qualifications specified.

Successful applicants then attend two days of initial training organised centrally by the BC/IDPA[3] with a trainer. Over these two days the trainee examiners (TEs) are introduced to the rating criteria, rating scales and scoring methods prescribed for all IELTS examining. The main focus is on standardisation of rating: TEs study a range of scripts which exemplify performance at particular band levels; they rate a range of scripts and discuss their ratings with fellow TEs and the trainer; they then study and discuss the standard ratings and profiles for these scripts. Differences between TEs'

Figure 10.1 IELTS examiner training and certification procedure

ratings and the standard ratings are discussed. For 'homework' at the end of the first day they complete a short rating task; their ratings for this are tabulated and discussed on day two. As they become more confident, TEs are asked to justify their ratings to the group.

At the end of initial training, TEs are told to consolidate their standardisation in the following weeks by means of the self-access training material in their local centre; when they find they are rating consistently to standard, they should apply to take the certification task. They are advised to attempt the certification task within six weeks of initial training.

For the certification task TEs receive a set of scripts and recorded interviews. They have to submit their ratings in writing to the BC/IDPA, who then determine whether they have achieved an acceptable level of standardisation. If TEs are found to be rating acceptably to standard for both the Writing and Speaking Modules, they are given certificated examiner status. TEs who are not successful on their first attempt are permitted to continue with self-access training and then attempt a different version of the certification task. The pass rate for the certification task at the first attempt is estimated to be between 40% and 50% (personal communication from BC source). Certificated examiner status lasts for two years, at the end of which the examiners have to complete a re-certification task successfully before they are permitted to continue examining.

3 Method

3.1 Participants

Twelve raters (seven women and five men) participated in the present study. They were among 25 trainee IELTS examiners who attended initial training in London in November/December 1999. One month before the training sessions, all 25 TEs had been sent a letter inviting them to take part in the present study. The letter made it clear that the study was quite separate from the IELTS training and certification procedure, and indicated that a small fee would be paid to those who participated as requested. Thirteen of the 25 TEs agreed to take part; 12 of the 13 went on to provide a full set of data. It cannot be assumed that they were typical of trainee examiners in general.

The participants were all working as English language teachers or directors, at UK colleges or universities or at British Council teaching centres outside the UK. All had recent EAP experience. They varied in the amount of English language examining they had done previously; some were senior examiners for other public exams, others had been involved only in testing within their institution.

3.2 Materials

The scripts used in the study were borrowed from the bank of 'certification scripts', which are selected by the IELTS Chief Examiner from time to time during regular sample monitoring of IELTS scripts and scores (IELTS 1998/9:19). The standard rating (or score) for each script was also made available; these scores had been agreed on by a team of senior examiners. Sixteen scripts (S01 to S16) were used in this study, ranging from band-level 3 to band-level 8. Eight of the scripts (S01, S02, S03, S04, S09, S10, S13, S14) were responses to IELTS Task 1, and the other eight (S05, S06, S07, S08, S11, S12, S15, S16) were responses to IELTS Task 2.

Raters were also provided with the two sets of 'global band descriptors' used by IELTS examiners, one set for assessing Task 1 scripts, the other for assessing Task 2 scripts. These scales provide a performance descriptor for each of the nine band levels. To rate a script, IELTS examiners follow a prescribed scoring method and decide which descriptor most accurately describes the candidate's performance; they then award a band score accordingly. The exam board does not make these descriptors publicly available.

3.3 Procedures

Data-collection would take place on four occasions over several months, from participants who were resident in different countries (two participants moved country between occasions). Given these requirements and practical constraints, it was decided that the data should be collected on paper by post.

On each occasion raters received a project task pack, which consisted of instructions, record sheets, two sets of global band descriptors, and eight scripts. There were two parts to the project task: for Part 1 the rater rated eight scripts and recorded the scores; for Part 2 he reflected on his rating of four of the scripts (two Task 1 scripts and two Task 2 scripts) and made notes in answer to the question *How did you arrive at this score for this script?* The detailed instructions given to raters are appended to this report (Appendix 10.1). Raters were instructed to complete both parts of the task in one sitting, and to return the pack with completed record sheets by a specified date two weeks after the pack had been sent out.

The retrospective written report procedure clearly brings certain limitations: the report reflects the rater's recollection of how they have decided on a score, but this recollection is inevitably subjective and incomplete. The verbal protocol procedure advocated by Green (1998) might have revealed more of the actual decision-making process, but it was not an option given the constraints of the present study. It was decided that, notwithstanding the above limitations, retrospective written reports on successive occasions could offer a valuable insight into changes in rater judgements and attitudes.

To make the task more easily manageable, the number of scripts was restricted to eight in Part 1 and four (of those eight) in Part 2. To permit direct comparison of scores across occasions, four of the sixteen scripts (S03, S04, S06, S07) were used on all four occasions, as shown in Figure 10.2. On occasions two and three, these four repeated scripts were interspersed with scripts used on one occasion only. The scripts used on the fourth occasion were identical to those used on the first occasion. It was thought that the intervening period of six months was long enough to minimise any practice effect. Raters did not have access to the standard ratings of the scripts, nor did they receive any feedback on their own ratings during the project.

Figure 10.2 Scripts used in the four project tasks

Project Task 1	Project Task 2	Project Task 3	Project Task 4
S01	S09	S13	S01
S02	S10	S14	S02
S03	S03	S03	S03
S04	S04	S04	S04
S05	S11	S15	S05
S06	S06	S06	S06
S07	S07	S07	S07
S08	S12	S16	S08

On each occasion raters were asked to make notes on just four of the eight scripts. It was thought that they would be more likely to make thoughtful, revealing notes on the smaller number of scripts, and would be able to do so at one sitting thus minimising the time between event and report, as recommended by Nisbett and Wilson (1977). The scripts in relation to which raters were asked to write notes are indicated in Figure 10.2 by shading.

Figure 10.3 shows the timing of the project tasks in relation to the raters' training as IELTS examiners. The first project task (PT1) preceded initial training; the second (PT2) was sent out immediately after initial training. Project Task 3 (PT3) was carried out two months after initial training, by which time TEs were expected to have done further training by self-access. The deadline for completing the final project task (PT4) was six months after initial training; it was expected that by that time at least some TEs would have applied for and possibly completed certification.

Figure 10.3 Timetable for data collection: timing of project tasks in relation to stages of the training process

Project Task	Completion deadline
PT1	One day before initial training
PT2	Three weeks after initial training
PT3	Two months after initial training
PT4	Six months after initial training

3.4 Data analysis

The project tasks produced two kinds of data: the scores awarded by raters to individual scripts, and the notes made by raters about how they arrived at those scores. The two kinds of data were analysed separately.

The scores given by raters were compared with the standard ratings for the same scripts, by subtracting the latter from the former. Thus, if a rater gave a particular script a score of 8, and the standard or 'official' band score for that script was 8, the difference was noted as zero; if a rater gave a score of 5, and the standard score was 6, the difference was noted as minus 1, and so on. The frequency with which the difference was zero (or minus 1, or minus 2, or plus 1, etc.) was counted for each rater on each occasion.

On each occasion during data collection raters were asked to make notes about their rating of four scripts – two Task 1 scripts and two Task 2 scripts. The 12 raters thus produced 24 sets of notes relating to Task 1 scripts and 24 sets relating to Task 2 scripts.

An initial reading of the notes was necessary before the analytical procedure could be finalised. It was evident on this first reading that the notes varied in quantity and style as well as content. For example, for Script 3 in PT1, raters TE01 and TE03 wrote as follows:

PT1 TE01 Script 3 (Score 6)
How did you arrive at this score for this script?
I felt it could have been more succinct.

PT1 TE03 Script 3 (Score 6)
How did you arrive at this score for this script?
Addressed the task more directly.
Fairly clear transfer of info into written word, covering main points. With nice turn of phrase 'Combining the two institutions . . .'
Not Band 7: sentences a little rambling i.e. not 'satisfactory range' (?)
Not Band 5: did not include a lot of 'irrelevant, inappropriate or inaccurate material'.

It was decided to analyse the notes in the following way: if a set of notes contained the name of a criterion (e.g. 'Task Fulfilment' or 'TF') or any of the key terms in the band descriptors relating to that criterion (e.g. '(ir)relevant', 'omits important information'), or cognates or clear paraphrases of those terms, it was recorded as referring to that criterion. On this basis TE01's notes above were recorded as referring to none of the criteria, and TE03's were recorded as referring to two criteria (TF and VSS). Two researchers working independently analysed the notes in this way and agreed on the results.

An incidental point evident on perusal of the notes was that at least one of the 'repeated scripts' was recognised as such by some raters. In PT2 this was the case with one rater (TE06) and one script (S07), in PT3 two raters (TE02, TE06) and one script (again S07), and in PT4 the same two raters (TE02, TE06) and the same script (S07). For example, TE06's notes on S07 include the following comment: 'I continue to have difficulty with this script (Is this the third time it has appeared?)' (PT3). As the raters did not at any time receive an indication of the standard ratings, nor any feedback on their own ratings, the researchers did not regard this recognition of a repeated script as being of particular significance for the present project.

4 Results

4.1 Scores

The results presented in this section are based on the scores given for the 'repeated' scripts (S03, S04, S06, S07), i.e. the four scripts which were used on all four occasions. The results of a similar analysis of the scores given for all eight scripts on each occasion are presented in Appendix 10.2 at the end of this report. The main trends are broadly similar in the two cases.

Table 10.1 shows the difference between the standard ratings and the scores given by raters in PT1, for the four repeated scripts. None of the scores is more than two bands from the standard rating. As a group raters tend to be rather more severe than the standard: 50% of their ratings are below the standard (either –1 or –2), while only 19% are above (+1 only). Individual raters differ in this respect: thus, the scores from rater TE01 are either on or above standard, while those from raters TE02, TE03, TE07, TE09 and TE10 are either on or below the standard rating.

Table 10.1 Project Task 1: Difference from standard rating (4 scripts)

Rater	Difference from standard rating							
	-3	-2	-1	0	$+1$	$+2$	$+3$	
TE01				3	1			4
TE02		2	1	1				4
TE03			3	1				4
TE04		1		1	2			4
TE05		1	1	1	1			4
TE06		1	1	1	1			4
TE07			3	1				4
TE08		2	1		1			4
TE09			1	3				4
TE10		1	3					4
TE12			1	2	1			4
TE13			1	1	2			4
Total	0	8	16	15	9	0	0	48
%	0	16.66	33.33	31.25	18.75	0	0	99.99

Table 10.2 shows the corresponding figures for PT2, which took place after raters had attended the two days of initial training. Again none of the scores is more than two bands from the standard rating. The group tends to be more lenient than in PT1: the percentage of ratings below the standard rating has gone down from 50% to 27%; the percentage above the standard rating has risen from 19% to 33% and this latter percentage now includes differences of +2 as well as +1. The percentage of ratings on standard has risen from 31% to 40%.

The figures for PT3 (Table 10.3) present a mixed picture. The percentage of ratings on standard has risen to 48%. For the first time, however, there are some differences of three bands between the scores given by raters and the standard rating. The percentage is relatively small (6%) but it involves three different raters and two different scripts (S04 and S07); it is not the result of one rogue script, nor of one rater having an off day.

Table 10.4 presents the figures for the final occasion (PT4), by which time eight of the TEs had applied to take the certification task (TE05, TE08, TE09 and TE12 had not yet applied). Ninety-two per cent of scores are now on or

Table 10.2 Project Task 2: Difference from standard rating (4 scripts)

	Difference from standard rating							
Rater	−3	−2	−1	0	+1	+2	+3	
TE01					3	1		4
TE02		1	1	1	1			4
TE03			3		1			4
TE04		1	1	1		1		4
TE05		1	1	2				4
TE06				2	2			4
TE07				3	1			4
TE08			1	3				4
TE09				2	1	1		4
TE10			1	3				4
TE12			1	1	1	1		4
TE13			1	1	1	1		4
Total	0	3	10	19	11	5	0	48
%	0	6.25	20.83	39.58	22.92	10.42	0	100

Table 10.3 Project Task 3: Difference from standard rating (4 scripts)

	Difference from standard rating							
Rater	−3	−2	−1	0	+1	+2	+3	
TE01				2	2			4
TE02			2	1	1			4
TE03	1	2			1			4
TE04			2	2				4
TE05		1		2	1			4
TE06			1	2	1			4
TE07				3	1			4
TE08	1			2	1			4
TE09				3	1			4
TE10				3	1			4
TE12	1	1	1	1				4
TE13			1	2	1			4
Total	3	4	7	23	11	0	0	48
%	6.25	8.33	14.58	47.92	22.92	0	0	100

within one band of the standard rating. None of the scores is more than two bands off the standard. Of the four instances (8%) that are two bands off the standard, three came from raters who had not yet applied for certification. Table 10.5 summarises the differences from standard in all four project tasks. It also shows how the overall severity/leniency of the ratings has evened out: in PT1 50 % were below the standard and 19% above it, whereas in PT4 33% were below and 31% above.

Table 10.4 Project Task 4: Difference from standard rating (4 scripts)

Rater			Difference from standard rating					
	-3	-2	-1	0	$+1$	$+2$	$+3$	
TE01				2	2			4
TE02			3		1			4
TE03		1		1	2			4
TE04			3		1			4
TE05			3	1				4
TE06			2		2			4
TE07				3	1			4
TE08		1		2		1		4
TE09			1	2	1			4
TE10				1	3			4
TE12		1		3				4
TE13			1	2	1			4
Total	0	3	13	17	14	1	0	48
%	0	6.25	27.08	35.42	29.17	2.08	0	100

Table 10.5 Summary of four occasions: scores in relation to standard (4 scripts)

	On standard	One band from standard	> one band from standard	Below standard	Above standard
PT1	15 (31%)	25 (52%)	8 (17%)	24 (50%)	9 (19%)
PT2	19 (40%)	21 (44%)	8 (17%)	13 (27%)	16 (33%)
PT3	23 (48%)	18 (38%)	7 (14%)	14 (29%)	11 (23%)
PT4	17 (35%)	27 (56%)	4 (8%)	16 (33%)	15 (31%)

4.2 Notes

In all four project tasks raters were instructed to rate the scripts using the IELTS band descriptors enclosed in the pack. It was not until after the first project task, however, at initial training, that raters were formally trained in the use of the IELTS descriptors and scoring method, which requires the rater to read the script a certain number of times taking the three criteria into account in a certain order. A change one might therefore expect to see over the four occasions is an increase in the number of sets of notes that contain references to all three prescribed criteria. Table 10.6 shows that this was in fact the case. On the first occasion, only six of the 24 sets (25%) of Task 1 notes referred to all three criteria. This increased after initial training to 37%, and again after the further self-access training period to 54%. There is a similar pattern with Task 2 scripts, where the figure doubled between PT1 and PT3 and then tailed off slightly in PT4.

Table 10.6 Reference to all three criteria

	T1 scripts	T2 scripts
PT1	6 (25%)	7 (29%)
PT2	9 (37%)	12 (50%)
PT3	13 (54%)	14 (58%)
PT4	12 (50%)	12 (50%)

The different criteria are not referred to equally frequently in the notes. As Table 10.7 shows, on the first occasion Vocabulary and Sentence Structure was the criterion most referred to in relation to Task 1 scripts, featuring in 21 of the 24 sets of notes; Task Fulfilment was referred to in 17 of the 24, and Coherence and Cohesion in only 11. References to TF increased fairly steadily over the four occasions, so that by the fourth occasion they feature in all but one of the 24 sets of notes. References to Coherence and Cohesion increased, but still feature in only 58% of the notes by the end.

Table 10.7 Reference to marking criteria (Task 1 scripts)

	TF	CC	VSS
PT1	17 (71%)	11 (46%)	21 (87%)
PT2	20 (83%)	15 (62%)	21 (87%)
PT3	21 (87%)	16 (67%)	24 (100%)
PT4	23 (96%)	14 (58%)	22 (92%)

Table 10.8 shows that, in the notes relating to Task 2 scripts, two criteria (AIE and VSS) featured prominently throughout. References to the third criterion (CQ) were relatively infrequent in PT1, and remained somewhat less frequent than the other two on the fourth occasion.

Table 10.8 Reference to marking criteria (Task 2 scripts)

	AIE	CQ	VSS
PT1	23 (96%)	10 (42%)	20 (83%)
PT2	20 (83%)	14 (58%)	24 (100%)
PT3	22 (92%)	18 (75%)	20 (83%)
PT4	20 (83%)	18 (75%)	20 (83%)

Examples of the notes have been appended to this article to indicate the variety of style and content which is not captured in the above analysis (Appendix 10.3). The idiosyncratic style of the notes was most marked before training: thus, on the first occasion, the only criterion referred to in TE01's very brief notes is 'succinctness', while TE08, in contrast, painstakingly lists the script's good and bad points as if preparing feedback for the writer and in the process refers to a range of criteria including coherence, communicative effectiveness and language accuracy. By the time of PT4, the notes from these two raters are closer to each other in style and content: they refer to similar criteria and appear to be following a similar scoring method. The notes from TE13 also seem to indicate a change of focus over the period of training: in PT1 his notes consisted almost exclusively of a list of language errors; in PT2 there is slightly more reference to the terms of the band descriptors; his PT3 notes suggest for the first time that he started by considering Task Fulfilment, as the scoring method requires; finally, in PT4, his notes refer to the three criteria in the prescribed order.

5 Discussion

The scores given by raters in PT1, i.e. before training, do not differ as grossly from the standard as might have been expected. The professional training and experience which IELTS examiners have more or less in common is no doubt a factor here. It may also be the case that the use of the rating scale, with its detailed band descriptors, can have a standardising effect whether or not raters have received formal training in its use. Certainly some raters in PT1, such as TE03 (see example of notes on p.430), appear to have studied the descriptors carefully, clarified for themselves what the marking criteria are, and proceeded systematically to base their rating on the detailed content of the descriptors.

The evidence from the scores and notes for PT2 suggests that initial training prompted some adjustment both in the criteria on which raters based their scores and also in the severity of their rating. As a group they rated significantly less severely in PT2, and this may be linked to the greater attention they appear to have given in PT2 to criteria such as CC and CQ, which had been relatively neglected in PT1. As far as standardisation of rating is concerned, the percentage of ratings on standard rose from 31% in PT1 to 40% in PT2; the percentage either on or within one band of standard is virtually unaltered in PT2 (83% in PT1, 84% in PT2).

There is a further small gain in standardisation of rating after PT2. Interpretation of the results from the last two project tasks, however, is complicated by the fact that raters varied in the amount of self-access training they did after PT2 and in their motivation to achieve certification. At the time of PT4 the majority of raters reported that they had completed their self-access training and applied for certification, but three raters (TE05, TE08 and TE12) reported that they still needed more time for the self-access training, and one rater (TE09) reported that she no longer intended to proceed with certification. There are also signs in the briefer, apparently more hurried notes from some raters in PT4 that they were by this time affected by 'participation fatigue'; the fact that the four successive project tasks were very similar, and that raters received no feedback on their scores or notes, is likely to have contributed to this. Certainly for a rater who was no longer motivated to standardise and certificate, the intervening period of six months would be long enough for the standardising effect of initial training to wane.

The gain in standardisation of rating over the period of training as a whole is not dramatic: the percentage of ratings on standard rose between PT1 and PT4 by just 4% to 35%; the percentage on or within one band of standard rose from 83% to 92%. There were only four instances (8%) in PT4 of a score more than one band off standard, and three of the four were given by raters who judged that they needed to do more training before attempting certification. As far as changes in relative severity/leniency are concerned, the results of this study are broadly in line with Weigle's finding that 'inexperienced raters tended to be . . . more severe in their ratings than the experienced ones' (1998:263). Evidence from the notes suggests that the relative severity of raters before training may have been associated with a predominant focus on language accuracy.

The limitations of retrospective written report data have been acknowledged in Section 3.3 and the small number of observations means that any conclusions must be tentative. Analysis of the notes suggests that raters paid more attention to some criteria than others. The criteria CC and CQ were referred to much less than the other criteria in PT1, and even in PT4 CC was referred to in only 58% of notes, in contrast to TF (96%) and VSS (92%). The reason for this is not clear – is it because CC is a more difficult concept to grasp and apply, or simply a more difficult criterion to make notes on?

The percentage of reports referring to all three relevant criteria doubled over the training period (see Table 10.6). This suggests that some raters at least adjusted their rating-procedure so as to conform to the prescribed scoring method. There is some evidence in the notes that the duration of the training programme (consisting of initial group sessions with a trainer, followed by a stage of self-access training which continues until the TE judges that he is ready to attempt the certification task) offers some TEs the opportunity they need to bring their rating procedure gradually into line with the prescribed method. The notes from TE13 (see Appendix 10.3) illustrate such a gradual evolution. It is worth noting, however, that despite these apparent changes in his rating procedure, TE13 gave the same score (one band below standard) on all four occasions. Indeed at the level of the individual rater no clear pattern emerged from the data to establish a link between changes in scoring procedure and standardised scoring.

Although the percentage of reports referring to all three relevant criteria doubled, it stood at only 50% at the end of the training period. This low figure may result in part from the method of data collection – the reports do not necessarily capture all the criteria that actually influenced the rating. However, it may also be a sign that, in spite of training, some raters have not adjusted their rating procedure to conform to the prescribed method. If further research confirms that some trained raters tend to neglect certain criteria, the following measures could be considered:

1. Additional feedback on their rating could be provided for trainee raters as part of the training programme. After initial training, TEs could be asked to complete a rating task, on which they would then receive feedback. The feedback could be based on a statistical analysis of their scores, of the kind investigated by Wigglesworth (1993). Alternatively, if TEs were asked to include a brief note explaining how they arrived at their scores, the feedback could be based more simply on those notes and whether the TE appeared to have given due attention to all three criteria.

2. The prescribed scoring method could be altered so as to require profile scoring of all scripts. At present the scoring method requires examiners to award a global band score or, if they find the script has a 'marked profile', a profile band score (i.e. a separate score for each of the three criteria). Profile scoring of all scripts would go some way to ensuring that raters pay due attention to the prescribed criteria.

6 Conclusions

The purpose of this study was to investigate the judgements made on successive occasions before and after training by trainee examiners for the IELTS Writing Module. It examined two kinds of data: the scores given by TEs, and their retrospective reports about how they arrived at a particular score for a script.

Analysis of the scores revealed that, in line with previous research, the examiners as a group became less severe in their rating after initial training. It also showed that for the group as a whole there was a modest gain in standardisation over the period, in that the percentage of ratings on standard rose from 31% to 35% and the percentage of aberrant ratings (more than one band from standard) fell from 17% to 8%.

The limitations of retrospective report data in general, and the small number of observations in this case, mean that conclusions based on this data must be tentative. Analysis of the reports suggested that raters' judgements on the whole tend to be influenced more by some of the prescribed criteria than others: the criterion of Coherence and Cohesion seems to be taken into account relatively little, even at the end of the training period. This is a matter for concern although it is not surprising given that the notion of coherence, in particular, has not received the attention it deserves until relatively recently. The fact that coherence is a semantic notion and not readily quantifiable makes it difficult for teachers and examiners to understand.

Coherence has not received attention until the relatively recent work of discourse scholars and the work of Halliday (and his Systemic Functional grammar). As a result, teachers preparing students for IELTS and IELTS examiners are unlikely to have had their consciousness raised about this notion. This may account for the lack of attention given to the criterion.

The percentage of reports referring to all three relevant criteria doubled over the training period; the fact that it stood at only 50% even at the end of training may arise in part from the method of data collection but may also point to a failure by some raters to follow the prescribed scoring method.

Further research is necessary to establish whether examiners consistently pay attention to the relevant criteria after training. Analysis of concurrent verbal protocols is likely to be more revealing for this purpose than retrospective written reports. If it is confirmed that some of the prescribed criteria are sometimes neglected by trained examiners, the exam board could consider either strengthening the training programme by providing additional feedback to trainee examiners on their rating, or altering the prescribed scoring method to require profile scoring of all IELTS scripts.

Notes

1   This section is based on information in the IELTS Handbook 2000, the IELTS Annual Review 1998/9 and the IELTS Guidelines for Examiner Trainers 1997.
2   Candidates opt to take either the Academic or the General Training version of the Writing Module. All materials used in this study were from the Academic version.
3   British Council/International Development Programme Australia.

APPENDIX 10.1
Instructions for Project Task 1

There are two parts to this task. Please set aside an hour to concentrate on the task and try to complete it in one sitting.

Part 1: Rating the scripts

1. Look at writing task A1. Read Script 1 and decide which band score (from 0 to 9) on rating-scale A is appropriate for this script. Write the score on the record sheet at the back of this booklet.
NB The score must be a single, whole number from 0 to 9. Do *not* award half marks or use other symbols.

2. Repeat the process for Scripts 2 to 4 (writing tasks A2 to A4).
Each script should take about 5 minutes to read and rate.

3. Repeat the process for Scripts 5 to 8 (writing tasks B5 and B6), but for these scripts use rating scale B.
Each of these scripts should take about 6 minutes to read and rate.

Part 2: Noting down how you arrived at a particular score

4. Look back at Script 1 and the score you awarded it. Think back to how you arrived at that score. In the appropriate box on the record sheet, write down any information that will help us understand the process by which you arrived at that score, and why you decided on that score rather than the one above or below. You may write in note-form. We are interested in any factors that were significant in your decision.
Line numbers have been added to the script to enable you to refer clearly to specific parts of the script as necessary.

5. Look back in the same way at the scores you awarded for Scripts 3, 5 and 7, and in each case note down how you arrived at the score. We realise that you may be able to write a fuller explanation in the case of some scripts than others.

6. Check that your record sheet is complete. Return it in the SAE, with the signed declaration, to Clare Furneaux by 19 November 1999.

Thank you.

APPENDIX 10.2
Tables 10.9–10.13

Table 10.9 PT1 Difference from standard rating (all eight scripts)

Rater			Difference from standard rating					
	−3	−2	−1	0	+1	+2	+3	
TE01				5	3			8
TE02		3	2	3				8
TE03			5	3				8
TE04		1		3	4			8
TE05		1	2	3	1	1		8
TE06		1	1	4	2			8
TE07			4	2	2			8
TE08		2	3	2	1			8
TE09			3	3	2			8
TE10	1	1	4	2				8
TE12			2	4	2			8
TE13			1	2	4	1		8
Total	1	9	27	36	21	2	0	96
%	1.04	9.37	28.12	37.50	21.87	2.08	0	99.98

Table 10.10 PT2 Difference from standard rating (all eight scripts)

Rater			Difference from standard rating					
	−3	−2	−1	0	+1	+2	+3	
TE01				1	5	2		8
TE02		1	1	5	1			8
TE03			3	2	3			8
TE04		1	1	3	2	1		8
TE05		1	1	4	2			8
TE06				5	3			8
TE07				6	2			8
TE08			1	6	1			8
TE09		1		3	2	2		8
TE10			1	5	2			8
TE12			1	4	2	1		8
TE13			1	4	2	1		8
Total	0	4	10	48	27	7	0	96
%	0	4.17	10.42	50	28.12	7.29	0	100

Table 10.11 PT3 Difference from standard rating (all eight scripts)

Rater	Difference from standard rating							
	−3	−2	−1	0	+1	+2	+3	
TE01		1		4	3			8
TE02		1	2	3	2			8
TE03	2	2	1	1	2			8
TE04	1		2	4		1		8
TE05	1	1		3	3			8
TE06		1	1	4	1	1		8
TE07			1	5	2			8
TE08	1		2	3	1	1		8
TE09			1	4	2	1		8
TE10		1		4	2	1		8
TE12	1	1	2	3		1		8
TE13		1	1	3	2		1	8
Total	6	9	13	41	20	6	1	96
%	6.25	9.37	13.54	42.71	20.83	6.25	1.04	99.99

Table 10.12 PT4 Difference from standard rating (all eight scripts)

Rater	Difference from standard rating							
	−3	−2	−1	0	+1	+2	+3	
TE01				3	5			8
TE02			4	1	3			8
TE03	1	1		3	3			8
TE04			3	3	2			8
TE05			4	3	1			8
TE06			3	3	2			8
TE07				4	2	2		8
TE08		1		4	2	1		8
TE09			2	3	3			8
TE10				3	5			8
TE12		1	1	4	1	1		8
TE13			1	4	3			8
Total	1	3	18	38	32	4	0	96
%	1.04	3.12	18.75	39.58	33.33	4.16	0	99.98

Table 10.13 Summary of four occasions: Scores in relation to standard (all 8 scripts)

	On standard	One band from standard	> one band from standard	Below standard	Above standard
PT1	36 (37.5%)	48 (50%)	12 (12.5%)	37 (38.5%)	23 (24%)
PT2	48 (50%)	37 (38.5%)	11 (11.5%)	14 (14.6%)	34 (35.4%)
PT3	41 (42.7%)	33 (34.4%)	22 (22.9%)	28 (29.2%)	27 (28.1%)
PT4	38 (39.6%)	50 (52.1%)	8 (8.3%)	22 (22.9%)	36 (37.5%)

APPENDIX 10.3
Examples of raters' notes explaining rationale for score awarded

---

PT1 TE01 Script 3 Score *6*
How did you arrive at this score for this script?
I felt it could have been more succinct.

PT2 TE01 Script 3 Score *8*
How did you arrive at this score for this script?
It was well organised and very clearly described the information in the table. I awarded the high mark despite the minor errors because it was easy to follow and didn't need a second read. I interpreted 'no significant errors' in the rating scale as allowing for one or two errors: Is that correct?

PT3 TE01 Script 3 Score *6*
How did you arrive at this score for this script?
Number of grammatical errors, even though it was easy to follow with a simple structure.

PT4 TE01 Script 3 Score *6*
How did you arrive at this score for this script?
Although there were grammatical errors, it included all relevant details but wasn't a Band 7 nor a Band 5. It was a case of deciding what it wasn't rather than what it was.

PT1 TE08 Script 3 Score *4*
How did you arrive at this score for this script?

Good points
- *legible*
- *attempts to organise work into some sort of coherent structure*
- *there is a message, albeit a rather limited one*
- *errors do not predominate (therefore not band 3)*

Bad points
- *Lines 11–13: Difficult to read/understand figures that are grouped together badly*
- *Lines 15–16: Not coherent: incomplete sentence*
- *Lines 18 and 22: Grammar incorrect – use and formation of tenses*

Attempt at conclusion is poor.
Difficult to follow the message.
Basic mistakes not expected at this level e.g. 'At 1983'

PT2 TE08 Script 3 Score 6
How did you arrive at this score for this script?
Message can be followed without difficulty, so not Band 5.
Range of vocabulary not satisfactory, so not Band 7.
Generally coherent and errors are not too intrusive, so Band 6.

PT3 TE08 Script 3 Score 6
How did you arrive at this score for this script?
Band 6 because writing mostly addresses the task.
Again, range of vocabulary is adequate but not really satisfactory, so not Band 7.
Very restricted range of expression and basic errors in word formation.

PT4 TE08 Script 3 Score 6
How did you arrive at this score for this script?
No irrelevant material, so therefore not Band 5.
More flaws than just 'minor', so not band 7.
Incorrect use of present perfect instead of past simple.
Inadequate conclusion.
Repetition of the word 'increase', so as in Band 6 'restricted range of vocabulary'.

PT1 TE13 Script 3   Score *5*
How did you arrive at this score for this script?
has given examples that x
and compare x
statistic show x
At 1983 x
which works x
statistics may be increasing x

Message clear, but language inaccuracies intrude and confuse.

PT2 TE13 Script 3   Score *5*
How did you arrive at this score for this script?
Line 4   'has given example that'
*   'compare'*
*   'change has increased'*
*   'whom went on the'*
*   'which has increased'*

Message can be followed, but constructions like above hinder the message.
Some irrelevant material.

PT3 TE13 Script 3   Score *5*
How did you arrive at this score for this script?
Relevant information is all present, but presentation is confused and confus-
ing, and the errors of vocabulary ('given examples that', 'the change has
increased', 'as a result') and grammar ('which work out', 'whom went')
make it difficult to follow. Last sentence is irrelevant.

PT4 TE13 Script 3   Score *5*
How did you arrive at this score for this script?
TF Band 6 : information quite well presented
CC and VSS Band 5 : too many errors of vocab and syntax ('given exam-
ples', 'the change has increased', 'combining the institutions which' , 'From
the info it proves').

Methodology evaluation of Chapter 10

This is a sound piece of work with interesting findings. However, nowadays, the analytical tools used in the chapter can be considered rather limited or low tech, especially in view of new analytical instruments such as multifaceted Rasch analysis (MFR), which are now available to researchers. The use of MFR enables researchers to use probabilistic methods to encompass a number of different variables. The reader can find a description of MFR in Chapter 1 (see page 61).

However, in spite of the availability of MFR, this does not mean that the analysis used in this chapter is without merit. The analysis is done painstakingly and thoroughly. Indeed, in many situations, such as an action research study in a school or institution, such methods of analysis would be relatively easy to replicate and could provide useful insights into the situation or problems being investigated. This study investigates an important topic – how raters develop their assessments during a training process.

A further point that researchers in language testing may wish to note concerns the issue of studies of inter-rating and intra-rating. This study focuses on the interesting topic of inter-rating: how raters change in their assessments of the Writing Module. It also allows for insights into the processes that raters use while assessing by the use of retrospective written reports. However, intra-rating studies have assumed importance too and it might have been interesting to consider changes in intra-rating reliability while the raters moved through the process of training.

11 Assessing the value of bias analysis feedback to raters for the IELTS Writing Module

Barry O'Sullivan and Mark Rignall

Abstract

Rater variation is potentially a serious weakness in performance testing, as it represents a significant source of construct-irrelevant variance. Rater training is widely used as a means of keeping this variation within acceptable limits, but concern is expressed in the literature about an apparent mismatch between, on the one hand, the critically important role assigned to rater training, and, on the other, the current state of knowledge of rater-training processes and effects.

While there have been a relatively small number of studies which have explored the effects on performance of particular aspects of rater training, only Wigglesworth (1993) has made specific reference to the role of feedback in training procedures by hypothesising that a formal feedback report based on multifaceted Rasch (MFR) bias interaction analysis might contribute to rater consistency. This project attempts to explore this hypothesis through an empirical study involving 20 trained IELTS examiners and the General Training (GT) Writing scripts from over 80 test candidates. Graphic feedback, similar to that provided by Wigglesworth, but with the addition of a brief written description, was given to a group of 10 examiners, based on their rating of a set of scripts. A second group received no such feedback. Following a second rating occasion, the performances of both groups were analysed, again using MFR. Results indicate that the feedback appears to have had only a very limited effect on the rating performance of the examiners. A questionnaire, completed by the examiners from the feedback group, yielded results which suggest that the feedback was seen by them as a very positive and beneficial addition to the marking of the examination.

It is concluded that a single 'one-shot' feedback will be of limited value, though its positive motivational effect suggests that feedback delivered systematically over a period of time may result in more consistent and reliable examiner performance.

1 Introduction

Rater variation is potentially the Achilles heel of performance testing, as it represents a significant source of construct-irrelevant variance. Rater training is widely used as a means of keeping this variation within acceptable limits, but concern is expressed in the literature about an apparent mismatch between, on the one hand, the critically important role assigned to rater training, and, on the other, the current state of knowledge of rater-training processes and effects:

> An understanding of the values, decision-making behaviour and even the idiosyncratic nature of the judgements markers make is of primary importance for both reliability and construct validity. Yet very little is known about the decision-making processes which are employed by the markers in making an assessment. Lack of knowledge in this area makes it more difficult to train markers to make valid and reliable assessments.
> (Milanovic, Saville and Shuhong 1996:93–4)

A number of studies in recent years have investigated the effect of training on rater behaviour. Although the datasets are mostly small, these studies give some indication as to which kinds of change can and cannot be brought about in rater behaviour by existing forms of training. Weigle (1994) examined verbal protocols from four inexperienced raters before and after training. She found that the post-training protocols of all the raters 'showed evidence, to a lesser or greater degree', of the three hypothesised effects of training (i.e. clarification of rating criteria, modification of the rater's expectations about candidates and task, and increased concern for inter-rater agreement). However, subsequent many-facet Rasch (MFR) analysis of the score data from eight experienced and eight inexperienced raters before and after training revealed that, while consistency had improved for most raters, 'significant differences in severity' remained between them (1998:263). George Rasch (1980) first proposed using probability theory as a basis for evaluating judgement-based tests, though it was not until the early 1990s, when the FACETS computer program was introduced, that the methodology came to be more widely recognised (see for example Bachman et al (1995) on validation of MFR and generalisability theory in a performance test context).

Other studies to investigate the area of rater variability include Lumley and McNamara (1995) and Tyndall and Kenyon (1995) who explored the ability of rater training to lead to convergence in terms of rater severity. Lumley and McNamara (1995) used MFR analysis to compare ratings given on three occasions, before and after training, by 13 experienced raters for the speaking subtest of the Occupational English Test (the data on the third occasion came from just four of the 13 raters). They found 'a substantial variation in rater harshness, which training has by no means eliminated, nor even reduced to a level which should permit reporting of raw scores for candidate performance' (p. 69). They also raise the question of the stability of rater characteristics over time, and conclude that the effects of training 'may not endure long after training'.

Tyndall and Kenyon (1995), when conducting a validation exercise on a newly devised holistic rating scale, observed that there were significant differences in the harshness of their ten raters – they also found that their raters were more inclined to work towards a more internalised scale than to use the scale provided, a finding supported by Brown (1995).

Furneaux and Rignall (2002; also earlier chapter) examined the scores and retrospective written reports given by 12 trainee examiners on four successive occasions before and during training. There was 'a modest gain in standardisation over the period: the number of ratings on standard rose by just 4% to 35%; the percentage on or within one band of the standard rating rose from 83% to 92%'. Analysis of the retrospective reports suggested that some individuals' rating procedures had evolved gradually over the training period to conform to the prescribed scoring method. There was also evidence that as a group raters continued to pay more attention to certain of the prescribed marking criteria than to others.

Reviewing the research evidence of differences in severity between raters after training, McNamara concludes that 'assessment procedures which rely on single ratings by trained and qualified raters are hard to defend' (1996:235). He argues that the traditional aim of rater training – 'to eliminate as far as possible differences between raters – is unachievable and possibly undesirable' (op cit: 232). The proper aim of training, he believes, is to get new raters to concentrate and to become self-consistent.

As far as content and methodology are concerned, much of the training referred to in the literature seems to follow the six steps which Bachman and Palmer outlined as 'a general procedure for training raters' (1996:222). This appears to be the case, for example, in the studies by Weigle (1994, 1998) of the UCLA placement test of writing, by Halleck (1996) of the American Council on the Teaching of Foreign Languages (ACTFL) oral proficiency interview and by Kenyon (1997). The literature contains very little critical discussion of the content and methods of rater training. It would be interesting to know, for example, whether rater training has evolved in recent years in keeping with the learner-centred approach adopted by many other instructional programmes. Nor is it clear how training procedures, which may have been devised originally for use among colleagues within one university/institution, have had to be adapted for large-scale, international testing. Of central focus in this study is one aspect of rater training that has received little attention in the literature, that is the effect of the provision of formal feedback to raters based on their rating, on the reasonable assumption that the quality of feedback to the trainee rater is likely to be an important factor in the success or failure of training.

In the one study that has addressed the matter, Wigglesworth (1993) experimented with a form of individualised feedback, based on MFR bias analysis, to 13 raters of an oral interaction test. She found some evidence of an improvement in rater consistency following the feedback, but points out that it might not be long-lasting. She does not discuss whether this feedback technique might be made more effective by adjusting its format or delivery.

Raters' own views about the rater training they received do not figure prominently in the literature. McDowell's study (2000) of the effectiveness of IELTS examiner training is an exception to this, as she surveyed both trainers and trainees, but it is a preliminary study only and its questionnaire mainly elicits scaled responses evaluating specific items of training material. Further investigation of the trainee's experience of rater training, i.e. from the trainee's point of view, might contribute to the continuing development of an effective training programme. It would also be in keeping with the call by Bachman (2000:19) for greater attention to be paid to the training of language testing professionals.

This study, however, will take as its focus, the post-training 'rater in action'. It aims to explore Wigglesworth's (1993) suggested use of bias analysis feedback to raters within the context of the IELTS Writing Module.

1.1 Research questions

The purpose of the present study is to assess the value of MFR-based feedback to raters of IELTS GT Writing. In particular it investigates the following questions:

1. What effect does MFR-based feedback have on rating performance in terms of internal consistency?
2a. How useful do raters find MFR-based feedback on their rating?
2b. What effect does this feedback have on their approach to rating?

2 Methodology

2.1 Raters

Twenty raters (fifteen women and five men) participated in the present study. They were recruited by means of a letter sent to all IELTS test centres in the UK and Ireland: it invited examiners to take part in the project as raters, indicating the work they would carry out and the fee they would receive on completion. Of the 35 examiners who replied positively, 20 were randomly selected to participate: all had been certificated IELTS examiners for at least one year and were currently active.

A short questionnaire was circulated to the raters early on in the project to obtain basic personal information, including their age and the extent of their examining experience. After the first round of rating this information was used in a random stratification procedure to divide raters into two groups of 10.

2.2 Scripts

UCLES provided 113 IELTS General Training Writing scripts for possible use in this project. They had been written by candidates at an IELTS centre in India in December 2000 and had already been through the usual marking procedure. The researchers selected 81 of these scripts for use in the present project. All were responses to the same version of the test (version number 42). Their official or standard scores ranged from Band 2 to Band 8 and were normally distributed across the 9-band scale. Care was also taken in selecting scripts to exclude those which were unlikely to photocopy clearly. The candidate details and examiner marks on each script were masked before multiple photocopies were made for distribution to raters.

To protect the security of the test materials used in the project, all raters were asked to sign a confidentiality declaration before Rating Occasion 1, and again before Rating Occasion 2.

2.3 Organisation of the batches

For purposes of MFR analysis, it is necessary to have a certain amount of overlap in the scripts marked by different raters, and in the scripts marked on different occasions. For this reason the scripts used in this project were organised into two cores of 15 scripts each (C1, C2) and five batches of 10 scripts each (B1, B2, B3, B4, B5), which were then assigned to individual raters as indicated in Figure 11.1. On each occasion each rater received a set of 25 scripts, which was made up of one core and one batch. Thus, for example, the set of 25 scripts received by Rater 1 on Rating Occasion 1 consisted of Core 1 and Batch 1, while Rater 2 on the same occasion received Core 1 and Batch 2.

This design ensured a high degree of overlap between the raters – all rated two core sets, a total of 30 scripts, while each rater was also connected to three other raters through their ratings of an additional batch. The scripts had also been selected and organised in such a way as to ensure that each core and each batch was representative of the range of performance of the entire group of candidates, thus exposing each rater to performance across the range.

Figure 11.1 Organisation of batches for Rating Occasions 1 and 2

	Rating Occasion 1			Rating Occasion 2		
Raters	Batches	Core	Batches	Batches	Core	Batches
1, 6, 11, 16	B1			B5		
2, 7, 12, 17			B2			B1
3, 8, 13, 18	B3	C1		B2	C2	
4, 9, 14, 19			B4			B3
5, 10, 15, 20	B5			B4		

2.4 Data collection

Two kinds of data were required in order to address the research questions for this project: the scores awarded by raters on successive rating occasions before and after feedback, and the views of raters on the feedback they received after the first rating occasion. The procedure for data collection therefore involved four main steps (Rating Occasion 1, feedback to raters, Rating Occasion 2, questionnaire completion by raters), which are described in turn below. See Appendix 11.1 for an outline of the project planning schedule.

2.4.1 Rating Occasion 1

Each rater received a set of 25 scripts (Core 1 and one of the five batches) and a copy of the relevant question paper. The rater was instructed to read and rate the scripts following all the usual IELTS procedures, to record global and profile marks for each script, and then to return the completed record sheet and all other materials within two weeks.

A database was devised using Microsoft Excel (2000), into which all data was entered and validated (through double entry and random spot checking). Specification files for use with FACETS (version 3.2) were then prepared from this dataset.

A random stratification procedure was used to create two groups of 10 raters (the 'Feedback' and 'Non-feedback' groups), which were equivalent in terms of the age of the raters, the extent of their examining experience and their performance in the first round of rating.

2.4.2 Feedback to raters

Two weeks after completion of the first round of rating, feedback was sent out to each member of the feedback group in the form of an individualised rating report. Members of the control group received no feedback.

The content of the rating report was based on what the analysis had revealed about the rater's performance in the first round of rating, in particular the degree of consistency in their rating (as indicated by the Infit and Outfit Mean Square figures) and any patterns of bias towards severity or leniency in their rating on the two tasks and on the different criteria (as indicated by the Z-scores generated through a multifaceted Rasch bias/interaction analysis). The purpose was to let raters know how they had performed, and to help them maintain or improve their performance in the second round.

The rating report was designed to be easily intelligible to all raters – no knowledge of MFR analysis was assumed, and statistical terms such as 'Z-score' were not used. Unlike Wigglesworth's 'assessment maps' (1993:309), the reports were designed to be self-explanatory as there would be no opportunity for further explanation or discussion of them with raters.

The reports followed a standard format, consisting of three sections:

1. A graph plotting the rater's Z-scores for each of the six marking criteria. Task 1: CC (Coherence and Cohesion), TF (Task Fulfilment), VSS (Vocabulary and Sentence Structure). Task 2: AIE (Arguments, Ideas and Evidence), CQ (Communicative Quality), VSS (Vocabulary and Sentence Structure). Task 1 is abbreviated to T1 and Task 2 to T2. Figure 11.2 shows an example of this kind of graph.

2. A section headed *Interpreting the Graph*, which explains the scale used in the graph, points out the criteria on which the rater tended to be severe or lenient, and whether the rater had used the breadth of the scale.

Figure 11.2 Graphical representation of rater bias indices used in feedback (based on Wigglesworth 1993)

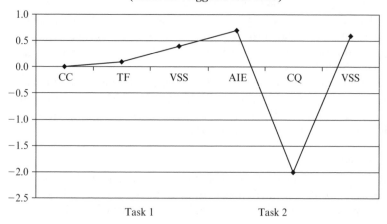

3. A section headed *Overall Comment*, which indicates the degree of consistency achieved by the rater and, if appropriate, suggests what the rater should focus on in the second round of rating.

Two examples of rating reports are included in Appendix 11.3. They illustrate the standard format and the way in which the content was tailored to individual raters. In the first example the Z-scores are low and as a result the scale on the graph only ranges from −1.5 to +2.0. The rater's slight tendencies to leniency (T1 VSS) and harshness (T2 CQ) are pointed out, as is a tendency not to use the entire scale. However, the gist of this report is that the rater should carry on broadly as before. In contrast, the second example is based on high Z-scores, ranging from −5.0 to +3.0. The rater's attention is drawn to the harshness of her TF ratings and the leniency of her AIE ratings, and she is encouraged to focus on these in the second round.

2.4.3 Rating Occasion 2

Again, each rater received a set of 25 scripts (Core 2 and one batch – a different batch from on the previous occasion) and a copy of the relevant question paper. As before, the rater was instructed to read and rate the scripts following all the usual IELTS procedures, to record global and profile marks for each script, and then to return the completed record sheet and all other materials within two weeks. The data from this second occasion was added to the Excel database and specification files were then prepared for use with FACETS as before.

2.4.4 Questionnaire

One week after Rating Occasion 2, a short questionnaire, consisting of a combination of closed and more open questions, was sent out to the 10 raters in the feedback group to elicit their views of the rating report and its effect on the second round of rating. The raters were asked to spend around 15 minutes completing the questionnaire and to return it within two weeks.

The design of the questionnaire (see Appendix 11.4) took account of the fact that the rating report had been an unfamiliar form of feedback for the raters. Feedback to IELTS examiners is usually given orally in the course of a group training session, and is based on the standard scores laid down by a team of senior examiners. The rating report in contrast provided more formal, written feedback, and was based on 'fair average' scores generated by MFR analysis. The questionnaire therefore asked raters whether they had found the report clear (Question 1), which aspects they had found most and least useful (Questions 5 and 6), and what changes might have made it more useful (Question 7).

A second consideration in designing the questionnaire was that the detailed content of the rating reports had varied considerably from rater to rater, according to their performance on the first round of rating. Thus, in two cases (R05 and R06) the reports drew attention to 'a serious level' of leniency or harshness on specific criteria in both T1 and T2; four other reports (R09, R11, R14, R20) pointed out a 'significant tendency' to leniency or harshness in either T1 or T2; the other four reports (R02, R03, R07, R19) indicated only a 'slight but not significant tendency' to leniency or harshness in T1 and/or T2. In view of this variation, it was decided that the questionnaire should contain two questions about the effect of the rating report: the first of these (Question 2) asks broadly about the effect on the rater's approach to the second round, while the second (Question 3) is aimed particularly at raters whose reports had recommended specific adjustments.

Finally, Questions 8 and 9 seek to elicit raters' views on the potential usefulness of this kind of rating report to IELTS examiners beyond this project.

2.5 Data analysis

For the score data, MFR bias analysis was used to generate the rating reports. As mentioned above MFR analysis allows the researcher to report candidate performance in terms of the effect of a number of variables or facets. An additional feature of the procedure is that all facets are reported on a true interval 'logit' scale – meaning that real comparisons can be made across these different variables. Bias interaction (an option within MFR) is roughly equivalent to ANOVA, in that it is possible to study the interaction of as many of the original facets as the researcher wishes in a single analysis. This means, for example, that we can explore the test data for instances of significant bias between say each rater and the different tasks used (allowing us to see if some raters show a tendency towards leniency or harshness on a particular task). By adding a third variable, the rating criteria, we can discover occasions of unpredicted bias on the part of individual raters when using specific rating criteria on individual tasks.

For the questionnaire data, responses to the closed questions were counted by category and tabulated, while the responses to each open question in turn were collated and their content analysed to identify common phrases or ideas.

3 Results and discussion

3.1 Rating Occasion 1

There were no problems with the way in which the raters responded to the first rating task. When the data was being input, no obvious changes to the procedure were noticed, i.e. all raters had awarded both analytic and global scores to all scripts. The summary table from the analysis of the rating occasion is presented in Figure 11.3.

Figure 11.3 All facet vertical summary

```
|Measr|+Candida  |-Raters     |-Tasks       |-Criteria    |S.1 |
-----------------------------------------------------------------------
       High scores Harsh Raters          Difficult tasks   Harshly Rated
+   6 +           +                      +                +            +(9) +
  |   |           |                      |                |            | ---  |
  |   |           |                      |                |            |      |
  |   | *         |                      |                |            |      |
+   5 +           +                      +                +            +      +
  |   |           |                      |                |            |      |
  |   |           |                      |                |            | 8    |
  |   |           |                      |                |            |      |
  |   |           |                      |                |            |      |
+   4 +           +                      +                +            +      +
  |   |           |                      |                |            |      |
  |   | *         |                      |                |            | ---  |
  |   | ****      |                      |                |            |      |
  |   | ****      |                      |                |            |      |
+   3 +           +                      +                +            +      +
  |   | **        |                      |                |            |      |
  |   | *****     |                      |                |            | 7    |
  |   | **        |                      |                |            |      |
  |   |           |                      |                |            |      |
+   2 + *         +                      +                +            + ---  +
  |   | *         |                      |                |            |      |
  |   | ******    |                      |                |            |      |
  |   | ***       | 15                   |                |            |      |
  |   | ***       | 8                    |                |            |      |
+   1 + *         +                      +                +            + 6    +
  |   | *         | 6                    |                |            |      |
  |   | ****      | 11    12             |                |            |      |
  |   | **        | 1                    |                | VSS        |      |
  |   | ****      | 20    17             |                | AIE   CQ   | ---  |
*   0 * **        * 19    4              * Task A  Task B *            *      *
  |   | **        | 10    14             |                | CC         |      |
  |   | **        | 18    9              |                |            |      |
  |   | ***       | 16    13    3    2   |                |            |      |
  |   | **        | 5                    |                | TF         |      |
+  -1 + *         + 7                    +                +            + 5    +
  |   | *         |                      |                |            |      |
  |   |           |                      |                |            |      |
  |   |           |                      |                |            |      |
+  -2 + *         +                      +                +            + ---  +
  |   | *         |                      |                |            |      |
  |   |           |                      |                |            |      |
  |   | *         |                      |                |            | 4    |
+  -3 +           +                      +                +            +      +
  |   | *         |                      |                |            |      |
  |   | ****      |                      |                |            | ---  |
  |   |           |                      |                |            |      |
+  -4 +           +                      +                +            +(2) +
       Low scores  Lenient raters        Easy Tasks       Leniently scored
-----------------------------------------------------------------------
|Measr| * = 1     |-Raters     |-Tasks       |-Criteria    |S.1 |
-----------------------------------------------------------------------
Metric maintained by + or |
```

The figure can be read as follows:

Column 1:   The measure in logits – a true interval scale upon which all facets are measured.

Column 2:   This column shows the candidates (high positive scores in logits represented higher-achieving candidates). This summary indicates that there is a range of almost 9 logits observed in the data.

Column 3: Here we see the raters (the higher the logit score the harsher the rater). The summary suggests that there is a range of harshness of 2.43 logits – corresponding to over 1 band scale level.

Column 4: This column shows the tasks (both of which appear to be of the same level of difficulty).

Column 5: These represent the rating criteria (there is approximately a half of one band scale difference between the average scores awarded to the most harshly and most leniently rated criteria, not altogether surprisingly, the harshest is for the VSS criterion).

Column 6: The final column is the actual scale used (we can see that the range of scores awarded is from 2 to 8).

Table 11.1 shows the results of the Raters Measurement Report. Here we can see that of the 20 raters, just one, number 6, was problematic. The relatively high infit mean square of 1.7 suggests that this rater was somewhat inconsistent in the way they applied the scale. Lunz and Wright (1997)

Table 11.1 Raters Measurement Report (arranged by rater ID number)

Obsvd Score	Obsvd Count	Obsvd Average	Fair Avrge	Measure Logit	Model Error	Infit MnSq	Std	Outfit MnSq	Std	Nu
848	150	5.7	5.3	0.35	0.11	0.8	−2	0.7	−2	1
926	150	6.2	5.7	−0.59	0.11	0.8	−1	0.8	−1	2
932	150	6.2	5.8	−0.66	0.11	1.4	3	1.4	3	3
882	150	5.9	5.5	−0.06	0.11	0.9	−1	0.9	−1	4
947	150	6.3	5.8	−0.79	0.11	0.8	−2	0.8	−2	5
808	147	5.5	5.0	0.80	0.11	1.7	5	1.7	5	6
968	150	6.5	6.0	−1.05	0.11	1.1	1	1.1	1	7
784	150	5.2	4.9	1.21	0.11	1.0	0	1.0	0	8
946	156	6.1	5.6	−0.37	0.11	1.0	0	1.0	0	9
885	150	5.9	5.5	−0.17	0.11	0.9	−1	0.8	−1	10
863	156	5.5	5.2	0.59	0.11	1.1	0	1.1	0	11
859	156	5.5	5.1	0.64	0.11	1.2	1	1.2	1	12
896	150	6.0	5.7	−0.60	0.11	0.7	−2	0.7	−2	13
856	150	5.7	5.5	−0.12	0.11	1.0	0	1.0	0	14
737	150	4.9	4.8	1.38	0.11	0.7	−3	0.7	−3	15
888	150	5.9	5.7	−0.50	0.11	1.3	2	1.3	2	16
868	150	5.8	5.4	0.15	0.11	1.3	2	1.3	2	17
913	150	6.1	5.6	−0.39	0.11	0.7	−3	0.7	−3	18
887	150	5.9	5.5	−0.07	0.11	0.6	−4	0.6	−4	19
860	150	5.7	5.3	0.26	0.11	0.9	0	0.9	−1	20
Obsvd Score	Obsvd Count	Obsvd Average	Fair Avrge	Measure Logit	Model Error	Infit MnSq	Std	Outfit MnSq	Std	Nu
877.7	150.8	5.8	5.4	0.00	0.11	1.0	−0.3	1.0	−0.3	Mean
55.0	2.3	0.4	0.3	0.65	0.00	0.3	2.4	0.3	2.4	S.D.

RMSE 0.11 Adj S.D. 0.64 Separation 5.82 Reliability 0.97
Fixed (all same) chi-square: 682.8 d.f.: 19 significance: .00
Random (normal) chi-square: 19.0 d.f.: 18 significance: .39

suggest that for a study in which judgements such as those made here are the focus of attention, an acceptable range for infit mean square is from 0.5 to 1.5, though McNamara (1995) uses a more conservative range of 0.7 to 1.3.

The spread of rater harshness was, as mentioned above, 2.43 logits. When we examine the range of candidate ability we see that it is 8.85, or 3.65 times greater than that for rater harshness. This suggests that the 'impact of individual differences in rater severity on examinees scores is likely to be very small' (Myford and Wolfe 2000:11). In fact the typical difference in range should be in the region of two to one (personal communication with J M Linacre, reported in Myford and Wolfe 2000:11).

There is also a possibility that the misfit may be at least partially due to the scripts rated, that is, there may well be unexpected variation on the actual performances and not just in the rating. Keeping this in mind, and noting the exploratory nature of this study, it was decided to continue with this rater in the study.

The relevant columns have been highlighted in the extract from the Bias/Interaction Calibration Report (Table 11.2). We are basically interested in the Z-scores for each rater on each task and on each criterion used to rate each task. This will indicate if there is any significant bias displayed by each rater towards a task/criterion. The bias can be negative, as shown here, meaning that the person awarded lower scores than would have been expected, or positive, meaning that the rater awarded higher scores than expected for this criterion when rating this particular task.

The results of this analysis were imported into the Excel program. Here, the data was sorted by rater, task and criterion (see Table 11.3) and a 'macro' (or mini-program) was written to generate graphs based on the six bias figures (three criteria by two tasks). These graphs then formed the basis for the feedback reports described below.

3.2 Rating Occasion 2

The second rating exercise took place in March 2001. This time the 20 raters who participated returned their scripts by the set date. As on the first occasion, there were no problems with the way in which the raters responded to the task.

Because the design meant that the two groups were essentially separate after the first rating occasion, the data from the second rating occasion was first analysed independently and later analysed as a group.

In order to explore fully the effect on the rating performance of the participating examiners a bias/interaction analysis will be performed on the merged data from the two rating occasions for each group (so two separate analyses will be undertaken). In each case the model used can be expressed as:

$$\text{Model} = ?, ?B, ?B, ?B, 1\text{-}5B, R9$$

Table 11.2 Bias/interaction calibration report (extract)

Obsvd Score	Exp. Score	Obsvd Count	Obs-Exp Average	Bias Logit	+ Error	Model Z-Score	Infit MnSq	Outfit MnSq	Sq	Raters	logit	N	Tasks	logit	N	Crit	logit
144	153.5	25	-0.38	0.68	0.27	2.5	0.8	0.8	20	20	0.26	1	Task A	0.04	1	TF	-0.70
134	142.4	25	-0.34	0.62	0.27	2.3	0.8	0.8	56	16	-0.50	1	Task A	0.04	3	VSS	0.44
153	160.0	26	-0.27	0.48	0.26	1.8	1.2	1.2	29	9	-0.37	1	Task A	0.04	2	CC	-0.13
156	162.5	25	-0.26	0.46	0.27	1.7	0.6	0.6	18	18	-0.39	1	Task A	0.04	1	TF	-0.70
151	157.2	25	-0.25	0.45	0.27	1.7	1.0	1.1	4	4	-0.06	1	Task A	0.04	1	TF	-0.70

Table 11.3 Example of data imported to Excel and sorted by rater, task, criterion

Z-score	Rater	Task	Criterion
1.1	17	Task A	CC
0.7	17	Task A	TF
−4.2	17	Task A	VSS
0.4	17	Task B	AIE
4.9	17	Task B	CQ
−2.9	17	Task B	VSS

where the facets included in the analysis are the rater, the task, the rating occasion and the rating criteria. Analysis of the data for the feedback group resulted in the following significant bias terms, Tables 11.4a and 11.4b.

Table 11.4a Bias/Interaction table for the feedback group (summary of positive significant interactions)

Z-Score	Rater	Task	Occasion	Criterion	Rater	Occ 1	Occ 2	Total
7.1	6	Task B	Occ 1	VSS	2	0	1	1
4.8	20	Task A	Occ 2	TF	3	0	3	3
3.4	5	Task B	Occ 1	AIE	5	2	0	2
3.3	9	Task A	Occ 2	CC	6	2	0	2
3.2	7	Task B	Occ 2	CQ	7	0	1	1
3.1	11	Task A	Occ 1	TF	9	1	2	3
2.8	14	Task A	Occ 2	VSS	11	1	0	1
2.7	9	Task A	Occ 2	TF	14	0	2	2
2.7	3	Task A	Occ 2	VSS	19	1	0	1
2.6	6	Task B	Occ 1	CQ	20	0	2	2
2.6	3	Task B	Occ 2	VSS				
2.5	3	Task B	Occ 2	CQ	Task			
2.5	14	Task B	Occ 2	VSS				
2.2	9	Task A	Occ 1	TF	Task A	3	7	10
2.1	5	Task B	Occ 1	CQ	Task B	4	4	8
2.1	20	Task A	Occ 2	CC				
2.0	2	Task A	Occ 2	TF	Criterion			
2.0	19	Task A	Occ 1	TF				
					TF	3	3	6
2.97	(2.73)	overall mean z-score (-the 7.1)			VSS	1	4	5
3.21	(2.56)	mean z-score for occasion 1			CQ	2	2	4
2.36		mean z-score for occasion 2			CC	0	2	2
					AIE	1	0	1
					Totals	7	11	18

Bias/Interactions observed
  Occasion 1-7
  Occasion 2-11

The results in Table 11.4a (which focuses on situations where examiners awarded scores that were lower than those predicted by the model), suggest that this group did not benefit from the feedback provided after the first rating occasion. Four of the 10 examiners did show a decrease in their tendency towards this type of bias, though the remaining six all demonstrated bias on more occasions during the second rating occasion. On the positive side, even using the more conservative estimation of the mean Z-score (calculated by removing the extreme score of 7.1), the degree of bias has lessened on the second rating occasion.

Table 11.4b Bias/Interaction table for the feedback group (summary of negative significant interactions)

Z-Score	Rater	Task	Occasion	Criterion	Rater	Occ 1	Occ 2	Total
-2.0	14	Task B	Occ 2	CQ	2	0	1	1
-2.1	3	Task A	Occ 1	TF	3	2	0	2
-2.2	19	Task A	Occ 2	CC	5	1	1	2
-2.2	19	Task B	Occ 2	CQ	6	0	2	2
-2.3	14	Task B	Occ 1	CQ	7	0	0	0
-3.0	2	Task B	Occ 2	CQ	9	1	1	2
-3.0	20	Task B	Occ 1	AIE	11	0	1	1
-3.0	9	Task B	Occ 2	VSS	14	1	1	2
-3.1	3	Task B	Occ 1	AIE	19	0	2	2
-3.2	9	Task B	Occ 1	AIE	20	2	0	2
-3.2	20	Task B	Occ 1	VSS				
-3.3	5	Task A	Occ 1	TF	**Task**			
-3.8	6	Task B	Occ 2	AIE				
-4.4	6	Task A	Occ 2	TF	Task A	2	4	6
-5.0	11	Task A	Occ 2	CC	Task B	5	5	10
-6.8	5	Task A	Occ 2	TF				

3.29	(3.05)	overall mean z-score (-the -6.8)	**Criterion**
2.89		mean z-score for occasion 1	
3.60	(3.20)	mean z-score for occasion 2	

Criterion	Occ 1	Occ 2	Total
TF	2	2	4
VSS	1	1	2
CQ	1	3	4
CC	0	2	2
AIE	3	1	4
Totals	7	9	16

Bias/Interactions observed
Occasion 1-7
Occasion 2-9

We can see from Table 11.4b that nine of the 10 examiners showed at least one bias/interaction over the two rating occasions. Again the tendency towards bias appears to be idiosyncratic, as there are occasions where examiners are more likely to show bias on either Occasion 1 or Occasion 2, and in the case of four examiners there appears to be no difference dependent on occasion. Interestingly, the mean Z-scores (again even when calculated using the more conservative method of removing the apparent outlier) show that there is indeed a major difference between the two rating occasions, but not in the direction predicted. Here, the examiners appear to be more likely to award unexpectedly high scores, at least compared to those predicted in the model.

The results of a similar bias/interaction analysis carried out on the scores awarded by the non-feedback group demonstrate that there are significantly fewer occasions of bias for this group. Similarly, the pattern of behaviour over the two rating occasions appears to be more idiosyncratic than group oriented – meaning that examiners are likely to behave in an essentially unpredictable manner in terms of their tendency towards bias. Although the number of occasions on which bias was observed was low, the actual degree of bias (as represented in the mean Z-scores) appears to be higher than with the feedback group.

In Table 11.5b it is clear that there is little difference between the performance of this group and that of the feedback group in terms of the overall number of bias interactions observed during the two rating occasions, though the criteria involved differ to a great extent.

Table 11.5a Bias/interaction table for the non-feedback group (summary of positive significant interactions)

Z-Score	Rater	Task	Occasion	Criterion	Rater	Occ 1	Occ 2	Total
5.8	17	Task B	Occ 1	CQ	1	1	0	1
5.2	12	Task A	Occ 2	VSS	4	0	0	0
4.7	12	Task A	Occ 1	VSS	8	0	0	0
4.2	18	Task B	Occ 2	AIE	10	0	0	0
3.4	12	Task A	Occ 2	TF	12	1	2	3
2.8	16	Task B	Occ 2	VSS	13	0	0	0
2.3	1	Task B	Occ 1	VSS	15	0	0	0
2.1	18	Task B	Occ 2	CQ	16	0	1	1
					17	1	0	1
3.81	(3.53)	overall mean z-score			18	0	2	2
		(-the 5.8)						
4.20	(3.40)	mean z-score for occasion 1						
4.43	(4.17)	mean z-score for occasion 2		**Task**			
			(-the 5.2)		Task A	1	2	3
					Task B	2	3	5
					Criterion			
					TF	0	1	1
					VSS	2	2	4
					CQ	1	1	2
Bias/Interactions observed					CC	0	0	0
					AIE	0	1	1
		Occasion 1-3						
		Occasion 2-5			Totals	3	4	8

3.3 Effects on reliability

Possibly the most obvious question to be asked is 'How does this impact on inter-rater reliability?' As ever, this is not an easy question to answer. The summary statistics from each of the analyses (shown in Table 11.6) indicate

Table 11.5b Bias/interaction table for the non-feedback group (summary of positive significant interactions)

Z-Score	Rater	Task	Occasion	Criterion	Rater	Occ 1	Occ 2	Total
−2.0	17	Task B	Occ 1	VSS	1	0	1	1
−2.1	1	Task B	Occ 2	AIE	4	0	0	0
−2.2	10	Task A	Occ 2	TF	8	0	2	2
−2.3	8	Task B	Occ 2	CQ	10	0	2	2
−2.3	17	Task A	Occ 2	VSS	12	1	1	2
−2.5	13	Task A	Occ 1	TF	13	1	0	1
−2.6	16	Task A	Occ 1	TF	15	0	0	0
−2.7	10	Task B	Occ 2	AIE	16	1	0	1
−3.2	12	Task B	Occ 2	CQ	17	2	2	4
−3.3	8	Task B	Occ 2	VSS	18	1	0	1
−3.4	18	Task A	Occ 1	VSS				
−3.4	17	Task B	Occ 2	VSS	Task			
−4.0	17	Task A	Occ 1	VSS				
−4.8	12	Task B	Occ 1	CQ	Task A	4	2	6
					Task B	2	6	8

3.29	overall mean z-score
2.89	mean z-score for occasion 1
3.60	mean z-score for occasion 2

Criterion	Occ 1	Occ 2	Total
TF	2	1	3
VSS	3	3	6
CQ	1	2	3
CC	0	0	0
AIE	0	2	2
Total	6	7	14

Bias/Interactions observed

       Occasion 1−6
       Occasion 2−8

that in each case the Fixed (all same) chi-square statistic, which tests the hypothesis 'Can these raters be thought of as equally severe?' supports the argument that they can be thus considered. The Random (normal) chi-square, which tests the hypothesis: 'Can these persons be thought of as sampled at random from a normally distributed population?' suggests that, in all cases they cannot. This is not at all surprising, as the raters have been carefully selected and trained, and any indication of randomness would be worrying. There appears to be a more clearly defined separation within the feedback group, though the difference may not be of particular relevance to this study.

One final analysis was made of the difference in rater profiles over the two occasions. Table 11.7 indicates that there appears to be a more individual or idiosyncratic nature to the differences in performance. We can see from this table that there appears to be a similar spread across the two groups in terms of consistency with 25% of the raters displaying an improvement over the two rating occasions, 10% (two raters, one from each group) showing a decline in consistency and 65% remaining the same. In terms of a tendency towards leniency, we can see that there is no systematic difference between the two groups.

Table 11.6 Summary statistics for the three analyses

```
------------------------------------------------------------------
Occasion 1 (all raters)

RMSE (Model) .14 Adj S.D. .71 Separation 5.06 Reliability .96
Fixed (all same) chi-square: 589.8 d.f.: 18 significance: .00
Random (normal) chi-square: 18.0 d.f.: 17 significance: .39
------------------------------------------------------------------
Occasion 2 (feedback group)

RMSE (Model) .11 Adj S.D. .70 Separation 6.24 Reliability .97
Fixed (all same) chi-square: 452.6 d.f.: 10 significance: .00
Random (normal) chi-square: 10.0 d.f.: 9 significance: .35
------------------------------------------------------------------
Occasion 2 (non-feedback group)

RMSE (Model) .11 Adj S.D. .63 Separation 5.56 Reliability .97
Fixed (all same) chi-square: 318.7 d.f.: 9 significance: .00
Random (normal) chi-square: 9.0 d.f.: 8 significance: .34
------------------------------------------------------------------
```

Table 11.7 Overview of rating performance across rating occasions

Rater	Infit MnSq Occasion		Outfit MnSq Occasion		Measure Occasion		Outcome	
	1	2	1	2	1	2	Consistent	Lenient
2	**0.8**	**1.2**	**0.8**	**1.2**	**−0.59**	**−0.05**	**Less**	**More**
4	0.9	0.5	0.9	0.4	−0.06	−0.38	Less	Less
5	**0.8**	**1.0**	**0.8**	**1.0**	**−0.79**	**−1.37**	**More**	**Less**
10	0.9	1.5	0.8	1.4	−0.17	−0.69	More	Less
15	0.7	1.0	0.7	1.1	1.38	1.19	More	Less
3	**1.4**	**0.8**	**1.4**	**0.8**	**−0.66**	**0.8**	**More**	**More**
17	**1.3**	**1.1**	**1.3**	**1.1**	**0.15**	**0.70**	**More**	**More**
1	0.8	0.8	0.7	0.8	0.35	−0.35	Same	Less
6	1.7	1.6	1.7	1.6	0.80	−0.86	Same	Less
8	1.0	0.8	1.0	0.8	1.21	0.45	Same	Less
11	**1.1**	**1.0**	**1.1**	**1.0**	**0.59**	**0.14**	**Same**	**Less**
19	**0.6**	**0.7**	**0.6**	**0.7**	**−0.07**	**−0.59**	**Same**	**Less**
20	**0.9**	**1.0**	**0.9**	**1.0**	**0.26**	**0.93**	**Same**	**Less**
9	**1.0**	**1.1**	**1.0**	**1.1**	**−0.37**	**−0.00**	**Same**	**More**
12	1.2	1.4	1.2	1.4	0.64	0.95	Same	More
13	0.7	0.6	0.7	0.6	−0.60	−0.28	Same	More
14	**1.0**	**0.9**	**1.0**	**0.9**	**−0.12**	**0.66**	**Same**	**More**
16	1.3	1.3	1.3	1.3	−0.50	−0.22	Same	More
18	0.7	0.7	0.7	0.7	−0.39	0.19	Same	More
7	**1.1**	**1.0**	**1.1**	**1.0**	**−1.05**	**−0.94**	**Same**	**Same**

Note: Bold type is the feedback group; + = Lenient; − = Harsh.

The mean severity measures on Rating Occasion 1, were .27 and -.27, for the feedback and non-feedback groups respectively. Further analysis of the results from Table 11.7 indicates that these both converged on 0 during the second rating occasion (0.03 and 0.00 for the feedback and non-feedback groups respectively). This essentially means that the two groups showed a tendency towards improving (in terms of consistency, and severity/leniency) during this second round of rating, and suggests that the relatively minor changes in rating behaviour were a function of this additional round, rather than a function of the intervention (the provision of feedback or not).

3.4 Questionnaire data

The 10 raters in the feedback group all completed and returned the questionnaire. The following analysis of their responses takes each question in turn.

Question 1 *Was the rating report clear?*
Eight of the 10 raters answered 'Yes' to this question. Of the two exceptions, R19 replied 'Mostly, yes', and asked for clarification of a specific line in her report; R06 replied 'Not totally' and explained that the scale on the graph had been difficult to interpret.

Question 2 *Did the rating report have any effect on the way you approached the second round of rating?*
All raters believed the rating report had had an effect on the way they approached the second round of rating. Two raters (R06, R11) mention that the rating report had prompted them to review some or all of their IELTS examiner materials: 'It made me re-read the Descriptors under the CC heading for Task 1 and consider the role and purpose of Coherence within the GT essays' (R11). It is clear that the rating report affected the quality of attention given by some raters in the second round of rating: in the words of R20, for example, 'I was hugely aware of the areas in which I had deviated from the norm – one doesn't like to think that one is grading students unfairly, be it too leniently or too harshly. I spent a lot of time over the first few scripts I graded' (R20). In contrast, R19 noted the morale-boosting effect of the rating report: 'On the whole it gave me a feeling of confidence that I am at least rating fairly consistently, if not perfectly'.

Question 3 *Where the rating report made specific recommendations, did you adjust the way you rated at all?*
Responses indicate the practical difficulty of acting on recommendations made in the rating reports: 'I tried to be less harsh on CQ on Task 2 but it was very difficult to adjust an assessment' (R14). R03 and R05 report taking action on the recommendations in their reports but they do not attempt to explain the process by which they did so (e.g. 'Marked less harshly in areas indicated and vice versa' R03 in Q2). The answers from R02 and R07 offer a little more detail about how they put recommendations into practice:

On those scripts in which I felt uncertain which of two adjacent bands to award for VSS on Task 1, I opted for the lower one in the second round of rating; conversely, where I was uncertain which of two adjacent bands to award for CQ on Task 2, I opted for the higher one.   (R02)

When I was wavering between two marks in an area in which I had been shown to be rather severe, I usually went for the more generous mark.   (R07)

Both R19 and R20, whose reports had indicated that their tendencies towards harshness or leniency were not significant, mention that they tried to make an appropriate adjustment in the second round of rating but were unsure how effectively they managed to do so:

I concentrated on trying to adjust the way I rated Task 2 according to the suggestions in the report. I also approached the scoring generally with a view to using a broader range of scores. However, in the end I felt that the latter probably had little effect on the scores I gave (is this because I am too set in my ways or because people read the descriptors differently?)   (R19)

I tried to internalise the information, but after a while it was difficult to say to what extent I had genuinely internalised and it was making a difference, or whether I had just lapsed into my previous standards.

(R20)

Question 4 *As a rater in this project, how useful did you find the Rating Report? Circle one number from 1 to 5 (1 = of little use; 5 = very useful)*

The most common response to this question was 5 or 'very useful', which was given by five raters. The lowest response was 3, given by two raters, whose comments were as follows: 'Good as far as it went, but needed comparison of other people's overall grades' (R03); and 'Please see previous answer – it's the Band Descriptors I find "not very useful"!' (R06).

Question 5 *Which aspect of the rating report did you find most useful?*

The aspect of the rating report most often singled out for favourable comment was the graph, which was referred to by seven raters. R20 provided a neat explanation of the graph's value to her: 'The graph. I'm a visual learner. More accessible and understandable for these purposes than text.' On the other hand, four raters (R02, R09, R14, R19) referred specifically to the written comments accompanying the graph.

Question 6 *Which aspect of the Rating Report did you find least useful?*

Seven raters did not specify a 'least useful' aspect; they responded either with '–' or an unspecific answer such as 'All useful' (R14) or 'Nothing, really'

(R20). Of the other three raters, R06's response is in fact concerned with the band descriptors, while R02 and R11 both specify an aspect which they had found not fully understandable: the scale on the graph (R02) and the source of the 'base-line marks' or fair average scores (R11).

Question 7 *Are there any changes or additions that would have improved the usefulness of the RR to you?*
    As far as possible improvements to the rating report are concerned, both R3 and R20 believe it would have been valuable to have had more information about the performance of the other raters in the group: '(I) needed to relate my global scores with those of other raters' (R3); 'Indicate the maximum deviations by a group of examiners. Could be therapeutic or terrifying!' (R20). Following up their replies to the previous question, R02 and R11 request respectively 'a representation of a full unit on the graph' and 'more explanation of how the base-line is established'. Other raters either mark the space with a '–' or give an unspecific answer, e.g. 'No suggestions – very useful exercise' (R09).

Question 8 *How useful would a RR of this kind be in your work as an IELTS examiner outside this project?*
    The nine raters who responded to this question gave either 4 or 5; seven of the nine believed that this kind of rating report was potentially 'very useful' to IELTS examiners. One rater (R06) failed to answer this question.

Question 9 *What do you see as the main benefits, if any, a rating report might bring to you in your work as an IELTS examiner outside this project?*
    The two benefits identified most frequently in response to this question are 'consistency' (of rating) and 'reassurance' for the rater, each of which is mentioned by four raters. In addition, 'accuracy' is referred to by three raters, 'reliability' and 'encouragement' by two raters each, and 'confidence' and 'feeling good' each by one rater. One other theme that appears in the responses to this question is the potential value of a rating report procedure as a means of combating the solitariness of IELTS examining (see R03, R19 and R20). To illustrate these themes, the responses of R05 and R19 are quoted in full below.

> a) Feedback would reassure examiners and/or encourage them to make adjustments to their ratings. b) A significant step in improving overall inter-rater reliability.
>   There are currently too few rater reliability training sessions. Once every two years is insufficient. They should be more frequent and they should be paid for by IELTS. Compare, for example, other Cambridge Exams! (R05)

> Although recertification takes place every couple of years, this is really only confirmation that one hasn't 'gone off the rails'. There is no feedback on one's ratings, either after recertification, or during the normal course of one's duties. Having the rating report meant that one was not operating in a vacuum. It lets you know how you are doing, and enables you to adjust where necessary. I would imagine therefore that it would lead to more accurate and consistent rating.   (R19)

To summarise the questionnaire data, it is clear that most raters judged this form of feedback to be of considerable potential value to IELTS examiners, but also that they experienced difficulty in putting certain feedback recommendations into practice. Comments such as that from R20 in response to Question 3 (quoted above) suggest that one cause of difficulty was that raters received feedback on only one occasion and therefore did not have the opportunity to monitor the effect of any adjustments they made following the feedback. Subsequent rounds of feedback would have enabled raters to find out whether they had made an appropriate adjustment, whether they had overcompensated, and to fine-tune their response. Another likely source of difficulty was the complex nature of some of the marking criteria, such as VSS or CC. If a rater is told, for example, that they are marking too severely on the criterion of VSS, they are faced with deciding whether to adjust the marking of vocabulary or of sentence structure or both, and how to do so in practice. This problem could be addressed either by simplifying the criteria, or by providing much more detailed feedback to engage with the complexity of the criteria in their present form.

Given the difficulties outlined above, it may seem surprising that raters valued the feedback as highly as they did. The explanation seems likely to be that their desire for feedback is motivated not merely by curiosity but by the sense of professional responsibility which is reflected in comments from many raters, such as R20's response to Question 2:

> I was hugely aware of the areas in which I had deviated from the norm – one doesn't like to think that one is grading students unfairly, be it too leniently or too harshly. I spent a lot of time over the first few scripts I graded.

Evidently raters are exercised by professional concerns, and it may be that they value feedback on their rating at least in part because it helps them to address 'ethical questions' of the kind proposed by Spolsky for language testers: 'How sure are you of your decision? How sure are you of the evidence that you're using to make that decision?' (1981, quoted in Bachman, 2000:23).

4 Conclusion

This study explored the potential value of a form of feedback to raters of the IELTS General Training Writing Module. The form of feedback, based on multifaceted Rasch bias analysis of the test results, was first suggested by Wigglesworth (1993) but had, to date, never been validated as a methodology. The results suggest that the approach used here may offer some additional support to raters. However, in the context of a single feedback (or one-shot) report, it is not at all clear that there is a lot of practical gain attached.

There are implications here for rater training and accreditation. Apart from the implications of using an MFR-based approach to test-data analysis, where the emphasis of rater training is on intra- rather then on inter-rater consistency, it is reasonable to question the long-term effects of any rater training exercise. Though the raters here were experienced, there were still instances of bias displayed by different raters, and the profile of this bias seems to have changed over a very short time, even where raters had not received any 'intervention' in the form of feedback. This, in addition to the observation that it is unlikely that candidates' scores will be significantly affected by differences in rater harshness, implies that we may need to reformulate our thinking on the rating process from an inter-rater agreement perspective to the more easily defended position (in terms of validity) of an intra-rater consistency approach.

There appears to be an acceptable level of correlation between the original scores awarded to the scripts and the scores suggested by the MFR analysis. However, the results do imply that there is some problem with the IELTS rating procedure. The fact that the non-feedback group displayed differences in rating performance over the two occasions suggests that there is a rater by performances interaction – this would suggest that further research is needed into the possible sources of the variability observed here.

The research reported here offers, we believe, an interesting perspective on one aspect of the rater training process. While the results of the score-data analysis appear to tell us that the type of feedback offered is limited in its effectiveness, the responses to the questionnaire items are overwhelmingly positive. It is certainly possible that these positive reactions may be a manifestation of the 'Hawthorn Effect'. The negative connotations associated with this effect suggest that the raters may have been telling us what they thought we wanted to hear, so these results should be treated with some degree of caution. On the other hand, there is another, more positive interpretation of the effect.

The term 'Hawthorn Effect' comes from a socio-economic study of the Hawthorn Plant of the Western Electric Company in Cicero, Illinois, in the 1920s–30s when researchers observed an increase in productivity among workers, which was explained by the fact that the workers liked being studied (Mayo 1945). Put very basically, the Hawthorn studies demonstrated that the mere act of intervention can produce positive changes, because the people involved in the social setting (here a rating procedure) may be encouraged or motivated by the additional and unusual amount of attention they are receiving. The implication for test rating is that raters may perform at a higher level (with more consistency and accuracy) when they are subjected to the kind of attention generated by a systematic feedback procedure. We believe that the results of this study may be interpreted as supporting the implementation of such a procedure and feel that further research is needed into the effects of a more systematic and longitudinal treatment (where a group of raters participate in a set of rating exercises over a period of time and where each exercise is followed by the sort of feedback suggested here).

APPENDIX 11.1
Planning schedule for the project

Date	Action
By 7 December 2000	Initial contact with UCLES re scripts
By 12 January 2001	Scripts in hand (begin review of scripts)
20 January 2001	Return of rater reply forms
By 24 January 2001	Review all rater replies
2 February 2001	Final decision on scripts to be used Final decision of raters to be used (& groups – Experimental & control)
By 9 February 2001	Contact all raters (Phone/email) to confirm participation
9 February 2001	Preparation of rating packs
12 February 2001	Post Scripts (round 1)
16 February 2001	Scripts received
By 19 February 2001	Decisions on type of feedback (& analyses)
1 March 2001	Scripts in post by raters (round 1)
5–9 March 2001	Input & Analyse all data
12–13 March 2001	Prepare feedback
14 March 2001	Post feedback
21 March 2001	Post Scripts (round 2)
26 March 2001	Scripts received
9 April 2001	Scripts in post by raters (round 2)
By April 11th 2001	Prepare questionnaire (experiences of rating/feedback etc.)
April 13th 2001	Post Questionnaire
By 20 April 2001	Input & Analyse all data (including comparison with round 1)
27 April 2001	Questionnaire returned
By 11 May 2001	Questionnaire processing
By 1 June 2001	Preliminary report (process, mechanics, outline of remaining project schedule)

APPENDIX 11.2
Rater confidentiality declaration

DECLARATION

I understand that the enclosed tasks and scripts have been issued to me for use solely in connection with the project being carried out by the University of Reading's Testing and Evaluation Research Unit for the IELTS Research Programme 2001. I understand that I must not copy or show the materials to any other person. I undertake to keep the materials secure for the two weeks they are in my possession and then to return them to Dr Barry O'Sullivan in the SAE provided.

Name: ....

Signature: ....

Date: ....

APPENDIX 11.3
Examples of feedback reports

Rater No. 2

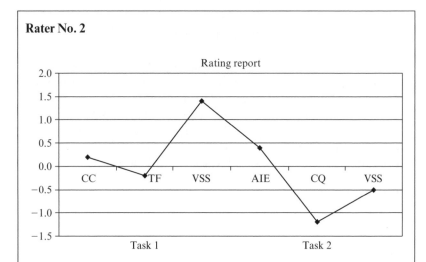

Interpreting the rating report graph:

It is important to realise that the scores on the vertical axis do not represent band-scale units. They are actually based on measurements of the degree of harshness (a negative score) and leniency (a positive score) of an examiner on each scale criterion for each task. Scores which vary by 2 units or more, in either direction, are considered problematic. Each full unit on this scale is equivalent to approximately 1/6 of a band scale.

The graph suggests that:

1. There is a slight (but not significant) tendency towards leniency for VSS on Task 1.
2. There is a slight (again not significant) tendency towards harshness for CQ on Task 2.

Additional analysis suggests that you are inclined not to use the entire breadth of the scale, limiting yourself somewhat to a relatively narrow band of scores (though this is not a significant trend).

Overall comment on your rating of this batch of scripts

Apart from these minor points, your rating was consistent both internally (meaning that you are consistent in the way you apply the scale) and with the group (meaning that your scores tend to agree with those of the other raters involved in this project).

Rater No. 5

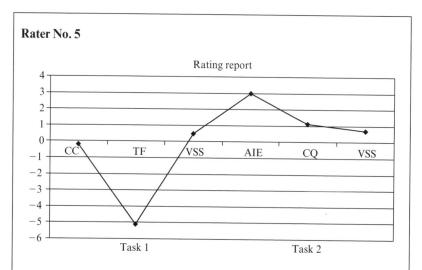

Interpreting the rating report graph:

It is important to realise that the scores on the vertical axis do not represent band-scale units. They are actually based on measurements of the degree of harshness (a negative score) and leniency (a positive score) of an examiner on each scale criterion for each task. Scores which vary by 2 units or more, in either direction, are considered problematic. Each full unit on this scale is equivalent to approximately 1/6 of a band scale.

The graph suggests that:

1. There is a serious level of harshness in your TF scores for Task 1.
2. There is a serious level of leniency in your AIE scores for Task 2.

Additional analysis suggests that you are inclined not to use the entire breadth of the scale, limiting yourself somewhat to a relatively narrow band of scores (though this is not a significant trend).

Overall comment on your rating of this batch of scripts

These analyses suggest that, on this occasion, you have tended to be somewhat inconsistent in your scoring. The up-and-down pattern of the graph suggests that you tend to be harsh on some criteria and lenient on others (specifically TF and AIE). This is probably the cause of the inconsistency. We suggest that you focus on these issues in particular in the next round of rating.

APPENDIX 11.4
IELTS Research Project –
Questionnaire

Question 1 *Was the rating report clear?*

Question 2 *Did the rating report have any effect on the way you approached the second round of rating?*

Question 3 *Where the rating report made specific recommendations, did you adjust the way you rated at all?*

Question 4 *As a rater in this project, how useful did you find the rating report? Circle one number from 1 to 5 (1=of little use; 5=very useful))*

1   2   3   4   5

Question 5 *Which aspect of the rating report did you find most useful?*

Question 6 *Which aspect of the rating report did you find least useful?*

Question 7 *Are there any changes or additions that would have improved the usefulness of the RR to you?*

Question 8 *How useful would a RR of this kind be in your work as an IELTS examiner outside this project?*

Question 9 *What do you see as the main benefits, if any, a rating report might bring to you in your work as an IELTS examiner outside this project?*

Methodology evaluation of Chapter 11

This chapter deals with an important and interesting topic for those engaged in performance testing. It is important, first, because of concerns about the reliability of raters in high-stakes tests when assessing spoken and written language and second, because of interest in the effectiveness of feedback to raters in helping them to be consistent and reliable in their assessments. The chapter is also interesting for its research design as it not only uses a mixture of quantitative and qualitative research tools but also explains their use very carefully. In addition, the qualitative data provides useful data for the training of future IELTS raters.

The methodology involves the application of multifaceted Rasch analysis (MFRA) using the software program FACETS to analyse the leniency or severity of raters when they applied the criteria for the IELTS written module to a sample of texts. The Rasch analysis is then employed to provide feedback on individual rater performance to an experimental group of raters. It then analyses the effects of such feedback on a second round of rating. This constitutes the first part of the research design. The second part uses qualitative methods by means of a questionnaire to gauge the raters' responses to the feedback after their rating exercise and how (or whether) it affected them in the second rating exercise.

Section 2 of the Chapter, the Methodology section provides a good example to new researchers with its meticulous description of all the elements in the study: the raters, the scripts that were used, the organisation of the batches of scripts, the data collection, the first rating, the feedback to raters and the second rating. In all of these, the reader receives a full description of what occurred and how it was planned. The final part of the Methodology section describes, again, with full explanations, the questions that were asked, the explanation for the approach taken (given that the feedback had been different from the feedback usually received by IELTS raters), and the reactions of the raters to the feedback.

Of particular interest to new researchers will be the way in which the results of the Rasch analysis are presented and explained. This is a very useful section and, given that many new researchers to testing and most other language researchers are unfamiliar with Rasch modelling, a very useful addition to the chapter. Researchers will often omit a description of the research tools and its application when presenting results. However, in the case of new research tools, an explanation of how the figures can be interpreted is never wasted.

The findings of the study should not be considered a failure in any way, even though they may appear disappointing to those who believe in the effectiveness of rater training and who would instinctively wish for a positive outcome. As was mentioned in the comments on research methodology in

Chapter 9, research is neutral. Studies are carried out by researchers in order to investigate whether commonly held beliefs have substance or not. Only in that way can the effects of prejudice and myth be dispelled.

The effect of publication of this chapter will almost certainly inspire replications of the research with more periods of feedback over a longer period of time. This is to be welcomed.

12

The impact of the joint-funded research studies on the IELTS Writing Module

Lynda Taylor

As explained in the introduction to this volume, the rationale for the IELTS Joint-funded Research Program is to promote and support research activity among test stakeholders which will contribute to the validation and ongoing development of the International English Language Testing System (IELTS).

The six funded research studies reported in Part 2 of this volume were all conducted between 1996 and 2001 and focus on the IELTS Writing test as it was operationalised during the period 1995–2004. Findings from these six studies provided the IELTS partners with valuable insights into candidate performance and rater behaviour in the IELTS Writing test as it was at that time, and gathered useful evidence relating to the validity, reliability, practicality and impact of the test; they also highlighted specific aspects of the test needing closer review and possible future revision. As a result, they directly informed the IELTS Writing Revision Project (2001–05) and, in combination with outcomes from other commissioned studies and internal validation investigations, had a significant impact on changes made to the assessment criteria and rating scales for the IELTS Writing test from January 2005. The specific contribution of each of these studies to the process of ongoing IELTS Writing test development and validation, as well as to the broader language testing field, is reviewed and evaluated in the sections which follow. (More detailed summaries of the work completed within the IELTS Writing Revision Project are reported in Cambridge ESOL's quarterly publication *Research Notes*, and a full project report is currently in preparation for web publication – Shaw and Falvey, forthcoming.)

Chapter 6: Authenticity in the IELTS Academic Module Writing test: a comparative study of Task 2 items and university assignments (Moore and Morton)

Moore and Morton's study was conducted in 1997 and first published in Volume 2 of the IELTS Research Reports 1999. This is one of a number focusing on test content validity through analysis of test task authenticity (Hale et al 1996, Lewkowicz 1997). Authentic test tasks are generally characterised as those which correspond closely to tasks the language user is likely to encounter in the target language use situation, in this case written tasks in the context of university study. Building on the early EAP needs analysis work of researchers like Weir (1983), extensive research over the past 20 years has led us to a much better understanding today of the nature of writing in higher education contexts.

The Moore and Morton study provides useful empirical evidence that Task 2 of the IELTS Writing test does indeed share features in common with the predominant written genre used in university study – the essay. The study also concludes that the demands of the IELTS Task 2 diverge in some respects from those of the university writing assignments analysed; it suggests that key differentiating features in the IELTS Writing tasks relate to: a need to draw upon prior knowledge; a restricted range of rhetorical functions; and an emphasis on 'real-world' rather than 'abstract' entities. The results of their study led Moore and Morton to make a number of interesting recommendations for changing the design of the IELTS Writing Module. These are worth considering and commenting on in some detail.

Their first recommendation is that the subject of Task 2 items be thematically linked to at least one passage from the IELTS Reading test and that candidates be given the option of making reference to this reading passage in their written response. Until April 1995 a strong thematic link did exist between the IELTS Reading and Writing Modules (for both Academic and General Training). This link was removed in the 1995 IELTS Revision Project on the grounds that the thematic link of the original test design, though desirable in some respects, increased the potential for confusing the assessment of writing ability with the assessment of reading ability (Charge and Taylor 1997). Monitoring of candidates' writing performance suggested that the extent to which candidates exploited the reading input varied considerably. Some candidates drew heavily on the written content of the reading texts, apparently treating the writing task as a measure of their reading ability; as a result, many risked masking their actual writing ability. Other candidates chose to articulate their own ideas on the topic, either making very little reference to the reading texts or forging artificial connections for the sake of the task. In some cases candidates were confused about whether it would be better to articulate their personal point of view on the topic or to reflect a more 'authoritative' view expressed in the reading text(s). This variation in candidates' treatment of the linked Writing task made the achievement of fair assessment at the marking stage a complex process; a more equitable form of task design was sought which removed the link between the IELTS Reading and Writing Modules for both Academic and General Training. Removal of the link also makes it easier to control comparability of task difficulty across the many different test versions which need to be produced for the IELTS Reading and Writing Modules each year. Interestingly, Moore and Morton themselves acknowledge that any recommendation for enhanced authenticity needs to take into account the inevitable constraints imposed upon the writing in the broad testing situation.

A second recommendation made by the authors is that 'a minimal number of Task 2 items' be framed around a *hortatory rhetoric*, i.e. the discussion of the desirability (or not) of a particular social practice, public policy, etc.; instead, they recommend that Task 2 items be designed to incorporate 'a diverse range of rhetorical functions' including: *description*; *summarisation*; *comparison*; *explanation*; *recommendation*. Several points are worth making in response to this recommendation.

First of all, it is important to remember that the IELTS Writing Module consists of more than just Task 2; there are *two* tasks – Task 1 (150 words) and Task 2 (250 words). The elicitation of two pieces of extended writing allows for broader domain sampling and contributes to increased reliability of the assessment. The Task 1 writing prompt presents candidates with some visual input (e.g. graph, diagram, bar chart) and asks them to describe this informa-tion in 150 words; performance on this task generally requires candidates to demonstrate skills of *description* and *summarisation*, and sometimes even *com-parison*, so these rhetorical functions are in fact provided for within the IELTS Writing test as a whole. In their study Moore and Morton made a conscious decision to focus only on IELTS Writing Task 2 and their reasons for restrict-ing the focus are understandable: 'it was considered too large an undertaking to investigate the authenticity of both tasks in the Writing test' (p. 199). The decision to focus on Task 2 was 'partly because this component carries a heavier weighting on the test and also because anecdotal evidence suggests that this task is given greater attention in test preparation classes' (p. 199).

Secondly, the researchers' conclusion that *hortatory rhetoric* is overused in the Task 2 prompts derives partly from the nature of the Task 2 corpus they used as the basis for their analysis. Unable to use 'live' or 'retired' Task 2 items, the researchers had to assemble a corpus of 20 Task 2 items drawn from sample test materials and commercially available test preparation materials. Of the 20 Task 2 items analysed, two came from the IELTS Handbook (1996) and the IELTS Specimen Materials (1995) – both pub-lished by the test producers; the remaining 18 were taken from a range of mostly commercially produced materials (six sources are listed in an appen-dix to their report). The researchers believed that the Task 2 items from these sources would reflect the nature of tasks used in the official versions of the IELTS test. Test prompts produced for commercial test preparation mater-ials tend to be modelled on (or cloned from) the limited number of sample tasks available in test handbooks and sample materials. This is the case for the 18 Task 2 prompts assembled by the researchers and in part explains the over-representation of hortatory tasks in their corpus. In addition, some of the 18 Task 2s are more representative than others of live IELTS writing test prompts; for example, Task 2 items 3, 4 and 5 (all taken from Source 3) involve much longer textual prompts than would normally be permitted in a live IELTS test.

Finally, many of the 18 Task 2s fail to include some of the additional rubric wording which often appears as part of the Task 2 writing prompt, e.g.

> *Discuss both these views and give your opinion . . .*
> *Do you think the advantages of this development/system outweigh the disadvantage s . . .?*
> *What do you think are the causes of this problem . . . and what measures could be taken to solve/reduce it?*

Such prompts invite test takers to use the rhetorical functions of *description*, *summarisation*, *comparison*, *explanation*, and *recommendation*.

Overall, therefore, the researchers' corpus of 20 Task 2 items is somewhat limited in its representativeness; a detailed survey of the IELTS writing prompts used in 'live' test versions of Tasks 1 and 2 would show the 'more diverse range of rhetorical functions' which they are advocating.

Moore and Morton's final recommendation is that some Task 2 items should be framed to include an attributed proposition in the task rubric; they suggest this could be either a generic attribution (e.g. *many psychologists argue*) or be attributed to a specific scholar. It is encouraging to be able to report that the design of the Task 2 prompt has evolved in recent years to include this format as the following example shows:

> *Some people believe that all zoos should be banned as they are cruel to animals and do not serve any useful purpose to society.*
> *To what extent do you agree or disagree with this opinion?*

In conclusion, it is perhaps worth reminding ourselves that IELTS is designed to test *readiness to enter* the world of university-level study in the English language and the ability to cope with the demands of that context immediately after entry. It does not necessarily assume that test takers have already mastered (or even partially acquired) the range of university-level writing skills which they are likely to need, in terms of genre and other techniques; indeed, they will probably need to develop many of these skills *during* their course of study, some in ways that are specific to their academic domain. The implication of this is that IELTS Writing tasks are not designed primarily to simulate the sort of university-level writing tasks which test takers will encounter in their studies. Instead, tasks are designed to be accessible to a wide range of test takers and to reflect features of writing activities that are already familiar to candidates from their previous study experience as well as some features of writing they may encounter in their subsequent study. One reason for including an essay for Task 2 is that it is a written genre widely used in both secondary and higher education contexts – a point acknowledged by Moore and Morton. It would perhaps be unreasonable to define the authenticity of IELTS Writing tasks solely in terms of 'simulated university-level writing tasks' and then to judge them against that criterion.

Chapter 7: A linguistic analysis of Chinese and Greek L1 scripts for IELTS Academic Writing Task 2 (Mayor, Hewings, North, Swann with Coffin)

The Mayor et al study was conducted in 2000 and has not been previously published. It set out to analyse linguistic features of test-taker performance in Task 2 of the IELTS Academic Writing Module and to explore the extent to which the features of analysis were associated with variables such as the test prompt, the task score awarded, and the test-taker's L1.

Results from the Mayor et al study provide useful validation evidence for several aspects of the IELTS test. First of all, they point to the comparability of the IELTS Task 2 test prompts; in other words, the different Writing test versions and the tasks within them appear to make similar demands on test-takers. This type of evidence is especially important in large-scale, high-stakes test contexts where multiple test versions need to be produced for security purposes but these must offer comparable opportunities to test takers; although the researchers observed that the different test versions appeared to elicit slightly different formal features, the results did not show a significant task effect. Findings from their study echo those from Cambridge ESOL's internal validation studies which help to confirm the comparability of IELTS Writing test prompts (see data reported in the IELTS Annual Review until 2002, and now on the IELTS website).

Secondly, the study provides support for claims about the discriminating power of IELTS Writing Task 2 and the rating scales. The descriptors appear to differentiate effectively between high-scoring and low-scoring scripts and the strongest predictors of high scores include high word length, low formal error rate and complexity in sentence structure – all of which appear in the IELTS band descriptors at the higher performance levels; other distinguishing features at higher levels include patterns of organisation and control of argument. Once again, the Mayor et al findings are consistent with internal qualitative analyses carried out on IELTS Writing performance as part of Cambridge ESOL's Common Scale for Writing Project which highlight features that differentiate performance across levels (see Hawkey and Barker 2004).

Finally, although Mayor et al observed some stylistic differences in the performance of the Greek and Chinese L1 groups (e.g. use of grammatical form, argumentative structure and cultural backgrounds), there seems to be no evidence of significant cultural bias due to task. This finding is encouraging since the test developers clearly design the IELTS Writing task prompts to cater for candidates' prior linguistic, cultural and educational experience irrespective of nationality or first language. The researchers comment that the IELTS marking criteria can be applied flexibly to allow for any cross-cultural variation in the use of English.

In their recommendations at the end of the study Mayor et al echo Moore and Morton's views on two points. First, they suggest that some sort of 'input' or background information should be (re)introduced for test takers to draw on in order to stimulate greater use of evidence; they believe this would achieve a closer correspondence between the task demands of IELTS and those which are commonly expected of students in higher education. Second, they express concern that test takers adopt an 'overly personal and hortatory style' and they suggest revising the generic task prompt wording to encourage a more neutral (less personal) tenor or style. Responses to both these recommendations were discussed earlier in relation to the Moore and Morton study (see above). Findings from the Mayor et al study, together with results from other studies included in this volume directly informed the revision of the IELTS assessment criteria and rating scale descriptors. The IELTS test developers rely heavily upon detailed qualitative analyses of IELTS Writing performance to gain a sound understanding of key features of performance across different proficiency levels and so reflect these in valid and reliable assessment criteria and scales.

Two other findings from the study are worth commenting on, relating to the rating approach and the influence of the task wording.

First, the Mayor et al study makes the interesting observation that 'markers appear to be responding to scripts in a holistic rather than strictly analytic way' (p. 297). It may be worth noting that the approach to rating which operated at the time of this study offered IELTS examiners a choice. They were encouraged to approach each script holistically to begin with, applying a 'global marking' scale; however, if the script presented an uneven profile making holistic rating problematic or inappropriate, then examiners could shift to 'profile marking', using a set of analytical scales derived from the global scale. Early on in the IELTS Writing Revision Project the relative merits of analytic and holistic approaches to assessment were reviewed to determine whether a standardised analytic approach might be more appropriate for the IELTS Writing test (Shaw 2002b). The benefits of analytical assessment were perceived to be: enhanced reliability through increased observations; greater discrimination across a wide range of assessment bands; provision of greater control over what informs the impressions of raters;

removal of the tendency to assess impressionistically; active discouragement of norm-referencing; and the provision of valuable research data/information. As previously discussed in this volume, the move to analytical scales for the Speaking test in 2001 was for reasons of consistent examiner focus and multiple observations. Consequently, it was decided that a move towards systematic analytic marking would also be appropriate for IELTS Writing and that any holistic approach to assessment amongst examiners should be actively discouraged. For this reason, profile (rather than global) marking became mandatory from July 2003 as an interim measure until the revised analytical scales were introduced in January 2005.

Second, the apparent influence of the topic or task wording on candidate output (i.e. that specific wording seemed to cue certain linguistic forms) is an interesting finding. In association with the revision of IELTS Writing assessment criteria and scales, several internal studies were conducted by Cambridge ESOL to investigate the transparency and effectiveness of the task rubrics. As a result, some minor adjustments may be made to the IELTS Task 2 rubrics in future. Though the fundamentally personal nature of the writing is unlikely to change (with candidates continuing to draw on their own knowledge and experience), the reduction of emphasis on 'you' and 'your' in the rubric may help to reduce the influence of the task wording on candidate output. The overall purpose of these changes is to ensure that the current rubrics come closer to fulfilling the three essential criteria laid down in the literature for instructions to test takers (e.g. Bachman and Palmer 1996): they must be simple enough for candidates and examiners to comprehend; short enough so as not to take up too much of the test administration time; and sufficiently explicit to allow candidates to know exactly what is expected of them.

Chapter 8: A corpus-based investigation of linguistic responses to an IELTS Academic Writing task (Kennedy and Thorp)

Recent years have seen growing interest among applied linguists and language testers in using corpus-based research methodology to gain insights into qualitative and quantitative features of L2 writing performance. The results of corpus-based investigations – whether these are studies of written or spoken language performance – are particularly valuable for test developers; they can help to shape test task and rubric design and can inform the definition of assessment criteria, performance level descriptors, and other marking criteria; as such, they make an important contribution to the development of examiner training programmes. Beyond the test development context, corpus-informed studies can help teachers and markers better understand key linguistic features of L2 writing performance and what characterises performance at different proficiency levels. For several years now, Cambridge ESOL has been directly involved in a variety of projects to enhance current linguistic and functional performance-level descriptions, including work on the Common Scale Projects (see for example Hawkey and Barker 2004) and on the Common European Framework of Reference (2001).

The Kennedy and Thorp project – carried out in 2000 and not previously published – was one of the first studies to apply corpus-based methodology to a set of IELTS Writing scripts in order to undertake a linguistic analysis of candidate performance; their study used IELTS Task 2 scripts generated by candidates in the live test context and these were analysed using a combination of manual and electronic tools to investigate specific features of performance at different levels of proficiency.

Like the Mayor et al study, Kennedy and Thorp's analysis provides useful evidence in support of claims about the discriminating power of IELTS Writing Task 2, especially the validity of the criteria and rating scales used by examiners to assess performance. It confirms that high-scoring scripts are characterised by features such as: more complex syntax; use of richer vocabulary; greater interactivity with the reader; complex organisation; and lower error rates. Lower-scoring scripts are characterised by: reduced word length; limited lexical range; heavy use of cohesive markers but poor content and organisation overall; and higher error rates. These features have always been reflected to some degree in the assessment criteria and band descriptors used by IELTS examiners.

Even though the results of this and other funded research studies suggested that the existing writing assessment criteria and band descriptors were functioning reasonably well, evidence from other sources – including an internal Cambridge ESOL validation survey of IELTS Writing examiners carried out in 2002 – pointed to the need to review and possibly revise the writing assessment criteria and scales; such a move is in line with Cambridge ESOL's Test Production Methodology (Weir and Milanovic 2003) and with the IELTS partners' strong commitment to ongoing improvement of the test in terms of its validity, reliability, impact and practicality. The content and conclusions of the Kennedy and Thorp study could thus feed directly into the IELTS Writing Revision Project (2001–05); its findings were instrumental in highlighting key features which characterise linguistic performance at different points on the L2 writing proficiency continuum and helped to redefine the assessment criteria and reformulate the band descriptors. The literature review sections on cohesion and coherence in the L1/L2, and on hedging, politeness and stance, were especially informative. In fact, it is worth noting that often one of the most valuable outcomes of reports from joint-funded projects is the surveys of recent literature they provide; these help the IELTS test developers stay up to date with theoretical and empirical work in a wide range of fields (including some that are only indirectly linked to language testing) allowing them to take account of these in their work.

Although the Kennedy and Thorp study concentrated on the Academic Writing component of IELTS, a follow-up funded study in 2000/01 (Kennedy and Thorp 2003) was able to replicate the approach with a corpus of General Training Writing scripts for Task 2; this meant that redevelopment of the assessment criteria and rating scales within the IELTS Writing Revision Project was able to benefit from corpus-based analyses of both the Academic and General Training Writing Modules. The revised assessment criteria and band level descriptors for both modules were redesigned to capture the essential qualities of IELTS written performance across the nine proficiency levels. In this way the new rating scales differentiated more effectively the features of language at different levels. Findings from both projects were also helpful in developing more detailed examiner training guidelines to deal with problems sometimes encountered in candidate performance, such as underlength scripts and non-use of paragraphing.

Chapter 9: Investigating task design in Academic Writing prompts (O'Loughlin and Wigglesworth)

The O'Loughlin and Wigglesworth study was conducted in 2000 and first published in Volume 4 of the IELTS Research Reports 2003. It set out to explore issues of task difficulty in IELTS Academic Writing Task 1. As such it provides a welcome complement to the three studies in this volume – Moore and Morton, Mayor et al, and Kennedy and Thorp – focusing on task-design issues for Task 2 of the IELTS Academic Writing Module. Task 2 tends to attract more research interest and enquiry, perhaps because it generates longer samples of extended writing performance (250 words) and because the task contributes more strongly towards the final band score; however, studies which investigate the shorter Task 1 are also important since they can help provide insights into effective task design and also inform guidelines for examiners when rating output from this task.

Academic Writing Task 1 requires candidates to consider information presented as a graph, table, chart or diagram and then to describe this information in at least 150 words. The volume and nature of the input material needs to be carefully controlled so that the task is accessible to test takers and is capable of generating sufficient written output for assessment purposes. In addition, test producers must control the level of difficulty across tasks so that tasks are comparable across multiple versions of a test; task comparability is especially important in high-stakes tests such as IELTS. Control of task effectiveness and comparability in IELTS Writing prompts is achieved through a variety of measures which include detailed task specification and guidance to test writers, as well as trialling of prompts on small but representative samples before they are used in live tests.

The last 15 years have seen a growing body of literature on the relationship between task design and linguistic output in classroom and other contexts, especially in regard to oral tasks (Ortega 1999, Skehan and Foster 1997); as O'Loughlin and Wigglesworth point out, some of the most productive work has been carried out in the context of assessment (Hamp-Lyons and Kroll 1996, Wigglesworth 1999). O'Loughlin and Wigglesworth set out to explore how far task difficulty may be affected by *amount* and *presentation* of information provided to the candidate; they used specially developed experimental tasks based on IELTS Writing test prompts and a mixed-method quantitative/qualitative approach to analyse both scores awarded and linguistic output produced. Their analyses of test scores suggested that there were no substantial differences in difficulty between the tasks, either in terms of amount of information presented or in terms of presentation of the information. This result provides validation evidence for the comparability of task difficulty and corroborates findings from internal validation studies conducted by Cambridge ESOL. It confirmed that task comparability could be achieved even though a variety of presentation types is used in Task 1 (i.e. bar charts, line graphs, tables, etc).

Interestingly, discourse analysis of the candidate output led the researchers to conclude that tasks which provide less information have the potential to elicit more complex language (defined in terms of structure, organisation, co-ordination, subordination and repetition of key words). The challenge for any test designer is to elicit as rich a sample of written language as possible from the test taker within the available time constraint; the researchers suggest that simpler rather than more complex tasks may well achieve this objective.

This study acknowledges the complex interactions which take place in writing assessment between task, test taker and rater (see Milanovic and Saville 1996 for a useful discussion of this) and it provides valuable insights for both task designers and task raters. The results complemented findings from other investigative studies, including the examiner survey conducted in 2001 by Cambridge ESOL, and alongside these fed directly into the IELTS Writing Revision Project to inform the redefinition of the assessment criteria, the redrafting of the rating scales, and enhanced guidelines for raters.

Chapter 10: The effect of standardisation-training on rater judgements for the IELTS Writing Module (Furneaux and Rignall)

Rater training is generally recognised as being essential to reliability and validity in the testing of second language performance (Alderson, Clapham and Wall 1995, Bachman and Palmer 1996, McNamara 1996); training also has an important role to play in the professionalisation of language testing which has been called for by some in the field (Bachman 2000). Cambridge

ESOL has for many years invested heavily in the initial training and ongoing standardisation of examiners for all its writing and speaking tests, including IELTS, through a comprehensive set of materials and procedures combined with a network of professional personnel.

Empirical research which can inform the development of effective rater training programmes has only more recently become available. Cambridge ESOL studies carried out in the early 1990s among writing and speaking markers were among the first to investigate rater strategies (Milanovic, Saville and Shuhong 1996, Pollitt and Murray 1996); such studies did much to advance our understanding of what raters pay attention to and how they arrive at their judgements. In addition to transparency of assessment criteria and applicability of rating descriptors, quality of feedback to examiners after rating is likely to be an important factor in the success, or otherwise, of training and standardisation. For example, Wigglesworth (1993) found evidence that examiner bias was reduced following feedback and that examiner–rater consistency improved. Interest in rater behaviour and the implications it has for the design of rater training programmes has grown steadily since the mid-1990s (see also the O'Sullivan and Rignall study, Chapter 11 in this volume).

The study by Furneaux and Rignall is an important contribution within a much larger and ongoing research programme which seeks to deepen our understanding of rater behaviour so we can refine our approaches to rater training and standardisation. Their study – conducted in 2000 and not previously published – set out to investigate the judgements made by a group of novice IELTS examiners rating the IELTS Academic Writing Module. The findings were encouraging in that they show an increase in the extent of 'marking to standard' over the training period and provide evidence of increasing attention to and dependence on the prescribed assessment criteria; they also help to identify which criteria raters find more or less salient, and which criteria they find difficult to interpret (e.g. Coherence and Cohesion); the researchers recommended that follow-up studies should explore further the extent to which examiners consistently pay attention to the prescribed criteria. This was done in a Cambridge ESOL writing examiner survey conducted as part of the first phase of the IELTS Writing Revision Project (2001–05). An in-depth review of IELTS examiner perceptions combined with a close analysis of candidates' actual writing performance, enabled the revision project team to redefine all the criteria, especially Coherence and Cohesion, so as to make them more transparent and interpretable by examiners.

One recommendation of the Furneaux and Rignall study was to consider replacing the mixed-mode holistic/profile marking approach with a single profile approach to ensure that all examiners would focus adequately on the key criteria for assessment. As mentioned above, this recommendation was implemented from July 2003 following similar findings from other studies; since then profile marking of IELTS writing performance using analytical scales has been standard practice, mirroring the practice for assessment of speaking performance.

As the overview of ELTS/IELTS Speaking and Writing test development in the introduction to this volume shows, the IELTS test developers have always sought to maximise the reliability of the subjectively assessed performance components within the available resources and practical constraints which operated at the time. At different stages of the test's history, the procedures for ELTS/IELTS examiner training and standardisation were reviewed and refined to increase their effectiveness and to reflect what had been learned. For example, the self-access approach to initial training, the limitations of which Furneaux and Rignall acknowledged in their study, eventually gave way to face-to-face training of all examiners. Concern for the stability of rater characteristics over time points to the importance of following up initial rater training with a regular programme of retraining/restandardisation activity; for this reason all IELTS examiners undergo systematic retraining and re-certification every two years. Some years ago, the IELTS partners implemented a sample monitoring programme which allows examiner performance to be formally evaluated and for examiners to receive feedback via their test centres. More recently, additional support has been provided by making available a self-access standardisation pack for examiners to use for purposes of 'corrective intervention' or 'top-up' practice at any time during the two-year period after initial face-to-face training and certification and before they are required to re-certificate. In 2006 the IELTS Professional Support Network (PSN) – a global system designed to integrate all aspects of IELTS examiner recruitment, training, certification, standardisation, monitoring and conduct – was introduced. This system is being developed and supported jointly by the IELTS partners to ensure that all stages of the IELTS examiner management process are comprehensive, transparent, ethical, and well supported with appropriate documentation; the aim is to create an effective global network of examiners, examiner-trainers and examiner support co-ordinators to support the efficient functioning of test centres worldwide. The PSN recognises the differing needs of new and experienced examiners, and one of its functions is to keep examiners informed about the IELTS test and their role as key stakeholders.

Chapter 11: Assessing the value of bias analysis feedback to raters for the IELTS Writing Module (O'Sullivan and Rignall)

The final study in this volume deals once again with the topic of reliability of rating – an issue of special concern in high-stakes tests of speaking and writing ability, such as IELTS. The O'Sullivan and Rignall study – conducted in 2001 and not previously published – is the second of the collected papers to explore issues of rater behaviour and training and is, in part, a follow-up study to the earlier project undertaken by Furneaux and Rignall. It explores the potential value of giving formal feedback to raters to encourage them to become more consistent and reliable in their rating behaviour. It was conducted in the context of rating written performance in IELTS General Training and complements other work done on the IELTS Academic Writing Module.

As with several of the studies in this volume, the results provided some validation support for the existing assessment criteria and rating scales and at the same time highlighted aspects needing review and revision. The level of correlation between the original scores assigned to the scripts and those assigned by raters in the experimental study provided encouraging evidence for rating reliability. At the same time, the raters' comments on perceived weaknesses or areas of confusion in the band descriptors corroborated findings from a worldwide survey of IELTS examiners carried out by Cambridge ESOL, and together these informed the process of redrafting assessment criteria and scales in the IELTS Writing Revision Project.

Although the findings of this study showed feedback to have only a limited effect on examiners' actual rating performance, it nevertheless provided some interesting and relevant insights into rater attitudes and behaviour, into their perspectives of the job they are asked to do and the support they need to do it well. Their concern for fairness, their desire to do a good job, their willingness to be evaluated – all point to a keen sense of professionalism and personal responsibility. Raters welcome positive feedback because it brings reassurance and boosts morale; but they also appreciate the chance to learn about any weaknesses so that these can be addressed. It is striking how often the words 'reassurance', 'consistency' and 'encouragement' appear in the questionnaire responses, along with the perception that rating can be a 'lonely' experience. Such insights into rater perceptions point to the importance of developing the professional cadre and can feed directly into rater training and development programmes. Bachman (2000) called for greater attention to be paid to the professionalisation of the language testing community, and this must surely apply as much to those involved in rating as to those involved in test design and development. Concerns about the long-term effect of rater training exercises point to the need to build and maintain an effective 'community' of raters, and the language testing community has much to learn from recent research on communities of practice (Lave and Wenger 1991, Wenger 1999). Research relating to assessment and communities of practice suggests that a tight network or team combined with good communication between examiners can facilitate the reliability of writing assessment (Wolf 1995). The IELTS partners take account of this work in designing the quality management systems relating to the rating process, including the implementation of the IELTS Examiner Professional Support Network (or PSN) which allows for ongoing and systematic examiner feedback over time rather than just a 'one-shot' approach.

This study set out to explore the value of giving raters bias analysis feedback derived from multifaceted Rasch (MFR) analysis; it may be worth noting that while the use of MFR in rater monitoring and feedback is an attractive option, it can really only be implemented operationally in situations where a multiple-rating model is used; traditional single and even double rating models do not easily lend themselves to use of MFR analysis under operational conditions in large-scale testing contexts because of the level of connectivity required and the turnaround times involved. Nevertheless, advances in technology, such as computer-based rating of written performance and electronic script management (ESM), will make it increasingly possible for MFR analysis to be used operationally in the future. University of Cambridge ESOL Examinations is actively exploring how new technologies can enable multiple marking of writing (and speaking) performances, and IELTS is likely to be one of the first large-scale tests to benefit from developments in this area.

References

Alderson, J C (1997) *Bands and Scores*, in Clapham C and Alderson J C (Eds) *Constructing and Trialling the IELTS Test*, IELTS Research Report 3, Cambridge: UCLES, The British Council and IDP Education Australia: IELTS Australia.

Alderson, J C and Clapham, C (1992) *Examining the ELTS Test: An account of the first stage of the ELTS revision project*, IELTS Research Report 2, The British Council/UCLES/International Development Program of Australian Universities and Colleges.

Alderson, J C and Wall, D (1993) Does washback exist? *Applied Linguistics* 14 (2), 115–29.

Alderson, J C, Clapham C and Wall, D (1995) *Language Test Construction and Evaluation*, Cambridge: Cambridge University Press.

American Educational Research Association, American Psychological Association, National Council on Measurement in Education (1999) *Standards for Educational and Psychological Testing*, Washington: American Educational Research Association.

Atari, O (1983) *A contrastive analysis of Arab and American university students in accomplishing written English discourse functions: Implications for EFL*, unpublished PhD dissertation, Georgetown University.

Atkinson, D (1999) TESOL and culture, *TESOL Quarterly* 33, 625–54.

Atkinson, D and Ramanathan, V (1995) Cultures of Writing: an ethnographic comparison of L1 and L2 university writing/language programs, *TESOL Quarterly* 29, 539–68.

Atkinson, D and Ramanathan, V (2000) On Peter Elbow's response to 'Individualism, Academic Writing, and ESL Writers', *Journal of Second Language Writing* 9, 71–6.

Bachman, L F (1988) Problems in examining the validity of the ACTFL oral proficiency interview, *Studies in Second Language Acquisition* 10, 149–64.

Bachman, L F (1990) *Fundamental Considerations in Language Testing*, Oxford: Oxford University Press.

Bachman, L F (2000) Modern language testing at the turn of the century: assuring that what we count counts, *Language Testing* 17 (1), 1–42.

Bachman, L F and Savignon, S (1986) The evaluation of communicative language proficiency: A critique of the ACTFL oral interview, *The Modern Language Journal* 70, 380–90.

Bachman, L F, Lynch, B K, and Mason, M (1995) Investigating variability in tasks and rater judgments in a performance test of foreign language speaking, *Language Testing* 12 (2), 238–57.

Bachman, L F and Palmer, A S (1996) *Language Testing in Practice*, Oxford: Oxford University Press.

Bazerman, C (1988) *Shaping Written Knowledge: The genre and activity of the experimental article in science*, Madison: University of Wisconsin Press.

References

Bazerman, C and Paradis, J (Eds) (1991) *Textual Dynamics of the Professions*, Madison: University of Wisconsin Press.

Becher, T (1989) *Academic Tribes and Territories: Intellectual enquiry and the cultures of disciplines*, Buckingham: Open University Press.

Bereiter, C and Scardamalia, M (1987) *The Psychology of Written Composition*, Hillsdale, NJ: Lawrence Erlbaum Associates.

Berkenkotter, C and Huckin, T N (1995) *Genre Knowledge in Disciplinary Communication: Cognition/culture/power*, New Jersey: Lawrence Erlbaum Associates.

Berry, M (1995) Thematic options and success in writing, in Ghadessy, M (Ed.) *Thematic Development in English Texts*, London: Pinter, 55–84.

Biber, D, Johansson, S, Leech, G, Conrad, S and Finegan, E (1999) *Longman Grammar of Spoken and Written English*, Harlow: Pearson Education Limited.

Braine, G (1995) Writing in the natural sciences and engineering, in D. Belcher and G. Braine (Eds) *Academic Writing in a Second Language*, Norwood, NJ: Ablex, 113–34.

Bridgeman, B and Carlson, S (1983) *Survey of academic tasks required of graduate and undergraduate foreign students*, TOEFL Research Report 15, Princeton, NJ: Educational Testing Service.

Bridges, G and Shaw, S D (2004) IELTS Writing: revising assessment criteria and scales (Phase 4), *Research Notes* 18, 8–12.

Brooks, L (2002) Functions observed in the old IELTS Speaking test versus those in the new Speaking test, Cambridge: internal UCLES Report.

Brooks, L (2003) Converting an observation checklist for use with the IELTS Speaking test, *Research Notes* 11, 20–21.

Brown, A (1995) The effect of rater variables in the development of an occupation-specific language performance test, *Language Testing* 12 (1), 1–15.

Brown, A and Hill, K (1998) Interviewer style and candidate performance in the IELTS oral interview, in Wood, S (Ed.) IELTS Research Reports 1, Sydney: ELICOS, 1–19.

Brown, A and Lumley, T (1997) Interviewer variability in specific-purpose language performance tests, in Kohonen, V, Huhta, A, Kurki-Suonio, L and Luoma, S (Eds) *Current Developments and Alternatives in Language Assessment: Proceedings of LTRC 96*, Jyväskylä: University of Jyväskylä and University of Tampere.

Buckingham, A (1997) Oral language testing: do the age, status and gender of the interlocutor make a difference? unpublished MA dissertation, University of Reading.

Butler, C (1985) *Statistics in Linguistics*, Oxford: Basil Blackwell.

Cafarella, C (1994) Assessor accommodation in the V.C.E. Italian oral test, *Australian Review of Applied Linguistics* 20, 21–41.

Canesco, G. and P. Byrd (1989) Writing requirements in graduate courses in business administration, *TESOL Quarterly* 23, 305–316.

Carlson, S, Bridgeman, B, Camp, R and Waanders, J (1985) *Relationship of admission test scores to writing performance of native and non native speakers of English*, TOEFL Research Report 19, Princeton NJ: Educational Testing Service.

Carrell, P (1982) Cohesion is not coherence, *TESOL Quarterly* 16, 479–87.

Carson, J, Chase, H, Gibson, S and Hargrove, M (1992) Literacy demands of the undergraduate curriculum, *Reading Research and Instruction* 31, 25–50.

Chalhoub-Deville, M (1995) Deriving oral assessment scales across different tests and rater groups, *Language Testing* 12, 16–35.

Channell, J (1994) *Vague Language*, Oxford: Oxford University Press.

Charge, N and Taylor, L B (1997) Recent developments in IELTS, *ELT Journal* 51 (4).

Cherry, R and Cooper, C (1980) *Cohesive ties and discourse structure: a study of average and superior texts at four grade levels*, unpublished manuscript, Dept. of Learning and Instruction, State University of New York at Buffalo.

Clapham, C (1993) Is ESP justified? in Douglas, D and Chapelle, C (Eds) *A New Decade of Language Testing Research*, Virginia: TESOL.

Clapham, C (1996) *The Development of IELTS: A study of the effect of background knowledge on reading comprehension*, Studies in Language Testing 4, Cambridge: UCLES/Cambridge University Press.

Clapham, C (1997) The Academic Modules: Reading, in Clapham C and Alderson, J C (Eds) *Constructing and Trialling the IELTS Test*, IELTS Research Report 3, Cambridge: UCLES, The British Council, IDP Australia.

Clapham, C and Alderson, J C (Eds) (1997) *Constructing and Trialling the IELTS Test*, IELTS Research Report 3, Cambridge: UCLES, The British Council, IDP Australia.

Coates, J (1993) *Women, Men and Language*, London: Longman.

Coffin, C (1997) Constructing and giving value to the past: an investigation into secondary school history, in Martin, J R and Christie, F (Eds) *Genres and Institutions: social processes in the workplace and school*, London: Pinter.

Coffin, C (2004) Arguing about how the world is or how the world should be: the role of argument in IELTS Tests, *Journal of English for Academic Purposes* 3 (3), 229–46.

Coffin, C (2006) *Historical Discourse: The language of time, cause and evaluation*, Continuum: London, UK.

Coffin, C and Mayor, B M (2004) Texturing writer and reader reference in novice academic writing, in Banks, D (Ed.) *Text and Texture*, Paris: L'Harmattan, 239–64.

Cohen, A D (1994) *Assessing Language Ability in the Classroom* (2nd ed.), Boston: Newbury House/Heinle and Heinle.

Cohen, A D and Hosenfeld, C (1981) Some uses of mentalistic data in second language research, *Language Learning* 31, 285–313.

Coniam, D and Falvey, P (2002) Does student language ability affect the assessment of teacher language ability? *Journal of Personnel Evaluation in Education* 16 (4), 269–85.

Connor, U (1984) A study of cohesion and coherence in English as a second language students' writing, *Papers in Linguistics*, 17 (3) 301–16.

Connor, U (1996) *Contrastive Rhetoric: Cross-cultural aspects of second-language writing*, Cambridge: Cambridge University Press.

Conrad, S and Biber, D (2000) Adverbial marking of stance in speech and writing, in Hunston, S and Thompson, G (Eds) *Evaluation in Text*, Oxford: Oxford University Press.

Cotton, F and Conrow, F (1998) An investigation of the predictive validity of IELTS amongst a group of international students studying at the University of Tasmania, *IELTS Research Report Vol. 1 1998*, Canberra: IELTS Australia Pty Limited.

Council of Europe (2001) *Common European Framework of Reference for Languages: Learning, teaching, assessment*, Cambridge: Cambridge University Press.

Crewe, W (1990) The illogic of logical connectors, *ELT Journal* 44 (4), 316–25.

Criper, C and Davies, A (1988) *ELTS Validation Project Report*, ELTS Research Report 1(i), Hertford, UK: The British Council/UCLES.

Crombie, W (1985a) *Discourse and Language Learning: A relational approach to syllabus design*, Oxford: Oxford University Press.

Crombie, W (1985b) *Process and Relation in Discourse and Language Learning*, Oxford: Oxford University Press.

Cronbach, L J (1970) *Essentials of psychological testing*, New York: Harper and Row.

Cronbach, L J (1971) Test validation, in Thorndike, R L (Ed.) *Educational measurement, Second edition*, Washington, DC: American Council on Education.

Crowhurst, M (1981) *Cohesion in argumentative prose*, paper presented at the meeting of the American Educational Research Association, Los Angeles, CA.

Cumming, A (forthcoming) Expertise in evaluating second language compositions, *Language Testing* 7, 31–51.

Davies, A (forthcoming) *Assessing Academic English: Testing English Proficiency, 1950–1989 – the IELTS solution*, Studies in Language Testing 23, Cambridge: UCLES/Cambridge University Press.

de Jong, J H A L and van Ginkel, LW (1992) Dimensions in oral foreign language proficiency, in Verhoeven, L and de Jong, J H A L (Eds) *The construct of language proficiency*, Amsterdam: John Benjamins, 187–205.

de Witt, R (1997) *How to Prepare for IELTS*, London: The British Council.

Deakin, G (1996) (Ed.) *Practice Tests for IELTS* (2nd edition), Hawthorn: LTS.

Deakin, G (1997) IELTS in context: Issues in EAP for overseas students, *EA Journal* 15, 7–28.

Delarulle, S (1997) Text type and rater decision-making in the writing module, in Brindley, G and Wigglesworth, G (Eds) *Access: Issues in English language test design and delivery*, Sydney: National Centre for English Language Teaching and Research, 215–42.

DiPardo, A (1994) Stimulated recall in research on writing: An antidote to 'I don't know, it was fine', in Smagorinsky, P (Ed) *Speaking about Writing: Reflections on research methodology*, Thousand Oaks, CA: Sage.

Douglas, D and Chapelle, C (1993) (Eds) *A New Decade of Language Testing Research*, Virginia: TESOL.

Drury, H and Webb, C (1991) Literacy at tertiary level: making explicit the writing requirements of a new culture, in Christie, F (Ed.) *Literacy in Social Processes: Papers from the inaugural Australian Systemics Network conference*, Deakin University, January 1990, Darwin: Centre for Studies of Language in Education, Northern Territory University.

Dudley-Evans, T and Henderson, W (Eds) (1990) *The Language of Economics: The analysis of economics discourse*, London: Modern English Publications/The British Council.

Eiler, M A (1979) *Meaning and choice in writing about literature: A study of cohesion in the expository texts of ninth graders*, doctoral dissertation, Illinois Institute of Technology, Dissertation Abstracts International 40, 4571A.

Ericsson, K and Simon, H (1984) *Protocol Analysis: Verbal reports as data*, Cambridge, MA: MIT Press.

Evans, C (1988) *Language People: The experience of teaching and learning modern languages in British universities,* Open University Press.

Evenson, L (1990) Pointers to superstructure in student writing, in Connor, U and Johns, A (Eds) *Coherence in Writing,* Virginia, USA: TESOL, 171–83.

Falvey, P and Coniam, D (2000) Establishing English language writing benchmarks for primary and secondary teachers of English language in Hong Kong, *Hong Kong Journal of Applied Linguistics* 5 (1), 128–59.

Field, Y and Yip, L (1992) A comparison of internal cohesive conjunction in the English essay writing of Cantonese speakers and native speakers of English, *RELC Journal* 23 (1), 15–28.

Filipi, A (1994) Interaction in an Italian oral test: The role of some expansion sequences, in Gardner, R (Ed.) *Spoken Interaction Studies in Australia,* Australian Review of Applied Linguistics Series S, 11, 119–36.

Flowerdew, L (1997) Interpersonal strategies: investigating interlanguage corpora, *RELC Journal* 28, 72–88.

Flowerdew, L (1998) Integrating 'expert' and interlanguage computer corpora findings on causality: discoveries for teachers and students, *ESP Journal* 17 (4), 329–245.

Foddy, W (1994) *Constructing Questions for Interviews and Questionnaires: Theory and practice in social research,* Cambridge: Cambridge University Press.

Foster, P (1996) Doing the task better: how planning time influences students' performance, in Willis, J and Willis, D (Eds) *Challenge and Change in Language Teaching,* London: Heinemann.

Foster, P and Skehan, P (1996) The influence of planning and task type on second language performances, *Studies in Second Language Acquisition* 18, 299–323.

Foster, P, Tonkyn, A, and Wigglesworth, G (2000) Measuring spoken language: a unit for all reasons, *Applied Linguistics* 21 (3), 354–75.

Freed, A F (1995) Language and gender, *Annual Review of Applied Linguistics* 15, 3–22.

Freed, A F and Greenwood, A (1996) Women, men, and type of talk: what makes the difference? *Language in Society,* 25, 1–26.

Freeman, R and McElhinny, B (1996) Language and gender, in McKay, S L and Hornberger, N H *Sociolinguistics and language teaching,* Cambridge: Cambridge University Press, 218–80.

Fries, P H (1994) 'On Theme, Rheme and discourse goals', in M. Coulthard (Ed.) *Advances in Written Text Analysis,* London: Routledge, 229–49.

Fulcher, G (1999) Assessment in English for Academic Purposes: Putting content validity in its place, *Applied Linguistics* 20 (2).

Fulcher, G (2003) *Testing Second Language Speaking,* Harlow: Pearson.

Furneaux, C and Rignall, M (2002) The effect of standardisation-training on rater-judgements for the IELTS Writing Module, London: British Council internal report.

Garbutt, M and O'Sullivan, K (1996) *IELTS Practice Tests,* Sydney, National Centre for English Language Teaching and Research.

Garman, M (1990) *Psycholinguistics,* Cambridge: Cambridge University Press.

Geoghegan, G (1983) *Non-Native Speakers of English at Cambridge University,* Cambridge: Bell Educational Trust.

Ghadessy, M (1999) Textual features and contextual factors for register identification, in Ghadessy, M (Ed.) *Text and Context in Functional Linguistics,* Amsterdam: John Benjamins, 125–39.

References

Grabe, W, and Kaplan, R B (1966) *Theory and Practice of Writing: An applied linguistic perspective*, London and New York: Longman.

Granger, S (1993) The International Corpus of Learner English, in Aarts, J, De Haan, P and Oostdijk, N (Eds) *English Language Corpora: Design, analysis and exploitation*, Amsterdam and Atlanta:Rodopi.

Granger, S and Tyson, S (1996) Connector usage in the English essay writing of native and non native EFL speakers of English, *World Englishes* 15 (1), 17–27.

Green, A (1998) *Verbal Protocol Analysis in Language Testing Research: A handbook*, Studies in Language Testing 5, Cambridge: UCLES/Cambridge University Press.

Griffin, P and McKay, P (1992) Assessment and reporting in the ESL Language and Literacy in Schools Project, in McKay, P (Ed.) *ESL development: Language and literacy in schools: Tapping the potential, Vol. 2*, Canberra: Commonwealth of Australia, 9–28.

Hadden, B L (1991) Teacher and nonteacher perceptions of second-language communication, *Language Learning* 41, 1–24.

Hale, G, Taylor, C, Bridgeman, B, Carson, J, Kroll, B and Kantor, R (1996) *A study of writing tasks assigned in academic degree programs*, TOEFL Research Report 54, Princeton, NJ: Educational Testing Service.

Halleck, G B (1996) Interrater reliability of the OPI: Using academic trainee raters, *Foreign Language Annals* 29 (2), 223–38.

Halleck, G and Reed, D (1996) Probing above the ceiling in oral interviews: What's up there, in Kohonen, V, Huhta, A, Kurki-Suonio, L and Luoma, S (Eds) *Current Developments and Alternatives in Language Assessment*, proceedings of LTRC 1996, Jyväskylä: University of Jyväskylä and University of Tampere, 225–238.

Halliday, M A K (1985 and 1994) *An Introduction to Functional Grammar*, London: Edward Arnold.

Halliday, M A K and Hasan, R (1976) *Cohesion in English*, London: Longman.

Hamp-Lyons, L (1986) The product-before: Task-related influences on the writer, in Robinson, P (Ed.) *Academic Writing: Process and product*, Norwood, NJ: Ablex, 87–110.

Hamp-Lyons, L (1990) Second language writing: assessment issues, in Kroll, B (Ed.) *Second Language Writing: Research insights for the classroom*, Cambridge: Cambridge University Press.

Hamp-Lyons, L and Clapham, C (1997) The Academic Modules: Writing, in Clapham, C and Alderson, J C (Eds) *Constructing and Trialling the IELTS Test*, IELTS Research Report 3, Cambridge: UCLES, The British Council and IDP Education Australia: IELTS Australia.

Hamp-Lyons, L and Kroll, B (1996) Issues in ESL writing assessment: An overview, *College ESL* 6 (1), 52–72.

Hartnett, C (1980) *Cohesion as a teachable measure of writing competence*, doctoral dissertation, Indiana University of Pennsylvania, Dissertation Abstracts International 41, 2086A.

Hartnett, C (1986) Static and dynamic cohesion: Signals of thinking in writing, in Couture, B (Ed.) *Functional Approaches to Writing: Research perspectives*, London: Frances Pinter.

Hawkey, R A (1982). *Investigation of Interrelationships between Cognitive/Affective and Social Factors and Language Learning*, unpublished PhD thesis, Institute of Education, University of London, London.

Hawkey, R A (2006) *Impact Theory and Practice: Studies of the IELTS test and Progetto Lingue 2000*, Studies in Language Testing 24, Cambridge: UCLES/Cambridge University Press.

Hawkey, R A and Barker, F (2004) Developing a common scale for the assessment of writing, *Assessing Writing* 9 (2), 122–159.

Hewings, A (1999a) *Disciplinary engagement in undergraduate writing: An investigation of clause-initial elements in geography essays*, unpublished PhD thesis, University of Birmingham, UK.

Hewings, A (1999b) The grammatical subject: a focus for enquiry into disciplinary differences, in Thompson, P (Ed.) *Current Issues in EAP Writing Instruction*, CALS, University of Reading.

Hewings, M and Hewings, A (2002) 'It is absolutely impossible . . .': a comparative study of *it*-clauses in student and published writing, *English for Specific Purposes* 21, 367–83.

Hill, K, Storch, N and Lynch, B (1999) A comparison of IELTS and TOEFL as predictors of academic success, in IELTS Research Reports 1999, Vol. 2, Canberra: IELTS Australia Pty Limited.

Hoey, M (1983) *On the surface of discourse*, London: George Allen and Unwin.

Hoey, M. (1986) Clause relations and the writer's communicative task, in Couture, B (Ed.) *Functional Approaches to Writing: Research perspectives*. London: Frances Pinter.

Holmes, J (1984) Modifying illocutionary force, *Journal of Pragmatics* 8, 345–65.

Holmes, J (1988) Doubt and certainty in ESL textbooks, *Applied Linguistics* 9 (1), 21–44.

Hopkins, D and Nettle, M (1998) *Passport to IELTS*, Hemel Hempstead: Prentice Hall ELT.

Horowitz, D (1986) What professors actually require of students: academic tasks for the ESL classroom, *TESOL Quarterly* 20, 445–62.

Huddleston, R (1982) *Introduction to the Grammar of English*, Cambridge: Cambridge University Press.

Hughes, A, Porter, D and Weir, C J (Eds) (1988) *ELTS Validation Project: Proceedings of a conference held to consider the ELTS Validation Project Report*, Research Report 1 (ii), London and Cambridge: The British Council/UCLES.

Hunston, S and Thompson, G (Eds) (2000) *Evaluation in Text: Authorial stance and the construction of discourse*, Oxford: Oxford University Press.

Huot, B (1990) Reliability, validity and holistic scoring: What we know and what we need to know, *College Composition and Communication* 41, 201–13.

Hyland, K (1994) Hedging in academic writing and EAP textbooks, *ESP Journal* 13 (3), 239–56.

Hyland, K (2000) Hedges, boosters and lexical invisibility: Noticing modifiers in academic texts, *Language Awareness*, 9 (4), 179–93.

Hyland, K (2001) 'Humble servants of the discipline? Self-mention in research articles', *English for Specific Purposes* 20 (3), 207–26.

Hymes, D (1972) *On Communicative Competence*, Philadelphia, PA: University of Pennsylvania Press.

Iedema, R, Feez, S and White, P (1995) *Literacy of Administration* (Write it Right: Literacy in Industry Research Project Stage 3), Issues in Education for the Socially and Economically Disadvantaged Monograph 7, New South Wales: Disadvantaged Schools Program, Metropolitan East Region.

IELTS (1995) *IELTS Specimen Materials*, UCLES/The British Council/IDP Education Australia Ltd.

IELTS (1996) *IELTS Handbook*, UCLES/The British Council/IDP Education Australia Ltd.

IELTS (2000) *IELTS Handbook*, UCLES/The British Council/IDP Education Australia Ltd.

ILTA (2000) Code of Ethics, downloaded from www.iltaonline.com

Ingram, D E (1997) The General Training Module, in Clapham, C and Alderson, J C (Eds) *Constructing and Trialling the IELTS Test*, IELTS Research Report 3, Cambridge: UCLES, The British Council and IDP Education Australia: IELTS Australia.

Ingram, D E and Wylie, E (1993) Assessing speaking proficiency in the International English Language Testing System, in Douglas, D and Chappelle, C (Eds) *A New Decade of Language Testing Research*, Virginia:TESOL.

Ingram, D E and Wylie, E (1997) The General Modules: Speaking, in Clapham, C and Alderson, J C (Eds) *Constructing and Trialling the IELTS Test*, IELTS Research Report 3, Cambridge: UCLES, The British Council and IDP Education Australia: IELTS Australia.

Ivanic, R (1998) *Writing and Identity*, Amsterdam: John Benjamins.

Jakeman, V and McDowell, C (1996) *Cambridge Practice Tests for IELTS*, Cambridge: Cambridge University Press.

Johns, A (1981) Necessary English: A faculty survey, *TESOL Quarterly* 15, 51–7.

Joyce, B and Showers, B (1980) Improving inservice training: The messages of research, *Educational Leadership* 37 (5), 379–85.

Kachru, Y (1995) Contrastive rhetoric in World Englishes, *English Today* 41 (11), 21–31.

Kachru, Y (1997) Cultural meaning and contrastive rhetoric in English Education, *World Englishes* 16 (3), 337–50.

Kelly, G A (1955) *The psychology of personal constructs*, Vols 1 and 2, Norton: New York.

Kennedy, C and Thorp, D (2003) *Investigating stance in an IELTS General Writing Task*, Cambridge: British Council/Cambridge ESOL internal report.

Kenyon, D (1997) Further research on the efficacy of rater self-training, in Huhta, A, Kohonen, V, Kurki-Suonio, L and Luoma, S (Eds) *Current Developments and Alternatives in Language Assessment*, Jyvaskyla: University of Jyvaskyla Press, 257–73.

Kerstjens, M and Nery, C (1999) Predictive validity in the IELTS test: A study of the relationship between minimum IELTS scores and students' academic success, in IELTS Research Reports 1999, Vol. 2, Canberra: IELTS Australia Pty Limited.

Khalil, A (1990) A study of cohesion and coherence in Arab EFL college students' writing, *System* 17 (3), 359–71.

Koyabashi, H and Rinnert, C (1992) Effects of first language on second language writing: Translation versus direct-composition, *Modern Language Journal* 42, 183–215.

Kroll, B (1990) What does time buy? ESL student performance on home versus class compositions, in Kroll, B (Ed.) *Second Language Writing: Research insights for the classroom*, Cambridge: Cambridge University Press.

Kroll, B (1998) Assessing writing abilities, *Annual Review of Applied Linguistics*, 18, 219–40.

Kunnan, A J (1995) *Test Taker Characteristics and Test Performance: A structural modelling approach*, Studies in Language Testing 2, Cambridge: UCLES/Cambridge University Press.

Kunnan, A J (2000) *Fairness and Validation in Language Assessment: Selected papers from the 19th Language Testing Research Colloquium, Orlando, Florida*, Studies in Language Testing 9, Cambridge: UCLES/Cambridge University Press.

Lackstrom, J, Selinker, L and Trimble, L (1973) Technical rhetorical principles and grammatical choice, *TESOL Quarterly* 7, 127–36.

Lave, J and Wenger, E (1991) *Situated learning: Legitimate peripheral participation*, Cambridge: Cambridge University Press.

Lawe Davies, R (1998) *Coherence in tertiary students writing*, unpublished PhD thesis, University of Western Australia, Perth, Western Australia.

Lazaraton, A (1993) *A qualitative approach to monitoring examiner conduct in the Cambridge Assessment of Spoken English (CASE)*, paper presented at 15th Language Testing Research Colloquium, Cambridge, England.

Lazaraton, A (1996a) Interlocutor support in oral proficiency interviews: The case of CASE, *Language Testing* 13 (2), 151–72.

Lazaraton, A (1996b) A qualitative approach to monitoring examiner conduct in the Cambridge Assessment of Spoken English (CASE), in Milanovic, M and Saville, N (Eds) *Performance Testing, Cognition and Assessment*, Studies in Language Testing 3, Cambridge: UCLES/Cambridge University Press, 18–33.

Lazaraton, A (1997) Preference organisation in oral proficiency interviews: The case of language ability assessments, *Research on Language and Social Interaction* 30 (1), 53–72.

Lazaraton, A (1998) *An analysis of differences in linguistic features of candidates at different levels of the IELTS Speaking Test*, Cambridge: internal UCLES report.

Lazaraton, A (2002) *A Qualitative Approach to the Validation of Oral Language Tests*, Studies in Language Testing 14, Cambridge: UCLES/Cambridge University Press.

Lazaraton, A and Saville, N (1994) *Processes and outcomes in oral assessment*, paper presented at 16th Language Testing Research Colloquium, Washington DC.

Lee, Y, Kantor, R and Mollaun, P (2002) Score dependability of the writing and speaking section of New TOEFL, paper presented at the annual meeting of National Council on Measurement in Education (NCME), New Orleans, LA.

Levelt, W (1989) *Speaking: from intention to articulation*, Cambridge, MA: MIT

Lewkowicz, J (1997) Investigating authenticity in language testing, unpublished PhD thesis, University of Lancaster.

Levinson, S (1979) Activity types and language, *Linguistics* 1 (7), 356–99.

Linacre, J M (1989) *Many-Facet Rasch Measurement*, Chicago: Mesa Press.

Linacre, J M (1989–1995) *FACETS: a computer program for many faceted Rasch measurement*, Chicago, IL: Mesa Press.

Locke, C (1984) *The influence of the interviewer on student performance in tests of foreign language oral/aural skills*, unpublished MA project, University of Reading.

Lumley, T (2000) *The process of the assessment of writing performance: The rater's perspective*, unpublished PhD dissertation, University of Melbourne, Australia.

Lumley, T and McNamara, T (1993) *The effect of interlocutor and assessment mode variables in offshore assessments of speaking skills in occupational settings*, paper presented at 15th Language Testing Research Colloquium, Cambridge.

Lumley, T and Brown, A (1996) Specific-purpose language performance tests: task and interaction, in Wigglesworth, G and Elder, C (Eds) *Australian Review of Applied Linguistics Series S*.

Lunz, Mary E, and Wright, Benjamin D (1997) Latent trait models for performance examinations, in Jürgen Rost and Rolf Langeheine (Eds) *Applications of Latent Trait and Latent Class Models in the Social Sciences*, http://www.ipn.uni-kiel.de/aktuell/buecher/rostbuch/ltlc.htm

Luoma, S (2004) *Assessing Speaking*, Cambridge: Cambridge University Press.

Lyons, J (1977) *Semantics* Vol. 2, Cambridge: Cambridge University Press.

Maltz, D and Borker, R (1982) A cultural approach to male-female miscommunication, in Gumperz, J (Ed.) *Language and Social Identity*, Cambridge: Cambridge University Press, 196–216.

Mann, W and Thompson, S (1989) Rhetorical structure theory: A theory of text organisation, in Polanyi, L (Ed.) *The Structure of Discourse*, Norwood NJ: Ablex.

Martin, J (1984) Language, register and genre, in Christie, F (Ed.) *Language Studies: Children's writing reader*, Geelong: Deakin University Press.

Martin, J R (1992) *English Text*, Philadelphia/Amsterdam: John Benjamins.

Martin, J R (1997) Analysing Genre: functional parameters, in Christie, F and Martin, J R (Eds) *Genres and Institutions: Social processes in the workplace and school*, London: Pinter, 3–39.

Martin, J R (2000) Beyond exchange: APPRAISAL Systems in English, in Hunston S and Thompson, G (Eds) *Evaluation in Text*, Oxford: Oxford University Press, 142–75.

Mayo, E (1945) *The Social Problems of an Industrial Civilization*, New Hampshire: Ayer.

Mayor, B M (2006) Dialogic and hortatory features in the writing of Chinese candidates for the IELTS test, *Journal of Language Culture and Curriculum* 19 (1), 104–21.

McCulley, G (1985) Writing quality, coherence, and cohesion, *Research in the Teaching of English* 19, 269–82.

McDowell C (2000) Monitoring IELTS examiner training effectiveness, in IELTS Research Reports 3, Sydney: ELICOS.

McNamara, T F (1990) Item response theory and the validation of an ESP test for health professionals, *Language Testing* 7, 52–76.

McNamara, T (1996) *Measuring Second Language Performance*, Harlow: Longman.

McNamara, T and Lumley, T (1997) The effect of interlocutor and assessment mode variables in overseas assessments of speaking skills in occupational settings, *Language Testing* 14, 140–56.

Mehnert, U (1998) The effects of different lengths of time for planning on second language performance, *Studies in Second Language Acquisition* 20 (1), 83–108.

Meiron, B E (1998) *Rating oral proficiency tests: a triangulated study of rater thought processes*, unpublished MA thesis, UCLA.

Meiron, B and Schick, L (2000) Ratings, raters and test performance: An exploratory study, in Kunnan, A J (Ed.) *Fairness and Validation in Language Assessment: Selected papers from the 19th Language Testing Research Colloquium, Orlando, Florida*, Studies in Language Testing 9, Cambridge: UCLES/Cambridge University Press.

Merrylees, B and McDowell, C (1999) An investigation of speaking test reliability with particular reference to examiner attitude to the speaking test format and candidate/examiner discourse produced, in Tulloh, R (Ed.) IELTS Research Reports 1999, Vol. 2, IELTS Australia Pty Limited.

Messick, S (1989) Validity, in Linn, R (Ed) *Educational Measurement* (3rd ed.), New York: ACE/Macmillan, 13–103.

Meyer, B (1975) *The Organisation of Prose and its Effects on Recall*, New York: North Holland.

Milanovic, M and Saville, N (1994) *An investigation of marking strategies using verbal protocols*, paper presented at 16th Language Testing Research Colloquium, Washington, DC, March 1994.

Milanovic, M and Saville, N (1996) Introduction, in Milanovic, M and Saville, N (Eds) *Performance Testing, Cognition and Assessment: Selected papers from the 15th Language Testing Research Colloquium, Cambridge and Arnhem*, Studies in Language Testing 3, Cambridge: UCLES/Cambridge University Press.

Milanovic, M, Saville, N, Pollitt, A, and Cook, A (1996) Developing rating scales for CASE: theoretical concerns and analyses, in Cumming, A and Berwick, A (Eds) *Validation in Language Testing*, Cleveland: Multilingual Matters, 15–37.

Milanovic, M, Saville, N and Shuhong, S (1996) A study of the decision-making behaviour of composition-markers, in Milanovic, M and Saville, N (Eds) *Performance Testing, Cognition and Assessment*, Studies in Language Testing 3, Cambridge: UCLES/Cambridge University Press, 92–114.

Morton, J, Wigglesworth, G and Williams, D (1997) Approaches to the evaluation of interviewer behaviour in oral tests, *Access: issues in language test design and delivery*. Sydney: National Centre for English Language Teaching and Research, 175–96.

Mosenthal, J and Tierney, R (1984) Cohesion: problems with talking about text, *Reading Research Quarterly* XIX (2), 240–44.

Munby, J (1978) *Communicative Syllabus Design*, Cambridge: Cambridge University Press.

Myers, B (1975) *The Organization of Prose and its Effect on Recall*, New York: New Holland.

Myers, G (1989) The pragmatics of politeness in scientific articles, *Applied Linguistics* 10 (1), 1–35.

Neeson, S (1985) *An exploratory study of the discourse structure of the Australian Second Language Proficiency Ratings test of oral proficiency*, unpublished MA thesis, University of Birmingham.

Neuner, J (1987) Cohesive ties and chains in good and poor freshman essays, *Research in the Teaching of English* 21 (1), 92–105.

Nisbett, R E and Wilson, T D (1977) Telling more than we can know: Verbal reports on mental processes, *Psychological Review* 84, 231–59.

O'Loughlin, K (2001) *The Equivalence of Direct and Semi-direct Speaking Tests*, Studies in Language Testing 13, Cambridge: UCLES/Cambridge University Press.

Ortega, L (1999) Planning and focus on form in L2 oral performance, *Studies in Second Language Acquisition* 21, 109–48.

Ostler, S (1980) A survey of academic needs for advanced ESL, *TESOL Quarterly* 14, 489–502.

O'Sullivan, B (2000) Exploring gender and oral proficiency interview performance, *System* 28, 373–86.

O'Sullivan, B, Weir, C and Saville, N (2002) Using observation checklists to validate speaking-test tasks, *Language Testing* 19 (1), 33–56.

Paltridge, B (1996) Genre, text type, and the language learning classroom, *ELT Journal* 50, 237–43.

Perrett, G (1990) The language testing interview: A reappraisal, in de Jong, J H A L and Stevenson, D K (Eds) *Individualising the Assessment of Language Abilities*, Clevedon, UK: Multilingual Matters, 225–37.

Polio, C (1997) Measures of linguistic accuracy in second language writing research, *Language Learning* 47 (1), 101–43.

Polio, C and Glew M, (1996) ESL writing assessment prompts: how students choose, *Journal of Second Language Learning* 5 (1), 35–49.

Pollitt, A and Murray, N L (1996) What raters really pay attention to, in Milanovic, M and Saville, N (Eds) *Performance Testing, Cognition and Assessment*, Studies in Language Testing 3, Cambridge: UCLES/Cambridge University Press, 74–91.

Porter, D (1991a) Affective factors in language testing, in Alderson, J C and North, B (Eds) *Language Testing in the 1990s*, London: Modern English Publications, 32–40.

Porter, D (1991b) Affective factors in the assessment of oral interaction: gender and status, in Arnivan, S (Ed.) *Current developments in Language Testing*, Anthology series 25, Singapore: SEAMEO Regional Language Centre, 92–102.

Porter, D and Shen Shu Hung (1991) Sex, status and style in the interview, *The Dolphin 21*, Aarhus University Press, Aarhu, 117–28.

Powers, D and Stansfield, C W (1983) *The Test of Spoken English as a Measure of Communicative Ability in the Health Professions*, TOEFL Research Report 13, Princeton, NJ: Educational Testing Service.

Pritchard, R (1980) *A study of the cohesive devices in the good and poor compositions of 11th graders*, unpublished PhD dissertation, University of Missouri-Columbia, Dissertation Abstracts International, 42, 688A.

Prosser, M and Webb, C (1994) Relating the process of undergraduate essay writing to the finished product, *Studies in Higher Education* 19, 125–38.

Quirk, R and Greenbaum, S (1973) *A University Grammar of English*, London: Longman.

Quirk, R, Greenbaum, S, Leech, G, and Svartvik, J (1985) *A Comprehensive Grammar of the English Language*, London: Longman.

Raffaldini, T (1988) The use of situation tests as measures of communicative ability, *Studies in Second Language Acquisition* 10, 197–216.

Rasch, G (1980) *Probabilistic models for some intelligence and attainment tests*, Chicago: University of Chicago Press.

Read, J and Nation, P (2004) *An investigation of the lexical dimension of the IELTS speaking test*, IDP Australia Research Report.

Ross, S (1992) Accommodative questions in oral proficiency interviews, *Language Testing* 9 (2), 173–86.

Ross, S (1996) Formulae and inter-interviewer variation in oral proficiency interview discourse, *Prospect* 11 (3), 3–16.

Ross, S and Berwick, R (1992) The discourse of accommodation in oral proficiency interviews, *Studies in Second Language Acquisition* 14, 159–76.

Saville, N (2002) The process of test development and revision within UCLES EFL, in Weir, C and Milanovic, M (Eds) *Continuity and Innovation: Revising the Cambridge Proficiency in English Examination 1913–2002*, Studies in Language Testing 15, Cambridge: UCLES/Cambridge University Press, 57–120.

Seedhouse, P and Egbert, M (2006) *The interactional organisation of the IELTS Speaking Test*, British Council IELTS Research Report.

Scott, M (1999) *WordSmith Tools*, version 3, Oxford: Oxford University Press.

Shaw, S D (2002a) IELTS Writing: revising assessment criteria and scales (Phase 1), *Research Notes* 9, 16–18.

Shaw, S D (2002b) IELTS Writing: revising assessment criteria and scales (Phase 2), *Research Notes* 10, 10–13.

Shaw, S D (2004a) IELTS Writing: revising assessment criteria and scales (concluding Phase 2), *Research Notes* 15, 9–11.

Shaw, S D (2004b) IELTS Writing: revising assessment criteria and scales (Phase 3), *Research Notes* 16, 3–7.

Shaw, S D and Falvey, P (2006) IELTS Writing: revising assessment criteria and scales (Phase 5), *Research Notes* 23, 7–12.

Shaw, S D and Falvey, P (forthcoming) *The IELTS Writing Assessment Revision Project: Towards a revised rating scale*, Cambridge: UCLES internal report.

Shen, F (1989) The classroom and the wider culture: identity as a key to learning English composition, *College Composition and Communication* 40 (4), 459–66.

Shohamy, E and Walton, A R (Eds) (1992) *Language Assessment for Feedback: Testing and other strategies*, Dubuque, Iowa: Kendall/Hunt.

Skehan, P (1998) *A Cognitive Approach to Language Learning*, Oxford: Oxford University Press.

Skehan, P and Foster, P (1997) Task type and task processing conditions as influences on foreign language performance, *Language Teaching Research* 13, 185–211.

Smagorinsky, P (1994) *Speaking about Writing: Reflections on research methodology*, California: Sage.

Stubbe, M (1998) Are you listening? Cultural influences on the use of supportive verbal feedback in conversation, *Journal of Pragmatics* 29, 257–89.

Stubbs, M. (1986) A matter of prolonged fieldwork: Notes towards a modal grammar of English, *Applied Linguistics* 7 (1), 1–25.

Sunderland, J (1995) Gender and language testing, *Language Testing Update* 17, 24–35.

Swales, J (1990) *Genre Analysis: English in academic and research settings*, Cambridge: Cambridge University Press.

Tannen, D (1984) *Conversational Style: Analysing talk among friends*, Norwood, NJ: Ablex.

Tannen, D (1990) *You just don't understand: Women and men in conversation*, New York: William Morrow.

Taylor, G (1989) *The Student's Writing Guide for the Arts and Social Sciences*, Cambridge: Cambridge University Press.

Taylor, L (2001a) Revising the IELTS speaking test: developments in test format and task design, *Research Notes* 5, 3–5.

Taylor, L (2001b) Revising the IELTS speaking test: retraining IELTS examiners worldwide, *Research Notes* 6, 9–11.

Taylor, L and Jones, N (2001) Revising the IELTS Speaking test, *Research Notes* 4, 9–12.

Thompson, G (1994) *Guide to Reporting*, London: Harper Collins.

Thompson, G (2001) Interaction in academic writing: Learning to argue with the reader, *Applied Linguistics* 22 (1).

Thompson, G and Ye, Y (1991) Evaluation in the reporting verbs used in academic papers, *Applied Linguistics* 12, 365–82.

Thompson, G and Thetela, P (1995) The sound of one hand clapping: the management of interaction in written discourse, *Text* 15 (1), 103–27.

Thompson, G and Hunston, S (2000) Evaluation: an introduction, in Hunston, S and Thompson G (Eds) *Evaluation in Text*, Oxford: Oxford University Press.

Thwaite, A (1993) Gender differences in spoken interaction in same dyadic conversations in Australian English, in Winter, J and Wigglesworth, G (Eds) *Language and gender in the Australian context*, Australian Review of Applied Linguistics Series S, 10, 149–79.

Tierney, R and Mosenthal, J (1983). Cohesion and textual coherence, *Research in the Teaching of English* 17 (3), 215–29.

Todd, V and Cameron, P (1996) *Prepare for IELTS Academic Modules*, Sydney: Insearch Language Centre.

Tonkyn, A and Wilson, J (2004) Revising the IELTS speaking test, in Sheldon, L E (Ed.) *Directions for the Future*, Oxford: Peter Lang, 191–203.

Trimble, L (1985) *English for Science and Technology: A discourse approach*, Cambridge: Cambridge University Press.

Tyndall, B, and Kenyon, D M (1995) Validation of a new holistic rating scale using Rasch multifaceted analysis, in Cumming, A and Berwick, R (Eds) *Validation in Language Testing*, Clevedon, England: Multilingual Matters.

UCLES (1995) *IELTS Specimen Materials*. Cambridge: UCLES.

UCLES (1996) *The IELTS handbook*. Cambridge: UCLES.

UCLES (1998) *The IELTS Handbook*, Cambridge: Cambridge University Press.

UCLES (2000) *The IELTS Handbook*, Cambridge: Cambridge University Press.

Van Bemmel, B and Tucker, J (1996) *IELTS to Success: Preparation tips and practice tests*, Brisbane: Jacaranda Wiley.

Van Lier, L (1989) Reeling, writhing, drawling, stretching and fainting in coils: oral proficiency interviews as conversations, *TESOL Quarterly* 23, 480–508.

Vassileva, I (2001) Commitment and detachment in English and Bulgarian academic writing, *English for Specific Purposes* 20 (1).

Vaughan, C (1991) Holistic assessment: what goes on in the rater's mind? in Hamp-Lyons, L (Ed.) *Assessing Second Language Writing in Academic Contexts* Norwood, NJ: Ablex Publishing Corporation, 111–25.

Wall, D, Clapham, C and Alderson, J C (1994) Evaluating a placement test, *Language Testing* 11, 321–44.

Weigle, S C (1994) Effects of training on raters of ESL compositions, *Language Testing* 10, 197–223.

Weigle, S C (1998) Using FACETS to model rater training effects, *Language Testing* 15 (2), 263–87.

Weir, C J (1983) *Identifying the language problems of overseas students in tertiary education in the United Kingdom*, unpublished PhD thesis, University of London.

Weir, C J and Milanovic, M (Eds) (2003) *Continuity and Innovation: The History of the CPE 1913–2002*, Studies in Language Testing 15, Cambridge: UCLES/Cambridge University Press.

Wenger, E (1999) *Communities of Practice: Learning, meaning, and identity*, Cambridge: Cambridge University Press.

White, P R R (1997) Death, Disruption and the Moral Order: the narrative impulse in mass-media hard news reporting, in Christie, F and Martin, J R (Eds) *Genres and Institutions: Social processes in the workplace and school*, London: Pinter, 101–33.

White, P R R (1998) *Telling Media Tales: The news story as rhetoric*, unpublished PhD thesis, Department of Linguistics, University of Sydney.

Wigglesworth, G (1993) Exploring bias analysis as a tool for improving rater consistency in assessing oral interaction, *Language Testing* 10 (3), 305–35.

Wigglesworth, G (1997) An investigation of planning time and proficiency level on oral test discourse, *Language Testing* 14 (1), 101–22.

Wigglesworth, G (1999) *Rating accuracy and complexity in written scripts*, paper presented at the Japanese Association of Language Teaching conference, Tokyo, October 8–10.

Wigglesworth, G (2001) Influences on performance in task-based oral assessments, in Bygate, M, Skehan, P and Swain, M *Task Based Learning*, London: Addison Wesley Longman, 186–209.

Winter, E (1977) A clause-relational approach to English texts: a study of some predictive lexical items in written discourse, *Instructional Science*, 6 (1), 1–92.

Winter, E (1978) A look at the role of certain words in information structure, *Informatics* 3 (1), 85–97.

Witte, S and Faigley, L (1981) Coherence, cohesion and writing quality, *College Composition and Communication* 32, 189–203.

Wolf, A (1995) *Competence-based assessment*, Milton Keynes: Open University Press.

Wolfe-Quintero, K, Inagaki, S, and Kim, H-Y (1998) *Second language development in writing: Measures of fluency, accuracy and complexity*, Technical Report 17, Second Language Teaching and Curriculum Center, University of Hawaii at Manao: University of Hawaii Press.

Wylie, E (1993) Report to the International Editing Committee of IELTS on a Study of the Inter-Rater Reliability of the Speaking Test, Cambridge: UCLES internal report.

Young, R and Milanovic, M (1992) Discourse variation in oral proficiency interviews, *Studies in Second Language Acquisition* 14, 403–24.